Copyright 2020 by Joshua Edward -All rights reserved.

No part of this book may be reproduced or transmitted in any form or by any means, electronic or mechanical, including photocopying and recording, or by any information storage and retrieval system, without permission in writing from the publisher. This is a work of fiction. Names, places, characters and incidents are either the product of the author's imagination or are used fictitiously, and any resemblance to any actual persons, living or dead, organizations, events or locales is entirely coincidental. The unauthorized reproduction or distribution of this copyrighted work is ilegal.

Disclaimer Notice:

Please note the information contained within this document is for educational and entertainment purposes only. All effort has been executed to present accurate, up to date, reliable, complete information. No warranties of any kind are declared or implied. Readers acknowledge that the author is not engaged in the rendering of legal, financial, medical, or professional advice. The content within this book has been derived from various sources. Please consult a licensed professional before attempting any techniques outlined in this book.

By reading this document, the reader agrees that under no circumstances is the author responsible for any losses, direct or indirect, that are incurred as a result of the use of the information contained within this document, including, but not limited to, errors, omissions, or inaccuracies.

CONTENTS

Introduction 10	Creamy Zucchini Pan 22
Ketogenic Instant Pot Breakfast Recipes 11	Breakfast Taco Omelet 22
Soft Eggs and Avocado Mix 11	Leeks and Pork Mix 22
Meat Sandwich 11	Keto Shakshuka 22
Blackberry Muffins 11	Cardamom Walnuts Pudding 23
Keto Cereal Bowl 11	Morning Bacon Bombs 23
Spinach Frittata 11	Basil Eggs Mix 23
Butter Crepes 12	Egg Muffins 23
Broccoli Casserole 12	Creamy Blueberries and Nuts 23
Soft Eggs 12	Egg Sandwich 23
Bell Peppers and Cauliflower Salad 12	Kale and Bok Choy Muffins 24
Cabbage Hash Browns 12	Keto Oatmeal 24
Cauliflower Hash 13	Spinach and Artichokes Muffins 24
Cabbage Hash Browns 13	Oregano Egg en Cocotte 24
Scallions and Broccoli Mix 13	Mozzarella and Kale Muffins 24
Meat Muffins with Quail Eggs 13	Hot Jalapeno Poppers Mix 25
Pork Hash 13	Chicken Bowls 25
Cinnamon Pancakes 13	Breakfast Stuffed Avocado 25
Creamy Eggs Ramekins 14	Coconut Pudding 25
Cinnamon Pancakes 14	Layered Casserole 25
Avocado and Broccoli Salad 14	Zucchini Spread 25
Paprika Eggs in Pepper Holes 14	Chili Casserole 26
Coconut Blueberry Pudding 14	Tomato and Zucchini Salad 26
Stuffed Pepper Halves with Omelet 15	Breakfast Hot Cacao 26
Bacon and Eggs 15	Turkey Bowls 26
Bacon Egg Cups 15	Zucchini Cheese Fritters 26
Broccoli and Cheese Pancake 15	Cheesy Tomato and Radish Salad 27
Zucchini Meat Cups 15	Cauliflower Fritters 27
Tomato and Peppers Salad 16	Pork and Kale Hash 27
Green Hash 16	Breakfast Spaghetti Squash Casserole 27
Chili Frittata 16	Sweet Zucchini Mix 27
Breakfast Avocado Bombs 16	Sweet Porridge 28
Cheesy Beef Casserole 16	Turkey Omelet 28
Spiced Hard-Boiled Eggs 16	Bacon Salad with Eggs 28
Asparagus and Eggs Mix 17	Strawberries and Nuts Salad 28
Minced Beef Pancakes 17	Classic Breakfast Casserole 28
Chia and Blueberries Bowls 17	Eggs, Leeks and Turkey Mix 29
Ham Roll 17	Low-Carb Flaxseed Brule 29
Almond Cocoa and Strawberries Mix 17	Sweet Berries Bowls 29
Fluffy Eggs 17	Mini Frittatas 29
Coconut Yogurt Mix 18	Mushroom and Okra Omelet 29
Bacon Eggs with Chives 18	Egg Benedict Sandwich 29
Artichokes Pudding 18	Cocoa Oatmeal 30
Avocado Boats with Omelet 18	Nutritious Taco Skillet 30
Scotch Eggs and Tomato Passata 18	Coconut Oatmeal 30
Breakfast Egg Hash 19	Wontons 30
Parsley Cauliflower Mix 19	Broccoli and Almonds Mix 30
Bacon Tacos 19	Breakfast Kale Bread 31
Pork Pie 19	Mushroom and Cauliflower Rice Salad 31
Mason Jar Omelet 19	Egg Scramble 31
Ginger Cauliflower Rice Pudding 20	Cinnamon Strawberry Oatmeal 31
Cauliflower Bake 20	Parmesan Chicken Balls 31
Bok Choy Bowls 20	Coconut Omelet 32
Cauliflower Toast 20	Blueberry Muffins 32
Mushroom and Avocado Salad 20	Leek Frittata 32
Sausage Casserole 20	Chicken Fritters 32
Salmon and Eggs Mix 21	Scallions and Peppers Bowls 32
Frittata with Greens 21	Crustless Egg Pie 32
Italian Beef and Green Beans Mix 21	Curry Cauliflower Rice Bowls 33
Cheese Egg Balls 21	Mini Casserole in Jars 33
Herbed Mushroom Mix 21	Ketogenic Instant Pot Lunch Recipes 34
Breakfast Crustless Quiche 22	Egg Salad 34

Provolone Chicken Soup	34
Green Beans and Rice Mix	34
Jalapeno Soup	34
Garlic Beef Mix	34
Aromatic Lasagna with Basil	35
Parsley Beef Bowls	35
Keto "Potato" Soup	35
Okra Soup	35
Egg Soup	35
Greek Turkey and Sauce	36
Beef Cabbage Soup	36
Lime Pork Bowls	36
Bacon Chowder	36
Coconut Broccoli Soup	36
Butternut Squash Soup	37
Pork Chops and Thyme Mushrooms	37
Tortilla Soup	37
Mexican Pork and Okra Salad	37
Asian Style Zucchini Soup	37
Pork and Kale Meatballs	38
Chili Verde	38
Pork and Baby Spinach	38
Keto Taco Soup	38
Cinnamon Turkey Curry	38
Chicken Enchilada Soup	39
Basil Shrimp and Eggplants	39
Creamy Cauliflower Soup	39
Mushroom and Chicken Soup	39
Kale Soup	39
Cod and Tomato Passata	40
Bone Broth Soup	40
Chicken and Mustard Sauce	40
Buffalo Chicken Soup	40
Chicken and Avocado Mix	40
Keto Lunch Bowl	41
Tomato and Pork Soup	41
Cobb Salad	41
Cayenne Pork and Artichokes Stew	41
Lobster Salad	41
Green Beans Soup	42
Italian Style Salad	42
Broccoli and Zucchini Soup	42
Egg & Cheese Salad with Dill	42
Beef Soup	42
Crab Salad	42
Curry Tomato Cream	43
Chicken Paprika	43
Spinach Soup	43
Sour Cauliflower Salad	43
Cabbage Soup	43
Warm Radish Salad	44
Cheesy Coconut Cream	44
Crack Chicken	44
Eggplant Soup	44
Salsa Chicken	44
Bell Pepper Cream	45
Lemon Carnitas	45
Chicken and Asparagus Soup	45
Smoky Pulled Pork	45
Hot Cod Stew	45
Chicken & Dumplings Soup	45
Lamb Stew	46
Zoodle Soup	46
Shrimp and Olives Stew	46
Hot Sausages Soup	46
Turkey Stew	46
Fajita Soup	47
Kale Stew	47
Kalua Chicken	47
Turmeric Cabbage Stew	47
Southwestern Chili	47
Chili Mushrooms Stew	48
Clam Chowder	48
Zucchini and Lamb Stew	48
Parsley Meatloaf	48
Beef and Cauliflower Stew	48
Pepper Pork Chops	49
Chicken and Brussels Sprouts Stew	49
Meat & Collard Greens Bowl	49
Cod and Shrimp Stew	49
Spinach Saag	49
Beef Meatballs Stew	50
Chicken & Mushroom Bowl	50
Salmon Stew	50
Cheddar Soup	50
Veggie Soup	50
Lunch Pot Roast	51
Artichokes Cream	51
Green Beans with Ham	51
Leek Soup	51
Spiral Ham	51
Sage Chicken and Turkey Stew	51
Coconut Soup	52
Bell Peppers and Kale Soup	52
Corned Beef with Cabbage	52
Tomato and Olives Stew	52
Lazy Meat Mix	52
Creamy Brussels Sprouts Stew	53
Shredded Chicken Salad	53
Ketogenic Instant Pot Side Dish Recipes	54
Ginger Cabbage and Radish Mix	54
Cauliflower Mac&Cheese	54
Chives Brussels Sprouts	54
Brussels Sprouts Casserole	54
Mozzarella Broccoli	54
Rosemary&Butter Mushrooms	54
Garlic Broccoli Mix	55
Bacon Brussels Sprouts	55
Balsamic Mushroom and Radish Mix	55
Spinach Mash with Bacon	55
Collard Greens and Tomatoes	55
Mashed Cauliflower	55
Balsamic Spinach	56
Fried Cauliflower Slices	56
Paprika Mushrooms	56
Mashed Brussel Sprouts	56
Coconut Spinach Mix	56
Cauliflower Rice	57
Chili Eggplant and Collard Greens	57
Soft Spinach with Dill	57
Chard and Mushrooms Mix	57
Mexican Style Keto Rice	57
Creamy Cauliflower	57
Kale&Parmesan Bowl	57
Creamy Green Beans	58
White Cabbage in Cream	58
Spinach and Radish Mix	58
Cauliflower Cheese	58

Recipe	Page
Lemon Cabbage Mix	58
Cauli-Tatoes	58
Herbed Radish Mix	59
Butter Spaghetti Squash	59
Asparagus Mix	59
Sliced Zucchini Casserole	59
Pine Nuts Savoy Cabbage	59
Green Beans Casserole	59
Spinach and Fennel Mix	60
Squash Casserole	60
Dill Cherry Tomatoes	60
Cheesy Zucchini Strips	60
Tomatoes and Cauliflower Mix	60
Turmeric Cabbage Rice	61
Green Beans and Herbs	61
Turnip Creamy Gratin	61
Cauliflower Rice and Olives	61
Parmesan Onion Rings	61
Rosemary Cauliflower	61
Rosemary Radish Halves	62
Lemon Artichokes	62
Sweet Baby Carrot	62
Celery and Broccoli Mix	62
Feta and Zucchini Bowl	62
Zucchini Mix	62
Herbed Asparagus	63
Dill Fennel Mix	63
Cheesy Radish	63
Mushrooms and Endives Mix	63
Turnip Cubes	63
Walnuts Green Beans and Avocado	63
Cilantro-Kale Salad	64
Thyme Brussels Sprouts	64
Cauliflower Gnocchi	64
Chives Broccoli Mash	64
Thyme Purple Cabbage Steaks	64
Creamy Endives	64
Smashed Cauliflower with Goat Cheese	65
Spinach and Kale Mix	65
Low Carb Fall Vegetables	65
Thyme Tomatoes	65
Steamed Broccoli	65
Lemon Brussels Sprouts and Tomatoes	65
Cheddar Tots with Broccoli	66
Creamy Fennel	66
Vegetable Fritters	66
Saffron Bell Peppers	66
Steamed Asparagus	66
Cabbage and Peppers	67
Roasted Cauliflower Steak	67
Green Beans and Kale	67
Cayenne Pepper Green Beans	67
Zucchinis and Bok Choy	67
Marinated Red Bell Peppers	67
Red Cabbage and Artichokes	68
Broccoli Nuggets	68
Balsamic Artichokes and Capers	68
Yellow Squash Noodles	68
Bell Peppers and Olives	68
Oregano Fennel Steaks	68
Tomatoes and Olives	69
Butter Shirataki Noodles	69
Balsamic Eggplant Mix	69
Asiago Cauliflower Rice	69
Buttery Eggplants	69
Spaghetti Squash Mac&Cheese	69
Bacon Artichokes	70
Sichuan Style Green Beans	70
Cabbage and Tomatoes	70
Cauliflower Tortillas	70
Balsamic Collard Greens	70
Gouda Vegetable Casserole	71
Cilantro Cauliflower Rice Mix	71
Warm Antipasto Salad	71
Leeks Sauté	71
Eggplant Gratin	71
Eggplant and Zucchini Mix	72
Beet Cubes with Pecans	72
Chili Cauliflower Rice	72
Jalapeno Popper Bread	72
Sage Eggplants and Green Beans	72
Baked Green Beans	72
Nutmeg Zucchini Rice	73
Spiced Zucchinis	73
Parmesan Broccoli Head	73
Leeks and Cabbage	73
Cauliflower Salad with Provolone Cheese	73
Cranberries Cauliflower Rice	74
Spiced Asparagus	74
Mint Zucchinis	74
Side Dish Cauliflower Ziti	74
Ketogenic Instant Pot Snack and Appetizer Recipes	75
Lemon Zucchini and Eggplant Spread	75
Zucchini Fries in Bacon	75
Oregano Green Beans Salsa	75
Bacon Bites with Asparagus	75
Basil Zucchini and Capers Dip	75
Bacon Onion Rings	75
Lime Spinach and Leeks Dip	76
Oregano Keto Bread Rounds	76
Chili Tomato and Zucchini Dip	76
Cabbage Chips	76
Parmesan Mushroom Spread	76
Soul Bread	77
Broccoli Dip	77
Tender Jicama Fritters	77
Ginger Cauliflower Spread	77
Spiced Chicken Carnitas	77
Radish Salsa	78
Cheese Almond Meal Bites	78
Mustard Greens Dip	78
Zucchini Parsley Tots	78
Spinach and Artichokes Spread	78
Paprika Deviled Eggs	79
Artichokes and Salmon Bowls	79
Parmesan Tomatoes Slices	79
Salmon and Cod Cakes	79
Mini Cheese Pepperoni Pizza	79
Green Beans and Cod Salad	80
Keto Queso Dip	80
Shrimp and Leeks Platter	80
Keto Jalapeno Bread	80
Balsamic Mussels Bowls	80
Turnip Fries	80
Tomato and Zucchini Salsa	81
Butternut Squash Fries	81
Sweet Shrimp Bowls	81
Popcorn Chicken	81

Parsley Clams Platter	81
Crunchy Green Beans	82
Zucchinis and Walnuts Salsa	82
Keto Breadsticks	82
Shrimp and Beef Bowls	82
Mini Chicken Skewers	82
Coconut Shrimp Platter	83
Parmesan Cauliflower Tots	83
Marinated Shrimp	83
Aromatic Swedish Meatballs	83
Eggplant and Spinach Dip	83
Kale Wraps	83
Balsamic Endives	84
Bread Twists	84
Italian Asparagus	84
Cheese Chips	84
Fennel and Leeks Platter	84
Butter Coffee	85
Nutmeg Endives	85
Pumpkin Spices Latte	85
Thyme Eggplants and Celery Spread	85
Salty Nuts Mix	85
Shrimp and Okra Bowls	85
Heart of Palm Dip	86
Mushrooms Salsa	86
Taco Shells	86
Cheesy Mushroom and Tomato Salad	86
Mini Margharita Pizzas in Mushroom Caps	86
Olives Spread	87
Keto Guacamole Deviled Eggs	87
Basil Stuffed Bell Peppers	87
Hot Tempeh	87
Mussels Salad	87
Garlic Aioli	87
Oregano Beef Bites	88
Pesto Wings	88
Watercress and Zucchini Salsa	88
Bacon Avocado Bombs	88
Basil Shallots and Peppers Dip	88
Bacon Sushi	89
Olives and Spinach Dip	89
Mint Salmon and Radish Salad	89
Keto Taquitos	89
Red Chard Spread	90
Chicken Celery Boats	90
Salmon and Swiss Chard Salad	90
Keto Nachos	90
Basil Peppers Salsa	90
Edamame Hummus	91
Pesto Chicken Salad	91
Crab Spread	91
Cabbage and Spinach Slaw	91
Bacon-Wrapped Shrimps	91
Cabbage, Tomato and Avocado Salsa	92
Tuna Steak Skewers	92
Shrimp and Mussels Salad	92
Marinated Olives	92
Beef, Arugula and Olives Salad	92
Chicharrones	92
Bacon Radish And Shrimp Salad	93
Keto Spanakopita Pie Slices	93
Cheesy Radish Spread	93
Dog Nuggets	93
Ketogenic Instant Pot Fish and Seafood Recipes	94
Cod and Tomatoes	94
Fish Saag	94
Cod and Cilantro Sauce	94
Brazilian Fish Stew	94
Salmon and Black Olives Mix	94
Fish Casserole	95
Coriander Cod Mix	95
Salmon Pie	95
Cod and Zucchinis	95
Pesto Salmon	95
Paprika Trout	96
Tuna Salad	96
Lime Shrimp	96
Tandoori Salmon	96
Trout and Radishes	96
Cheese Melt	96
Cod and Broccoli	97
Prosciutto Shrimp Skewers	97
Rosemary Trout and Cauliflower	97
Lime Salmon Burger	97
Cinnamon Cod Mix	97
Curry Fish	98
Trout and Eggplant Mix	98
Fried Salmon	98
Salmon and Tomato Passata	98
Spicy Mackerel	98
Salmon and Artichokes	98
Salmon in Fragrant Sauce	99
Trout and Spinach Mix	99
Shrimp Salad with Avocado	99
Sea Bass and Sauce	99
Seafood Omelet	99
Sea Bass and Pesto	100
Shrimp Tacos	100
Tuna and Mustard Greens	100
Shrimp Cocktail	100
Salmon and Salsa	100
Mussels Casserole	101
Saffron Chili Cod	101
Skagenrora	101
Salmon and Endives	101
Butter Scallops	101
Chili Tuna	102
Cajun Crab Casserole	102
Mackerel and Shrimp Mix	102
Crab Melt with Zucchini	102
Mackerel and Basil Sauce	102
Baked Snapper	102
Oregano Tuna	103
Salmon Salad	103
Creamy Shrimp and Radish Mix	103
Butter Cod Loin	103
Marjoram Tuna	103
Cod in Cream Sauce	103
Bacon Trout Mix	104
Salmon and Kohlrabi Gratin	104
Tuna and Fennel Mix	104
Mussel Chowder	104
Tilapia Salad	104
Paprika Salmon Skewers	105
Salmon and Dill Sauce	105
Tuscan Shrimps	105
Tilapia and Olives Salsa	105
Parmesan Scallops	106

Catfish and Avocado Mix	106
Seafood Bisque	106
Tilapia and Capers Mix	106
Lobster Bisque	106
Glazed Salmon	107
Tarragon Lobster	107
Spicy Tilapia and Kale	107
Mussels Mariniere	107
Lime Glazed Salmon	107
Tuna Cakes	107
Tilapia and Zucchini Noodles	108
Salmon under Parmesan Blanket	108
Salmon and Coconut Mix	108
Salmon Poppers	108
Haddock and Cilantro Sauce	109
Tuna Rolls	109
Tilapia and Red Sauce	109
Fish Sticks	109
Lime Cod Mix	109
Crab Rangoon Dip	110
Salmon and Shrimp Mix	110
Coriander Seabass	110
Salmon and Green Beans	110
Dill Halibut	110
Cod and Asparagus	110
Spinach and Tilapia Casserole	111
Turmeric Shrimp Mix	111
Fish Pie	111
Cod and Basil Tomato Passata	111
Mackerel Pate	111
Shrimp and Lemon Green Beans Mix	112
Crab Rangoon Fat Bombs	112
Herbed Haddock Mix	112
Crab&Broccoli Casserole	112
Salmon and Garlic Spinach	112
Tuna and Bacon Cups	113
Thyme Crab and Spinach	113
Halibut Ceviche	113
Smoked Crab and Cod Mix	113
Parchment Fish	113
Rosemary Tilapia and Pine Nuts	114
Poached Cod	114
Crab, Spinach and Chives	114
Light Shrimp Pad Thai	114
Chili Haddock and Tomatoes	114
Coated Coconut Shrimps	115
Tuna and Green Beans Mix	115
Steamed Crab Legs	115
Chipotle Tilapia Mix	115
Salmon with Lemon	115
Ginger Halibut	115
Zingy Fish	116
Halibut and Brussels Sprouts	116
Thyme Cod	116
Creamy Catfish	116
Mussels Mariniere	116
Ketogenic Instant Pot Poultry Recipes	117
Oregano Chicken	117
Chicken Tonnato	117
Spiced Chicken Bites	117
Paprika Chicken Wings	117
Coconut Chicken and Peppers	117
Garlic Chicken Drumsticks	118
Basil Chili Chicken	118
Chicken Provencal	118
Chicken and Oregano Sauce	118
Chicken with Blue Cheese Sauce	118
Balsamic Curry Chicken	119
Flying Jacob Casserole	119
Chicken and Eggplant Mix	119
Chicken Caprese Casserole	119
Sesame Chicken	119
Cajun Chicken Salad	119
Turkey and Spring Onions Mix	120
Caesar Salad	120
Italian Paprika Chicken	120
Hoagie Bowl	120
Tomato Turkey and Sprouts	121
BLT Chicken Wrap	121
Chicken, Kale and Artichokes	121
Pizza Stuffed Chicken	121
Sage Chicken and Broccoli	121
Chicken Patties	122
Turkey and Cabbage Mix	122
Mozzarella Chicken Fillets	122
Balsamic Turkey and Zucchini	122
Bruschetta Chicken	122
Ginger Balsamic Chicken	123
Greek Chicken	123
Tarragon Chicken Mix	123
Chicken Rendang	123
Duck and Fennel	123
Chicken Zucchini Enchiladas	124
Chicken and Herbs Sauce	124
Chicken Cacciatore	124
Turkey and Lime Dill Sauce	124
Coconut Chicken Tenders	125
Hot Curry Turkey	125
Balsamic Roast Chicken	125
Duck and Hot Eggplant Mix	125
Chicken & Snap Pea Salad	125
Chicken, Cabbage and Leeks	126
Spinach Stuffed Chicken	126
Turkey and Spicy Okra	126
Chicken Scarpariello	126
Chicken and Balsamic Mushrooms	127
Chicken Divan Casserole	127
Creamy Turkey and Chard	127
Orange Chicken	127
Duck and Coriander Sauce	128
Chicken Stroganoff	128
Chicken, Baby Kale and Spinach Mix	128
Pecan Chicken	128
Chicken and Cauliflower Rice	128
Cayenne Pepper Chicken Meatballs	129
Turkey and Mustard Greens Mix	129
Chicken Cheese Calzone	129
Turkey and Rocket Mix	129
Butter Chicken Stew	130
Chicken and Watercress Mix	130
Chicken Cauliflower Rice	130
Duck, Leeks and Asparagus	130
Chicken Crust Pizza	130
Chicken and Garlic Spinach	131
Asiago Chicken Drumsticks	131
Turmeric Duck Mix	131
Chicken Stuffed Avocado	131
Turkey and Hot Lemon Sauce	131

Chicken Cordon Bleu	132
Oregano Chicken and Dates	132
Herbed Whole Chicken	132
White Duck Chili	132
Ground Chicken Mix	132
Chicken, Radish and Green Beans	133
Bacon-Wrapped Chicken Tenders	133
Cinnamon Turkey and Celery Mix	133
Chicken and Spinach Bowl	133
Salsa Verde Turkey	133
Keto Chicken Burger	134
Basil Chicken Mix	134
Chicken Liver Pate	134
Chicken and Hot Endives	134
Coconut Chicken Cubes	134
Indian Chicken and Sauce	135
Chicken Lettuce Rolls	135
Turkey and Creamy Garlic Mix	135
Turkey Bolognese Sauce	135
Chicken Casserole	135
Turkey Stuffed Mushrooms	136
Turkey and Cilantro Tomato Salsa	136
Cornish Game Hens	136
Chicken and Green Sauté	136
Blackened Chicken	136
Chicken Meatballs and Spinach	137
Anniversary Chicken	137
Cheesy Turkey	137
Ajiaco	137
Creamy Chicken Wings	138
Ground Turkey Chili	138
Turkey and Blackberries Sauce	138
Ethiopian Spicy Doro Wat Soup	138
Thyme Duck and Coconut	138
Turkey Soup	139
Tuscan Chicken	139
Chicken Fricassee	139
Marinated Turkey Mix	139
Chicken Steamed Balls	139
Tabasco Chicken and Kale	140
South American Garden Chicken	140
Chicken, Peppers and Mushrooms	140
Chicken Moussaka	140
Cheddar Turkey	140
Fajita Chicken Casserole	141
Chicken and Almonds Mix	141
Chicken with Black Olives	141
Turkey, Brussels Sprouts and Walnuts	141
Indian Chicken Korma	141
Ketogenic Instant Pot Meat Recipes	143
Garlic and Parsley Pork	143
Rosemary Barbecue Pork Chops	143
Rosemary and Cinnamon Pork	143
Kalua Pork	143
Curry Pork and Kale	143
Parmesan Pork	143
Pork and Cilantro Tomato Mix	144
Garlic Pork Loin	144
Mustard Pork and Chard	144
Fragrant Pork Belly	144
Pork, Spinach and Green Beans	144
Parmesan Pork Tenderloins	144
Pork, Kale and Capers Mix	145
Keto Ham	145
Pork and Lemon Basil Sauce	145
Jalapeno Pulled Pork	145
Pork and Cauliflower Rice	146
Char Siu	146
Spicy Pork, Zucchinis and Eggplants	146
Chili Spare Ribs	146
Pork Meatballs and Spring Onions Sauce	146
Taiwanese Braised Pork Belly	147
Raspberry Pork Mix	147
Korean Style Pork Ribs	147
Chili Pork Chops	147
Pork and Turnip Cake	147
Rosemary Pork Chops	148
Kalua Pig	148
Pork Chops and Green Chilies Mix	148
Greek Style Pork Chops	148
Sage and Tarragon Pork	148
Curry Pork Sausages	148
Coconut Pork Mix	149
Sage Pork Loin	149
Beef, Cauliflower Rice and Shrimp Mix	149
Spinach and Fennel Pork Stew	149
Spiced Beef	149
Garlic Smoky Ribs	150
Beef, Sprouts and Bok Choy Mix	150
Ground Meat Stew	150
Lamb and Broccoli Mix	150
Pork&Mushrooms Ragout	150
Dill Lamb and Tomatoes	151
Mesquite Ribs	151
Curry Lamb and Cauliflower	151
Keto Pork Posole	151
Garlic Lamb and Chard	151
Hoisin Meatballs	151
Coriander Beef and Pork Mix	152
Tender Pork Satay	152
Pork Ribs and Green Beans	152
Ham and Cheese Dinner Casserole	152
Lime Pork Chops	153
Blackberry Pork Chops	153
Pesto Pork and Mustard Greens	153
Pork and Celery Curry	153
Paprika Lamb Chops	153
Beef and Squash Ragu	153
Pork and Olives	154
Beef Loin with Acorn Squash	154
Beef and Herbed Radish	154
Beef Tips	154
Beef and Endives Mix	155
Onion Baby Back Ribs	155
Beef and Mushroom Rice	155
Beef & Cabbage Stew	155
Feta Cheese Lamb Mix	155
Tender Salisbury Steak	156
Mustard and Sage Beef	156
Cumin Kielbasa	156
Spiced Lamb Meatballs	156
Prosciutto and Eggs Salad	156
Mint Lamb Chops	157
Mississippi Roast	157
Lamb Chops, Fennel and Tomatoes	157
Keto Oxtail Goulash	157
Italian Leg of Lamb	157
Italian Beef	158

Recipe	Page
Hot Curry Lamb and Green Beans	158
Thyme Braised Beef	158
Lamb and Sun-dried Tomatoes Mix	158
Butter Lamb	158
Cumin Lamb and Capers	158
Coriander Leg of Lamb	159
Herbed Crusted Lamb Cutlets	159
Dhansak Curry Meat	159
Pine Nuts Lamb Meatballs	159
Mint Lamb Cubes	159
Lamb Shoulder Roast	160
Pork Chops in Sweet Sauce	160
Moroccan Lamb	160
Kalua Pork	160
Spinach Pork Meatloaf	160
Spoon Lamb	161
Ginger Lamb and Basil	161
Rogan Josh	161
Coconut Lamb Chops	161
mb Shank	161
Spicy Beef, Sprouts and Avocado Mix	162
White Pork Soup	162
Beef and Creamy Sauce	162
Lamb Pulao	162
Pork and Chives Asparagus	163
Meat&Cheese Pie	163
Oregano and Thyme Beef	163
Burger Casserole	163
Almond Lamb Meatloaf	164
Cauliflower Shepherd's Pie	164
Pork and Bok Choy	164
Big Mac Bites	164
Smoked Paprika Lamb	164
Zoodle Pork Casserole	165
Cajun Beef and Leeks Sauce	165
Ground Beef Skewers	165
Beef and Savoy Cabbage Mix	165
Pastrami	165
Pork and Mint Zucchinis	166
Pork Belly Salad	166
Beef and Walnuts Rice	166
Pork Salad with Kale	166
Ketogenic Instant Pot Vegetable Recipes	**167**
Lime and Paprika Asparagus	167
Garlic and Cheese Baked Asparagus	167
Basil Spicy Artichokes	167
Brussels Sprouts in Heavy Cream	167
Coconut Leeks and Sprouts	167
Wrapped Bacon Carrot	167
Mozzarella Artichokes and Capers	168
Caprese Zoodles	168
Asparagus and Tomatoes	168
Cauliflower Florets Mix	168
Asparagus and Chives Dressing	168
Balsamic Brussels Sprouts	168
Creamy Asparagus Mix	169
Tender Sautéed Vegetables	169
Parmesan Radishes and Asparagus	169
Spaghetti Squash Nests	169
Artichokes and Bacon Mix	169
Lemongrass Green Beans	170
Balsamic Green Beans and Capers	170
Cucumbers and Zucchini Noodles	170
Brussels Sprouts and Sauce	170
Eggs and Mushrooms Cups	170
Bell Peppers and Chives	170
Kale Skillet with Nuts	171
Cayenne Peppers and Sauce	171
Shredded Spaghetti Squash with Bacon	171
Bell Peppers and Brussels Sprouts	171
Green Peas Salad	171
Bell Peppers and Mustard Greens	171
Cauliflower Risotto	172
Parmesan Radish	172
Collard Greens with Cherry Tomatoes	172
Cheddar Tomatoes	172
Cauliflower Gratin	172
Creamy Tomatoes	172
Scalloped Cabbage	173
Garlic Celery and Kale	173
Hash Brown Casserole	173
Creamy Eggplant Mix	173
Stuffed Mushrooms	173
Spicy Eggplant and Kale Mix	174
Green Beans Salad	174
Tomato and Dill Sauté	174
Tuscan Mushrooms Sauce	174
Mustard Greens and Cabbage Sauté	174
Thyme Cauliflower Head	174
Dill Zucchini, Tomatoes and Eggplants	175
Stuffed Spaghetti Squash	175
Balsamic Okra	175
Shallot Mushrooms	175
Creamy Okra and Collard Greens	175
Baked Kabocha Squash	176
Balsamic Savoy Cabbage	176
Sautéed Kohlrabi	176
Cilantro Red Cabbage and Artichokes	176
Butter Edamame Beans	176
Dill Fennel and Brussels Sprouts	176
Marinated Tomatillos Paste	176
Cinnamon Green Beans Mix	177
Tender Rutabaga	177
Okra and Olives Mix	177
Zucchini Goulash	177
Olives, Capers and Kale	177
Cheddar Mushrooms	177
Eggplants and Cabbage Mix	178
Garlic Eggplant Rounds	178
Eggplants, Cucumber and Olives	178
Vegetable Soup	178
Lemon Peppers and Bok Choy	178
Cream of Celery	179
Tomato Bok Choy Mix	179
Steamed Rutabaga Mash	179
Garlic Cabbage and Watercress	179
Fragrant Artichoke Hearts	179
Mint and Basil Eggplant	179
Steamed Broccoli Raab (Rabe)	180
Broccoli and Watercress Mix	180
Avocado Pie	180
Balsamic Bok Choy and Onions	180
Zucchini Pasta with Blue Cheese	180
Balsamic and Coconut Cabbage	181
Lemon Artichoke	181
Buttery Turmeric Brussels Sprouts	181
Zucchini Boats	181
Lemon and Pesto Broccoli	181

Zucchini Fettuccine	182
Bok Choy and Parmesan Mix	182
Keto Club Salad	182
Milky Fennel	182
Bell Pepper Pizza	182
Minty Green Beans	182
Peppers & Cheese Salad	183
Almonds Green Beans Mix	183
Bok Choy Salad	183
Mixed Peppers and Parsley	183
Avocado Pesto Zoodles	183
Peppers, Green Beans and Olives Mix	183
Collard Wraps	184
Lemon Tomato and Green Beans	184
Portobello Toasts	184

Ketogenic Instant Pot Dessert Recipes 185

Sweet Zucchini Pudding	185
Chocolate Pudding	185
Almond Strawberry Bread	185
Pumpkin Pie Cups	185
Coconut Zucchini Cake	185
Keto Custard	186
Vanilla Blackberries Bowls	186
Pumpkin Spices Pudding	186
Plums and Raisins Mix	186
Molten Brownies Cups	186
Berry Chocolate Cream	186
Almond Tart	187
Strawberries and Pecans Cream	187
Chocolate Pudding Cake	187
Coconut and Macadamia Chocolate Cream	187
Spice Pie	187
Cantaloupe Pudding	188
Keto Cheesecake	188
Coconut Raspberries Bowls	188
Butter Cake	188
Watermelon Cream	189
Cinnamon Mini Rolls	189
Lemon Strawberries Stew	189
Lava Cake	189
Egg and Cantaloupe Pudding	189
Rhubarb Custard	190
Cocoa Strawberries Mix	190
Chocolate Mousse	190
Lime Cherry Bowls	190
Cocoa-Vanilla Pudding	190
Zucchini Rice Pudding	190
Keto Carrot Pie	191
Creamy Rice Pudding	191
Pecan Pie	191
Berries and Nuts Pudding	191
Keto Crème Brulee	191
Lime Coconut Vanilla Cream	192
Lavender Pie	192
Plums Jam	192
Blueberry Parfait	192
Raspberries and Coconut Puddings	192
Pandan Custard	193
Cinnamon Cream	193
Mug Cake	193
Lemon Cantaloupe Stew	193
Coconut Cake	193
Ginger Chocolate Cream	194
Walnut pie	194
Macadamia Blackberry Stew	194
Keto Chip Cookies	194
Plums and Berries Compote	194
Keto Vanilla Crescent Cookies	194
Lime Watermelon Compote	195
Vanilla Muffins	195
Heavy Cream and Raspberries Ramekins	195
Fat Bomb Jars	195
Coconut Pecans Cream	195
Blueberry Clusters	195
Chocolate and Brazil Nuts Bread	196
Strawberry Cubes	196
Greek Pudding	196
Avocado Brownies	196
Pecans and Plums Bread	196
Cheesecake Bites	197
Chocolate Cheesecake	197
Coconut Crack Bars	197
Plums and Rice Pudding	197
Keto Blondies	197
Cinnamon Berries Custard	198
Low Carb Nutella	198
Ginger and Cardamom Plums Mix	198
Cheesecake Fat Bombs	198
Chocolate Cake	198
Peanut Butter Balls	199
Chocolate Cookies	199
Cinnamon Muffins	199
Coffee Cake	199
Keto Fudge	199
Nutmeg Pudding	200
Fluffy Donuts	200
Chocolate Chips Balls	200
Coconut Muffins	200
Coconut and Cocoa Doughnuts	200
Raspberry Pie	201
Chocolate Balls	201
Mint Cookies	201
Vanilla and Cocoa Cream	201
Coconut Clouds	201
Plums Pie	202
Shortbread Cookies	202
Vanilla Cream Mix	202
Lime Bars	202
Mascarpone Cheesecake	202
Peppermint Cookies	203
Creamy Chocolate Avocado Mix	203
Macadamia Cookies	203
Vanilla Chocolate Cupcakes	203
Keto Pralines	203
Cream Cheese and Blackberries Mousse	204
Blueberry Crisp	204

Appendix : Recipes Index 205

Introduction

Are you looking for an easy way to cook healthy meals in the comfort of your own home? Are you searching for simple kitchen tools that will help you prepare some rich and delicious dishes for you and your loved ones? Well, if that's the case, then this is the best guide you could use.

This cooking guide presents to you the best and most innovative cooking tool available these days. We're talking about the instant pot. This original and useful pot has gained so many fans all over the world due to the fact that it's so easy to use and because it can help you cook so many delicious meals. You can prepare easy breakfasts, lunch dishes, snacks, appetizers, side dishes, fish and seafood, meat, poultry, vegetable and dessert recipes instant pot

This brings us to the second part of this guide. This journal focuses on using the instant pot to make the best Ketogenic dishes. The Ketogenic diet is much more than a simple weight loss program. It's a lifestyle that will improve your health and the way you look.

This low-carb and high-fat diet will get your body to a state of ketosis. The diet help you produce more ketones and therefore it will improve your metabolism and your energy levels.

The Ketogenic diet will show its multiple benefits in a matter of minutes and it will help you look and feel better. All you need to do now is to get your hands on a copy of this great recipes collection because it brings you the best Ketogenic meals made in an instant pot.

You will enjoy each of these great dishes.

So, let's start this culinary trip right away. Have fun cooking in your instant pot and enjoy the multiple benefits of the Ketogenic diet.

Ketogenic Instant Pot Breakfast Recipes

Soft Eggs and Avocado Mix

Preparation time: 5 minutes
Cooking time: 3 minutes
Servings: 2
Ingredients:
- 2 cups water
- 4 eggs
- 1 avocado, peeled and cubed
- 1 tomato, cubed
- 2 teaspoons avocado oil
- A pinch of salt and black pepper
- 1 teaspoon balsamic vinegar

Directions:
Put the water in the instant pot, add the steamer basket, add the eggs inside, put the lid on and cook on Low for 3 minutes. Release the pressure fast for 5 minutes, cool the eggs down, peel, cut them into quarters and put them in a bowl. Add the avocado and the rest of the ingredients, toss a bit, divide between plates and serve.
Nutrition: calories 170, fat 14.7, fiber 3.2, carbs 5.5, protein 6

Meat Sandwich

Preparation time: 10 minutes
Cooking time: 12 minutes
Servings: 2
Ingredients:
- 1 cup minced beef
- ½ teaspoon chili flakes
- 1 tablespoon water
- ½ teaspoon garlic powder
- ¼ teaspoon salt
- 2 eggs, beaten
- 2 cheddar cheese slices
- 1 teaspoon butter

Directions:
In the mixing bowl combine together the minced beef, chili flakes, water, salt, and garlic powder. Then make 4 meatballs and press them gently with the help of the fingertips. Wrap every ball in paper foil. Pour water in the instant pot and insert the steamer rack Place the meatballs on the rack and cook them on Manual (high pressure) for 8 minutes. After this, remove the meatballs from the instant pot and remove them from the paper foil. Clean the instant pot and remove the steamer rack. Preheat the instant pot on Saute mode and add butter. Melt it. Add beaten egg and cook them for 2 minutes. Then flip on another side. Place the one slice of cheese in the center egg and wrap it. Repeat the same steps with remaining cheese and egg. Then place the first wrapped cheese on 1 meatball and cove rit with the second meatball to get the sandwich. Repeat the same steps with the remaining ingredients. Pierce the cooked sandwiches with toothpicks if needed.
Nutrition: calories 353, fat 20.9, fiber 0.1, carbs 1.2, protein 38.5

Blackberry Muffins

Preparation time: 10 minutes
Cooking time: 20 minutes
Servings: 4
Ingredients:
- 1 and ½ tablespoons flaxseed meal
- ½ cup coconut flour
- 4 tablespoons swerve
- 1 teaspoon baking powder
- ½ cup almond milk
- ¼ teaspoon baking soda
- 2 eggs, whisked
- 1 and ½ tablespoons ghee, melted
- 1 teaspoon vanilla extract
- ½ cup blackberries
- 1 cup water

Directions:
In a bowl, combine the flaxmeal with the flour, swerve and the rest of the ingredients except the water and whisk well. Divide this into a muffin pan. Put the water in the instant pot, add the steamer basket, put the muffin pan inside, put the lid on and cook on High for 20 minutes. Release the pressure naturally for 10 minutes, cool the muffins down and serve for breakfast.
Nutrition: calories 112, fat 9.1, fiber 1.1, carbs 4.2, protein 4.8

Keto Cereal Bowl

Preparation time: 10 minutes
Cooking time: 10 minutes
Servings: 2
Ingredients:
- 1 tablespoon flaxseeds
- 1 tablespoon sesame seeds
- ¼ cup walnuts, chopped
- ¼ cup almonds, chopped
- ¼ teaspoon ground cinnamon
- ½ teaspoon vanilla extract
- 1 tablespoon coconut oil
- 1 egg white, whisked

Directions:
In the mixing bowl combine together flaxseeds, sesame seeds, walnuts, almonds, ground cinnamon, and vanilla extract. Then add coconut oil and whisked egg white. Mix up the mixture. Preheat the instant pot on Saute mode. Then place the nut mixture in the instant pot bowl and flatten it gently. Cook the cereals for 10 minutes. Stir them every 2 minutes. Then cool the cereals well.
Nutrition: calories 281, fat 25.3, fiber 4.2, carbs 6.6, protein 9.5

Spinach Frittata

Preparation time: 10 minutes
Cooking time: 10 minutes
Servings: 4
Ingredients:
- 6 eggs, whisked
- 1 cup baby spinach
- 1 spring onion, minced
- ½ teaspoon garlic powder
- A pinch of salt and black pepper
- 1 cup water
- Cooking spray

Directions:

In a bowl, combine the eggs with the spinach and the rest of the ingredients except the water and the cooking spray and whisk well. Grease a pan with the cooking spray and pour the frittata mix inside. Put the water in the instant pot, add the trivet, put the pan inside, put the lid on and cook on High for 10 minutes. Release the pressure naturally for 10 minutes, divide the frittata between plates and serve.
Nutrition: calories 103, fat 6.4, fiber 1.1, carbs 2.5, protein 8.4

Butter Crepes

Preparation time: 10 minutes
Cooking time: 15 minutes
Servings: 4
Ingredients:
- ½ cup of coconut milk
- 1 egg, beaten
- 1 tablespoon butter, melted
- ½ teaspoon baking powder
- 1 teaspoon lemon juice
- 1 teaspoon vanilla extract
- ½ cup almond meal
- 4 tablespoons ground coconut flour
- ½ teaspoon coconut oil, melted
- ¼ teaspoon salt

Directions:
In the mixing bowl mix up together coconut milk, eggs, melted butter, baking powder, lemon juice, vanilla extract, and salt. Then add the almond meal and ground coconut flour. Stir the mixture until you get the thick liquid. Grease the instant pot bowl with coconut oil. Preheat the instant pot on Saute mode for 3 minutes. After this, ladle 1 ladle of the crepe batter in the instant pot bowl in the shape of crepe. Cook the crepe on Saute mode for 1 minute from each side. Cook the crepes additional time if you prefer the golden-brown crust. Repeat the same steps with the remaining crepe batter.
Nutrition: calories 204, fat 17.8, fiber 2.8, carbs 8.4, protein 5.2

Broccoli Casserole

Preparation time: 10 minutes
Cooking time: 40 minutes
Servings: 4
Ingredients:
- 3 broccoli stalks, grated
- 2 tablespoons avocado oil
- 2 garlic cloves, minced
- A pinch of salt and black pepper
- 6 eggs, whisked
- ¼ cup heavy cream
- 1 cup cheddar cheese, grated
- 1 green onion, chopped

Directions:
Set the instant pot on Sauté mode, add the oil, heat it up, add the garlic and the broccoli, stir and sauté for 4 minutes. In a bowl, mix the eggs with the cream, salt and pepper, whisk well and pour over the broccoli mix in the pot. Put the lid on and cook on High for 35 minutes. Release the pressure naturally for 10 minutes, sprinkle the cheese and the onion all over, leave aside for a few minutes more, divide between plates and serve.
Nutrition: calories 247, fat 19, fiber 0.5, carbs 2.3, protein 15

Soft Eggs

Preparation time: 10 minutes
Cooking time: 4 minutes
Servings: 2
Ingredients:
- ¼ teaspoon ground black pepper
- ¼ teaspoon salt
- ½ teaspoon butter, melted
- 2 eggs
- 1 cup water, for cooking

Directions:
Pour water in the instant pot and insert the steamer rack. Place the eggs on the rack and close the instant pot lid. Cook the eggs on Manual mode (Low pressure) for 4 minutes. Then cool the eggs in the ice water and peel them. Cut the eggs into halves and sprinkle with salt, ground black pepper, and melted butter.
Nutrition: calories 72, fat 5.3, fiber 0.1, carbs 0.5, protein 5.6

Bell Peppers and Cauliflower Salad

Preparation time: 10 minutes
Cooking time: 20 minutes
Servings: 4
Ingredients:
- 1 cauliflower head, florets separated
- 1 tablespoon avocado oil
- 2 spring onions, chopped
- ¼ red bell pepper, sliced
- ¼ yellow bell pepper, sliced
- ¼ green bell pepper, sliced
- A pinch of salt and black pepper
- 2 eggs

Directions:
Set the instant pot on Sauté mode, add the oil, heat it up, add the bell peppers and sauté them for 4 minutes. Add the rest of the ingredients, toss a bit, put the lid on and cook on High for 15 minutes. Release the pressure naturally for 10 minutes, divide the mix into bowls and serve for breakfast.
Nutrition: calories 63, fat 3, fiber 2.3, carbs 6, protein 4.5

Cabbage Hash Browns

Preparation time: 10 minutes
Cooking time: 16 minutes
Servings: 2
Ingredients:
- 1 cup white cabbage, shredded
- 1 teaspoon onion powder
- 1 egg, beaten
- ¾ cup onion, minced
- 1 teaspoon ground paprika
- ½ teaspoon coconut oil, melted

Directions:
Mix up together cabbage with onion powder, egg, minced onion, and ground paprika. Then preheat the instant pot on manual mode. Brush the instant pot bowl with coconut oil. With the help of the spoon make the small hash brown fritters from the cabbage mixture and place them in the instant pot. Cook 2 hash browns per 1 time. Cook the meal for 4 minutes from each side.
Nutrition: calories 74, fat 3.6, fiber 2.3, carbs 7.8, protein 4

Cauliflower Hash

Preparation time: 10 minutes
Cooking time: 15 minutes
Servings: 4
Ingredients:
- A pinch of salt and black pepper
- 2 cups cauliflower, riced
- 1 teaspoon red bell pepper, chopped
- 1 teaspoon green bell pepper, chopped
- ½ tablespoon olive oil
- 1 cup black olives, pitted and chopped
- 1 cup cheddar cheese, shredded

Directions:
Set your instant pot on sauté mode, add the oil, heat it up, add the cauliflower rice and cook it for 2-3 minutes. Add the rest of the ingredients except the cheese, toss a bit, put the lid on and cook on High for 12 minutes. Release the pressure naturally for 10 minutes, divide the hash between plates and serve.
Nutrition: calories 199, fat 14.9, fiber 3, carbs 7.6, protein 8.9

Cabbage Hash Browns

Preparation time: 10 minutes
Cooking time: 16 minutes
Servings: 2
Ingredients:
- 1 cup white cabbage, shredded
- 1 teaspoon onion powder
- 1 egg, beaten
- ¾ cup onion, minced
- 1 teaspoon ground paprika
- ½ teaspoon coconut oil, melted

Directions:
Mix up together cabbage with onion powder, egg, minced onion, and ground paprika. Then preheat the instant pot on manual mode. Brush the instant pot bowl with coconut oil. With the help of the spoon make the small hash brown fritters from the cabbage mixture and place them in the instant pot. Cook 2 hash browns per 1 time. Cook the meal for 4 minutes from each side.
Nutrition: calories 74, fat 3.6, fiber 2.3, carbs 7.8, protein 4

Scallions and Broccoli Mix

Preparation time: 10 minutes
Cooking time: 20 minutes
Servings: 4
Ingredients:
- 1 pound broccoli florets, roughly chopped
- 4 eggs, whisked
- 1 tablespoon sweet paprika
- 1 tablespoon avocado oil
- 2 scallions, chopped
- 1 cup cheddar cheese, shredded

Directions:
Set the instant pot on Sauté mode, add the oil, heat it up, add the scallions and the broccoli, toss, and sauté for 5 minutes. Add the eggs and the paprika, toss, put the lid on and cook on High for 15 minutes more. Release the pressure naturally for 10 minutes, sprinkle the cheese on top, leave the mix aside for a couple more minutes, divide it between plates and serve for breakfast.
Nutrition: calories 227, fat 14.8, fiber 4, carbs 6.7, protein 16

Meat Muffins with Quail Eggs

Preparation time: 10 minutes
Cooking time: 22 minutes
Servings: 4
Ingredients:
- 4 quail eggs
- 1 cup ground pork
- ¼ cup onion, diced
- 1 teaspoon garlic, diced
- ½ teaspoon salt
- ½ teaspoon chili flakes
- ½ teaspoon ground turmeric
- 1 teaspoon dried dill
- 2 tablespoons coconut flour
- 1 tablespoon ketchup
- 1 teaspoon olive oil
- 1 cup water, for cooking

Directions:
In the mixing bowl combine together ground pork, onion, garlic, salt, chili flakes, ground turmeric, dried dill, coconut flour, and ketchup. Then brush the muffin molds with olive oil gently. Fill every muffin mold with ground meat mixture and flatten the surface of prepared muffins well. Then pour water in the instant pot and insert the steamer rack. Arrange the muffins on the rack and close the lid. Cook the meat muffins for 20 minutes on Manual mode (high pressure). Then make a quick pressure release and open the lid. Crac the quail eggs on the surface of every muffin and close the lid. Cook the meal for 2 minutes more on Manual mode (high pressure). Use the quick pressure release.
Nutrition: calories 144, fat 8, fiber 4.5, carbs 9.1, protein 8.8

Pork Hash

Preparation time: 10 minutes
Cooking time: 20 minutes
Servings: 4
Ingredients:
- 2 tablespoons olive oil
- 1 spring onion, chopped
- 2 garlic cloves, minced
- 1 pound pork meat, ground
- 1 red bell pepper, chopped
- 1 green bell pepper, chopped
- ½ teaspoon Italian seasoning
- 2 tablespoons veggie stock
- 1 tablespoon cilantro, chopped

Directions:
Set your instant pot on sauté mode, add the oil, heat it up, add the onion and the garlic and sauté for 2 minutes. Add the meat and brown it for 3 minutes more. Add the rest of the ingredients, put the lid on and cook on High for 15 minutes more. Release the pressure naturally for 10 minutes, divide the hash between plates and serve for breakfast.
Nutrition: calories 104, fat 7.4, fiber 0.9, carbs 5.4, protein 1

Cinnamon Pancakes

Preparation time: 10 minutes
Cooking time: 45 minutes

Servings: 3
Ingredients:
- 2 eggs, beaten
- 1 teaspoon matcha green tea powder
- 1 teaspoon vanilla extract
- 1 teaspoon ground cinnamon
- 1 teaspoon baking powder
- 1 tablespoon apple cider vinegar
- 1 tablespoon Erythritol
- 1 tablespoon sesame oil
- 1 cup almond flour
- ¼ cup cream

Directions:
In the big bowl mix up together eggs, vanilla extract, apple cider vinegar, baking powder, and cream. Then add matcha green tea powder, ground cinnamon, Erythritol, and almond flour. Whisk the liquid until smooth. Brush the instant pot bowl with ½ tablespoon of sesame oil and pour the 1/3 part of all liquid inside. Cook it for 15 minutes on Manual mode (low pressure). Cook the pancake for an additional 5 minutes for the golden-brown crust. Repeat the same steps with the remaining batter. In the end, you should get 3 pancakes.
Nutrition: calories 157, fat 13.3, fiber 1.5, carbs 9.5, protein 5.9

Creamy Eggs Ramekins

Preparation time: 10 minutes
Cooking time: 5 minutes
Servings: 4
Ingredients:
- 2 tablespoons ghee, melted
- ¼ cup cream cheese
- 2 tablespoons heavy cream
- 4 eggs, whisked
- 1 teaspoon hot paprika
- 1 tablespoon chives, chopped
- A pinch of salt and black pepper
- 1 cup water

Directions:
In a bowl, combine the cream cheese with the eggs and the rest of the ingredients except the chives and the water and whisk well. Divide this into 4 ramekins and sprinkle the chives on top. Put the water in the instant pot, add the steamer basket inside, put the ramekins in the pot, put the lid on and cook on High for 5 minutes. Release the pressure naturally for 10 minutes and serve the eggs hot.
Nutrition: calories 196, fat 18.6, fiber 0, carbs 1, protein 6.8

Cinnamon Pancakes

Preparation time: 10 minutes
Cooking time: 45 minutes
Servings: 3
Ingredients:
- 2 eggs, beaten
- 1 teaspoon matcha green tea powder
- 1 teaspoon vanilla extract
- 1 teaspoon ground cinnamon
- 1 teaspoon baking powder
- 1 tablespoon apple cider vinegar
- 1 tablespoon Erythritol
- 1 tablespoon sesame oil
- 1 cup almond flour
- ¼ cup cream

Directions:
In the big bowl mix up together eggs, vanilla extract, apple cider vinegar, baking powder, and cream. Then add matcha green tea powder, ground cinnamon, Erythritol, and almond flour. Whisk the liquid until smooth. Brush the instant pot bowl with ½ tablespoon of sesame oil and pour the 1/3 part of all liquid inside. Cook it for 15 minutes on Manual mode (low pressure). Cook the pancake for an additional 5 minutes for the golden-brown crust. Repeat the same steps with the remaining batter. In the end, you should get 3 pancakes.
Nutrition: calories 157, fat 13.3, fiber 1.5, carbs 9.5, protein 5.9

Avocado and Broccoli Salad

Preparation time: 10 minutes
Cooking time: 16 minutes
Servings: 4
Ingredients:
- 2 cup broccoli florets
- ¼ cup coconut milk
- ½ cup cheddar cheese, shredded
- A pinch of salt and black pepper
- 1 tablespoon chives, chopped
- 1 tablespoon avocado oil
- 1 tablespoon balsamic vinegar
- 1 avocado, peeled, pitted and cubed
- 1 cup baby arugula

Directions:
In your instant pot, combine the broccoli with the except the milk, cheese, salt and pepper, toss, put the lid on and cook on High for 12 minutes. Release the pressure naturally for 10 minutes, cool the broccoli mix a bit, transfer it to a bowl, add the avocado and the remaining ingredients, toss and serve.
Nutrition: calories 216, fat 18.7, fiber 5, carbs 7.6, protein 7

Paprika Eggs in Pepper Holes

Preparation time: 20 minutes
Cooking time: 5 minutes
Servings: 4
Ingredients:
- 2 bell pepper
- 4 eggs
- 4 Cheddar cheese sliced
- ½ teaspoon salt
- 1 teaspoon olive oil
- 1 cup water, for cooking

Directions:
Slice the bell pepper into the rings. Then pour water in the instant pot and insert the steamer rack. Brush the instant pot pan with olive oil and insert the pepper rings inside. Crack the eggs in the pepper rings. Then sprinkle every eg with salt and top with cheese slice. Place the instant pot pan in the instant pot. Cook breakfast for 5 minutes on low pressure.
Nutrition: calories 172, fat 12.7, fiber 0.8, carbs 4.8, protein 11.2

Coconut Blueberry Pudding

Preparation time: 10 minutes
Cooking time: 25 minutes
Servings: 4
Ingredients:

- 1 and ½ cups coconut flour
- Zest of 1 lime, grated
- 2 teaspoons baking powder
- ½ cup ghee, melted
- ¾ cup swerve
- 1 teaspoon vanilla extract
- 1 egg, whisked
- ½ cup coconut milk
- 2 cups blueberries
- 1 cup water

Directions:
In a bowl, mix all the ingredients except the water, whisk well and divide into 4 ramekins. Add the water to your instant pot, add the steamer basket, add the ramekins inside, put the lid on and cook on High for 25 minutes. Release the pressure naturally for 10 minutes, and serve the puddings for breakfast.
Nutrition: calories 356, fat 34, fiber 2.5, carbs 10, protein 2.7

Stuffed Pepper Halves with Omelet

Preparation time: 15 minutes
Cooking time: 6 minutes
Servings: 4
Ingredients:
- 4 bell peppers
- 2 eggs, beaten
- 1 oz Mozzarella, shredded
- ¼ teaspoon chili powder
- 1 cup water, for cooking

Directions:
Cut the bell peppers into halves and remove the seeds. Then in the mixing bowl combine together eggs, chili powder, and Mozzarella cheese. Pour water in the instant pot and insert the steamer rack. Pour egg mixture in every pepper half and transfer the vegetables in the instant pot. Cook the meal for 6 minutes on low pressure.
Nutrition: calories 90, fat 3.8, fiber 1.7, carbs 9.5, protein 6

Bacon and Eggs

Preparation time: 10 minutes
Cooking time: 15 minutes
Servings: 4
Ingredients:
- 1 shallot, chopped
- 1 and ½ cups bacon, chopped
- 2 cups cheddar cheese, shredded
- 4 eggs, whisked
- 1 cup almond milk
- 1 tablespoon avocado oil
- A pinch of salt and black pepper

Directions:
Set the instant pot on Sauté mode, add the oil, heat it up, add the bacon and the shallot and cook for 2-3 minutes. Add the rest of the ingredients, toss, put the lid on and cook on High for 12 minutes. Release the pressure naturally for 10 minutes, divide the mix between plates and serve.
Nutrition: calories 392, fat 37, fiber 1.4, carbs 4.6, protein 21

Bacon Egg Cups

Preparation time: 15 minutes
Cooking time: 15 minutes
Servings: 2
Ingredients:
- 2 eggs
- 4 bacon slices
- ¼ teaspoon dried parsley
- 1 teaspoon butter, soften
- ¼ teaspoon salt

Directions:
Brush the muffin molds with butter. Then place the bacon slices in the muffin molds to cover the muffin molds sides. Crack the eggs in the muffin molds and sprinkle them with parsley and salt. Cover the molds with foil and arrange it in the instant pot. Cook the meal for 15 minutes on Saute mode.
Nutrition: calories 240, fat 20.3, fiber 0, carbs 0.4, protein 15.6

Broccoli and Cheese Pancake

Preparation time: 10 minutes
Cooking time: 25 minutes
Servings: 4
Ingredients:
- 2 cups coconut flour
- A pinch of salt and black pepper
- 3 eggs, whisked
- 1 teaspoon baking soda
- 1 and ½ cups almond milk
- 1 cup mozzarella, shredded
- 1 cup broccoli florets, grated
- Cooking spray

Directions:
In a bowl, mix the eggs with the eggs and the rest of the ingredients except the cooking spray and whisk well. Grease the instant pot with the cooking spray, add the pancake mix, spread, put the lid on and cook on High for 25 minutes. Release the pressure naturally for 10 minutes, divide the pancake between plates and serve for breakfast.
Nutrition: calories 76, fat 4.8, fiber 0.6, carbs 2, protein 6.8

Zucchini Meat Cups

Preparation time: 10 minutes
Cooking time: 15 minutes
Servings: 4
Ingredients:
- 1 cup zucchini, grated
- ½ cup ground beef
- 1.4 cup carrot, grated
- 1 teaspoon onion powder
- ½ teaspoon salt
- ¼ cup Cheddar cheese, shredded
- 1 tablespoon sesame oil
- ½ teaspoon ground black pepper
- 1 cup water, for cooking

Directions:
Squeeze the grated zucchini, if needed and place it in the big mixing bowl. Add ground beef, carrot, onion powder, salt, cheese, and ground black pepper. Then brush the muffin molds (cups) with sesame oil. Place the zucchini-meat mixture in the muffin molds. Pour water in the instant pot. Insert the steamer rack. Place the muffin molds with the meat-zucchini mixture in the instant pot. Cook the meal for 15 minutes on Manual (High pressure). Then allow the natural pressure release for 10 minutes.

Nutrition: calories 121, fat 7.1, fiber 1.4, carbs 5.5, protein 9

Tomato and Peppers Salad

Preparation time: 10 minutes
Cooking time: 10 minutes
Servings: 4
Ingredients:
- A pinch of salt and black pepper
- 3 cups baby spinach, chopped
- 1 pound cherry tomatoes, cubed
- 3 green onions, chopped
- 1 tablespoon olive oil
- 1 tablespoon balsamic vinegar
- ½ pound mixed bell peppers, cut into strips

Directions:
Set the instant pot on Sauté mode, add the oil, heat it up, add the onions and sauté for 2 minutes. Add the tomatoes and the rest of the ingredients, put the lid on and cook on High for 8 minutes. Release the pressure naturally for 10 minutes, divide the mix into bowls and serve for breakfast.
Nutrition: calories 60, fat 8.1, fiber 2, carbs 6.1, protein 1.9

Green Hash

Preparation time: 10 minutes
Cooking time: 10 minutes
Servings: 2
Ingredients:
- ½ cup fresh spinach, chopped
- ½ cup fresh parsley, chopped
- ¼ cup cauliflower, shredded
- 2 eggs, beaten
- 1 teaspoon avocado oil
- ½ teaspoon ground black pepper
- ½ teaspoon salt
- ½ cup Cheddar cheese, shredded

Directions:
Brush the instant pot bowl with avocado oil. After this, in the mixing bowl mix up together eggs, parsley, spinach, cauliflower, ground black pepper, salt, and cheese. Stir the mixture until homogenous and transfer in the instant pot bowl. Flatten the mixture with the help of the wooden spatula and close the lid. Cook the green hash for 10 minutes on High pressure (Manual mode). Then make a quick pressure release and open the lid. Cool the green hash to the room temperature and cut into servings.
Nutrition: calories 191, fat 14.2, fiber 1.2, carbs 3.1, protein 13.6

Chili Frittata

Preparation time: 10 minutes
Cooking time: 30 minutes
Servings: 4
Ingredients:
- 1 cup heavy cream
- 4 eggs, whisked
- 10 ounces canned green chilies
- A pinch of salt and black pepper
- ½ teaspoon sweet paprika
- 1 teaspoon chili powder
- 1 tablespoon cilantro, chopped
- 1 tablespoon avocado oil

Directions:
In a bowl, mix the eggs with the rest of the ingredients except the oil and whisk well. Grease the instant pot with the oil, pour the eggs mixture, spread, put the lid on and cook on High for 30 minutes. Release the pressure naturally for 10 minutes, divide the frittata between plates and serve for breakfast.
Nutrition: calories 404, fat 20.2, fiber 8.9, carbs 11.1, protein 14.6

Breakfast Avocado Bombs

Preparation time: 20 minutes
Cooking time: 8 minutes
Servings: 2
Ingredients:
- 1 avocado, peeled, halved, pitted
- 5 bacon slices
- 1 oz Cheddar cheese, shredded
- ½ teaspoon avocado oil
- ¼ teaspoon white pepper
- 1 cup water, for cooking

Directions:
Mix up together cheese with white pepper. Then fill every avocado half with cheese mixture and stick them together. Wrap the avocado in the bacon slices and brush with avocado oil. Wrap the avocado in foil. Pour water in the instant pot and insert the steamer rack. Place the wrapped avocado in the instant pot and cook for 8 minutes on Manual mode (high pressure). Then allow natural pressure release for 10 minutes. Remove the cooked avocado from the foil, cut it into halves and transfer in the serving plates.
Nutrition: calories 540, fat 46.5, fiber 6.8, carbs 9.7, protein 23.1

Cheesy Beef Casserole

Preparation time: 10 minutes
Cooking time: 25 minutes
Servings: 6
Ingredients:
- 1 pound beef, ground
- 4 eggs, whisked
- 1 red bell pepper, chopped
- ½ cup green onions, chopped
- 1 tablespoon olive oil
- 1 cup mozzarella cheese, shredded
- 1 tablespoon cilantro, chopped

Directions:
Set your instant pot on sauté mode, add the oil, heat it up, add the meat and brown for 5 minutes. Add the rest of the ingredients except the cheese and the cilantro and toss. Sprinkle the cheese on top, put the lid on and cook on High for 20 minutes. Release the pressure naturally for 10 minutes, divide the mix between plates, sprinkle the cilantro on top and serve.
Nutrition: calories 224, fat 10.9, fiber 0.5, carbs 2.5, protein 28.2

Spiced Hard-Boiled Eggs

Preparation time: 15 minutes
Cooking time: 10 minutes
Servings: 4
Ingredients:
- 4 eggs
- ½ teaspoon dried sage

- ¼ teaspoon chili flakes
- 1 teaspoon butter, softened
- ¼ teaspoon dried parsley
- ¼ teaspoon dried thyme
- 1 cup water, for cooking

Directions:
Pour water in the instant pot and insert the steamer rack. Place the eggs on the rack and close the lid. Cook the eggs on Manual (high pressure) for 5 minutes. Then make a quick pressure release. Cool the eggs in ice water for 10 minutes. Meanwhile, churn together sage, butter, chili flakes, parsley, and thyme. Then peel the eggs and cut them into halves. Spread every egg half with a spiced butter mixture.
Nutrition: calories 72 fat 5.3, fiber 0.1, carbs 0.5, protein 5.6

Asparagus and Eggs Mix

Preparation time: 5 minutes
Cooking time: 20 minutes
Servings: 6
Ingredients:
- 1 asparagus stalk, halved
- 6 eggs, whisked
- ¼ cup scallions, chopped
- 1 red chili pepper, chopped
- A pinch of salt and black pepper
- ¼ teaspoon chili powder
- 1 tablespoon olive oil

Directions:
Set the instant pot on Sauté mode, add the oil, heat it up, add the asparagus and the scallions and cook for 2-3 minutes. Add the eggs and the rest of the ingredients, toss, put the lid on and cook on High for 15 minutes. Release the pressure fast for 5 minutes, divide the mix between plates and serve.
Nutrition: calories 85, fat 6.7, fiber 0.2, carbs 0.8, protein 5.6

Minced Beef Pancakes

Preparation time: 10 minutes
Cooking time: 14 minutes
Servings: 2
Ingredients:
- 7 oz minced beef
- 1 egg, beaten
- 1 tablespoon coconut flour
- 1 teaspoon ground black pepper
- ½ teaspoon ground turmeric
- 1 teaspoon garlic powder
- 1 teaspoon coconut oil
- 1 teaspoon dried parsley

Directions:
Mix up together minced beef and egg. Add ground black pepper, coconut flour, and turmeric. After this, add garlic powder and dried parsley. Grease the instant pot bowl with coconut oil. After this, transfer the meat mixture in the instant pot and flatten it well in the shape of a pancake. Cook the meat pancake on Saute mode for 7 minutes from each side. Transfer the cooked beef pancake on the paper towel to get rid of extra oil. Cut the cooked meal into halves.
Nutrition: calories 260, fat 11.1, fiber 2.1, carbs 4.8, protein 33.8

Chia and Blueberries Bowls

Preparation time: 5 minutes
Cooking time: 10 minutes
Servings: 4
Ingredients:
- ¼ cup chia seeds
- 1 cup blueberries
- 1/3 cup almonds, chopped
- 1 and ½ cup almond milk
- 1 teaspoon vanilla extract
- 2 tablespoons stevia

Directions:
In your instant pot, combine the chia seeds with the rest of the ingredients, put the lid on and cook on High for 10 minutes. Release the pressure fast for 5 minutes, divide the mix into bowls and serve for breakfast.
Nutrition: calories 70, fat 4.1, fiber 1.9, carbs 4.3, protein 2

Ham Roll

Preparation time: 15 minutes
Cooking time: 3 hours
Servings: 4
Ingredients:
- 1-pound spiral ham, raw, sliced
- ½ cup Mozzarella, shredded
- 1 teaspoon salt
- 1 teaspoon ground paprika
- ½ teaspoon dried thyme
- ½ teaspoon dried rosemary
- 1 teaspoon avocado oil
- 1 tablespoon mustard
- 1 cup water, for cooking

Directions:
Sprinkle the sliced ham with salt, ground paprika, thyme, and rosemary. Then place the ham on the chopping board in one layer. Sprinkle the surface of the ham with shredded Mozzarella and roll it. Brush the ham roll with mustard and wrap in the foil. Pour water in the instant pot and insert the steamer rack. Place the wrapped ham roll in the instant pot and cook it on Manual mode (Low pressure) for 3 hours.
Nutrition: calories 148, fat 4.6, fiber 0.8, carbs 2.5, protein 23.2

Almond Cocoa and Strawberries Mix

Preparation time: 10 minutes
Cooking time: 10 minutes
Servings: 4
Ingredients:
- 3 cups almond milk
- ½ cup coconut cream
- 2 and ½ tablespoon cocoa powder
- 2 cups strawberries, halved
- 1 teaspoon vanilla extract
- 1 teaspoon cinnamon powder

Directions:
In your instant pot, combine the almond milk with the rest of the ingredients, toss, put the lid on and cook on High for 10 minutes. Release the pressure naturally for 10 minutes, divide the strawberry mix into bowls and serve for breakfast.
Nutrition: calories 312, fat 14.5, fiber 4.6, carbs 7.9, protein 5.6

Fluffy Eggs

Preparation time: 10 minutes
Cooking time: 5 minutes
Servings: 1
Ingredients:
- 2 eggs
- ¼ teaspoon chives
- ½ teaspoon chili flakes
- 1 teaspoon sesame oil

Directions:
Brush the instant pot bowl with sesame oil. Then crack eggs in the bowl and separate the egg whites and egg yolks. Whisk the egg whites until you get soft peaks. Preheat the instant pot on Saute mode for 3 minutes. With the help of the spoon make 2 rounds from the egg whites in the instant pot and cook them on Saute mode for 2 minutes. After this, place the egg yolks in the center of every egg white round. Sprinkle them with chives and chili flakes. Close the lid and cook the eggs on Saute mode for 3 minutes more or until the egg yolks are solid.
Nutrition: calories 166, fat 13.3, fiber 0, carbs 0.7, protein 11.1

Coconut Yogurt Mix

Preparation time: 5 minutes
Cooking time: 5 minutes
Servings: 2
Ingredients:
- 1 cup coconut milk
- ½ cup coconut, unsweetened and flaked
- 1 cup yogurt
- ½ teaspoon stevia
- ¼ teaspoon vanilla extract
- ½ teaspoon cinnamon powder

Directions:
In your instant pot, combine the coconut milk with the coconut and the rest of the ingredients, toss, put the lid on and cook on High for 5 minutes. Release the pressure fast for 5 minutes, divide the yogurt mix into bowls and serve.
Nutrition: calories 218, fat 18.4, fiber 2.2, carbs 6.7, protein 5.2

Bacon Eggs with Chives

Preparation time: 7 minutes
Cooking time: 10 minutes
Servings: 2
Ingredients:
- 2 eggs
- 1 tablespoon chives
- 2 bacon slices, chopped
- ¼ teaspoon almond butter
- ¼ teaspoon salt
- ¼ teaspoon ground black pepper

Directions:
Preheat the instant pot on Saute mode for 4 minutes. Then place the chopped bacon inside and cook it for 3 minutes. Stir the bacon and crack the eggs over it. Add almond butter. Sprinkle the eggs with salt and ground black pepper. Close the lid. Cook the eggs for 2 minutes on Saute mode. Then open the lid and sprinkle the eggs with chives. Cook them for 1 minute more.
Nutritiosn: calories 179, fat 13.5, fiber 0.3, carbs 1.2, protein 13.1

Artichokes Pudding

Preparation time: 10 minutes
Cooking time: 15 minutes
Servings: 4
Ingredients:
- 2 cups almond milk
- ¼ cup coconut cream
- 1 and ½ cups canned artichokes, drained and chopped
- 1 teaspoon sweet paprika
- A pinch of salt and black pepper
- 1 tablespoon chives, chopped

Directions:
In your instant pot, mix the almond milk with cream and the rest of the ingredients, put the lid on and cook on High for 15 minutes. Release the pressure naturally for 10 minutes, divide the mix between plates and serve.
Nutrition: calories 312, fat 23.4, fiber 3.2, carbs 7.3, protein 3.2

Avocado Boats with Omelet

Preparation time: 15 minutes
Cooking time: 10 minutes
Servings: 2
Ingredients:
- 1 avocado, halved, pitted
- 2 eggs, beaten
- 1 tablespoon cream
- 1 teaspoon fresh dill
- 1 oz Parmesan, grated
- 1 cup water, for cooking

Directions:
Remove ½ part of avocado meat with the help of the scooper. You will get avocado boats. In the mixing bowl combine together eggs, cream, dill, and Parmesan. Pour the egg mixture in the prepared avocado boats. Pour water and insert the steamer rack in the instant pot. Carefully arrange the avocado boats in the instant pot. You can cover the surface of every avocado boat with foil if desired. Cook the meal for 10 minutes on Steam mode.
Nutrition: calories 319, fat 27.4, fiber 6.8, carbs 10, protein 10

Scotch Eggs and Tomato Passata

Preparation time: 6 minutes
Cooking time: 18 minutes
Servings: 4
Ingredients:
- 1 pound pork, ground
- A pinch of salt and black pepper
- 1 teaspoon cilantro, chopped
- 1 teaspoon hot paprika
- 4 eggs, hard boiled and peeled
- 1 tablespoon avocado oil
- 1 cup tomato passata

Directions:
In a bowl, mix the pork with the rest of the ingredients except the eggs, tomato passata and the oil and stir well. Divide the mix into 4 balls and flatten them on a working surface. Divide the eggs on each pork ball and wrap them well. Set the instant pot on Sauté mode, add the oil, heat it up, add the scotch eggs and brown them for 2 minutes on each side. Add the tomato passata, put the lid on and cook

on High for 12 minutes. Release pressure fast for 6 minutes, divide the mix between plates and serve for breakfast.
Nutrition: calories 245, fat 8.9, fiber 1.1, carbs 3.9, protein 36

Breakfast Egg Hash

Preparation time: 10 minutes
Cooking time: 20 minutes
Servings: 4
Ingredients:
- 4 eggs, beaten
- 6 oz celery stalk, chopped
- 1 cup bok choy, chopped
- ¼ white onion, diced
- 1 teaspoon ground paprika
- ½ teaspoon salt
- 1 tablespoon butter
- ½ teaspoon dried basil

Directions:
Preheat the instant pot on Saute mode for 3 minutes. Then add butter and melt it on the same cooking mode. Add chopped bok choy and celery stalk. Then add onion and mix up the vegetable mixture well. After this, close the lid and sauté the ingredients for 5 minutes. Open the lid and mix up the mixture one more time. In the mixing bowl combine together eggs with salt and ground paprika. Pour the egg mixture over the vegetables and stir gently. Close the lid and cook the hash brown for 10 minutes pr until eggs are firm.
Nutrition: calories 102, fat 7.4, fiber 1.2, carbs 2.9, protein 6.3

Parsley Cauliflower Mix

Preparation time: 10 minutes
Cooking time: 20 minutes
Servings: 4
Ingredients:
- 2 cups cauliflower florets
- 2 ounces cheddar cheese, shredded
- 1 teaspoon garlic powder
- 1 teaspoon chili powder
- 2 eggs, whisked
- 1 tablespoon parsley, chopped
- 1 tablespoon avocado oil
- ½ cup heavy cream
- A pinch of salt and black pepper

Directions:
Set your instant pot on sauté mode, add the oil, heat it up, add the cauliflower, garlic and chili powder and cook for 5 minutes. Add the rest of the ingredients, toss, put the lid on and cook on High for 15 minutes. Release the pressure naturally for 10 minutes, divide the mix into bowls and serve for breakfast.
Nutrition: calories 164, fat 13.1, fiber 1.7, carbs 4.6, protein 7.9

Bacon Tacos

Preparation time: 15 minutes
Cooking time: 5 minutes
Servings: 4
Ingredients:
- 10 bacon slices
- ½ cup Cheddar cheese, shredded
- ½ cup white cabbage, shredded
- 1 tablespoon taco seasonings
- 1 teaspoon coconut oil
- 8 oz chicken breast, skinless, boneless
- 1 tomato, chopped

Directions:
Rub the chicken breast with Taco seasonings well and place it in the instant pot. Add coconut oil and cook the chicken for 20 minutes on Saute mode. Flip the chicken breast after 10 minutes of cooking. Then remove the cooked chicken from the instant pot and chop it. Line the table with paper foil. Put the bacon crosswise on it to get the shape of the net. Then with the help of the round cutter make 4 rounds (tortillas). Preheat the instant pot on Saute mode well. Then place the first bacon round. Cook it for 3 minutes from each side. Repeat the same steps with all bacon rounds. After this, place the cooked bacon "net" on the plate. Top every bacon "net" with chopped chicken, cheese, and tomato. Fold it in the shape of tacos.
Nutrition: calories 401, fat 27.1, fiber 0.4, carbs 3.5, protein 33.4

Pork Pie

Preparation time: 10 minutes
Cooking time: 30 minutes
Servings: 4
Ingredients:
- ½ cup heavy cream
- A pinch of salt and black pepper
- 4 eggs, whisked
- 2 cups pork meat, ground and browned
- 2 green onions, chopped
- 1 cup cheddar cheese, shredded
- 1 cup water

Directions:
In a bowl, mix the eggs with the rest of the ingredients except the water, whisk well and spread into a pie pan. Add the water to your instant pot, add the trivet, add the pan inside, put the lid on and cook on High for 30 minutes. Release the pressure naturally for 10 minutes, divide the mix between plates and serve hot for breakfast.
Nutrition: calories 231, fat 19.3, fiber 0.2, carbs 1.7, protein 13

Mason Jar Omelet

Preparation time: 10 minutes
Cooking time: 8 minutes
Servings: 2
Ingredients:
- 2 eggs, beaten
- ¼ cup heavy cream
- ¼ cup Mozzarella, shredded
- ½ teaspoon salt
- 1 teaspoon ground black pepper
- 1 tablespoon fresh dill, chopped
- 1 teaspoon coconut oil, melted
- 1 cup water, for cooking

Directions:
Mix up together eggs with heavy cream, salt, cheese, ground black pepper, and dill. Then brush every mason jar with coconut oil gently. Pour the egg mixture in every mason jar. Pour water in the instant pot and insert the steamer rack. Arrange the mason jars on the rack and close the lid. Cook the omelet for 8 minutes on Manual mode (High pressure). Then

make quick pressure release and remove the mason jars from the instant pot.
Nutrition: calories 151, fat 12.9, fiber 0.5, carbs 2.4, protein 7.3

Ginger Cauliflower Rice Pudding
Preparation time: 10 minutes
Cooking time: 15 minutes
Servings: 4
Ingredients:
- 2 cups almond milk
- 1 cup cauliflower rice
- 1 teaspoon cinnamon powder
- 1 tablespoon ginger, grated
- 3 tablespoons stevia
- 1 teaspoon vanilla extract

Directions:
In your instant pot, mix the cauliflower rice with the milk and the other ingredients, toss, put the lid on and cook on High for 15 minutes. Release the pressure naturally for 10 minutes, stir the pudding, divide it into bowls and serve.
Nutrition: calories 284, fat 28.7, fiber 2.8, carbs 7.7, protein 2.9

Cauliflower Bake
Preparation time: 15 minutes
Cooking time: 2 minutes
Servings: 4
Ingredients:
- 1-pound cauliflower, chopped
- ½ teaspoon ground black pepper
- 3 oz Parmesan, grated
- ½ cup cream
- 1 teaspoon dried cilantro
- 1 teaspoon garlic powder
- 1 teaspoon mustard
- 1 cup water, for cooking

Directions:
Pour water in the instant pot and insert the steamer rack. Place the cauliflower in the rack and cook it on Manual mode (High pressure) for 2 minutes. Make a quick pressure release. After this, place the hot cauliflower in the big bowl. Add cheese, ground black pepper, cilantro, cream, garlic powder, and mustard. Mix up the cauliflower well until cheese is melted.
Nutrition: calories 123, fat 6.6, fiber 3.1, carbs 8.7, protein 9.7

Bok Choy Bowls
Preparation time: 10 minutes
Cooking time: 20 minutes
Servings: 4
Ingredients:
- 1 and ½ cups veggie stock
- 2 cups bok choy, roughly torn
- 2 tablespoons ginger, grated
- 2 garlic cloves, minced
- 1 tablespoon coconut aminos
- 1 tablespoon sweet paprika
- 2 tomatoes, cubed
- A pinch of salt and black pepper

Directions:
In your instant pot, mix the bok choy with the stock and the rest of the ingredients, toss, put the lid on and cook on High for 20 minutes. Release the pressure naturally for 10 minutes, divide the mix into bowls and serve for breakfast.
Nutrition: calories 89, fat 6.8, fiber 2.1, carbs 6.1, protein 1.7

Cauliflower Toast
Preparation time: 15 minutes
Cooking time: 8 minutes
Servings: 2
Ingredients:
- ½ cup cauliflower, shredded
- ½ cup ground chicken
- 1 teaspoon butter
- 1 tablespoon coconut flour, ground
- ½ teaspoon salt
- ¼ cup Cheddar cheese

Directions:
Mix up together shredded cauliflower and ground chicken. Add coconut flour and salt. Make balls from the mixture. After this, press them gently to get the shape of toasts. Place butter in the instant pot and melt it on Saute mode. Then arrange the prepared cauliflower toast in the instant pot. Cook the toasts for 4 minutes from each side or until they are light brown. Place the cooked toasts in the plate and top with Cheddar cheese.
Nutrition: calories 156, fat 9.4, fiber 0.9, carbs 3.2, protein 14.5

Mushroom and Avocado Salad
Preparation time: 10 minutes
Cooking time: 20 minutes
Servings: 4
Ingredients:
- 2 avocados, pitted, peeled and cubed
- 1 tablespoon olive oil
- 1 tablespoon chives, chopped
- A pinch of salt and black pepper
- ½ pound white mushrooms, sliced
- 1 tablespoon balsamic vinegar
- ½ cup veggie stock
- 1 cup baby arugula

Directions:
Set the instant pot on Sauté mode, add the oil, heat it up, add the mushrooms and cook for 4 minutes. Add the rest of the ingredients except the avocado and the arugula, put the lid on and cook on High for 15 minutes. Release the pressure naturally for 10 minutes, transfer the mix to a bowl, add the avocado and the arugula, toss and serve for breakfast.
Nutrition: calories 250, fat 23.3, fiber 6.4, carbs 7.6, protein 3.8

Sausage Casserole
Preparation time: 10 minutes
Cooking time: 50 minutes
Servings: 5
Ingredients:
- 10 ground Italian sausages
- 1 teaspoon Italian seasonings
- 4 eggs, beaten
- ½ teaspoon salt
- 1 teaspoon sesame oil
- ¼ cup Cheddar cheese, shredded
- 1 cup water, for cooking

Directions:

Preheat the instant pot on Sauté mode for 5 minutes. Then pour sesame oil inside, add Italian sausages. Cook them for 10 minutes on sauté mode. Stir the sausages every 2 minutes. Meanwhile, mix up together eggs, salt, Italian seasonings, and Cheddar cheese. When the ground sausages are cooked, add them in the egg mixture and stir. Transfer the mixture in the baking pan and flatten it. Then clean the instant pot bowl and pour water inside. Insert the steamer rack. Place the baking pan with casserole in the instant pot. Cook it for 35 minutes on Sauté mode.
Nutrition: calories 424, fat 32.6, fiber 0, carbs 2.4, protein 25.8

Salmon and Eggs Mix

Preparation time: 10 minutes
Cooking time: 12 minutes
Servings: 4
Ingredients:
- 4 ounces smoked salmon, skinless, boneless and cut into strips
- 4 eggs
- A pinch of salt and black pepper
- ½ cup coconut cream
- 1 tablespoon chives, chopped
- 1 tablespoon cilantro, chopped
- Cooking spray

Directions:
In a bowl, mix the salmon with the eggs and the rest of the ingredients except the cooking spray and whisk well. Grease the instant pot with the cooking spray, pour the salmon mix, spread, put the lid on and cook on High for 12 minutes. Release the pressure naturally for 10 minutes, divide the mix between plates and serve.
Nutrition: calories 167, fat 12.9, fiber 0.7, carbs 2.1, protein 11.4

Frittata with Greens

Preparation time: 10 minutes
Cooking time: 10 minutes
Servings: 2
Ingredients:
- 2 eggs, beaten
- 2 tablespoons heavy cream
- 1/3 cup fresh spinach, chopped
- ¼ cup fresh arugula, chopped
- 1 teaspoon coconut oil, melted
- ½ teaspoon ground paprika
- ¼ teaspoon salt
- 1 cup water, for cooking

Directions:
In the mixing bowl mix up together eggs, heavy cream, arugula, spinach, salt, and ground paprika Then brush the baking pan with melted coconut oil. Pour the egg mixture in the baking pan. Pour water and insert the steamer rack in the instant pot. Place the baking pan with frittata on the rack and close the lid. Cook the frittata for 10 minutes on Manual mode (high pressure).
Nutrition: calories 138, fat 12.3, fiber 0.4, carbs 1.3, protein 6.1

Italian Beef and Green Beans Mix

Preparation time: 10 minutes
Cooking time: 30 minutes
Servings: 6
Ingredients:
- 2 spring onions chopped
- 1 red bell pepper, chopped
- 1 pound beef, ground
- ½ cup veggie stock
- A pinch of salt and black pepper
- 1 tablespoon Italian seasoning
- 1 tablespoon cilantro, chopped
- 1 teaspoon olive oil
- ½ pound green beans, trimmed and halved

Directions:
Set your instant pot on sauté mode, add the oil, heat it up, add the meat Italian seasoning, salt and pepper and brown for 5 minutes. Add the rest of the ingredients, toss, put the lid on and cook on High for 25 minutes. Release the pressure naturally for 10 minutes, divide everything between plates and serve for breakfast.
Nutrition: calories 259, fat 9.4, fiber 2.4, carbs 6.7, protein 35.8

Cheese Egg Balls

Preparation time: 10 minutes
Cooking time: 14 minutes
Servings: 4
Ingredients:
- 4 eggs, beaten
- ½ cup Mozzarella, shredded
- 1 teaspoon dried basil
- 1 tablespoon heavy cream
- 1 cup water, for cooking

Directions:
Mix up together eggs, dried basil, and heavy cream. Then pour the liquid in the silicone egg molds. Top every mold with Mozzarella. Then pour water in the instant pot and insert the trivet. Place the silicone egg molds on the trivet. Cook the egg balls for 7 minutes on Manual mode (High pressure). Then allow the natural pressure release for 7 minutes more. Cool the egg balls to the room temperature and remove from the silicone molds.
Nutrition: calories 86, fat 6.4, fiber 0, carbs 0.6, protein 6.6

Herbed Mushroom Mix

Preparation time: 10 minutes
Cooking time: 20 minutes
Servings: 4
Ingredients:
- 1 and ½ pounds brown mushrooms, chopped
- 2 tablespoons chicken stock
- A pinch of salt and black pepper
- 1 tablespoon olive oil
- ½ teaspoon garlic powder
- ½ teaspoon basil, dried
- 1 teaspoon rosemary, chopped
- 1 red bell pepper, cut into strips

Directions:
Set your instant pot on sauté mode, add the oil, heat it up, add the mushrooms, stir and sauté for 5 minutes. Add the rest of the ingredients, put the lid on and cook on High for 15 minutes. Release the pressure naturally for 10 minutes, divide the mix between plates and serve for breakfast.

Nutrition: calories 42, fat 3.7, fiber 0.6, carbs 2.7, protein 0.4

Breakfast Crustless Quiche

Preparation time: 10 minutes
Cooking time: 25 minutes
Servings: 8
Ingredients:
- 7 eggs, beaten
- 3 oz Gouda cheese, shredded
- 6 oz Feta cheese, crumbled
- ½ teaspoon white pepper
- 1 tablespoon fresh dill, chopped
- ¼ cup dried tomatoes, chopped
- ¼ cup heavy cream
- 1 cup fresh spinach, chopped
- 1 teaspoon sesame oil
- ½ teaspoon salt
- 1 cup water, for cooking

Directions:
Pour water in the instant pot and insert the trivet. After this, in the mixing bowl combine together eggs, Gouda and Feta cheese, white pepper, fresh dill, dried tomatoes, heavy cream, spinach, and salt. Brush the round baking pan with sesame oil from inside and pour egg mixture inside. Insert the baking pan on the trivet and close the lid. Cook the quiche for 25 minutes on manual mode (High pressure). Allow the natural pressure release. Cool the cooked quiche for 5-10 minutes and then cut into the servings.
Nutrition: calories 170, fat 13.3, fiber 0.2, carbs 2.2, protein 10.8

Creamy Zucchini Pan

Preparation time: 10 minutes
Cooking time: 20 minutes
Servings: 4
Ingredients:
- 4 zucchinis, sliced
- 1 tablespoon avocado oil
- 1 shallot, minced
- ¼ cup heavy cream
- 2 tablespoons parsley, chopped
- 6 eggs, whisked
- 2 tablespoons cheddar, grated
- A pinch of salt and black pepper

Directions:
Set the instant pot on Sauté mode, add the oil, heat it up, add the shallot and sauté for 2-3 minutes. Add the zucchinis and the rest of the ingredients, toss, put the lid on and cook on High for 15 minutes. Release the pressure naturally for 10 minutes, divide the mix between plates and serve for breakfast.
Nutrition: calories 163, fat 10.4, fiber 2.4, carbs 7.7, protein 11.8

Breakfast Taco Omelet

Preparation time: 10 minutes
Cooking time: 35 minutes
Servings: 2
Ingredients:
- 1 cup ground beef
- 1 teaspoon taco seasonings
- 3 eggs, beaten
- ¼ cup heavy cream
- 1 teaspoon dried basil
- ¼ teaspoon dried oregano
- 1 teaspoon butter

Directions:
Preheat the instant pot on sauté mode for 2 minutes. Then place the butter in the hot instant pot and melt it. Add ground beef and taco seasonings. Mix up well. Sauté the meat mixture for 10 minutes. Stir it every 2 minutes. Meanwhile, in the mixing bowl mix up together eggs, cream, dried basil, and dried oregano. Pour the egg mixture over the cooked meat and cook on sauté mode for 25 minutes or until the omelet is firm.
Nutrition: calories 298, fat 22.2, fiber 0.1, carbs 2.1, protein 21.7

Leeks and Pork Mix

Preparation time: 10 minutes
Cooking time: 30 minutes
Servings: 4
Ingredients:
- 1 pound pork meat, ground
- ¼ cup coconut cream
- 2 leeks, chopped
- 4 eggs, whisked
- 1 tablespoon sweet paprika
- 1 tablespoon chives, chopped
- A pinch of salt and black pepper
- ¼ teaspoon garlic powder
- 1 tablespoon olive oil

Directions:
Set your instant pot on sauté mode, add the oil, heat it up, add the leeks and sauté for 5 minutes. Add the meat and brown for 4-5 minutes more. Add the eggs and the rest of the ingredients, toss, put the lid on and cook on High for 20 minutes. Release the pressure naturally for 10 minutes, divide the mix between plates and serve for breakfast.
Nutrition: calories 160, fat 11.8, fiber 1.8, carbs 7.1, protein 6.9

Keto Shakshuka

Preparation time: 5 minutes
Cooking time: 20 minutes
Servings: 2
Ingredients:
- 2 eggs
- 1 bell pepper, chopped
- 1 garlic clove, diced
- ½ white onion, diced
- ¼ teaspoon salt
- 1 tablespoon marinara sauce
- 1 teaspoon tomato paste
- ¼ cup of water
- 1 tablespoon coconut oil
- ½ cup kale, chopped
- ½ teaspoon ground cumin

Directions:
Preheat the instant pot on sauté mode. Then add coconut oil and melt it. When the oil starts shimmering, add diced onion and garlic. Saute the vegetables for 3 minutes. Then add salt, marinara sauce, tomato paste, water, and kale. Sprinkle the mixture with ground cumin and bell pepper. Mix up well. Saute the vegetables for 5 minutes or until they are soft. After this, crack the eggs over the vegetables and close the lid. Saute the meal for 10 minutes more.

Nutrition: calories 173, fat 11.7, fiber 2, carbs 11.5, protein 7.4

Cardamom Walnuts Pudding

Preparation time: 5 minutes
Cooking time: 10 minutes
Servings: 2
Ingredients:
- 1 teaspoon cardamom, ground
- ½ cup walnuts, chopped
- 1 teaspoon swerve
- 1 and ½ cups coconut cream
- 2 tablespoons almond meal

Directions:
In your instant pot, mix the cream with the cardamom and the rest of the ingredients, toss, put the lid on and cook on High for 10 minutes. Release the pressure fast for 5 minutes, divide everything into bowls and serve.
Nutrition: calories 231, fat 21.9, fiber 3.2, carbs 5.1, protein 8.9

Morning Bacon Bombs

Preparation time: 15 minutes
Cooking time: 1 minute
Servings: 4
Ingredients:
- 8 oz cauliflower
- 2 tablespoons cream cheese
- 4 bacon slices, cooked, chopped
- 1 teaspoon fresh parsley, chopped
- ½ teaspoon ground black pepper
- ¼ teaspoon garlic powder
- ½ teaspoon chili flakes
- 1 cup water, for cooking

Directions:
Pour water in the instant pot and insert trivet. Then place cauliflower on the trivet and cook for 1 minute on Manual (high pressure). Then make a quick pressure release. Remove the cauliflower from the instant pot and chop it into the tiny pieces or just mash with the help of the fork. Place the prepared cauliflower in the bowl. Add cream cheese, parsley, ground black pepper, garlic powder, and chili flakes. Mix up the mixture with the help of the spoon until you get a smooth mixture. After this, with the help of the scooper, make cauliflower balls. Coat every ball in the bacon mixture. Store the bacon balls in the fridge for up to 1 day.
Nutrition: calories 136, fat 9.8, fiber 1.5, carbs 3.7, protein 8.6

Basil Eggs Mix

Preparation time: 5 minutes
Cooking time: 15 minutes
Servings: 4
Ingredients:
- 2 tablespoons basil, chopped
- Cooking spray
- A pinch of salt and black pepper
- 4 eggs, whisked
- 1 cup cheddar cheese, shredded
- 1 teaspoon chili powder

Directions:
Grease the instant pot with the cooking spray, add the eggs and the rest of the ingredients, toss, put the lid on and cook on High for 15 minutes. Release the pressure fast for 5 minutes, divide the mix between plates and serve for breakfast.
Nutrition: calories 180, fat 14, fiber 0.3, carbs 1.1, protein 12.7

Egg Muffins

Preparation time: 10 minutes
Cooking time: 5 minutes
Servings: 4
Ingredients:
- 4 eggs, beaten
- 1 bell pepper, chopped
- ¼ cup fresh parsley, chopped
- ¼ teaspoon ground paprika
- ¼ teaspoon salt
- ¼ cup cream cheese
- 1 cup water, for cooking

Directions:
In the mixing bowl combine together eggs, bell pepper, parsley, ground paprika, salt, and cream cheese. When the mixture is homogenous, pour it in the silicone muffin molds. Pour water in the instant pot and insert trivet. Place the muffin molds on the trivet and close the lid. Cook the egg muffins on Manual mode (high pressure) for 5 minutes. Then make a quick pressure release and remove the muffins from the instant pot.
Nutrition: calories 125, fat 9.6, fiber 0.6, carbs 3.3, protein 7.1

Creamy Blueberries and Nuts

Preparation time: 5 minutes
Cooking time: 8 minutes
Servings: 6
Ingredients:
- ½ cup walnuts, chopped
- ½ cups almonds, chopped
- 2 teaspoons swerve
- 1 cup blueberries
- 1 teaspoon vanilla extract
- 1 cup coconut cream

Directions:
In your instant pot, combine the walnuts with the almonds and the rest of the ingredients, toss, put the lid on and cook on High for 8 minutes. Release the pressure fast for 5 minutes, divide the mix into bowls and serve for breakfast.
Nutrition: calories 218, fat 19.7, fiber 3.2, carbs 5.8, protein 5.3

Egg Sandwich

Preparation time: 15 minutes
Cooking time: 15 minutes
Servings: 4
Ingredients:
- 4 bacon slices
- 4 eggs
- 1 cup water, for cooking

Directions:
Pour water in the instant pot and insert trivet. Place the eggs on the trivet and cook them for 5 minutes on Manual mode (High pressure). Then make a quick pressure release and transfer the eggs in the ice water. Leave them there for 10 minutes. Meanwhile, clean the instant pot and discard the trivet. Preheat

the instant pot on sauté mode for 3 minutes. Then place the bacon slices inside and cook them on sauté mode for 2 minutes from each side. Meanwhile, peel the eggs and cut into halves. Place the cooked bacon on the egg halves and cover with the remaining egg halves to make the sandwiches. Pierce the egg sandwiches with toothpicks for convenience.
Nutrition: calories 166, fat 12.3, fiber 0, carbs 0.6, protein 12.6

Kale and Bok Choy Muffins
Preparation time: 10 minutes
Cooking time: 20 minutes
Servings: 4
Ingredients:
- ½ cup almond milk
- 4 eggs, whisked
- 1 tablespoon avocado oil
- A pinch of salt and black pepper
- ½ cup bok choy, chopped
- ½ cup kale, chopped
- 1 tablespoon chives, chopped
- 1 and ½ cups water

Directions:
In a bowl, mix the almond milk with the eggs and the rest of the ingredients except the water and the oil and stir well. Grease a muffin tray with the oil and pour the muffin mix inside. Add the water to your instant pot, add the trivet, add muffin tray inside, put the lid on and cook on High for 20 minutes. Release the pressure naturally for 10 minutes, cool the muffins down and serve for breakfast.
Nutrition: calories 142, fat 12, fiber 1.1, carbs 3.3, protein 6.7

Keto Oatmeal
Preparation time: 5 minutes
Cooking time: 1.5 hours
Servings: 2
Ingredients:
- 2 tablespoons coconut flakes
- 1 tablespoon flax seeds
- 2 tablespoons hemp seeds
- ½ cup of coconut milk
- 1 tablespoon almond meal
- 1 teaspoon Erythritol
- 1 teaspoon vanilla extract
- ¼ cup of water

Directions:
Combine together all ingredients in the instant pot and stir well with the spoon. Close the lid and cook Keto oatmeal for 1.5 hours on Low pressure (Manual mode). Stir the cooked meal well before serving.
Nutrition: calories 239, fat 22, fiber 3.3, carbs 9, protein 5.3

Spinach and Artichokes Muffins
Preparation time: 10 minutes
Cooking time: 20 minutes
Servings: 12
Ingredients:
- 1 cup baby spinach, chopped
- 1 cup canned artichoke hearts, drained and chopped
- A pinch of salt and black pepper
- 1 and ½ cups water
- Cooking spray
- 3 cups almond flour
- 1 teaspoon baking soda
- 4 eggs

Directions:
In a bowl, mix the spinach with the artichokes and the rest of the ingredients except the water and the cooking spray and stir well. Grease a muffin tray with the cooking spray and pour the muffin mix inside. Add the water to your instant pot, add the trivet, add the muffin tray inside, put the lid on and cook on High for 20 minutes. Release the pressure naturally for 10 minutes, cool the muffins down and serve for breakfast.
Nutrition: calories 66, fat 4.5, fiber 0.2, carbs 0.6, protein 5.8

Oregano Egg en Cocotte
Preparation time: 8 minutes
Cooking time: 2 minutes
Servings: 1
Ingredients:
- 1 egg
- 1 teaspoon cream
- ½ teaspoon butter, softened
- ¼ teaspoon chives, chopped
- ¼ teaspoon salt
- 1 teaspoon dried oregano
- 1 cup water, for cooking

Directions:
Grease the ramekin with butter. Add cream in the ramekin. Then crack the egg. After this, top the cracked egg with salt, oregano, ground black pepper, and chives. Pour water in the instant pot and insert trivet. Place the ramekin with egg on the trivet and close the lid. Cook the meal on Manual mode (Low pressure) for 2 minutes. When the meal is cooked, remove it from the instant pot. Remove the cooked egg from the ramekin.
Nutrition: calories 84, fat 6.5, fiber 0.2, carbs 0.8, protein 5.7

Mozzarella and Kale Muffins
Preparation time: 10 minutes
Cooking time: 20 minutes
Servings: 4
Ingredients:
- Cooking spray
- 2 cups water
- 1 cup mozzarella cheese, grated
- 4 eggs, whisked
- ½ teaspoon basil, dried
- ¼ teaspoon baking soda
- 1 cup almond flour
- ¼ cup kale, chopped
- A pinch of salt and black pepper
- ½ cup almond milk

Directions:
In a bowl, mix the mozzarella with the eggs and the rest of the ingredients except the water and the cooking spray and whisk well. Grease a muffin tray with the cooking spray and pour the muffins mix inside. Add the water to your instant pot, add the trivet, add the muffin tray inside, put the lid on and cook on High for 20 minutes. Release the pressure

naturally for 10 minutes, divide the muffins between plates and serve for breakfast.
Nutrition: calories 155, fat 12.9, fiber 0.7, carbs 2.7, protein 8.4

Hot Jalapeno Poppers Mix

Preparation time: 10 minutes
Cooking time: 11 minutes
Servings: 2
Ingredients:
- 5 oz chicken fillet
- 2 jalapeno peppers, sliced
- ½ teaspoon ranch seasonings
- 2 teaspoons cream cheese
- ½ teaspoon sesame oil
- ¼ cup heavy cream
- 1 oz Parmesan, grated

Directions:
Chop the chicken fillet and sprinkle it with ranch seasonings. Then preheat the instant pot on sauté mode for 2 minutes and add sesame oil. Then add chicken and sauté it for 3 minutes from each side. After this, place the cooked chicken in the bowl and shred it with the help of the fork. Return the chicken back in the instant pot and add cream cheese, heavy cream, sliced jalapeno, and Parmesan. Mix up well. Sauté the meal for 3 minutes more or until the cheese is melted.
Nutrition: calories 262, fat 16.3, fiber 0.6, carbs 2.1, protein 25.8

Chicken Bowls

Preparation time: 10 minutes
Cooking time: 15 minutes
Servings: 4
Ingredients:
- 1 avocado, peeled and cut into wedges
- 2 tomatoes, cubed
- 1 and ½ cups baby spinach
- A pinch of salt and black pepper
- 2 chicken breasts, skinless, boneless and cubed
- 2 tablespoons olive oil
- 2 tablespoons chicken stock
- ¼ cup tomato passata
- 1 shallot, chopped

Directions:
Set your instant pot on sauté mode, add the oil, heat it up, add the shallot and sauté for 2 minutes. Add the chicken, stock and tomato passata, put the lid on and cook on High for 13 minutes. Release the pressure naturally for 10 minutes, transfer the chicken mix to a bowl, add the remaining ingredients, toss and serve for breakfast.
Nutrition: calories 1, fa78t 17, fiber 4.6, carbs 7.6, protein 1.7

Breakfast Stuffed Avocado

Preparation time: 10 minutes
Cooking time: 3 minutes
Servings: 2
Ingredients:
- 1 avocado, halved, pitted
- 1 egg, beaten
- 1 teaspoon cream cheese
- 1 oz bacon, crumbled
- 2 oz Parmesan, grated
- 1 cup water, for cooking

Directions:
Pour water in the instant pot and insert the steamer rack. Mix up together cream cheese, egg, bacon, and cheese. The fill the avocado holes with egg mixture. Place the avocado in the instant pot. Close the lid and cook the meal for 3 minutes on Manual mode (high pressure). Then make a quick pressure release.
Nutrition: calories 410, fat 34.4, fiber 6.7, carbs 10.1, protein 19.2

Coconut Pudding

Preparation time: 5 minutes
Cooking time: 5 minutes
Servings: 6
Ingredients:
- 2 cups coconut milk
- 1 cup coconut cream
- ¼ cup walnuts, chopped
- ½ cup coconut, unsweetened and shredded
- 4 teaspoons swerve

Directions:
In your instant pot, combine the coconut milk with the rest of the ingredients, toss, put the lid on and cook on High for 5 minutes. Release the pressure fast for 5 minutes, divide the pudding into bowls and serve.
Nutrition: calories 332, fat 33.8, fiber 3.6, carbs 7.8, protein 4.2

Layered Casserole

Preparation time: 10 minutes
Cooking time: 15 minutes
Servings: 4
Ingredients:
- 1 cup ground chicken
- 1 cup Cheddar cheese, shredded
- 2 tablespoons cream cheese
- 1 teaspoon butter, melted
- ½ teaspoon taco seasonings
- ½ teaspoon salt
- 1 cup leek, chopped
- ¼ cup of water

Directions:
Grease the instant pot bowl with butter. In the mixing bowl combine together ground chicken and taco seasonings. Then place the ground chicken in the instant pot and flatten it to make the chicken layer. After this, top the chicken with leek and salt. Then top the leek with cheese. Mix up together cream cheese and water. Pour the liquid over the casserole and close the lid. Cook the casserole on Saute mode for 15 minutes.
Nutrition: calories 222, fat 14.7, fiber 0.4, carbs 4.1, protein 17.9

Zucchini Spread

Preparation time: 10 minutes
Cooking time: 12 minutes
Servings: 4
Ingredients:
- 4 zucchinis, sliced
- A pinch of salt and black pepper
- ½ cup heavy cream
- ½ cup cream cheese, soft

- 2 garlic cloves, minced
- ½ cup veggie stock
- 1 tablespoon avocado oil
- 1 tablespoon dill, chopped

Directions:
In your instant pot, mix the zucchinis with the stock, salt and pepper, put the lid on and cook on High for 12 minutes. Release the pressure naturally for 10 minutes, drain the zucchinis, transfer them to a blender, add the rest of the ingredients, pulse, divide into bowls and serve as a morning spread.
Nutrition: calories 193, fat 16.5, fiber 2.5, carbs 7.8, protein 5.2

Chili Casserole

Preparation time: 10 minutes
Cooking time: 20 minutes
Servings: 2
Ingredients:
- ½ cup ground beef
- 1 teaspoon tomato paste
- ½ white onion, diced
- ½ teaspoon ground cumin
- ½ teaspoon ground thyme
- ¼ teaspoon salt
- 1/3 cup Cheddar cheese, shredded
- 1 chili pepper, chopped
- 1 teaspoon coconut oil, melted
- 1 cup water, for cooking

Directions:
In the mixing bowl combine together ground beef, tomato paste, white onion, ground cumin, thyme, salt, and chili pepper. Then brush the baking pan with coconut oil. Place the ground beef mixture in the baking pan. Flatten the surface of the mixture. After this, top the meat mixture with Cheddar cheese. Pour water in the instant pot and insert the trivet. Cover the baking pan with foil and place it on the trivet. Cook the chili casserole for 20 minutes o Manual mode (High pressure). Then make a quick pressure release.
Nutrition: calories 177, fat 12.8, fiber 0.9, carbs 3.9, protein 11.8

Tomato and Zucchini Salad

Preparation time: 10 minutes
Cooking time: 10 minutes
Servings: 4
Ingredients:
- 2 spring onions, chopped
- 1 pound cherry tomatoes, roughly cubed
- 2 zucchinis, sliced
- 1 tablespoon olive oil
- 2 garlic cloves, minced
- 1 tablespoon rosemary, chopped
- 1 tablespoon basil, chopped
- ½ cup tomato passata
- 1 tablespoon chives, chopped
- A pinch of sea salt and black pepper

Directions:
Set your instant pot on sauté mode add the oil, heat it up, add the spring onions and the garlic and sauté for 2-3 minutes. Add tomatoes, zucchinis and the rest of the ingredients except the chives, put the lid on and cook on High for 8 minutes. Release the pressure naturally for 10 minutes, divide the mix into bowls and serve for breakfast with the chives sprinkled on top.
Nutrition: calories 86, fat 4.1, fiber 3.6, carbs 5.8, protein 3

Breakfast Hot Cacao

Preparation time: 5 minutes
Cooking time: 15 minutes
Servings: 2
Ingredients:
- 1 cup heavy cream
- ½ cup of water
- 1 tablespoon cocoa powder
- 1 teaspoon butter
- 1 tablespoon Erythritol

Directions:
In the mixing bowl mix up together cocoa powder and heavy cream. When the liquid is smooth, pour it in the instant pot bowl. Add water and sauté the liquid for 5 minutes. After this, add butter and Erythritol. Stir well. Saute the hot cacao for 10 minutes more.
Nutrition: calories 153, fat 16.3, fiber 0.5, carbs 7.1, protein 1.2

Turkey Bowls

Preparation time: 10 minutes
Cooking time: 20 minutes
Servings: 2
Ingredients:
- 1 tablespoon olive oil
- 2 cups okra, sliced
- ½ cup chicken stock
- 2 cups yellow bell pepper, chopped
- A pinch of salt and black pepper
- 1 turkey breast, skinless, boneless and cubed
- 2 tablespoons oregano, chopped
- 1 tablespoon thyme, chopped
- ½ cup balsamic vinegar

Directions:
Set the instant pot on sauté mode, add the oil, heat it up, add the turkey and brown for 5 minutes. Add the okra and the rest of the ingredients, put the lid on and cook on High for 15 minutes. Release the pressure naturally for 10 minutes, divide the mix into bowls and serve for breakfast.
Nutrition: calories 171, fat 8.2, fiber 2.6, carbs 7.8, protein 3.9

Zucchini Cheese Fritters

Preparation time: 10 minutes
Cooking time: 10 minutes
Servings: 4
Ingredients:
- 2 zucchini, grated
- 1/3 cup Mozzarella, shredded
- 1 egg, beaten
- 2 tablespoons almond flour
- 1 teaspoon butter, melted
- ½ teaspoon salt
- ½ teaspoon ground turmeric
- ¼ teaspoon dried sage

Directions:
Mix up together grated zucchini and egg. When the mixture is homogenous, add shredded Mozzarella

and almond flour. After this, add salt, ground turmeric, and dried sage. Mix up the mixture. Preheat the instant pot on sauté mode for 2 minutes. Then toss butter inside and melt it. With the help of the spoon make the fritters and place them in the hot butter. Saute the fritters for 3 minutes from each side.
Nutrition: calories 69, fat 4.4, fiber 1.5, carbs 4.4, protein 4

Cheesy Tomato and Radish Salad
Preparation time: 10 minutes
Cooking time: 10 minutes
Servings: 4
Ingredients:
- ¼ cup radishes, sliced
- 1 pound cherry tomatoes, halved
- 1 tablespoon basil, chopped
- 1 tablespoon olive oil
- 1 tablespoon chives, chopped
- ½ cup mozzarella, shredded
- A pinch of salt and black pepper

Directions:
In your instant pot, mix the radishes with the tomatoes and the rest of the ingredients except the mozzarella and toss. Sprinkle the cheese on top, put the lid on and cook on High for 10 minutes. Release the pressure naturally for 10 minutes, divide the salad into bowls and serve for breakfast.
Nutrition: calories 62, fat 4.4, fiber 1.5, carbs 4.9, protein 2.1

Cauliflower Fritters
Preparation time: 10 minutes
Cooking time: 7 minutes
Servings: 4
Ingredients:
- 2 cups cauliflower, shredded
- ½ cup Cheddar cheese, shredded
- 2 eggs, beaten
- 1 teaspoon olive oil
- ½ teaspoon chili powder

Directions:
In the mixing bowl combine together shredded cauliflower and Cheddar cheese. Add eggs and chili powder. With the help of the fork stir the mixture until homogenous. Preheat the instant pot on sauté mode for 2 minutes. Add olive oil and heat it for 1 minute. With the help of 2 spoons make the medium size fritters and arrange them in the instant pot. Cook the cauliflower fritters for 2 minutes from each side. If you want a golden-brown crust, cook the fritters for 2 additional minutes from each side.
Nutrition: calories 112, fat 8.2, fiber 1.4, carbs 3.2, protein 7.3

Pork and Kale Hash
Preparation time: 10 minutes
Cooking time: 15 minutes
Servings: 4
Ingredients:
- 1 tablespoon avocado oil
- 1 spring onion, chopped
- 2 cups pork meat, ground
- 2 garlic cloves, minced
- ½ cup beef stock
- A pinch of salt and black pepper
- 1 pound kale, torn

Directions:
Set your instant pot on sauté mode, add the oil, heat it up, add the onion, garlic and the meat and brown for 5 minutes. Add the rest of the ingredients, toss, put the lid on and cook on High for 10 minutes. Release the pressure naturally for 10 minutes, divide the mix between plates and serve.
Nutrition: calories 66, fat 5.3, fiber 2, carbs 6.5, protein 3.8

Breakfast Spaghetti Squash Casserole
Preparation time: 15 minutes
Cooking time: 25 minutes
Servings: 4
Ingredients:
- 10 oz spaghetti squash, trimmed
- ½ cup ground beef
- 1 teaspoon onion powder
- ½ teaspoon garlic powder
- 1 teaspoon dried dill
- 1 teaspoon dried parsley
- ½ teaspoon salt
- 1 teaspoon dried oregano
- ½ cup mozzarella, shredded
- 1 tablespoon marinara sauce
- 1 cup water, for cooking

Directions:
Cut the spaghetti squash into the halves and clean it. Then pour water and insert the trivet in the instant pot. Place the spaghetti squash on the trivet and cook it on Manual mode (high pressure) for 10 minutes. Then make a quick pressure release. After this, remove the squash from the instant pot. Clean the instant pot and remove the trivet. Place ground beef in the instant pot. Add garlic powder, dried dill, dried parsley, salt, dried oregano, and marinara sauce. Mix up the mixture well and sauté it for 10 minutes. Stir it with the help of the spatula from time to time to avoid burning. Meanwhile, shred the spaghetti squash with the help of the forks. Top the cooked ground beef with shredded spaghetti squash. Then top the squash with mozzarella. Close the lid and sauté the casserole for 5 minutes or until the cheese is melted.
Nutrition: calories 73, fat 3.2, fiber 0.4, carbs 6.7, protein 5

Sweet Zucchini Mix
Preparation time: 10 minutes
Cooking time: 10 minutes
Servings: 4
Ingredients:
- 1 and ½ cups coconut cream
- 1 teaspoon nutmeg, ground
- 4 zucchinis, sliced
- 2 tablespoons swerve
- ¼ cup walnuts, chopped

Directions:
In your instant pot, combine the cream with the zucchinis and the rest of the ingredients, put the lid on and cook on High for 10 minutes. Release the pressure naturally for 10 minutes, divide the mix into bowls and serve.

Nutrition: calories 83, fat 8.2, fiber 2.8, carbs 7.6, protein 4.3

Sweet Porridge

Preparation time: 10 minutes
Cooking time: 10 minutes
Servings: 2
Ingredients:
- ¾ cup of coconut milk
- ¼ cup of organic almond milk
- ¾ cup of water
- 1 tablespoon almond butter
- 2 teaspoons chia seeds
- 1 teaspoon hemp seeds
- 1 tablespoon toasted coconut
- 2 tablespoons walnuts, chopped
- 1 teaspoon vanilla extract
- 1 teaspoon liquid stevia

Directions:
Preheat the instant pot on sauté mode for 5 minutes. Then pour coconut milk, organic almond milk, and water inside. On sauté mode bring the liquid to boil and switch off the instant pot. Stirring constantly add chia seeds, hemp seeds, toasted coconut, and walnuts. Then add almond butter, vanilla extract, and liquid stevia. Stir the mixture for 1 minute or until it will be thick. Then transfer it in the serving bowls. The porridge is recommended to serve warm/hot.

Nutrition: calories 380, fat 35.3, fiber 6.1, carbs 11.4, protein 8.3

Turkey Omelet

Preparation time: 10 minutes
Cooking time: 15 minutes
Servings: 4
Ingredients:
- 1 cup turkey breast, skinless, boneless and cut into strips
- 1 tomato, chopped
- 2 bacon slices, cooked and crumbled
- 4 eggs, whisked
- 1 small avocado, pitted, peeled and chopped
- A pinch of salt and black pepper
- 2 tablespoons olive oil

Directions:
Set your instant pot on sauté mode, add half of the oil, heat it up, add the meat and cook for 5 minutes. Add the rest of the ingredients, toss, spread the mix into the pot, put the lid on and cook on High for 10 minutes. Release the pressure naturally for 10 minutes, divide the omelet between plates and serve.

Nutrition: calories 228, fat 21.2, fiber 3.6, carbs 5.3, protein 6.6

Bacon Salad with Eggs

Preparation time: 10 minutes
Cooking time: 15 minutes
Servings: 4
Ingredients:
- 4 eggs
- 6 bacon slices
- 1 tablespoon lemon juice
- 1 pecan, chopped
- ½ teaspoon ground paprika
- ¼ teaspoon cayenne pepper
- ¼ teaspoon salt
- 1 cup arugula, chopped
- ½ cup lettuce, chopped
- 1 cup water, for cooking

Directions:
Pour water and insert the trivet in the instant pot. Place the eggs on the trivet and cook on manual mode (high pressure) for 5 minutes. Then make a quick pressure release. Remove the eggs from the instant pot and cool them in the ice/cold water for 10 minutes. Meanwhile, clean the instant pot and remove the trivet. Preheat it on manual mode for 1 minute. Then place the bacon in the instant pot in one layer. Cook it for 3 minutes from each side or until crunchy. Meanwhile, peel the eggs and chop them. Place the chopped eggs in the salad bowl. Add arugula and lettuce. When the bacon is cooked, cool it to the room temperature and chop roughly. Add bacon in the salad mixture. Then sprinkle it with lemon juice, ground paprika, salt, and cayenne pepper. Add pecans. Shake the salad gently.

Nutrition: calories 246, fat 18.9, fiber 0.6, carbs 1.9, protein 16.7

Strawberries and Nuts Salad

Preparation time: 10 minutes
Cooking time: 10 minutes
Servings: 4
Ingredients:
- ½ cup almonds, chopped
- ½ cup walnuts, chopped
- 2 cups strawberries, halved
- 1 tablespoon stevia
- ½ teaspoon nutmeg, ground
- 1 cup coconut cream

Directions:
In your instant pot, mix the strawberries with the cream and the rest of the ingredients, put the lid on and cook on Low for 10 minutes. Release the pressure naturally for 10 minutes, divide the mix into bowls and serve.

Nutrition: calories 328, fat 29.8, fiber 5.4, carbs 7.6, protein 8.1

Classic Breakfast Casserole

Preparation time: 10 minutes
Cooking time: 20 minutes
Servings: 4
Ingredients:
- 7 oz breakfast sausages, chopped
- 4 oz Monterey Jack cheese, shredded
- ½ red onion, sliced
- 1 bell pepper, diced
- 2 oz avocado, chopped
- 4 eggs, beaten
- ¼ cup heavy cream
- ½ teaspoon salt
- ½ teaspoon cayenne pepper
- 1 teaspoon coconut oil

Directions:
Toss the coconut oil in the instant pot and melt it on sauté mode. Then add onion and chopped breakfast sausages. Cook them on sauté mode for 5 minutes. Stir them from time to time. Then add bell pepper and cook the ingredients for 3 minutes more. Meanwhile, mix up together cheese, eggs, avocado, cayenne pepper, salt, and heavy cream. Pour the liquid over the breakfast sausages and close the lid.

Cook the casserole on sauté mode for 10 minutes or until the egg mixture is solid.
Nutrition: calories 417, fat 33.8, fiber 1.7, carbs 5.6, protein 23

Eggs, Leeks and Turkey Mix
Preparation time: 10 minutes
Cooking time: 15 minutes
Servings: 4
Ingredients:
- 2 leeks, chopped
- ½ cup chicken stock
- 2 tablespoons olive oil
- 2 garlic cloves, minced
- 8 eggs, whisked
- 1 turkey breast, skinless, boneless and cut into strips

Directions:
Set your instant pot on Sauté mode, add the oil, heat it up, add the leeks, garlic and the meat and brown for 5 minutes. Add the rest of the ingredients, toss, put the lid on and cook on High for 10 minutes. Release the pressure naturally for 10 minutes, divide the mix between plates and serve.
Nutrition: calories 216, fat 16, fiber 0.8, carbs 7.6, protein 11.9

Low-Carb Flaxseed Brule
Preparation time: 15 minutes
Cooking time: 20 minutes
Servings: 2
Ingredients:
- 2 egg yolks
- ½ cup heavy whipped cream
- 1 teaspoon vanilla extract
- 1 teaspoon Erythritol
- 1 teaspoon flaxseeds
- ½ teaspoon chia seeds
- 1 cup water, for cooking

Directions:
Pour water and insert the steamer rack in the instant pot. After this, in the mixing bowl whisk together egg yolks, heavy whipped cream, vanilla extract, Erythritol, flaxseeds, and chia seeds. When you get a smooth batter, pour it in the ramekin and cover with foil. Arrange the ramekin in the instant pot. Cook it on Manual mode (Low pressure) for 20 minutes. Then allow natural pressure release for 10 minutes and remove the cooked meal from the instant pot.
Nutrition: calories 187, fat 17.1, fiber 1.5, carbs 6, protein 4.1

Sweet Berries Bowls
Preparation time: 10 minutes
Cooking time: 12 minutes
Servings: 6
Ingredients:
- 3 tablespoons coconut flakes, unsweetened
- 1 cup strawberries
- 1 cup blackberries
- 2 cups almond milk
- 1 teaspoon vanilla extract
- 1 teaspoon swerve

Directions:
In your instant pot, mix the berries with the coconut and the rest of the ingredients, put the lid on and cook on Low for 12 minutes. Release the pressure naturally for 10 minutes, divide the mix into bowls and serve.
Nutrition: calories 213, fat 20.1, fiber 3.7, carbs 6.7, protein 2.4

Mini Frittatas
Preparation time: 15 minutes
Cooking time: 15 minutes
Servings: 4
Ingredients:
- 6 oz ground sausages
- 1 cup broccoli, shredded
- 2 oz Parmesan, grated
- 4 eggs, beaten
- 1 tablespoon coconut milk
- ½ teaspoon ghee
- 1 cup water, for cooking

Directions:
In the mixing bowl combine together broccoli, ground sausages, grated cheese, and coconut milk. Then add eggs and stir the frittata mixture gently. Grease the silicone egg molds with ghee. Pour the egg mixture in every silicone mold. After this, pour water in the instant pot and insert the steamer rack. Place the silicone molds with frittatas on the rack and close the lid. Cook the breakfast on Manual (High pressure) for 15 minutes. Then allow the natural pressure release for 10 minutes. Cool the frittatas little and remove them from the molds.
Nutrition: calories 274, fat 21, fiber 0.7, carbs 2.6, protein 19.1

Mushroom and Okra Omelet
Preparation time: 10 minutes
Cooking time: 15 minutes
Servings: 2
Ingredients:
- 1 pound white mushrooms, sliced
- 2 spring onions, chopped
- 2 garlic cloves, minced
- 1 tablespoon avocado oil
- 2 chili peppers, minced
- 1 cup okra
- ½ cup cilantro, chopped
- 4 eggs, whisked

Directions:
Set your instant pot on sauté mode, add the oil, heat it up, add the onions and garlic and sauté for 2 minutes. Add the mushrooms and sauté for 2 minutes more. Add the rest of the ingredients, toss, spread the mix into the instant pot, put the lid on and cook on High for 10 minutes. Release the pressure naturally for 10 minutes, divide the omelet between plates and serve.
Nutrition: calories 108, fat 5.2, fiber 2.4, carbs 4.7, protein 9.9

Egg Benedict Sandwich
Preparation time: 15 minutes
Cooking time: 2 minutes
Servings: 1
Ingredients:
- 2 egg whites
- 1 egg
- 1 tablespoon almond meal

- ¼ teaspoon salt
- 1 teaspoon butter, melted
- 1/3 teaspoon baking powder
- 1 spinach leaf
- 1 cup water, for cooking

Directions:
Put the melted butter in the ramekin. Add salt, almond meal, and baking powder. Whisk the mixture. Then add egg whites and whisk the mixture. Pour the water in the instant pot and insert trivet. Place the ramekin with egg white mixture on the trivet and cook it for 1 minute on High pressure (Manual mode). Then make a quick pressure release. Crack the egg in the silicone egg mold. Remove the ramekin with cooked egg whites from the instant pot. Insert the silicone mold with egg on the trivet and cook it for 1 minute –High pressure – Quick pressure release. Remove the cooked egg white from the ramekin and cut it into halves (crosswise). When the egg is cooked, remove it from the instant pot. Place the cooked egg on one half of the baked egg white. Top with spinach leaf and remaining baked egg white half.

Nutrition: calories 261, fat 20, fiber 1, carbs 3.4, protein 18.2

Cocoa Oatmeal

Preparation time: 10 minutes
Cooking time: 10 minutes
Servings: 6
Ingredients:
- 1 cup almond milk
- 1 cup coconut cream
- 1 cup coconut flakes, unsweetened
- 2 tablespoons stevia
- 1 teaspoon cocoa powder
- 2 teaspoons vanilla extract

Directions:
In your instant pot, mix the almond milk with the rest of the ingredients, put the lid on and cook on High for 10 minutes. Release the pressure naturally for 10 minutes, divide the mix into bowls and serve.

Nutrition: calories 236, fat 23.6, fiber 3.1, carbs 6.5, protein 2.3

Nutritious Taco Skillet

Preparation time: 10 minutes
Cooking time: 35 minutes
Servings: 2
Ingredients:
- 1 ½ cup ground beef
- 1 teaspoon taco seasonings
- ½ cup Mexican cheese, shredded
- 1 teaspoon chili powder
- ½ teaspoon onion powder
- ½ white onion, diced
- ¼ teaspoon ground cumin
- 1 egg, beaten
- 1 teaspoon tomato paste
- ¼ cup of water
- 1 teaspoon coconut oil

Directions:
Toss coconut oil in the instant pot and preheat it on sauté mode until it is melted. Add ground beef. Sprinkle the meat with Taco seasonings, chili powder, onion powder, ground cumin, and diced onion. Stir the mixture with the help of a spatula. Saute the ground beef mixture for 10 minutes. Stir it from time to time. After this, add shredded Mexican cheese, tomato paste, and water. Mix up well. Saute the taco mixture for 5 minutes more. Then pour the beaten egg over the ground beef. Stir the meal well and cook on sauté mode for 5 minutes more.

Nutrition: calories 298, fat 19.3, fiber 1.2, carbs 6.1, protein 24.5

Coconut Oatmeal

Preparation time: 5 minutes
Cooking time: 10 minutes
Servings: 6
Ingredients:
- 1 cup coconut, unsweetened and shredded
- 1 cup coconut milk
- 1 cup walnuts, chopped
- ½ cup almonds, chopped
- 1 cup coconut cream
- Seeds from 1 pomegranate

Directions:
In your instant pot, mix the coconut with the milk and the rest of the ingredients, toss, put the lid on and cook on High for 10 minutes. Release the pressure fast for 5 minutes, divide the mix into bowls and serve for breakfast.

Nutrition: calories 406, fat 30.2, fiber 5.4, carbs 6.8, protein 9

Wontons

Preparation time: 20 minutes
Cooking time: 12 minutes
Servings: 2
Ingredients:
- 5 oz ground pork
- 1 tablespoon chives, chopped
- 1 tablespoon dried cilantro
- ¼ teaspoon oyster sauce
- ½ teaspoon soy sauce
- ½ teaspoon garlic powder
- 1 egg, beaten
- 1 cup water, for cooking

Directions:
In the mixing bowl combine together ground pork, chives, cilantro, oyster sauce, soy sauce, and garlic powder. Then add egg and mix up the mixture until homogenous. Pour water in the instant pot and insert the steamer rack. Then transfer the ground pork mixture in the silicone egg molds and transfer the mold in the instant pot. Cook the wontons on Manual mode (high pressure) for 12 minutes. Then allow the natural pressure release for 10 minutes more.

Nutrition: calories 136, fat 4.7, fiber 0.1, carbs 0.9, protein 21.6

Broccoli and Almonds Mix

Preparation time: 5 minutes
Cooking time: 15 minutes
Servings: 4
Ingredients:
- 1 cup broccoli florets
- ½ cup coconut flakes
- 1 cup heavy cream
- ½ cup almonds, toasted and chopped
- 2 eggs, whisked
- Cooking spray

Directions:

Grease the instant pot with the cooking spray, add the broccoli and almonds and the pour the eggs mixed with the heavy cream on top. Sprinkle the coconut on top, put the lid on and cook on High for 15 minutes. Release the pressure fast for 5 minutes, divide the mix between plates and serve.
Nutrition: calories 248, fat 22.8, fiber 3, carbs 6.6, protein 6.9

Breakfast Kale Bread

Preparation time: 25 minutes
Cooking time: 60 minutes
Servings: 6
Ingredients:
- 1 egg, beaten
- 1 teaspoon baking powder
- 1 teaspoon lemon juice
- 1 cup kale, grinded
- 1 tablespoon flaxseeds meal
- ½ cup coconut flour
- ¼ cup almond meal
- ¼ teaspoon salt
- 2 tablespoons sesame oil
- ½ teaspoon dried sage
- 1/3 cup water
- 1 teaspoon pumpkin seeds, chopped
- 1 cup water, for cooking

Directions:
Mix up together beaten egg, baking powder, lemon juice, 1/3 cup of water, dried sage, sesame oil, salt, almond meal, and coconut flour. Then add flaxseeds meal and grinded kale. Knead the soft and non-sticky dough. After this, line the round baking pan with paper foil and put the kneaded dough inside. Press it little. Sprinkle the surface of dough with pumpkin seeds. Pour water in the instant pot and insert the trivet. Arrange the baking pan with dough on the trivet and close the lid. Cook the kale bread 45 minutes on manual (high pressure). Then allow the natural pressure release for 15 minutes more. Open the instant pot lid and remove the baking pan with bread from it. Cool the bread for 10-15 minutes.
Nutrition: calories 129, fat 8.9, fiber 5.1, carbs 9.7, protein 3.8

Mushroom and Cauliflower Rice Salad

Preparation time: 10 minutes
Cooking time: 20 minutes
Servings: 4
Ingredients:
- 2 shallots, chopped
- 2 tablespoons avocado oil
- 2 cups white mushrooms, sliced
- 2 tablespoons lemon juice
- A pinch of salt and black pepper
- 4 garlic cloves, minced
- 1 cup cauliflower rice
- 1 cup veggie stock
- 1 tablespoon chives, chopped

Directions:
Set your instant pot on sauté mode, add the oil, heat it up, add the shallots, garlic and mushrooms, stir and sauté for 5 minutes. Add the rest of the ingredients, toss, put the lid on and cook on High for 15 minutes.

Release the pressure naturally for 10 minutes, divide the mix into bowls and serve for breakfast.
Nutrition: calories 23, fat 3.1, fiber 0.8, carbs 2.7, protein 1.5

Egg Scramble

Preparation time: 5 minutes
Cooking time: 5 minutes
Servings: 2
Ingredients:
- ¼ teaspoon ground paprika
- ¼ teaspoon ground turmeric
- ¼ teaspoon chili flakes
- 1 tablespoon butter
- 1 tablespoon heavy cream
- 2 eggs, beaten
- ¼ teaspoon salt

Directions:
Set sauté mode and place butter in the instant pot. Melt the butter and add beaten eggs and heavy cream. Cook it for 1 minute and add chili flakes Scramble the eggs with the help of the fork well. Then cook the scrambled eggs for 2 minutes more. Transfer the cooked egg scramble in the plates and sprinkle with ground paprika and ground turmeric.
Nutrition: calories 142, fat 13, fiber 0.2, carbs 0.9, protein 5.8

Cinnamon Strawberry Oatmeal

Preparation time: 5 minutes
Cooking time: 10 minutes
Servings: 6
Ingredients:
- 2 cups almond milk
- ½ cup coconut cream
- 1 tablespoon cinnamon powder
- 1 cup coconut flakes
- 1 cup strawberries, halved

Directions:
In your instant pot, mix the almond milk with the rest of the ingredients, toss a bit, put the lid on and cook on High for 10 minutes. Release the pressure fast for 5 minutes, divide the mix into bowls and serve.
Nutrition: calories 285, fat 28.4, fiber 3.9, carbs 7.5, protein 2.9

Parmesan Chicken Balls

Preparation time: 15 minutes
Cooking time: 20 minutes
Servings: 6
Ingredients:
- 2 cups ground chicken
- ½ cup Parmesan, grated
- 1 teaspoon onion powder
- ¼ teaspoon ground cumin
- ½ teaspoon ground thyme
- 1 teaspoon dried parsley
- 2 tablespoons almond meal
- 1 cup water, for cooking

Directions:
Mix up together ground chicken, Parmesan, onion powder, ground cumin, thyme, dried parsley, and almond meal. With the help of the scooper make the balls or use the fingertips for this step. Pour water in the instant pot and insert the steamer rack. Place the

chicken balls on the steamer rack and close the lid. Cook the meal on Steam mode for 20 minutes.
Nutrition: calories 103, fat 4.5, fiber 0.3, carbs 0.9, protein 14.1

Coconut Omelet

Preparation time: 10 minutes
Cooking time: 10 minutes
Servings: 4
Ingredients:
- 1 cup coconut flakes
- ½ cup coconut milk
- 4 eggs, whisked
- A pinch of salt and black pepper
- 1 tablespoon sweet paprika
- Cooking spray

Directions:
In a bowl, combine the eggs with the rest of the ingredients except the cooking spray and whisk really well. Grease the instant pot with the cooking spray, pour the omelet mix inside, spread, put the lid on and cook on High for 10 minutes. Release the pressure naturally for 10 minutes, divide the omelet between plates and serve.
Nutrition: calories 209, fat 18.6, fiber 3.1, carbs 6, protein 7.2

Blueberry Muffins

Preparation time: 10 minutes
Cooking time: 18 minutes
Servings: 7
Ingredients:
- 1 cup almond flour
- ¼ cup coconut flour
- ½ teaspoon baking powder
- 2 tablespoons coconut oil, melted
- 2 tablespoons Erythritol
- ¼ cup blueberries
- 2 eggs, beaten
- ½ teaspoon vanilla extract
- 1 cup water, for cooking

Directions:
In the mixing bowl combine together almond flour and coconut flour. Add Erythritol and baking powder. After this, add coconut oil, eggs, and vanilla extract. Stir the mixture until homogenous with the help of the spatula. Then add blueberries and mix up the mixture until homogenous. Transfer the muffin mixture in the muffin molds and arrange them on the steamer rack. Cover the muffins with foil. Pour water in the instant pot and arrange the steamer rack inside. Cook the muffins on Manual mode – high pressure (more) for 18 minutes. Then make a quick pressure release. Cool the muffins well and then remove them from the molds.
Nutrition: calories 169, fat 13.2, fiber 3.6, carbs 11.6, protein 5.6

Leek Frittata

Preparation time: 10 minutes
Cooking time: 15 minutes
Servings: 4
Ingredients:
- 4 eggs, whisked
- 2 leeks, sliced
- 1 shallot, chopped
- 1 tablespoon sweet paprika
- A pinch of salt and black pepper
- 1 red bell pepper, chopped
- Cooking spray

Directions:
Grease your instant pot with the cooking spray, add leeks, shallot and the rest of the ingredients, toss, spread well into the pot, put the lid on and cooking o High for 15 minutes. Release the pressure naturally for 10 minutes, divide the frittata between plates and serve.
Nutrition: calories 106, fat 9.4, fiber 1.9, carbs 6.6, protein 6.8

Chicken Fritters

Preparation time: 10 minutes
Cooking time: 10 minutes
Servings: 2
Ingredients:
- ½ cup broccoli, shredded
- 1 cup ground chicken
- ¼ cup fresh cilantro, blended
- 1 egg, beaten
- ½ teaspoon ground black pepper
- 1 tablespoon flaxseed meal
- 1 cup water, for cooking

Directions:
Mix up together shredded broccoli and blended cilantro. Add ground chicken, egg, ground black pepper, and flaxseed meal. Stir it will. With the help of the fingertips make the medium fritters. Pour water in the instant pot. Line the steamer rack with foil. Place the fritters on the rack and insert them in the instant pot. Cook the chicken fritters for 10 minutes on manual mode (high pressure). Then make a quick pressure release and remove the fritters from the instant pot.
Nutrition: calories 193, fat 8.6, fiber 1.7, carbs 3.1, protein 24.4

Scallions and Peppers Bowls

Preparation time: 10 minutes
Cooking time: 15 minutes
Servings: 4
Ingredients:
- 1 red bell pepper, cut into strips
- 1 green bell pepper, cut into strips
- 3 garlic cloves, minced
- 4 scallions, chopped
- 2 teaspoons olive oil
- 2 tablespoons veggie stock
- 4 eggs, whisked
- 2 tablespoons red pepper sauce
- 1 tablespoon cilantro, chopped

Directions:
Set your instant pot on sauté mode, add the oil, heat it up, add the scallions and the garlic and cook for 2 minutes. Add the bell peppers and the rest of the ingredients, toss, put the lid on and cook on High for 10 minutes. Release the pressure naturally for 10 minutes, divide the mix into bowls and serve for breakfast.
Nutrition: calories 110, fat 6.9, fiber 1.3, carbs 6.7, protein 6.6

Crustless Egg Pie

Preparation time: 15 minutes
Cooking time: 25 minutes
Servings: 6
Ingredients:
- 4 eggs, beaten
- 7 oz chicken fillet, shredded, cooked
- ¼ cup heavy cream
- ¼ cup coconut flour
- 1 cup green beans, chopped
- ½ teaspoon salt
- ½ teaspoon ground nutmeg
- ½ teaspoon butter, softened
- 1 cup water, for cooking

Directions:
Grease the baking pan with butter. Then place the green beans in the pan in one layer. Top the green beans with shredded chicken. After this, in the mixing bowl combine together beaten eggs, heavy cream, coconut flour, salt, and ground nutmeg. Pour the egg mixture over the shredded chicken. Cover the baking pan with foil. Pour water and insert the rack in the instant pot. Place the baking pan with pie in the instant pot and close the lid. Cook the pie on High pressure (manual mode) for 25 minutes. Then make a quick pressure release. Cool the cooked pie to the room temperature and cut it into the servings.
Nutrition: calories 151, fat 8.1, fiber 2.7, carbs 5.1, protein 14.4

Curry Cauliflower Rice Bowls

Preparation time: 10 minutes
Cooking time: 12 minutes
Servings: 6
Ingredients:
- 1 broccoli head, florets separated
- 4 tomatoes, cubed
- 1 cup veggie stock
- 1 cup cauliflower rice
- 1 tablespoon ginger, grated
- 2 teaspoons curry powder
- 1 teaspoon chili flakes

Directions:
In your instant pot, mix the broccoli with the tomatoes and the rest of the ingredients, toss, put the lid on and cook on High for 12 minutes. Release the pressure naturally for 10 minutes, divide the mix into bowls and serve for breakfast.
Nutrition: calories 30, fat 5, fiber 2, carbs 4.5, protein 1.3

Mini Casserole in Jars

Preparation time: 20 minutes
Cooking time: 15 minutes
Servings: 4
Ingredients:
- 1 cup ground pork
- ¼ onion, diced
- 1 garlic clove, diced
- ½ cup Cheddar cheese, shredded
- ½ cup kale, chopped
- 1 teaspoon coconut oil, melted
- ½ teaspoon salt
- 1 cup water, for cooking

Directions:
Mix up together ground pork, diced onion, garlic, and salt. Then brush the mason jars with coconut oil. After this, fill every jar with ground pork mixture. Top the ground pork with kale and Cheddar cheese and place the jars on the trivet. Cover every jar with foil. Pour water in the instant pot and insert the trivet. Cook the casseroles on Manual (High pressure) for 15 minutes. Then allow the natural pressure release for 10 minutes and remove the casserole from the instant pot.
Nutrition: calories 307, fat 22.1, fiber 0.3, carbs 0.2, protein 24

Ketogenic Instant Pot Lunch Recipes

Egg Salad

Preparation time: 10 minutes
Cooking time: 5 minutes
Servings: 4
Ingredients:
- 6 eggs
- 2 tablespoon avocado mayonnaise
- 2 cucumbers, sliced
- 1 avocado, peeled, pitted and cubed
- 2 spring onions, chopped
- 1 tablespoon cheddar cheese, grated
- 1 tablespoon mustard powder
- 1 tablespoon parsley, chopped
- A pinch of salt and black pepper
- 2 cups water

Directions:
Put the water in the instant pot, add the steamer basket and put the eggs inside. Put the lid on, cook on High for 5 minutes and then release the pressure naturally for 10. Cool the eggs down, peel, cut them into quarters and put them in a bowl. Add the cucumber, avocado and the rest of the ingredients, toss and serve for lunch.
Nutrition: calories 243, fat 18, fiber 4.8, carbs 8.7, protein 11.5

Provolone Chicken Soup

Preparation time: 10 minutes
Cooking time: 18 minutes
Servings: 4
Ingredients:
- 3 oz bacon, chopped
- 10 oz chicken fillet, chopped
- 3 oz Provolone cheese, grated
- 1 tablespoon cream cheese
- 1 white onion, diced
- ½ teaspoon salt
- ½ teaspoon ground black pepper
- 1 teaspoon dried parsley
- 1 garlic clove, diced
- 4 cups of water

Directions:
Place the chopped bacon in the instant pot and cook it for 5 minutes on sauté mode. Stir it from time to time to avoid burning. After this, transfer the cooked bacon in the plate and dry little with the paper towel. Then add onion and diced garlic in the instant pot. Sauté the vegetables for 2 minutes and add chicken and cream cheese. Stir well and sauté the ingredients for 5 minutes. After this, add salt, ground black pepper, dried parsley, water, and Provolone cheese. Stir the soup mixture well. Close the lid and cook the soup for 5 minutes on manual mode (high pressure). Then make a quick pressure release. Add the cooked bacon in the soup. Stir the cooked soup well before serving.
Nutrition: calories 346, fat 20.7, fiber 0.7, carbs 3.8, protein 34.4

Green Beans and Rice Mix

Preparation time: 10 minutes
Cooking time: 25 minutes
Servings: 4
Ingredients:
- 1 shallot, chopped
- 1 red bell pepper, chopped
- 3 garlic cloves, minced
- 3 celery stalks, chopped
- 1 pound green beans, trimmed and halved
- A pinch of salt and black pepper
- 1 teaspoon hot sauce
- 1 tablespoon thyme, chopped
- 2 cups veggie stock
- 2 cups cauliflower rice

Directions:
In your instant pot, mix the shallot with the bell pepper and the rest of the ingredients, put the lid on and cook on High for 25 minutes. Release the pressure naturally for 10 minutes, divide the mix between plates and serve for lunch.
Nutrition: calories 52, fat 5.3, fiber 3.1, carbs 4.6, protein 2.7

Jalapeno Soup

Preparation time: 10 minutes
Cooking time: 20 minutes
Servings: 4
Ingredients:
- ½ cup ground pork
- 1 teaspoon garlic powder
- 1 bell pepper, diced
- 1 jalapeno pepper, sliced
- 1 teaspoon coconut oil
- 1 tomato, chopped
- ½ teaspoon salt
- 1 teaspoon thyme
- 4 cups of water

Directions:
Put the coconut oil in the instant pot and preheat it on Saute mode. When the coconut oil starts shimmering, add bell pepper and jalapeno pepper. Cook the vegetables for 1 minute and stir them. Add ground pork, garlic powder, tomato, salt, and thyme. Stir well and sauté the ingredients for 2 minutes. Then add water and close the lid. Cook the jalapeno soup for 5 minutes on Manual mode (high pressure). Then allow the natural pressure release for 5 minutes.
Nutrition: calories 142, fat 9.4, fiber 0.9, carbs 3.7, protein 10.7

Garlic Beef Mix

Preparation time: 10 minutes
Cooking time: 20 minutes
Servings: 6
Ingredients:
- 2 pounds beef, cubed
- 1 tablespoon olive oil
- ½ cup okra
- 3 spring onions, chopped
- A pinch of salt and black pepper
- 1 cup chicken stock
- 1 cup tomato passata
- 2 tablespoons mustard
- 1 cup cheddar cheese, shredded

Directions:
Set the instant pot on Sauté mode, add the oil, heat it up, add the meat and brown for 5 minutes. Add the

rest of the ingredients except the cheese, put the lid on and cook on High for 15 minutes. Release the pressure naturally for 10 minutes, sprinkle the cheese on top, leave the mix aside for 10 minutes, divide it into bowls and serve.
Nutrition: calories 411, fat 19.3, fiber 1.6, carbs 5, protein 52.4

Aromatic Lasagna with Basil

Preparation time: 15 minutes
Cooking time: 10 minutes
Servings: 6
Ingredients:
- 2 eggplants, peeled, sliced
- 1 cup ground pork
- 3 tablespoons marinara sauce
- 1 white onion, diced
- 1 oz fresh basil, chopped
- ½ cup Ricotta cheese
- ½ cup Mozzarella, shredded
- ½ teaspoon dried oregano
- ¼ teaspoon salt
- 1 cup water, for cooking

Directions:
In the mixing bowl combine together ground pork, diced onion, basil, and dried oregano. Add salt and stir the meat mixture well with the help of the spoon. Line the baking pan with paper foil. Then place the sliced eggplants in the baking pan to make the layer. Sprinkle the eggplants with marinara sauce. Top the marinara sauce with ground pork mixture. Then spread the mixture with Ricotta cheese and shredded Mozzarella. Cover the lasagna with foil. Pour water in the instant pot and insert the trivet. Place the lasagna on the trivet and close the lid. Cook the lasagna for 10 minutes on manual mode (high pressure). Then make a quick pressure release. Cool the cooked lasagna little before serving.
Nutrition: calories 251, fat 13.5, fiber 7.2, carbs 14.9, protein 18.7

Parsley Beef Bowls

Preparation time: 10 minutes
Cooking time: 20 minutes
Servings: 6
Ingredients:
- 2 pounds beef roast, thinly sliced
- 1 tablespoon parsley, chopped
- 3 garlic cloves, minced
- A pinch of salt and black pepper
- ½ cup veggie stock
- 1 tablespoon lemon juice
- 2 tablespoons olive oil
- 1 teaspoon balsamic vinegar
- 1 cup feta cheese, crumbled

Directions:
Set the instant pot on Sauté mode, add the oil, heat it up, add the meat and garlic and brown for 5 minutes. Add salt, pepper and the rest of the ingredients except the cheese, put the lid on and cook on High for 15 minutes. Release the pressure naturally for 10 minutes, divide the mix into bowls, sprinkle the cheese on top and serve for lunch.
Nutrition: calories 390, fat 19.4, fiber 0.1, carbs 1.6, protein 9.5

Keto "Potato" Soup

Preparation time: 15 minutes
Cooking time: 4 minutes
Servings: 2
Ingredients:
- 1 cup cauliflower, chopped
- 1 oz bacon, chopped, cooked
- 2 oz Cheddar cheese, shredded
- 2 tablespoons cream cheese
- 1 oz leek, chopped
- 1 cup of water
- ½ teaspoon salt
- ½ teaspoon cayenne pepper

Directions:
Pour water in the instant pot. Add cauliflower, cream cheese, leek, salt, and cayenne pepper. Close the lid and cook soup mixture for 4 minutes on Manual mode (high pressure). Allow the natural pressure release for 10 minutes. Then add cheese and stir the soup until it is melted. With the help of the immersion blender, blend the soup until you get the creamy texture. Then ladle the soup in the serving bowls and top with bacon.
Nutrition: calories 248, fat 19, fiber 1.6, carbs 5.7, protein 14.3

Okra Soup

Preparation time: 10 minutes
Cooking time: 15 minutes
Servings: 4
Ingredients:
- 2 tablespoons olive oil
- 1 spring onion, chopped
- 3 cups okra
- 3 cups chicken stock
- 1 teaspoon garlic powder
- A pinch of salt and black pepper
- 1 cup cheddar cheese, shredded
- ½ cup coconut milk

Directions:
Set your instant pot on sauté mode, add the oil, heat it up, add the onion, stir and cook for 2 minutes. Add the rest of the ingredients, toss, put the lid on and cook on High for 13 minutes. Release the pressure naturally for 10 minutes, stir the soup again, divide it into bowls and serve.
Nutrition: calories 284, fat 24.1, fiber 3.2, carbs 7, protein 9.9

Egg Soup

Preparation time: 5 minutes
Cooking time: 15 minutes
Servings: 2
Ingredients:
- 2 eggs, beaten
- 2 cups chicken broth
- 1 tablespoon chives, chopped
- ½ teaspoon salt
- ½ teaspoon chili flakes

Directions:
Pour chicken broth in the instant pot. Add chives, salt, and chili flakes. Saute the liquid for 10 minutes. Then add beaten eggs and stir the soup well. Cook the soup for 5 minutes more.
Nutrition: calories 102, fat 5.8, fiber 0.1, carbs 1.3, protein 10.5

Greek Turkey and Sauce

Preparation time: 10 minutes
Cooking time: 25 minutes
Servings: 4
Ingredients:
- 1 turkey breast, skinless, boneless and cubed
- 1 tablespoon lime juice
- 1 cup Greek yogurt
- 1 cup tomato passata
- 1 tablespoon avocado oil
- 1 tablespoon garam masala
- ¼ teaspoon ginger, grated
- A pinch of salt and black pepper

Directions:
Set the instant pot on Sauté mode, add the oil, heat it up, add the turkey, ginger and garam masala, stir and brown for 5 minutes. Add the rest of the ingredients, toss, put the lid on and cook on High for 20 minutes. Release the pressure naturally for 10 minutes, divide the mix between plates and serve.
Nutrition: calories 20, fat 4.6, fiber 1.1, carbs 3.6, protein 0.9

Beef Cabbage Soup

Preparation time: 10 minutes
Cooking time: 15 minutes
Servings: 6
Ingredients:
- 1 cup white cabbage, shredded
- ½ cup kale, chopped
- 11 oz beef sirloin, chopped
- ½ teaspoon salt
- 1 teaspoon dried basil
- ½ teaspoon fennel seeds
- ½ teaspoon ground black pepper
- 1 garlic clove, diced
- 1 teaspoon almond butter
- 5 cups of water

Directions:
Put almond butter in the instant pot and melt it on sauté mode. Add white cabbage and diced garlic. Cook the vegetables for 5 minutes. Stir them occasionally. Then add chopped beef sirloin, fennel seeds, ground black pepper, salt, and stir well. Add basil and water. Then add kale and close the lid. Cook the soup on Manual mode (high pressure) for 5 minutes. Then make a quick pressure release.
Nutrition: calories 120, fat 4.8, fiber 0.8, carbs 2.1, protein 16.7

Lime Pork Bowls

Preparation time: 10 minutes
Cooking time: 20 minutes
Servings: 6
Ingredients:
- 2 pounds pork stew meat, cubed
- 1 teaspoon garlic, minced
- 1 shallot, chopped
- 1 tablespoon beef stock
- 2 teaspoon lime juice
- ½ teaspoon chili powder
- 1 teaspoon sweet paprika
- ½ cup tomato passata
- 1 tablespoon olive oil
- A pinch of salt and black pepper

Directions:
Set your instant pot on sauté mode, add the oil, heat it up, add the shallot, garlic and the meat and brown for 5 minutes. Add the rest of the ingredients, put the lid on and cook on High for 15 minutes. Release the pressure naturally for 10 minutes, divide the mix between plates and serve.
Nutrition: calories 351, fat 17.1, fiber 0.6, carbs 2.4, protein 20

Bacon Chowder

Preparation time: 10 minutes
Cooking time: 20 minutes
Servings: 4
Ingredients:
- 1 cup fresh spinach, chopped
- ½ cup heavy cream
- 4 oz bacon, chopped, cooked
- 1 teaspoon dried dill
- ½ teaspoon salt
- 4 chicken thighs, skinless, boneless, chopped
- ½ teaspoon cayenne pepper
- ½ teaspoon ground thyme
- 1 teaspoon coconut oil
- 1 teaspoon minced garlic
- 4 cups of water
- ½ cup mushrooms, chopped

Directions:
Put coconut oil in the instant pot and melt it on sauté mode. Then add chopped chicken thighs, salt, dill, cayenne pepper, and ground thyme. Stir the chicken well and sauté for 5 minutes. After this, add minced garlic and chopped mushrooms. Stir well and cook for 5 minutes more. Then add heavy cream and water. Then add chopped spinach and bacon. Close the lid and cook the chowder on Manual mode (high pressure) for 10 minutes. Then make a quick pressure release and open the lid. Cool the chowder for 10-15 minutes before serving.
Nutrition: calories 249, fat 19.4, fiber 0.4, carbs 2, protein 16.4

Coconut Broccoli Soup

Preparation time: 10 minutes
Cooking time: 15 minutes
Servings: 4
Ingredients:
- 1 broccoli head, florets separated
- 4 cups chicken stock
- A pinch of salt and white pepper
- ¼ teaspoon garlic powder
- 1 tablespoon chives, chopped
- 2 cups cheddar cheese, shredded
- 1 cup coconut cream

Directions:
In your instant pot, combine the broccoli with the stock and the rest of the ingredients except the cheese and the cream, stir, put the lid on and cook o High for 10 minutes. Release the pressure naturally for 10 minutes, set the pot on Sauté mode again, add the cheese and the cream, stir, blend using an immersion blender, cook for 5 minutes more, divide into bowls and serve.
Nutrition: calories 376, fat 33.5, fiber 1.4, carbs 4.9, protein 16.2

Butternut Squash Soup

Preparation time: 10 minutes
Cooking time: 25 minutes
Servings: 6
Ingredients:
- 2 cups butternut squash, chopped
- 2 garlic cloves, peeled, diced
- 1 teaspoon curry powder
- ½ teaspoon ginger, minced
- 1 white onion, diced
- 1 teaspoon salt
- 1 teaspoon ground paprika
- 1 tablespoon butter
- 5 cups chicken broth
- 2 tablespoons Ricotta cheese

Directions:
Melt butter in sauté mode. Then add garlic and onion. Saute the vegetables until they are golden brown. Then add butternut squash, ginger, salt, ground paprika, and ricotta cheese. Then add curry powder and chicken broth. Close the lid and cook the soup on manual mode (high pressure) for 15 minutes. Then make a quick pressure release. Blend the soup with the help of the immersion blender.
Nutrition: calories 87, fat 3.6, fiber 1.4, carbs 8.7, protein 5.5

Pork Chops and Thyme Mushrooms

Preparation time: 10 minutes
Cooking time: 25 minutes
Servings: 4
Ingredients:
- 3 garlic cloves, minced
- 1 tablespoon olive oil
- 1 spring onion, chopped
- 10 white mushrooms, sliced
- 4 pork chops, bone-in
- 1 cup beef stock
- 1 tablespoon thyme, chopped
- 1 cup coconut cream

Directions:
Set your instant pot on sauté mode, add oil, heat it up, add the garlic and the mushrooms and sauté for 2 minutes. Add the meat and brown it for 2-3 minutes more. Add the rest of the ingredients, put the lid on and cook on High for 20 minutes. Release the pressure naturally for 10 minutes, divide everything between plates and serve.
Nutrition: calories 444, fat 38, fiber 2.2, carbs 6.3, protein 21.6

Tortilla Soup

Preparation time: 10 minutes
Cooking time: 30 minutes
Servings: 2
Ingredients:
- ½ Poblano pepper, chopped
- ¼ teaspoon minced garlic
- ¼ teaspoon ground coriander
- ½ cup tomatoes, canned
- 1 tablespoon dried cilantro
- ¼ teaspoon salt
- 2 cups chicken broth
- 8 oz chicken breast, skinless, boneless
- 1 tablespoon lemon juice
- 1 teaspoon butter
- ¼ cup Cheddar cheese, shredded
- 2 low carb tortillas, chopped

Directions:
Melt butter in sauté mode. When the butter is melted, add chopped Poblano pepper, minced garlic, ground coriander, and dried cilantro. Add chicken breast and cook the ingredients for 10 minutes. Stir them from time to time. After this, add canned tomatoes, salt, and chicken broth. Close the lid and cook the soup on manual mode (high pressure) for 15 minutes. Then make a quick pressure release and open the lid. Add lemon juice and sauté the soup for 5 minutes more. Ladle the soup into the bowls and top with Cheddar cheese and chopped low carb tortillas.
Nutrition: calories 336, fat 13, fiber 8.3, carbs 16.1, protein 36.2

Mexican Pork and Okra Salad

Preparation time: 10 minutes
Cooking time: 30 minutes
Servings: 4
Ingredients:
- 2 pounds pork sirloin, cubed
- A pinch of salt and black pepper
- 2 teaspoons garlic powder
- 1 tablespoon olive oil
- 1 and ½ cups okra
- 1 cup tomato passata
- 2 garlic cloves, minced
- 1 tablespoon smoked paprika

Directions:
Set the instant pot on Sauté mode, add the oil, heat it up, add the meat, garlic, salt and pepper and brown for 5 minutes. Add the remaining ingredients, toss, put the lid on and cook on High for 25 minutes. Release the pressure naturally for 10 minutes, divide everything between plates and serve for lunch.
Nutrition: calories 66, fat 3.9, fiber 2, carbs 2.7, protein 1.6

Asian Style Zucchini Soup

Preparation time: 10 minutes
Cooking time: 25 minutes
Servings: 4
Ingredients:
- ½ teaspoon minced ginger
- ¼ teaspoon minced garlic
- 1 teaspoon coconut oil
- 10 oz beef sirloin steak, chopped
- ½ cup cremini mushrooms, sliced
- 4 cups chicken broth
- ½ teaspoon salt
- 1 zucchini, trimmed
- 1 teaspoon chives, chopped

Directions:
Heat up instant pot on sauté mode. Toss coconut oil and melt it. Then add minced ginger and minced garlic. Stir well and add chopped steak. Sauté the mixture for 5 minutes. Meanwhile, with the help of the spiralizer make the zucchini noodles. Add mushrooms in the beef mixture. Then sprinkle it with salt. Add chicken broth and cook the soup on Manual mode (high pressure) for 12 minutes. Then make a quick pressure release and open the lid. Add spiralized noodles and stir the soup. Let it rest for 5 minutes. Top the cooked soup with chives.

Nutrition: calories 191, fat 7, fiber 0.6, carbs 3.2, protein 27.2

Pork and Kale Meatballs

Preparation time: 10 minutes
Cooking time: 20 minutes
Servings: 6
Ingredients:
- 2 pounds pork stew meat, ground
- ¼ cup cheddar, grated
- 1 cup kale, chopped
- ¼ cup green onions, chopped
- 1 egg, whisked
- A pinch of salt and black pepper
- 1 tablespoon garlic, minced
- 1 tablespoon avocado oil
- 1 cup tomato passata
- ½ cup beef stock

Directions:
In a bowl, combine the meat with the cheese, kale, green onions, the egg, garlic, salt and pepper, stir well and shape medium meatballs out of this mix. Set the instant pot on Sauté mode, add the oil, heat it up, add the meatballs and brown them for 2 minutes on each side. Add the sauce and the stock, toss gently, put the lid on and cook on High for 15 minutes. Release the pressure naturally for 10 minutes, divide everything between plates and serve for lunch.
Nutrition: calories 362, fat 16.1, fiber 1, carbs 4.4, protein 26.7

Chili Verde

Preparation time: 10 minutes
Cooking time: 3 hours 5 minutes
Servings: 2
Ingredients:
- 9 oz pork shoulder, chopped
- ½ cup salsa Verde
- 1 teaspoon sesame oil
- ½ cup chicken broth
- ¼ teaspoon cayenne pepper
- ¼ teaspoon salt

Directions:
Pour sesame oil in the instant pot and preheat it on sauté mode for 3 minutes. Meanwhile, mix up together pork shoulder, cayenne pepper, and salt. Add the pork shoulder in the hot oil and sauté the meat for 2 minutes. Then stir it with the help of the spatula and add chicken broth and salsa Verde. Close the lid. Cook the meal on manual (low pressure) for 3 hours. When the time is over, shred the meat.
Nutrition: calories 418, fat 30.1, fiber 0.3, carbs 2.9, protein 31.7

Pork and Baby Spinach

Preparation time: 10 minutes
Cooking time: 20 minutes
Servings: 4
Ingredients:
- 1 pound pork stew meat, cubed
- 1 tablespoon olive oil
- ½ cup shallots, chopped
- 1 cup red bell peppers, chopped
- 2 garlic cloves, minced
- 1 cup beef stock
- 1 teaspoon chili powder
- 4 cups baby spinach

Directions:
Set your instant pot on sauté mode, add the oil, heat it up, add the meat and shallots and brown for 5 minutes. Add the rest of the ingredients except the spinach, put the lid on and cook on High for 10 minutes. Release the pressure naturally for 10 minutes, set the pot on Sauté mode again, add the spinach, toss, cook everything for 5 minutes more, divide between plates and serve.
Nutrition: calories 310, fat 14.9, fiber 1.3, carbs 7.6, protein 35.3

Keto Taco Soup

Preparation time: 10 minutes
Cooking time: 25 minutes
Servings: 5
Ingredients:
- 2 cups ground beef
- 1 teaspoon onion powder
- 1 teaspoon taco seasonings
- 1 garlic clove, diced
- 1 teaspoon chili flakes
- 1 teaspoon ground cumin
- 1 tablespoon tomato paste
- ½ cup heavy cream
- 5 cups of water
- 1 teaspoon coconut oil
- 1 tablespoon cream cheese
- 1 jalapeno pepper, sliced

Directions:
Toss the coconut oil in the instant pot and melt it on sauté mode. Add ground beef and onion powder. After this, add taco seasonings and diced garlic. Mix up the ingredients well. Then sprinkle the meat mixture with chili flakes and ground cumin. Saute the ground beef for 10 minutes. Mix it up with the help of the spatula every 3 minutes. Then add tomato paste, heavy cream, and water. Add sliced jalapeno pepper and close the lid. Cook the soup on Manual (high pressure) for 10 minutes. Then allow the natural pressure release for 10 minutes and ladle the soup into the bowls.
Nutrition: calories 170, fat 12.7, fiber 0.3, carbs 2.4, protein 11.2

Cinnamon Turkey Curry

Preparation time: 10 minutes
Cooking time: 30 minutes
Servings: 4
Ingredients:
- 3 tomatoes, chopped
- 1 bug turkey breast, skinless, boneless and cubed
- 2 tablespoons avocado oil
- 1 cup chicken stock
- 14 ounces canned coconut milk
- 2 garlic cloves, minced
- 3 red chilies, chopped
- 1 tablespoon ginger, grated
- 1 teaspoon cinnamon, ground
- 1 teaspoon turmeric, ground
- 1 tablespoon lemon juice
- A pinch of salt and black pepper

Directions:

Set your instant pot on sauté mode, add the oil, heat it up, add the meat and brown for 5 minutes. Add the tomatoes and the rest of the ingredients, put the lid on and cook on High for 25 minutes. Release the pressure naturally for 10 minutes, divide everything between plates and serve.
Nutrition: calories 268, fat 25, fiber 4.3, carbs 7.9, protein 3.7

Chicken Enchilada Soup

Preparation time: 10 minutes
Cooking time: 32 minutes
Servings: 4
Ingredients:
- 1-pound chicken fillet
- ½ white onion, chopped
- 1 bell pepper, chopped
- 1 jalapeno pepper, chopped
- 1 tablespoon avocado oil
- 1 tablespoon tomato paste
- 1 teaspoon apple cider vinegar
- 1 teaspoon chipotle pepper
- ½ teaspoon garlic powder
- ½ teaspoon ground cumin
- ½ teaspoon ground coriander
- ½ teaspoon ground paprika
- 1/3 teaspoon salt
- 1 teaspoon dried oregano
- 4 cups of water

Directions:
Pour avocado oil in the instant pot. Add white onion, bell pepper, and jalapeno pepper. Saute the vegetables on sauté mode for 5 minutes. Meanwhile, in the shallow bowl combine together garlic powder, cumin, coriander, paprika, salt, and dried oregano. Add the spices in the vegetables. Then add tomato paste, chipotle pepper, and apple cider vinegar. Add water and chicken fillet. Close the lid and cook enchilada soup on Manual mode (high pressure) for 25 minutes. Then make a quick pressure release and open the lid. With the help of 2 forks shred the chicken fillet and stir the soup.
Nutrition: calories 244, fat 9.1, fiber 1.4, carbs 5.5, protein 33.7

Basil Shrimp and Eggplants

Preparation time: 10 minutes
Cooking time: 10 minutes
Servings: 4
Ingredients:
- 2 eggplants, cubed
- 2 tablespoons veggie stock
- 2 tablespoons olive oil
- A pinch of salt and black pepper
- 4 garlic cloves, minced
- 1 pound shrimp, peeled and deveined
- Juice of 1 lime
- ½ teaspoon sweet paprika
- 2 tablespoons basil, chopped

Directions:
Set your instant pot on sauté mode, add the oil, heat it up, add the garlic and the eggplants and sauté for 2 minutes. Add the shrimp and the rest of the ingredients, put the lid on and cook on Low for 8 minutes. Release the pressure naturally for 10 minutes, divide everything into bowls and serve for lunch.
Nutrition: calories 269, fat 9.5, fiber 5.4, carbs 6.7, protein 28.8

Creamy Cauliflower Soup

Preparation time: 10 minutes
Cooking time: 15 minutes
Servings: 2
Ingredients:
- 1 tablespoon cream cheese
- 1 oz bacon, chopped, cooked
- 2 oz Cheddar cheese, shredded
- 2 cups cauliflower, chopped
- ½ teaspoon salt
- 1 teaspoon dried oregano
- 2 cups chicken broth
- ½ teaspoon ground nutmeg
- ½ medium white onion, diced

Directions:
Place onion and cream cheese in the instant pot. Cook the ingredients on sauté mode until onion is light brown. Then add chopped cauliflower, salt, dried oregano, and ground nutmeg. Cook the vegetables for 3 minutes. Then stir them well and add chicken broth. Cook the soup on Manual (High pressure) for 4 minutes. Then make a quick pressure release and open the lid. With the help of immersion blender, blend the soup until smooth. Ladle the soup in the bowls and top with Cheddar cheese and cook bacon.
Nutrition: calories 286, fat 18.8, fiber 3.2, carbs 9.7, protein 19.9

Mushroom and Chicken Soup

Preparation time: 10 minutes
Cooking time: 20 minutes
Servings: 4
Ingredients:
- 1 shallot, chopped
- 1 quart chicken stock
- 1 pound mushrooms, sliced
- 1 tablespoon olive oil
- A pinch of salt and black pepper
- 2 tablespoons ginger, minced
- 1 pound chicken breast, skinless, boneless and cubed

Directions:
Set your instant pot on sauté mode, add the oil, heat it up, add the shallot and the mushrooms and cook for 4 minutes. Add the rest of the ingredients, put the lid on and cook on High for 15 minutes. Release the pressure naturally for 10 minutes, divide everything into bowls and serve.
Nutrition: calories 203, fat 7.4, fiber 1.5, carbs 6.4, protein 28.5

Kale Soup

Preparation time: 10 minutes
Cooking time: 17 minutes
Servings: 4
Ingredients:
- 3 cups of water
- 9 oz sausages, chopped
- 2 oz Parmesan
- ½ cup heavy cream
- 2 cups kale, chopped
- ½ teaspoon ground black pepper

- ¼ onion, diced
- 1 teaspoon dried basil
- 1 tablespoon olive oil

Directions:
Pour olive oil in the instant pot and add the onion. Saute the onion for 3 minutes. Then stir well and add sausages. Mix up well and cook them for 3 minutes. After this, add water, kale, basil, and ground black pepper. Saute the mixture for 8 minutes. Then add heavy cream and Parmesan. Close the lid and cook the soup on manual mode (high pressure) for 3 minutes. Then make a quick pressure release. Let the cooked kale soup cool for 10-15 minutes before serving.
Nutrition: calories 364, fat 30.2, fiber 0.7, carbs 5.3, protein 18.4

Cod and Tomato Passata

Preparation time: 10 minutes
Cooking time: 12 minutes
Servings: 4
Ingredients:
- 4 cod fillets, boneless and skinless
- A pinch of salt and black pepper
- 2 tablespoons chives, chopped
- 2 tablespoons olive oil
- 2 teaspoons lime juice
- 1 cup tomato passata
- 1 tablespoon basil, chopped

Directions:
Set your instant pot on sauté mode, add the oil, heat it up, add the cod and cook for 1 minute on each side. Add the rest of the ingredients, put the lid on and cook on High for 10 minutes. Release the pressure naturally for 10 minutes, divide everything between plates and serve.
Nutrition: calories 75, fat 7.1, fiber 1, carbs 3.4, protein 0.9

Bone Broth Soup

Preparation time: 7 minutes
Cooking time: 10 minutes
Servings: 2
Ingredients:
- 1 eggplant, trimmed, chopped
- 2 cups bone broth
- ¼ cup carrot, grated
- 1 tablespoon butter
- ½ teaspoon salt
- 1 teaspoon dried dill

Directions:
In the mixing bowl combine together eggplants and salt. Leave the vegetables for 5 minutes. Meanwhile, toss the butter in the instant pot and melt it on sauté mode. Add grated carrot and cook it for 2 minutes. Meanwhile, dry the eggplants. Add them in the carrot and stir. Sprinkle the vegetables with dried dill. Then add bone broth and close the lid. Cook the soup for 5 minutes on Manual mode (high pressure). Then make a quick pressure release.
Nutrition: calories 200, fat 6.2, fiber 8.5, carbs 15.1, protein 22.5

Chicken and Mustard Sauce

Preparation time: 10 minutes
Cooking time: 15 minutes
Servings: 4
Ingredients:
- 2 chicken breasts, skinless, boneless and halved
- 1 tablespoon olive oil
- Salt and black pepper to the taste
- ½ teaspoon onion powder
- ½ teaspoon garlic powder
- ½ cup chicken stock
- 1 teaspoon Dijon mustard
- 1 tablespoon basil, chopped

Directions:
Set your instant pot on sauté mode, add the oil, heat it up, add the chicken and brown for 2-3 minutes. Add the rest of the ingredients, put the lid on and cook on High for 12 minutes. Release the pressure naturally for 10 minutes, divide everything between plates and serve.
Nutrition: calories 34, fat 3.6, fiber 0.1, carbs 0.7, protein 0.3

Buffalo Chicken Soup

Preparation time: 10 minutes
Cooking time: 15 minutes
Servings: 5
Ingredients:
- 1 white onion, diced
- ½ cup celery stalk, chopped
- ½ teaspoon minced garlic
- 1 teaspoon olive oil
- 1-pound chicken breast, cooked, shredded
- 4 cups chicken broth
- 1 tablespoon buffalo sauce

Directions:
In the instant pot bowl mix up together onion, minced garlic, and olive oil. Cook the ingredients on sauté mode for 4 minutes. Then stir them well and add shredded chicken breast. Add chicken broth and buffalo sauce. Mix up well. Cook the soup on soup mode for 10 minutes.
Nutrition: calories 154, fat 4.3, fiber 0.7, carbs 3.4, protein 23.4

Chicken and Avocado Mix

Preparation time: 10 minutes
Cooking time: 17 minutes
Servings: 8
Ingredients:
- 2 chicken breasts, skinless, boneless and halved
- 2 cups tomato passata
- A pinch of salt and black pepper
- 2 avocados, peeled, pitted and cubed
- 1 cup cheddar cheese, shredded
- 1 tablespoon olive oil

Directions:
Set your instant pot on sauté mode, add the oil, heat it up, add the chicken and brown for 5 minutes. Add the rest of the ingredients except the cheese and toss. Sprinkle the cheese on top, put the lid on and cook on High for 12 minutes. Release the pressure naturally for 10 minutes, divide everything between plates and serve.
Nutrition: calories 198, fat 16.4, fiber 4.6, carbs 6.6, protein 5.4

Keto Lunch Bowl
Preparation time: 10 minutes
Cooking time: 25 minutes
Servings: 2
Ingredients:
- ½ cup broccoli, chopped
- 8 oz chicken fillet, chopped
- 1 green bell pepper, chopped
- 1 teaspoon ground black pepper
- ½ teaspoon dried cilantro
- 1 cup chicken broth
- ½ teaspoon salt
- ½ teaspoon almond butter

Directions:
Place almond butter, bell pepper, and broccoli in the instant pot. Cook the ingredients on sauté mode for 5 minutes. Stir them with the help of the spatula from time to time. After this, add chopped chicken fillet, ground black pepper, salt, and cilantro. Add chicken broth and mix up the meal well. Close the lid and cook it on stew mode for 20 minutes. When the meal is cooked, let it rest for 10 minutes before serving.
Nutrition: calories 289, fat 11.6, fiber 2.1, carbs 7.9, protein 37.4

Tomato and Pork Soup
Preparation time: 10 minutes
Cooking time: 25 minutes
Servings: 4
Ingredients:
- 1 and ½ pounds pork stew meat, cubed
- 8 cups chicken stock
- 15 ounces tomatoes, chopped
- A pinch of salt and black pepper
- 1 tablespoon chives, chopped

Directions:
In your instant pot, mix all the ingredients except the chives, put the lid on and cook on High for 25 minutes. Release the pressure naturally for 10 minutes, divide the soup into bowls and serve.
Nutrition: calories 39, fat 4.3, fiber 1.2, carbs 3.4, protein 2.4

Cobb Salad
Preparation time: 10 minutes
Cooking time: 21 minutes
Servings: 4
Ingredients:
- 1-pound chicken breast, skinless, boneless
- 1 avocado, pitted, peeled
- 4 eggs
- 1 cup lettuce, chopped
- 1 tablespoon lemon juice
- ¼ teaspoon salt
- ½ teaspoon white pepper
- ½ cup white cabbage, shredded
- 4 oz Feta cheese, crumbled
- 1 tablespoon coconut oil
- ½ teaspoon chili flakes
- 1 tablespoon heavy cream
- 1 tablespoon apple cider vinegar
- ½ teaspoon garlic powder
- 1 cup water, for cooking

Directions:
Pour water and insert the trivet in the instant pot. Place the eggs on the trivet and close the lid. Cook them in manual mode (high pressure) for 5 minutes. Then make a quick pressure release. Cool the eggs in ice water. Then peel the eggs. Cut the eggs and avocado into the wedges. After this, rub the chicken breast with lemon juice, salt, and coconut oil. Place the chicken breast in the instant pot and cook it on sauté mode for 7 minutes from each side. The cooked chicken should be light brown. Make the sauce: whisk together chili flakes, olive oil, heavy cream, apple cider vinegar, and garlic powder. In the big salad bowl combine together lettuce, eggs, avocado, white pepper, white cabbage, and crumbled feta. Chop the cooked chicken roughly and add in the salad. Shake the salad well. Then sprinkle the cooked cobb salad with sauce.
Nutrition: calories 417, fat 27.9, fiber 3.8, carbs 7.4, protein 34.9

Cayenne Pork and Artichokes Stew
Preparation time: 10 minutes
Cooking time: 25 minutes
Servings: 4
Ingredients:
- 1 spring onion, chopped
- 2 and ½ pounds pork stew meat, cubed
- 15 ounces canned tomatoes, chopped
- 2 red chilies, chopped
- 1 and ½ cups canned artichoke hearts, chopped
- 2 garlic cloves, minced
- 2 tablespoons avocado oil
- 1 tablespoon cayenne pepper
- A pinch of salt and black pepper
- 1 teaspoon basil, dried

Directions:
Set your instant pot on sauté mode, add the oil, heat it up add the onion and the meat and brown for 5 minutes. Add the rest of the ingredients, put the lid on and cook on High for 20 minutes. Release the pressure naturally for 10 minutes, divide the stew into bowls and serve.
Nutrition: calories 36, fat 6.4, fiber 2.1, carbs 3.5, protein 1.4

Lobster Salad
Preparation time: 10 minutes
Cooking time: 4 minutes
Servings: 4
Ingredients:
- 4 lobster tails, peeled
- 1 teaspoon avocado oil
- ¼ teaspoon salt
- 2 cucumbers, chopped
- ¼ cup whipped cream
- 1 tablespoon apple cider vinegar
- 1 teaspoon dried dill
- ½ cup celery stalk, chopped
- 1 cup water, for cooking

Directions:
Pour water and insert the trivet in the instant pot. Arrange the lobster tails on the trivet and cook them on Manual mode (high pressure) for 4 minutes. Then make a quick pressure release. Cool the cooked lobster tails little and chop them roughly. Place the chopped lobster tails in the salad bowl. Add cucumbers, dried ill, and celery stalk. After this, make

the salad sauce: in the shallow bowl combine together salt, avocado oil, whipped cream, dill, and apple cider vinegar. Sprinkle the salad with sauce and mix up it well with the help of 2 spoons.
Nutrition: calories 139, fat 3.7, fiber 1, carbs 6.3, protein 1.3

Green Beans Soup

Preparation time: 10 minutes
Cooking time: 15 minutes
Servings: 4
Ingredients:
- 2 tablespoons olive oil
- 1 shallot, chopped
- 1 teaspoon garlic, minced
- 1 red bell pepper, chopped
- 8 cups chicken stock
- 1 and ½ pounds green beans, trimmed and halved
- 1 cup tomatoes, chopped
- 1 tablespoon chili powder
- 1 cup coconut cream

Directions:
Set your instant pot on sauté mode, add the oil, heat it up, add the shallot and the garlic and sauté for 2 minutes. Add the rest of the ingredients, put the lid on and cook on High for 13 minutes. Release the pressure naturally for 10 minutes, divide the soup into bowls and serve.
Nutrition: calories 242, fat 22.9, fiber 2.8, carbs 8.9, protein 3.7

Italian Style Salad

Preparation time: 5 minutes
Cooking time: 5 minutes
Servings: 2
Ingredients:
- 8 oz shrimps, peeled
- 1 teaspoon Italian seasonings
- 1 teaspoon olive oil
- ½ cup cherry tomatoes, halved
- ¼ teaspoon chili flakes
- ½ teaspoon coconut oil

Directions:
Toss coconut oil in the instant pot. Melt it on sauté mode and add peeled shrimps. Cook the shrimps for 1 minute from each side. Then place the shrimps in the bowl. Add chili flakes, Italian seasonings, halved cherry tomatoes, and olive oil. Shake the salad before serving.
Nutrition: calories 173, fat 5.5, fiber 0.5, carbs 3.5, protein 26.2

Broccoli and Zucchini Soup

Preparation time: 10 minutes
Cooking time: 15 minutes
Servings: 4
Ingredients:
- 1 shallot, chopped
- 2 teaspoons avocado oil
- 1 pound broccoli florets
- 1 pound zucchinis, sliced
- 4 cups chicken stock
- 1 teaspoon basil, dried
- 1 tablespoon cilantro, chopped

Directions:
Set your instant pot on sauté mode, add the oil, heat it up, add the shallot and sauté for 2 minutes. Add the broccoli and the rest of the ingredients, put the lid on and cook on High for 12 minutes. Release the pressure naturally for 10 minutes, ladle the soup into bowls and serve.
Nutrition: calories 70, fat 11.3, fiber 4.3, carbs 6.7, protein 5.3

Egg & Cheese Salad with Dill

Preparation time: 15 minutes
Cooking time: 4 minutes
Servings: 3
Ingredients:
- 3 eggs
- 2 tablespoons cream cheese
- 1 tablespoon dried dill
- ½ cup Cheddar cheese, shredded
- ¼ teaspoon minced garlic
- 1 cup water, for cooking

Directions:
Pour water and insert rack in the instant pot. Place the eggs in the instant pot, close the lid and cook them for 4 minutes on Manual mode (high pressure) Then make a quick pressure release. Cool the eggs in cold water for 10 minutes. After this, peel the eggs and grate them. In the mixing bowl combine together grated eggs, shredded cheese, minced garlic, dill, and cream cheese. Mix up the salad well.
Nutrition: calories 165, fat 13, fiber 0.1, carbs 1.4, protein 11

Beef Soup

Preparation time: 10 minutes
Cooking time: 25 minutes
Servings: 4
Ingredients:
- 1 and ½ pound beef meat, cubed
- 2 tablespoons olive oil
- A pinch of salt and black pepper
- 1 cup scallions, chopped
- 1 tablespoon sweet paprika
- 6 cups veggie stock
- 1 tablespoon parsley, chopped

Directions:
Set your instant pot on sauté mode, add the oil, heat it up, add the meat and the scallions and brown for 5 minutes. Add the rest of the ingredients, put the lid on and cook on High for 20 minutes. Release the pressure naturally for 10 minutes, ladle the soup into bowls and serve.
Nutrition: calories 73, fat 7.3, fiber 1.3, carbs 2.9, protein 0.8

Crab Salad

Preparation time: 10 minutes
Cooking time: 2 minutes
Servings: 2
Ingredients:
- 10 oz crab meat
- 1 tablespoon sour cream
- 1 tablespoon cream
- ¼ teaspoon minced garlic
- 1 tablespoon cream cheese
- ½ teaspoon lime juice
- ½ red onion, diced

- ¼ cup fresh cilantro, chopped
- ¼ cup fresh spinach, chopped
- ¼ teaspoon salt
- ¼ teaspoon ground cumin
- 1 cup water, for cooking

Directions:
Pour water in the instant pot. Line the trivet with the paper foil and insert the instant pot. Place the crab meat on the trivet and cook it on Manual mode (high pressure) for 2 minutes. Then make a quick pressure release and remove the crab meat from the instant pot. Chop it and place it in the salad bowl. Add diced onion, spinach, and cilantro. In the shallow bowl make the salad dressing: whisk together sour cream, cream, minced garlic, cream cheese, and lime juice. Then add salt and ground cumin. Add the dressing in the salad and stir it well.
Nutrition: calories 175, fat 6, fiber 0.8, carbs 6.4, protein 18.9

Curry Tomato Cream

Preparation time: 10 minutes
Cooking time: 20 minutes
Servings: 4
Ingredients:
- 1 pound tomatoes, peeled and chopped
- A pinch of salt and black pepper
- 3 garlic cloves, minced
- 1 tablespoon cilantro, chopped
- 2 cups coconut cream
- 2 cups chicken stock
- 1 tablespoon red curry paste
- 2 tablespoons chives, chopped

Directions:
In your instant pot, combine the tomatoes with salt, pepper, garlic and the stock, put the lid on and cook on High for 20 minutes. Release the pressure naturally for 10 minutes, transfer the soup to a blender, add the cream and curry paste, pulse well, divide into bowls and serve with the chives and cilantro sprinkled on top.
Nutrition: calories 320, fat 30.2, fiber 4.1, carbs 8.1, protein 4.2

Chicken Paprika

Preparation time: 10 minutes
Cooking time: 25 minutes
Servings: 2
Ingredients:
- 2 chicken thighs, skinless, boneless
- 2 tablespoons ground paprika
- 1 tablespoon almond meal
- 1 teaspoon tomato paste
- ½ teaspoon dried celery root
- ½ cup heavy cream
- 1 tablespoon butter
- ½ teaspoon salt
- ½ teaspoon white pepper
- ¼ teaspoon ground nutmeg
- 1 tablespoon lemon juice

Directions:
Melt butter in sauté mode. Meanwhile, rub the chicken thighs with salt and white pepper. Cook the chicken thighs on sauté mode for 4 minutes from each side. Meanwhile, in the mixing bowl combine together almond meal, dried celery root, and ground nutmeg. In the separated bowl combine together heavy cream, tomato paste, and lemon juice. Pour the heavy cream liquid in the chicken. Then add almond meal mixture and stir gently. Cook the meal on meat mode for 15 minutes.
Nutrition: calories 476, fat 30.3, fiber 3.3, carbs 6.5, protein 44.8

Spinach Soup

Preparation time: 10 minutes
Cooking time: 20 minutes
Servings: 4
Ingredients:
- 2 teaspoons olive oil
- 1 scallion, chopped
- 1 celery stalk, chopped
- 4 cups baby spinach
- 4 garlic cloves, minced
- 2 teaspoons cumin, ground
- 6 cups veggie stock
- 1 teaspoon basil, dried

Directions:
Set your instant pot on sauté mode, add the oil, heat it up, add the scallion and garlic and sauté for 5 minutes. Add the celery, cumin and the basil and sauté for 4 minutes more. Add the spinach and the stock, put the lid on and cook on High for 10 minutes. Release the pressure naturally for 10 minutes, ladle the soup into bowls and serve.
Nutrition: calories 37, fat 3.1, fiber 1, carbs 3, protein 1.4

Sour Cauliflower Salad

Preparation time: 10 minutes
Cooking time: 9 minutes
Servings: 2
Ingredients:
- 1 cup cauliflower, chopped
- 2 eggs
- 1/3 teaspoon salt
- ½ cup purple cabbage, shredded
- 1 tablespoon lemon juice
- 1 tablespoon cream cheese
- 4 oz bacon, chopped, cooked
- 1 cup water, for cooking

Directions:
Pour water and insert the trivet in the instant pot. Place the eggs on the trivet and cook them on manual mode (high pressure) for 5 minutes. Then make a quick pressure release. Cool the eggs. Place the cauliflower on the trivet and cook on steam mode for 4 minutes. Make a quick pressure release. Peel and chop the eggs. Place the eggs in the mixing bowl. Add cooked cauliflower, salt, shredded purple cabbage, lemon juice, cream cheese, and bacon. Mix up the salad.
Nutrition: calories 406, fat 29.9, fiber 1.7, carbs 5.1, protein 28.2

Cabbage Soup

Preparation time: 6 minutes
Cooking time: 15 minutes
Servings: 4
Ingredients:
- 1 shallot, chopped
- 1 pound green cabbage, shredded
- 12 cups chicken stock

- 1 celery stalk, chopped
- 1 tablespoon olive oil
- A pinch of salt and black pepper
- 2 tablespoons dill, chopped

Directions:
Set your instant pot on sauté mode, add oil, heat it up, add the shallot and sauté for 2 minutes. Add the rest of the ingredients, put the lid on and cook on High for 13 minutes. Release the pressure fast for 6 minutes, ladle the soup into bowls and serve.
Nutrition: calories 92, fat 5.4, fiber 3.1, carbs 5.7, protein 3.9

Warm Radish Salad

Preparation time: 10 minutes
Cooking time: 11 minutes
Servings: 4
Ingredients:
- 3 cups radish, sliced
- 7 oz chicken fillet, chopped
- 1 tablespoon lemon juice
- 1 teaspoon olive oil
- ¼ teaspoon salt
- 1 teaspoon butter
- 1 tablespoon dried parsley
- ½ teaspoon sesame oil

Directions:
Mix up together chopped chicken fillet with lemon juice, olive oil, and salt. Place the chicken in the instant pot and cook it on sauté mode for 3 minutes from each side. Then add radish and butter, and sauté the ingredients for 5 minutes. Transfer the cooked salad in the bowl. Add dried parsley and sesame oil. Mix up the salad.
Nutrition: calories 133, fat 6.5, fiber 1.4, carbs 3.1, protein 15

Cheesy Coconut Cream

Preparation time: 5 minutes
Cooking time: 20 minutes
Servings: 4
Ingredients:
- 2 tablespoons olive oil
- ½ cup spring onions, chopped
- 6 cups chicken stock
- A pinch of salt and black pepper
- 2 tablespoons parsley, chopped
- 2 cups coconut cream
- 1 cup cheddar cheese, grated

Directions:
Set your instant pot on Sauté mode, add the oil, heat it up, add the spring onions and sauté for 2-3 minutes. Add the rest of the ingredients, whisk, put the lid on and cook on High for 15 minutes. Release the pressure naturally for 10 minutes, divide the soup into bowls and serve.
Nutrition: calories 313, fat 30.5, fiber 2, carbs 6.1, protein 7.4

Crack Chicken

Preparation time: 10 minutes
Cooking time: 10 minutes
Servings: 4
Ingredients:
- 1-pound chicken breast
- 1 teaspoon salt
- 1 teaspoon garlic powder
- ½ teaspoon ground black pepper
- 1 teaspoon sesame oil
- ½ cup chicken broth
- 2 tablespoons cream cheese
- ½ teaspoon ground cumin
- ½ teaspoon ground coriander
- ½ teaspoon onion powder
- ½ teaspoon chives

Directions:
Cut the chicken breast into 4 servings. Then sprinkle the chicken with salt, garlic powder, sesame oil, and ground black pepper. Place the chicken in the instant pot and cook it on sauté mode for 2 minutes from each side. Then add chicken broth and cream cheese. Sprinkle the ingredients with ground cumin, coriander, onion powder, and chives. Stir the chicken with the help of the spatula and close the lid. Cook the crack chicken on poultry mode for 5 minutes.
Nutrition: calories 167, fat 6, fiber 0.2, carbs 1.3, protein 25.3

Eggplant Soup

Preparation time: 10 minutes
Cooking time: 15 minutes
Servings: 4
Ingredients:
- 1 tablespoon avocado oil
- 1 celery stalk, chopped
- 1 shallot chopped
- 3 eggplants, cubed
- 2 tomatoes, chopped
- 8 cups chicken stock
- A pinch of salt and black pepper
- 2 tablespoons rosemary, chopped

Directions:
Set your instant pot on Sauté mode, add the oil, heat it up, add the shallot and celery, stir and sauté for 3 minutes. Add the eggplants and the rest of the ingredients, put the lid on and cook on High for 12 minutes. Release the pressure naturally for 10 minutes, ladle the soup into bowls and serve.
Nutrition: calories 144, fat 5.7, fiber 0.2, carbs 5.3, protein 6.1

Salsa Chicken

Preparation time: 15 minutes
Cooking time: 17 minutes
Servings: 2
Ingredients:
- ¼ cup hot salsa
- 10 oz chicken breast, skinless, boneless
- 1 teaspoon taco seasoning
- ¼ teaspoon salt
- ¼ teaspoon chili flakes
- 1 tablespoon cream cheese
- ¼ cup chicken broth

Directions:
Place the chicken breast in the instant pot. Sprinkle the poultry with taco seasoning, salt, and chili flakes. Then add cream cheese, salsa, and chicken broth. Close and seal the lid. Cook the meal on manual mode (high pressure) for 17 minutes. Then allow the natural pressure release for 10 minutes and shred the chicken. Serve the shredded chicken with hot sauce from the instant pot.

Nutrition: calories 198, fat 5.5, fiber 0.5, carbs 3.3, protein 31.5

Bell Pepper Cream

Preparation time: 10 minutes
Cooking time: 20 minutes
Servings: 4
Ingredients:
- 1 shallot, chopped
- 2 tablespoons olive oil
- 4 red bell peppers, roughly chopped
- 2 tomatoes, cubed
- 3 tablespoons tomato paste
- 6 cups chicken stock
- ½ teaspoon red pepper flakes
- 1 teaspoon chives, chopped

Directions:
Set the instant pot on Sauté mode, add the oil, heat it up, add the shallot and cook for 2 minutes Add the rest of the ingredients except the chives, put the lid on and cook on High for 18 minutes. Release the pressure naturally for 10 minutes, blend the soup using an immersion blender, divide it into bowls and serve.
Nutrition: calories 134, fat 8.4, fiber 2.8, carbs 5.4, protein 3.3

Lemon Carnitas

Preparation time: 10 minutes
Cooking time: 30 minutes
Servings: 4
Ingredients:
- 13 oz pork butt, chopped
- ¼ cup white onion, diced
- 1 teaspoon ghee
- ½ teaspoon garlic powder
- 1 tablespoon lemon juice
- ¼ teaspoon grated lemon zest
- ½ teaspoon chipotle powder
- 1 cup of water
- ½ teaspoon salt
- 1 cup lettuce leaves

Directions:
Put pork butt, white onion, ghee, garlic powder, lemon juice, grated lemon zest, and chipotle powder in the instant pot. Saute the ingredients for 5 minutes. Then mix up the meat mixture with the help of the spatula and add salt and water. Close and seal the lid and cook ingredients on manual mode (high pressure) for 25 minutes. When the time is over, make a quick pressure release and open the lid. Shred the cooked pork with the help of the fork. Then fill the lettuce leaves with shredded pork.
Nutrition: calories 194 fat 7.3, fiber 0.3, carbs 1.4, protein 28.9

Chicken and Asparagus Soup

Preparation time: 10 minutes
Cooking time: 20 minutes
Servings: 4
Ingredients:
- 1 asparagus stalk, trimmed and halved
- A pinch of salt and black pepper
- 2 chicken breasts, skinless, boneless and cubed
- 2 scallions, chopped
- 1 tablespoon avocado oil
- 1 tablespoon sweet chili sauce
- ¼ cup parsley, chopped
- 5 cups chicken stock

Directions:
Set the instant pot on Sauté mode, add the oil, heat it up, add the scallions and the chili sauce and cook for 3 minutes. Add the chicken and brown for 2 minutes more. Add the rest of the ingredients, put the lid on and cook on High for 15 minutes. Release the pressure naturally for 10 minutes, ladle the soup into bowls and serve.
Nutrition: calories 108, fat 4.4, fiber 0.5, carbs 3.1, protein 1.1

Smoky Pulled Pork

Preparation time: 10 minutes
Cooking time: 20 minutes
Servings: 4
Ingredients:
- 1-pound pork loin
- 1 teaspoon smoked paprika
- ½ teaspoon liquid smoke
- ½ teaspoon ground coriander
- ½ teaspoon salt
- 1 teaspoon onion powder
- 1 teaspoon tomato paste
- 1 cup chicken broth

Directions:
Put the pork loin in the instant pot. Add smoked paprika, liquid smoke, ground coriander, salt, onion powder, tomato paste, and chicken broth. Close the lid and cook the pork on manual mode (high pressure) for 20 minutes. When the time is over, make a quick pressure release and open the lid. Remove the pork loin from the instant pot and shred it. Place the cooked pulled pork in the bowl and sprinkle it with ½ part of liquid from the instant pot.
Nutrition: calories 233, fat 8, fiber 0.3, carbs 1.3, protein 36.7

Hot Cod Stew

Preparation time: 5 minutes
Cooking time: 12 minutes
Servings: 4
Ingredients:
- 1 pound cod fillets, boneless, skinless and cubed
- 1 cup chicken stock
- 1 tablespoon hot sauce
- 1 tablespoon hot paprika
- A pinch of salt and black pepper
- 1 tablespoon cilantro, chopped

Directions:
In your instant pot, combine the cod with the rest of the ingredients, put the lid on and cook on High for 12 minutes. Release the pressure fast for 5 minutes, divide the stew into bowls and serve.
Nutrition: calories 100, fat 4.3, fiber 1, carbs 3.2, protein 1.4

Chicken & Dumplings Soup

Preparation time: 10 minutes
Cooking time: 25 minutes
Servings: 4
Ingredients:

- 4 cups chicken broth
- 4 chicken wings
- ½ onion, diced
- 1 tablespoon dried dill
- ½ teaspoon salt
- ¼ cup coconut flour
- 2 tablespoons water
- 1 teaspoon ghee

Directions:
In the mixing bowl combine together water and coconut flour. Knead the non-sticky dough. Add more coconut flour if the dough is sticky. Then make the log from the dough and cut it into pieces. After this, place the ghee in the instant pot and preheat it on sauté mode. When the ghee is melted, add diced onion and cook it until light brown. After this, add chicken wings, dried ill, and salt. Add chicken broth and close the lid. Cook the soup on manual mode (high pressure) for 10 minutes. Then make a quick pressure release. Open the lid and add prepared dough pieces (dumplings). Sauté the soup for 5 minutes more.
Nutrition: calories 179, fat 9.5, fiber 3.5, carbs 10.8, protein 11.9

Lamb Stew

Preparation time: 10 minutes
Cooking time: 30 minutes
Servings: 4
Ingredients:
- 1 tablespoon avocado oil
- 1 and ½ pound lamb shoulder, cubed
- 1 cup black olives, pitted and sliced
- 2 tomatoes, cubed
- A pinch of salt and black pepper
- 1 cup beef stock
- 1 cup tomato passata
- 2 tablespoons basil, chopped

Directions:
Set your instant pot on Sauté mode, add the oil, heat it up, add the meat and brown for 5 minutes. Add the rest of the ingredients except the basil, put the lid on and cook on High for 25 minutes. Release the pressure naturally for 10 minutes, divide the stew into bowls and serve with the basil, sprinkled on top.
Nutrition: calories 251, fat 5.6, fiber 2.7, carbs 4.7, protein 8.3

Zoodle Soup

Preparation time: 10 minutes
Cooking time: 25 minutes
Servings: 2
Ingredients:
- 2 cups chicken broth
- ½ teaspoon salt
- ½ teaspoon chili flakes
- 1 teaspoon dried oregano
- 1 teaspoon butter
- 8 oz chicken tenderloins
- 1 zucchini, spiralized

Directions:
Melt the butter in sauté mode. Then add chicken tenderloins. Sprinkle them with chili flakes, dried oregano, and salt. Cook the chicken for 3 minutes. Then add chicken broth and close the lid. Cook the soup on manual mode (high pressure) for 10 minutes. When the time is over, make a quick pressure release and open the lid. Add spiralized zucchini and stir the soup. Leave it to rest for 10 minutes.
Nutrition: calories 170, fat 4.1, fiber 1.4, carbs 4.7, protein 29.1

Shrimp and Olives Stew

Preparation time: 10 minutes
Cooking time: 10 minutes
Servings: 4
Ingredients:
- 1 and ½ pounds shrimp, peeled and deveined
- 1 cup black olives, pitted and halved
- 2 tablespoons olive oil
- 2 scallions, chopped
- 2 tomatoes, cubed
- 1 tablespoon sweet paprika
- ½ cup chicken stock

Directions:
Set your instant pot on Sauté mode, add the oil, heat it up, add the scallions and cook for 2 minutes. Add the rest of the ingredients, put the lid on and cook on Low for 8 minutes. Release the pressure naturally for 10 minutes, divide the stew into bowls and serve.
Nutrition: calories 118, fat 11, fiber 2.7, carbs 6.1, protein 1.3

Hot Sausages Soup

Preparation time: 10 minutes
Cooking time: 23 minutes
Servings: 3
Ingredients:
- 2 cups spinach, chopped
- 2 cups beef broth
- 7 oz sausages, chopped
- 1 teaspoon ghee
- ½ teaspoon salt
- ½ teaspoon ground cumin
- ½ teaspoon ground coriander
- ½ teaspoon dried celery
- ½ teaspoon onion powder
- 2 bell peppers, chopped

Directions:
Preheat the instant pot on sauté mode and place ghee inside. Melt it and add sausages. Cook the sausages for 10 minutes. Stir them from time to time with the help of the spatula. After this, sprinkle the sausages with salt, ground cumin, coriander, dried celery, and onion powder. Add beef broth and bell peppers. Close and seal the lid. Cook the soup on manual mode (high pressure) for 5 minutes. Then make a quick pressure release and open the lid. Stir the soup and add spinach. Cook the soup for 5 minutes more on sauté mode.
Nutrition: calories 295, fat 21.4, fiber 1.6, carbs 7.8, protein 17.6

Turkey Stew

Preparation time: 10 minutes
Cooking time: 20 minutes
Servings: 4
Ingredients:
- 1 turkey breast, skinless, boneless and cubed
- 1 teaspoon olive oil
- A pinch of salt and black pepper

- 1 tablespoon avocado oil
- 1 celery stalk, chopped
- 2 cups chicken stock
- 2 cups tomatoes, chopped
- 1 tablespoons cilantro, chopped

Directions:
Set your instant pot on Sauté mode, add the oil, heat it up, add the meat and cook for 5 minutes. Add the rest of the ingredients, put the lid on and cook on High for 15 minutes. Release the pressure naturally for 10 minutes, divide the stew into bowls and serve.
Nutrition: calories 81, fat 4.3, fiber 1.5, carbs 6, protein 8.6

Fajita Soup

Preparation time: 10 minutes
Cooking time: 20 minutes
Servings: 4
Ingredients:
- ¼ cup cream cheese
- 12 oz chicken fillet
- ½ teaspoon taco seasonings
- 2 bell peppers, chopped
- ½ cup canned tomatoes
- 3 cups beef broth
- ½ teaspoon salt
- ¼ cup heavy cream
- 1 jalapeno pepper, sliced
- 1 chili pepper, sliced
- 1 tablespoon butter
- ½ teaspoon minced garlic

Directions:
Melt the butter in sauté mode and add chicken fillet. Sprinkle it with taco seasonings, salt, and minced garlic. Cook it for 4 minutes from each side. After this, add cream cheese, canned tomatoes, cream, and bell peppers. Close the lid and cook the soup on manual mode (high pressure) for 10 minutes. Then make a quick pressure release and open the lid. Shred the chicken with the help of the fork. Add sliced chili pepper and jalapeno pepper in the soup and cook it on sauté mode for 5 minutes more.
Nutrition: calories 320, fat 18.3, fiber 1.2, carbs 7.6, protein 30.4

Kale Stew

Preparation time: 10 minutes
Cooking time: 20 minutes
Servings: 4
Ingredients:
- 1 shallot, chopped
- 2 garlic cloves, minced
- 1 pound kale, torn
- 20 ounces canned tomatoes, chopped
- 2 tablespoons olive oil
- A pinch of salt and black pepper
- ½ teaspoon cayenne pepper
- 1 tablespoon parsley, chopped

Directions:
Set the instant pot on Sauté mode, add the oil, heat it up, add the shallot and garlic and cook for 2 minutes. Add the other ingredients, put the lid on and cook on High for 18 minutes. Release the pressure naturally for 10 minutes, divide the stew into bowls and serve.
Nutrition: calories 145, fat 7.3, fiber 3.5, carbs 5.2, protein 4.8

Kalua Chicken

Preparation time: 15 minutes
Cooking time: 15 minutes
Servings: 3
Ingredients:
- 3 bacon slices
- ¼ teaspoon salt
- ¼ teaspoon of liquid smoked
- 6 chicken thighs, skinless, boneless
- 1/3 cup water

Directions:
Place the bacon at the bottom of the instant pot bowl. Sprinkle the chicken thighs with salt and liquid smoker and place over the bacon. Then add water, close and seal the lid. Cook the chicken on manual mode (high pressure) for 15 minutes. When the time is over, allow the natural pressure release and transfer the chicken tights on the chopping board. Shred the chicken and transfer it in the serving plates. Chop the cooked bacon. Sprinkle the cooked chicken with instant pot liquid and cooked bacon.
Nutrition: calories 363, fat 21.9, fiber 0, carbs 0.3, protein 45

Turmeric Cabbage Stew

Preparation time: 10 minutes
Cooking time: 20 minutes
Servings: 4
Ingredients:
- 3 garlic cloves, chopped
- 1 celery stalk, chopped
- 2 cups green cabbage, shredded
- 1 cup veggie stock
- ½ tablespoon avocado oil
- 14 ounces canned tomatoes, chopped
- A pinch of salt and black pepper
- 1 teaspoon turmeric powder

Directions:
Set your instant pot on Sauté mode, add the oil, heat it up, add the celery and garlic and sauté for 2 minutes. Add the rest of the ingredients, put the lid on and cook on High for 15 minutes. Release the pressure naturally for 10 minutes, divide the stew into bowls and serve.
Nutrition: calories 35, fat 4.2, fiber 2.4, carbs 3.2, protein 1.6

Southwestern Chili

Preparation time: 5 minutes
Cooking time: 25 minutes
Servings: 2
Ingredients:
- 1 cup ground beef
- ¼ cup celery stalk, chopped
- ¼ onion, chopped
- 1 teaspoon chili powder
- ¼ teaspoon salt
- 1 tablespoon tomato paste
- 1 cup chicken stock
- 1 teaspoon butter
- ½ teaspoon smoked paprika
- 1 tablespoon salsa

Directions:
Put the butter in the instant pot bowl. Add ground beef and cook it on sauté mode for 5 minutes. Then

stir the ground beef and sprinkle it with chili powder, salt, smoked paprika, and salsa. Add tomato paste, onion, and celery stalk. Add chicken stock. Close the lid and cook chili on stew mode for 20 minutes.
Nutrition: calories 173, fat 10.7, fiber 1.6, carbs 5.1, protein 14.3

Chili Mushrooms Stew
Preparation time: 10 minutes
Cooking time: 15 minutes
Servings: 4
Ingredients:
- 2 spring onions, chopped
- 2 teaspoons avocado oil
- 2 garlic cloves, minced
- 1 teaspoon chili powder
- A pinch of salt and black pepper
- 6 cups mushrooms, sliced
- 2 cups veggie stock
- 1 cup tomato passata
- 1 tablespoon chives, chopped

Directions:
Set your instant pot on Sauté mode, add the oil, heat it up, add the onions and the garlic and sauté for 2 minutes. Add the mushrooms and sauté for 2 minutes more. Add the rest of the ingredients except the cilantro, put the lid on and cook on High for 10 minutes. Release the pressure naturally for 10 minutes, divide the stew into bowls and serve with the chives sprinkled on top.
Nutrition: calories 56, fat 4.5, fiber 2.2, carbs 3.7, protein 4.7

Clam Chowder
Preparation time: 10 minutes
Cooking time: 22 minutes
Servings: 5
Ingredients:
- 8 oz clams, canned
- ¼ cup clam juice
- ½ cup celery stalk, chopped
- 2 cups cauliflower, chopped
- 2 oz bacon, chopped
- ½ white onion, diced
- ½ teaspoon ground coriander
- ½ teaspoon ground thyme
- ¼ teaspoon salt
- ¼ teaspoon ground black pepper
- ½ teaspoon coconut oil
- 3 cups of water
- ½ cup heavy cream

Directions:
Set sauté mode and put the bacon in the instant pot. Cook it for 5 minutes. Stir it from time to time. After this, transfer the cooked bacon on the plate. Put coconut oil in the instant pot and add the onion. Cook it for 4 minutes or until it is light brown. Then add cauliflower, celery stalk, water, ad clam juice. Close and seal the lid and cook the chowder for 5 minutes on Manual mode (high pressure). When the time is over, make a quick pressure release and open the lid. Blend the mixture with the help of the immersion blender. Then add canned clams, ground coriander, thyme, salt, ground black pepper, and heavy cream. Cook the chowder on sauté mode for 5 minutes more.

Ladle the cooked chowder in the bowls and sprinkle with bacon.
Nutrition: calories 145, fat 9.8, fiber 1.7, carbs 9, protein 5.8

Zucchini and Lamb Stew
Preparation time: 10 minutes
Cooking time: 30 minutes
Servings: 4
Ingredients:
- 2 tablespoons olive oil
- 2 zucchinis, sliced
- A pinch of salt and black pepper
- 1 pound lamb shoulder, cubed
- 2 tablespoons tomato passata
- ¼ cup veggie stock
- 1 teaspoon sweet paprika
- 1 tablespoon dill, chopped

Directions:
Set your instant pot on Sauté mode, add the oil, heat it up, add the meat and brown for 5 minutes. Add the rest of the ingredients, put the lid on and cook on High for 25 minutes. Release the pressure naturally for 10 minutes, divide the stew into bowls and serve.
Nutrition: calories 292, fat 15.6, fiber 1.5, carbs 4.5, protein 33.4

Parsley Meatloaf
Preparation time: 15 minutes
Cooking time: 30 minutes
Servings: 7
Ingredients:
- 2 cups ground beef
- 1 tablespoon parsley, chopped
- 1 teaspoon minced garlic
- 1 egg, beaten
- 1 teaspoon chili powder
- 2 oz Parmesan, grated
- 1 teaspoon butter, melted
- 1 tablespoon pork rinds
- 1 cup water, for cooking

Directions:
In the big bowl combine together ground beef, parsley, minced garlic, egg, chili powder, Parmesan, and pork rinds. Mix up the mixture until smooth. After this, pour water and insert the rack in the instant pot. Line the rack with foil and place the ground beef mixture on it. Make the shape of the meatloaf with the help of the fingertips. Then brush the surface of meatloaf with butter and close the lid. Cook the meatloaf for 30 minutes on Manual mode (high pressure). Then make a quick pressure release. Cool the meatloaf well.
Nutrition: calories 127, fat 8.4, fiber 0.2, carbs 0.7, protein 12.2

Beef and Cauliflower Stew
Preparation time: 10 minutes
Cooking time: 25 minutes
Servings: 4
Ingredients:
- 1 tablespoon olive oil
- 2 shallots, chopped
- A pinch of salt and black pepper
- 1 pound beef stew meat, cubed
- 15 ounces canned tomatoes, chopped

- 5 cups chicken stock
- 1 tablespoon cilantro, chopped

Directions:
Set your instant pot on Sauté mode, add the oil, heat it up, add the shallot and the meat and brown for 5 minutes. Add the rest of the ingredients, put the lid on and cook on High for 20 minutes.. Release the pressure naturally for 10 minutes, divide the stew into bowls and serve.
Nutrition: calories 272, fat 11.5, fiber 1.3, carbs 5.1, protein 35.6

Pepper Pork Chops

Preparation time: 10 minutes
Cooking time: 25 minutes
Servings: 4
Ingredients:
- 16 oz pork chops
- ½ teaspoon ground black pepper
- ½ teaspoon salt
- ½ teaspoon chili flakes
- ¼ teaspoon cayenne pepper
- 1 tablespoon sesame oil
- 1 teaspoon lemon juice
- ½ teaspoon dried rosemary
- 1 cup water, for cooking

Directions:
In the bowl combine together salt, ground black pepper, chili flakes, cayenne pepper, sesame oil, lemon juice, and dried rosemary. Rub the pork chops with oily mixture and wrap in the foil. Pour water and insert the trivet in the instant pot. Place the wrapped pork chops in the instant pot and cook on manual mode (high pressure) for 25 minutes. When the time is over, make a quick pressure release.
Nutrition: calories 395, fat 31.6, fiber 0.2, carbs 0.4, protein 25.5

Chicken and Brussels Sprouts Stew

Preparation time: 10 minutes
Cooking time: 25 minutes
Servings: 4
Ingredients:
- 1 tablespoon avocado oil
- 2 scallions, chopped
- 1 pound chicken breasts, skinless, boneless and cubed
- ½ pound Brussels sprouts, halved
- 1 teaspoon basil, chopped
- 1 and ½ cups chicken stock
- A pinch of salt and black pepper
- 1 tablespoon tomato paste

Directions:
Set your instant pot on Sauté mode, add the oil, heat it up, add the scallions and the chicken and brown for 5 minutes. Add the remaining ingredients, put the lid on and cook on High for 20 minutes. Release the pressure naturally for 10 minutes, divide the stew into bowls and serve.
Nutrition: calories 250, fat 9.1, fiber 2.7, carbs 6.7, protein 35.1

Meat & Collard Greens Bowl

Preparation time: 10 minutes
Cooking time: 18 minutes
Servings: 4
Ingredients:
- 1 cup ground pork
- 2 cups collard greens, chopped
- 1 tablespoon butter
- ½ teaspoon salt
- 1 teaspoon minced garlic
- 1 teaspoon ground paprika
- 1 teaspoon ground turmeric
- ¼ cup chicken broth

Directions:
Melt the butter in sauté mode and add ground pork. Sprinkle it with salt, minced garlic, ground paprika, and ground turmeric. Cook the ground pork on sauté mode for 10 minutes. Stir it from time to time to avoid burning. After this, add collard greens and chicken broth. Cook the meal on manual mode (high pressure) for 5 minutes. When the time is finished, make a quick pressure release. Mix up the cooked meal well before serving.
Nutrition: calories 271, fat 19.5, fiber 1.1, carbs 2.2, protein 21.1

Cod and Shrimp Stew

Preparation time: 5 minutes
Cooking time: 14 minutes
Servings: 4
Ingredients:
- 1 and ½ pounds shrimp, peeled and deveined
- 1 and ½ pounds cod fillets, boneless, skinless and cubed
- 20 ounces canned tomatoes, chopped
- 3 garlic cloves, minced
- 2 tablespoons parsley, chopped
- 2 cups veggie stock
- 1 tablespoon basil, dried
- A pinch of salt and black pepper

Directions:
In your instant pot, mix the shrimp with the cod and the rest of the ingredients, put the lid on and cook on High for 14 minutes. Release the pressure fast for 5 minutes, divide the stew into bowls and serve.
Nutrition: calories 130, fat 7.5, fiber 1.8, carbs 6.4, protein 1.5

Spinach Saag

Preparation time: 5 minutes
Cooking time: 10 minutes
Servings: 4
Ingredients:
- 1-pound spinach, chopped
- 2 tablespoons ghee
- 1 teaspoon garam masala
- ½ teaspoon ground coriander
- 1 teaspoon salt
- ½ teaspoon ground thyme
- ½ teaspoon cayenne pepper
- ½ teaspoon ground turmeric
- 1 teaspoon minced garlic
- ¼ cup of water

Directions:
Place ghee in the instant pot and melt it on sauté mode. After this, add garam masala, ground coriander, salt, thyme, cayenne pepper, turmeric, and minced garlic. Stir the mixture and cook it for 1 minute. Then add spinach and water. Mix up the greens well with the help of the spatula. Close the lid

and cook the meal on sauté mode for 5 minutes. Switch off the instant pot. Open the lid and blend the spinach until you get a smooth puree. Place the spinach saag in the serving plates.
Nutrition: calories 114, fat 9.2, fiber 3.6, carbs 6.3, protein 4.5

Beef Meatballs Stew

Preparation time: 10 minutes
Cooking time: 15 minutes
Servings: 4
Ingredients:
- 1 and ½ pounds beef meat, ground
- 1 egg
- 2 tablespoons cilantro, chopped
- 2 garlic cloves, minced
- A pinch of salt and black pepper
- ¾ cup beef stock
- ½ cup tomato passata
- ½ teaspoon sweet paprika
- 2 tablespoons olive oil
- 1 tablespoon parsley, chopped

Directions:
In a bowl, mix the beef with the egg, salt, pepper, garlic and the cilantro, stir and shape medium meatballs out of this mix. Set the instant pot o Sauté mode, add the oil, heat it up, add the meatballs and brown for 2 minutes on each side. Add the rest of the ingredients, put the lid on and cook on High for 10 minutes. Release the pressure naturally for 10 minutes, divide the mix between plates and serve.
Nutrition: calories 90, fat 8.3, fiber 0.6, carbs 2.5, protein 2.4

Chicken & Mushroom Bowl

Preparation time: 10 minutes
Cooking time: 20 minutes
Servings: 2
Ingredients:
- 1 cup cremini mushrooms, sliced
- 10 oz chicken breast, skinless, boneless, chopped
- ½ cup heavy cream
- 1 teaspoon salt
- ½ teaspoon ground paprika
- ½ teaspoon cayenne pepper
- 1 tablespoon coconut oil

Directions:
Melt coconut oil in the instant pot on sauté mode. Add cremini mushrooms and sauté them for 5 minutes. After this, add chopped chicken breast. Sprinkle the ingredients with salt, ground paprika, and cayenne pepper. Cook them for 5 minutes more. Then add heavy cream and close the lid. Cook the meal on poultry mode for 10 minutes.
Nutrition: calories 336, fat 21.6, fiber 0.5, carbs 2.9, protein 31.7

Salmon Stew

Preparation time: 10 minutes
Cooking time: 15 minutes
Servings: 4
Ingredients:
- 4 salmon fillets, boneless and cubed
- 2 cups chicken stock
- 2 tablespoons olive oil
- 2 shallots, chopped
- 2 tomatoes, cubed
- 1 tablespoon sweet paprika
- ½ teaspoon chili powder
- 1 zucchini, chopped
- 1 eggplant, chopped
- A pinch of salt and black pepper

Directions:
Set the instant pot on Sauté mode, add the oil, heat it up, add the shallots and cook for 2 minutes. Add the salmon and the rest of the ingredients, put the lid on and cook on High for 13 minutes. Release the pressure naturally for 10 minutes, divide the stew into bowls and serve.
Nutrition: calories 354, fat 19, fiber 6.1, carbs 7.6, protein 34.2

Cheddar Soup

Preparation time: 20 minutes
Cooking time: 5 minutes
Servings: 3
Ingredients:
- 1 cup chicken broth
- 1 cup heavy cream
- 1 teaspoon xanthan gum
- 2 cups broccoli, chopped
- ½ cup cheddar cheese, shredded
- ½ teaspoon salt
- 1 teaspoon ground black pepper
- ½ teaspoon chili flakes
- 1 teaspoon ground cumin

Directions:
Pour chicken broth and heavy cream in the instant pot. Add broccoli, salt, ground black pepper, chili flakes, and ground cumin. Close and seal the lid. Cook the mixture on manual mode (high pressure) for 5 minutes. Then allow the natural pressure release for 10 minutes and open the lid. Add xanthan gum and blend the soup with the help of the immersion blender. Ladle the soup in the bowls and top with cheddar cheese.
Nutrition: calories 252, fat 21.9, fiber 1.8, carbs 6.5, protein 9

Veggie Soup

Preparation time: 10 minutes
Cooking time: 15 minutes
Servings: 4
Ingredients:
- 1 tablespoon avocado oil
- 1 celery stalk, chopped
- 2 tomatoes, chopped
- 1 shallot, chopped
- 1 zucchini, chopped
- 2 garlic cloves, minced
- 6 cups chicken stock
- A pinch of salt and black pepper
- 1 teaspoon basil, dried
- 2 cups kale, chopped
- 2 tablespoons basil, chopped

Directions:
Set your instant pot on Sauté mode, add oil, heat it up, add the shallot and the garlic and sauté for 2 minutes. Add the rest of the ingredients except the basil, put the lid on and cook on High for 13 minutes. Release the pressure naturally for 10 minutes, ladle into bowls and serve with the basil sprinkled on top.

Nutrition: calories 58, fat 3.1, fiber 1.2, carbs 2.4, protein 3.4

Lunch Pot Roast

Preparation time: 10 minutes
Cooking time: 60 minutes
Servings: 4
Ingredients:
- 1-pound beef chuck pot roast, chopped
- 1 cup turnip, chopped
- 1 cup zucchini, chopped
- 1 garlic clove, diced
- 1 teaspoon salt
- 1 teaspoon coconut aminos
- 1 teaspoon ground black pepper
- 1 teaspoon butter
- 2 cups of water

Directions:
Put all ingredients in the instant pot and close the lid. Set meat mode and cook the meal for 60 minutes. When the time is over, open the lid and stir the ingredients carefully with the help of the spoon.
Nutrition: calories 269, fat 10.5, fiber 1.1, carbs 3.6, protein 38.2

Artichokes Cream

Preparation time: 10 minutes
Cooking time: 15 minutes
Servings: 4
Ingredients:
- 2 cups artichoke hearts, chopped
- 3 tablespoons ghee
- 6 cups chicken stock
- 1 shallot, chopped
- ¼ teaspoon lime juice
- 1 teaspoon rosemary, dried
- ½ cup coconut cream
- A pinch of salt and black pepper

Directions:
Set your instant pot on Sauté mode, add the ghee, heat it up, add the shallot and cook for 2 minutes. Add the rest of the ingredients, put the lid on and cook on High for 13 minutes. Release the pressure naturally for 10 minutes, blend the soup using an immersion blender, ladle into bowls and serve.
Nutrition: calories 169, fat 17.6, fiber 0.3, carbs 3, protein 1.8

Green Beans with Ham

Preparation time: 10 minutes
Cooking time: 6 minutes
Servings: 3
Ingredients:
- 2 cups green beans, chopped
- 7 oz ham, chopped
- ½ white onion, chopped
- 1 teaspoon olive oil
- ½ teaspoon salt
- ½ teaspoon ground nutmeg
- 1 cup water, for cooking

Directions:
Pour water and insert the steamer rack in the instant pot. Place the green bean, ham, and onion in the rack and close the lid. Cook the ingredients on steam mode for 6 minutes. Then make a quick pressure release and transfer the ingredients in the big bowl. Sprinkle them with ground nutmeg, salt, and olive oil. Stir well.
Nutrition: calories 153, fat 7.5, fiber 3.8, carbs 9.7, protein 12.5

Leek Soup

Preparation time: 10 minutes
Cooking time: 15 minutes
Servings: 4
Ingredients:
- 4 cups chicken stock
- 2 leeks, chopped
- 1 tablespoon olive oil
- 1 shallot, minced
- 1 tablespoon sweet paprika
- 1 tablespoon tomato paste
- A pinch of salt and black pepper
- 1 tablespoon cilantro, chopped

Directions:
Set the instant pot on Sauté mode, add the oil, heat it up, add the shallot and the leeks and sauté for 2 minutes. Add the rest of the ingredients, put the lid on and cook on High for 13 minutes. Release the pressure naturally for 10 minutes, ladle the soup into bowls and serve.
Nutrition: calories 75, fat 4.4, fiber 1.6, carbs 3.4, protein 1.8

Spiral Ham

Preparation time: 10 minutes
Cooking time: 12 minutes
Servings: 5
Ingredients:
- 1-pound spiral ham, sliced
- 1 tablespoon Erythritol
- 2 tablespoons butter, melted
- ½ teaspoon minced ginger
- 1 teaspoon mustard
- 1 cup water, for cooking

Directions:
In the shallow bowl combine together Erythritol, butter, minced ginger, and mustard. Then pour water and insert the trivet in the instant pot. Line the trivet with foil. Brush the spiral ham with butter mixture generously and transfer the ham in the instant pot. Cook the ham on manual mode (high pressure) for 12 minutes. When the time is over, make a quick pressure release and open the lid. Place the cooked spiral ham in the serving plate.
Nutrition: calories 237, fat 16.6, fiber 0.1, carbs 7.6, protein 17.3

Sage Chicken and Turkey Stew

Preparation time: 10 minutes
Cooking time: 25 minutes
Servings: 4
Ingredients:
- ½ pound turkey breast, skinless, boneless and cubed
- ½ pound chicken breast, skinless, boneless and cubed
- 1 tablespoon sage, chopped
- 1 teaspoon olive oil
- ¼ pound tomatoes, cubed
- 1 shallot, chopped
- A pinch of salt and black pepper

- 2 tablespoons tomato paste
- 2 and ½ cups chicken stock
- 1 tablespoon cilantro, chopped

Directions:
Set your instant pot on Sauté mode, add oil, heat it up, add the turkey, chicken and the shallots, and brown for 5 minutes. Add the rest of the ingredients except the cilantro, put the lid on and cook on High for 20 minutes. Release the pressure naturally for 10 minutes, divide the stew into bowls, sprinkle the cilantro on top and serve.
Nutrition: calories 147, fat 3.7, fiber 1.2, carbs 2.5, protein 22.4

Coconut Soup

Preparation time: 10 minutes
Cooking time: 13 minutes
Servings: 4
Ingredients:
- 2 cups of coconut milk
- 2 cups of water
- 1 teaspoon dried lemongrass
- 1 tablespoon lemon juice
- 1 teaspoon curry paste
- ½ cup white mushrooms, chopped
- 1 teaspoon butter

Directions:
Melt the butter in sauté mode. Add mushrooms and sauté them for 3 minutes. Then stir the vegetables and add lemongrass, lemon juice, and curry paste. Add water and coconut milk. Stir the mixture until the curry paste is dissolved. Close the lid and cook the soup on soup mode for 10 minutes.
Nutrition: calories 296, fat 30.4, fiber 2.8, carbs 7.5, protein 3.1

Bell Peppers and Kale Soup

Preparation time: 10 minutes
Cooking time: 15 minutes
Servings: 4
Ingredients:
- 4 red bell peppers, deseeded and roughly chopped
- ½ pound kale, torn
- A pinch of salt and black pepper
- 1 cup tomato passata
- 4 cups chicken stock
- 1 tablespoon cilantro, chopped

Directions:
In your instant pot, mix the bell peppers with the kale and the rest of the ingredients, put the lid on and cook on High for 15 minutes. Release the pressure naturally for 10 minutes, ladle the soup into bowls and serve.
Nutrition: calories 100, fat 6.3, fiber 2.2, carbs 3.7, protein 21.2

Corned Beef with Cabbage

Preparation time: 10 minutes
Cooking time: 43 minutes
Servings: 2
Ingredients:
- 10 oz corned beef
- ½ teaspoon ground nutmeg
- ¼ teaspoon ground black pepper
- ¼ teaspoon ground paprika
- ¾ teaspoon salt
- 1 teaspoon dried cilantro
- 1 cup chicken broth
- 1 cup cabbage, chopped
- 1 teaspoon butter

Directions:
Rub the corned beef with ground nutmeg, ground black pepper, ground paprika, salt, and dried cilantro. Place the meat in the instant pot. Add chicken broth and cook it on manual mode (high pressure) for 40 minutes. When the time is over, make a quick pressure release and open the lid. Shred the corned beef with the help of the fork and add chopped cabbage and butter. Cook the meal on manual (high pressure) for 3 minutes more. When the time is over, make a quick pressure release. Stir the cooked meal well.
Nutrition: calories 290, fat 20.6, fiber 1.2, carbs 3.1, protein 22

Tomato and Olives Stew

Preparation time: 5 minutes
Cooking time: 15 minutes
Servings: 4
Ingredients:
- 1 pound tomatoes, cubed
- 1 tablespoon olive oil
- A pinch of salt and black pepper
- 1 cup kalamata olives, pitted
- 1 teaspoon thyme, dried
- 1 cup chicken stock
- 1 tablespoon oregano, chopped

Directions:
Set your instant pot on Sauté mode, add the oil, heat it up, add the tomatoes and cook them for 2 minutes. Add the rest of the ingredients except the oregano, put the lid on and cook on High for 15 minutes Release the pressure fast for 5 minutes, add the oregano, stir, divide the stew into bowls and serve right away.
Nutrition: calories 96, fat 7.6, fiber 3, carbs 6.8, protein 1.6

Lazy Meat Mix

Preparation time: 10 minutes
Cooking time: 45 minutes
Servings: 2
Ingredients:
- 3 oz chicken fillet, chopped
- 4 oz pork chops, chopped
- 4 oz beef sirloin, chopped
- 1 onion, chopped
- 1 teaspoon tomato paste
- 1 teaspoon dried rosemary
- 1 cup of water
- ½ teaspoon salt
- 1 teaspoon olive oil

Directions:
Preheat the olive oil on sauté mode. Then add chicken, pork chops, and beef sirloin. Add onion and cook the ingredients for 3 minutes. Then stir them well and add tomato paste, dried rosemary, water, and salt. Stir it well until tomato paste is dissolved. Then close the lid and cook the meat mix on meat mode for 40 minutes.
Nutrition: calories 414, fat 23.3, fiber 1.6, carbs 6, protein 43

Creamy Brussels Sprouts Stew

Preparation time: 5 minutes
Cooking time: 25 minutes
Servings: 4
Ingredients:
- 1 tablespoon olive oil
- 2 shallots, chopped
- 1 pound Brussels sprouts, halved
- A pinch of salt and black pepper
- 1 cup chicken stock
- 1 cup coconut cream
- 1 tablespoon chives, chopped

Directions:
Set your instant pot on Sauté mode, add the oil, heat it up, add the shallots and sauté for 5 minutes. Add the rest of the ingredients except the chives, put the lid on and cook on High for 20 minutes. Release the pressure fast for 5 minutes, add the chives, stir the stew, divide it into bowls and serve.
Nutrition: calories 220, fat 16.7, fiber 5.6, carbs 6.8, protein 5.4

Shredded Chicken Salad

Preparation time: 10 minutes
Cooking time: 12 minutes
Servings: 4
Ingredients:
- 9 oz Chinese cabbage, shredded
- 10 oz chicken fillet
- ½ teaspoon lemon juice
- ¼ cup heavy cream
- 1 teaspoon white pepper
- ½ cup of water
- ½ teaspoon salt
- ½ teaspoon ground turmeric
- ¼ teaspoon dried sage
- 1 tablespoon cream cheese
- 1 tablespoon sour cream
- ½ teaspoon dried dill

Directions:
Rub the chicken fillet with white pepper, salt, ground turmeric, and dried sage. Place it in the instant pot. Add water and heavy cream. Close and seal the lid Cook the chicken on manual mode (high pressure) for 12 minutes. Then make a quick pressure release. Remove the chicken fillet from the instant pot and shred it. Put the shredded chicken in the salad bowl. Add sour cream and cream cheese in the instant pot (to the cream mixture). Then add dill and stir it. Sprinkle the salad with lemon juice and ½ of the cream mixture from the instant pot. Mix up the salad well.
Nutrition: calories 187, fat 9.7, fiber 0.9, carbs 2.4, protein 22

Ketogenic Instant Pot Side Dish Recipes

Ginger Cabbage and Radish Mix

Preparation time: 10 minutes
Cooking time: 15 minutes
Servings: 4
Ingredients:
- 1 red cabbage head, shredded
- 2 tablespoons veggie stock
- 1 cup radish, sliced
- 3 garlic cloves, minced
- 1 tablespoon coconut aminos
- 1 tablespoon olive oil
- ½ inch ginger, grated

Directions:
Set the instant pot on Sauté mode, add the oil, heat it up, add the garlic and the ginger and sauté for 3 minutes. Add the rest of the ingredients, put the lid on and cook on High for 12 minutes. Release the pressure naturally for 10 minutes, divide the mix between plates and serve as a side dish.
Nutrition: calories 83, fat 4.4, fiber 2.1, carbs 3.3, protein 2.6

Cauliflower Mac&Cheese

Preparation time: 15 minutes
Cooking time: 5 minutes
Servings: 4
Ingredients:
- 2 cups cauliflower, shredded
- ½ cup Provolone cheese, grated
- 1 tablespoon cream cheese
- ¼ cup of coconut milk
- ¼ teaspoon salt
- ½ teaspoon white pepper

Directions:
Put shredded cauliflower in the instant pot bowl. Top it with Provolone cheese. After this, in the mixing bowl combine together cream cheese, coconut milk, salt, and white pepper. Pour the liquid over the cheese and close the lid. Cook the side dish on manual mode (high pressure) for 5 minutes. When the time is over, allow the natural pressure release for 5 minutes more. Broil the surface of the cooked meal with the help of the kitchen torch.
Nutrition: calories 114, fat 8.9, fiber 1.7, carbs 4.1, protein 5.8

Chives Brussels Sprouts

Preparation time: 10 minutes
Cooking time: 10 minutes
Servings: 4
Ingredients:
- 1 pound Brussels sprouts, halved
- ¼ cup chicken stock
- A pinch of salt and black pepper
- 1 tablespoon green onions, chopped
- 2 tablespoons olive oil
- 1 tablespoon tomato passata
- 1 tablespoon chives, chopped

Directions:
In your instant pot, combine the sprouts with the stock and the rest of the ingredients, put the lid on and cook on High for 10 minutes. Release the pressure naturally for 10 minutes, divide the mix between plates and serve as a side dish.
Nutrition: calories 112, fat 7.5, fiber 2.4, carbs 4.5, protein 4

Brussels Sprouts Casserole

Preparation time: 10 minutes
Cooking time: 4 hours
Ingredients:
- 1 cup Brussels sprouts, halved
- ½ cup heavy cream
- ½ teaspoon ground black pepper
- ½ cup mushrooms, sliced
- 1 teaspoon salt
- 1 oz Monterey Jack cheese, shredded

Directions:
In the mixing bowl combine together cheese with heavy cream, salt, and ground black pepper. Place the Brussel sprouts in the instant pot in one layer. Then top it with sliced mushrooms. Pour the heavy cream mixture over the mushrooms and close the lid. Cook the casserole on manual mode (low pressure) for 4 hours.
Nutrition: calories 120, fat 10.4, fiber 1.3, carbs 3.9, protein 4.1

Mozzarella Broccoli

Preparation time: 10 minutes
Cooking time: 10 minutes
Servings: 4
Ingredients:
- 1 pound broccoli florets
- ½ cup veggie stock
- 2 shallots, chopped
- A pinch of salt and black pepper
- 1 cup mozzarella, shredded
- 1 tablespoon cilantro, chopped
- 3 tablespoons olive oil

Directions:
Set the instant pot on Sauté mode, add the oil, heat it up, add the shallots and sauté for 2 minutes. Add the rest of the ingredients except the mozzarella and toss. Sprinkle the mozzarella on top, put the lid on and cook on High for 8 minutes. Release the pressure naturally for 10 minutes, divide the mix between plates and serve.
Nutrition: calories 149, fat 12.1, fiber 3, carbs 7.8, protein 5.2

Rosemary&Butter Mushrooms

Preparation time: 5 minutes
Cooking time: 7 minutes
Servings: 2
Ingredients:
- 8 oz white mushrooms, chopped
- 1 teaspoon dried rosemary
- 2 tablespoons butter
- ½ teaspoon salt
- 1 cup chicken broth
- ¼ cup of coconut milk
- ½ teaspoon dried oregano

Directions:
Put mushrooms and butter in the instant pot and cook them on sauté mode for 4 minutes. Then add chicken broth, dried oregano, salt, and coconut milk

Close the lid and cook the side dish on manual mode (high pressure) for 3 minutes. When the time is over, make a quick pressure release. Serve the mushrooms with coconut-butter gravy.
Nutrition: calories 182, fat 13, fiber 3.4, carbs 9.8, protein 10.2

Garlic Broccoli Mix

Preparation time: 10 minutes
Cooking time: 15 minutes
Servings: 4
Ingredients:
- 2 tablespoons ghee, melted
- 3 garlic cloves, minced
- 1 pound broccoli florets
- ½ cup coconut cream
- 3 tablespoons lime juice
- 1 tablespoon dill, chopped
- ½ cup chicken stock
- A pinch of salt and black pepper

Directions:
Set your instant pot on sauté mode, add the ghee, heat it up, add the garlic and cook for 2 minutes. Add the broccoli and the rest of the ingredients, toss, put the lid on and cook on High for 12 minutes. Release the pressure naturally for 10 minutes, divide the mix between plates and serve.
Nutrition: calories 170, fat 14, fiber 3.8, carbs 6.5, protein 4.3

Bacon Brussels Sprouts

Preparation time: 10 minutes
Cooking time: 10 minutes
Servings: 6
Ingredients:
- 12 oz Brussels sprouts
- 3oz leek, chopped
- 2 oz bacon, chopped
- 1 teaspoon avocado oil
- ½ teaspoon salt
- 1 cup water, for cooking

Directions:
Pour water and insert the steamer rack in the instant pot. Then trim Brussel sprouts and cut them into halves. Arrange the vegetables in the steamer rack and cook on high pressure for 3 minutes. Then make a quick pressure release. Remove the Brussel sprouts from the instant pot. Clean the instant pot and rid of the steamer rack. Put bacon in the instant pot. Add avocado oil and cook the ingredients on sauté mode for 4 minutes. Stir them halfway of cooking. Then add leek and cook the mixture for 2 minutes more. Add the Brussel sprouts, mix up well and sauté the meal for 1 minute.
Nutrition: calories 85, fat 4.3, fiber 2.4, carbs 7.3, protein 5.7

Balsamic Mushroom and Radish Mix

Preparation time: 10 minutes
Cooking time: 15 minutes
Servings: 4
Ingredients:
- 2 tablespoons avocado oil
- A pinch of salt and black pepper
- 1 pound white mushrooms, sliced
- ¼ cup chicken stock
- 1 cup radishes, sliced
- 2 tablespoons balsamic vinegar
- 1 tablespoon parsley, chopped

Directions:
Set the instant pot on sauté mode, add the oil, heat it up, add the mushrooms and sauté for 5 minutes. Add the rest of the ingredients, put the lid on and cook on High for 10 minutes. Release the pressure naturally for 10 minutes, divide the mix between plates and serve.
Nutrition: calories 41, fat 4.3, fiber 1.9, carbs 3.5, protein 3.9

Spinach Mash with Bacon

Preparation time: 10 minutes
Cooking time: 8 minutes
Servings: 3
Ingredients:
- 1 oz bacon, chopped, cooked
- 1 cup spinach, chopped
- 1 tablespoon cream cheese
- ¼ teaspoon minced garlic
- ¼ cup Provolone cheese, grated
- ¼ cup heavy cream
- ¼ cup onion, diced
- ½ teaspoon white pepper
- 1 teaspoon cayenne pepper
- ½ teaspoon salt
- 1 cup water, for cooking

Directions:
Put all ingredients in the instant pot baking pan. Pour water and insert the trivet in the instant pot. Place the baking pan with spinach mixture in the instant pot. Cook the dip on manual (high pressure) 8 minutes. When the time is over, allow the natural pressure release for 10 minutes and open the lid. Mix up the spinach mash carefully with the help of the spoon.
Nutrition: calories 145, fat 11.9, fiber 0.7, carbs 2.7, protein 7.3

Collard Greens and Tomatoes

Preparation time: 10 minutes
Cooking time: 15 minutes
Servings: 4
Ingredients:
- 2 tablespoons avocado oil
- 1 pound collard greens
- ¼ cup chicken stock
- 1 tablespoon lime juice
- 2 cups cherry tomatoes, chopped
- 2 spring onions, chopped
- A pinch of salt and black pepper
- 1 tablespoon chives, chopped

Directions:
Set your instant pot on sauté mode, add the oil, heat it up, add the onions and sauté for 2 minutes. Add the rest of the ingredients, put the lid on and cook on High for 13 minutes. Release the pressure naturally for 10 minutes, divide the mix between plates and serve.
Nutrition: calories 60, fat 4.6, fiber 1.4, carbs 3.2, protein 3.6

Mashed Cauliflower

Preparation time: 10 minutes

Cooking time: 4 minutes
Servings: 1
Ingredients:
- 1 cup cauliflower, chopped
- ¼ teaspoon salt
- 1 tablespoon butter
- 1 cup water, for cooking

Directions:
Pour water and insert the steamer rack in the instant pot. Place the chopped cauliflower on the rack and close the lid. Cook the vegetables for 4 minutes on Steam mode. When the time is over, make a quick pressure release. Transfer the cooked cauliflower in the bowl. Add butter and salt. With the help of the potato masher mash the vegetables until smooth. Add ¼ cup of water from the instant pot. If the mash is not soft enough – add more water. Mix up the mashed cauliflower well.
Nutrition: calories 127, fat 11.6, fiber 2.5, carbs 5.3, protein 2.1

Balsamic Spinach

Preparation time: 5 minutes
Cooking time: 7 minutes
Servings: 4
Ingredients:
- ¼ cup veggie stock
- 1 and ½ pound baby spinach
- 1 tablespoon balsamic vinegar
- 1 tablespoon walnuts, chopped
- 1 tablespoon chives, chopped

Directions:
In your instant pot, mix the spinach with the stock and the rest of the ingredients, put the lid on and cook on High for 7 minutes. Release the pressure fast for 5 minutes, divide the mix between plates and serve.
Nutrition: calories 13, fat 1.2, fiber 0.2, carbs 0.3, protein 0.5

Fried Cauliflower Slices

Preparation time: 10 minutes
Cooking time: 5 minutes
Servings: 3
Ingredients:
- 9 oz cauliflower head, trimmed
- 1 teaspoon ground nutmeg
- ½ teaspoon ground paprika
- ½ teaspoon ground turmeric
- ½ teaspoon dried oregano
- 1 tablespoon lemon juice
- 1 tablespoon avocado oil
- ¼ teaspoon minced garlic
- 1 tablespoon heavy cream
- 1 cup water, for cooking

Directions:
Slice the cauliflower into the steaks. Then pour water in the instant pot. Insert the steamer rack. Place the cauliflower steaks on the rack and close the lid. Cook the vegetables on manual mode (high pressure) for 2 minutes. Then make a quick pressure release. Remove the cauliflower steaks and clean the instant pot. In the shallow bowl combine together ground nutmeg, paprika, turmeric, oregano, lemon juice, avocado oil, minced garlic, and heavy cream. Carefully brush the cauliflower slices with spice mixture from both side and place in the instant pot in one layer. Cook the cauliflower on sauté mode for 1 minute from each side or until it light brown. Repeat the same steps with remaining cauliflower slices.
Nutrition: calories 53, fat 3, fiber 2.8, carbs 6.1, protein 2

Paprika Mushrooms

Preparation time: 10 minutes
Cooking time: 15 minutes
Servings: 4
Ingredients:
- and ½ pound white mushrooms, sliced
- A pinch of salt and black pepper
- 1 tablespoon sweet paprika
- 1 cup veggie stock
- 1 tablespoon dill, chopped
- 1 tablespoon rosemary, chopped
- 1 tablespoon avocado oil

Directions:
Set your instant pot on sauté mode, add the oil, heat it up, add the mushrooms and sauté them for 5 minutes. Add the rest of the ingredients, put the lid on and cook on High for 10 minutes. Release the pressure naturally for 10 minutes, divide the mix between plates and serve.
Nutrition: calories 14, fat 2.3, fiber 1.3, carbs 2.1, protein 0.5

Mashed Brussel Sprouts

Preparation time: 10 minutes
Cooking time: 5 minutes
Servings: 4
Ingredients:
- 2 cups Brussel sprouts
- ½ teaspoon onion powder
- ¼ cup heavy cream, hot
- ¼ teaspoon salt
- 1 cup water, for cooking

Directions:
Pour water and insert the steamer rack in the instant pot. Place the Brussel sprouts in the rack and cook it on manual mode (high pressure) for 5 minutes. When the time is over, make a quick pressure release. Transfer the cooked vegetables in the food processor. Add cream, salt, and onion powder. Blend the mixture until is smooth. Put the cooked mashed Brussel sprouts in the bowls. It is recommended to serve the side dish warm or hot.
Nutrition: calories 46, fat 2.9, fiber 1.7, carbs 4.5, protein 1.7

Coconut Spinach Mix

Preparation time: 5 minutes
Cooking time: 7 minutes
Servings: 4
Ingredients:
- 1 and ½ pounds baby spinach
- ¼ cup coconut cream
- 1 tablespoon chili powder
- A pinch of salt and black pepper
- 1 tablespoon cilantro, chopped

Directions:
In your instant pot, combine the spinach with the rest of the ingredients, put the lid on and cook on High for 7 minutes. Release the pressure fast for 5

minutes, divide the mix between plates and serve as a side dish.
Nutrition: calories 41, fat 3.9, fiber 1, carbs 1.9, protein 0.6

Cauliflower Rice

Preparation time: 2 minutes
Cooking time: 1 minute
Servings: 2
Ingredients:
- 1 cup cauliflower, shredded
- 5 oz chicken broth

Directions:
Put cauliflower and chicken broth in the instant pot. Set manual mode (high pressure) and cook cauliflower for 1 minute. Then make a quick pressure release. Add salt and ground black pepper if desired.
Nutrition: calories 24, fat 0.5, fiber 1.3, carbs 2.9, protein 2.4

Chili Eggplant and Collard Greens

Preparation time: 10 minutes
Cooking time: 15 minutes
Servings: 4
Ingredients:
- 1 big eggplant, cubed
- 1 pound collard greens, halved
- 2 tablespoons avocado oil
- 2 teaspoons chili paste
- ½ cup chicken stock
- 1 tablespoon cilantro, chopped
- 4 green onions, chopped

Directions:
Set your instant pot on sauté mode, add the oil, heat it up, add the spring onions and the eggplants, stir and cook for 4 minutes. Add the rest of the ingredients, put the lid on and cook on High for 10 minutes. Release the pressure naturally for 10 minutes, divide everything between plates and serve.
Nutrition: calories 84, fat 2.4, fiber 2, carbs 6, protein 4.2

Soft Spinach with Dill

Preparation time: 5 minutes
Cooking time: 10 minutes
Servings: 2
Ingredients:
- 2 cup fresh spinach, chopped
- 1 teaspoon avocado oil
- 1 tablespoon fresh dill, chopped
- 1 teaspoon lemon juice
- ¼ teaspoon salt
- 1 teaspoon butter
- ¼ teaspoon onion powder

Directions:
Set instant pot on sauté mode and adjust 10 minutes. Pour avocado oil and add chopped spinach. Sprinkle the greens with dill, lemon juice, salt, and onion powder. Add butter. Stir the spinach every 2 minutes.
Nutrition: calories 32, fat 2.4, fiber 1, carbs 2.4, protein 1.3

Chard and Mushrooms Mix

Preparation time: 10 minutes
Cooking time: 12 minutes
Servings: 4
Ingredients:
- 2 tablespoons olive oil
- 1 pound white mushrooms, sliced
- 1 red chard bunch, roughly chopped
- ¼ cup chicken stock
- 1 teaspoon garlic powder
- A pinch of salt and black pepper
- 3 tablespoons parsley, chopped

Directions:
Set your instant pot on sauté mode, add the oil, heat it up, add the mushrooms and sauté for 2 minutes. Add the rest of the ingredients, put the lid on and cook on High for 10 minutes. Release the pressure naturally for 10 minutes, divide the mix between plates and serve as a side dish.
Nutrition: calories 88, fat 7.4, fiber 1.3, carbs 4.5, protein 3.8

Mexican Style Keto Rice

Preparation time: 5 minutes
Cooking time: 4 minutes
Servings: 5
Ingredients:
- 3 cups cauliflower, shredded
- ½ teaspoon taco seasonings
- ½ teaspoon garlic powder
- 1 teaspoon lime juice
- 1 teaspoon dried cilantro
- 1 bell pepper, diced
- 2 cups chicken broth
- ½ teaspoon salt

Directions:
In the shallow bowl combine together taco seasonings, garlic powder, salt, and dried cilantro. Then put shredded cauliflower in the instant pot bowl. Add spice mixture. After this, add lime juice, bell pepper, and chicken broth. Gently mix up the vegetables with the help of the spoon. Close the lid of the instant pot and cook the meal on manual (high pressure) for 4 minutes. When the time is over, make a quick pressure release. Stir the side dish well.
Nutrition: calories 42, fat 0.7, fiber 1.9, carbs 6.2, protein 3.4

Creamy Cauliflower

Preparation time: 10 minutes
Cooking time: 15 minutes
Servings: 4
Ingredients:
- 1 pound cauliflower florets
- 1 cup red onion, chopped
- ¼ cup chicken stock
- A pinch of salt and black pepper
- 2 tablespoons balsamic vinegar
- 1 cup coconut cream

Directions:
In your instant pot, mix the cauliflower with the rest of the ingredients, put the lid on and cook on High for 15 minutes. Release the pressure naturally for 10 minutes, divide the mix between plates and serve.
Nutrition: calories 180, fat 14.5, fiber 4.5, carbs 7.5, protein 4

Kale&Parmesan Bowl

Preparation time: 5 minutes
Cooking time: 10 minutes

Servings: 3
Ingredients:
- 3 pecans
- 7 oz curly kale, chopped
- 2 oz Parmesan, grated
- 2 tablespoon cream cheese

Directions:
Put the pecans in the grinder and grind until you get smooth mass. Then mix up together grinded pecans with cream cheese. Heat up the instant pot on sauté mode for 2 minutes. Add cream cheese mixture and kale. Cook the ingredients for 4 minutes. Stir them halfway of cooking. Then add cheese. Cook the meal for 4 minutes more or until the kale is tender.
Nutrition: calories 214, fat 17, fiber 3.9, carbs 8.7, protein 10.9

Creamy Green Beans
Preparation time: 10 minutes
Cooking time: 15 minutes
Servings: 4
Ingredients:
- 10 ounces green beans, trimmed and halved
- A pinch of salt and black pepper
- 1/3 cup parmesan, grated
- 2 ounces cream cheese
- 1/3 cup coconut cream
- 1 tablespoon dill, chopped

Directions:
In your instant pot, mix the green beans with the cream cheese and the rest of the ingredients, put the lid on and cook on High for 15 minutes. Release the pressure naturally for 10 minutes, divide the mix between plates and serve as a side dish.
Nutrition: calories 119, fat 9.8, fiber 3, carbs 6, protein 3

White Cabbage in Cream
Preparation time: 5 minutes
Cooking time: 7 hours
Servings: 4
Ingredients:
- 12 oz white cabbage, roughly chopped
- 1 cup cream
- 1 tablespoon cream cheese
- 1 teaspoon salt
- 1 teaspoon chili powder

Directions:
Put all ingredients in the instant pot bowl and close the lid. Cook the vegetables for 7 minutes on manual mode (high pressure). When the time is over, make a quick pressure release. Open the instant pot lid and stir the cooked side dish well.
Nutrition: calories 71, fat 4.4, fiber 2.4, carbs 7.2, protein 1.8

Spinach and Radish Mix
Preparation time: 5 minutes
Cooking time: 7 minutes
Servings: 4
Ingredients:
- 1 pound spinach, torn
- 2 cups radishes, sliced
- A pinch of salt and black pepper
- ¼ cup veggie stock
- 1 teaspoon chili powder
- 1 tablespoon parsley, chopped

Directions:
In your instant pot, mix the spinach with the radishes and the rest of the ingredients, put the lid on and cook on High for 7 minutes. Release the pressure fast for 5 minutes, divide the mix between plates and serve.
Nutrition: calories 70, fat 4.4, fiber 3.7, carbs 4, protein 3.7

Cauliflower Cheese
Preparation time: 5 minutes
Cooking time: 15 minutes
Servings: 2
Ingredients:
- ½ cup cauliflower, cut into florets
- ½ teaspoon dried dill
- ¼ teaspoon dried cilantro
- ¼ teaspoon dried sage
- 3 oz Parmesan, grated
- ¼ cup of organic almond milk

Directions:
Put cauliflower in the instant pot bowl. Sprinkle it with dried dill, cilantro, and sage. In the separated bowl mix up together almond milk and Parmesan. Pour the liquid over the cauliflower and close the lid. Cook the meal on sauté mode for 15 minutes. Stir the cauliflower every 5 minutes to avoid burning.
Nutrition: calories 164, fat 10.7, fiber 1.2, carbs 4, protein 14.7

Lemon Cabbage Mix
Preparation time: 10 minutes
Cooking time: 10 minutes
Servings: 4
Ingredients:
- 1 pound green cabbage, shredded
- ½ cup chicken stock
- A pinch of salt and black pepper
- 1 tablespoon lemon juice
- 1 tablespoon chives, chopped
- 1 tablespoon lemon zest, grated

Directions:
In your instant pot, mix the cabbage with the stock and the rest of the ingredients, put the lid on and cook on High for 10 minutes. Release the pressure naturally for 10 minutes, divide the mix between plates sand serve.
Nutrition: calories 34, fat 2.4, fiber 1, carbs 1.9, protein 1.6

Cauli-Tatoes
Preparation time: 10 minutes
Cooking time: 5 minutes
Servings: 2
Ingredients:
- 1 teaspoon cream cheese
- ½ teaspoon salt
- ½ teaspoon ground turmeric
- ½ teaspoon white pepper
- 2 cups cauliflower
- ½ teaspoon garlic powder
- 1 cup water, for cooking

Directions:
Pour water and insert the trivet in the instant pot. Put the cauliflower on the trivet and cook it for 5

minutes on steam mode. Then make a quick pressure release. Open the lid and transfer cooked cauliflower in the food processor. Add salt, ground turmeric, cream cheese, white pepper, and garlic powder. Then add ¾ cup of the remaining water from the instant pot. Blend the mixture until it is smooth (appx for 3-5 minutes).
Nutrition: calories 36, fat 0.8, fiber 2.8, carbs 6.6, protein 2.3

Herbed Radish Mix

Preparation time: 10 minutes
Cooking time: 12 minutes
Servings: 4
Ingredients:
- 3 cups red radishes, halved
- ½ cup veggie stock
- 2 tablespoons basil, chopped
- 1 tablespoon oregano, chopped
- 1 tablespoon chives, chopped
- 1 tablespoon green onion, chopped
- A pinch of salt and black pepper

Directions:
In your instant pot, combine the radishes with the stock and the rest of the ingredients, put the lid on and cook on High for 12 minutes. Release the pressure naturally for 10 minutes, divide the mix between plates and serve.
Nutrition: calories 30, fat 1.3, fiber 0.1, carbs 1, protein 0.8

Butter Spaghetti Squash

Preparation time: 10 minutes
Cooking time: 6 minutes
Servings: 3
Ingredients:
- 2 cups spaghetti squash, cubed
- 2 tablespoons butter
- ½ teaspoon salt
- 1 cup water, for cooking

Directions:
Pour water and insert the steamer rack in the instant pot. Arrange the spaghetti squash cubes in the instant pot and cook them on manual mode (high pressure) for 6 minutes. Then make a quick pressure release and open the lid. Transfer the cooked squash cube sin the serving plates and top them with butter and salt. Wait till butter and salt dissolve.
Nutrition: calories 89, fat 2, fiber 8.1, carbs 4.7, protein 0.5

Asparagus Mix

Preparation time: 5 minutes
Cooking time: 8 minutes
Servings: 4
Ingredients:
- 1 pound asparagus, trimmed and halved
- 2 teaspoons mustard
- ¼ cup coconut cream
- 2 garlic cloves, minced
- 1 tablespoon chives, chopped
- Salt and black pepper to the taste

Directions:
In your instant pot, combine the asparagus with the rest of the ingredients, put the lid on and cook on High for 8 minutes. Release the pressure fast for 5 minutes, divide the mix between plates and serve.
Nutrition: calories 67, fat 4.2, fiber 3, carbs 3.9, protein 3.4

Sliced Zucchini Casserole

Preparation time: 10 minutes
Cooking time: 5 minutes
Servings: 4
Ingredients:
- 2 zucchini, sliced
- 1 tomato, sliced
- ½ cup kohlrabi, chopped
- ½ cup chicken broth
- 1 teaspoon salt
- 1 teaspoon ground paprika
- 1 tablespoon nuts, chopped
- ½ cup Mozzarella, chopped
- ½ teaspoon sesame oil

Directions:
Brush the instant pot bowl with sesame oil. Place the zucchini slices in the instant pot. Then top them with sliced tomato and chopped kohlrabi. After this, mix up together chicken broth, salt, and ground paprika. Pour the liquid over the ingredients. Then sprinkle the casserole mixture with nuts and Mozzarella. Close the lid and cook the casserole on High pressure (manual mode) for 5 minutes. When the time is over, make a quick pressure release. Cool the cooked casserole to the room temperature.
Nutrition: calories 57, fat 2.8, fiber 2.3, carbs 6, protein 3.7

Pine Nuts Savoy Cabbage

Preparation time: 10 minutes
Cooking time: 15 minutes
Servings: 4
Ingredients:
- 1 Savoy cabbage, shredded
- 2 tablespoons avocado oil
- 1 tablespoon balsamic vinegar
- ¼ cup pine nuts, toasted
- ½ cup veggie stock
- Salt and black pepper to the taste

Directions:
Set your instant pot on sauté mode, add the oil, heat it up, add the cabbage and sauté for 2 minutes. Add the rest of the ingredients, put the lid on and cook on High for 15 minutes. Release the pressure naturally for 10 minutes, divide the mix between plates and serve as a side dish.
Nutrition: calories 67, fat 6.7, fiber 0.5, carbs 1.5, protein 1.3

Green Beans Casserole

Preparation time: 10 minutes
Cooking time: 20 minutes
Servings: 6
Ingredients:
- 1-pound green beans, chopped
- 1 cup button mushrooms, chopped
- 1 garlic clove, diced
- ½ white onion, diced
- 1 teaspoon butter
- 1/3 cup heavy cream
- ½ teaspoon salt

- 2 tablespoons almond meal
- 1 teaspoon Italian seasonings
- 1 teaspoon coconut oil, melted

Directions:
Toss butter in the instant pot and melt it on sauté mode. Add onion and cook it for 2 minutes. Then stir it and add mushrooms. Cook the mixture for 2 minutes more. Stir the ingredients again and add garlic clove, green beans, and salt. Mix up well. In the mixing bowl combine together coconut oil, Italian seasonings, almond meal, and cream. Pour the liquid over the casserole mixture and close the lid. Cook it on sauté mode for 16 minutes.
Nutrition: calories 79, fat 5.2, fiber 3.2, carbs 7.5, protein 2.5

Spinach and Fennel Mix

Preparation time: 10 minutes
Cooking time: 10 minutes
Servings: 4
Ingredients:
- 2 fennel bulbs, sliced
- 2 tablespoons olive oil
- 4 garlic cloves, chopped
- 2 tablespoons balsamic vinegar
- 2 and ½ cups baby spinach
- ½ teaspoon nutmeg, ground
- ¼ cup veggie stock

Directions:
In your instant pot, combine the fennel with the spinach and the rest of the ingredients, put the lid on and cook on High for 10 minutes. Release the pressure naturally for 10 minutes, divide the mix between plates and serve.
Nutrition: calories 104, fat 7.4, fiber 3.6, carbs 6.4, protein 1.7

Squash Casserole

Preparation time: 10 minutes
Cooking time: 5 minutes
Servings: 3
Ingredients:
- 7 oz spaghetti squash, chopped
- 1 zucchini, grated
- ½ cup Cheddar cheese
- 1 tablespoon cream cheese
- ½ teaspoon salt
- 1 teaspoon ground black pepper
- 1 cup water, for cooking

Directions:
Make the layer of spaghetti squash in the baking pan and top it with grated zucchini. After this, sprinkle the zucchini with Cheddar cheese. In the mixing bowl combine together cream cheese, salt, and ground black pepper. Spread the mixture over the Cheddar cheese. Pour water and insert the trivet in the instant pot. Place the baking pan with casserole in the instant pot and cook it on manual mode (high pressure) for 6 minutes. Then make a quick pressure release. Let the cooked casserole rest for 10 minutes before serving.
Nutrition: calories 120, fat 7.9, fiber 0.9, carbs 7.5, protein 6.2

Dill Cherry Tomatoes

Preparation time: 10 minutes
Cooking time: 12 minutes
Servings: 4
Ingredients:
- 4 garlic cloves, minced
- A pinch of salt and black pepper
- 2 pounds cherry tomatoes, halved
- 2 tablespoons olive oil
- 1 tablespoon dill, chopped
- ½ cups chicken stock
- ¼ cup basil, chopped

Directions:
Set your instant pot on sauté mode, add the oil, heat it up, add the garlic and sauté for 2 minutes. Add the rest of the ingredients, put the lid on and cook on High for 10 minutes. Release the pressure naturally for 10 minutes, divide the mix between plates and serve.
Nutrition: calories 109, fat 7.6, fiber 2.9, carbs 6.8, protein 2.5

Cheesy Zucchini Strips

Preparation time: 10 minutes
Cooking time: 8 minutes
Servings: 2
Ingredients:
- 1 zucchini, trimmed
- 1/3 cup Mozzarella, shredded
- 1 teaspoon avocado oil
- 1 tablespoon almond meal
- ¼ teaspoon salt

Directions:
Cut the zucchini into the strips and sprinkle them with salt and almond meal. Then heat up the instant pot on sauté mode for 2-3 minutes. Add avocado oil. Arrange the zucchini strips in one layer in the instant pot and cook them for 2 minutes from each side or until they are light brown. Repeat the same steps with remaining zucchini strips (if you use small instant and can't arrange all vegetables per one time of cooking). Then top the cooked zucchini strips with Mozzarella and close the lid. Cook the side dish on sauté mode for 3 minutes or until the cheese is melted.
Nutrition: calories 49, fat 2.8, fiber 1.6, carbs 4.2, protein 3.2

Tomatoes and Cauliflower Mix

Preparation time: 10 minutes
Cooking time: 12 minutes
Servings: 4
Ingredients:
- ½ cup scallions, chopped
- 1 tablespoon avocado oil
- 1 pound cauliflower florets
- ½ cup chicken stock
- 2 cups cherry tomatoes, halved
- 1 tablespoon chives, chopped
- 2 tablespoons parsley, chopped

Directions:
Set your instant pot on Sauté mode, add the oil, heat it up, add the scallions and sauté for 2 minutes. Add the rest of the ingredients, put the lid on and cook on High for 10 minutes. Release the pressure naturally for 10 minutes, divide the mix between plates and serve as a side dish.

Nutrition: calories 55, fat 1.6, fiber 0.4, carbs 1.5, protein 3.5

Turmeric Cabbage Rice

Preparation time: 10 minutes
Cooking time: 35 minutes
Servings: 5
Ingredients:
- 1 ½ cup white cabbage, shredded
- 1 teaspoon salt
- 1 cup of coconut milk
- 1 teaspoon ground turmeric
- 1 white onion, diced
- 1 tablespoon coconut oil

Directions:
In the mixing bowl combine together salt and shredded cabbage. Leave the vegetables for 5 minutes. Meanwhile, heat up the instant pot bowl on sauté mode for 2 minutes. Add coconut oil and diced onion. Cook the onion for 3 minutes. Then stir it with the help of the spatula and add cabbage. After this, in the bowl combine together ground turmeric and coconut milk. When the liquid starts to be yellow, pour it over the cabbage. Stir the cabbage and close the lid. Cook the cabbage rice on sauté mode for 30 minutes. Stir ti from time to time to avoid burning.
Nutrition: calories 149, fat 14.2, fiber 2.2, carbs 6.2, protein 1.6

Green Beans and Herbs

Preparation time: 10 minutes
Cooking time: 12 minutes
Servings: 4
Ingredients:
- 2 tablespoons avocado oil
- ½ teaspoon chili powder
- 1 pound green beans, trimmed and halved
- 1 and ½ cups chicken stock
- 1 tablespoon rosemary, chopped
- 1 tablespoon basil, chopped
- 1 tablespoon dill, chopped
- A pinch of salt and black pepper
- ½ cup almonds, chopped

Directions:
In your instant pot, combine the green beans with the chili and the rest of the ingredients. put the lid on and cook on High for 12 minutes. Release the pressure naturally for 10 minutes, divide the mix between plates and serve as a side dish.
Nutrition: calories 119, fat 7.2, fiber 3.4, carbs 5.3, protein 4.9

Turnip Creamy Gratin

Preparation time: 5 minutes
Cooking time: 7 minutes
Servings: 2
Ingredients:
- 1 cup turnip, sliced
- 1/3 cup heavy cream
- ¼ teaspoon salt
- ¼ teaspoon dried sage
- 1 teaspoon butter
- 1/3 teaspoon garlic powder
- ½ cup Cheddar cheese, shredded

Directions:
Toss butter in the instant pot and melt it on sauté mode (approx.2-3 minutes). Then add sliced turnip and cook it on sauté mode for 1 minute from each side. Sprinkle the vegetables with salt, dried sage, and garlic powder. Then add heavy cream. Top the turnip with Cheddar cheese and close the lid. Cook the meal on manual mode (high pressure) for 3 minutes. Then make a quick pressure release.
Nutrition: calories 220, fat 18.8, fiber 1.3, carbs 5.5, protein 8.1

Cauliflower Rice and Olives

Preparation time: 10 minutes
Cooking time: 15 minutes
Servings: 4
Ingredients:
- 1 cup cauliflower rice
- 1 and ½ cup chicken stock
- 1 cup black olives, pitted and sliced
- 1 tablespoon chives, chopped
- A pinch of salt and black pepper
- ½ cup cilantro, chopped

Directions:
In your instant pot, mix the cauliflower rice with the rest of the ingredients, put the lid on and cook on High for 15 minutes. Release the pressure naturally for 10 minutes, divide the mix between plates and serve.
Nutrition: calories 40, fat 3.6, fiber 1.2, carbs 2.2, protein 0.3

Parmesan Onion Rings

Preparation time: 10 minutes
Cooking time: 5 minutes
Servings: 4
Ingredients:
- 1 big white onion
- 1 egg, beaten
- 1 teaspoon cream cheese
- 2 oz Parmesan, grated
- 2 tablespoons almond meal
- 1 tablespoon butter

Directions:
Trim and peel the onion. Then slice it roughly and separate every onion slice into the rings. In the mixing bowl combine together Parmesan and almond meal. Then take a separated bowl and mix up cream cheese and egg in it. Dip the onion rings in the egg mixture and then coat well in cheese mixture. Toss butter in the instant pot and melt it on sauté mode. Then arrange the onion rings in the melted butter in one layer. Cook the onion rings for 2 minutes from each side on sauté mode.
Nutrition: calories 122, fat 8.8, fiber 1.2, carbs 4.8, protein 7.1

Rosemary Cauliflower

Preparation time: 10 minutes
Cooking time: 12 minutes
Servings: 4
Ingredients:
- 1 pound cauliflower florets
- 1 cup chicken stock
- 2 garlic cloves, minced
- A pinch of salt and black pepper
- 1 tablespoon rosemary, chopped

- 1 teaspoon hot chili sauce

Directions:
In your instant pot, combine the cauliflower with the stock and the rest of the ingredients, put the lid on and cook on High for 12 minutes. Release the pressure naturally for 10 minutes, divide the mix between plates and serve.
Nutrition: calories 36, fat 2.4, fiber 1.5, carbs 2.3, protein 3.6

Rosemary Radish Halves

Preparation time: 10 minutes
Cooking time: 10 minutes
Servings: 4
Ingredients:
- 3 cups radish, trimmed
- 1 tablespoon olive oil
- 1 teaspoon dried rosemary
- ½ teaspoon salt

Directions:
Cut the radishes into the halves and sprinkle with salt. In the shallow bowl whisk together olive oil and dried rosemary. After this, sprinkle the radish halves with fragrant oil and shake the vegetables well. Transfer the radishes in the instant pot and cook the on sauté mode for 10 minutes. Stir the vegetables every 2 minutes.
Nutrition: calories 45, fat 3.6, fiber 1.5, carbs 3.2, protein 0.6

Lemon Artichokes

Preparation time: 10 minutes
Cooking time: 12 minutes
Servings: 4
Ingredients:
- 4 artichokes, trimmed
- 1 tablespoon olive oil
- 1 tablespoon lemon juice
- 1 tablespoon chives, chopped
- 1 tablespoon sweet paprika
- 1 tablespoon parsley, chopped
- 2 cups water

Directions:
In a bowl, mix the artichokes with the oil and the other ingredients except the water and toss. Put the water in your instant pot, add the steamer basket, put the artichokes inside, put the lid on and cook on High for 12 minutes. Release the pressure naturally for 10 minutes, divide the artichokes between plates and serve.
Nutrition: calories 113, fat 4, fiber 2.4, carbs 3.5, protein 5.6

Sweet Baby Carrot

Preparation time: 10 minutes
Cooking time: 4 minutes
Servings: 4
Ingredients:
- 1 cup baby carrot
- 1 tablespoon Erythritol
- ½ teaspoon dried thyme
- 2 tablespoons butter, melted
- 1 cup water, for cooking

Directions:
Wash the baby carrot carefully and trim if needed. Then pour water in the instant pot and insert the trivet, Put the prepared baby carrots in the baking pan. Add dried thyme, Erythritol, and butter. Mix up the vegetables well and place over the trivet. Close the lid. Cook the carrot for 4 minutes on manual mode (high pressure). When the time is over make a quick pressure release.
Nutrition: calories 69, fat 5.8, fiber 1.1, carbs 7.8, protein 0.6

Celery and Broccoli Mix

Preparation time: 10 minutes
Cooking time: 12 minutes
Servings: 4
Ingredients:
- 2 garlic cloves, minced
- 1 tablespoon olive oil
- 1 and ½ cups broccoli florets
- 1 celery stalk, chopped
- ½ cups veggie stock
- A pinch of salt and black pepper
- 2 tablespoons lime juice

Directions:
Set your instant pot on sauté mode, add the oil, heat it up, add the garlic and celery and cook for 2 minutes. Add the rest of the ingredients, put the lid on and cook on High for 10 minutes. Release the pressure naturally for 10 minutes, divide the mix between plates and serve.
Nutrition: calories 33, fat 3.5, fiber 0.1, carbs 0.7, protein 0.1

Feta and Zucchini Bowl

Preparation time: 5 minutes
Cooking time: 3 minutes
Servings: 4
Ingredients:
- 2 zucchini, chopped
- 1 teaspoon olive oil
- ½ teaspoon chili flakes
- ½ teaspoon paprika
- 2 oz Feta, crumbled

Directions:
Place olive oil, zucchini, chili flakes, and paprika in the instant pot. Stir the ingredients gently and close the lid. Cook zucchini on sauté mode for 2 minutes. Then open the lid and mix up them well with the help of the spatula. Keep cooking zucchini for 1 minute more. Transfer the cooked zucchini into the serving bowls and top with feta cheese.
Nutrition: calories 64, fat 4.4, fiber 1.2, carbs 4, protein 3.2

Zucchini Mix

Preparation time: 10 minutes
Cooking time: 20 minutes
Servings: 4
Ingredients:
- ½ cup veggie stock
- 3 zucchinis, sliced
- A pinch of salt and black pepper
- 1 tablespoon dill, chopped
- ½ teaspoon nutmeg, grated
- 2 tablespoons sweet paprika

Directions:
In your instant pot, mix the zucchinis with the rest of the ingredients, put the lid on and cook on Low for 20

minutes. Release the pressure naturally for 10 minutes, divide the mix between plates and serve.
Nutrition: calories 40, fat 2.3, fiber 1.5, carbs 1.9, protein 2.5

Herbed Asparagus

Preparation time: 5 minutes
Cooking time: 5 minute
Servings: 2
Ingredients:
- 6 oz asparagus, trimmed
- ¼ teaspoon dried thyme
- ¼ teaspoon salt
- ¼ teaspoon ground black pepper
- ¼ teaspoon dried oregano
- ¼ teaspoon ground nutmeg
- 2 tablespoons butter
- ¼ cup chicken broth

Directions:
In the mixing bowl combine together dried thyme, salt, ground black pepper, oregano, and nutmeg. Then put the asparagus in the instant pot. Sprinkle the vegetables with spice mixture. Stir them gently. Then add butter and chicken broth. Close the lid and cook asparagus on manual mode (high pressure) for 5 minutes. Then make the quick pressure release, open the lid, and shake the asparagus gently.
Nutrition: calories 127, fat 11.9, fiber 2.1, carbs 3.9, protein 2.7

Dill Fennel Mix

Preparation time: 10 minutes
Cooking time: 10 minutes
Servings: 4
Ingredients:
- 2 fennel bulbs, sliced
- ¼ cup chicken stock
- A pinch of salt and black pepper
- 1 tablespoon dill, chopped
- 1 tablespoon parsley, chopped

Directions:
In your instant pot, mix the fennel with the stock and the rest of the ingredients, put the lid on and cook on High for 10 minutes. Release the pressure naturally for 10 minutes, divide the mix between plates and serve.
Nutrition: calories 39, fat 3.2, fiber 1, carbs 2.9, protein 1.7

Cheesy Radish

Preparation time: 8 minutes
Cooking time: 3 minutes
Servings: 3
Ingredients:
- 1 ½ cup radish, sliced
- ½ teaspoon minced garlic
- 1 teaspoon sesame oil
- ¼ cup Monterey Jack cheese, shredded
- ¼ cup heavy cream
- 1 tablespoon cream cheese

Directions:
Put radish minced garlic, sesame oil, heavy cream, and cream cheese in the instant pot. Mix up the radish mixture well. Then top it with shredded cheese and close the lid. Cook the radish for 3 minutes on Manual mode (high pressure). Then make a quick pressure release.
Nutrition: calories 105, fat 9.3, fiber 0.9, carbs 2.6, protein 3.2

Mushrooms and Endives Mix

Preparation time: 10 minutes
Cooking time: 15 minutes
Servings: 4
Ingredients:
- 1 pound white mushrooms, sliced
- 2 spring onions, chopped
- 1 garlic clove, minced
- 2 endives, trimmed and halved
- 1 tablespoon balsamic vinegar
- 1 tablespoon chives, chopped
- 1 cup chicken stock

Directions:
In your instant pot, mix the mushrooms with the rest of the ingredients, put the lid on and cook on High for 15 minutes. Release the pressure naturally for 10 minutes, divide the mix between plates and serve.
Nutrition: calories 31, fat 3.1, fiber 1.3, carbs 2.3, protein 3.9

Turnip Cubes

Preparation time: 10 minutes
Cooking time: 3 minutes
Servings: 6
Ingredients:
- 1-pound turnip, cubed
- 1 teaspoon salt
- ½ teaspoon ground black pepper
- 1 teaspoon avocado oil
- 1 cup water, for cooking

Directions:
Pour water and insert the steamer rack in the instant pot. In the mixing bowl mix up together turnip cubes, salt, and ground black pepper. Sprinkle the vegetables with avocado oil and place them in the steamer rack. Close and seal the lid. Cook the turnip on Manual mode (high pressure) for 3 minutes. Then allow the natural pressure release for 5 minutes.
Nutrition: calories 23, fat 0.2, fiber 1.4, carbs 5, protein 0.7

Walnuts Green Beans and Avocado

Preparation time: 10 minutes
Cooking time: 15 minutes
Servings: 6
Ingredients:
- 2 cups green beans, halved
- ½ cup chicken stock
- ½ cup walnuts, chopped
- 1 avocado, peeled, pitted and cubed
- ¼ teaspoon sweet paprika
- A pinch of salt and black pepper
- 2 teaspoons balsamic vinegar

Directions:
In your instant pot, mix the green beans with the stock and the rest of the ingredients, put the lid on and cook on High for 15 minutes. Release the pressure naturally for 10 minutes, divide the mix between plates and serve.
Nutrition: calories 146, fat 12.8, fiber 2.5, carbs 6.7, protein 3.9

Cilantro-Kale Salad

Preparation time: 10 minutes
Cooking time: 2 minutes
Servings: 2
Ingredients:
- 2 cups kale, chopped
- ½ cup fresh cilantro, chopped
- 1 pecan, chopped
- ½ teaspoon ground paprika
- ¼ teaspoon salt
- 1 tablespoon avocado oil
- 1 cucumber, chopped
- 1 cup water, for cooking

Directions:
Pour water and insert the steamer rack in the instant pot. Place the kale in the steamer. Close and seal the lid. Cook the greens for 2 minutes on Manual mode (high pressure). Then make a quick pressure release and transfer the kale in the salad bowl. Add chopped cilantro, pecan, and cucumber. After this, sprinkle the salad with ground paprika, salt, and avocado oil. Mix up the salad well.
Nutrition: calories 98, fat 6.2, fiber 3.1, carbs 9.2, protein 3

Thyme Brussels Sprouts

Preparation time: 10 minutes
Cooking time: 12 minutes
Servings: 4
Ingredients:
- 2 and ½ pounds Brussels sprouts, halved
- 2 tablespoons olive oil
- A pinch of salt and black pepper
- 2 shallots, chopped
- ½ cups beef stock
- 1 tablespoon thyme, chopped

Directions:
Set your instant pot on Sauté mode, add the oil, heat it up, add the shallots and sauté for 2 minutes. Add the rest of the ingredients, put the lid on and cook on High or 10 minutes. Release the pressure naturally for 10 minutes, divide the mix between plates and serve as a side dish.
Nutrition: calories 64, fat 7.1, fiber 0.3, carbs 0.5, protein 0.4

Cauliflower Gnocchi

Preparation time: 15 minutes
Cooking time: 8 minutes
Servings: 6
Ingredients:
- 2 cups cauliflower, boiled
- 1 egg yolk
- ¼ cup coconut flour
- ½ cup almond meal
- 1 tablespoon cream cheese
- 2 oz Parmesan, grated
- 1 teaspoon dried basil
- 2 tablespoons butter

Directions:
Place the boiled cauliflower in the food processor and blend it until smooth. Then add egg yolk, coconut flour, almond meal, cream cheese, and grated Parmesan. Blend the cauliflower mixture for 15 seconds more. Then transfer the mixture on the chopping board and knead it into the ball. Then cut the dough ball into 3 parts. After this, make 3 logs from the dough. Cut the logs into the small gnocchi with the help of the cutter. Toss the butter in the instant pot and melt it for 2 minutes on sauté mode. Add dried basil and bring the butter to boil (it will take around 1 minute). After this, add prepared gnocchi and cook them for 5 minutes. Stir the gnocchi from time to time.
Nutrition: calories 155, fat 11.7, fiber 3.8, carbs 7.3, protein 7.1

Chives Broccoli Mash

Preparation time: 10 minutes
Cooking time: 12 minutes
Servings: 4
Ingredients:
- 1 broccoli, florets separated
- A pinch of salt and black pepper
- ½ teaspoon turmeric powder
- ½ cup chicken stock
- 1 tablespoon ghee, melted
- 1 tablespoon chives, chopped

Directions:
In your instant pot, mix the broccoli with the rest of the ingredients except the ghee and the chives, put the lid on and cook on High for 12 minutes. Release the pressure naturally for 10 minutes, drain the broccoli, transfer it to a blender, add the ghee, pulse well, divide between plates, sprinkle the chives on top and serve.
Nutrition: calories 31, fat 3.3, fiber 0.1, carbs 0.3, protein 0.1

Thyme Purple Cabbage Steaks

Preparation time: 10 minutes
Cooking time: 4 minutes
Servings: 4
Ingredients:
- 10 oz purple cabbage
- 1 teaspoon apple cider vinegar
- 1 teaspoon olive oil
- ½ teaspoon salt
- ½ teaspoon lemon juice
- 1 cup water, for cooking

Directions:
Cut the purple cabbage into 4 cabbage steaks. Pour water and insert the steamer rack in the instant pot. Place the cabbage steaks on the rack and close the lid. Cook the vegetables for 4 minutes on Manual mode (high pressure). Then allow the natural pressure release for 5 minutes. Place the cabbage steaks in the serving plates. In the shallow bowl whisk together apple cider vinegar, olive oil, salt, and lemon juice. Sprinkle every cabbage steak with apple cider vinegar mixture.
Nutrition: calories 28, fat 1.3, fiber 1.8, carbs 4.1, protein 0.9

Creamy Endives

Preparation time: 10 minutes
Cooking time: 10 minutes
Servings: 4
Ingredients:
- 4 endives, trimmed and halved
- ½ cup chicken stock
- ¼ cup coconut cream

- 1 tablespoon dill, chopped
- 1 tablespoon smoked paprika

Directions:
In your instant pot, mix the endives with the rest of the ingredients, put the lid on and cook on High for 10 minutes. Release the pressure naturally for 10 minutes, divide the mix between plates and serve as a side dish.
Nutrition: calories 43, fat 3.9, fiber 1.1, carbs 2.3, protein 0.9

Smashed Cauliflower with Goat Cheese

Preparation time: 15 minutes
Cooking time: 5 minutes
Servings: 3
Ingredients:
- 1 ½ cup cauliflower, chopped
- ½ teaspoon salt
- 2 oz Goat cheese, crumbled
- 1 tablespoon cream cheese
- 1 cup water, for cooking

Directions:
Pour water and insert the steamer rack in the instant pot. Place the cauliflower in the steamer rack and close the lid. Cook the vegetables on manul mode (high pressure) for 5 minutes. Make a quick pressure release. Place the cooked cauliflower in the food processor and blend it until smooth. Transfer the cauliflower into the bowl. Add salt and cream cheese. Mix up the cauliflower mass well. Place the cooked meal on the plate and top with goat cheese.
Nutrition: calories 110, fat 7.9, fiber 1.3, carbs 3.2, protein 7

Spinach and Kale Mix

Preparation time: 5 minutes
Cooking time: 10 minutes
Servings: 4
Ingredients:
- 1 and ½ pounds baby spinach
- ½ pound kale, torn
- 1 tablespoon ghee, melted
- A pinch of salt and black pepper
- 1 cup veggie stock
- 1 teaspoon nutmeg, ground
- 1 tablespoon chives, chopped

Directions:
In your instant pot, mix the spinach with the kale and the rest of the ingredients, toss, put the lid on and cook on High for 10 minutes. Release the pressure fast for 5 minutes, divide the mix between plates and serve.
Nutrition: calories 59, fat 3.4, fiber 1, carbs 2.4, protein 1.8

Low Carb Fall Vegetables

Preparation time: 10 minutes
Cooking time: 8 minutes
Servings: 5
Ingredients:
- 1 cup mushrooms, chopped
- 1 cup zucchini, chopped
- 1/2 cup bell pepper, chopped
- 1 eggplant, chopped
- 3 tablespoons butter
- ½ teaspoon salt
- 1 teaspoon dried basil
- 1 teaspoon dried thyme
- ½ teaspoon ground black pepper
- ½ teaspoon cayenne pepper
- 1 cup water, for cooking

Directions:
Pour water and insert the trivet in the instant pot. Put all vegetables in the instant pot baking pan. Sprinkle them with salt, dried basil, thyme, ground black pepper, and cayenne pepper. Mix up the vegetables and top with butter. Arrange the baking pan with vegetables in the instant pot. Close the lid and cook the side dish for 8 minutes on Manual mode (high pressure). Make a quick pressure release.
Nutrition: calories 96, fat 7.2, fiber 4, carbs 7.9, protein 1.9

Thyme Tomatoes

Preparation time: 10 minutes
Cooking time: 10 minutes
Servings: 4
Ingredients:
- ½ cup veggie stock
- 1 pound cherry tomatoes, halved
- 1 tablespoon thyme, chopped
- A pinch of salt and black pepper
- 1 teaspoon chili powder
- 1 shallot, chopped
- 1 tablespoon olive oil

Directions:
Set the instant pot on Sauté mode, add the oil, heat it up, add the shallot and sauté for 2 minutes. Add the tomatoes and the rest of the ingredients, put the lid on and cook on High for 8 minutes. Release the pressure naturally for 10 minutes, divide the mix between plates and serve.
Nutrition: calories 54, fat 3.9, fiber 1.8, carbs 2.4, protein 1.1

Steamed Broccoli

Preparation time: 10 minutes
Cooking time: 1 minute
Servings: 2
Ingredients:
- 1 cup broccoli florets
- ½ teaspoon garlic, diced
- ¼ teaspoon salt
- 1 teaspoon sesame oil
- 1 cup water, for cooking

Directions:
Pour water and insert the steamer rack in the instant pot. Place the broccoli florets in the steamer rack and close the lid. Cook the vegetables on Manual mode (high pressure) for 1 minute. Then make a quick pressure release and transfer the cooked broccoli florets in the serving plates. Sprinkle vegetables with garlic, salt, and sesame oil.
Nutrition: calories 37, fat 2.4, fiber 1.2, carbs 3.3, protein 1.3

Lemon Brussels Sprouts and Tomatoes

Preparation time: 10 minutes
Cooking time: 15 minutes
Servings: 4

Ingredients:
- 1 pound Brussels sprouts, trimmed and halved
- ½ pound cherry tomatoes, halved
- 1 tablespoon lemon juice
- 1 tablespoon lemon zest, grated
- ¼ cup veggie stock
- 1 tablespoon rosemary, chopped
- A pinch of salt and black pepper

Directions:
In your instant pot, mix the Brussels sprouts with the tomatoes and the remaining ingredients, put the lid on and cook on High for 15 minutes. Release the pressure naturally for 10 minutes, divide the mix between plates and serve as a side dish.
Nutrition: calories 64, fat 2.7, fiber 1.5, carbs 2, protein 4.5

Cheddar Tots with Broccoli

Preparation time: 10 minutes
Cooking time: 5 minutes
Servings: 4
Ingredients:
- 1 cup broccoli, shredded
- ¼ cup Cheddar cheese, shredded
- ¼ teaspoon garlic powder
- ¼ teaspoon salt
- 2 tablespoon almond meal
- ¼ teaspoon ground black pepper
- 1 teaspoon coconut oil
- 1 teaspoon dried dill

Directions:
In the mixing bowl combine together shredded broccoli, cheese, garlic powder, salt, almond meal, ground black pepper, and dried dill. Mix up the mixture with the help of the spoon until homogenous. After this, make the small tots from the mixture. Heat up instant pot bowl on sauté mode for 3 minutes. Then toss coconut oil and melt it (appx.1 minute). Then arrange the tots in the instant pot in one layer and cook tots for 1 minute from each side.
Nutrition: calories 65, fat 5.1, fiber 1, carbs 2.6, protein 3.1

Creamy Fennel

Preparation time: 5 minutes
Cooking time: 8 minutes
Servings: 4
Ingredients:
- 2 big fennel bulbs, sliced
- 2 tablespoons avocado oil
- 2 spring onions, chopped
- 2 shallots, minced
- 1 garlic clove, minced
- 1 and ½ cups coconut cream
- ¼ teaspoon nutmeg, ground
- A pinch of salt and black pepper

Directions:
Set your instant pot on Sauté mode, add the oil, heat it up, add spring onions, shallots and the garlic and sauté for 2 minutes. Add the fennel and the rest of the ingredients, toss, put the lid on and cook on High for 6 minutes. Release the pressure fast for 5 minutes, divide the mix between plates and serve as a side dish.
Nutrition: calories 58, fat 3.2, fiber 1, carbs 2.7, protein 0.3

Vegetable Fritters

Preparation time: 10 minutes
Cooking time: 6 minutes
Servings: 4
Ingredients:
- ½ cup turnip, boiled
- ½ cup cauliflower, boiled
- 1 egg, beaten
- 1 teaspoon dried parsley
- 3 tablespoons coconut flour
- 1 teaspoon avocado oil
- 1/3 teaspoon salt
- 1 teaspoon ground turmeric

Directions:
Mash turnip and cauliflower with the help of the potato masher. Then add egg, dried parsley, coconut flour, salt, and ground turmeric in the mashed mixture and stir well. Make the medium side fritters and place them in the instant pot. Add avocado oil. Cook the fritters on sauté mode for 3 minutes from each side.
Nutrition: calories 50, fat 1.9, fiber 3, carbs 6, protein 2.6

Saffron Bell Peppers

Preparation time: 10 minutes
Cooking time: 10 minutes
Servings: 4
Ingredients:
- 2 yellow bell peppers, cut into strips
- 2 red bell peppers, thinly sliced
- 3 garlic cloves, minced
- 1 shallots, chopped
- A pinch of salt and black pepper
- 1 teaspoon saffron powder
- ¼ cup chicken stock
- 1 tablespoon cilantro, chopped

Directions:
In your instant pot, mix the peppers with the garlic and the rest of the ingredients, put the lid on and cook on High for 10 minutes. Release the pressure naturally for 10 minutes, divide the mix between plates and serve.
Nutrition: calories 64, fat 2.4, fiber 1.7, carbs 1.9, protein 1.4

Steamed Asparagus

Preparation time: 5 minutes
Cooking time: 1 minute
Servings: 2
Ingredients:
- 6 oz asparagus, chopped
- ¼ teaspoon salt
- 1 cup water, for cooking

Directions:
Pour water and insert the steamer rack in the instant pot. Place the chopped asparagus in the steamer rack and close the lid. Cook the vegetables on Manual (high pressure) for 1 minute. Then make a quick pressure release and open the lid. Sprinkle the asparagus with salt.
Nutrition: calories 17, fat 0.1, fiber 1.8, carbs 3.3, protein 1.9

Cabbage and Peppers

Preparation time: 10 minutes
Cooking time: 15 minutes
Servings: 4
Ingredients:
- 2 red bell peppers, cut into strips
- 1 green cabbage head, shredded
- ½ cup chicken stock
- 1 tablespoon avocado oil
- 1 tablespoon sweet paprika
- A pinch of salt and black pepper
- 2 garlic cloves, minced
- 1 teaspoon lime zest, grated
- 1 teaspoon lime juice
- 1 tablespoon dill, chopped

Directions:
Set the instant pot on Sauté mode, add the oil, heat it up, add the garlic, lime zest and lime juice and sauté for 2 minutes. Add the peppers and the rest of the ingredients, put the lid on and cook on High for 12 minutes. Release the pressure naturally for 10 minutes, divide the mix between plates and serve.
Nutrition: calories 79, fat 2.6, fiber 0.4, carbs 1.4, protein 3.5

Roasted Cauliflower Steak

Preparation time: 10 minutes
Cooking time: 4 minutes
Servings: 2
Ingredients:
- 8 oz cauliflower
- 1 teaspoon olive oil
- ½ teaspoon apple cider vinegar
- ¼ teaspoon chili flakes
- ¼ teaspoon salt
- ¼ teaspoon onion powder
- ¼ teaspoon ground turmeric
- 1 cup water, for cooking

Directions:
Cut the cauliflower into medium steaks. In the shallow bowl combine together olive oil, apple cider vinegar, chili flakes, salt, onion powder, and ground turmeric. Then brush the cauliflower steaks with oily mixture form both sides. Pour water and insert the trivet in the instant pot. Arrange the cauliflower steaks in the instant pot in one layer. Cook the vegetables for 4 minutes on manual mode (high pressure). Then make a quick pressure release. Cool the cauliflower steaks for 2-5 minutes before serving.
Nutrition: calories 51, fat 2.5, fiber 2.9, carbs 6.5, protein 2.3

Green Beans and Kale

Preparation time: 10 minutes
Cooking time: 8 minutes
Servings: 4
Ingredients:
- 2 cups kale, torn
- 1 tablespoon avocado oil
- 1 garlic clove, minced
- 1 pound green beans, trimmed
- 1 tablespoon chives, chopped
- 1 tablespoon oregano, chopped
- ¼ cup chicken stock
- 1 teaspoon chili powder

Directions:
Set your instant pot on Sauté mode, add the oil, heat it up, add the garlic and cook for 1 minute. Add the rest of the ingredients, put the lid on and cook on High for 7 minutes. Release the pressure naturally for 10 minutes, divide the mix between plates and serve.
Nutrition: calories 64, fat 1.9, fiber 0.5, carbs 1.4, protein 3.4

Cayenne Pepper Green Beans

Preparation time: 10 minutes
Cooking time: 3 minutes
Servings: 4
Ingredients:
- 2 cups green beans, chopped
- 1 teaspoon cayenne pepper
- 1 tablespoon nut oil
- ¼ teaspoon salt
- 1 cup water, for coking

Directions:
Pour water and insert the steamer rack in the instant pot. Place the green beans in the steamer rack. Cook the vegetables for 3 minutes on Manual mode (high pressure). Make a quick pressure release and cool the green beans in ice water for 4 minutes. Transfer the green beans in the mixing bowl and sprinkle with nut oil and salt. Mix up the beans well.
Nutrition: calories 48, fat 3.5, fiber 2, carbs 4.2, protein 1.1

Zucchinis and Bok Choy

Preparation time: 10 minutes
Cooking time: 10 minutes
Servings: 4
Ingredients:
- 2 bunches bok choy
- 3 zucchinis, sliced
- ¼ cup veggie stock
- 2 garlic cloves, minced
- 1 teaspoon ginger, grated
- 1 tablespoon avocado oil
- 1 tablespoon smoked paprika
- A pinch of salt and black pepper
- 1 tablespoon dill, chopped

Directions:
Set the instant pot on Sauté mode, add the oil, heat it up, add the ginger and the garlic and sauté for 2 minutes Add the bok choy and the rest of the ingredients, put the lid on and cook on High for 8 minutes. Release the pressure naturally for 10 minutes, divide everything between plates and serve as a side dish.
Nutrition: calories 49, fat 1, fiber 0.2, carbs 0.3, protein 2.4

Marinated Red Bell Peppers

Preparation time: 15 minutes
Cooking time: 3 minutes
Servings: 4
Ingredients:
- 4 red bell peppers
- 1 tablespoon apple cider vinegar
- 1 teaspoon olive oil
- 1 teaspoon Italian seasonings
- ¼ teaspoon minced garlic
- 1 cup of water

Directions:
Cut the bell peppers into the strips and put them in the instant pot. Add water and close the lid. Cook the bell peppers on manual (high pressure) for 3 minutes. Then make a quick pressure release and remove the bell peppers from water. Transfer the vegetables in the bowl and sprinkle with olive oil, Italian seasonings, minced garlic, and apple cider vinegar. Mix up the peppers. Leave the cooked meal for 10 minutes to marinate.
Nutrition: calories 40, fat 1.5, fiber 2, carbs 6.2, protein 1

Red Cabbage and Artichokes
Preparation time: 10 minutes
Cooking time: 15 minutes
Servings: 4
Ingredients:
- 4 garlic cloves, minced
- ½ cup spring onions, chopped
- 1 tablespoon avocado oil
- 1 red cabbage head, shredded
- ¼ cup veggie stock
- 1 cup canned artichokes hearts, drained and chopped
- 1 tablespoon balsamic vinegar
- 1 tablespoon dill, chopped

Directions:
Set your instant pot on Sauté mode, add the oil, heat it up, add the garlic and the onions and sauté for 2 minutes. Add the rest of the ingredients, put the lid on and cook on High for 13 minutes. Release the pressure naturally for 10 minutes, divide the mix between plates and serve.
Nutrition: calories 69, fat 2.3, fiber 1.9, carbs 2, protein 2.9

Broccoli Nuggets
Preparation time: 10 minutes
Cooking time: 10 minutes
Servings: 4
Ingredients:
- 1 cup broccoli, chopped
- 1 egg, beaten
- ¼ teaspoon salt
- 3 tablespoons almond meal
- ¼ cup Provolone cheese, grated
- 1 teaspoon butter

Directions:
Put broccoli in the blender and blend until smooth. Then transfer the smooth mixture in the bowl. Add egg and 2 tablespoons of almond meal. Then add cheese and salt. Stir the mixture with the help of the spoon until homogenous. Toss butter in the instant pot and melt it on sauté mode for 1 minute. Make the medium size nuggets and place them in the instant pot. Cook the broccoli nuggets for 3 minutes from each side.
Nutrition: calories 87, fat 6.6, fiber 1.2, carbs 2.7, protein 5.1

Balsamic Artichokes and Capers
Preparation time: 10 minutes
Cooking time: 15 minutes
Servings: 4
Ingredients:
- 4 artichokes, trimmed
- 1 cup water
- 2 tablespoons balsamic vinegar
- 2 tablespoons capers, drained and chopped
- 1 tablespoon chives, chopped
- A pinch of salt and black pepper
- 1 tablespoon avocado oil

Directions:
In a bowl, mix the artichokes with the rest of the ingredients except the water and the capers and toss. Put the water in the instant pot, add the steamer basket, put the artichokes inside, put the lid on and cook on High for 15 minutes. Release the pressure naturally for 10 minutes, divide the artichokes between plates, sprinkle the capers on top and serve.
Nutrition: calories 84, fat 1.9, fiber 1, carbs 1.5, protein 5.5

Yellow Squash Noodles
Preparation time: 15 minutes
Cooking time: 1 minute
Servings: 4
Ingredients:
- 1-pound yellow squash, peeled
- 1 teaspoon sesame oil
- ½ teaspoon ground cinnamon
- ¼ teaspoon salt
- 1 cup water, for cooking

Directions:
With the help of the spiralizer make the spirals from the squash. Then pour water and insert the steamer rack in the instant pot. Place the squash spirals in the steamer rack and close the lid. Cook the vegetables for 1 minute on Manual mode (high pressure). Transfer the cooked squash spirals (noodles) in the serving plates and sprinkle withs alt, ground nutmeg, and sesame oil.
Nutrition: calories 29, fat 1.3, fiber 1.4, carbs 4, protein 1.4

Bell Peppers and Olives
Preparation time: 10 minutes
Cooking time: 12 minutes
Servings: 4
Ingredients:
- 1 and ½ pounds mixed bell peppers, cut into strips
- 2 teaspoons lemon zest, grated
- 2 tablespoons lemon juice
- 2 scallions, chopped
- 1 cup black olives, pitted and halved
- ¼ cup veggie stock

Directions:
In your instant pot, mix the peppers with the lemon zest and the rest of the ingredients, put the lid on and cook on High for 12 minutes. Release the pressure naturally for 10 minutes, divide the mix between plates and serve.
Nutrition: calories 44, fat 3.7, fiber 1.4, carbs 3, protein 0.5

Oregano Fennel Steaks
Preparation time: 10 minutes
Cooking time: 15 minutes
Servings: 4
Ingredients:

- 1-pound fennel bulb
- ½ teaspoon ground black pepper
- ¼ teaspoon salt
- 1 teaspoon coconut oil
- 2 tablespoons almond meal
- 1 cup organic almond milk

Directions:
Slice the fennel bulb into the steaks and rub with salt and ground black pepper. Heat up the instant pot on sauté mode. Put coconut oil inside and melt it for 1 minute. Place the fennel slices in the instant pot and cook them for 1 minute. Then flip the fennel steaks on another side and sprinkle with almond meal. After this, pour the almond milk over the fennel steaks and close the lid. Cook the fennel steaks for 10 minutes on Manual mode (low pressure). Serve the fennel steaks with a small amount of almond milk sauce from the instant pot.
Nutrition: calories 70, fat 3.5, fiber 4.1, carbs 9.2, protein 2.3

Tomatoes and Olives

Preparation time: 10 minutes
Cooking time: 15 minutes
Servings: 4
Ingredients:
- 1 pound cherry tomatoes, halved
- 1 cup kalamata olives, pitted and halved
- 2 tablespoons goat cheese, crumbled
- 1 tablespoon balsamic vinegar
- ¼ cup veggie stock
- 1 tablespoon chives, chopped
- A pinch of salt and black pepper

Directions:
In your instant pot, mix the tomatoes with the olives and the rest of the ingredients except the cheese and the stock, put the lid on and cook o High for 15 minutes. Release the pressure naturally for 10 minutes, divide the mix between plates, sprinkle the cheese and the chives on top and serve.
Nutrition: calories 60, fat 3.8, fiber 2.1, carbs 3.5, protein 1.3

Butter Shirataki Noodles

Preparation time: 10 minutes
Cooking time: 3 minutes
Servings: 2
Ingredients:
- 7 oz shirataki noodles
- 1 cup chicken broth
- ½ teaspoon salt
- 1 tablespoon butter

Directions:
Pour chicken broth in the instant pot. Add shirataki noodles and salt. Close the lid and cook the side dish for 3 minutes in Manual mode (high pressure). Then make a quick pressure release and open the lid. Drain the chicken broth. Add butter in the noodles and carefully mix them up.
Nutrition: calories 91, fat 6.4, fiber 10.5, carbs 0.5, protein 3.2

Balsamic Eggplant Mix

Preparation time: 10 minutes
Cooking time: 12 minutes
Servings: 4
Ingredients:
- 2 eggplants, sliced
- ¼ cup veggie stock
- 1 tablespoon olive oil
- 6 garlic cloves, minced
- 1 tablespoon balsamic vinegar
- 1 tablespoon chives, chopped
- A pinch of salt and black pepper

Directions:
Set the instant pot on Sauté mode, add the oil, heat it up, add the garlic and sauté for 2 minutes. Add the eggplants and the rest of the ingredients, put the lid on and cook on High for 10 minutes. Release the pressure naturally for 10 minutes, divide the mix between plates and serve.
Nutrition: calories 106, fat 4, fiber 1.9, carbs 2.7, protein 3

Asiago Cauliflower Rice

Preparation time: 10 minutes
Cooking time: 10 minutes
Servings: 4
Ingredients:
- 2 cups cauliflower, shredded
- 1 tablespoon almond butter
- ½ white onion, diced
- 1 teaspoon apple cider vinegar
- 2 oz Asiago cheese, shredded
- 1 cup chicken broth
- ¼ teaspoon dried tarragon

Directions:
Heat up the instant pot on sauté mode for 3 minutes. Add almond butter and melt it. Then add shredded cauliflower and diced onion. Cook the vegetables on sauté mode for 2 minutes. Then sprinkle the mixture with apple cider vinegar and dried tarragon, Add chicken broth and close the lid. Cook the meal on manual mode (high pressure) for 4 minutes. Then make a quick pressure release and open the lid. Add Asiago cheese and mix up the meal well.
Nutrition: calories 102, fat 6.7, fiber 1.9, carbs 4.9, protein 6.7

Buttery Eggplants

Preparation time: 5 minutes
Cooking time: 12 minutes
Servings: 4
Ingredients:
- 1 pound eggplants, sliced
- A pinch of salt and black pepper
- 2 shallots, chopped
- 1 cup chicken stock
- 1 tablespoon ghee, melted
- 2 tablespoons parsley, chopped

Directions:
Set your instant pot on Sauté mode, add the ghee, heat it up, add the shallots and cook for 2 minutes. Add the eggplants and the rest of the ingredients, put the lid on and cook on High for 10 minutes. Release the pressure fast for 5 minutes, divide the mix between plates and serve.
Nutrition: calories 60, fat 3.5, fiber 1.8, carbs 3, protein 1.4

Spaghetti Squash Mac&Cheese

Preparation time: 10 minutes

Cooking time: 15 minutes
Servings: 4
Ingredients:
- 9 oz spaghetti squash, cleaned, seeded
- 3 teaspoons butter
- ¼ teaspoon ground black pepper
- ¼ teaspoon onion power
- 2 oz Parmesan, grated
- ½ cup Edam cheese, grated
- 1 cup water, for cooking

Directions:
Pour water and insert the steamer rack in the instant pot. Place the spaghetti squash in the instant pot and close the lid. Cook the vegetables on manual mode (high pressure) for 10 minutes. Then make a quick pressure release and open the lid. Cool the spaghetti squash till the room temperature. With the help of the fork shred the spaghetti squash. Put the shredded squash in the instant pot. Add butter, ground black pepper, and onion powder. Stir it well. Set sauté mode. Top the shredded squash with Edam cheese and Parmesan and close the lid. Saute the meal for 5 minutes or until the cheese is melted.
Nutrition: calories 179, fat 13.1, fiber 0, carbs 5.4, protein 11.2

Bacon Artichokes
Preparation time: 10 minutes
Cooking time: 12 minutes
Servings: 4
Ingredients:
- 1 cup bacon, chopped
- 1 pound canned artichokes hearts, drained
- ¼ teaspoon nutmeg, ground
- A pinch of salt and black pepper
- 1 cup coconut milk
- 2 tablespoons parsley, chopped

Directions:
In your instant pot, combine the artichokes with the rest of the ingredients, put the lid on and cook on High for 12 minutes. Release the pressure naturally for 10 minutes, divide the mix between plates and serve as a side dish.
Nutrition: calories 140, fat 14.2, fiber 1.4, carbs 3.5, protein 1.4

Sichuan Style Green Beans
Preparation time: 15 minutes
Cooking time: 7 minutes
Servings: 4
Ingredients:
- 1 tablespoon apple cider vinegar
- ½ teaspoon chili flakes
- ½ teaspoon minced garlic
- 1 tablespoon sesame oil
- ½ teaspoon minced ginger
- 12 oz green beans, trimmed
- 1 cup water, for cooking

Directions:
Pour water and insert the steamer rack in the instant pot. Put the green beans in the rack and close the lid. Cook the vegetables for 7 minutes on steam mode. Then make a quick pressure release. Put the cooked green beans in the bowl. Sprinkle them with chili flakes, minced garlic, minced ginger, sesame oil, and apple cider vinegar. Mix up the green beans and leave for 10 minutes to marinate.
Nutrition: calories 59, fat 3.5, fiber 2.9, carbs 6.4, protein 1.6

Cabbage and Tomatoes
Preparation time: 10 minutes
Cooking time: 15 minutes
Servings: 4
Ingredients:
- 1 green cabbage, shredded
- 1 pound cherry tomatoes, halved
- 1 shallot, chopped
- 1 tablespoon olive oil
- ¼ cup balsamic vinegar
- ¼ cup veggie stock
- A pinch of cayenne pepper
- 1 tablespoon dill, chopped

Directions:
Set your instant pot on Sauté mode, add the oil, heat it up, add the shallot and sauté for 2 minutes. Add the cabbage and the rest of the ingredients, put the lid on and cook on High for 13 minutes. Release the pressure naturally for 10 minutes, divide the mix between plates and serve.
Nutrition: calories 56, fat 3.8, fiber 1.5, carbs 3, protein 1.2

Cauliflower Tortillas
Preparation time: 15 minutes
Cooking time: 5 minutes
Servings: 4
Ingredients:
- 1 cup cauliflower, shredded
- 1 egg, beaten
- ½ teaspoon dried cilantro
- 1 teaspoon lemon juice
- ½ teaspoon lemon zest, grated
- ¼ teaspoon ground black pepper
- ¼ teaspoon salt
- 1 tablespoon coconut flour
- 1 teaspoon olive oil

Directions:
Place the shredded cauliflower in the cheesecloth and squeeze well. Then transfer the squeezed cauliflower in the bowl. Add egg, dried cilantro, lemon juice, lemon zest, ground black pepper, salt, and coconut flour. Mix up the cauliflower mixture until smooth. After this, make the small balls from the cauliflower mixture. With the help of the rolling pin roll up the cauliflower balls into the tortillas. Brush the instant pot with olive oil from inside. Place the cauliflower tortillas in the instant pot (cook 2 tortillas per one cooking) and cook them on sauté mode for 2 minutes from each side.
Nutrition: calories 30, fat 1.3, fiber 1.4, carbs 2.8, protein 2.2

Balsamic Collard Greens
Preparation time: 10 minutes
Cooking time: 15 minutes
Servings: 4
Ingredients:
- 1 bunch collard greens, trimmed
- 2 tablespoons avocado oil
- ½ cup chicken stock
- 2 tablespoons balsamic vinegar
- 3 garlic cloves, minced

- A pinch of salt and black pepper
- 1 tablespoon chives, chopped

Directions:
Set the instant pot on Sauté mode, add the oil, heat it up, add the garlic and cook for 2 minutes. Add the collard greens and the rest of the ingredients, put the lid on and cook on High for 13 minutes. Release the pressure naturally for 10 minutes, divide everything between plates and serve as a side dish.
Nutrition: calories 73, fat 2.1, fiber 0.3, carbs 1.4, protein 0.3

Gouda Vegetable Casserole

Preparation time: 15 minutes
Cooking time: 5 minutes
Servings: 4
Ingredients:
- 1 cup collard greens, chopped
- ½ cup white mushrooms, chopped
- 1 cup celery stalk, chopped
- ½ white onion, sliced
- 2 bacon slices, chopped
- 1 teaspoon olive oil
- 1 teaspoon ground black pepper
- 1 teaspoon fresh basil, chopped
- ½ teaspoon salt
- 3 oz Gouda cheese, grated
- 1 tablespoon cream cheese

Directions:
Put chopped bacon in the instant pot and cook it on sauté mode for 3 minutes. Stir the bacon. Add sliced onion and white mushrooms. Cook the vegetables for 2 minutes more. After this, add celery stalk. Sprinkle the mixture with ground black pepper, olive oil, basil, salt, and cream cheese. Close the lid and cook the meal on manual mode (high pressure) for 3 minutes. Then allow the natural pressure release for 10 minutes. After this, open the lid and transfer the casserole in the serving plates. Top the casserole with Gouda cheese.
Nutrition: calories 162, fat 12.1, fiber 1.3, carbs 3.8, protein 9.9

Cilantro Cauliflower Rice Mix

Preparation time: 10 minutes
Cooking time: 15 minutes
Servings: 4
Ingredients:
- 1 shallot, chopped
- 1 teaspoon garlic, minced
- 1 tablespoon avocado oil
- 1 and ½ cups cauliflower rice
- 1 and ½ cups chicken stock
- A pinch of salt and black pepper
- 2 tablespoons chives, chopped

Directions:
Set your instant pot on Sauté mode, add the oil, heat it up, add the shallot and the garlic and sauté for 2 minutes Add the rest of the ingredients except the chives, put the lid on and cook on High for 13 minutes Release the pressure naturally for 10 minutes, divide the mix between plates and serve as a side dish.
Nutrition: calories 55, fat 2.3, fiber 0.2, carbs 0.3, protein 0.1

Warm Antipasto Salad

Preparation time: 10 minutes
Cooking time: 5 minutes
Servings: 4
Ingredients:
- 2 cups lettuce, chopped
- 3 mozzarella balls, sliced
- 4 oz ham, chopped
- 2 oz artichoke hearts, chopped, canned
- 1 tomato, chopped
- 1 teaspoon fresh basil, chopped
- ¼ chili pepper, chopped
- 1 tablespoon olive oil
- ¼ teaspoon salt
- 1 kalamata olive, chopped

Directions:
Pour ½ tablespoon of olive oil in the instant pot. Add chopped ham and cook it on sauté mode for 5 minutes. Stir it from time to time. Meanwhile, in the mixing bowl combine together sliced mozzarella, lettuce, chopped artichoke hearts, tomato, basil, chili pepper, and kalamata olive. Add remaining olive oil and salt. Then add hot ham and mix up the salad well.
Nutrition: calories 181, fat 12.9, fiber 1.6, carbs 4.1, protein 13

Leeks Sauté

Preparation time: 10 minutes
Cooking time: 10 minutes
Servings: 4
Ingredients:
- 2 scallions, chopped
- 4 leeks, sliced
- A pinch of salt and black pepper
- 1 teaspoon chili powder
- ¼ cup chicken stock
- 2 tablespoons parsley, chopped
- 1 tablespoon lemon zest, grated

Directions:
In your instant pot, combine the leeks with the rest of the ingredients, put the lid on and cook on High for 10 minutes. Release the pressure naturally for 10 minutes, divide the mix between plates and serve.
Nutrition: calories 61, fat 2.5, fiber 1.1, carbs 2.1, protein 1.7

Eggplant Gratin

Preparation time: 15 minutes
Cooking time: 10 minutes
Servings: 3
Ingredients:
- 1 eggplant, sliced
- ¼ cup heavy cream
- ¼ cup Cheddar cheese, shredded
- 1 teaspoon coconut oil
- ¼ teaspoon salt
- ¼ teaspoon chili powder
- ½ teaspoon garlic powder
- 1 teaspoon fresh parsley, chopped
- 3 oz kohlrabi, chopped

Directions:
Melt coconut oil on sauté mode. Add eggplants and kohlrabi. Sprinkle the vegetables with salt, chili powder, and garlic powder. Mix up well and sauté them for 5 minutes. After this, mix up the vegetables one more time. In the mixing bowl combine together

heavy cream, Cheddar cheese, garlic powder, and fresh parsley. Pour the liquid over the sauteed vegetables and close the lid. Cook the gratin for 5 minutes on manual mode (high pressure). Then allow the natural pressure release for 10 minutes.
Nutrition: calories 134, fat 8.7, fiber 6.6, carbs 11.6, protein 4.7

Eggplant and Zucchini Mix

Preparation time: 10 minutes
Cooking time: 12 minutes
Servings: 4
Ingredients:
- 2 eggplants, cubed
- 2 zucchinis, roughly cubed
- 1 tablespoon chives, chopped
- ¼ cup chicken stock
- 1 teaspoon chili powder
- 1 tablespoon oregano, chopped
- A pinch of salt and black pepper
- 2 tablespoons parsley, chopped

Directions:
In your instant pot, combine the eggplants with the zucchinis and the rest of the ingredients, put the lid on and cook on High for 12 minutes. Release the pressure naturally for 10 minutes, divide the mix between plates and serve.
Nutrition: calories 91, fat 1, fiber 0.2, carbs 0.3, protein 4.2

Beet Cubes with Pecans

Preparation time: 15 minutes
Cooking time: 15 minutes
Servings: 4
Ingredients:
- 7 oz beet, peeled
- 2 pecans, chopped
- ½ teaspoon olive oil
- ¼ teaspoon salt
- 1 cup water, for cooking

Directions:
Cut the beet into the cubes. Pour water and insert the steamer rack in the instant pot. Put the beet cubes in the instant pot and close the lid. Cook the vegetables for 15 minutes on high-pressure mode. Then allow the natural pressure release for 10 minutes. Open the lid and transfer the cooked beet cubes in the serving plates. Sprinkle the vegetables with pecans, salt, and olive oil.
Nutrition: calories 76, fat 5.7, fiber 1.7, carbs 5.9, protein 1.6

Chili Cauliflower Rice

Preparation time: 10 minutes
Cooking time: 20 minutes
Servings: 4
Ingredients:
- A pinch of salt and black pepper
- ½ teaspoon cayenne pepper
- 1 teaspoon chili powder
- 2 tablespoons green onions, chopped
- 1 cup chicken stock
- 2 cups cauliflower rice

Directions:
In your instant pot, mix the cauliflower rice with the stock and the rest of the ingredients, put the lid on and cook on Low for 20 minutes. Release the pressure naturally for 10 minutes, divide the mix between plates and serve.
Nutrition: calories 52, fat 1.5, fiber 0.2, carbs 0.3, protein 0.7

Jalapeno Popper Bread

Preparation time: 10 minutes
Cooking time: 8 minutes
Servings: 4
Ingredients:
- 5 eggs, beaten
- 1 oz bacon, chopped, cooked
- 1 jalapeno pepper, chopped
- ½ teaspoon avocado oil
- ½ cup Cheddar cheese, shredded
- 1 cup water, for cooking

Directions:
In the mixing bowl whisk together eggs, bacon, jalapeno pepper, and cheese. Then brush the instant pot baking pan with avocado oil. Pour the egg mixture in the baking pan. Pour water and insert the trivet in the instant pot. Place the baking pan on the trivet and close the lid. Cook the bread on manual (high pressure) for 8 minutes. Then allow the natural pressure release for 5 minutes. Cool the cooked bread well and then remove it from the baking pan. Slice the bread.
Nutrition: calories 176, fat 13.2, fiber 0.1, carbs 0.9, protein 13.1

Sage Eggplants and Green Beans

Preparation time: 10 minutes
Cooking time: 15 minutes
Servings: 4
Ingredients:
- 2 cups green beans, trimmed and halved
- 1 cup chicken stock
- 2 garlic cloves, minced
- 2 eggplants, roughly cubed
- 2 tablespoon olive oil
- 2 tablespoons sage, chopped
- 2 tablespoons parmesan, grated

Directions:
Set your instant pot on Sauté mode, add the oil, heat it up, add the garlic and cook for 2 minutes. Add the green beans and the rest of the ingredients except the parmesan, put the lid on and cook on High for 13 minutes. Release the pressure naturally for 10 minutes, divide the mix between plates, sprinkle the parmesan on top and serve.
Nutrition: calories 152, fat 7.8, fiber 2.1, carbs 4.3, protein 4.1

Baked Green Beans

Preparation time: 5 minutes
Cooking time: 6 minutes
Servings: 1
Ingredients:
- 4 oz green beans, chopped
- ½ teaspoon butter
- 1 tablespoon almond meal
- 1 oz Provolone cheese, grated
- 1 cup water, for cooking

Directions:

Pour water and insert the steamer rack in the instant pot. Place the green beans on the rack and cook them on manual mode (high pressure) for 1 minute. After this, make a quick pressure release and open the lid. Place the cooked green beans in the bowl. Add almond meal and grated Provolone cheese. Then clean the instant pot and remove the rack. Put the green beans mixture in the instant pot bowl. Add butter and close the lid. Cook the baked green beans for 5 minutes.
Nutrition: calories 186, fat 12.6, fiber 4.6, carbs 10, protein 10.6

Nutmeg Zucchini Rice
Preparation time: 10 minutes
Cooking time: 15 minutes
Servings: 4
Ingredients:
- 2 tablespoons avocado oil
- 1 shallot, chopped
- 2 garlic cloves, minced
- 2 cups cauliflower rice
- 1 and ½ cups chicken stock
- 1 big zucchini, grated
- ½ teaspoon allspice, ground
- 1 tablespoon parsley, chopped

Directions:
Set your instant pot on Sauté mode, add the oil, heat it up, add the shallot and the garlic and sauté for 2 minutes. Add the rest of the ingredients, toss, put the lid on and cook on High for 13 minutes. Release the pressure naturally for 10 minutes, divide the mix between plates and serve as a side dish.
Nutrition: calories 62, fat 1.7, fiber 1, carbs 1.4, protein 1.2

Garlic Bread
Preparation time: 15 minutes
Cooking time: 6 minutes
Servings: 6
Ingredients:
- 5 oz Parmesan, grated
- ½ cup almond meal
- 1 tablespoon cream cheese
- 1 egg, beaten
- 1 teaspoon chives
- 1 tablespoon sesame oil
- 1 teaspoon minced garlic

Directions:
In the mixing bowl mix up together Parmesan, almond meal, and cream cheese. Microwave the mixture for 10 seconds. Then mix it well until smooth and add an egg. Stir it until homogenous. Brush the instant pot bowl with ½ tablespoon of sesame oil. Then place the cheese dough in the instant pot and flatten it in the shape of the pancake. Brush the bread with remaining sesame oil and sprinkle with minced garlic and chives. Cook the bread on sauté mode for 6 minutes. Flip the bread on another side after 5 minutes of cooking.
Nutrition: calories 159, fat 12.6, fiber 1, carbs 2.8, protein 10.4

Spiced Zucchinis
Preparation time: 5 minutes
Cooking time: 15 minutes
Servings: 4
Ingredients:
- 1 teaspoon ginger, grated
- 3 garlic cloves, minced
- 2 zucchinis, sliced
- 1 tablespoon olive oil
- 1 tablespoon cumin, ground
- 1 teaspoon cardamom, ground
- 1 teaspoon sweet paprika
- A pinch of salt and black pepper

Directions:
Set the instant pot on sauté mode, add the oil, heat it up, add the garlic and the ginger and sauté for 2 minutes. Add the remaining ingredients, put the lid on and cook on High for 13 minutes. Release the pressure fast for 5 minutes, divide the mix between plates and serve.
Nutrition: calories 59, fat 4.2, fiber 1.5, carbs 2.4, protein 1.9

Parmesan Broccoli Head
Preparation time: 10 minutes
Cooking time: 4 minutes
Servings: 4
Ingredients:
- 9 broccoli head
- 2 oz Parmesan, grated
- 1 teaspoon sesame oil
- ½ teaspoon chili flakes
- 1 cup water, for cooking

Directions:
Pour water and insert the trivet in the instant pot. Sprinkle the broccoli head with sesame oil and chili flakes. Then top it with parmesan and wrap in the foil. Place the wrapped broccoli in the instant pot and close the lid. Cook the vegetable for 4 minutes on Manual mode (high pressure). Make a quick pressure release and open the lid. Remove the broccoli from the foil.
Nutrition: calories 56, fat 4.2, fiber 0, carbs 0.5, protein 4.6

Leeks and Cabbage
Preparation time: 10 minutes
Cooking time: 10 minutes
Servings: 4
Ingredients:
- 2 garlic cloves, minced
- 3 leeks, sliced
- 1 green cabbage, shredded
- A pinch of salt and black pepper
- ½ teaspoon rosemary, dried
- ½ teaspoon thyme dried
- ½ cup chicken stock

Directions:
In your instant pot, mix the leeks with the cabbage and the rest of the ingredients, put the lid on and cook on High for 10 minutes. Release the pressure naturally for 10 minutes, divide the mix between plates and serve as a side dish.
Nutrition: calories 55, fat 1.6, fiber 0.7, carbs 1.1, protein 1.2

Cauliflower Salad with Provolone Cheese
Preparation time: 10 minutes
Cooking time: 3 minutes
Servings: 2

Ingredients:
- 4 oz cauliflower florets
- ½ teaspoon apple cider vinegar
- ¼ teaspoon chili flakes
- ¼ teaspoon chives
- 1 oz Provolone cheese, chopped
- 1 teaspoon olive oil
- 1 cup water, for cooking

Directions:
Pour water and insert the steamer rack in the instant pot. Place the cauliflower florets in the rack and close the lid. Cook the vegetables for 3 minutes on Manual mode (high pressure). Then make a quick pressure release and open the lid. Place the cauliflower florets in the salad bowl. Sprinkle them with apple cider vinegar, chili flakes, chives, and olive oil. Add chopped Provolone cheese and mix up well.
Nutrition: calories 84, fat 6.2, fiber 1.4, carbs 3.3, protein 4.7

Cranberries Cauliflower Rice

Preparation time: 10 minutes
Cooking time: 15 minutes
Servings: 4
Ingredients:
- 2 tablespoons avocado oil
- 2 shallots, chopped
- ½ cup cranberries
- 1 and ½ cups cauliflower rice
- 1 cup veggie stock
- A pinch of salt and black pepper
- ½ cup cilantro, chopped

Directions:
Set your instant pot on Sauté mode, add the oil, heat it up, add the shallots and sauté for 2 minutes Add the rest of the ingredients, stir, put the lid on and cook on High for 13 minutes. Release the pressure naturally for 10 minutes, divide the mix between plates and serve as a side dish.
Nutrition: calories 34, fat 2, fiber 0.2, carbs 1.7, protein 1

Spiced Asparagus

Preparation time: 10 minutes
Cooking time: 4 minutes
Servings: 6
Ingredients:
- 1-pound asparagus, trimmed
- 1 teaspoon olive oil
- 1 teaspoon lemon juice
- ½ teaspoon chili powder
- 1 teaspoon chili flakes
- 1 teaspoon ground black pepper
- ½ teaspoon ground coriander
- 1 teaspoon butter, melted
- 1 cup water, for cooking

Directions:
Insert trivet in the instant pot. Add water. Put the asparagus on the trivet, add chili powder, chili flakes, ground black pepper, and butter. Close the lid. Cook the asparagus for 4 minutes on manual mode (high pressure). Then make a quick pressure release and open the lid. Transfer the cooked asparagus in the serving plates and sprinkle with lemon juice, olive oil, and butter. Gently mix the cooked vegetables.
Nutrition: calories 29, fat 1.6, fiber 1.8, carbs 3.3, protein 1.8

Mint Zucchinis

Preparation time: 10 minutes
Cooking time: 12 minutes
Servings: 4
Ingredients:
- 1 tablespoon balsamic vinegar
- 2 zucchinis, sliced
- 1 teaspoon lime juice
- A pinch of salt and black pepper
- ¼ cup chicken stock
- 1 tablespoon olive oil
- ½ cup green onions, chopped
- 2 tablespoons mint, chopped

Directions:
Set the instant pot on Sauté mode, add the oil, heat it up, add the onions and sauté for 2 minutes. Add the rest of the ingredients, put the lid on and cook on High for 10 minutes. Release the pressure naturally for 10 minutes, divide the mix between plates and serve.
Nutrition: calories 52, fat 3.8, fiber 1.6, carbs 2.3, protein 1.6

Side Dish Cauliflower Ziti

Preparation time: 10 minutes
Cooking time: 5 minutes
Servings: 4
Ingredients:
- 1 cup cauliflower, chopped
- ¼ teaspoon garlic, diced
- 1/3 onion, diced
- ½ teaspoon chili pepper
- ½ teaspoon salt
- 1 teaspoon tomato paste
- ½ cup cream
- 1 teaspoon olive oil
- 1 tablespoon ricotta cheese
- ½ cup Mozzarella cheese, shredded

Directions:
Mix up together cauliflower and onion. Add garlic, chili pepper, salt, and ricotta cheese. Mix up the vegetables well. Then in the separated bowl mix up together tomato paste and cream. Brush the instant pot bowl with olive oil and put the vegetable mixture inside. Pour the cream mixture over the vegetables. Then top the meal with Mozzarella and close the lid. Cook the cauliflower ziti for 5 minutes on Manual mode (high pressure). When the time is over, allow the natural pressure release for 5 minutes.
Nutrition: calories 114, fat 8.4, fiber 0.9, carbs 4.2, protein 6

Ketogenic Instant Pot Snack and Appetizer Recipes

Lemon Zucchini and Eggplant Spread

Preparation time: 10 minutes
Cooking time: 15 minutes
Servings: 4
Ingredients:
- 2 and ½ teaspoons lemon zest, grated
- 3 tablespoons lemon juice
- 2 zucchinis, chopped
- 2 eggplants, chopped
- 1 tablespoon olive oil
- ½ cup veggie stock
- 2 tablespoons dill, chopped

Directions:
In your instant pot, the zucchinis with the eggplants and the rest of the ingredients, except the dill, put the lid on and cook on High for 15 minutes. Release the pressure naturally for 10 minutes, blend the mix with an immersion blender, divide into bowls, sprinkle the dill on top and serve.
Nutrition: calories 121, fat 4.3, fiber 1, carbs 1.4, protein 4.3

Zucchini Fries in Bacon

Preparation time: 10 minutes
Cooking time: 10 minutes
Servings: 6
Ingredients:
- 2 zucchini, trimmed
- 2 oz Parmesan, grated
- 2 tablespoons almond meal
- 1 teaspoon olive oil
- 1 egg, beaten

Directions:
Cut the zucchini into fries shape and place it in the bowl. Then add egg and shake the vegetables well. In the separated bowl combine together Parmesan and almond meal. Coat the zucchini fries in the cheese mixture. Then heat up the instant pot on sauté mode for 3 minutes. Sprinkle the instant pot bowl with olive oil and arrange the zucchini in one layer. Cook the fries for 1 minute from each side or until they are light brown. Then place the cooked fries on the paper towel and dry little to get rid of oil. Repeat the same steps with the remaining zucchini.
Nutrition: calories 69, fat 4.6, fiber 1, carbs 3, protein 5.2

Oregano Green Beans Salsa

Preparation time: 10 minutes
Cooking time: 10 minutes
Servings: 4
Ingredients:
- 1 pound green beans, trimmed and halved
- ¼ cup veggie stock
- 1 tablespoon olive oil
- 2 garlic cloves, minced
- A pinch of salt and black pepper
- 2 tomatoes, cubed
- 2 cucumbers, cubed
- 1 avocado, peeled, pitted and cubed
- 2 tablespoons balsamic vinegar
- 1 tablespoon oregano, chopped

Directions:
In your instant pot mix the green beans with the stock, garlic, salt and pepper, put the lid on and cook on High for 10 minutes. Release the pressure naturally for 10 minutes, transfer the green beans to a bowl, add the rest of the ingredients, toss, divide the salsa into cups and serve.
Nutrition: calories 209, fat 11.2, fiber 3, carbs 4.4, protein 4.8

Bacon Bites with Asparagus

Preparation time: 10 minutes
Cooking time: 4 minutes
Servings: 5
Ingredients:
- 4 oz asparagus, trimmed
- 3 oz bacon, sliced
- ½ teaspoon salt
- ¼ teaspoon chili powder
- 1 cup water, for cooking

Directions:
Wrap every asparagus in the bacon and sprinkle with salt and chili powder. After this, pour water in the instant pot and insert the steamer rack. Place the wrapped asparagus in the rack and close the lid. Cook the snack on manual mode (high pressure) for 4 minutes. When the time is over, make a quick pressure release.
Nutrition: calories 97, fat 7.2, fiber 0.5, carbs 1.2, protein 6.8

Basil Zucchini and Capers Dip

Preparation time: 10 minutes
Cooking time: 10 minutes
Servings: 4
Ingredients:
- 1 shallot, chopped
- 1 and ½ pounds zucchinis, chopped
- 1 tablespoon olive oil
- 2 garlic cloves, minced
- A pinch of salt and black pepper
- 1 tablespoon capers, drained and chopped
- ¼ cup veggie stock
- 1 bunch basil, chopped

Directions:
Set your instant pot on Sauté mode, add the oil, heat it up, add the shallot and the garlic, stir and sauté for 2 minutes. Add the zucchinis and the rest of the ingredients, put the lid on and cook on High for 8 minutes. Release the pressure naturally for 10 minutes, blend everything using an immersion blender, divide into bowls and serve.
Nutrition: calories 75, fat 2.5, fiber 0.1, carbs 0.6, protein 1.2

Bacon Onion Rings

Preparation time: 10 minutes
Cooking time: 7 minutes
Servings: 4
Ingredients:
- 1 large white onion, peeled
- 4 bacon slices
- 1 teaspoon olive oil
- ¼ teaspoon dried thyme
- ¼ teaspoon salt
- 1 cup water, for cooking

Directions:
Slice the onion into thick rings. Then wrap every onion ring in the bacon. Pour water and insert the steamer rack in the instant pot. Place the onion rings on the rack and close the lid. Cook the snack for 3 minutes on manual mode (high pressure). Make a quick pressure release and open the lid. Transfer the onion rings on the plate and clean the instant pot. Sprinkle the snack with salt and dried thyme. Then brush with olive oil. Place the onion rings back in the instant pot and cook for 2 minutes from each side on sauté mode.
Nutrition: calories 128, fat 9.2, fiber 0.8, carbs 3.8, protein 7.5

Lime Spinach and Leeks Dip
Preparation time: 10 minutes
Cooking time: 20 minutes
Servings: 4
Ingredients:
- 1 shallot, chopped
- 2 tablespoons avocado oil
- 2 leeks, chopped
- 2 garlic cloves, minced
- 4 cups spinach, torn
- ¼ cup veggie stock
- ¼ cup lime juice
- 1 bunch basil, chopped
- A pinch of salt and black pepper

Directions:
Set your instant pot on Sauté mode, add the oil, heat it up, add the shallot, leeks and garlic and sauté for 5 minutes. Add the rest of the ingredients, put the lid on and cook on High for 15 minutes. Release the pressure naturally for 10 minutes, blend the mix using an immersion blender, transfer to bowls and serve as a snack.
Nutrition: calories 56, fat 1.8, fiber 0.5, carbs 1.6, protein 1.7

Oregano Keto Bread Rounds
Preparation time: 10 minutes
Cooking time: 35 minutes
Servings: 6
Ingredients:
- ½ cup Cheddar cheese, shredded
- 4 tablespoons almond meal
- ½ teaspoon baking powder
- 2 eggs, beaten
- 1 teaspoon coconut oil
- 1 teaspoon dried oregano

Directions:
In the mixing bowl combine together shredded cheese with almond meal. Add baking powder and dried oregano. Stir the ingredients with the help of the fork. Then add beaten eggs and knead the non-sticky dough. Add more almond meal if needed. Make 6 balls from the cheese mixture and roll them up with the help of the rolling pin. Preheat the instant pot on sauté mode for 2 minutes. Then add coconut oil and melt it. After this, place the first keto bread round in the instant pot and cook it for 3 minutes. Then flip it on another side and cook for 2 minutes more. Remove the cooked keto bread from the instant pot and cool little. Repeat the same steps with remaining keto bread rounds.

Nutrition: calories 90, fat 7.4, fiber 0.6, carbs 1.4, protein 5.1

Chili Tomato and Zucchini Dip
Preparation time: 10 minutes
Cooking time: 15 minutes
Servings: 4
Ingredients:
- 2 cups tomatoes, cubed
- 2 cups zucchinis, cubed
- 1 tablespoon hot paprika
- 2 red chilies, chopped
- ¼ cup veggie stock
- 1 tablespoon basil, chopped
- A pinch of salt and black pepper
- 2 scallions, chopped
- 1 tablespoon olive oil

Directions:
Set the instant pot on Sauté mode, add the oil, heat it up, add the chilies and the scallions and sauté for 2 minutes. Add the tomatoes and the rest of the ingredients except the basil, put the lid on and cook on High for 12 minutes. Release the pressure naturally for 10 minutes, blend the mix with an immersion blender, divide into bowls, sprinkle the basil on top and serve.
Nutrition: calories 58, fat 3.5, fiber 1.9, carbs 2.3, protein 1.6

Cabbage Chips
Preparation time: 10 minutes
Cooking time: 20 minutes
Servings: 10
Ingredients:
- 1-pound cabbage
- 1 oz Parmesan, grated
- 1 teaspoon ground paprika
- 1 teaspoon sesame oil

Directions:
Separate the cabbage leaves into the petals. Tear the petals and sprinkle with ground paprika and grated Parmesan. Shake the torn leaves. Heat up the instant pot on sauté mode for 3 minutes. Then place the cabbage petals in one layer in the instant pot. Cook the chips for 2 minutes from each side. Then cook the cabbage chips for 2 minutes more from each side or until they are light crunchy. Repeat the same steps with remaining torn cabbage petals.
Nutrition: calories 25, fat 1.1, fiber 1.2, carbs 2.9, protein 1.5

Parmesan Mushroom Spread
Preparation time: 10 minutes
Cooking time: 20 minutes
Servings: 4
Ingredients:
- 1 shallot chopped
- 2 tablespoons olive oil
- 1 tablespoon rosemary, chopped
- A pinch of salt and black pepper
- 3 garlic cloves, minced
- 1 cup chicken stock
- 2 pounds white mushrooms, sliced
- ½ cup parmesan, grated
- ½ cup coconut cream
- 1 tablespoons parsley, chopped

Directions:
Set your instant pot on Sauté mode, add the oil, heat it up, add the shallot and garlic and sauté for 2 minutes. Add the mushrooms and sauté for 5 minutes. Add the rest of the ingredients, put the lid on and cook on High for 15 minutes. Release the pressure naturally, divide the mix into bowls and serve as a party spread.
Nutrition: calories 187, fat 12.4, fiber 2.1, carbs 4.5, protein 8.2

Soul Bread
Preparation time: 15 minutes
Cooking time: 35 minutes
Servings: 10
Ingredients:
- 1 cup of protein powder
- ¼ teaspoon salt
- ½ teaspoon baking powder
- ½ teaspoon xanthan gum
- 2 tablespoons cream cheese
- 2 eggs, beaten
- 2 tablespoons sesame oil
- 4 tablespoons whipped cream
- 1 tablespoon butter, melted
- 3 tablespoons coconut flour
- 1 cup water, for cooking

Directions:
In the big mixing bowl combine together protein powder, salt, baking powder, xanthan gum, and coconut flour. Then add cream cheese, eggs, sesame oil, whipped cream, and melted butter. With the help of the hand blender whisk the mixture until you get a smooth batter. Then pour water and insert the rack in the instant pot. Pour the bread batter in the instant pot baking pan and transfer it in the instant pot. Close the lid and cook the soul bread on manual (high pressure) for 35 minutes. When the time is over, make a quick pressure release and open the lid. Cook the cooked bread to the room temperature and remove it from the baking pan. Slice the soul bread into the servings.
Nutrition: calories 117, fat 7.7, fiber 3.5, carbs 6.8, protein 7

Broccoli Dip
Preparation time: 10 minutes
Cooking time: 15 minutes
Servings: 6
Ingredients:
- 2 tablespoons avocado oil
- 8 garlic cloves, minced
- 2 cups veggie stock
- 6 cups broccoli florets
- 1 cup Greek yogurt
- 1 tablespoon dill, chopped
- A pinch of salt and black pepper
- ½ cup coconut cream

Directions:
Set your instant pot on Sauté mode, add the oil, heat it up, add the garlic and cook for 2 minutes. Add the rest of the ingredients except the dill and the yogurt, put the lid on and cook on High for 13 minutes. Release the pressure naturally for 10 minutes, add the yogurt, blend the mix with an immersion blender, divide into bowls, sprinkle the dill on top and serve.
Nutrition: calories 136, fat 8.6, fiber 4.8, carbs 5.6, protein 5.1

Tender Jicama Fritters
Preparation time: 10 minutes
Cooking time: 18 minutes
Servings: 4
Ingredients:
- 4 oz jicama, peeled, grated
- 1 egg, beaten
- 2 tablespoons Cheddar cheese, shredded
- ½ teaspoon ground coriander
- 1 teaspoon almond butter
- 2 tablespoons coconut flakes
- 1 tablespoon almond flour
- ½ teaspoon baking powder
- ½ teaspoon apple cider vinegar

Directions:
Mix up together jicama, egg, cheese, ground coriander, coconut flakes, baking powder, apple cider vinegar, and almond flour. Stir the mixture with the help of the spoon until homogenous. Then heat up the instant pot on sauté mode for 4 minutes or until it is hot. Add almond butter and melt it. Separate the jicama mixture into 4 parts. With the help of the spoon arrange the fritters in the instant pot (2 fritters per one cooking). Cook them for 3 minutes from each side. The cooked fritters should be golden brown. Dry the fritters with the help of the paper towel if needed.
Nutrition: calories 85, fat 6.2, fiber 2.2, carbs 4.5, protein 3.8

Ginger Cauliflower Spread
Preparation time: 10 minutes
Cooking time: 15 minutes
Servings: 4
Ingredients:
- 1 shallot, chopped
- 1 tablespoon avocado oil
- 2 tablespoons ginger, minced
- 1 pound cauliflower florets
- ¼ cup chicken stock
- 2 red hot chilies, chopped
- 1 and ¼ tablespoon balsamic vinegar

Directions:
Set your instant pot on Sauté mode, add the oil, heat it up, add the ginger and the shallot and sauté for 2 minutes. Add the rest of the ingredients, put the lid on and cook on High for 13 minutes. Release the pressure naturally for 10 minutes, blend the mix a bit with an immersion blender, divide into bowls and serve as a party spread.
Nutrition: calories 45, fat 2.5, fiber 1.3, carbs 2, protein 2.6

Spiced Chicken Carnitas
Preparation time: 20 minutes
Cooking time: 10 minute
Servings: 8
Ingredients:
- 1-pound chicken fillet
- ½ teaspoon ground coriander
- ½ teaspoon ground paprika
- ½ teaspoon ground turmeric
- ½ teaspoon salt

- ½ teaspoon dried cilantro
- ½ teaspoon dried oregano
- ½ teaspoon dried thyme
- 1 teaspoon butter
- 1 teaspoon minced garlic
- 1 tablespoon lemon juice
- 1 jalapeno pepper, chopped
- 1 cup chicken broth

Directions:
Put the chicken fillet in the instant pot. Sprinkle it with ground coriander, paprika, turmeric, salt, dried cilantro, oregano, thyme, butter, and minced garlic. Add jalapeno pepper and chicken broth. Close the lid and cook the chicken for 10 minutes on steam mode. When the time is over, allow the natural pressure release for 10 minutes. Open the lid and shred the chicken with the help of the fork. Sprinkle the cooked chicken with lemon juice and stir gently.
Nutrition: calories 120, fat 4.9, fiber 0.2, carbs 0.6, protein 17.1

Radish Salsa

Preparation time: 10 minutes
Cooking time: 15 minutes
Servings: 4
Ingredients:
- 2 cups red radishes, sliced
- 1 shallot, chopped
- 2 spring onions, chopped
- 2 tomatoes, cubed
- 1 avocado, peeled and cubed
- 1 tablespoon olive oil
- ¼ cup chicken stock
- A pinch of salt and black pepper
- 1 tablespoon oregano, chopped
- 1 tablespoon chives, chopped

Directions:
In your instant pot, combine the radishes with the stock, oregano, salt and pepper, put the lid on and cook on Low for 15 minutes. Release the pressure naturally for 10 minutes, transfer the radishes to a bowl, add the rest of the ingredients, toss, divide into small cups and serve as an appetizer.
Nutrition: calories 160, fat 13.7, fiber 5.5, carbs 10.1, protein 2.2

Cheese Almond Meal Bites

Preparation time: 10 minutes
Cooking time: 2 minutes
Servings: 4
Ingredients:
- ½ cup Cheddar cheese
- 1 egg, beaten
- ½ teaspoon salt
- 1 cup almond meal
- 1 teaspoon coconut oil

Directions:
Grate the cheese and combine it with egg and salt. When you get a homogenous mixture, make the small balls with the help of the medium scooper. After this, coat the balls in the almond meal. Toss the coconut oil in the instant pot and melt it on sauté mode. Then place the balls in the instant pot and cook for 30 seconds from each side. The almond meal bites have to be served warm.

Nutrition: calories 220, fat 18.8, fiber 3, carbs 5.4, protein 9.9

Mustard Greens Dip

Preparation time: 5 minutes
Cooking time: 14 minutes
Servings: 4
Ingredients:
- 6 ounces mustard greens, chopped
- 1 tablespoon olive oil
- 1 tablespoon basil, chopped
- 1 garlic clove, minced
- ¼ cup veggie stock
- 1 tablespoon balsamic vinegar
- 2 tablespoon coconut cream
- A pinch of salt and black pepper

Directions:
Set your instant pot on Sauté mode, add the oil, heat it up, add the garlic and cook for 1 minute Add the rest of the ingredients, put the lid on and cook on High for 13 minutes. Release the pressure fast for 5 minutes, blend the mix with an immersion blender, divide into bowls and serve.
Nutrition: calories 60, fat 5.4, fiber 1.6, carbs 2.8, protein 1.4

Zucchini Parsley Tots

Preparation time: 10 minutes
Cooking time: 10 minutes
Servings: 6
Ingredients:
- 1 zucchini, grated
- ½ teaspoon ground black pepper
- ¼ teaspoon salt
- 1 oz pumpkin, grated
- 3 tablespoons coconut flour
- 2 oz Provolone cheese, grated
- 1 teaspoon dried parsley
- 1 tablespoon butter

Directions:
Squeeze the grated zucchini to get rid of zucchini juice and place it in the big bowl. Add ground black pepper, salt, grated cheese, and dried parsley. With the help of the fork mix up the mixture. Then add grated pumpkin and coconut flour Stir the mixture. If the zucchini mixture is dry, add a small amount of zucchini liquid. With the help of the fingertips make the zucchini tots (small-sized tots). Toss butter in the instant pot and heat it up on sauté mode. Then arrange the zucchini tots in the instant pot in one layer and cook them for 2 minutes. Then flip the zucchini tots with the help of the spatula and cook for 1 minute more.
Nutrition: calories 73, fat 4.9, fiber 2.1, carbs 4.3, protein 3.4

Spinach and Artichokes Spread

Preparation time: 10 minutes
Cooking time: 15 minutes
Servings: 6
Ingredients:
- 14 ounces canned artichoke hearts, drained
- 8 ounces mozzarella cheese, shredded
- 1 pound spinach, torn
- 1 teaspoon garlic powder
- ½ cup chicken stock

- ½ cup coconut cream
- A pinch of salt and black pepper

Directions:
In your instant pot, mix the artichokes with the rest of the ingredients, put the lid on and cook on High for 15 minutes. Release the pressure naturally for 10 minutes, blend the mix using an immersion blender, stir well, transfer to a bowl and serve as a snack.
Nutrition: calories 204, fat 11.5, fiber 3.1, carbs 4.2, protein 5.9

Paprika Deviled Eggs

Preparation time: 10 minutes
Cooking time: 5 minutes
Servings: 2
Ingredients:
- 2 eggs
- 1 teaspoon ground paprika
- ½ teaspoon cream cheese
- ¼ teaspoon salt
- 1 cup water, for cooking

Directions:
Pour water and insert the steamer rack in the instant pot. Place the eggs on the rack and cook them on steamer mode for 5 minutes. Then make a quick pressure release and open the lid. Cool the eggs in the cold water for 5 minutes. Peel the eggs and cut them into halves. Remove the egg yolks and place them in the bowl. Smash the egg yolks with the help of the fork. Add cream cheese and ½ teaspoon of ground paprika. Stir well and fill the egg whites with egg yolk mixture. Top the deviled eggs with remaining paprika.
Nutrition: calories 69, fat 4.8, fiber 0.4, carbs 1, protein 5.8

Artichokes and Salmon Bowls

Preparation time: 5 minutes
Cooking time: 8 minutes
Servings: 4
Ingredients:
- 1 cup canned artichoke hearts, drained
- 1 pound smoked salmon, skinless, boneless and cubed
- 1 tablespoon olive oil
- A pinch of salt and black pepper
- 1 cup cherry tomatoes, cubed
- ¼ cup coconut cream
- 1 tablespoon chives, chopped

Directions:
In your instant pot, mix the artichoke hearts with the salmon and the rest of the ingredients, toss, put the lid on and cook on High for 8 minutes. Release the pressure fast for 5 minutes, divide the mix into small bowls and serve as an appetizer.
Nutrition: calories 206, fat 12.4, fiber 0.9, carbs 2.6, protein 21.5

Parmesan Tomatoes Slices

Preparation time: 10 minutes
Cooking time: 10 minutes
Servings: 8
Ingredients:
- 2 tomatoes
- 1 teaspoon basil, chopped
- 2 oz Parmesan, grated
- 1 teaspoon sesame oil

Directions:
Slice the tomatoes into 8 thick slices. Then brush the instant pot bowl with sesame oil and preheat it on sauté mode for 3 minutes or until it is hot. Then put the sliced tomatoes in one layer in instant pot and cook for 1 minute. Then flip the tomatoes on another side and top with ½ teaspoon of fresh basil and half of grated Parmesan. Close the lid and sauté the tomatoes for 4 minutes. Carefully transfer the tomatoes on the plate. Repeat the same steps with remaining tomatoes.
Nutrition: calories 33, fat 2.2, fiber 0.4, carbs 1.5, protein 2.6

Salmon and Cod Cakes

Preparation time: 10 minutes
Cooking time: 10 minutes
Servings: 4
Ingredients:
- 1 tablespoon olive oil
- 1 egg, whisked
- 1 cup tomato passata
- 4 tablespoons almond flour
- ½ pound cod fillets, boneless and chopped
- 1 pound salmon meat, minced
- 1 tablespoon parsley, chopped
- 2 tablespoons lime zest
- A pinch of salt and black pepper

Directions:
In a bowl, combine the cod and salmon meat with the rest of the ingredients except the oil and tomato passata, stir and shape medium cakes out of this mix Set your instant pot on sauté mode, add the oil, heat it up, add the patties and cook them for 2 minutes on each side. Add the tomato passata, put the lid on and cook on High for 8 minutes Release the pressure naturally for 10 minutes, arrange the cakes on a platter and serve as an appetizer.
Nutrition: calories 62, fat 4.7, fiber 1.3, carbs 3.9, protein 2.3

Mini Cheese Pepperoni Pizza

Preparation time: 10 minutes
Cooking time: 6 minutes
Servings: 4
Ingredients:
- 8 pepperoni slices
- ¼ cup Mozzarella, shredded
- 1 tablespoon low-carb marinara sauce
- 1 kalamata olive, sliced
- 1 cup water, for cooking

Directions:
Pour water in the instant pot and insert the steamer rack. Then arrange 2 pepperoni slices in one muffin mold to get the "pepperoni cups". Repeat the same step with the remaining pepperoni. After this, put Marinara sauce inside the pepperoni cups. Top them with Mozzarella cheese and sliced olive. Place the muffin molds with mini pizzas in the instant pot and close the lid. Cook the meal on manual mode (high pressure) for 6 minutes. When the time is over, make a quick pressure release and remove the mold from the instant pot. Cool the cooked pizzas little before serving.
Nutrition: calories 62, fat 5.3, fiber 0.1, carbs 0.4, protein 3

Green Beans and Cod Salad

Preparation time: 10 minutes
Cooking time: 15 minutes
Servings: 4
Ingredients:
- 1 pound cod fillets, skinless, boneless and cubed
- 2 tablespoons parsley, chopped
- 2 teaspoons lime juice
- 2 cups green beans, trimmed and halved
- A pinch of salt and black pepper
- 1 cup coconut cream
- 1 tablespoon oregano, chopped
- 1 tablespoon chives, chopped

Directions:
In your instant pot, combine the cod with the green beans and the rest of the ingredients except the oregano and chives, put the lid on and cook o High for 15 minutes. Release the pressure naturally for 10 minutes, divide the mix into small bowls, sprinkle the oregano and the chives on top and serve as an appetizer.
Nutrition: calories 160, fat 14.5, fiber 3.8, carbs 8.1, protein 2.6

Keto Queso Dip

Preparation time: 10 minutes
Cooking time: 3 hours
Servings: 6
Ingredients:
- 1 teaspoon garlic powder
- 1 tablespoon almond butter
- 1 tablespoon chili, chopped
- 2 cups Mexican cheese, shredded
- 2 tablespoons cream cheese
- ¼ cup heavy cream
- 1 cup water, for cooking

Directions:
Put shredded Mexican cheese in the baking pan. Add garlic powder, almond butter, chili, cream cheese, and heavy cream. Stir the mixture well. Then pour water and insert the steamer rack in the instant pot. Place the baking pan with cheese mixture in the instant pot and close the lid. Close the lid and cook the queso dip for 3 hours on manual mode (low pressure). When the dip is cooked, mix it up well and transfer it in the serving bowl.
Nutrition: calories 76, fat 6.7, fiber 0.4, carbs 1.7, protein 3.8

Shrimp and Leeks Platter

Preparation time: 5 minutes
Cooking time: 5 minutes
Servings: 6
Ingredients:
- 2 pounds shrimp, peeled and deveined
- 2 leeks, sliced
- 1 tablespoon sweet paprika
- 1 tablespoon olive oil
- 1 tablespoon chives, chopped
- ½ cup veggie stock
- 2 garlic cloves, minced

Directions:
Set instant pot on Sauté mode, add the oil, heat it up, add the leeks and garlic and sauté for 1 minute. Add the rest of the ingredients except the chives, put the lid on and cook on High for 4 minutes. Release the pressure fast for 5 minutes, arrange the shrimp and leeks on a platter and serve as an appetizer.
Nutrition: calories 224, fat 5.1, fiber 1, carbs 3.9, protein 35.1

Keto Jalapeno Bread

Preparation time: 20 minutes
Cooking time: 35 minutes
Servings: 8
Ingredients:
- ½ cup coconut flour
- ½ cup almond flour
- ½ teaspoon baking powder
- 4 eggs, beaten
- ½ teaspoon lemon juice
- 2 jalapeno peppers, sliced
- 1 teaspoon butter
- ½ teaspoon salt
- 1 oz Jarlsberg cheese, shredded
- 1 cup water, for cooking

Directions:
In the mixing bowl mix up together coconut flour and almond flour. Add baking powder and lemon juice. Then add eggs and salt. Stir the mixture until smooth. Brush the instant pot baking pan with butter and place the prepared bread dough inside. Then add sliced jalapeno and stir it. Top the bread with shredded cheese. Cover the bread with paper foil. Pour the water in the instant pot and insert the steamer rack. Place the baking pan in the rack and close the lid. Cook the jalapeno bread for 35 minutes on manual mode (high pressure). When the time is over, make a quick pressure release and open the lid. Remove the paper foil from the bread and cool meal well.
Nutrition: calories 119, fat 7.6, fiber 3.9, carbs 7.1, protein 6

Balsamic Mussels Bowls

Preparation time: 10 minutes
Cooking time: 10 minutes
Servings: 4
Ingredients:
- 2 cups tomato passata
- 2 pounds mussels, scrubbed
- 2 chili peppers, chopped
- ¼ cup veggie stock
- 1 tablespoon olive oil
- ¼ cup balsamic vinegar
- 2 garlic cloves, minced
- A pinch of salt and black pepper
- ½ cup oregano, chopped

Directions:
Set your instant pot on Sauté mode, add oil heat it up, add the chili peppers and the garlic and cook for 2 minutes. Add the rest of the ingredients, put the lid on and cook on High for 8 minutes. Release the pressure naturally for 10 minutes, divide the mix into bowls and serve as an appetizer.
Nutrition: calories 306, fat 9.8, fiber 4.8, carbs 6.5, protein 20.5

Turnip Fries

Preparation time: 10 minutes
Cooking time: 12 minutes

Servings: 4
Ingredients:
- 7 oz turnip, peeled
- ½ teaspoon salt
- ¼ teaspoon ground turmeric
- 1 tablespoon avocado oil

Directions:
Cut the turnip into the French fries shape and sprinkle with avocado oil. Mix up the turnip fries well and place them in the instant pot in one layer. Cook the turnip fries on sauté mode for 3 minutes from each side. Then transfer the cooked turnip fries in the plate and sprinkle with ground turmeric.
Nutrition: calories 19, fat 0.5, fiber 1.1, carbs 3.5, protein 0.5

Tomato and Zucchini Salsa

Preparation time: 10 minutes
Cooking time: 10 minutes
Servings: 4
Ingredients:
- 1 pound tomatoes, cubed
- 2 zucchinis, cubed
- 2 tablespoons olive oil
- ¼ cup chicken stock
- ½ teaspoon red pepper flakes
- 2 teaspoons garlic, minced
- 2 teaspoons ginger, chopped
- 1 tablespoon cilantro, chopped
- 2 teaspoons oregano, dried

Directions:
Set your instant pot on Sauté mode, add the oil, heat it up, add the pepper flakes, garlic and ginger and sauté for 2 minutes. Add the rest of the ingredients, put the lid on and cook on High for 8 minutes. Release the pressure naturally for 10 minutes, divide the salsa into bowls and serve cold.
Nutrition: calories 105, fat 7.6, fiber 3, carbs 6.7, protein 2.5

Butternut Squash Fries

Preparation time: 10 minutes
Cooking time: 10 minutes
Servings: 10
Ingredients:
- 1-pound butternut squash, peeled
- ½ teaspoon dried thyme
- ½ teaspoon salt
- 1 teaspoon sesame oil
- 1 cup water, for cooking

Directions:
Cut the peeled butternut squash into French fries shape. Sprinkle the vegetables with dried thyme, salt, and sesame oil. After this, pour water and insert the steamer rack in the instant pot. Place the butternut squash in the rack and close the lid. Cook the fries for 6 minutes on Manual mode (high pressure). When the time is over, make a quick pressure release and transfer the cooked butternut squash fries in the tray in one layer. Broil the fries for 4 minutes at 400F in the oven.
Nutrition: calories 25, fat 0.5, fiber 0.9. carbs 5.3, protein 0.5

Sweet Shrimp Bowls

Preparation time: 5 minutes
Cooking time: 5 minutes
Servings: 6
Ingredients:
- 2 pounds shrimp, peeled and deveined
- 2 scallions, chopped
- 1 cup veggie stock
- 1 tablespoon olive oil
- 2 garlic cloves, minced
- 1 avocado, peeled, pitted and cubed
- 1 tablespoon sweet paprika

Directions:
Set your instant pot on Sauté mode, add the oil, heat it up, add the scallions and the ginger, stir and cook for 1 minute. Add the rest of the ingredients, put the lid on and cook on High for 4 minutes. Release the pressure fast for 5 minutes, divide the mix into bowls and serve as an appetizer.
Nutrition: calories 274, fat 11.6, fiber 2.8, carbs 6.5, protein 35.4

Popcorn Chicken

Preparation time: 10 minutes
Cooking time: 12 minutes
Servings: 4
Ingredients:
- 9 oz chicken fillet
- 1 teaspoon chili powder
- 1 teaspoon ground paprika
- ½ teaspoon salt
- 1 tablespoon sesame oil
- 1 teaspoon coconut oil
- 1 teaspoon lemon juice
- 1 tablespoon almond meal

Directions:
Chop the chicken fillet into the small cubes (popcorn cubes). Then place it in the zip lock bag and add chili powder, ground paprika, salt, sesame oil, and lemon juice. Shake the chicken mixture well and transfer it in the bowl. Sprinkle the chicken with almond meal and shake well. After this, toss the coconut oil in the instant pot and melt it on sauté mode for 2-3 minutes. Then place the chicken popcorn in the instant pot and cook it for 10 minutes. Stir the chicken popcorn every 2 minutes.
Nutrition: calories 173, fat 10.2, fiber 0.6, carbs 1, protein 18.9

Parsley Clams Platter

Preparation time: 10 minutes
Cooking time: 12 minutes
Servings: 4
Ingredients:
- 20 clams, scrubbed
- 2 spring onions, chopped
- 1 and ½ cups veggie stock
- 2 tablespoons parsley, chopped
- 2 teaspoons lime zest, grated
- 1 tablespoon lime juice

Directions:
In your instant pot, combine the clams with the stock and the rest of the ingredients, put the lid on and cook on High for 12 minutes. Release the pressure naturally for 10 minutes, arrange the clams on a platter and serve.
Nutrition: calories 224, fat 4.5, fiber 1.2, carbs 2.7, protein 1.3

Crunchy Green Beans

Preparation time: 10 minutes
Cooking time: 10 minutes
Servings: 10
Ingredients:
- 1-pound green beans
- 2 eggs, beaten
- 1/3 cup coconut flakes
- ½ teaspoon salt
- ½ teaspoon ground black pepper
- 1 tablespoon coconut oil
- 1 cup water, for cooking

Directions:
Pour water and insert the steamer rack in the instant pot. Place the green beans in the rack and close the lid. Cook the vegetables on Manual mode (high pressure) for 4 minutes. Then make a quick pressure release and cool the green beans in ice water. After this, clean the instant pot and remove the steamer rack. Mix up together eggs with salt and ground black pepper. Then dip green beans in the egg mixture. After this, coat them in coconut flakes. Put the coconut oil in the instant pot and melt it on sauté mode. Place the green beans in one layer and cook for 1 minute from each side or until the green beans are light brown. Repeat the same steps with remaining green beans.
Nutrition: calories 48, fat 3.2, fiber 1.8, carbs 3.8, protein 2

Zucchinis and Walnuts Salsa

Preparation time: 10 minutes
Cooking time: 12 minutes
Servings: 4
Ingredients:
- 4 zucchinis, sliced
- ½ cup veggie stock
- 3 garlic cloves, minced
- 1 tablespoon ghee, melted
- 1 cup walnuts, chopped
- ¼ cup parsley, chopped
- ¼ cup parmesan cheese, grated
- 1 teaspoon oregano, dried
- 1 teaspoon balsamic vinegar

Directions:
In your instant pot, combine the zucchinis with the stock and the rest of the ingredients except the parmesan, put the lid on and cook on High for 12 minutes. Release the pressure naturally for 10 minutes, divide the mix into bowls, sprinkle the parmesan on top and serve as an appetizer.
Nutrition: calories 259, fat 22.1, fiber 4.6, carbs 5.9, protein 10.2

Keto Breadsticks

Preparation time: 15 minutes
Cooking time: 13 minutes
Servings: 8
Ingredients:
- ½ cup Mozzarella cheese, shredded
- 3 tablespoons cream cheese
- 1 egg, beaten
- 1 cup almond flour

Directions:
Mix up together shredded Mozzarella and almond flour. Then add egg and cream cheese. Mix up the cheese mixture well and then knead it in the dough ball. Preheat the instant pot on saute mode for 3 minutes. Meanwhile, place the dough ball on the baking paper and cover it with the second baking paper sheet. Roll up the dough into the flatbread shape. Remove the baking paper that covers the dough and transfer the dough in the instant pot. Close the lid and cook the meal for 10 minutes. Then open the lid and remove the meal with the baking paper from the instant pot. Let it cool well and then cut it into the sticks.
Nutrition: calories 110, fat 8.8, fiber 1.5, carbs 3.2, protein 4.5

Shrimp and Beef Bowls

Preparation time: 10 minutes
Cooking time: 10 minutes
Servings: 4
Ingredients:
- 1 and ½ pounds shrimp, peeled and deveined
- ½ pound beef, cut into strips
- 1 tablespoon Italian seasoning
- 1 cup chicken stock
- A pinch of salt and black pepper
- 1 tablespoon olive oil
- 1 tablespoon sweet paprika
- 1 tablespoon cilantro, chopped
- 1 teaspoon red pepper flakes, crushed

Directions:
Set the instant pot on Sauté mode, add the oil, heat it up, add the beef and brown for 2 minutes. Add the rest of the ingredients, put the lid on and cook on High for 8 minutes. Release the pressure naturally fro 10 minutes, divide the mix into bowls and serve as an appetizer.
Nutrition: calories 155, fat 8.5, fiber 0.8, carbs 1.8, protein 17.7

Mini Chicken Skewers

Preparation time: 15 minutes
Cooking time: 8 minutes
Servings: 4
Ingredients:
- 10 oz chicken fillet
- 1 teaspoon apple cider vinegar
- ¼ teaspoon lemon zest, grated
- ¼ teaspoon ground paprika
- ¼ teaspoon tomato paste
- ¼ tablespoon olive oil
- ¼ teaspoon salt
- 1 cup water, for cooking

Directions:
Chop the chicken into the medium cubes. In the shallow bowl combine together apple cider vinegar, lemon zest, ground paprika, tomato paste, salt, and olive oil. Then mix up together chicken cubes and tomato mixture. After this, string chicken into the wooden skewers. Pour water in the instant pot and insert the trivet. Arrange the chicken skewers in the trivet and close the lid. Cook the meal for 8 minutes on manual mode (high pressure). When the time is over, make a quick pressure release. It is recommended to serve the chicken skewers immediately.
Nutrition: calories 143, fat 6.2, fiber 0.1, carbs 0.2, protein 20.5

Coconut Shrimp Platter

Preparation time: 10 minutes
Cooking time: 4 minutes
Servings: 4
Ingredients:
- 2 pounds shrimp, peeled and deveined
- 2 tablespoons coconut aminos
- 3 tablespoons balsamic vinegar
- ¾ cup veggie stock
- 1 tablespoon chives, chopped
- 1 tablespoon basil, chopped
- 1 tablespoon chervil, chopped

Directions:
In your instant pot, combine the shrimp with the aminos and the rest of the ingredients, put the lid on and cook on High for 5 minutes. Release the pressure naturally for 10 minutes, arrange the shrimp on a platter and serve.
Nutrition: calories 273, fat 3.9, fiber 0.1, carbs 3.8, protein 17.8

Parmesan Cauliflower Tots

Preparation time: 15 minutes
Cooking time: 5 minutes
Servings: 2
Ingredients:
- 1 oz Parmesan, grated
- ¼ cup cauliflower, shredded
- 1 egg white
- ¼ teaspoon ground paprika
- 1 tablespoon almond flour
- 1 teaspoon butter
- ¼ teaspoon ground black pepper

Directions:
Whisk the egg white little and combine it with Parmesan and shredded cauliflower. Then add ground paprika and ground black pepper. Stir the mixture. Add almond flour and stir the mixture until it is homogenous and non-sticky. Make the small tots with the help of the fingertips. Melt butter in the instant pot on sauté mode. Place the cauliflower tots in the instant pot and cook them for 2 minutes from each side. If you prefer crunchy crust – increase the time of cooking to 3 minutes per one side.
Nutrition: calories 97, fat 6.7, fiber 0.9, carbs 2.4, protein 7.4

Marinated Shrimp

Preparation time: 10 minutes
Cooking time: 6 minutes
Servings: 4
Ingredients:
- 1 and ½ pounds shrimp, peeled and deveined
- ¼ cup chicken stock
- 1 tablespoon avocado oil
- Juice of ½ lemon
- 4 garlic cloves, minced
- 2 thyme springs, chopped
- 1 tablespoon rosemary, chopped
- Salt and black pepper to the taste

Directions:
In your instant pot, combine the shrimp with the stock and the rest of the ingredients, put the lid on and cook on High for 6 minutes. Release the pressure naturally for 10 minutes, arrange the shrimp on a platter and serve as an appetizer.
Nutrition: calories 282, fat 4.5, fiber 0.6, carbs 2.3, protein 30.4

Aromatic Swedish Meatballs

Preparation time: 15 minutes
Cooking time: 11 minutes
Servings: 6
Ingredients:
- ½ cup ground beef
- ½ cup ground pork
- ¼ cup of water
- ½ teaspoon ground black pepper
- ½ white onion, diced
- ½ teaspoon all spices
- 3 tablespoons almond meal
- ½ cup heavy cream
- 1 teaspoon dried dill
- ½ teaspoon minced garlic
- 1 egg yolk
- ½ teaspoon cilantro, chopped
- 1/3 cup chicken broth
- 1 teaspoon avocado oil
- ½ teaspoon salt

Directions:
In the mixing bowl, mix up together ground beef, ground pork, water, ground black pepper, diced onion, all spices, almond meal, dried dill, minced garlic, and egg yolk. Stir the ground meat mixture well. Then make the small meatballs. Place them in the instant pot and add avocado oil. Cook them on sauté mode for 3 minutes from each side. Then add chicken broth, salt, cilantro, and heavy cream. Close the lid and cook the meatballs for 5 minutes on manual mode (high pressure). Then make a quick pressure release. Cool the meatballs to the room temperature.
Nutrition: calories 168, fat 12.9, fiber 0.7, carbs 2.3, protein 10.6

Eggplant and Spinach Dip

Preparation time: 10 minutes
Cooking time: 15 minutes
Servings: 4
Ingredients:
- 2 eggplants, cubed
- 1 cup baby spinach
- ¼ cup veggie stock
- ¼ cup coconut cream
- A pinch of salt and black pepper
- 2 garlic cloves, minced
- 1 tablespoon lemon juice

Directions:
In your instant pot, combine the eggplants with the spinach and the rest of the ingredients, put the lid on and cook on High for 15 minutes. Release the pressure naturally for 10 minutes, blend the mix with an immersion blender, divide into bowls and serve as a party dip.
Nutrition: calories 108, fat 4.1, fiber 2.6, carbs 3.7, protein 3.5

Kale Wraps

Preparation time: 10 minutes
Cooking time: 15 minutes

Servings: 4
Ingredients:
- 4 kale leaves
- ½ cup ground chicken
- ¼ teaspoon chili flakes
- ¼ teaspoon salt
- ¼ teaspoon onion powder
- ¼ teaspoon garlic powder
- 1 teaspoon butter
- 1 teaspoon chives, chopped

Directions:
Toss butter in the instant pot. Set instant pot on sauté mode for 15 minutes. Add ground chicken. Sprinkle it with chili flakes, salt, onion powder, and garlic powder. Stir well and sauté the mixture for 5 minutes. Then stir it well and cook for 10 minutes more. When the ground chicken is cooked, switch off the instant pot. Fill the kale leaves with chicken and wrap.
Nutrition: calories 53, fat 2.3, fiber 0.4, carbs 2.5, protein 5.8

Balsamic Endives

Preparation time: 10 minutes
Cooking time: 12 minutes
Servings: 4
Ingredients:
- 4 endives, trimmed and halved lengthwise
- A pinch of salt and black pepper
- 2 tablespoons lime juice
- ¼ cup olive oil
- 2 teaspoons balsamic vinegar
- 1 teaspoon thyme, dried
- 2 cups water

Directions:
Put the water in the instant pot, add steamer basket, add the endives inside, put the lid on and cook on High for 12 minutes. Release the pressure naturally for 10 minutes, transfer the endives to a bowl, add the rest of the ingredients, toss gently, arrange everything on a platter and serve.
Nutrition: calories 109, fat 12.6, fiber 0.1, carbs 0.2, protein 1

Bread Twists

Preparation time: 15 minutes
Cooking time: 20 minutes
Servings: 7
Ingredients:
- 4 tablespoons almond flour
- 4 tablespoons coconut flour
- ¼ teaspoon salt
- ½ teaspoon baking powder
- 1 teaspoon apple cider vinegar
- 1 tablespoon butter
- ¾ cup Cheddar cheese, shredded
- 1 egg, beaten
- 1 tablespoon water
- 1 cup water, for cooking

Directions:
In the mixing bowl combine together butter and Cheddar cheese. Place the mixture in the microwave and heat it up for 30 seconds. Stir the mixture until smooth. In the separated bowl combine together almond flour, coconut flour, salt, baking powder, apple cider vinegar, and egg. When the mixture is smooth, add cheese mixture and knead the dough. After this, roll up the dough and cut it into the triangles. Twist every triangle. Pour water and insert the steamer rack in the instant pot. Line the rack with baking paper. Arrange the twists in the rack in one layer and brush with 1 tablespoon of water. Then close the lid and cook the meal for 20 minutes on manual mode (high pressure). Then make a quick pressure release and remove the twists from the instant pot.
Nutrition: calories 114, fat 8.6, fiber 2.2, carbs 4.1, protein 5.3

Italian Asparagus

Preparation time: 4 minutes
Cooking time: 4 minutes
Servings: 4
Ingredients:
- 1 cup water
- 1 pound asparagus, trimmed
- ½ tablespoon Italian seasoning
- A pinch of salt and black pepper
- 1 tablespoon cilantro, chopped
- 1 tablespoon lemon juice
- 1 teaspoon olive oil

Directions:
Put the water in your instant pot, add steamer basket, add the asparagus, put the lid on and cook on High for 4 minutes. Release the pressure fast for 4 minutes, transfer the asparagus to a bowl, add the rest of the ingredients, toss, arrange everything on a platter and serve.
Nutrition: calories 39, fat 2.1, fiber 1.1, carbs 1.3, protein 2.5

Cheese Chips

Preparation time: 5 minutes
Cooking time: 30 minutes
Servings: 5
Ingredients:
- 5 Cheddar cheese slices

Directions:
Line the instant pot with baking paper. Then place Cheddar cheese slices inside in one layer (put 2 Cheddar slices). The close the lid and cook cheese chips for 15 minutes on sauté mode or until the chips are dry (it depends on your instant pot type). When the time is over, open the lid and remove the cheese chips with baking paper. Cool the chips and then remove them from the baking paper with the help of the metal spatula. Repeat the same steps with remaining cheese slices.
Nutrition: calories 113, fat 9.3, fiber 0, carbs 0.4, protein 7

Fennel and Leeks Platter

Preparation time: 5 minutes
Cooking time: 8 minutes
Servings: 4
Ingredients:
- 4 leeks, roughly sliced
- 2 fennel bulbs, halved
- 1 tablespoon smoked paprika
- 1 teaspoon chili sauce
- A pinch of salt and black pepper
- 1 tablespoon ghee, melted
- ½ cup chicken stock

Directions:
In your instant pot, combine the leeks with the fennel, salt, pepper and the stock, put the lid on and cook on High for 8 minutes. Release the pressure fast for 5 minutes, arrange the leeks and fennel on a platter, sprinkle the paprika on top, drizzle the chili sauce and the ghee and serve as an appetizer.
Nutrition: calories 124, fat 4, fiber 2.1, carbs 3.3, protein 3.2

Butter Coffee
Preparation time: 10 minutes
Cooking time: 10 minutes
Servings: 2
Ingredients:
- 2 teaspoons instant coffee
- 2 tablespoons butter
- 1 cup of water
- ¼ cup heavy cream

Directions:
Pour water in the instant pot and bring it to boil on sauté mode. Then add instant coffee and stir it until coffee is dissolved. Then add butter and switch off the instant pot. Let the butter melts. Then pour the cooked butter coffee in the serving cups.
Nutrition: calories 154, fat 17.1, fiber 0, carbs 0.4, protein 0.4

Nutmeg Endives
Preparation time: 10 minutes
Cooking time: 10 minutes
Servings: 4
Ingredients:
- 4 endives, trimmed and halved
- 1 cup water
- Salt and black pepper to the taste
- 2 tablespoons olive oil
- 1 teaspoon nutmeg, ground
- 1 tablespoon chives, chopped

Directions:
Add the water to your instant pot, add steamer basket, add the endives inside, put the lid on and cook on High for 10 minutes. Release the pressure naturally for 10 minutes, arrange the endives on a platter, drizzle the oil, season with salt, pepper and nutmeg, sprinkle the chives at the end and serve as an appetizer.
Nutrition: calories 63, fat 7.2, fiber 0.1, carbs 0.3, protein 0.1

Pumpkin Spices Latte
Preparation time: 10 minutes
Cooking time: 10 minutes
Servings: 2
Ingredients:
- ½ cup of coconut milk
- ¼ cup of water
- 2 teaspoons instant coffee
- 1 teaspoon pumpkin spices
- 1 teaspoon pumpkin puree

Directions:
Pour water in the instant pot. Add instant coffee and stir the liquid until it is dissolved. Then set sauté mode and bring the liquid to boil (it will take appx.3-5 minutes). Add pumpkin spices and pumpkin puree. Saute the liquid for 2 minutes more. Meanwhile, whisk the coconut milk with the help of the hand whisker until you get big foam. Pour hot coffee in the serving cups. Add coconut milk with foam.
Nutrition: calories 142, fat 14.4, fiber 1.5, carbs 4.1, protein 1.5

Thyme Eggplants and Celery Spread
Preparation time: 10 minutes
Cooking time: 12 minutes
Servings: 4
Ingredients:
- 2 pounds eggplant, roughly chopped
- A pinch of salt and black pepper
- 2 celery stalks, chopped
- 2 tablespoons olive oil
- 4 garlic cloves, minced
- ½ cup veggie stock
- 2 tablespoons lime juice
- 1 bunch thyme, chopped

Directions:
Set your instant pot on sauté mode, add the oil, heat it up, add the celery stalks and the garlic and sauté for 2 minutes. Add the rest of the ingredients, put the lid on and cook on High for 10 minutes. Release the pressure naturally for 10 minutes, blend the mix using an immersion blender, divide into cups and serve as a spread.
Nutrition: calories 123, fat 7.4, fiber 1.8, carbs 3.7, protein 2.5

Salty Nuts Mix
Preparation time: 10 minutes
Cooking time: 7 minutes
Servings: 5
Ingredients:
- 1 teaspoon coconut aminos
- 1 teaspoon coconut oil
- ½ teaspoon sesame oil
- ¼ teaspoon chili powder
- 1 teaspoon salt
- 2 tablespoons walnuts
- 5 pecans
- 1 tablespoon pistachios
- 1 tablespoon cashew

Directions:
Place coconut oil and sesame oil in the instant pot. Heat up the oils on sauté mode for 1 minute. Then add coconut aminos, chili powder, walnuts, pecans, pistachios, and cashew. Mix up the nuts and cook them for 5 minutes. Stir the nuts every 1 minute. Add salt and mix up the mixture. Transfer the nut mix in the paper bag.
Nutrition: calories 144, fat 14.4, fiber 1.9, carbs 3.3, protein 2.7

Shrimp and Okra Bowls
Preparation time: 10 minutes
Cooking time: 12 minutes
Servings: 4
Ingredients:
- 1 pound okra, trimmed
- ½ pound shrimp, peeled and deveined
- A pinch of salt and black pepper
- 2 tablespoons olive oil
- 1 cup tomato passata, chopped
- 1 tablespoon cilantro, chopped

Directions:
In your instant pot, combine the okra with the shrimp and the rest of the ingredients, put the lid on and cook on High for 12 minutes. Release the pressure fast for 5 minutes, divide the mix into bowls and serve as an appetizer.
Nutrition: calories 188, fat 8.3, fiber 4.6, carbs 6.1, protein 15.6

Heart of Palm Dip

Preparation time: 10 minutes
Cooking time: 8 minutes
Servings: 8
Ingredients:
- 1-pound heart of palm, chopped
- 1 garlic clove, diced
- 1 tablespoon avocado oil
- 1 teaspoon lemon juice
- ½ teaspoon salt
- ¼ teaspoon ground black pepper
- ¼ teaspoon fennel seeds
- ¼ cup heavy cream
- 1 oz Provolone cheese, grated

Directions:
Pour avocado oil in the instant pot and heat it up. Add diced garlic, ground black pepper, and fennel seeds. Cook the ingredients for 2 minutes or until they become aromatic. Meanwhile, put the heart of palms in the blender. Add lemon juice. Blend the mixture until smooth. Add heavy cream and cheese in the hot oil mixture and bring it to boil. Remove the liquid from the heat and add it in the blender heart of palm. Stir well. Store the dip in the fridge for up to 8 hours.
Nutrition: calories 45, fat 2.9, fiber 1.5, carbs 3.1, protein 2.5

Mushrooms Salsa

Preparation time: 10 minutes
Cooking time: 10 minutes
Servings: 4
Ingredients:
- 1 pound white mushrooms, halved
- A pinch of salt and black pepper
- 1 tablespoon ghee, melted
- ¼ cup chicken stock
- 1 tablespoon rosemary, chopped
- 1 tablespoon basil, chopped
- 1 tablespoon oregano, chopped
- 2 tomatoes, cubed
- 1 avocado, peeled, pitted and cubed

Directions:
In your instant pot, combine the mushrooms with salt, pepper and the rest of the ingredients, put the lid on and cook on High for 10 minutes. Release the pressure naturally for 10 minutes, divide the salsa into bowls and serve as an appetizer.
Nutrition: calories 173, fat 13.7, fiber 6.2, carbs 7.7, protein 5.3

Taco Shells

Preparation time: 15 minutes
Cooking time: 50 minutes
Servings: 4
Ingredients:
- 4 lettuce leaves
- ¼ cup radish, chopped
- 10 oz beef sirloin
- ½ teaspoon dried cilantro
- ½ teaspoon salt
- ½ teaspoon dried oregano
- 1 teaspoon taco seasoning
- 1 teaspoon green chile
- ½ cup chicken broth
- 1 teaspoon ground paprika
- 1 teaspoon cream cheese

Directions:
Put beef sirloin, dried cilantro, salt, oregano, taco seasonings, green chile, ground paprika, and chicken broth in the instant pot. Close the lid and cook meat on stew/meat mode for 50 minutes. When the time is over, remove the meat from the instant pot and shred it. Then mix up together 3 tablespoons chicken broth from instant pot and cream cheese. Stir the liquid in the shredded meat and stir well. Then fill the lettuce leaves with shredded beef.
Nutrition: calories 146, fat 5, fiber 0.4, carbs 1.5, protein 22.4

Cheesy Mushroom and Tomato Salad

Preparation time: 10 minutes
Cooking time: 10 minutes
Servings: 4
Ingredients:
- 4 tomatoes, cubed
- ½ cup veggie stock
- A pinch of salt and black pepper
- 1 tablespoon ghee, melted
- 1 pound mushrooms, halved
- 1 cup mozzarella, shredded
- 1 tablespoon parsley, chopped

Directions:
Set your instant pot on sauté mode, add the ghee, heat it up, add the mushrooms, stir and sauté for 2 minutes. Add the rest of the ingredients except the mozzarella and toss. Sprinkle the mozzarella on top, put the lid on and cook on High for 8 minutes. Release the pressure naturally for 10 minutes, divide the mix into bowls and serve as an appetizer.
Nutrition: calories 95, fat 5, fiber 2.3, carbs 4.7, protein 6.7

Mini Margharita Pizzas in Mushroom Caps

Preparation time: 15 minutes
Cooking time: 10 minutes
Servings: 4
Ingredients:
- 4 Portobello mushroom caps
- 1/3 cup Mozzarella, shredded
- 1 teaspoon fresh basil, chopped
- 1 teaspoon cream cheese
- ¼ teaspoon dried oregano
- 1 teaspoon tomato sauce
- 1 cup water, for cooking

Directions:
Pour water and insert the trivet in the instant pot. Then mix up together shredded Mozzarella, basil, cream cheese, and dried oregano. Fill the mushroom caps with the Mozzarella mixture. Top every Portobello cap with tomato sauce and transfer in the trivet. Close the lid and cook pizzas for 10 minutes on

manual mode (high pressure). When the time is over, make a quick pressure release and transfer the cooked Margharita pizzas on the plate.
Nutrition: calories 10, fat 0.7, fiber 0.1, carbs 0.3, protein 0.8

Olives Spread
Preparation time: 10 minutes
Cooking time: 15 minutes
Servings: 4
Ingredients:
- 2 cups black olives, pitted and haled
- 2 garlic cloves, minced
- 1 tablespoon lemon juice
- 1 tablespoon olive oil
- A pinch of salt and black pepper
- 1 tablespoon parsley, chopped
- ¼ cup chicken stock

Directions:
In your instant pot, combine the black olives with the stock, salt and the rest of the ingredients, put the lid on and cook on High for 10 minutes. Release the pressure naturally for 10 minutes, blend the mix using an immersion blender, divide into bowls and serve as a party spread.
Nutrition: calories 111, fat 10.8, fiber 2.2, carbs 4.9, protein 0.8

Keto Guacamole Deviled Eggs
Preparation time: 20 minutes
Cooking time: 5 minutes
Servings:6
Ingredients:
- 6 eggs
- 1 avocado, pitted, peeled
- 2 tablespoons lemon juice
- ¼ teaspoon salt
- 1 tablespoon cream cheese
- 1 teaspoon chives, chopped
- 1 cup water, for cooking

Directions:
Pour water and insert the steamer rack in the instant pot. Place the eggs in the trivet and close the lid. Cook them on Manual (high pressure) for 5 minutes. Then allow the natural pressure release for 5 minutes. Cool the eggs in ice water and peel. Then cut them into halves and remove the egg yolks. Place the egg yolks in the bowl. Chop the avocado and add it in the egg yolks. Smash the mixture with the fork until smooth. Then add cream cheese, salt, and lemon juice. Mix up well and add chives. Stir the guacamole mixture little. Fill the egg whites with guacamole mass.
Nutrition: calories 138, fat 11.5, fiber 2.3, carbs 3.4, protein 6.4

Basil Stuffed Bell Peppers
Preparation time: 10 minutes
Cooking time: 15 minutes
Servings: 4
Ingredients:
- 4 red bell peppers, tops cut off and deseeded
- 2 tablespoons parsley, chopped
- 2 cups basil, chopped
- ¼ cup mozzarella, shredded
- 1 tablespoon garlic, minced
- 2 teaspoons lemon juice
- 1 cup baby spinach, torn
- 2 cups water

Directions:
In a bowl, mix all the ingredients except the water and the peppers, stir well and stuff the peppers with this mix. Add the water to your instant pot, add the trivet inside, arrange the bell peppers in the pot, put the lid on and cook on High for 15 minutes. Release the pressure naturally for 10 minutes, arrange the peppers on a platter and serve as an appetizer.
Nutrition: calories 52, fat 4.8, fiber 2.4, carbs 3.6, protein 2.5

Hot Tempeh
Preparation time: 10 minutes
Cooking time: 9 minutes
Servings:4
Ingredients:
- 8 oz tempeh
- 1 teaspoon chili powder
- ¼ teaspoon ground paprika
- ¼ teaspoon ground turmeric
- 1 teaspoon avocado oil

Directions:
Cut the tempeh into 4 servings. After this, in the shallow bowl mix up together chili powder, ground paprika, turmeric, and avocado oil. Rub the tempeh with chili powder mixture from each side. Preheat the instant pot on sauté mode for 3 minutes. Then add tempeh and cook it for 3 minutes from each side.
Nutrition: calories 114, fat 6.4, fiber 0.4, carbs 5.9, protein 10.6

Mussels Salad
Preparation time: 10 minutes
Cooking time: 6 minutes
Servings: 4
Ingredients:
- 1 pound mussels, scrubbed
- 2 cups baby spinach
- ½ cup chicken stock
- 1 tablespoon balsamic vinegar
- 2 scallions, chopped
- ½ teaspoon olive oil
- ½ teaspoon chili powder
- ½ teaspoon oregano, chopped
- A pinch of salt and black pepper

Directions:
In your instant pot, mix the mussels with the stock, salt and pepper, put the lid on and cook on High for 6 minutes. Release the pressure naturally for 10 minutes, transfer the mussels to a bowl, add the rest of the ingredients, toss, and serve as an appetizer.
Nutrition: calories 112, fat 3.4, fiber 0.7, carbs 1.7, protein 14.1

Garlic Aioli
Preparation time: 15 minutes
Cooking time: 4 minutes
Servings:4
Ingredients:
- 4 garlic cloves, peeled
- 1 teaspoon lime juice
- 1 teaspoon mustard
- ½ cup heavy cream

- ¼ teaspoon ground black pepper
- ¼ teaspoon salt
- 1 cup water, for cooking

Directions:
Wrap the garlic in the foil. Then pour water and insert the steamer rack in the instant pot. Place the wrapped garlic in the rack and close the lid. Cook it on manual (high pressure) for 4 minutes. Then allow the natural pressure release for 5 minutes and open the lid. Remove the garlic from the foil and transfer it in the bowl. Smash it with the help of the fork until you get puree texture. After this, add lime juice, mustard, ground black pepper, salt. Stir the mixture. Whip the heavy cream. Then combine together whipped cream and garlic mixture. Store the meal in the fridge for up to 4 days.
Nutrition: calories 61, fat 5.8, fiber 0.2, carbs 2, protein 0.7

Oregano Beef Bites

Preparation time: 10 minutes
Cooking time: 15 minutes
Servings: 4
Ingredients:
- 1 tablespoon lime juice
- 2 tablespoons avocado oil
- 1 pound beef stew meat, cubed
- 2 garlic cloves, minced
- 1 tablespoon smoked paprika
- 1 tablespoon oregano, chopped
- 1 tablespoon lime zest, grated
- 1 cup beef stock

Directions:
Set the instant pot on Sauté mode, add the oil, heat it up, add the meat and brown for 5 minutes. Add the rest of the ingredients, put the lid on and cook on High for 10 minutes. Release the pressure naturally for 10 minutes, arrange the beef bites on a platter and serve.
Nutrition: calories 236, fat 8.4, fiber 1.6, carbs 2.8, protein 34.5

Pesto Wings

Preparation time: 10 minutes
Cooking time: 15 minutes
Servings: 6
Ingredients:
- 6 chicken wings
- 1 teaspoon ground paprika
- 1 teaspoon butter
- 4 teaspoons pesto sauce
- 2 tablespoons cream cheese

Directions:
Rub the chicken wings with ground paprika. Toss butter in the instant pot and heat it up on sauté mode. When the butter is melted, place the chicken wings inside (in one layer) and cook them for 3 minutes from each side or until you get light brown color. Then add pesto sauce and cream cheese. Coat the chicken wings in the mixture well, bring to boil, and close the lid. Saute the wings for 4 minutes.
Nutrition: calories 127, fat 9.6, fiber 0.3, carbs 3.7, protein 6.4

Watercress and Zucchini Salsa

Preparation time: 5 minutes
Cooking time: 12 minutes
Servings: 4
Ingredients:
- 1 bunch watercress, trimmed
- Juice of 1 lime
- ¼ cup chicken stock
- 2 teaspoons thyme, dried
- 2 tablespoons avocado oil
- 1 cup tomato, cubed
- 1 avocado, peeled, pitted and cubed
- 2 zucchinis, cubed
- 2 spring onions, chopped
- 3 garlic cloves, minced
- ¼ cup cilantro, chopped
- 1 tablespoon balsamic vinegar

Directions:
Set the instant pot on Sauté mode, add the oil, heat it up, add the garlic and sauté for 2 minutes. Add the rest of the ingredients, put the lid on and cook on High for 10 minutes. Release the pressure fast for 5 minutes, divide the salsa into cups and serve as an appetizer.
Nutrition: calories 144, fat 11.1, fiber 4.4, carbs 5.3, protein 3

Bacon Avocado Bombs

Preparation time: 20 minutes
Cooking time: 10 minutes
Servings: 8
Ingredients:
- 1 avocado, pitted, peeled
- 3 eggs
- 2 bacon slices, chopped
- 4 tablespoons cream cheese
- ½ teaspoon green onion, minced
- 1 cup water, for cooking

Directions:
Pour water and insert the steamer rack in the instant pot. Place the egg on the rack and close the lid. Cook them for 5 minutes on steam mode. When the time is over, allow the natural pressure release for 5 minutes more. Then cool the eggs in ice water and peel. Clean the instant pot and remove the steamer rack. Put the chopped bacon slices in the instant pot and cook them on sauté mode for minutes or until crunchy. Stir the bacon every minute. Meanwhile, chop the avocado and eggs into tiny pieces and place the ingredients in the big bowl. Add minced green onion and cream cheese. With the help of the fork mix up the mixture and smash it gently (we don't need smooth texture).Then add cooked bacon and stir until homogenous. With the help of the scopper make the balls and refrigerate them for 10-15 minutes. Store the bacon avocado bombs in the fridge in the closed vessel for up to 8 days.
Nutrition: calories 118, fat 10.3, fiber 1.7, carbs 2.5, protein 4.7

Basil Shallots and Peppers Dip

Preparation time: 5 minutes
Cooking time: 15 minutes
Servings: 2
Ingredients:
- ½ cup lemon juice
- 3 shallots, minced
- ½ teaspoon hot sauce

- 1 tablespoon balsamic vinegar
- 1 and ½ pounds mixed peppers, roughly chopped
- ¼ cup chicken stock
- 1 tablespoon olive oil
- 2 tablespoons basil, chopped

Directions:
Set the instant pot on Sauté mode, add the oil, heat it up, add the shallots and sauté for 2 minutes. Add the rest of the ingredients, put the lid on and cook on High for 13 minutes. Release the pressure fast for 5 minutes, blend the mix using an immersion blender, divide into bowls and serve.
Nutrition: calories 78, fat 7.6, fiber 0.3, carbs 1.5, protein 0.7

Bacon Sushi

Preparation time: 15 minutes
Cooking time: 4 minutes
Servings: 6
Ingredients:
- 6 bacon slices
- 1 cucumber
- 3 teaspoons cream cheese
- ¼ teaspoon ground black pepper
- ¼ teaspoon salt
- ¼ teaspoon dried thyme
- ½ teaspoon coconut oil

Directions:
Sprinkle the bacon slices with dried thyme, salt, and ground black pepper. Put coconut oil in the instant pot. Melt it on sauté mode. Then arrange the bacon in one layer. Cook it for 1 minute and flip on another side. Cook the bacon for 1 minute more. Then transfer the bacon on the paper towel and dry well. Place the dried bacon on the sushi mat in the shape of the net. Then spread the bacon net with cream cheese. Cut the cucumber into the sticks. Place the cucumber sticks over the cream cheese. Roll the bacon in the shape of sushi and cut into 6 servings.
Nutrition: calories 120, fat 9, fiber 0.3, carbs 2.2, protein 7.5

Olives and Spinach Dip

Preparation time: 5 minutes
Cooking time: 10 minutes
Servings: 4
Ingredients:
- 4 cups baby spinach
- ½ cup coconut cream
- A pinch of salt and black pepper
- 2 tablespoons avocado oil
- 4 garlic cloves, roasted and minced
- 2 tablespoons lime juice
- 1 tablespoon chives, chopped
- 1 cup kalamata olives, pitted and halved

Directions:
In your instant pot, combine all the ingredients except the chives, put the lid on and cook on High for 10 minutes. Release the pressure fast for 5 minutes, blend the mix using an immersion blender, add chives, stir, divide into bowls and serve as a party dip.
Nutrition: calories 129, fat 11.8, fiber 2.8, carbs 6.3, protein 2.1

Ranch Poppers
Preparation time: 15 minutes
Cooking time: 4 minute
Servings: 8
Ingredients:
- ½ cup ground chicken
- ¼ cup zucchini, grated
- 1 teaspoon dried cilantro
- ¼ teaspoon garlic powder
- 1 teaspoon almond flour
- 1 teaspoon olive oil
- ½ teaspoon salt

Directions:
Mix up together ground chicken, grated zucchini, cilantro, garlic powder, and almond flour. Add salt and stir the mas until homogenous. Make the small balls (poppers) with the help of the fingertips. Pour olive oil in the instant pot. Arrange the ranch poppers in the instant pot and cook them for 1.5 minutes from each side.
Nutrition: calories 43, fat 3, fiber 0.4, carbs 0.9, protein 3.3

Mint Salmon and Radish Salad

Preparation time: 10 minutes
Cooking time: 15 minutes
Servings: 4
Ingredients:
- 1 pound salmon fillets, boneless, skinless and cubed
- 2 cups red radishes, sliced
- 1 shallot, sliced
- ½ tablespoons avocado oil
- 2 tablespoons mint leaves, chopped
- ½ cup coconut cream
- A pinch of salt and black pepper

Directions:
Set the instant pot on Sauté mode, add the oil, heat it up, add the shallot and sauté for 2 minutes. Add the salmon and cook for 2 minutes more. Add the rest of the ingredients, put the lid on and cook on High for 10 minutes. Release the pressure naturally for 10 minutes, divide the mix into bowls and serve as an appetizer.
Nutrition: calories 232, fat 14.5, fiber 1.9, carbs 4, protein 23.2

Keto Taquitos

Preparation time: 15 minutes
Cooking time: 20 minutes
Servings: 6
Ingredients:
- 3 low carb tortillas
- ¼ teaspoon onion powder
- ¼ cup Cheddar cheese, shredded
- 5 oz chicken breast, skinless, boneless
- ½ teaspoon ground black pepper
- ¼ teaspoon salt
- ½ teaspoon cayenne pepper
- 1 teaspoon butter
- 1 cup water, for cooking

Directions:
Rub the chicken breast with salt, cayenne pepper, and ground black pepper. Pour water and insert the steamer rack in the instant pot. Arrange the chicken in the steamer rack and close the lid. Cook it on manual mode (high pressure) for 15 minutes. Then make a quick pressure release and transfer the chicken on the chopping board. Shred the chicken.

Place the shredded chicken in the mixing bowl. Add onion powder and shredded Cheddar cheese. Mix up the mixture well. Then spread tortillas with chicken mixture and roll. Clean the instant pot and remove the rack. Toss the butter in the instant pot, melt it on sauté mode. Arrange the rolled tortillas in the instant pot in one layer. Cook them for 2 minutes from each side. When taquitos are cooked, remove them from the instant pot and cut into 6 servings.
Nutrition: calories 93, fat 3.8, fiber 3.6, carbs 6.3, protein 7.7

Red Chard Spread

Preparation time: 10 minutes
Cooking time: 15 minutes
Servings: 4
Ingredients:
- 1 pound red chard
- 1 cup spring onions, chopped
- 1 cup veggie stock
- 1 tablespoon sweet paprika
- 1 tablespoon lime juice
- 2 tablespoons olive oil
- 2 garlic cloves, minced
- ½ cup coconut cream
- 1 tablespoon chives, chopped

Directions:
In your instant pot, combine chard with the rest of the ingredients except the cream and the chives, put the lid on and cook on High for 15 minutes. Release the pressure naturally for 10 minutes, add the cream, blend everything using an immersion blender, divide into bowls, sprinkle the chives on top and serve.
Nutrition: calories 144, fat 14.4, fiber 2, carbs 5, protein 1.5

Chicken Celery Boats

Preparation time: 10 minutes
Cooking time: 10 minutes
Servings: 2
Ingredients:
- 2 celery stalks
- 3 oz chicken fillet
- ¼ teaspoon minced garlic
- ¼ teaspoon salt
- 1 teaspoon cream cheese
- 1 cup water, for cooking

Directions:
Pour water and insert the steamer rack in the instant pot. Put the chicken on the rack and close the lid. Cook it on manual mode (high pressure) for 10 minutes. Then make a quick pressure release and remove the chicken from the instant pot. Shred the chicken and mix it up with minced garlic, salt, and cream cheese. Fill the celery stalks with chicken mixture.
Nutrition: calories 90, fat 3.8, fiber 0.3, carbs 0.7, protein 12.6

Salmon and Swiss Chard Salad

Preparation time: 10 minutes
Cooking time: 15 minutes
Servings: 4
Ingredients:
- 1 teaspoon olive oil
- 1 pound salmon fillets, boneless, skinless and cubed
- A pinch of salt and black pepper
- ¼ pound Swiss chard, torn
- 1 tablespoon rosemary, chopped
- 1 tablespoon lime juice
- 1 spring onion, chopped
- ¼ cup chicken stock

Directions:
Set the instant pot on Sauté mode, add the oil, heat it up, add the spring onion and sauté for 2 minutes. Add the salmon and cook for 2 minutes on each side. Add the rest of the ingredients, put the lid on and cook on High for 10 minutes. Release the pressure naturally for 10 minutes, divide the mix into bowls and serve as an appetizer.
Nutrition: calories 170, fat 8.4, fiber 0.9, carbs 1.9, protein 22.7

Keto Nachos

Preparation time: 10 minutes
Cooking time: 27 minutes
Servings: 2
Ingredients:
- ½ cup mini bell peppers
- ½ cup ground beef
- ¼ teaspoon chili powder
- ¼ teaspoon ground cumin
- ¼ teaspoon dried thyme
- ¼ teaspoon onion powder
- ¼ teaspoon garlic powder
- 2 oz Provolone cheese, grated
- 1 teaspoon coconut oil

Directions:
Put coconut oil in the instant pot and preheat it on sauté mode until it is melted. Then add ground beef, chili powder, ground cumin, thyme, onion powder, and garlic powder. Mix up the mixture well with the help of a spatula and cook on sauté mode for 15 minutes. Stir it from time to time. When the time is over, cut the mini bell peppers into halves and place them in the instant pot. Cook the keto nachos for 10 minutes more. The cooked bell peppers shouldn't be soft.
Nutrition: calories 213, fat 14, fiber 1.2, carbs 6.5, protein 15

Basil Peppers Salsa

Preparation time: 10 minutes
Cooking time: 12 minutes
Servings: 4
Ingredients:
- 1 and ½ pounds mixed bell peppers, cut into strips
- 2 tablespoons parsley, chopped
- 2 tablespoons basil, chopped
- 2 teaspoons lime juice
- 1 tablespoon avocado oil
- ½ cup tomato passata
- 2 tomatoes, cubed
- 1 avocado, peeled, pitted and cubed
- A pinch of salt and black pepper

Directions:
In your instant pot, combine all the ingredients, put the lid on and cook o High for 12 minutes. Release

the pressure naturally for 10 minutes, transfer the mix to small bowls, toss and serve as an appetizer.
Nutrition: calories 127, fat 10.5, fiber 4.8, carbs 7.8, protein 2

Edamame Hummus

Preparation time: 15 minutes
Cooking time: 5 minutes
Servings: 8
Ingredients:
- 1 ½ cup edamame beans, shelled
- 1 teaspoon salt
- ½ teaspoon harissa
- 1 garlic clove, peeled
- 4 tablespoons olive oil
- 1 tablespoon lemon juice
- 1 avocado, pitted, peeled, chopped
- 1 cup water, for cooking

Directions:
Pour water in the instant pot. Add edamame beans and garlic, and close the lid. Cook the beans on manual mode (high pressure) for 2 minutes. Then make a quick pressure release and open the lid. Transfer the edamame beans and garlic in the blender. Add 1/3 cup of water from the instant pot. Then add harissa, salt, lemon juice, and avocado. Blend the mixture until it is smooth and soft. Add more water if the texture of the hummus is very thick. Then add olive oil and pulse the hummus for 10 seconds. Transfer the cooked edamame hummus in the serving bowl.
Nutrition: calories 99, fat 9, fiber 2.2, carbs 3.5, protein 2.5

Pesto Chicken Salad

Preparation time: 10 minutes
Cooking time: 20 minutes
Servings: 4
Ingredients:
- 1 pound chicken breast, skinless, boneless and cubed
- 2 tablespoons basil pesto
- 2 tablespoons olive oil
- 2 spring onions, chopped
- 2 tablespoons garlic, chopped
- 1 cup chicken stock
- 1 cup tomatoes, crushed
- 1 tablespoon oregano, chopped

Directions:
Set your instant pot on Sauté mode, add the oil, heat it up, add the chicken and the onions and brown for 5 minutes. Add the rest of the ingredients except the basil, put the lid on and cook on High for 15 minutes. Release the pressure naturally for 10 minutes, divide the mix into bowls and serve right away.
Nutrition: calories 212, fat 10.2, fiber 1.3, carbs 4.6, protein 25.2

Crab Spread

Preparation time: 10 minutes
Cooking time: 4 minutes
Servings: 6
Ingredients:
- ½ cup cauliflower, chopped
- 10 oz crab meat
- 1 teaspoon minced garlic
- ½ cup cream cheese
- 1 tablespoon fresh cilantro, chopped
- 1 cup water, for cooking

Directions:
Place crab meat and cauliflower in the instant pot. Add water and close the lid. Cook the ingredients for 4 minutes on manual mode (high pressure). Then remove the cooked cauliflower and crab meat from the instant pot. Chop the crab meat into small pieces. Then smash the cauliflower with the help of the fork. The smashed mixture shouldn't be smooth. Mix up together cauliflower, crab meat, minced garlic, cream cheese, and cilantro. Mix up the spread well and store it in the fridge for up to 3 days.
Nutrition: calories 112, fat 7.6, fiber 0.2, carbs 2, protein 7.6

Cabbage and Spinach Slaw

Preparation time: 10 minutes
Cooking time: 15 minutes
Servings: 4
Ingredients:
- 2 cups red cabbage, shredded
- 1 tablespoon avocado mayonnaise
- 1 spring onion, chopped
- 1 pound baby spinach
- ½ cup chicken stock
- 1 teaspoon chili powder
- 1 tablespoon sweet paprika
- 1 tablespoon chives, chopped
- 1 tablespoon avocado oil

Directions:
Set instant pot on Sauté mode, add the oil, heat it up, add the onion and cook for 2 minutes. Add the rest of the ingredients except the spinach, avocado mayonnaise and the chives, put the lid on and cook on High for 12 minutes. Release the pressure naturally for 10 minutes, transfer the mix to a bowl, add the remaining ingredients, toss and serve as an appetizer.
Nutrition: calories 72, fat 3.8, fiber 1.2, carbs 2.6, protein 4.3

Bacon-Wrapped Shrimps

Preparation time: 15 minutes
Cooking time: 8 minutes
Servings: 4
Ingredients:
- 4 king shrimps, peeled
- 4 bacon slices
- ¼ teaspoon chili flakes
- ¼ teaspoon ground black pepper
- ¼ teaspoon salt
- ½ teaspoon avocado oil
- 1 cup water, for cooking

Directions:
Brush the instant pot bowl with avocado oil and heat it up for 2 minutes on sauté mode. Arrange the bacon slices in one layer and cook for 2 minutes from each side. Cool the cooked bacon. Clean the instant pot. Place the steamer rack and pour water in the instant pot. Place the shrimps in the mixing bowl. Add chili flakes, ground black pepper, and salt. Mix up the spices and shrimps. Then wrap every shrimp in cooked bacon. Secure them with toothpicks. Place the shrimps on the rack and close the lid. Cook the seafood for 2 minutes on manual mode (high

pressure). When the time is over, make a quick pressure release.
Nutrition: calories 127, fat 8.3, fiber 0.1, carbs 0.4, protein 12.4

Cabbage, Tomato and Avocado Salsa

Preparation time: 5 minutes
Cooking time: 12 minutes
Servings: 4
Ingredients:
- 1 and ½ pound cherry tomatoes, cubed
- ¼ cup veggie stock
- 2 tablespoons olive oil
- ¼ cup balsamic vinegar
- 2 spring onions, chopped
- 1 red cabbage head, shredded
- 1 tablespoon basil, chopped
- 1 tablespoon parsley, chopped
- 1 tablespoon chives, chopped
- 1 avocado, peeled, pitted and cubed

Directions:
In your instant pot, combine the tomatoes the rest of the ingredients, put the lid on and cook on High for 12 minutes. Release the pressure fast for 5 minutes, transfer the mix to small bowls and serve as an appetizer.
Nutrition: calories 254, fat 17.3, fiber 2.5, carbs 5.5, protein 5.4

Tuna Steak Skewers

Preparation time: 15 minutes
Cooking time: 5 minutes
Servings:4
Ingredients:
- 2 tuna steaks
- ¼ teaspoon salt
- 1 teaspoon ground paprika
- ¾ teaspoon dried sage
- 1 cup water, for cooking

Directions:
Chop the tuna steaks into medium cubes and sprinkle with salt, ground paprika, and dried sage. Then string the meat on the skewers. Pour water and insert the steamer rack in the instant pot. Arrange the tuna steak skewers on the rack and close the lid. Cook the snack for 5 minutes on manual mode (high pressure). Then allow the natural pressure release for 10 minutes.
Nutrition: calories 158, fat 5.4, fiber 0.3, carbs 0.4, protein 25.5

Shrimp and Mussels Salad

Preparation time: 6 minutes
Cooking time: 12 minutes
Servings: 4
Ingredients:
- 1 pound mussels, scrubbed
- ½ cup tomato passata
- ¼ cup chicken stock
- 1 pound shrimp, peeled and deveined
- 1 and ½ cups baby spinach
- 2 tablespoons olive oil
- 1 teaspoon hot paprika
- 2 teaspoons oregano, dried
- 1 tablespoon parsley, chopped

Directions:
In your instant pot, combine the mussels with the rest of the ingredients except the parsley and the spinach, put the lid on and cook on High for 10 minutes. Release the pressure fast for 6 minutes, set the pot on Sauté mode again, add the spinach and the parsley, toss, cook for 2 minutes more, divide into bowls and serve as an appetizer.
Nutrition: calories 303, fat 11.7, fiber 0.8, carbs 7.8, protein 39.3

Marinated Olives

Preparation time: 10 minutes
Cooking time: 4 minutes
Servings:7
Ingredients:
- 7 kalamata olives
- 2 tablespoons lemon juice
- ¼ teaspoon peppercorns
- ¼ teaspoon minced garlic
- ¼ teaspoon fennel seeds
- ¼ teaspoon thyme
- 1 bay leaf
- 4 tablespoons avocado oil

Directions:
Pour avocado oil in the instant pot. Add bay leaf, thyme, fennel seeds, minced garlic, peppercorns, and lemon juice. Cook the ingredients on sauté mode for 4 minutes or until it is brought to boil. Then add olives and coat them in the oil mixture well. Switch off the instant pot. Transfer the cooked olives in the glass can and let them cool to room temperature. Marinate the olives for 2-3 days in the fridge.
Nutrition: calories 18, fat 1.5, fiber 0.6, carbs 1, protein 0.2

Beef, Arugula and Olives Salad

Preparation time: 10 minutes
Cooking time: 20 minutes
Servings: 4
Ingredients:
- 1 and ½ pounds beef, cut into strips
- 2 tomatoes, cubed
- ¼ cup beef stock
- ½ cup black olives, pitted and sliced
- 1 tablespoon avocado oil
- 2 spring onions, chopped
- ½ cup cilantro chopped
- 2 cups tomatoes, chopped
- 1 tablespoon basil, chopped
- A pinch of salt and black pepper
- 1 cup baby arugula

Directions:
Set your instant pot on Sauté mode, add the oil, heat it up, add the onions and the meat and brown for 5 minutes. Add the rest of the ingredients except the arugula, put the lid on and cook on High for 15 minutes. Release the pressure naturally for 10 minutes, transfer the mix to a bowl, add the arugula, toss and serve as an appetizer.
Nutrition: calories 378, fat 16.7, fiber 2.8, carbs 7.8, protein 24.3

Chicharrones

Preparation time: 15 minutes
Cooking time: 35 minutes
Servings:4

Ingredients:
- 8 oz pork skin
- ¼ teaspoon salt
- ½ teaspoon avocado oil
- 1 cup water, for cooking

Directions:
Pour water in the instant pot. Add pork skin and close the lid. Cook it on manual mode (high pressure) for 25 minutes. Then allow the natural pressure release for 10 minutes. Remove the pork skin from the instant pot. Clean the instant pot. Chop the pork skin into small pieces and return back in the instant pot. Add oil and salt. Mix up well. Cook the meal on sauté mode for 10 minutes. Stir it from time to time to avoid burning.
Nutrition: calories 309, fat 17.8, fiber 0, carbs 0, protein 34.8

Bacon Radish And Shrimp Salad

Preparation time: 5 minutes
Cooking time: 15 minutes
Servings: 4
Ingredients:
- 1 pound shrimp, peeled and deveined
- 1 shallot, chopped
- 2 cups radishes, sliced
- 1 cup bacon, cooked and crumbled
- 1 tablespoon olive oil
- 1 teaspoon sweet paprika
- 1 tablespoon oregano, chopped
- A pinch of salt and black pepper
- 1 cup veggie stock

Directions:
Set your instant pot on Sauté mode, add the oil, heat it up, add the shallot and sauté for 2 minutes. Add the rest of the ingredients except the oregano and the bacon, put the lid on and cook on High for 13 minutes. Release the pressure fast for 5 minutes, transfer the mix to small bowls, sprinkle the oregano and the bacon on top and serve as an appetizer.
Nutrition: calories 179, fat 5.7, fiber 1.6, carbs 4.5, protein 26.5

Keto Spanakopita Pie Slices

Preparation time: 20 minutes
Cooking time: 50 minutes
Servings: 6
Ingredients:
- 4 tablespoons butter, softened
- 4 tablespoons coconut flour
- 4 tablespoons almond flour
- ¼ teaspoon baking powder
- ¼ teaspoon ground nutmeg
- ¼ teaspoon salt
- 3 eggs
- 1 cups fresh spinach, chopped
- 1 cup cheddar cheese, shredded
- 2 tablespoons cream cheese
- 1 cup water, for cooking

Directions:
Make the spanakopita crust: mix up together butter, coconut flour, almond flour, baking powder, ground nutmeg, and salt. Crack 1 egg inside the mixture and knead the non-sticky dough. Then line the instant pot baking pan with baking paper and place the dough inside. Flatten it in the shape of the pie crust. In the mixing bowl combine together cream cheese, shredded Cheddar cheese, spinach, and cracked remaining eggs. Stir it well. Place the mixture over the pie crust and flatten it. Cover the surface of spanakopita with baking paper. Pour water and insert the rack in the instant pot. Place the pan with spanakopita in the instant pot and close the lid. Cook the spanakopita for 50 minutes on manual (high pressure). Then make a quick pressure release. Cool the cooked meal to room temperature and slice.
Nutrition: calories 319, fat 27.5, fiber 4.1, carbs 7.8, protein 12.9

Cheesy Radish Spread

Preparation time: 10 minutes
Cooking time: 10 minutes
Servings: 4
Ingredients:
- 2 cups radishes, sliced
- 4 ounces cream cheese, soft
- 1 cup cheddar cheese, grated
- ½ cup chicken stock
- ½ cup coconut cream
- A pinch of salt and black pepper
- 2 shallots, minced
- 1 teaspoon sweet paprika

Directions:
In your instant pot, combine all the ingredients, stir, put the lid on and cook on High for 12 minutes. Release the pressure naturally for 10 minutes, blend everything using an immersion blender, divide into bowls and serve.
Nutrition: calories 294, fat 20.6, fiber 1.8, carbs 5.4, protein 10.4

Dog Nuggets

Preparation time: 10 minutes
Cooking time: 20 minutes
Servings: 6
Ingredients:
- 5 oz Piza keto dough
- 3 pork sausages
- 1 cup water, for cooking

Directions:
Roll up the dough and cut it into 6 strips. Then cut every pork sausage into halves. Roll every sausage half in the doughs trip. Pour water in the instant pot and insert the steamer rack. Line the rack with baking paper. Place the dog nuggets on the baking paper and close the lid. Cook the snack for 20 minutes on manual mode (high pressure). Then make a quick pressure release and transfer the meal in the serving plate.
Nutrition: calories 199, fat 10.2, fiber 3.2, carbs 6.7, protein 20.1

Ketogenic Instant Pot Fish and Seafood Recipes

Cod and Tomatoes

Preparation time: 10 minutes
Cooking time: 15 minutes
Servings: 4
Ingredients:
- 4 cod fillets, boneless and skinless
- ¼ cup chicken stock
- 2 tablespoons olive oil
- Juice of 1 lemon
- 2 shallots, chopped
- 3 tomatoes, cubed
- 4 thyme springs, chopped
- A pinch of salt and black pepper

Directions:
Set the instant pot on Sauté mode, add the oil, heat it up, add the shallots and cook for 2 minutes. Add the rest of the ingredients, put the lid on and cook on High for 12 minutes. Release the pressure naturally for 10 minutes, divide everything between plates and serve.
Nutrition: calories 232, fat 16.5, fiber 1.1, carbs 4.8, protein 16.5

Fish Saag

Preparation time: 10 minutes
Cooking time: 5 minutes
Servings: 4
Ingredients:
- 1 teaspoon tomato paste
- ½ white onion, diced
- 4 tablespoons coconut milk
- ½ teaspoon ginger, minced
- ¼ teaspoon garlic powder
- ½ teaspoon garam masala
- ½ teaspoon ground turmeric
- 1 cup spinach, chopped
- ¼ teaspoon salt
- ½ cup of water
- 12 oz haddock fillet
- 1 teaspoon olive oil
- ¼ teaspoon ground black pepper

Directions:
Put in the blender: tomato paste, diced onion, ginger, garlic powder, garam masala, ground turmeric, and chopped spinach. Blend the mixture until is smooth (appx.2 minutes). Then add water and pulse it for 10 seconds. Pour the liquid in the instant pot. Insert the steamer rack over it. Brush the haddock fillet with olive oil and sprinkle with salt and ground black pepper. Place the fish on the foil. Fold the foil to get the fish package and transfer it on the steamer rack. Close and seal the lid. Cook the fish saag for 5 minutes on steam mode (high pressure). When the time is over, make a quick pressure release and remove the fish. Cut the haddock fillet into the servings and place it on the plate. Top every fish serving with spinach sauce (from the instant pot).
Nutrition: calories 151, fat 5.6, fiber 1, carbs 3.2, protein 21.5

Cod and Cilantro Sauce

Preparation time: 5 minutes
Cooking time: 15 minutes
Servings: 4
Ingredients:
- 4 cod fillets, boneless
- ¼ cup chicken stock
- 1 tablespoon ghee, melted
- 1 tablespoon ginger, grated
- Salt and black pepper to the taste
- Juice of 1 lemon
- 2 tablespoons cilantro, chopped

Directions:
In a blender, combine the ghee with the ginger, lemon juice and cilantro and blend well. In your instant pot, combine the cod with the cilantro sauce, salt, pepper and the stock, put the lid on and cook on High for 15 minutes. Release the pressure fast for 5 minutes, divide everything between plates and serve.
Nutrition: calories 188, fat 12.8, fiber 0.2, carbs 2.2, protein 16.8

Brazilian Fish Stew

Preparation time: 10 minutes
Cooking time: 14 minutes
Servings: 6
Ingredients:
- 6 halibut fillet, chopped (6 oz each fish fillet)
- 1 tablespoon almond butter
- 1 tablespoon lemon juice
- 1 teaspoon fresh parsley, chopped
- 1 white onion, diced
- 1 green bell pepper, chopped
- 2 garlic cloves, diced
- 1 teaspoon tomato paste
- 1 cup chicken broth
- 3 tablespoons coconut milk
- 1 teaspoon ground coriander
- 1 teaspoon paprika
- ½ teaspoon white pepper
- ¼ teaspoon chili powder

Directions:
Make the stew sauce: combine together almond butter, lemon juice, parsley, onion, bell pepper, diced garlic, tomato paste, chicken broth, coconut milk, ground coriander, paprika, white pepper, and chili powder. Then transfer the mixture in the instant pot and close the lid. Cook the ingredients for 8 minutes on manual mode (high pressure). Then allow the natural pressure release and open the lid. Stir the stew sauce well and set sauté mode for 6 minutes. Cook the stew on sauté mode for 1 minute and then add chopped halibut fillets. Close the lid and sauté the stew for the remaining 5 minutes.
Nutrition: calories 247, fat 7.7, fiber 1.2, carbs 4.8, protein 38.1

Salmon and Black Olives Mix

Preparation time: 5 minutes
Cooking time: 15 minutes
Servings: 4
Ingredients:
- 1 pound salmon fillets, boneless, skinless and cubed
- 1 cup black olives, pitted and chopped
- 1 cup kalamata olives, pitted and chopped
- 2 garlic cloves, minced
- 1 tablespoon olive oil
- A pinch of salt and black pepper

- ¼ cup chicken stock
- 1 tablespoon parsley, chopped

Directions:
Set the instant pot on Sauté mode, add the oil, heat it up, add the fish and sear for 2 minutes on each side. Add the rest of the ingredients, put the lid on and cook on High for 10 minutes. Release the pressure fast for 5 minutes, divide everything between plates and serve.
Nutrition: calories 261, fat 17.6, fiber 2.2, carbs 4.8, protein 22.5

Fish Casserole

Preparation time: 5 minutes
Cooking time: 15 minutes
Servings: 6
Ingredients:
- 1 cup white mushrooms, chopped
- 1 tablespoon coconut oil
- 1 teaspoon ground black pepper
- 1 tablespoon fresh cilantro, chopped
- 1 cup whipped cream
- 1-pound cod, chopped
- 2 oz Parmesan, grated
- 1 teaspoon dried oregano

Directions:
Toss coconut oil in the instant pot and melt it on sauté mode. Then add chopped white mushrooms and cook for 5 minutes. Stir them from time to time. After this, add ground black pepper, dried oregano, and chopped cod. Stir the ingredients with the help of the spatula and cook for 2 minutes. Then add fresh cilantro and whipped cream. Mix up the casserole and cook it for 3 minutes. Then top the meal with Parmesan and close the lid.
Cook the casserole for 5 minutes.
Nutrition: calories 192, fat 11.2, fiber 0.3, carbs 1.7, protein 21.2

Coriander Cod Mix

Preparation time: 5 minutes
Cooking time: 15 minutes
Servings: 4
Ingredients:
- 4 cod fillets, boneless and skinless
- 1 cup coconut cream
- 2 spring onions, sliced
- 2 garlic cloves, minced
- 2 tablespoons coriander, chopped
- A pinch of salt and black pepper
- 2 tablespoons lime juice

Directions:
In your instant pot, combine the trout with the cream and the rest of the ingredients, put the lid on and cook on High for 15 minutes. Release the pressure fast for 5 minutes, divide everything between plates and serve.
Nutrition: calories 297, fat 24.3, fiber 1.6, carbs 5.4, protein 17.6

Salmon Pie

Preparation time: 15 minutes
Cooking time: 20 minutes
Servings: 4
Ingredients:
- 10 oz salmon fillet, chopped
- ½ teaspoon ground coriander
- ½ teaspoon salt
- ½ cup green peas
- ½ cup heavy cream
- 1 teaspoon coconut oil
- 1 teaspoon sesame oil
- ½ cup almond meal
- 2 tablespoons butter, softened
- 1 cup water, for cooking

Directions:
Toss the coconut oil in the instant pot bowl and melt it on sauté mode. When the oil is melted, add chopped salmon fillet. Sprinkle it with coriander and cook for 1 minute from each side. After this, add salt, green peas, and heavy cream. Close the lid and sauté the fish for 3 minutes. Meanwhile, make the pie dough: mix up together almond meal and butter. Knead the dough. Brush the instant pot baking pan with sesame oil. Then place the dough inside and flatten it in the shape of the pie crust. Put the salmon fillet mixture (stuffing) inside the pie crust and flatten it. Cover the pie with foil and secure the edges. Then clean the instant pot and pour water inside. Arrange the steamer rack and put the pie on it. Cook the salmon pie for 15 minutes on Manual mode (high pressure). When the time is over, make a quick pressure release and open the lid. Remove the foil and let the pie cool for 10-15 minutes. Cut it into the servings. Transfer the serving in the table with the help of the spatula.
Nutrition: calories 300, fat 24, fiber 2.4, carbs 5.6, protein 17.6

Cod and Zucchinis

Preparation time: 5 minutes
Cooking time: 15 minutes
Servings: 4
Ingredients:
- 4 cod fillets, boneless and skinless
- 2 zucchinis, sliced
- 1 tablespoon avocado oil
- 2 garlic cloves, minced
- 1 tablespoon sweet paprika
- Salt and black pepper to the taste
- 1 tablespoon parsley, chopped
- ½ cup veggie stock

Directions:
Set the instant pot on Sauté mode, add the oil, heat it up, add the garlic and sauté for 2 minutes. Add the rest of the ingredients, put the lid on and cook on High for 12 minutes. Release the pressure naturally for 5 minutes, divide the mix between plates and serve.
Nutrition: calories 182, fat 10.4, fiber 1.9, carbs 6.2, protein 17.5

Pesto Salmon

Preparation time: 10 minutes
Cooking time: 10 minutes
Servings: 3
Ingredients:
- 9 oz salmon fillet (3 oz every salmon fillet)
- 3 teaspoons pesto sauce
- 1 teaspoon butter
- 2 tablespoons organic almond milk

Directions:

Melt butter in sauté mode. Meanwhile, mix up together almond milk and pesto sauce. Brush the salmon fillets with pesto mixture from both sides and put in the melted butter. Cook the fish for 3 minutes from each side on sauté mode.
Nutrition: calories 166, fat 9.9, fiber 0.1, carbs 3, protein 17.3

Paprika Trout
Preparation time: 5 minutes
Cooking time: 12 minutes
Servings: 4
Ingredients:
- 4 trout fillets, boneless and skinless
- ½ cup chicken stock
- A pinch of salt and black pepper
- ½ teaspoon oregano, dried
- 2 teaspoons sweet paprika
- 1 tablespoon chives, chopped

Directions:
In your instant pot, combine the trout with the rest of the ingredients, put the lid on and cook on High for 12 minutes. Release the pressure fast for 5 minutes, divide the mix between plates and serve.
Nutrition: calories 132, fat 5.5, fiber 0.5, carbs 0.9, protein 16.8

Tuna Salad
Preparation time: 15 minutes
Cooking time: 5 minutes
Servings: 5
Ingredients:
- 3 eggs
- ½ red onion, diced
- ½ teaspoon minced garlic
- 1 avocado, pitted, peeled, chopped
- 1 celery stalk, chopped
- 3 tablespoons ricotta cheese
- 1 teaspoon lemon juice
- ½ teaspoon ground paprika
- 8 oz tuna, canned
- 1 cup water, for cooking

Directions:
Pour water and insert the steamer rack in the instant pot. Put eggs on the rack and close the lid. Cook the eggs on steam mode for 5 minutes. Allow the natural pressure release for 5 minutes. The cool the eggs in cold water. Peel the eggs. Meanwhile, make the salad sauce: mix up together ricotta cheese, lemon juice, minced garlic, and ground paprika. In the salad bowl combine together, onion, avocado, and celery stalk. Shred the canned tuna and add it in the salad bowl too. After this, add salad sauce. Chop the eggs and add in the salad too. Mix up the cooked meal.
Nutrition: calories 223, fat 14.9, fiber 3.1, carbs 5.5, protein 17.4

Lime Shrimp
Preparation time: 5 minutes
Cooking time: 8 minutes
Servings: 4
Ingredients:
- 1 pound shrimp, peeled and deveined
- Zest of 1 lime, grated
- Juice of 1 lime
- 1 cup chicken stock
- ¼ cup cilantro, chopped
- A pinch of salt and black pepper

Directions:
In your instant pot, combine the shrimp with the rest of the ingredients, put the lid on and cook on High for 8 minutes. Release the pressure fast for 5 minutes, divide the shrimp between plates and serve with a side salad.
Nutrition: calories 138, fat 3.8, fiber 0, carbs 2, protein 26

Tandoori Salmon
Preparation time: 15 minutes
Cooking time: 3 minutes
Servings: 2
Ingredients:
- ½ teaspoon garam masala
- ½ teaspoon ground paprika
- 1 teaspoon minced ginger
- ½ teaspoon ground turmeric
- ½ teaspoon salt
- ½ teaspoon chili powder
- ½ teaspoon minced garlic
- 1 tablespoon lemon juice
- 1 tablespoon olive oil
- 10 oz salmon fillet
- 1 cup water, for cooking

Directions:
Cut the salmon fillet into 2 servings. After this, in the mixing bowl combine together garam masala, paprika, minced ginger, ground turmeric, salt, chili powder, minced garlic, lemon juice, and olive oil. Stir the mixture until smooth. Rub the salmon fillets with the spice mixture and arrange it in the steamer rack. Pour water in the instant pot and insert the steamer rack with salmon inside. Close the lid and cook the meal for 3 minutes on steam mode (high pressure). When the time is over, make a quick pressure release and open the lid.
Nutrition: calories 259, fat 16.1, fiber 0.7, carbs 2.1, protein 27.9

Trout and Radishes
Preparation time: 5 minutes
Cooking time: 12 minutes
Servings: 4
Ingredients:
- 4 trout fillets, boneless and skinless
- A pinch of salt and black pepper
- 1 tablespoon parsley, chopped
- 2 tablespoons tomato passata
- 2 cups red radishes, sliced

Directions:
In your instant pot, combine all the ingredients, put the lid on and cook on High for 12 minutes. Release the pressure fast for 5 minutes, divide everything between plates and serve.
Nutrition: calories 129, fat 5.3, fiber 1.1, carbs 2.5, protein 17

Cheese Melt
Preparation time: 10 minutes
Cooking time: 6 minutes
Servings: 2
Ingredients:
- 2 low carb tortillas

- ¼ cup Cheddar cheese, shredded
- 4 oz tuna, canned
- 1 teaspoon cream cheese
- ½ teaspoon Italian seasonings
- 1 teaspoon sesame oil

Directions:
Shred the tuna and mix it with Italian seasonings and cream cheese. Then spread the mixture over the tortillas. Top the mixture with Cheddar cheese and fold into the shape of pockets. Pour sesame oil in the instant pot and heat it up on sauté mode for 2 minutes. Then arrange the cheese pockets in the instant pot and cook them for 2 minutes from each side. Transfer the cooked meal in the serving plates. It is recommended to eat the cheese melts immediately after cooking.
Nutrition: calories 272, fat 14.5, fiber 7, carbs 12.4, protein 21.7

Cod and Broccoli

Preparation time: 5 minutes
Cooking time: 15 minutes
Servings: 4
Ingredients:
- 4 cod fillets, boneless and skinless
- A pinch of salt and black pepper
- 1 pound broccoli florets
- 2 tablespoon tomato passata
- 1 cup chicken stock
- 1 tablespoon cilantro, chopped

Directions:
In your instant pot, combine all the ingredients, put the lid on and cook on High for 15 minutes. Release the pressure fast for 5 minutes, divide the mix between plates and serve.
Nutrition: calories 197, fat 10, fiber 3.1, carbs 4.3, protein 19.4

Prosciutto Shrimp Skewers

Preparation time: 15 minutes
Cooking time: 4 minutes
Servings: 7
Ingredients:
- 1-pound shrimps, peeled
- 4 oz prosciutto, sliced
- ½ teaspoon olive oil
- ¼ teaspoon chili powder
- 1 cup water, for cooking

Directions:
Wrap every shrimp in prosciutto and string on the skewers. Then sprinkle the shrimps with olive oil and chili powder. Pour water in the instant pot and arrange the steamer rack. Place the shrimp skewers in the steamer and close the lid. Cook the meal for 4 minutes on manual mode (high pressure). When the time is over, make a quick pressure release and open the lid. Transfer the cooked shrimp skewers on the plate.
Nutrition: calories 104, fat 2.4, fiber 0, carbs 1.3, protein 18.2

Rosemary Trout and Cauliflower

Preparation time: 10 minutes
Cooking time: 15 minutes
Servings: 4
Ingredients:
- 4 trout fillets, boneless and skinless
- ½ cup veggie stock
- 2 garlic cloves, minced
- 2 cups cauliflower florets
- 1 tablespoon avocado oil
- A pinch of salt and black pepper
- 1 tablespoon rosemary, chopped

Directions:
Set the instant pot on Sauté mode, add the oil, heat it up, add the garlic and sauté for 2 minutes. Add the rest of the ingredients, put the lid on and cook on High for 13 minutes. Release the pressure naturally for 10 minutes, divide the mix between plates and serve.
Nutrition: calories 140, fat 5.9, fiber 1.8, carbs 3.9, protein 17.7

Lime Salmon Burger

Preparation time: 10 minutes
Cooking time: 8 minutes
Servings: 6
Ingredients:
- 14 oz salmon fillet
- 1 teaspoon mustard
- ½ teaspoon lime zest, grated
- 1 tablespoon lime juice
- ½ teaspoon chives, chopped
- ½ teaspoon ground black pepper
- ½ teaspoon cayenne pepper
- 1 teaspoon olive oil
- ¼ teaspoon ground coriander
- 12 Cheddar cheese slices

Directions:
Chop the salmon fillet and put it in the blender. Blend the fish until smooth and transfer it in the mixing bowl. Add mustard, lime zest, lime juice, chives, ground black pepper, cayenne pepper, and ground coriander. Stir the mixture with the help of the spoon and make 6 burgers, Brush the instant pot with olive oil. Place the salmon burgers in the instant pot in one layer. Set sauté mode and cook them for 5 minutes. Then flip the burgers on another side and cook for 3 minutes more. When the fish burgers are cooked, transfer them on the plate and cool for 5 minutes. Then place every salmon burger on the cheese slice and top with the remaining cheese slice. Pierce every burger with a toothpick.
Nutrition: calories 324, fat 23.6, fiber 0.2, carbs 1.2, protein 27

Cinnamon Cod Mix

Preparation time: 5 minutes
Cooking time: 12 minutes
Servings: 4
Ingredients:
- 4 cod fillets, boneless and skinless
- 1 tablespoon cinnamon powder
- 1 cup cherry tomatoes, cubed
- Juice of ½ lemon
- ½ cup veggie stock
- A pinch of salt and black pepper
- 1 tablespoon cilantro, chopped

Directions:
In your instant pot, mix the fish with the rest of the ingredients, put the lid on and cook on High for 12

minutes. Release the pressure fast for 5 minutes, divide everything between plates and serve.
Nutrition: calories 162, fat 9.6, fiber 0.3, carbs 3, protein 16.5

Curry Fish
Preparation time: 15 minutes
Cooking time: 4 minutes
Servings: 4
Ingredients:
- 1-pound cod fillet
- 1 teaspoon curry paste
- 2 tablespoons coconut milk
- ½ teaspoon sesame oil
- 1 cup water, for cooking

Directions:
In the shallow bowl whisk together coconut milk and curry paste. Add sesame oil and stir the liquid. After this, chop the cod fillet into the big cubes. Pour the curry mixture over the fish and mix up. Then pour water and insert the steamer rack. Put the fish cubes in the steamer rack and close the lid. Cook the meal on steam mode for 4 minutes. When the time is over, allow the natural pressure release for 5 minutes.
Nutrition: calories 122, fat 4.1, fiber 0.2, carbs 0.8, protein 20.5

Trout and Eggplant Mix
Preparation time: 10 minutes
Cooking time: 15 minutes
Servings: 4
Ingredients:
- 4 trout fillets, boneless
- 2 scallions, chopped
- 2 eggplants, cubed
- ½ cup chicken stock
- 2 tablespoons parsley, chopped
- 3 tablespoons olive oil
- A pinch of salt and black pepper
- 2 tablespoons smoked paprika

Directions:
Set the instant pot on Sauté mode, add the oil, heat it up, add the scallions and the eggplant and cook for 2 minutes, Add the rest of the ingredients except the parsley, put the lid on and cook on High for 13 minutes. Release the pressure naturally for 10 minutes, divide the mix between plates and serve with the parsley sprinkled on top.
Nutrition: calories 291, fat 16.8, fiber 4.5, carbs 6.4, protein 20

Fried Salmon
Preparation time: 10 minutes
Cooking time: 7 minutes
Servings: 4
Ingredients:
- 1 teaspoon Erythritol
- ¼ teaspoon lemongrass
- ¼ teaspoon ground nutmeg
- ½ teaspoon cayenne pepper
- ¼ teaspoon salt
- 1-pound salmon fillet
- 1 tablespoon coconut oil

Directions:
Cut the salmon fillet into 4 fillets. In the shallow bowl combine together spices: lemongrass, ground nutmeg, cayenne pepper, and salt. Rub every salmon fillet with spices. Then toss coconut oil in the instant pot and melt it on sauté mode (approximately 2-3 minutes). Place the salmon fillets in one layer and cook them for 2 minutes from each side. Then sprinkle the salmon fillets with Erythritol and flip on another side. Cook the fish for 1 minute more and transfer in the plate.
Nutrition: calories 181, fat 10.5, fiber 0.1, carbs 1.5, protein 22

Salmon and Tomato Passata
Preparation time: 10 minutes
Cooking time: 15 minutes
Servings: 4
Ingredients:
- 1 tablespoon olive oil
- 4 salmon fillets, boneless, skinless and cubed
- 1 tablespoon rosemary, chopped
- 1 shallot, chopped
- 1 cup tomato passata
- 1 teaspoon chili powder
- 1 tablespoon chives, chopped
- A pinch of salt and black pepper

Directions:
Set the instant pot on Sauté mode, add the oil, heat it up, add the shallot and sauté for 2 minutes. Add the rest of the ingredients, put the lid on and cook on High for 12 minutes. Release the pressure naturally for 10 minutes, divide the mix between plates and serve.
Nutrition: calories 291, fat 16.8, fiber 4.5, carbs 7.4, protein 20

Spicy Mackerel
Preparation time: 15 minutes
Cooking time: 8 minutes
Servings: 4
Ingredients:
- 1-pound fresh mackerel, trimmed
- 1 teaspoon dried oregano
- ½ teaspoon chili powder
- ¼ teaspoon ground black pepper
- ½ teaspoon salt
- ¼ teaspoon chili flakes
- ½ teaspoon dried sage
- 1 teaspoon dried basil
- 1 tablespoon olive oil
- 1 cup water, for cooking

Directions:
In the mixing bowl mix up together dried oregano, chili powder, ground black pepper, salt, chili flakes, dried sage, and dried basil. Then rub the fish with spicy mixture generously. After this, brush it with olive oil and place in the steamer rack, Pour water and insert the steamer rack in the instant pot Close the lid and cook the fish for 8 minutes on Manual mode (high pressure). When the time is over, make a quick pressure release.
Nutrition: calories 330, fat 23.8, fiber 0.3, carbs 0.6, protein 27.2

Salmon and Artichokes
Preparation time: 10 minutes
Cooking time: 15 minutes

Servings: 4
Ingredients:
- 1 pound salmon, skinless, boneless and cubed
- 2 spring onions, chopped
- 12 ounces canned artichokes, roughly chopped
- 1 and ½ cups chicken stock
- A pinch of salt and black pepper
- 1 tablespoon cilantro, chopped

Directions:
In your instant pot, combine all the ingredients, put the lid on and cook on High for 15 minutes. Release the pressure naturally for 10 minutes, divide everything between plates and serve.
Nutrition: calories 193, fat 7.1, fiber 4.1, carbs 6.4, protein 24.5

Salmon in Fragrant Sauce
Preparation time: 10 minutes
Cooking time: 5 minutes
Servings: 2
Ingredients:
- 10 oz salmon fillet
- 1 teaspoon fresh parsley, chopped
- ½ teaspoon lime zest, grated
- 1 teaspoon minced garlic
- 1 jalapeno pepper, diced
- 1 teaspoon Erythritol
- 2 tablespoons avocado oil
- 1 teaspoon ground paprika
- ½ teaspoon ground coriander
- 2 tablespoons lemon juice
- 1 cup water, for cooking

Directions:
Cut the salmon fillet into 2 servings. Pour water and insert the steamer rack in the instant pot. Place the salmon fillets on the rack and close the lid. Steam the fish for 5 minutes on Steam mode. When the time is over make a quick pressure release and transfer the fish on the plates. While the fish is cooking, make the fragrant sauce: in the bowl combine together parsley, lime zest, minced garlic, diced jalapeno pepper, Erythritol, avocado oil, paprika, ground coriander, and lemon juice. Pour the sauce over the cooked salmon.
Nutrition: calories 218, fat 10.8, fiber 1.4, carbs 5.2, protein 28.2

Trout and Spinach Mix
Preparation time: 5 minutes
Cooking time: 15 minutes
Servings: 4
Ingredients:
- 6 trout fillets, boneless
- 2 tablespoons avocado oil
- 2 scallions, minced
- 2 garlic cloves, minced
- 2 tablespoons cilantro, chopped
- 1 cup baby spinach
- A pinch of salt and black pepper
- 2 tablespoons balsamic vinegar

Directions:
Set the instant pot on Sauté mode, add the oil, heat it up, add the scallions and the garlic and sauté for 2 minutes. Add the rest of the ingredients, put the lid on and cook on High for 12 minutes. Release the pressure fast for 5 minutes, divide the mix between plates and serve.
Nutrition: calories 194, fat 8.8, fiber 0.7, carbs 1.8, protein 25.4

Shrimp Salad with Avocado
Preparation time: 10 minutes
Cooking time: 7 minutes
Servings: 4
Ingredients:
- ½ avocado, chopped
- 7 oz shrimps, peeled
- 1 cup lettuce, chopped
- 2 bacon slices, chopped
- 2 tablespoons heavy cream
- 1 teaspoon peanuts, chopped
- ½ teaspoon ground black pepper
- ¼ teaspoon Pink salt
- 1 cup water, for cooking

Directions:
Pour water and insert the steamer rack in the instant pot. Place the shrimps in the rack and close the lid. Cook them on manual mode (high pressure) for 1 minute. Then make quick pressure release and transfer the shrimps in the salad bowl. Remove the steamer rack and clean the instant pot bowl. Place the bacon in the instant pot and cook it on sauté mode for 6 minutes. Stir it every minute to avoid burning. Then transfer the cooked bacon to the shrimps. Add chopped bacon, lettuce, and peanuts. Then in the shallow bowl mix up together heavy cream, peanuts, ground black pepper, and Pink salt. Pour the liquid over the salad and shake it gently.
Nutrition: calories 194, fat 12.9, fiber 1.9, carbs 4, protein 15.7

Sea Bass and Sauce
Preparation time: 10 minutes
Cooking time: 15 minutes
Servings: 4
Ingredients:
- 4 sea bass fillets, boneless and skinless
- 2 tablespoons lime juice
- 2 garlic cloves, minced
- 1 shallot, chopped
- 1 cup chicken stock
- 1 cup tomato passata
- A pinch of salt and black pepper

Directions:
In your instant pot, combine the fish with the rest of the ingredients, put the lid on and cook on High for 15 minutes. Release the pressure naturally for 10 minutes, divide the mix between plates and serve.
Nutrition: calories 154, fat 2.9, fiber 1.3, carbs 2.5, protein 25

Seafood Omelet
Preparation time: 15 minutes
Cooking time: 10 minutes
Servings: 4
Ingredients:
- 4 eggs, beaten
- 2 tablespoons cream cheese
- ½ teaspoon chili flakes
- 1 oz Parmesan, grated

- 5 oz crab meat, canned, chopped
- ½ teaspoon butter, melted
- 1 teaspoon chives, chopped
- 1 cup water, for cooking

Directions:
In the mixing bowl combine together eggs, cream cheese, chili flakes, and chives. Brush the instant pot baking pan with butter and pour the egg mixture inside. Top the egg mixture with chopped crab meat and grated Parmesan. Whisk the mixture gently with the help of the fork. Pour water and insert the steamer rack in the instant pot. Place the instant pot baking pan in the rack and close the lid. Cook the omelet on steam mode for 10 minutes. When the time is over, allow the natural pressure release for 5 minutes.
Nutrition: calories 139, fat 8.7, fiber 0, carbs 1.4, protein 12.7

Sea Bass and Pesto

Preparation time: 5 minutes
Cooking time: 12 minutes
Servings: 4
Ingredients:
- 4 sea bass fillets, skinless, boneless
- 2 tablespoons olive oil
- 2 tablespoons garlic, chopped
- 1 cup basil, chopped
- 2 tablespoons pine nuts
- A pinch of salt and black pepper
- 1 cup tomato passata
- 1 tablespoon parsley, chopped

Directions:
In your blender, combine the oil with the garlic, basil, pine nuts, slat and pepper and pulse well. In your instant pot, combine the sea bass with the pesto, salt, pepper, tomato passata and the parsley, put the lid on and cook on High for 12 minutes. Release the pressure fast for 5 minutes, divide the mix between plates and serve.
Nutrition: calories 237, fat 12.7, fiber 1.3, carbs 5.5, protein 25.8

Shrimp Tacos

Preparation time: 10 minutes
Cooking time: 1 minute
Servings: 5
Ingredients:
- 5 low carb tortillas
- ½ cup white cabbage, shredded
- 2 oz Cotija cheese, crumbled
- 1 tablespoon lemon juice
- ½ teaspoon ground cumin
- ½ teaspoon cayenne pepper
- ¼ teaspoon garlic powder
- ¼ teaspoon onion powder
- ½ teaspoon chili powder
- 1 tablespoon green onions, chopped
- 1 tablespoon fresh cilantro, chopped
- 2 tablespoons avocado oil
- 3 tablespoons heavy cream
- 1-pound shrimps, peeled
- 1 cup water, for cooking

Directions:
Pour water and insert the steamer rack in the instant pot. In the mixing bowl combine together lemon juice, ground cumin, cayenne pepper, garlic powder, onion powder, and chili powder. Coat the shrimps in the mixture and transfer in the steamer rack. Close the lid and cook them for 1 minute on Manual mode (high pressure). Make a quick pressure release and open the lid. Make the taco sauce: mix up together heavy cream, avocado oil, cilantro, and green onions. Then mix up together shredded white cabbage and sauce. Place the cooked shrimps on the tortillas. Add shredded cabbage mixture and Cotija cheese. Fold the tortillas into the tacos.
Nutrition: calories 272, fat 10.9, fiber 7.7, carbs 15, protein 27

Tuna and Mustard Greens

Preparation time: 10 minutes
Cooking time: 10 minutes
Servings: 4
Ingredients:
- 2 cups mustard greens
- 1 tablespoon olive oil
- 1 cup tomato passata
- 1 shallot, chopped
- 1 tablespoon basil, chopped
- A pinch of salt and black pepper
- 14 ounces tuna fillets, boneless, skinless and cubed

Directions:
Set your instant pot on Sauté mode, add the oil, heat it up, add the shallot and sauté for 2 minutes. Add rest of the ingredients, put the lid on and cook on High for 8 minutes. Release the pressure naturally for 10 minutes, divide the mix between plates and serve.
Nutrition: calories 124, fat 3.7, fiber 1.9, carbs 2.6, protein 1.6

Shrimp Cocktail

Preparation time: 10 minutes
Cooking time: 1 minute
Servings: 6
Ingredients:
- 16 oz shrimps, peeled
- 1 cup low carb ketchup
- ½ tablespoon lemon juice
- 1 teaspoon horseradish, grated
- ¼ teaspoon white pepper
- ½ teaspoon salt
- 1 cup water, for cooking

Directions:
Pour water and insert the steamer rack in the instant pot. Sprinkle the shrimps with salt and place in the steamer rack. Cook the seafood for 0 minutes on manual mode (high pressure). Make a quick pressure release and transfer the shrimps in the serving plate. Then make shrimp cocktail sauce: in the sauce bowl, mix up together low carb ketchup, lemon juice, horseradish, and white pepper. Dip the shrimps in the sauce.
Nutrition: calories 99, fat 1.3, fiber 0.1, carbs 1.3, protein 17.3

Salmon and Salsa

Preparation time: 10 minutes
Cooking time: 8 minutes
Servings: 4
Ingredients:
- 4 salmon fillets, boneless

- ½ cup veggie stock
- 1 cup black olives, pitted
- 1 cup tomatoes, cubed
- 1 tablespoon basil, chopped
- 1 tablespoon olive oil
- 1 tablespoon balsamic vinegar
- A pinch of salt and black pepper
- 1 tablespoon chives, chopped

Directions:
In your instant pot, combine the fish with the stock, salt and pepper, put the lid on and cook on High for 8 minutes. Release the pressure naturally for 10 minutes and divide the salmon between plates. In a bowl, mix the olives with the rest of the ingredients, toss, add next to the salmon and serve.
Nutrition: calories 313, fat 18.2, fiber 1.7, carbs 4, protein 35.4

Mussels Casserole

Preparation time: 10 minutes
Cooking time: 13 minutes
Servings: 4
Ingredients:
- 9 oz mussels, canned
- 1 cup cauliflower, chopped
- ½ cup Cheddar cheese, shredded
- ½ cup heavy cream
- 1 teaspoon Italian seasonings
- 1 teaspoon olive oil
- 1 teaspoon salt
- 1 tablespoon fresh dill, chopped
- 1 cup water, for cooking

Directions:
Pour water and insert the trivet in the instant pot. Place the cauliflower on the trivet and cook it on manual mode (high pressure) for 3 minutes. Then make a quick pressure release. Transfer the cauliflower in the instant pot casserole mold. Add canned mussels, cheese, heavy cream, Italian seasonings, olive oil, salt, and dill. Mix up the casserole and cover it with foil. Place the casserole mold on the trivet and close the lid. Cook the casserole for 10 minutes on manual mode (high pressure). When the time is over, make a quick pressure release. Mix up the casserole with the help of the spoon before serving.
Nutrition: calories 185, fat 13.2, fiber 0.7, carbs 4.9, protein 12.1

Saffron Chili Cod

Preparation time: 5 minutes
Cooking time: 12 minutes
Servings: 4
Ingredients:
- 4 cod fillets, boneless and skinless
- 3 garlic cloves, minced
- 1 teaspoon turmeric powder
- 1 tablespoon chili paste
- 1 cup tomato passata

Directions:
In your instant pot, combine the cod with the rest of the ingredients, put the lid on and cook on High for 12 minutes. Release the pressure fast for 5 minutes, divide everything between plates and serve.
Nutrition: calories 244, fat 12, fiber 1.6, carbs 4.5, protein 14.6

Skagenrora

Preparation time: 10 minutes
Cooking time: 1 minute
Servings: 4
Ingredients:
- 11 oz shrimps, peeled
- ½ cup of coconut milk
- 1 tablespoon ricotta cheese
- 2 tablespoons fresh parsley, chopped
- 1 teaspoon lime juice
- ¼ teaspoon chili powder
- ¼ teaspoon ground black pepper
- 1 red onion, chopped
- 1 cup water, for cooking

Directions:
Pour water and insert the steamer rack in the instant pot. Put the shrimps in the rack and close the lid. Cook them on manual mode (high pressure) for 1 minute. When the time is over, make a quick pressure release and transfer the shrimps in the salad bowl. In the separated bowl mix up together coconut milk, ricotta cheese, fresh parsley, lime juice, chili powder, and ground black pepper. The sauce is cooked. Combine together shrimps with chopped red onion. Add sauce and mix it up.
Nutrition: calories 180, fat 8.9, fiber 1.4, carbs 6, protein 19.3

Salmon and Endives

Preparation time: 10 minutes
Cooking time: 15 minutes
Servings: 4
Ingredients:
- 4 salmon fillets, boneless
- 1 cup tomato passata
- 1 shallot, sliced
- 2 endives, trimmed and halved
- 1 tablespoon balsamic vinegar
- A pinch of salt and black pepper
- 1 tablespoon parsley, chopped

Directions:
In your instant pot, combine the salmon with the rest of the ingredients, put the lid on and cook on High for 15 minutes. Release the pressure naturally for 10 minutes, divide the mix between plates and serve.
Nutrition: calories 251, fat 11.1, fiber 1, carbs 3.4, protein 35.4

Butter Scallops

Preparation time: 10 minutes
Cooking time: 7 minutes
Servings: 4
Ingredients:
- 1-pound scallops
- 3 tablespoons butter
- ½ teaspoon dried rosemary
- ¼ teaspoon salt

Directions:
Put butter in the instant pot. Set sauté mode and melt butter (it will take approximately 3 minutes. Add dried rosemary and salt. Stir the butter. Then place the scallops in the hot butter in one layer. Cook them on sauté mode for 2 minutes. Then flip the scallops on another side and cook for 2 minutes more. Serve the scallops with hot butter.

Nutrition: calories 177, fat 9.5, fiber 0.1, carbs 2.8, protein 19.1

Chili Tuna

Preparation time: 5 minutes
Cooking time: 15 minutes
Servings: 4
Ingredients:
- 1 pound tuna, skinless, boneless and cubed
- Juice of 1 lemon
- 1 tablespoon chili powder
- 1 cup tomato passata
- A pinch of salt and black pepper
- 1 shallot, chopped
- 1 tablespoon chives, chopped
- 1 tablespoon cilantro, chopped

Directions:
In your instant pot, combine the tuna with the lemon juice and the rest of the ingredients, put the lid on and cook on High for 15 minutes. Release the pressure fast for 5 minutes, divide the chili into bowls and serve.
Nutrition: calories 232, fat 9.6, fiber 1.6, carbs 4.4, protein 31.2

Cajun Crab Casserole

Preparation time: 10 minutes
Cooking time: 15 minutes
Servings: 6
Ingredients:
- ½ cup celery stalks, chopped
- ½ white onion, diced
- 3 eggs, beaten
- 1 tablespoon dried parsley
- 10 oz crab meat, chopped, canned
- 1 teaspoon Cajun seasonings
- ½ cup white Cheddar cheese, shredded
- ½ teaspoon salt
- ½ teaspoon ground black pepper
- ½ teaspoon cayenne pepper
- ½ cup heavy cream
- 1 teaspoon sesame oil

Directions:
Heat up the instant pot on sauté mode for 3 minutes and add sesame oil. Add diced onion and cook it for 2 minutes. Stir it well. Switch off the instant pot. Add celery stalk in the onion and mix up. Then add beaten eggs, dried parsley, crab meat, Cajun seasonings, cheese, salt, ground black pepper, cayenne pepper, and heavy cream. Stir the casserole carefully with the help of a spatula and close the lid. Cook the meal on stew mode for 10 minutes.
Nutrition: calories 159, fat 9.7, fiber 0.4, carbs 2.8, protein 11.5

Mackerel and Shrimp Mix

Preparation time: 5 minutes
Cooking time: 12 minutes
Servings: 6
Ingredients:
- 1 pound shrimp, peeled and deveined
- 1 pound mackerel, skinless, boneless and cubed
- 1 cup radishes, cubed
- ½ cup chicken stock
- 2 garlic cloves, minced
- 1 tablespoon olive oil
- 1 cup tomato passata

Directions:
Set instant pot on Sauté mode, add the oil, heat it up, add the radishes and the garlic and sauté for 2 minutes. Add the rest of the ingredients, put the lid on and cook on High for 10 minutes. Release the pressure fast for 5 minutes, divide the mix into bowls and serve.
Nutrition: calories 332, fat 17.4, fiber 0.9, carbs 4.4, protein 36.4

Crab Melt with Zucchini

Preparation time: 15 minutes
Cooking time: 8 minutes
Servings: 4
Ingredients:
- 1 large zucchini
- 1 teaspoon avocado oil
- ½ cup Monterey Jack cheese, shredded
- 1 green bell pepper, finely chopped
- 9 oz crab meat, chopped
- 2 tablespoons ricotta cheese
- 1 cup water, for cooking

Directions:
Trim the ends of zucchini and slice it lengthwise into 4 slices. Then pour water in the instant pot and insert the trivet. Place the zucchini slices in the baking mold. Brush them with avocado oil gently. After this, in the mixing bowl combine together Monterey Jack cheese, bell pepper, crab meat, and ricotta cheese. Spread the mixture over the zucchini and transfer it on the trivet. Close the instant pot lid and cook the meal on manual mode (high pressure) for 8 minutes. When the time is over, make a quick pressure release.
Nutrition: calories 144, fat 6.4, fiber 1.3, carbs 6.7, protein 13.6

Mackerel and Basil Sauce

Preparation time: 10 minutes
Cooking time: 15 minutes
Servings: 4
Ingredients:
- 1 cup veggie stock
- 2 chili peppers, chopped
- 2 tablespoons olive oil
- 1 pound mackerel, skinless, boneless and cubed
- 2 teaspoons red pepper flakes
- A pinch of salt and black pepper
- ½ cup basil, chopped

Directions:
Set your instant pot on Sauté mode, add the oil, heat it up, add the chili peppers and the pepper flakes and cook for 2 minutes. Add the rest of the ingredients, put the lid on and cook on High for 12 minutes. Release the pressure naturally for 10 minutes, divide everything between plates and serve.
Nutrition: calories 362, fat 14.7, fiber 0.4, carbs 0.8, protein 27.5

Baked Snapper

Preparation time: 10 minutes
Cooking time: 10 minutes
Servings: 4
Ingredients:

- 1-pound snapper, trimmed, cleaned
- 1 tablespoon lemongrass
- 1 tablespoon sage
- 1 teaspoon avocado oil
- 1 teaspoon salt
- 1 teaspoon red pepper
- 1 cup water, for cooking

Directions:
Pour water and insert trivet in the instant pot. Rub the fish with salt and red pepper. Then fill it with sage and lemongrass. Brush the fish with avocado oil and transfer on the trivet. Close the lid and cook the snapper for 10 minutes on manual mode (high pressure). When the time is over, make a quick pressure release and open the lid. Remove the sage and lemongrass from the fish.
Nutrition: calories 151, fat 2.2, fiber 0.7, carbs 2.9, protein 27.9

Oregano Tuna

Preparation time: 10 minutes
Cooking time: 12 minutes
Servings: 4
Ingredients:
- 1 pound tuna, skinless, boneless and cubed
- 1 cup black olives, pitted and sliced
- 2 tablespoon avocado oil
- 1 shallot, chopped
- 14 ounces tomatoes, chopped
- 2 tablespoons oregano, chopped

Directions:
Set your instant pot on Sauté mode, add the oil, heat it up, add the shallot and sauté for 2 minutes. Add the tuna and the rest of the ingredients, put the lid on and cook on High for 10 minutes. Release the pressure naturally for 10 minutes, divide the mix between plates and serve.
Nutrition: calories 284, fat 14.1, fiber 3.5, carbs 6.7, protein 31.4

Salmon Salad

Preparation time: 10 minutes
Cooking time: 8 minutes
Servings: 2
Ingredients:
- ½ cup curly kale, chopped
- 7 oz salmon fillet, chopped
- 1 teaspoon onion flakes
- ½ teaspoon salt
- 1 teaspoon coconut oil
- 1 teaspoon olive oil
- ½ teaspoon chili flakes
- ¼ cup cherry tomatoes, halved

Directions:
Place coconut oil in the instant pot and heat it up on sauté mode. When the coconut oil is melted, add salmon fillet. Sprinkle the fish with salt and chili flakes. Cook it for 2 minutes from each side on sauté mode. Then transfer the cooked salmon in the salad bowl. Add curly kale, onion flakes, salt, olive oil, and halved cherry tomatoes. Shake the salad.
Nutrition: calories 202, fat 11.2, fiber 2.2, carbs 6, protein 21.7

Creamy Shrimp and Radish Mix

Preparation time: 5 minutes
Cooking time: 6 minutes
Servings: 4
Ingredients:
- 1 and ½ pound shrimp, peeled and deveined
- 1 cup red radishes, sliced
- ½ cup black olives, pitted
- 2 spring onions, chopped
- 1 and ½ cups coconut cream
- 1 tablespoon cilantro, chopped
- 1 tablespoon sweet paprika

Directions:
In your instant pot, combine the shrimp with the rest of the ingredients, put the lid on and cook on High for 6 minutes. Release the pressure fast for 5 minutes, divide the mix into bowls and serve.
Nutrition: calories 301, fat 5.9, fiber 1.9, carbs 6.4, protein 52.4

Butter Cod Loin

Preparation time: 10 minutes
Cooking time: 15 minutes
Servings: 2
Ingredients:
- 8 oz cod loin
- 1 tablespoon oregano
- ¼ teaspoon chili flakes
- 3 tablespoons butter
- ½ teaspoon salt
- ¼ teaspoon minced ginger

Directions:
Put butter and chili flakes in the instant pot bowl. Set sauté mode and melt the mixture. Add minced ginger, salt, oregano, and stir it. Then arrange the cod loin inside. Cook it on sauté mode for 6 minutes from each side. Serve the fish topped with hot butter mixture from the instant pot.
Nutrition: calories 251, fat 18.5, fiber 1, carbs 1.6, protein 20.5

Marjoram Tuna

Preparation time: 10 minutes
Cooking time: 15 minutes
Servings: 4
Ingredients:
- 1 and ½ pounds tuna, skinless, boneless and cubed
- 2 spring onions, chopped
- 1 tablespoon avocado oil
- 3 garlic cloves, minced
- ½ cup basil, chopped
- ½ cup chicken stock
- 2 tablespoons tomato passata
- 1 tablespoon marjoram, chopped
- A pinch of salt and black pepper

Directions:
Set your instant pot on Sauté mode, add the oil, heat it up, add the garlic and the spring onions, stir and sauté for 3 minutes. Add the rest of the ingredients, put the lid on and cook on High for 12 minutes. Release the pressure naturally for 10 minutes, divide the mix between plates and serve.
Nutrition: calories 345, fat 16.9, fiber 0.7, carbs 2.4, protein 26.6

Cod in Cream Sauce

Preparation time: 5 minutes
Cooking time: 15 minutes
Servings: 4
Ingredients:
- 16 oz salmon fillet
- 1 cup heavy cream
- 1 teaspoon minced garlic
- 1 tablespoon fresh parsley, chopped
- 1 teaspoon chives, chopped
- 1 oz Parmesan, grated
- 1 cup water, for cooking

Directions:
Mix up together water and minced garlic and pour the liquid in the instant pot. Insert trivet and place a salmon fillet in it. Close the lid and cook the fish on steam mode for 5 minutes. Then allow the natural pressure release for 5 minutes and transfer the fish on the plate. Cut it into servings. After this, remove the liquid from the instant pot. Discard the trivet. Pour heavy cream in the instant pot. Add parsley and chives. Bring the liquid to boil on sauté mode. Then add cheese and switch off the instant pot. Stir the liquid carefully until the cheese is melted. Pour the cooked cream sauce over the salmon.
Nutrition: calories 278, fat 19.6, fiber 0.1, carbs 1.4, protein 25

Bacon Trout Mix

Preparation time: 10 minutes
Cooking time: 15 minutes
Servings: 4
Ingredients:
- 1 cup bacon, cooked and crumbled
- 4 trout fillets, boneless and skinless
- 10 ounces tomato passata
- 2 tablespoons cilantro, chopped
- 1 shallot, chopped
- 1 tablespoon olive oil
- 1 tablespoon lemon juice

Directions:
Set your instant pot on Sauté mode, add the oil, heat it up, add the shallot and sauté for 2 minutes. Add the rest of the ingredients, put the lid on and cook on High for 13 minutes. Release the pressure naturally for 10 minutes, divide the mix between plates and serve.
Nutrition: calories 166, fat 8.9, fiber 1.1, carbs 3.8, protein 17.5

Salmon and Kohlrabi Gratin

Preparation time: 10 minutes
Cooking time: 14 minutes
Servings: 3
Ingredients:
- 8 oz salmon fillet, chopped
- ¼ teaspoon ground black pepper
- ½ teaspoon salt
- 4 oz kohlrabi, chopped
- ½ cup heavy cream
- 1 tablespoon almond meal
- 1 teaspoon lemon juice
- 1 teaspoon sesame oil
- 3 oz Provolone cheese, grated
- 1 cup water, for cooking

Directions:
Pour water and insert the steamer rack in the instant pot. Place kohlrabi in the steamer and cook it on steam mode for 4 minutes. Then make a quick pressure release. Brush the instant pot pan mold with sesame oil. Place the salmon in it. Then sprinkle the fish with salt and ground black pepper. Top the fish with kohlrabi. After this, sprinkle the mixture with lemon juice, almond meal, heavy cream, and Provolone cheese. Place the mold in the steamer rack and close the lid. Cook the gratin on manual mode (high pressure) for 10 minutes. Then make quick pressure realize.
Nutrition: calories 304, fat 22.2, fiber 1.7, carbs 4.1, protein 23.4

Tuna and Fennel Mix

Preparation time: 10 minutes
Cooking time: 15 minutes
Servings: 4
Ingredients:
- 1 tablespoon avocado oil
- 1 pound tuna, skinless, boneless and cubed
- 2 tuna fillets, boneless, skinless and cubed
- 3 garlic cloves, minced
- ¼ cup parsley, chopped
- ½ cup chicken stock
- 2 fennel bulbs, sliced
- 1 tablespoon sweet paprika

Directions:
Set the instant pot on Sauté mode, add the oil, heat it up, add the garlic and cook for 2 minutes. Add the tuna, fennel and the rest of the ingredients, put the lid on and cook on High for 13 minutes, Release the pressure naturally for 10 minutes, divide everything between plates and serve.
Nutrition: calories 263, fat 10.2, fiber 2.4, carbs 4.8, protein 23.5

Mussel Chowder

Preparation time: 10 minutes
Cooking time: 30 minutes
Servings: 4
Ingredients:
- 1 cup heavy cream
- 1 cup chicken broth
- 6 oz mussels, canned
- 1 zucchini, chopped
- 1 teaspoon paprika
- ½ teaspoon salt
- 1 onion, diced
- 1 teaspoon coconut oil

Directions:
Toss coconut oil in the instant pot. Add onion and cook the ingredients on sauté mode for 5 minutes. Then stir well and cook for 3 minutes more. After this, add zucchini and salt. Saute the ingredients for 2 minutes more. Add paprika, salt, chicken stock, and heavy cream. Close the lid and cook the chowder on soup mode for 20 minutes. Then open the lid and with the help of the immersion blender, blend the chowder until it gets the creamy texture. Add mussels and cook the chowder for 5 minutes more on sauté mode.
Nutrition: calories 180, fat 13.7, fiber 1.3, carbs 7.2, protein 7.9

Tilapia Salad

Preparation time: 5 minutes

Cooking time: 12 minutes
Servings: 4
Ingredients:
- 1 and ½ pounds tilapia fillets, boneless, skinless and cubed
- 1 cup black olives, pitted
- 1 cup zucchinis, cubed
- 1 cup baby spinach
- 1 tablespoon olive oil
- 1 tablespoon balsamic vinegar
- A pinch of salt and black pepper
- 2 tomatoes, cubed
- ½ cup chicken stock
- 1 tablespoon lemon juice
- 1 tablespoon sweet paprika

Directions:
In your instant pot, combine the fish with the olives, zucchinis, tomatoes, stock, paprika, salt and pepper, toss, put the lid on and cook on High for 12 minutes. Release the pressure fast for 5 minutes, transfer the mix to a bowl, add the remaining ingredients, toss and serve.
Nutrition: calories 187, fat 8.6, fiber 3, carbs 6.9, protein 22.8

Paprika Salmon Skewers

Preparation time: 15 minutes
Cooking time: 5 minutes
Servings: 4
Ingredients:
- 1-pound salmon fillet, fresh, cubed
- 1 tablespoon paprika
- ½ teaspoon salt
- ½ teaspoon ground turmeric
- 1 teaspoon avocado oil
- ½ teaspoon lemon juice
- 1 cup water, for cooking

Directions:
Make the sauce: mix up together paprika, salt, ground turmeric, avocado oil, and lemon juice. Then coat the salmon cubes in the sauce well and string on the wooden skewers. Pour water and insert trivet in the instant pot. Arrange the salmon skewers on the trivet and close the lid. Cook the meal on manual mode (high pressure) for 5 minutes. Then make a quick pressure release and remove the fish from the instant pot.
Nutrition: calories 158, fat 7.4, fiber 0.8, carbs 1.2, protein 22.3

Salmon and Dill Sauce

Preparation time: 10 minutes
Cooking time: 20 minutes
Servings: 6
Ingredients:
- 6 salmon fillets, boneless
- ½ teaspoon lemon pepper
- 1 spring onion, chopped
- Juice of ½ lemon
- A pinch of salt and black pepper
- 1 tablespoon chives, chopped
- ½ cup avocado mayonnaise
- ½ cup heavy cream
- 1 teaspoon dill, chopped

Directions:
Set the instant pot on Sauté mode, add the cream, dill and the rest of the ingredients except the salmon and the mayonnaise, whisk and cook for 5 minutes. Add the fish, put the lid on and cook on High for 15 minutes. Release the pressure naturally for 10 minutes, add the avocado mayonnaise, toss gently, divide everything between plates and serve.
Nutrition: calories 399, fat 22.1, fiber 0.2, carbs 1.1, protein 23.8

Tuscan Shrimps

Preparation time: 10 minutes
Cooking time: 25 minutes
Servings: 4
Ingredients:
- 1-pound shrimps, peeled
- ¼ teaspoon minced garlic
- 1 teaspoon butter
- 1 teaspoon coconut oil
- ½ white onion, diced
- 1 teaspoon apple cider vinegar
- 1 cup heavy cream
- ¼ teaspoon salt
- ½ teaspoon ground black pepper
- 2 cups spinach, chopped
- 3 oz Provolone cheese, grated
- 1 tablespoon almond flour
- 1 teaspoon Italian seasonings
- 1 teaspoon dried cilantro
- ¼ cup of water

Directions:
Heat up instant pot on sauté mode for 3 minutes. Then place butter and coconut oil inside. Heat up the ingredients for 2 minutes and add minced garlic and diced onion. Add apple cider vinegar and stir the ingredients. Sauté them for 5 minutes. Stir the mixture from time to time. Then add salt, ground black pepper, cilantro, Italian seasonings, and stir well. Add water and bring the mixture to boil on sauté mode. Add spinach and almond flour. Stir it well and cook for 3 minutes. Then add heavy cream and shrimps. Cook the meal on sauté mode for 10 minutes.
Nutrition: calories 385, fat 24.7, fiber 1.4, carbs 6.7, protein 34

Tilapia and Olives Salsa

Preparation time: 10 minutes
Cooking time: 15 minutes
Servings: 4
Ingredients:
- 4 tilapia fillets, boneless
- 1 tablespoon olive oil
- A pinch of salt and black pepper
- 12 ounces tomato passata
- 2 tablespoon sweet red pepper, chopped
- 2 tablespoon green onions, chopped
- ½ tablespoons Italian seasoning
- 1 and ½ cups black olives, pitted
- 1 tablespoon balsamic vinegar

Directions:
Set the instant pot on Sauté mode, add the oil, heat it up, add the fish and cook for 2 minutes on each side. Add salt, pepper and the tomato passata, put the lid on and cook on High for 10 minutes. Release the pressure naturally for 10 minutes and divide the fish between plates. In a bowl, mix the red pepper with

the remaining ingredients, toss, divide next to the fish and serve.
Nutrition: calories 155, fat 4.6, fiber 2.5, carbs 3.4, protein 7.4

Parmesan Scallops

Preparation time: 8 minutes
Cooking time: 11 minutes
Servings: 4
Ingredients:
- 11 oz scallops
- 4 oz Parmesan, grated
- 1 tablespoon butter, melted
- ½ teaspoon avocado oil
- 1 teaspoon garlic powder

Directions:
Brush scallops with butter and sprinkle with garlic powder. Brush the instant pot bowl with avocado oil and heat it up for 3 minutes on sauté mode. Then place the scallops in the instant pot in one layer and cook them for 3 minutes. Flip the scallops and top with grated Parmesan. Close the lid and sauté the meal for 5 minutes more.
Nutrition: calories 188, fat 6.9, fiber 0.1, carbs 3.4, protein 22.4

Catfish and Avocado Mix

Preparation time: 10 minutes
Cooking time: 16 minutes
Servings: 4
Ingredients:
- 4 catfish fillets, boneless
- 2 teaspoons olive oil
- 2 tablespoons lime juice
- 2 tablespoons cilantro, chopped
- A pinch of salt and black pepper
- 2 teaspoons sweet paprika
- 1/3 cup spring onions, chopped
- 2 teaspoons oregano, dried
- 2 teaspoons cumin, dried
- ½ cup tomato passata
- 1 avocado, peeled, pitted and cubed

Directions:
Set the instant pot on Sauté mode, add the oil, heat it up, add the onions and cook for 2 minutes. Add the fish and cook for 1 minute on each side. Add the rest of the ingredients, put the lid on and cook on High for 12 minutes more. Release the pressure naturally for 10 minutes, divide everything between plates and serve.
Nutrition: calories 353, fat 23.4, fiber 2.6, carbs 6.4, protein 15.3

Seafood Bisque

Preparation time: 5 minutes
Cooking time: 10 minutes
Servings: 3
Ingredients:
- 1 tablespoon coconut oil
- 1 oz leek, chopped
- ½ red onion, diced
- 1 teaspoon celery, chopped
- ½ teaspoon ground thyme
- ½ teaspoon lemon zest, grated
- 3 tablespoons cream cheese
- 1 cup chicken broth
- 1 tablespoon scallions, chopped
- 1 oz bacon, chopped, cooked
- ½ teaspoon salt
- 9 oz shrimps, peeled

Directions:
Put coconut oil in the instant pot and melt it on sauté mode for 2 minutes. Then add leek, red onion, and celery. Sprinkle the ingredients with ground thyme, lemon zest, and salt. Mix up well and cook on sauté mode for 4 minutes. Then add cream cheese and stir well until homogenous. Then and chicken stock and shrimps. Mix up the meal well and close the lid. Cook it on manual mode (high pressure) for 2 minutes. When the time is over, make a quick pressure release. Top the cooked meal with bacon and scallions.
Nutrition: calories 253, fat 13.9, fiber 0.7, carbs 5.4, protein 25.7

Tilapia and Capers Mix

Preparation time: 10 minutes
Cooking time: 15 minutes
Servings: 4
Ingredients:
- 4 tilapia fillets, boneless
- 3 tablespoons lemon juice
- 2 tablespoons ghee, melted
- A pinch of salt and black pepper
- ½ teaspoon oregano, dried
- 2 tablespoons capers, drained and chopped
- 1 teaspoon sweet paprika
- ½ teaspoon garlic powder
- ½ cup chicken stock

Directions:
Set the instant pot on Sauté mode, add the ghee, melt it, add the fish and sear for 2 minutes on each side. Add salt, pepper and the rest of the ingredients, put the lid on and cook on High for 10 minutes. Release the pressure naturally for 10 minutes, divide the mix between plates and serve.
Nutrition: calories 173, fat 7.2, fiber 0.5, carbs 2.3, protein 4.7

Lobster Bisque

Preparation time: 10 minutes
Cooking time: 15 minutes
Servings: 4
Ingredients:
- 1 teaspoon tomato paste
- 1 tablespoon celery, grated
- 1 white onion, diced
- ¼ teaspoon minced garlic
- 1 tablespoon butter
- 3 cups chicken broth
- 1 tablespoon ground paprika
- ½ teaspoon ground black pepper
- ½ cup heavy cream
- 4 lobster tails
- ½ teaspoon salt
- 1 tablespoon chives, chopped

Directions:
Melt the butter in the instant pot on sauté mode for 3 minutes. Then add celery and onion. Cook the vegetables for 2 minutes. After this, stir them well and add minced garlic. Mix up well. Add lobster tails and cook them for 1 minute from each side. After this, mix up together tomato paste and heavy cream. Add the liquid in the instant pot. Then add chicken broth,

ground black pepper, ground paprika, and salt. Close the lid. Cook the bisque for 3 minutes on manual mode (high pressure). When the time is over, make a quick pressure release. Top the meal with chopped chives.
Nutrition: calories 170, fat 9.7, fiber 1.4, carbs 5.2, protein 4.7

Glazed Salmon

Preparation time: 10 minutes
Cooking time: 15 minutes
Servings: 4
Ingredients:
- 4 salmon fillets, boneless
- A pinch of salt and black pepper
- 4 teaspoons mustard
- 1 tablespoon coconut aminos
- 1 teaspoon balsamic vinegar
- 3 tablespoons swerve

Directions:
Set the instant pot on Sauté mode, add the mustard, the aminos and the rest of the ingredients except the salmon, whisk well and cook for 3 minutes. Add the salmon, put the lid on and cook on High for 12 minutes. Release the pressure naturally for 10 minutes, divide the salmon between plates, drizzle the glaze all over and serve.
Nutrition: calories 251, fat 11.9, fiber 0.5, carbs 1.2, protein 35.4

Tarragon Lobster

Preparation time: 10 minutes
Cooking time: 8 minutes
Servings: 3
Ingredients:
- 12 oz lobster tails
- 1 tablespoon tarragon
- 1 tablespoon lemon juice
- 2 tablespoons butter, melted
- ¼ teaspoon salt
- 1 cup water, for cooking

Directions:
With the help of the scissors and knife trim and clean the lobster tails from shells. Then pour water and insert the steamer rack in the instant pot. Arrange the lobster tails on the rack and close the lid. Cook the seafood for 3 minutes on manual mode (high pressure). When the time is over, make a quick pressure release and open the lid. Transfer the lobsters on the plate and clean the instant pot. Remove the steamer rack from the instant pot. Put the melted butter, tarragon, lemon juice, and salt in the instant pot and cook it for 3 minutes on sauté mode. Top every lobster tail with fragrant butter liquid.
Nutrition: calories 172, fat 8.7, fiber 0.1, carbs 0.4, protein 21.8

Spicy Tilapia and Kale

Preparation time: 10 minutes
Cooking time: 20 minutes
Servings: 4
Ingredients:
- 4 tilapia fillets, boneless
- A pinch of salt and black pepper
- 3 tablespoons olive oil
- 2 garlic cloves, minced
- 1 teaspoon fennel seed
- 14 ounces canned tomatoes, crushed
- 1 bunch kale, chopped
- ½ teaspoon red pepper flakes

Directions:
Set the instant pot on Sauté mode, add the oil, heat it up, add the garlic and fennel seed and cook for 3 minutes. Add the rest of the ingredients except the fish, toss and sauté for 4 minutes more. Add the fish, put the lid on and cook on High for 12 minutes. Release the pressure naturally for 10 minutes, divide the mix between plates and serve.
Nutrition: calories 138, fat 11.2, fiber 1.5, carbs 4.8, protein 6.3

Mussels Mariniere

Preparation time: 10 minutes
Cooking time: 8 minutes
Servings: 5
Ingredients:
- 2 garlic cloves, diced
- 1 white onion, diced
- 1 tablespoon fresh parsley, chopped
- 1 cup chicken broth
- ¼ cup of coconut milk
- 1 tablespoon avocado oil
- 1 tablespoon lemon juice
- 1-pound fresh mussels

Directions:
Pour avocado oil in the instant pot. Add diced garlic and onion. Cook the vegetables on sauté mode for 4 minutes. Stir them after 2 minutes of cooking. Then add parsley, lemon juice, and coconut milk. Mix up the mixture and cook it for 1 minute. Add mussels and chicken broth, Close the lid and cook the meal on manual mode (high pressure) for 3 minutes. When the time is over, make a quick pressure release.
Nutrition: calories 129, fat 5.6, fiber 0.9, carbs 6.9, protein 12.4

Lime Glazed Salmon

Preparation time: 10 minutes
Cooking time: 15 minutes
Servings: 4
Ingredients:
- 4 salmon fillets, boneless
- A pinch of salt and black pepper
- 1 tablespoon ginger, grated
- 1 tablespoon coconut aminos
- 1 tablespoon sesame seeds
- 1 teaspoon lime zest, grated
- 1 tablespoon lime juice
- ½ cup chicken stock

Directions:
Set the instant pot on Sauté mode, add the stock, lime juice and the rest of the ingredients except the salmon and the sesame seeds, whisk and cook for 3 minutes. Add the salmon, put the lid on and cook on High for 12 minutes. Release the pressure naturally for 10 minutes, divide the salmon mix between plates, sprinkle the sesame seeds on top and serve.
Nutrition: calories 255, fat 12.3, fiber 0.5, cabs 1.7, protein 35.4

Tuna Cakes

Preparation time: 15 minutes
Cooking time: 4 minutes
Servings: 4
Ingredients:
- 10 oz tuna, canned
- 1 egg, beaten
- 1 teaspoon dried oregano
- ½ teaspoon salt
- 1 teaspoon ground coriander
- 3 tablespoons coconut flour
- ½ teaspoon chili flakes
- 1 cup water, for cooking

Directions:
Place the canned tuna in the bowl and smash it with the help of the fork. When the tuna is smooth, add egg, dried oregano, salt, ground coriander, coconut flour, and chili flakes. Stir the tuna cakes mixture well. After this, pour water and insert the steamer rack in the instant pot. With the help of the scooper make the medium size tuna cakes and place them on the trivet on one layer. Close the lid and cook the meal on manual mode (high pressure) for 5 minutes. Then allow the natural pressure release for 5 minutes more and transfer the tuna cakes on the plate.
Nutrition: calories 175, fat 7.8, fiber 2.4, carbs 3.7, protein 21.4

Tilapia and Zucchini Noodles

Preparation time: 10 minutes
Cooking time: 15 minutes
Servings: 4
Ingredients:
- 4 tilapia fillets, boneless
- ¼ teaspoon garlic powder
- 2 zucchinis, cut with a spiralizer
- ½ teaspoon cumin, ground
- 2 garlic cloves, minced
- ½ teaspoon smoked paprika
- A pinch of salt and black pepper
- 2 teaspoons olive oil
- ½ cup tomato passata

Directions:
Set the instant pot on Sauté mode, add the oil, heat it up, add the garlic, cumin, garlic powder, paprika, salt and pepper, stir and cook for 3 minutes. Add the rest of the ingredients, put the lid on and cook on High for 12 minutes. Release the pressure naturally for 10 minutes, divide the whole mix between plates and serve.
Nutrition: calories 259, fat 13.9, fiber 2.2, carbs 4.9, protein 15.2

Salmon under Parmesan Blanket

Preparation time: 10 minutes
Cooking time: 11 minutes
Servings: 4
Ingredients:
- 1-pound salmon fillet
- 1 teaspoon chili flakes
- ¼ teaspoon cayenne pepper
- 1 teaspoon olive oil
- ½ teaspoon ground paprika
- ½ teaspoon dried thyme
- 4 oz Parmesan, grated
- 1 cup water, for cooking

Directions:
In the shallow bowl combine together chili flakes, cayenne pepper, ground paprika, and dried thyme. Then rub the salmon fillet with spices. After this, brush the fish fillet with olive oil. Heat up the instant pot on sauté mode for 3 minutes. Then place the salmon fillet in the hot instant pot and cook for 2 minutes from each side. Then remove the fish from the instant pot. Clean the instant pot and pour water inside. Insert the steamer rack and line it with foil. Place the salmon fillet in the instant pot and top with grated Parmesan. Close the lid and cook the meal on manual (high pressure) for 5 minutes. Then make a quick pressure release. Transfer the cooked fish on the plate and cut it into servings.
Nutrition: calories 253, fat 14.3, fiber 0.2, carbs 1.3, protein 31.2

Salmon and Coconut Mix

Preparation time: 10 minutes
Cooking time: 20 minutes
Servings: 4
Ingredients:
- 4 salmon fillets, boneless
- 3 tablespoons avocado mayonnaise
- 1 teaspoon lime zest, grated
- ¼ cup coconut cream
- ¼ cup lime juice
- ½ cup coconut, unsweetened and shredded
- 2 teaspoons Cajun seasoning
- A pinch of salt and black pepper

Directions:
Set the instant pot on Sauté mode, add the coconut cream and the rest of the ingredients except the fish, whisk and cook for 5 minutes. Add the fish, put the lid on and cook on High for 10 minutes. Release the pressure naturally for 10 minutes, divide the salmon and the sauce between plates and serve.
Nutrition: calories 306, fat 17.5, fiber 1.4, carbs 2.5, protein 25.3

Salmon Poppers

Preparation time: 15 minutes
Cooking time: 10 minutes
Servings: 6
Ingredients:
- 10 oz salmon fillet, chopped
- 3 eggs, beaten
- 1 tablespoon pork rinds
- 1 jalapeno pepper, chopped
- 1 tablespoon cream cheese
- ¼ teaspoon garlic powder
- 1 teaspoon dried oregano
- ½ teaspoon salt
- 1 tablespoon coconut oil
- ½ teaspoon onion powder

Directions:
Put the salmon fillet in the food processor. Add egg, pork rinds, jalapeno pepper, cream cheese, garlic powder, dried oregano, salt, and onion powder. Blend the mixture until smooth. Then with the help of the scooper make the small poppers. Toss the coconut oil in the instant pot and melt it on sauté mode. Then place the salmon poppers in the instant pot in one layer. Cook the meal for 3 minutes from each side or until it is light brown. Dry the cooked salmon poppers with the help of the paper towels if needed.

Nutrition: calories 135, fat 8.8, fiber 0.2, carbs 0.8, protein 13.7

Haddock and Cilantro Sauce

Preparation time: 10 minutes
Cooking time: 15 minutes
Servings: 4
Ingredients:
- 4 haddock fillets, skinless, boneless and cubed
- 3 teaspoons Italian seasoning
- 2 tablespoons cilantro, chopped
- 2 tomatoes, cubed
- 1 cup heavy cream
- 1 tablespoon lemon juice
- 1 tablespoon avocado oil

Directions:
Set the instant pot on Sauté mode, add the oil, heat it up, add the cilantro, tomatoes, and the rest of the ingredients except the fish, whisk and simmer for 4 minutes. Add the fish, put the lid on and cook on High for 10 minutes. Release the pressure naturally for 10 minutes, divide everything between plates and serve.
Nutrition: calories 299, fat 14.1, fiber 0.9, carbs 3.9, protein 36.7

Tuna Rolls

Preparation time: 20 minutes
Cooking time: 20 minutes
Servings: 4
Ingredients:
- 4 kale leaves
- 10 oz tuna, canned
- ½ white onion, minced
- 1 teaspoon ground coriander
- ½ teaspoon salt
- ½ teaspoon ground paprika
- ¼ teaspoon ground nutmeg
- 2 oz leek, chopped
- 1 teaspoon avocado oil
- 1 cup water, for cooking

Directions:
Pour avocado oil in the instant pot. Add chopped leek and minced white onion. Cook the vegetables on sauté mode for 5 minutes. Stir the mixture from time to time with the help of the spatula. Then add tuba, salt, ground coriander, ground paprika, ground nutmeg, and mix up well. Then transfer the mixture in the bowl and clean the instant pot. Pour water and insert the steamer rack in the instant pot. Then fill every kale leaf with tuna mix tuna mixture and roll. Arrange the tuna rolls on the rack and close the lid. Cook the tuna rolls on manual mode (high pressure) for 15 minutes. Then allow the natural pressure release for 10 minutes.
Nutrition: calories 157, fat 6, fiber 1, carbs 5.3, protein 19.7

Tilapia and Red Sauce

Preparation time: 10 minutes
Cooking time: 20 minutes
Servings: 4
Ingredients:
- 4 tilapia fillets, boneless
- A pinch of salt and black pepper
- 2 tablespoons avocado oil
- 1 tablespoon lemon juice
- 2 spring onions, minced
- ½ cup chicken stock
- ¼ cup tomato passata
- 1 teaspoon garlic powder
- 1 teaspoon oregano, dried
- 1 cup roasted red peppers, chopped
- 10 ounces canned tomatoes and chilies, chopped

Directions:
Set the instant pot on Sauté mode, add the oil, heat it up, add the onions and cook for 2 minutes. Add the rest of the ingredients except the fish and simmer everything for 8 minutes more. Add the fish, put the lid on and cook on High for 10 minutes. Release the pressure naturally for 10 minutes, divide everything between plates and serve.
Nutrition: calories 184, fat 2.2, fiber 1.6, carbs 1.9, protein 22.2

Fish Sticks

Preparation time: 15 minutes
Cooking time: 7 minutes
Servings: 2
Ingredients:
- 8 oz tilapia fillet
- ¼ cup coconut flakes
- 1 egg, beaten
- ¼ teaspoon chili flakes
- ¼ teaspoon ground nutmeg
- 1 tablespoon sesame oil
- 1 cup water, for cooking

Directions:
Cut the tilapia fillet into 2 sticks. Then pour water and insert the steamer rack in the instant pot. Line the rack with foil and place the tilapia sticks on it. Close the lid and cook them for 3 minutes on manual mode (high pressure). When the time is over, make a quick pressure release and open the lid. Dip the cooked fish sticks in the egg and then coat in the coconut flakes. Clean the instant pot and remove the steamer rack. Pour sesame oil in the instant pot and place the tilapia sticks. Cook them for 1 minute from each side on sauté mode or until the fish sticks are light brown.
Nutrition: calories 222, fat 13.5, fiber 1, carbs 1.8, protein 24.2

Lime Cod Mix

Preparation time: 10 minutes
Cooking time: 15 minutes
Servings: 4
Ingredients:
- 4 cod fillets, boneless
- ½ teaspoon cumin, ground
- A pinch of salt and black pepper
- 1 tablespoon olive oil
- ½ cup chicken stock
- 3 tablespoons cilantro, chopped
- 2 tablespoons lime juice
- 2 teaspoons lime zest, grated

Directions:
Set the instant pot on Sauté mode, add the oil, heat it up, add the cod and cook for 1 minute on each side. Add the remaining ingredients, put the lid on and cook on High for 13 minutes. Release the pressure

naturally for 10 minutes, divide the mix between plates and serve.
Nutrition: calories 187, fat 13.1, fiber 0.2, carbs 1.6, protein 16.1

Crab Rangoon Dip

Preparation time: 10 minutes
Cooking time: 1.5 hours
Servings: 4
Ingredients:
- 1 teaspoon Erythritol
- 3 tablespoons cream cheese
- 1 tablespoon chives, chopped
- ½ cup whipped cream
- 6 oz crab meat, chopped
- ¼ teaspoon garlic powder

Directions:
Place all ingredients in the instant pot and stir well. Close the lid and cook the dip on manual (low pressure) for 1.5 hours.
Nutrition: calories 109, fat 8, fiber 0, carbs 2.8, protein 6.3

Salmon and Shrimp Mix

Preparation time: 5 minutes
Cooking time: 20 minutes
Servings: 4
Ingredients:
- 4 salmon fillets, boneless
- 1 pound shrimp, peeled and deveined
- 1 teaspoon Cajun seasoning
- A pinch of salt and black pepper
- 2 tablespoons olive oil
- Juice of 1 lemon
- ½ cup chicken stock
- 2 tablespoons tomato passata

Directions:
Set the instant pot on Sauté mode, add the oil, heat it up, add the rest of the ingredients except the salmon and the shrimp and cook for 3 minutes. Add the salmon and cook for 2 minutes on each side. Add the shrimp, put the lid on and cook on High for 10 minutes. Release the pressure fast for 5 minutes, divide the mix between plates and serve.
Nutrition: calories 393, fat 20, fiber 0.1, carbs 2.2, protein 25

Coriander Seabass

Preparation time: 7 minutes
Cooking time: 5 minutes
Servings: 4
Ingredients:
- 1 teaspoon ground coriander
- ½ teaspoon salt
- ½ teaspoon ground black pepper
- 12 oz Seabass fillet
- 1 cup water, for cooking

Directions:
In the shallow bowl combine together salt, ground coriander, and ground black pepper. Cut the fish fillet into 4 servings. Pour water and insert the steamer rack in the instant pot. Line the steamer rack with baking paper and place the Seabass on it. Sprinkle the fish with coriander mixture and close the lid. Cook the Seabass on manual mode (high pressure) for 5 minutes. When the time is over, make a quick pressure release.
Nutrition: calories 106, fat 6.3, fiber 0.7, carbs 5.2, protein 8

Salmon and Green Beans

Preparation time: 10 minutes
Cooking time: 20 minutes
Servings: 4
Ingredients:
- 4 salmon fillets, boneless
- A pinch of salt and black pepper
- ½ teaspoon sweet paprika
- ½ teaspoon mustard
- ½ teaspoon garlic powder
- 1 tablespoon olive oil
- 1 teaspoon tarragon, dried
- A pinch of salt and black pepper
- ¼ teaspoon dill, chopped
- 1 tablespoons ghee, melted
- ½ cup chicken stock
- 1 pound green beans, trimmed and halved

Directions:
Set the instant pot on Sauté mode, add the oil, heat it up, add the rest of the ingredients except the fish and cook for 5 minutes. Add the fish, put the lid on and cook on High for 15 minutes. Release the pressure naturally for 10 minutes, divide everything between plates and serve.
Nutrition: calories 334, fat 18, fiber 4.3, carbs 5.6, protein 23.7

Dill Halibut

Preparation time: 15 minutes
Cooking time: 8 minutes
Servings: 2
Ingredients:
- 1 tablespoon dried dill
- 2 tablespoons butter, softened
- 10 oz halibut steaks (5 oz each steak)
- ¼ teaspoon salt
- ¼ teaspoon ground paprika
- ¼ cup heavy cream

Directions:
Place butter and dill in the instant pot. Add salt and ground paprika. Melt the mixture on sauté mode. Then add heavy cream and halibut steaks. Close and seal the lid. Cook the fish on manual mode (high pressure) for 2 minutes. When the time is over, allow the natural pressure release for 10 minutes. Serve the fish with hot dill-butter sauce.
Nutrition: calories 348, fat 21.2, fiber 0.3, carbs 1.4, protein 36.8

Cod and Asparagus

Preparation time: 10 minutes
Cooking time: 15 minutes
Servings: 4
Ingredients:
- 4 cod fillets, boneless and skinless
- 2 tablespoons lemon juice
- A pinch of salt and black pepper
- 1 tablespoon parsley, chopped
- 2 tablespoons ghee, melted
- ¼ cup chicken stock
- 1 pound asparagus, trimmed

- ½ teaspoon garlic powder
- 2 teaspoons capers, drained

Directions:
Set the instant pot on Sauté mode, add the ghee, heat it up, add the asparagus and the rest of the ingredients except the fish, and cook for 5 minutes. Add the fish, put the lid on and cook on High for 10 minutes. Release the pressure naturally for 10 minutes, divide everything between plates and serve.
Nutrition: calories 237, fat 16.1, fiber 2.5, carbs 6.2, protein 18.6

Spinach and Tilapia Casserole

Preparation time: 20 minutes
Cooking time: 8 minutes
Servings: 6
Ingredients:
- 1-pound tilapia fillet
- 2 cups fresh spinach, chopped
- 4 teaspoons butter
- ¼ cup cream cheese
- 1 cup Cheddar cheese, shredded
- ½ cup heavy cream
- 1 teaspoon salt
- 1 teaspoon ground black pepper
- ½ teaspoon cayenne pepper
- 1 teaspoon dried oregano

Directions:
Chop the tilapia fillet roughly. In the mixing bowl combine together dried oregano, cayenne pepper, ground black pepper, and salt. Then grease the instant pot bowl with butter and place fresh spinach inside. After this, add cream cheese and chopped tilapia. Sprinkle the fish with Cheddar cheese and heavy cream. Close the lid and cook casserole on manual mode (high pressure) for 8 minutes. When the time is over, allow the natural pressure release for 10 minutes.
Nutrition: calories 233, fat 16.6, fiber 0.5, carbs 1.6, protein 20.1

Turmeric Shrimp Mix

Preparation time: 5 minutes
Cooking time: 8 minutes
Servings: 4
Ingredients:
- 2 pounds shrimp, peeled and deveined
- A pinch of salt and black pepper
- ½ cup chicken stock
- 1 tablespoon avocado oil
- 1 teaspoon turmeric powder
- 1 tablespoon parsley, chopped

Directions:
Set the instant pot on Sauté mode, add the oil, heat it up, add all the ingredients, toss, put the lid on and cook on High for 8 minutes. Release the pressure fast for 5 minutes, divide the mix between plates and serve.
Nutrition: calories 278, fat 4.4, fiber 0.3, carbs 3.4, protein 27.5

Fish Pie

Preparation time: 15 minutes
Cooking time: 21 minutes
Servings: 5
Ingredients:
- 12 oz Pollock, chopped
- ½ cup heavy cream
- ½ white onion, diced
- 3 celery stalks, chopped
- 1 bay leaf
- ½ cup broccoli, chopped
- ¼ cup green peas
- ½ teaspoon salt
- ½ teaspoon ground black pepper
- 1 tablespoon dried parsley
- 1 teaspoon butter
- ½ cup almond meal
- 1 egg, beaten
- 1 tablespoon coconut oil, melted

Directions:
In the mixing bowl combine together egg, almond meal, and coconut oil Knead the dough. Place it in the freezer. After this, place all remaining ingredients in the instant pot and stir well. Close the lid and cook the mixture on sauté mode for 15 minutes. Then stir it well. Grate the frozen almond dough with the help of the grated. Then top the fish mixture with the grated dough and close the lid. Cook the fish pie on manual (high pressure) for 6 minutes. When the time is over, make a quick pressure release and open the lid. Cool the fish pie little and only after this cut it into the servings.
Nutrition: calories 236, fat 14.5, fiber 2.3, carbs 5.8, protein 21.2

Cod and Basil Tomato Passata

Preparation time: 10 minutes
Cooking time: 12 minutes
Servings: 4
Ingredients:
- 1 pound cod, skinless, boneless and cubed
- 2 tablespoons avocado oil
- 2 garlic cloves, minced
- 10 ounces canned tomatoes, chopped
- 2 tablespoons basil, chopped
- ½ cup veggie stock

Directions:
Set your instant pot on Sauté mode, add the oil, heat it up, add the garlic, stir and brown for 2 minutes. Add the rest of the ingredients, put the lid on and cook on High for 10 minutes. Release the pressure naturally for 10 minutes, divide the mix into bowls and serve.
Nutrition: calories 240, fat 10.7, fiber 1.2, carbs 3.7, protein 31.1

Mackerel Pate

Preparation time: 10 minutes
Cooking time: 5 minutes
Servings: 5
Ingredients:
- 12 oz mackerel fillet
- 1 teaspoon mustard
- 1 teaspoon lemon juice
- 2 tablespoons cream cheese
- 1 teaspoon butter, softened
- 1 cup water, for cooking

Directions:
Pour water and insert the steamer rack in the instant pot. Place the mackerel fillet on the rack and close the lid. Cook the fish on manual mode (high pressure) for 5 minutes. Then make a quick pressure release

and open the lid. Transfer the cooked mackerel in the food processor. Add mustard, lemon juice, cream cheese, and butter. Blend the mixture until smooth. Transfer the cooked pate in the bowl and store it in the fridge for up to 4 days.
Nutrition: calories 202, fat 14.5, fiber 0.1, carbs 0.4, protein 16.7

Shrimp and Lemon Green Beans Mix
Preparation time: 10 minutes
Cooking time: 12 minutes
Servings: 4
Ingredients:
- 1 pound shrimp, peeled and deveined
- ½ cup chicken stock
- ½ pound green beans, trimmed and halved
- 1 tablespoon lemon zest, grated
- 1 cup tomato passata
- 1 tablespoon oregano, chopped
- A pinch of salt and black pepper
- 1 tablespoon lemon juice

Directions:
In your instant pot, combine all the ingredients, put the lid on and cook on Low for 12 minutes. Release the pressure naturally for 10 minutes, divide the mix between plates and serve.
Nutrition: calories 174, fat 2.3, fiber 1.2, carbs 1.5, protein 28

Crab Rangoon Fat Bombs
Preparation time: 10 minutes
Cooking time: 7 minutes
Servings: 2
Ingredients:
- 2 bacon slices, chopped
- 5 oz crab meat, canned, chopped
- ¼ cup Cheddar cheese, shredded
- ½ teaspoon garlic powder
- ¼ teaspoon onion powder
- ¼ teaspoon ground black pepper

Directions:
Put the chopped bacon in the instant pot and cook it on sauté mode until golden brown (appx. 5-7 minutes). Stir the bacon from time to time. Meanwhile, in the mixing bowl combine together crab meat, Cheddar cheese, garlic powder, onion powder, and ground black pepper. Stir the mixture with the help of the spoon until homogenous. Cool the cooked bacon to the room temperature. With the help of the scooper make the small balls from the crab meat mixture. Coat every crab ball in the chopped bacon.
Nutrition: calories 227, fat 13.9, fiber 0.2, carbs 2.6, protein 19.6

Herbed Haddock Mix
Preparation time: 10 minutes
Cooking time: 15 minutes
Servings: 4
Ingredients:
- 2 tablespoons olive oil
- 2 garlic cloves, minced
- ½ cup chicken stock
- 2 tablespoons tomato passata
- A pinch of salt and black pepper
- 1 pound haddock fillets, boneless
- 1 cup red bell pepper, chopped
- ¼ cup tarragon, chopped
- ¼ cup parsley, chopped

Directions:
Set your instant pot on Sauté mode, add the oil, heat it up, add the garlic and the rest of the ingredients except the haddock, stir and cook for 5 minutes. Add the fish, put the lid on and cook on High for 10 minutes. Release the pressure naturally for 10 minutes, divide everything between plates and serve.
Nutrition: calories 209, fat 8.4, fiber 0.8, carbs 4.4, protein 28.6

Crab&Broccoli Casserole
Preparation time: 20 minutes
Cooking time: 10 minutes
Servings: 3
Ingredients:
- ½ cup broccoli florets
- 6 oz crab meat, chopped
- 1 cup Cheddar cheese
- 2 tablespoons ricotta cheese
- ½ teaspoon dried dill
- ½ teaspoon dried parsley
- ½ teaspoon dried oregano
- ½ teaspoon ground black pepper
- ¼ cup of coconut milk
- ½ teaspoon salt
- 1 cup water, for cooking

Directions:
Mix up together crab meat with ricotta cheese. Then place the mixture in the instant pot casserole mold in one layer. Top it with broccoli florets and sprinkle with dill, parsley, oregano, ground black pepper, and salt. Then top the vegetables with Cheddar cheese and coconut milk. Pour water and insert the steamer rack in the instant pot. Place the casserole mold over the rack and close the lid. Cook the meal on manual mode (high pressure) for 10 minutes. Then allow the natural pressure release for 10 minutes and remove it from the instant pot.
Nutrition: calories 270, fat 19.2, fiber 1.1, carbs 4.6, protein 18.6

Salmon and Garlic Spinach
Preparation time: 10 minutes
Cooking time: 15 minutes
Servings: 4
Ingredients:
- 1 and ½ pounds salmon fillets, boneless, skinless
- 1 pound baby spinach
- 3 garlic cloves, minced
- 1 cup tomato passata
- A pinch of salt and black pepper
- 2 tablespoon avocado oil
- 1 tablespoon sage, chopped

Directions:
Set the instant pot on Sauté mode, add the oil, heat it up, add the garlic and the rest of the ingredients except the fish and the spinach, whisk and cook for 5 minutes. Add the fish and the spinach, put the lid on and cook on High for 10 minutes. Release the pressure naturally for 10 minutes, divide everything between plates and serve.

Nutrition: calories 355, fat 15.4, fiber 3.6, carbs 4.6, protein 26.5

Tuna and Bacon Cups

Preparation time: 15 minutes
Cooking time: 7 minutes
Servings: 4
Ingredients:
- 4 bacon slices
- 10 oz tuna, chopped
- 1 egg, beaten
- 1 teaspoon cream cheese
- ½ teaspoon ground nutmeg
- 2 oz Mozzarella, shredded
- 1 cup water, for cooking

Directions:
In the mixing bowl combine together tuna, egg, cream cheese, ground nutmeg, and Mozzarella. Stir the mixture until homogenous. Arrange the bacon in the shape of the cups in the muffin molds. Then fill every bacon cup with tuna mixture. Pour water and insert the steamer rack in the instant pot. Place the muffin molds with bacon cups in the instant pot and close the lid. Cook the meal on manual mode (high pressure) for 7 minutes. When the time is over, make a quick pressure release and open the lid. Cool the meal little and remove it from the molds.

Nutrition: calories 295, fat 17.7, fiber 0.1, carbs 1, protein 31.3

Thyme Crab and Spinach

Preparation time: 5 minutes
Cooking time: 14 minutes
Servings: 4
Ingredients:
- 1 tablespoon avocado oil
- 3 cups crab meat
- 1 cup chicken stock
- 2 tablespoons tomato passata
- ½ pound baby spinach
- 1 cup green bell pepper, chopped
- 4 garlic cloves, chopped
- 1 cup tomatoes, cubed
- 2 teaspoons thyme, dried
- A pinch of salt and black pepper

Directions:
Set the instant pot on Sauté mode, add the oil, heat it up, add the garlic, bell pepper and the rest of the ingredients except the crab and the spinach, stir and simmer for 4 minutes. Add the crab and the spinach, put the lid on and cook on High for 10 minutes. Release the pressure fast for 5 minutes, divide the mix between plates and serve.

Nutrition: calories 64, fat 1.4, fiber 0.2, carbs 0.4, protein 5.5

Halibut Ceviche

Preparation time: 20 minutes
Cooking time: 1 minute
Servings: 2
Ingredients:
- 6 oz halibut fillet
- 1 tomato, chopped
- ¼ red onion, diced
- 1 tablespoon fresh cilantro, chopped
- ½ jalapeno pepper, chopped
- ¼ teaspoon minced garlic
- 2 tablespoons lemon juice
- ¼ teaspoon salt
- ¼ teaspoon ground black pepper
- 1 teaspoon avocado oil
- 1 cup water, for cooking

Directions:
Pour water and insert the steamer rack in the instant pot. Line it with the baking paper and place the halibut fillet on it. Close the lid and cook fish for 1 minute on manual mode (high pressure). When the time is over, make a quick pressure release and open the lid. Cool the fish well. Meanwhile, in the mixing bowl combine together tomato, onion, cilantro, jalapeno pepper, and minced garlic. Then sprinkle the halibut with lemon juice, avocado oil, and ground black pepper. Massage the fish gently and leave for 10 minutes to marinate. Then chop the halibut roughly and add in the mixing bowl. Shake the cooked meal gently and transfer in the serving glasses.

Nutrition: calories 115, fat 2.5, fiber 1, carbs 3.5, protein 18.7

Smoked Crab and Cod Mix

Preparation time: 10 minutes
Cooking time: 12 minutes
Servings: 6
Ingredients:
- 1 pound crab meat
- 1 cup chicken stock
- 1 pound cod fillets, boneless, skinless and cubed
- 2 tablespoons olive oil
- 1 tablespoon smoked paprika
- A pinch of salt and black pepper
- 2 garlic cloves, minced
- 1 tablespoon oregano, chopped
- ½ cup tomato passata

Directions:
Set the instant pot on Sauté mode, add the oil, heat it up, add the garlic and the rest of the ingredients except the cod and the crab, whisk and cook for 5 minutes. Add the crab and the rest of the ingredients, put the lid on and cook on High for 7 minutes. Release the pressure naturally for 10 minutes, divide the mix between plates and serve.

Nutrition: calories 300, fat 15.7, fiber 1.6, carbs 3.5, protein 21.5

Parchment Fish

Preparation time: 15 minutes
Cooking time: 10 minutes
Servings: 4
Ingredients:
- 1-pound salmon fillet
- 4 lemon slices
- ½ teaspoon salt
- 1 teaspoon dried thyme
- ½ teaspoon dried rosemary
- ½ white onion, sliced
- 1 tablespoon avocado oil
- 1 teaspoon butter
- ½ teaspoon cayenne pepper
- 1 cup water, for cooking

Directions:

Pour water and insert the steamer rack in the instant pot. Then place the sliced onion on the parchment. Top it with a salmon fillet. Sprinkle the fish with dried thyme, rosemary, and salt. Then top the fish with lemon slices, cayenne pepper, and butter. Sprinkle the ingredients with avocado oil and wrap in the shape of the packet. Place the fish packet on the rack and close the lid. Cook the meal on manual (high pressure) for 10 minutes. When the time is over, allow the natural pressure release for 10 minutes. Remove the cooked meal from the instant pot.
Nutrition: calories 173, fat 8.5, fiber 0.9, carbs 2.5, protein 22.3

Rosemary Tilapia and Pine Nuts

Preparation time: 10 minutes
Cooking time: 15 minutes
Servings: 4
Ingredients:
- 4 tilapia fillets, skinless and boneless
- ¼ cup avocado oil
- Juice of 1 lime
- 1 tablespoon lime zest, grated
- 4 garlic cloves, minced
- ½ cup pine nuts
- 1 tablespoon rosemary, chopped
- A pinch of salt and black pepper
- 1 cup chicken stock
- 1 teaspoon sweet paprika

Directions:
Set the instant pot on Sauté mode, add the oil, heat it up, add the garlic and the rest of the ingredients except the fish, whisk and cook for 5 minutes. Add the fish, put the lid on and cook on High for 10 minutes. Release the pressure naturally for 10 minutes, divide the mix between plates and serve.
Nutrition: calories 170, fat 14, fiber 2, carbs 5.3, protein 8.3

Poached Cod

Preparation time: 15 minutes
Cooking time: 10 minutes
Servings: 4
Ingredients:
- 1-pound cod fillet
- 1 tablespoon avocado oil
- ¾ teaspoon salt
- 1 teaspoon Italian seasonings
- 1 teaspoon ground black pepper
- 1 cup of water

Directions:
In the shallow bowl combine together avocado oil, salt, Italian seasonings, and ground black pepper. Then rub the cod fillet with a spice mixture from both sides and leave for 10 minutes to marinate. Meanwhile, pour water and insert the steamer rack in the instant pot. Line the rack with baking paper. Then place the cod on the rack and close the lid. Cook the fish on steam mode for 10 minutes. Then make a quick pressure release.
Nutrition: calories 101, fat 1.8, fiber 0.3, carbs 0.7, protein 20.4

Crab, Spinach and Chives

Preparation time: 10 minutes
Cooking time: 10 minutes
Servings: 4
Ingredients:
- 1 pound crab meat
- 1 cup baby spinach
- 1 cup chicken stock
- ¼ cup tomato passata
- 1 tablespoon olive oil
- 1 tablespoon chives, chopped

Directions:
In your instant pot, combine the crab meat with the spinach and the rest of the ingredients, put the lid on and cook on High for 10 minutes. Release the pressure naturally for 10 minutes, divide the mix between plates and serve.
Nutrition: calories 139, fat 5.7, fiber 0.4, carbs 3.3, protein 14.2

Light Shrimp Pad Thai

Preparation time: 10 minutes
Cooking time: 12 minutes
Servings: 4
Ingredients:
- ½ white onion, diced
- 1 egg, beaten
- 1 teaspoon coconut oil
- 1-pound shrimps, peeled
- 1 teaspoon dried cilantro
- 1 tablespoon walnuts, chopped
- 1 teaspoon minced garlic
- 1 teaspoon apple cider vinegar
- 1 teaspoon stevia

Directions:
Toss coconut oil in the instant pot and melt it for 2 minutes on sauté mode. Then add onion and cook it on sauté mode for 4 minutes or until onion is light brown. Then add shrimps and mix up well. Cook the ingredients for 2 minutes more. Stir well and sprinkle with cilantro, minced garlic, and stevia. Stir well and cook for 2 minutes more. After this, add the apple cider vinegar. Stir well. Then add walnuts and beaten egg. Whisk the mixture and cook for 3 minutes.
Nutrition: calories 179, fat 5.3, fiber 0.4, carbs 3.5, protein 27.9

Chili Haddock and Tomatoes

Preparation time: 10 minutes
Cooking time: 15 minutes
Servings: 4
Ingredients:
- 4 haddock fillets, boneless
- 1 tablespoon red chili powder
- A pinch of salt and black pepper
- ½ cup chicken stock
- 1 cup tomatoes, cubed
- 4 garlic cloves, minced
- 2 tablespoons avocado oil
- 1 tablespoon chives, chopped

Directions:
Set the instant pot on Sauté mode, add the oil, heat it up, add the garlic and the rest of the ingredients except the fish and the chives, whisk and cook for 5 minutes. Add the fish, put the lid on and cook on High for 10 minutes. Release the pressure naturally for 10

minutes, divide the mix into bowls and serve with the chives sprinkled on top.
Nutrition: calories 197, fat 2.8, fiber 1.5, carbs 2.2, protein 26.4

Coated Coconut Shrimps

Preparation time: 10 minutes
Cooking time: 10 minutes
Servings: 4
Ingredients:
- 4 king shrimps, peeled
- 1 egg, beaten
- 1 teaspoon cream cheese
- ¼ teaspoon cayenne pepper
- ½ cup coconut flakes
- ½ teaspoon salt
- 2 tablespoons coconut oil

Directions:
Mix up together coconut flakes with cayenne pepper and salt. In the separated bowl mix up together the egg with cream cheese. Then dip the shrimps in the egg mixture and coat in the coconut mixture. Repeat the same step one more time. Toss the coconut oil in the instant pot and melt it for minutes on sauté mode. Then arrange the prepared shrimps and cook them on sauté mode for 3 minutes from each side or until they are light brown.
Nutrition: calories 134, fat 11.5, fiber 0.9, carbs 1.7, protein 6.2

Tuna and Green Beans Mix

Preparation time: 10 minutes
Cooking time: 12 minutes
Servings: 4
Ingredients:
- 1 pound tuna, skinless, boneless and cubed
- 1 pound green beans, trimmed
- 1 and ½ cups tomato passata
- 1 tablespoons olive oil
- ½ teaspoon sweet paprika
- 1 teaspoon oregano, dried
- Salt and black pepper to the taste

Directions:
Set your instant pot on Sauté mode, add the oil, heat it up, add the green beans and the rest of the ingredients except the tuna, stir and cook for 5 minutes. Add the tuna, put the lid on and cook on High for 7 minutes. Release the pressure naturally for 10 minutes, divide the mix into bowls and serve.
Nutrition: calories 278, fat 12.7, fiber 3.6, carbs 4.5, protein 27.5

Steamed Crab Legs

Preparation time: 12 minutes
Cooking time: 5 minutes
Servings: 3
Ingredients:
- 10 oz crab legs
- 1 cup water, for cooking

Directions:
Pour water and insert the trivet in the instant pot. Arrange the crab legs on the trivet and close the lid. Cook the meal on steam mode for 5 minutes. When the time is over, allow the natural pressure release for 10 minutes. Remove the cooked crab legs from the instant pot.
Nutrition: calories 95, fat 1.4, fiber 0, carbs 0, protein 18.1

Chipotle Tilapia Mix

Preparation time: 10 minutes
Cooking time: 15 minutes
Servings: 4
Ingredients:
- 4 tilapia fillets, boneless
- 2 garlic cloves, minced
- 1 teaspoon chipotle chili powder
- 2 spring onions, chopped
- ½ tablespoon lime juice
- A pinch of salt and black pepper
- 1 tablespoon olive oil
- 1 cup chicken stock
- 1 tablespoon parsley, chopped
- 2 tablespoons tomato passata

Directions:
Set your instant pot on Sauté mode, add the oil, heat it up, add the garlic, chili powder and the rest of the ingredients except the tilapia and the parsley, stir and cook for 5 minutes. Add the fish, put the lid on and cook on High for 10 minutes. Release the pressure naturally for 10 minutes, divide the mix between plates and serve with the parsley sprinkled on top.
Nutrition: calories 250, fat 14.9, fiber 0.4, carbs 5.5, protein 13.9

Salmon with Lemon

Preparation time: 15 minutes
Cooking time: 10 minutes
Servings: 2
Ingredients:
- 10 oz salmon fillet
- 4 lemon slices
- 1 teaspoon salt
- 1 teaspoon butter, softened
- 1 cup water, for cooking

Directions:
Rub the salmon fillet with salt and softened butter. Then pour water and insert the trivet in the instant pot. Line the trivet with baking paper and place the salmon fillet on it. Top the salmon with the lemon slices and close the lid. Cook the meal for 10 minutes on Steam mode. When the time is over, allow the natural pressure release and open the lid. Cut the cooked salmon into the servings.
Nutrition: calories 208, fat 10.7, fiber 0.4, carbs 1.3, protein 27.7

Ginger Halibut

Preparation time: 10 minutes
Cooking time: 15 minutes
Servings: 4
Ingredients:
- 4 halibut fillets, boneless
- 1 cup tomatoes, chopped
- 1 tablespoon ginger, grated
- ¼ cup chicken stock
- 1 tablespoon sweet paprika
- 1 tablespoon chives, chopped

Directions:
Set the instant pot on Sauté mode, add the ginger and the rest of the ingredients except the fish, toss and

cook for 3 minutes. Add the fish, put the lid on and cook on High for 12 minutes. Release the pressure naturally for 10 minutes, divide the mix between plates and serve.
Nutrition: calories 337, fat 7.1, fiber 1.4, carbs 3.8, protein 18.6

Zingy Fish
Preparation time: 10 minutes
Cooking time: 15 minutes
Servings: 4
Ingredients:
- 1 cup broccoli florets
- 1-pound coley fillet, chopped
- 3 tablespoons apple cider vinegar
- 1 orange slice
- 1 tablespoon olive oil
- 1 cup water, for cooking

Directions:
In the mixing bowl combine together broccoli florets, coley fillet, apple cider vinegar, and olive oil. Chop the orange slice and add it in the fish mixture. Shake the fish mixture well and place it in the instant pot mold. Pour water and insert the steamer rack. Place the mold with the fish mixture in the instant pot and close the lid. Cook the meal on steam mode for 15 minutes. When the time is over, make a quick pressure release
Nutrition: calories 169, fat 4.7, fiber 0.6, carbs 4, protein 26.7

Halibut and Brussels Sprouts
Preparation time: 5 minutes
Cooking time: 12 minutes
Servings: 4
Ingredients:
- 4 halibut fillets, boneless and skinless
- 1 pound Brussels sprouts, halved
- 2 garlic cloves, minced
- 1 tablespoon avocado oil
- 1 cup tomato passata
- A pinch of salt and black pepper
- 1 tablespoon parsley, chopped

Directions:
Set the instant pot on Sauté mode, add the oil, heat it up, add the garlic and cook for 2 minutes Add the rest of the ingredients, put the lid on and cook on High for 10 minutes. Release the pressure fast for 5 minutes, divide everything between plates and serve.
Nutrition: calories 389, fat 7.7, fiber 5.4, carbs 6.1, protein 18.7

Thyme Cod
Preparation time: 10 minutes
Cooking time: 10 minutes
Servings: 2
Ingredients:
- 8 oz cod fillet
- 1 teaspoon dried thyme
- ½ teaspoon garlic powder
- 1 teaspoon sesame oil
- 1 cup water, for cooking

Directions:
Rub the cod fillet with dried thyme, and garlic powder. Then sprinkle the fish with sesame oil. Wrap it in the foil. Pour water and insert the steamer rack in the instant pot. Place the wrapped fish in the instant pot and close the lid. Cook the meal on manual mode (high pressure) for 10 minutes. When the time is over, make a quick pressure release and remove it from the instant pot.
Nutrition: calories 115, fat 3.3, fiber 0.3, carbs 0.8, protein 20.4

Creamy Catfish
Preparation time: 10 minutes
Cooking time: 12 minutes
Servings: 4
Ingredients:
- 1 pound catfish fillets, boneless, skinless and cubed
- 1 and ½ cups coconut milk
- 2 garlic cloves, minced
- 1 tablespoon ginger, grated
- ½ teaspoon yellow curry paste
- A pinch of salt and black pepper
- 2 tablespoons lime juice
- 1 tablespoon parsley, chopped

Directions:
In your instant pot, mix the fish with the coconut milk and the rest of the ingredients except the parsley, put the lid on and cook on High for 12 minutes. Release the pressure naturally for 10 minutes, divide everything into bowls and serve.
Nutrition: calories 274, fat 14.4, fiber 0.9, carbs 4.5, protein 16.9

Mussels Mariniere
Preparation time: 10 minutes
Cooking time: 8 minutes
Servings: 5
Ingredients:
- 2 garlic cloves, diced
- 1 white onion, diced
- 1 tablespoon fresh parsley, chopped
- 1 cup chicken broth
- ¼ cup of coconut milk
- 1 tablespoon avocado oil
- 1 tablespoon lemon juice
- 1-pound fresh mussels

Directions:
Pour avocado oil in the instant pot. Add diced garlic and onion. Cook the vegetables on sauté mode for 4 minutes. Stir them after 2 minutes of cooking. Then add parsley, lemon juice, and coconut milk. Mix up the mixture and cook it for 1 minute. Add mussels and chicken broth, Close the lid and cook the meal on manual mode (high pressure) for 3 minutes. When the time is over, make a quick pressure release.
Nutrition: calories 129, fat 5.6, fiber 0.9, carbs 6.9, protein 12.4

Ketogenic Instant Pot Poultry Recipes

Oregano Chicken

Preparation time: 10 minutes
Cooking time: 20 minutes
Servings: 4
Ingredients:
- 2 chicken breasts, skinless, boneless and cubed
- 1 cup tomato passata
- ½ cup chicken stock
- 1 tablespoon oregano, chopped
- A pinch of salt and black pepper
- 1 teaspoon sweet paprika
- 1 tablespoon cilantro, chopped

Directions:
In your instant pot, combine all the ingredients, toss, put the lid on and cook on High for 20 minutes. Release the pressure naturally for 10 minutes, divide the mix between plates and serve.
Nutrition: calories 183, fat 2.5, fiber 1.2, carbs 1.5, protein 13.4

Chicken Tonnato

Preparation time: 20 minutes
Cooking time: 15 minutes
Servings: 4
Ingredients:
- 1 teaspoon capers
- 2 oz tuna, canned
- ½ teaspoon minced garlic
- 1 teaspoon dried oregano
- 1 teaspoon lemon juice
- 1 tablespoon fresh basil, chopped
- 4 tablespoons ricotta cheese
- 2 tablespoons avocado oil
- ¼ teaspoon salt
- ½ teaspoon ground black pepper
- 1-pound chicken breast, skinless, boneless
- 1 cup water, for cooking

Directions:
Pour water in the instant pot and add chicken breast. Close and seal the lid and cook the chicken on manual (high pressure) for 15 minutes. When the time is over, allow the natural pressure release for 10 minutes. Meanwhile, place all remaining ingredients from the list above in the food processor. Blend the mixture until smooth. When the chicken is cooked, remove it from the instant pot and slice into servings. Then arrange the chicken in the plate and top with blended sauce.
Nutrition: calories 189, fat 6.2, fiber 0.6, carbs 1.8, protein 29.8

Spiced Chicken Bites

Preparation time: 10 minutes
Cooking time: 24 minutes
Servings: 4
Ingredients:
- 2 chicken breasts, skinless, boneless and cubed
- 2 tablespoons avocado oil
- ½ teaspoon turmeric powder
- ½ teaspoon cumin, ground
- ½ teaspoon allspice, ground
- ½ teaspoon cinnamon powder
- 1 teaspoon sweet paprika
- 2 tablespoons tomato paste
- 1 cup chicken stock

Directions:
Set your instant pot on Sauté mode, add the oil, heat it up, add the chicken and brown for 2 minutes on each side. Add the rest of the ingredients, put the lid on and cook on High for 20 minutes Release the pressure naturally for 10 minutes, divide the mix between plates and serve.
Nutrition: calories 238, fat 9.7, fiber 1, carbs 2.9, protein 33.3

Paprika Chicken Wings

Preparation time: 10 minutes
Cooking time: 17 minutes
Servings: 4
Ingredients:
- 11 oz chicken wings
- 1 tablespoon ground paprika
- 1 tablespoon avocado oil
- 1 teaspoon ground nutmeg
- 1 teaspoon sage
- 1 cup water, for cooking

Directions:
Place the chicken wings in the bowl and sprinkle with ground paprika, sage, and ground nutmeg. Then sprinkle the chicken wings with avocado oil and mix up with the help of the fingertips. After this, heat up the instant pot on sauté mode for 3 minutes. Then place the chicken wings in the instant pot in one layer. Cook the chicken wings for 2 minutes from each side or until they are light brown. After this, remove the chicken wings and clean the instant pot. Pour water and insert the steamer rack in instant pot. Line the steamer rack with foil and arrange the chicken wings. Cook the chicken on manual mode (high pressure) for 10 minutes. When the time is over, make a quick pressure release.
Nutrition: calories 161, fat 6.7, fiber 1, carbs 1.5, protein 22.9

Coconut Chicken and Peppers

Preparation time: 10 minutes
Cooking time: 24 minutes
Servings: 4
Ingredients:
- 1 cup chicken stock
- A pinch of salt and black pepper
- 1 pound chicken breast, skinless, boneless and cubed
- 1 tablespoon coconut, unsweetened and shredded
- 1 tablespoon oregano, chopped
- ½ pound mixed peppers, cut into strips
- 1 tablespoon chives, chopped
- 1 tablespoon olive oil

Directions:
Set your instant pot on Sauté mode, add the oil, heat it up, add the onion and the chicken and brown for 2 minutes on each side Add the rest of the ingredients, put the lid on and cook on High for 20 minutes Release the pressure naturally for 10 minutes, divide everything between plates and serve.

Nutrition: calories 256, fat 12.6, fiber 0.6, carbs 1.2, protein 33.2

Garlic Chicken Drumsticks

Preparation time: 10 minutes
Cooking time: 25 minutes
Servings: 4
Ingredients:
- 4 chicken drumsticks
- 1 teaspoon minced garlic
- 1 teaspoon garlic powder
- 3 tablespoons butter, melted
- 1 teaspoon dried parsley
- 1 oz Parmesan, grated
- 1 cup water, for cooking

Directions:
Pour water and insert the trivet in the instant pot. Then line it with baking paper. Rub the chicken drumsticks with minced garlic, parsley, and garlic powder. Then brush with butter and place on the trivet. Close the lid and cook the chicken for 15 minutes on manual mode (high pressure. Meanwhile, preheat the instant pot to 365F and line the baking tray with baking paper. When the time is over, make a quick pressure release and transfer the cooked chicken drumsticks in the tray. Top the chicken with Parmesan and place in the preheated oven. Cool the meal for 10 minutes more or until cheese is light brown.

Nutrition: calories 180, fat 12.8, fiber 0.1, carbs 1, protein 15.2

Basil Chili Chicken

Preparation time: 5 minutes
Cooking time: 24 minutes
Servings: 4
Ingredients:
- 1 pound chicken breast, skinless, boneless and cubed
- A pinch of salt and black pepper
- 1 tablespoon chili powder
- 1 cup coconut cream
- 2 teaspoons sweet paprika
- ½ cup chicken stock
- 2 tablespoons basil, chopped

Directions:
In your instant pot, combine the chicken with the rest of the ingredients, toss a bit, put the lid on and cook on High for 24 minutes Release the pressure naturally for 10 minutes, divide the mix between plates and serve.

Nutrition: calories 364, fat 23.2, fiber 2.3, carbs 5.1, protein 35.4

Chicken Provencal

Preparation time: 10 minutes
Cooking time: 17 minutes
Servings: 4
Ingredients:
- 1 tablespoon coconut oil
- 2 oz pancetta, chopped
- 3 oz leek, chopped
- 1-pound chicken fillet, chopped
- ½ teaspoon ground thyme
- ½ teaspoon salt
- ½ teaspoon ground black pepper
- 2 tablespoons apple cider vinegar
- ½ cup mushrooms, sliced
- 1 cup chicken broth

Directions:
Place the coconut oil in the instant pot and melt it on sauté mode. Add pancetta and cook it for 5 minutes. Stir it from time to time. After this, add leek and mix up well. Cook the ingredients for 3 minutes. Then add chicken. Sprinkle the mixture with ground thyme, salt, and ground black pepper. Mix up the ingredients well and cook for 2 minutes. After this, add mushrooms and apple cider vinegar. Add chicken broth and close the lid. Cook the meal on manual mode (high pressure) for 7 minutes. When the time is over, make a quick pressure release and transfer the meal in the serving bowls.

Nutrition: calories 348, fat 18.2, fiber 0.6, carbs 4.1, protein 39.9

Chicken and Oregano Sauce

Preparation time: 10 minutes
Cooking time: 20 minutes
Servings: 4
Ingredients:
- 2 chicken breasts, skinless, boneless and halved
- 1 tablespoon lemon juice
- 2 tablespoons olive oil
- 2 tablespoons oregano, chopped
- 1 cup tomato passata
- 1 teaspoon ginger, grated

Directions:
Set the instant pot on Sauté mode, add the oil, heat it up, add tomato passata and the rest of the ingredients except the chicken, whisk and cook for 5 minutes. Add the chicken, put the lid on and cook on High for 15 minutes. Release the pressure naturally for 10 minutes, divide the mix between plates and serve.

Nutrition: calories 300, fat 15.8, fiber 2, carbs 5.2, protein 33.9

Chicken with Blue Cheese Sauce

Preparation time: 10 minutes
Cooking time: 15 minutes
Servings: 3
Ingredients:
- 12 oz chicken fillet
- 1 teaspoon butter
- ½ teaspoon salt
- ½ teaspoon ground paprika
- ½ teaspoon cayenne pepper
- ½ cup heavy cream
- 2 oz Blue cheese, crumbled
- 1 teaspoon dried cilantro

Directions:
Cut the chicken fillet into 3 servings. Rub every chicken fillet with salt, ground paprika, and cayenne pepper. Then place butter in the instant pot and add chicken fillets. Cook the chicken on sauté mode for 5 minutes from each side. Then add heavy cream and dried cilantro. Cook the mixture for 3 minutes. After this, add Blue cheese and carefully stir the meal. Cook it for 2 minutes.

Nutrition: calories 364, fat 22.6, fiber 0.2, carbs 1.4, protein 37.4

Balsamic Curry Chicken

Preparation time: 10 minutes
Cooking time: 20 minutes
Servings: 4
Ingredients:
- 1 pound chicken breast, skinless, boneless and cubed
- A pinch of salt and black pepper
- 1 cup chicken stock
- 1 cup coconut cream
- 3 garlic cloves, minced
- 1 and ½ tablespoon balsamic vinegar
- 1 tablespoon chives, chopped

Directions:
In your instant pot, combine the chicken with the rest of the ingredients, put the lid on and cook on High for 20 minutes. Release the pressure naturally for 10 minutes, divide the mix between plates and serve.
Nutrition: calories 360, fat 22.1, fiber 1.4, carbs 4.3, protein 34.5

Flying Jacob Casserole

Preparation time: 15 minutes
Cooking time: 25 minutes
Servings: 6
Ingredients:
- 1-pound chicken breast, cooked, chopped
- 1 cup heavy cream
- 4 egg whites, whisked
- ½ cup chili pepper, chopped
- 1 teaspoon Italian seasonings
- 1 tablespoon peanuts, chopped
- ½ teaspoon salt
- 1 teaspoon dried parsley
- 1 cup water, for cooking

Directions:
In the mixing bowl combine together heavy cream with Italian seasonings and dried parsley. Add salt and stir gently. Then place the chopped chicken in the instant pot casserole mold. Flatten it to make the layer. Pour whisked egg mixture over the chicken and flatten it with the help of the spatula. After this, top the mixture with heavy cream mixture and chopped peanuts. Top the meal with chili pepper and cover with the foil. Pour water and insert the steamer rack in the instant pot. Place the casserole on the rack and close the lid. Cook it on manual mode (high pressure) for 25 minutes. When the time is over, make a quick pressure release and open the lid. Remove the foil and cool the casserole for 10-15 minutes.
Nutrition: calories 188, fat 10.5, fiber 1, carbs 3.2, protein 19.6

Chicken and Eggplant Mix

Preparation time: 10 minutes
Cooking time: 20 minutes
Servings: 4
Ingredients:
- 2 chicken breasts, skinless, boneless and halved
- A pinch of salt and black pepper
- 2 eggplants, roughly cubed
- 2 tablespoons olive oil
- 1 cup tomato passata
- 1 tablespoon oregano, dried

Directions:
In your instant pot, combine all the ingredients, put the lid on and cook on High for 20 minutes. Release the pressure naturally for 10 minutes, divide between plates and serve.
Nutrition: calories 362, fat 16.1, fiber 4.4, carbs 5.4, protein 36.4

Chicken Caprese Casserole

Preparation time: 15 minutes
Cooking time: 10 minutes
Servings: 4
Ingredients:
- 11 oz chicken breast, skinless, boneless, chopped
- 1 tablespoon fresh basil, chopped
- 3 teaspoons pesto sauce
- 1 cup Mozzarella cheese, shredded
- 3 tablespoons cream cheese
- ½ cup cherry tomatoes, halved
- ½ teaspoon salt
- ½ teaspoon white pepper
- 1 cup water, for cooking

Directions:
In the mixing bowl combine together chicken breast, basil, salt, white pepper, pesto sauce, and shredded Mozzarella. Add cream cheese and mix up the mixture well. Then place mixture in the casserole mold for instant pot. Then top the mixture with cherry tomatoes and cover with foil. Pour water and insert the steamer rack in the instant pot. Place the casserole on the rack and close the lid. Cook the meal for 10 minutes on steam mode. When the time is over, make a quick pressure release and open the lid. Remove the foil from the casserole. Cool the meal for 10-15 minutes.
Nutrition: calories 157, fat 7.5, fiber 0.4, carbs 1.8, protein 19.7

Sesame Chicken

Preparation time: 10 minutes
Cooking time: 20 minutes
Servings: 4
Ingredients:
- 2 chicken breasts, skinless, boneless and cubed
- A pinch of salt and black pepper
- 1 teaspoon sesame seeds
- 4 garlic cloves, minced
- 1 cup tomato passata
- 1 tablespoon parsley, chopped
- 1 tablespoon oregano, chopped

Directions:
In your instant pot, mix all the ingredients except the sesame seeds, put the lid on and cook on High for 20 minutes. Release the pressure naturally for 10 minutes, divide everything between plates and serve with the sesame seeds sprinkled on top.
Nutrition: calories 243, fat 9, fiber 1.6, carbs 5.4, protein 34.1

Cajun Chicken Salad

Preparation time: 10 minutes
Cooking time: 25 minutes
Servings: 2
Ingredients:
- 8 oz chicken fillet

- 1 teaspoon Cajun seasonings
- 1 teaspoon tomato paste
- ¼ teaspoon salt
- ½ cup chicken broth
- 1 cup radish, chopped
- 1 tablespoon fresh parsley, chopped
- 1 cup lettuce, chopped
- 1 tablespoon olive oil
- ½ teaspoon chili flakes
- 1 teaspoon apple cider vinegar

Directions:
Rub the chicken with Cajun seasonings and place it in the instant pot. Add tomato paste and chicken broth. Stir the mixture gently. Close the lid and cook the chicken on stew mode for 25 minutes. Meanwhile, in the salad bowl combine together chopped radish and lettuce. Sprinkle the vegetables with salt, olive oil, and chili flakes. Add apple cider vinegar and mix up well. When the chicken is cooked, remove it from the instant pot, cool little and chop. Add chopped chicken in the salad bowl. Mix up the salad well with the help of the spoon.
Nutrition: calories 302, fat 15.9, fiber 1.3, carbs 3.7, protein 34.8

Turkey and Spring Onions Mix
Preparation time: 10 minutes
Cooking time: 25 minutes
Servings: 4
Ingredients:
- 1 turkey breast, skinless, boneless and cubed
- 2 tablespoons avocado oil
- 4 spring onions, chopped
- 1 cup tomato passata
- A handful cilantro, chopped
- A pinch of salt and black pepper

Directions:
Set your instant pot on Sauté mode, add the oil, heat it up, add the meat and brown for 5 minutes. Add the rest of the ingredients, put the lid on and cook on High for 20 minutes. Release the pressure naturally for 10 minutes between plates, divide the turkey mix between plates, and serve.
Nutrition: calories 222, fat 6.7, fiber 1.6, carbs 4.8, protein 34.4

Caesar Salad
Preparation time: 10 minutes
Cooking time: 15 minutes
Servings:6
Ingredients:
- 1-pound chicken breast, skinless, boneless
- 1 teaspoon sesame oil
- 2 bacon slices, chopped
- 2 cups lettuce, chopped
- 2 oz Parmesan, grated
- 1 tablespoon heavy cream
- 1 teaspoon cream cheese
- ½ teaspoon mustard
- ¼ teaspoon lemon zest, grated
- ½ garlic clove, diced
- 1 cup water, for cooking

Directions:
Pour water and insert the trivet in the instant pot. Place the chicken on the trivet and close the lid. Cook the chicken for 10 minutes and when the time is over, make a quick pressure release. Open the lid and cool the chicken well. Clean the instant pot and remove the trivet. Place the chopped bacon in the instant pot and cook it on sauté mode for 4 minutes or until crunchy. Stir the bacon from time to time to avoid burning. Meanwhile, chop the chicken roughly and place in the salad bowl. Add lettuce, garlic, and sesame oil. Mix up well. Make the dressing: mix up together heavy cream, mustard, and lemon zest. Add cooked bacon and dressing in the salad. Mix up the salad well. Top the cooked meal with grated Parmesan.
Nutrition: calories 172, fat 8.6, fiber 0.2, carbs 1.3, protein 21.7

Italian Paprika Chicken
Preparation time: 10 minutes
Cooking time: 20 minutes
Servings: 4
Ingredients:
- 1 pound chicken breasts, skinless, boneless and cubed
- A pinch of salt and black pepper
- 1 tablespoon olive oil
- 1 tablespoon sweet paprika
- 1 tablespoon Italian seasoning
- 2 garlic cloves, minced
- 1 and ½ cups chicken stock

Directions:
Set your instant pot on Sauté mode, add the oil, heat it up, add the meat and brown for 5 minutes. Add the rest of the ingredients, put the lid on and cook on High for 15 minutes. Release the pressure naturally for 10 minutes, divide between plates and serve.
Nutrition: calories 264, fat 13.2, fiber 0.7, carbs 1.9, protein 33.2

Hoagie Bowl
Preparation time: 20 minutes
Cooking time: 10 minutes
Servings: 4
Ingredients:
- 4 oz turkey breast, skinless, boneless
- 2 oz salami, chopped
- 3 oz deli ham, chopped
- 4 oz Cheddar cheese, chopped
- ½ cup lettuce, chopped
- 1 tomato, chopped
- 1 pickled banana pepper, chopped
- ¾ red onion, chopped
- 2 tablespoon heavy cream
- 1 teaspoon apple cider vinegar
- 1 teaspoon avocado oil
- ½ teaspoon dried oregano
- ½ teaspoon salt
- 1 cup water, for cooking

Directions:
Pour water and insert the trivet in the instant pot. Place the turkey on the trivet and close the lid. Cook it on manual (high pressure) for 10 minutes. When the time is over, allow the natural pressure release for 10 minutes. Then remove the turkey from the instant pot and cool it well. After this, chop it and transfer it in the mixing bowl. Add salami, deli ham, Cheddar cheese, lettuce, tomato, chopped pickled banana pepper, and onion. Shake the salad gently. In the shallow bowl make the dressing: whisk together

heavy cream, apple cider vinegar, avocado oil, and salt. Then pour the dressing over the salad and mix up well with the help of the spoon.
Nutrition: calories 257, fat 17.9, fiber 1.5, carbs 6, protein 17.9

Tomato Turkey and Sprouts

Preparation time: 10 minutes
Cooking time: 25 minutes
Servings: 4
Ingredients:
- 1 big turkey breast, skinless, boneless and cubed
- 1 tablespoon avocado oil
- 1 pound Brussels sprouts
- 1 teaspoon chili powder
- 1 and ½ cups tomato passata
- 2 tablespoons cilantro, chopped
- A pinch of salt and black pepper

Directions:
Set the instant pot on Sauté mode, add the oil, heat it up, add the meat and brown for 5 minutes. Add the rest of the ingredients, put the lid on and cook on High for 20 minutes. Release the pressure naturally for 10 minutes, divide the mix between plates and serve.
Nutrition: calories 249, fat 6.6, fiber 2.5, carbs 4.5, protein 37.3

BLT Chicken Wrap

Preparation time: 10 minutes
Cooking time: 10 minutes
Servings: 4
Ingredients:
- 4 low carb tortillas
- 4 bacon slices
- 1 cup lettuce, chopped
- 10 oz chicken fillet
- ½ teaspoon salt
- ¼ teaspoon cayenne pepper
- 2 oz Parmesan, grated
- 1 tablespoon heavy cream
- 1 tablespoon lemon juice
- 1 cup water, for cooking

Directions:
Place the bacon in the instant pot and cook it on sauté mode for 3 minutes. Then flip it on another side and cook for 2 minutes more. Place the cooked bacon on the tortillas. Then clean the instant pot and pour water inside. Insert the trivet. Rub the chicken with salt and cayenne pepper and put it in the instant pot. Close the lid. Cook it on steam mode for 10 minutes. Then make a quick pressure release and open the lid. Chop the chicken and put it over the bacon. Add lettuce and Parmesan. In the mixing bowl, mix up together lemon juice and heavy cream. Pour the mixture over Parmesan. Roll the tortillas into the wraps.
Nutrition: calories 379, fat 19.7, fiber 7.1, carbs 13.4, protein 35.3

Chicken, Kale and Artichokes

Preparation time: 10 minutes
Cooking time: 25 minutes
Servings: 4
Ingredients:
- 1 pound chicken breast, skinless, boneless and cubed
- 1 shallot, minced
- 4 garlic cloves, minced
- 1 pound kale, torn
- A pinch of salt and black pepper
- 1 cup canned artichoke hearts, drained
- 1 cup chicken stock
- 2 tablespoons avocado oil

Directions:
Set your instant pot on Sauté mode, add the oil, heat it up, add the shallot, garlic and the chicken and sauté for 5 minutes. Add the rest of the ingredients, toss, put the lid on and cook on High for 20 minutes. Release the pressure naturally for 10 minutes, divide the mix between plates and serve.
Nutrition: calories 288, fat 9.5, fiber 2.1, carbs 5.6, protein 38.6

Pizza Stuffed Chicken

Preparation time: 15 minutes
Cooking time: 12 minutes
Servings:5
Ingredients:
- 1-pound chicken breast, skinless, boneless
- 1 teaspoon minced garlic
- 1 teaspoon Italian seasonings
- 1/3 teaspoon onion powder
- ¼ teaspoon ground black pepper
- 1 tablespoon tomato paste
- ½ cup chicken broth
- ½ cup Mozzarella cheese, shredded

Directions:
Cut the chicken into 5 servings and beat them gently with the help of the kitchen hammer. Then rub every piece with Italian seasonings, onion powder, minced garlic, and ground black pepper. Then sprinkle every chicken piece with Mozzarella and roll them to make the pockets. Secure every roll with a toothpick. Pour chicken broth in the instant pot. Add tomato paste and stir well. Place the chicken rolls in the instant pot and close the lid. Cook them on manual mode (high pressure) for 12 minutes. When the time is over, make a quick pressure release and open the lid. If you like the golden-brown crust, broil the rolls in the preheated to 400F oven for 4 minutes.
Nutrition: calories 122, fat 3.2, fiber 0.2, carbs 1.3, protein 20.7

Sage Chicken and Broccoli

Preparation time: 10 minutes
Cooking time: 30 minutes
Servings: 4
Ingredients:
- 1 pound chicken breast, skinless, boneless and cubed
- 1 cup broccoli florets
- 3 garlic cloves, minced
- 1 cup tomato passata
- A pinch of salt and black pepper
- 2 tablespoons olive oil
- 1 tablespoon sage, chopped

Directions:
Set pot on Sauté mode, add the oil, heat it up, add the garlic and the chicken and sauté for 5 minutes. Add the rest of the ingredients, put the lid on and cook on

High for 25 minutes. Release the pressure naturally for 10 minutes, divide the mix between plates and serve.
Nutrition: calories 217, fat 10.1, fiber 1.8, carbs 5.9, protein 25.4

Chicken Patties

Preparation time: 10 minutes
Cooking time: 8 minutes
Servings: 3
Ingredients:
- 9 oz chicken fillet, cooked
- 3 tablespoons coconut flour
- 1 teaspoon cream cheese
- 1 egg, beaten
- 1 teaspoon minced onion
- ¼ teaspoon garlic powder
- ¾ teaspoon chili flakes
- ½ teaspoon salt
- 1 tablespoon avocado oil

Directions:
Shred the chicken and put it in the mixing bowl. Add coconut flour, egg, cream cheese, minced onion, garlic powder, chili flakes, and salt. Stir the chicken mixture until homogenous. Then place the avocado oil in the instant pot and heat it up on sauté mode for 2 minutes. With the help of the spoon make the medium size patties and place them in the hot oil. Cook the patties for 3 minutes from each side on sauté mode or until they are light brown.
Nutrition: calories 224, fat 9.5, fiber 3.3, carbs 5.7, Protein 27.7

Turkey and Cabbage Mix

Preparation time: 10 minutes
Cooking time: 30 minutes
Servings: 4
Ingredients:
- 2 turkey breasts, skinless, boneless and cubed
- 1 red cabbage, shredded
- 1 cup chicken stock
- 2 tablespoons tomato puree
- ½ teaspoon chili powder
- A pinch of salt and black pepper

Directions:
In your instant pot, combine the turkey meat with the rest of the ingredients, put the lid on and cook on High for 30 minutes. Release the pressure naturally for 10 minutes, divide everything between plates and serve.
Nutrition: calories 392, fat 11.6, fiber 0.3, carbs 1.1, protein 24.2

Mozzarella Chicken Fillets

Preparation time: 10 minutes
Cooking time: 20 minutes
Servings: 4
Ingredients:
- 12 oz chicken fillet
- ½ cup white mushrooms, chopped
- 3 oz leek, chopped
- 1 cup chicken broth
- ½ teaspoon salt
- 2 tablespoons apple cider vinegar
- ½ teaspoon ground paprika
- ½ teaspoon sage
- 1 teaspoon sesame oil
- 5 oz Mozzarella cheese, shredded

Directions:
Pour sesame oil in the instant pot and heat it up on sauté mode for 1 minute. Then add white mushrooms and cook them for 4 minutes. Stir the vegetables well and add leek, salt, ground paprika, and sage, Mix up well and sauté the mixture for 5 minutes more. After this, add chicken broth and apple cider vinegar. Add chicken fillet and close the lid. Cook the chicken on manual (high pressure) for 10 minutes. When the time is over, make a quick pressure release and open the lid. Top the chicken fillet with Mozzarella and close the lid. Leave the meal for 5-10 minutes or until the cheese is melted.
Nutrition: calories 288, fat 13.5, fiber 0.6, carbs 4.8, protein 35

Balsamic Turkey and Zucchini

Preparation time: 10 minutes
Cooking time: 25 minutes
Servings: 4
Ingredients:
- 1 big turkey breast, skinless, boneless and cubed
- 1 and ½ cups chicken stock
- A pinch of salt and black pepper
- 2 zucchinis, sliced
- 3 garlic cloves, minced
- 1 tablespoon balsamic vinegar
- 1 tablespoon olive oil
- 1 tablespoon chili powder
- ½ teaspoon sweet paprika

Directions:
Set the instant pot on Sauté mode, add the oil, heat it up, add the garlic, chili powder, paprika and the meat and brown for 5 minutes. Add the rest of the ingredients, put the lid on and cook on High for 20 minutes. Release the pressure naturally for 10 minutes, divide the mix between plates and serve.
Nutrition: calories 249, fat 9.7, fiber 1.9, carbs 5.3, protein 34.3

Bruschetta Chicken

Preparation time: 10 minutes
Cooking time: 8 minutes
Servings: 2
Ingredients:
- 8 oz chicken fillet
- ¼ teaspoon ground black pepper
- 1/3 teaspoon salt
- ¼ teaspoon sage
- ¼ teaspoon minced garlic
- 1/3 cup chicken broth
- 3 tablespoons apple cider vinegar
- ½ teaspoon Italian seasonings
- 2 teaspoons coconut oil
- ¼ cup cherry tomatoes, halved
- 1 teaspoon fresh basil, chopped
- ½ teaspoon sesame oil
- 1 oz Provolone cheese grated

Directions:
Toss coconut oil in the instant pot and heat it up for 2 minutes on sauté mode. Then cut the chicken fillet into 2 servings. Place the chicken in the hot coconut oil and sprinkle with salt, sage, and Italian seasonings.

Cook the chicken fillets for 3 minutes and then flip on another side. Cook the fillets for 3 minutes more. After this, add minced garlic, chicken broth, and apple cider vinegar. Close the lid and cook the meal on manual mode (high pressure) for 10 minutes. When the time is over, make a quick pressure release and open the lid. Transfer the chicken in the plate In the mixing bowl combine together cherry tomatoes, basil, and sesame oil. Mix up the ingredients. Top the chicken with tomato mixture. Then sprinkle the meal with grated cheese.
Nutrition: calories 336, fat 19, fiber 0.4, carbs 1.7, protein 53.7

Ginger Balsamic Chicken

Preparation time: 10 minutes
Cooking time: 25 minutes
Servings: 4
Ingredients:
- 2 chicken breasts, skinless, boneless and cubed
- 2 spring onions, chopped
- 1 tablespoon balsamic vinegar
- 1 tablespoon ginger, grated
- 1 tablespoon olive oil
- 3 garlic cloves, minced
- A pinch of salt and black pepper
- 1 cup chicken stock
- 2 tablespoons sweet paprika
- 1 tablespoon cilantro, chopped

Directions:
Set the instant pot on Sauté mode, add the oil, heat it up, add the spring onions, ginger, garlic and the meat and brown for 5 minutes. Add the rest of the ingredients, put the lid on and cook on High for 20 minutes. Release the pressure naturally for 10 minutes, divide the mix between plates and serve.
Nutrition: calories 269, fat 12.6, fiber 1.7, carbs 4.4, protein 33.9

Greek Chicken

Preparation time: 10 minutes
Cooking time: 10 minutes
Servings: 3
Ingredients:
- 10 oz chicken breast, skinless, boneless, chopped
- ½ oz jumbo olives, chopped
- 1 tablespoon olive oil
- ¼ teaspoon cayenne pepper
- 1 teaspoon dried oregano
- 1 teaspoon dried thyme
- ½ teaspoon salt
- ¼ teaspoon chili flakes
- 1/3 cup water
- 1 cucumber, chopped
- 3 tablespoons heavy cream
- ¼ teaspoon garlic powder
- 1 tablespoon lemon juice
- ½ teaspoon dried dill
- 3 oz Feta cheese, crumbled

Directions:
Sprinkle the chopped chicken with cayenne pepper, dried oregano, thyme, salt, and chili flakes. Then sprinkle the chicken with olive oil and place it in the instant pot. Set sauté mode and cook the chicken for 5 minutes. Stir it from time to time. Then add water and close the lid. Cook the chicken for 5 minutes on manual mode (high pressure). Then make a quick pressure release and open the lid. Transfer the cooked chicken in the serving bowls. Add chopped cucumber in every bowl. In the shallow bowl mix up together heavy cream, garlic powder, lemon juice, and dried dill. Pour the liquid over the cucumbers. Top the meal with crumbled Feta cheese.
Nutrition: calories 299, fat 19.2, fiber 1.1, carbs 6.5, protein 25.3

Tarragon Chicken Mix

Preparation time: 5 minutes
Cooking time: 25 minutes
Servings: 4
Ingredients:
- 2 chicken breasts, skinless and halved
- 1 shallot, chopped
- 1 and ½ teaspoon tarragon, dried
- 1 cup tomato passata
- A pinch of salt and black pepper
- 1 cup tomatoes, cubed
- ½ cup red cabbage, shredded

Directions:
In your instant pot, mix the chicken with the rest of the ingredients, put the lid on and cook on High for 25 minutes. Release the pressure fast for 5 minutes, divide the mix between plates and serve.
Nutrition: calories 241, fat 8.6, fiber 1.5, carbs 5.6, protein 34.1

Chicken Rendang

Preparation time: 15 minutes
Cooking time: 20 minutes
Servings: 4
Ingredients:
- ¾ teaspoon Galang, chopped
- ¼ white onion, chopped
- 1 teaspoon lemongrass, chopped
- ½ teaspoon garlic, diced
- ¾ teaspoon minced ginger
- ¼ teaspoon chili pepper, minced
- 1 tablespoon nut oil
- 1/3 cup coconut milk
- ½ teaspoon cardamom pods
- ¼ teaspoon ground cinnamon
- 1 anise star
- 1 tablespoon coconut flakes
- 4 chicken thighs
- ¼ cup of water

Directions:
Place Galang, white onion, garlic, minced ginger, and chili pepper in the instant pot. Add nut oil and cook the mixture on sauté mode for 4 minutes. Stir the mixture from time to time. Then add coconut milk, cardamom pods, anise star, and coconut flakes. Stir well. Put the chicken thighs in the mixture and coat them well with the help of the spoon. Close the lid and cook the chicken on manual mode (high pressure) for 15 minutes. When the time is over, allow the natural pressure release for 10 minutes.
Nutrition: calories 343, fat 15.2, fiber 2.7, carbs 7.1, protein 43.3

Duck and Fennel

Preparation time: 10 minutes

Cooking time: 25 minutes
Servings: 4
Ingredients:
- 2 duck breasts, boneless and skin scored
- 1 cup chicken stock
- 2 fennel bulbs, sliced
- Juice of 1 lime
- 1 tablespoon avocado oil
- 1 cup tomato passata
- 1 tablespoon parsley, chopped

Directions:
Set the instant pot on Sauté mode, add the oil, heat it up, add the duck breasts skin side down and cook for 5 minutes. Add the rest of the ingredients except the parsley, put the lid on and cook on High for 20 minutes. Release the pressure naturally for 10 minutes, divide the mix between plates and serve with the parsley sprinkled on top.
Nutrition: calories 260, fat 7.7, fiber 3.4, carbs 4.5, protein 34.5

Chicken Zucchini Enchiladas

Preparation time: 15 minutes
Cooking time: 13 minutes
Servings: 6
Ingredients:
- 1 tablespoon avocado oil
- ½ white onion, diced
- 1 green bell pepper, chopped
- 1 chili pepper, chopped
- ½ teaspoon ground cumin
- ½ teaspoon ground coriander
- 1 garlic clove, diced
- 1-pound chicken breast, cooked, shredded
- 1 cup Cheddar cheese, shredded
- 2 zucchini, trimmed
- ½ cup heavy cream
- 1 tablespoon Enchilada sauce

Directions:
Put onion and bell pepper in the instant pot. Add avocado oil, ground cumin, coriander, and diced garlic. Cook the ingredients on sauté mode for 5 minutes. Stir them from time to time. Then add shredded chicken and Enchilada sauce. Mix up the mixture well and cook it for 3 minutes more. Transfer the cooked mixture into the mixing bowl. After this, clean the instant pot. Slice the zucchini lengthwise. You should get 18 slices. Place the layer of 3 zucchini slices on the chopping board and spread it with chicken mixture. Roll it and transfer in the instant pot. Repeat the same step with all remaining zucchini and chicken mixture. Then top the zucchini rolls with Cheddar cheese and heavy cream. Close and seal the lid. Cook enchiladas for 5 minutes on manual mode (high pressure). When the time is over, make a quick pressure release.
Nutrition: calories 225, fat 12.4, fiber 1.6, carbs 6.2, protein 22.2

Chicken and Herbs Sauce

Preparation time: 10 minutes
Cooking time: 25 minutes
Servings: 4
Ingredients:
- 2 chicken breasts, skinless, boneless and halved
- 2 tablespoons ghee, melted
- 1 cup chicken stock
- 2 bay leaves
- A pinch of salt and black pepper
- 1 tablespoon chervil, chopped
- 1 tablespoon chives, chopped
- 1 tablespoon cilantro, chopped
- 1 tablespoon thyme, chopped

Directions:
Set your instant pot on Sauté mode, add the ghee, heat it up, add the chervil, chives, cilantro, bay leaves and thyme and cook for 2 minutes. Add the meat and brown for 3 minutes more. Add the rest of the ingredients, put the lid on and cook on High for 20 minutes. Release the pressure naturally for 10 minutes, divide the mix between plates and serve.
Nutrition: calories 277, fat 15, fiber 0.3, carbs 0.9, protein 33.2

Chicken Cacciatore

Preparation time: 15 minutes
Cooking time: 25 minutes
Servings: 5
Ingredients:
- 5 chicken thighs, boneless
- ½ teaspoon salt
- ½ teaspoon ground black pepper
- 2 garlic cloves, diced
- ¼ onion, diced
- ¼ cup bell pepper, chopped
- ½ cup cremini mushrooms, chopped
- ¼ cup tomatoes, canned
- ½ teaspoon dried rosemary
- ½ teaspoon dried cumin
- ½ teaspoon dried thyme
- ¼ teaspoon ground coriander
- ½ cup kale, chopped
- 1 tablespoon coconut oil
- ½ cup chicken broth

Directions:
Toss the coconut oil in the instant pot and melt it on sauté mode. Then place the chicken thighs in the hot oil and cook them for 3 minutes from each side or until the chicken is light brown. After this, sprinkle the chicken with salt and ground black pepper. Add garlic, onion, and bell pepper. Add mushrooms and stir the ingredients. Then add canned tomatoes, rosemary, cumin, thyme, and ground coriander. Stir the ingredients with the help of the spatula well and add chicken broth. Close and seal the lid. Cook the meal on manual mode (high pressure) for 15 minutes. When the time is over, make a quick pressure release and open the lid. Add kale and close the lid. Cook the meal for 2 minutes more on manual mode (high pressure). Then make a quick pressure release and open the lid. Stir the meal well before serving.
Nutrition: calories 319, fat 13.8, fiber 0.7, carbs 3.2, protein 43.5

Turkey and Lime Dill Sauce

Preparation time: 5 minutes
Cooking time: 30 minutes
Servings: 4
Ingredients:
- 1 big turkey breast, skinless, boneless and cubed

- 1 tablespoon ghee, melted
- 1 and ½ tablespoons lime zest, grated
- 1 tablespoon lime juice
- 1 cup chicken stock
- 1 tablespoon dill, chopped
- 1 tablespoon smoked paprika
- A pinch of salt and black pepper

Directions:
Set the instant pot on Sauté mode, add the ghee, heat it up, add lime zest, juice, stock, dill and paprika, whisk and cook for 5 minutes. Add the meat, salt and pepper, put the lid on and cook on High for 25 minutes. Release the pressure fast for 5 minutes, divide the mix between plates and serve.
Nutrition: calories 230, fat 9.2, fiber 0.8, carbs 1.6, protein 33.8

Coconut Chicken Tenders

Preparation time: 10 minutes
Cooking time: 7 minutes
Servings: 4
Ingredients:
- 11 oz chicken fillet
- ½ cup coconut flour
- 2 eggs, beaten
- 1 oz Parmesan, grated
- ¼ teaspoon ground black pepper
- 1 tablespoon cream cheese
- 1 cup water, for cooking

Directions:
Cut the chicken fillet into the tenders. Then sprinkle them with ground black pepper. In the mixing bowl combine together Parmesan and coconut flour. After this, in the separated mixing bowl mix up together cream cheese and eggs. Dip every chicken tender in the egg mixture and then coat them well in the coconut flour mixture. Pour water and insert the steamer rack in the instant pot. Line the steamer rack with baking paper. Place the chicken tenders on the rack and close the lid. Cook the meal for 7 minutes on manual mode (high pressure). When the time is over, make a quick pressure release and open the lid. Transfer the cooked chicken tenders on the plate. If you prefer golden-brown crust – broil the cooked chicken tenders in the preheated to 400F oven for 5 minutes.
Nutrition: calories 219, fat 10.6, fiber 0.7, carbs 1.6, protein 28.1

Hot Curry Turkey

Preparation time: 5 minutes
Cooking time: 30 minutes
Servings: 4
Ingredients:
- 1 big turkey breast, skinless, boneless and cubed
- 2 curry leaves
- 1 tablespoon green curry paste
- 4 tablespoons hot sauce
- 1 cup chicken stock
- 2 tablespoons tomato passata
- 1 tablespoon chives, chopped

Directions:
In your instant pot, combine the turkey with the rest of the ingredients, put the lid on and cook on High for 30 minutes. Release the pressure fast for 5 minutes, discard curry leaves, divide the mix into bowls and serve.
Nutrition: calories 210, fat 6.6, fiber 0.2, carbs 2, protein 33.6

Balsamic Roast Chicken

Preparation time: 15 minutes
Cooking time: 16 minutes
Servings: 2
Ingredients:
- 2 chicken thighs, skinless, boneless
- 3 tablespoons balsamic vinegar
- 3 tablespoons avocado oil
- ¼ teaspoon salt
- ¼ teaspoon cayenne pepper
- ¼ teaspoon chili flakes
- ¼ teaspoon ground paprika
- ½ cup chicken broth
- 1 teaspoon peppercorns

Directions:
In the mixing bowl mix up together chicken thighs, balsamic vinegar, avocado oil, salt, cayenne pepper, chili flakes, and ground paprika. Leave the chicken or 10 minutes to marinate. Preheat the instant pot on sauté mode for 3 minutes. Then place the chicken thighs and all liquid from them in the instant pot and cook for 3 minutes from each side. Add chicken broth and peppercorns. Close and seal the lid. Cook the chicken for 10 minutes on manual mode (high pressure). When the time is over, make a quick pressure release. Transfer the chicken in the plate and shred it gently. Sprinkle the meal with the chicken broth liquid from the instant pot.
Nutrition: calories 324, fat 13.9, fiber 1.4, carbs 2.6, protein 43.9

Duck and Hot Eggplant Mix

Preparation time: 10 minutes
Cooking time: 30 minutes
Servings: 4
Ingredients:
- 2 duck legs, skinless, boneless and cubed
- 1 tablespoon olive oil
- 2 eggplants, sliced
- A pinch of salt and black pepper
- 1 tablespoon hot paprika
- 2 tablespoons tomato paste
- 2 cups chicken stock
- 1 and ½ teaspoons chili powder
- 1 tablespoon cilantro, chopped

Directions:
Set your instant pot on Sauté mode, add the oil, heat it up, add the meat and the rest of the ingredients except the eggplants, stock and cilantro, toss and cook for 5 minutes. Add the eggplant and stock, put the lid on and cook on High for 25 minutes. Release the pressure naturally for 10 minutes, divide the mix between plates and serve with the cilantro sprinkled on top.
Nutrition: calories 338, fat 17, fiber 2.6, carbs 6.6, protein 30

Chicken & Snap Pea Salad

Preparation time: 15 minutes
Cooking time: 14 minutes
Servings: 8

Ingredients:
- 1 teaspoon Erythritol
- 1 teaspoon mustard
- 1 tablespoon sesame oil
- ¼ teaspoon ground black pepper
- ¼ teaspoon ground paprika
- ¼ teaspoon ground turmeric
- ¼ teaspoon garlic powder
- ½ teaspoon onion powder
- 3 tablespoons olive oil
- ½ red onion, sliced
- 1-pound chicken breast, skinless, boneless
- 1 bell pepper, chopped
- 2 cup green peas
- 1 cup water, hot

Directions:
Make the salad dressing: whisk together Erythritol, mustard, sesame oil, and paprika. Then in the shallow bowl combine together ground black pepper, turmeric, garlic powder, and onion powder. Sprinkle the chicken breast with spice mixture and massage well with the help of the fingertips. Brush the chicken with olive oil and place it in the instant pot. Cook the chicken breast for 4 minutes on sauté mode. Then flip it on another side and cook for 5 minutes more. After this, add hot water and insert the trivet. Place the green peas and bell pepper on the trivet and close the lid. Cook the ingredients on manual mode (high pressure) for 4 minutes. When the time is over, allow the natural pressure release for 5 minutes. Transfer the green peas and bell pepper in the salad bowl. Add red onion. Then chop the chicken and add it in the salad bowl too. Shake the salad and sprinkle with dressing.
Nutrition: calories 165, fat 8.7, fiber 2.3, carbs 8.1, protein 14.4

Chicken, Cabbage and Leeks

Preparation time: 10 minutes
Cooking time: 30 minutes
Servings: 4
Ingredients:
- 2 chicken breasts, skinless, boneless and cubed
- A pinch of salt and black pepper
- 1 tablespoon ghee, melted
- 1 red cabbage, shredded
- 2 leeks, sliced
- 1 cup chicken stock
- 1 tablespoon tomato passata
- 1 tablespoon basil, chopped
- 1 tablespoon balsamic vinegar

Directions:
Set the instant pot on Sauté mode, add the ghee, heat it up, add the meat and the leeks and brown for 5 minutes. Add the rest of the ingredients except the basil, toss, put the lid on and cook on High for 25 minutes Release the pressure naturally for 10 minutes, divide the mix between plates, sprinkle the basil on top and serve.
Nutrition: calories 275, fat 11.9, fiber 0.6, carbs 6.7, protein 33.7

Spinach Stuffed Chicken

Preparation time: 15 minutes
Cooking time: 18 minutes
Servings: 2
Ingredients:
- 10 oz chicken breast, skinless, boneless
- 3 oz Goat cheese, crumbled
- 1 cup spinach, chopped
- ½ teaspoon salt
- ½ teaspoon onion powder
- ¼ teaspoon ground turmeric
- ¼ teaspoon dried thyme
- 1 teaspoon apple cider vinegar
- 1 tablespoon olive oil
- 1 cup water, for cooking

Directions:
Pour olive oil in the instant pot and heat it up on sauté mode for 2-3 minutes. Add spinach. Sprinkle it with salt, onion powder, ground turmeric, and dried thyme. Stir the ingredients well and sauté for 5 minutes. Stir with the help of the spatula from time to time. When the time is over, add crumbled Goat cheese and apple cider vinegar and mix up. Transfer the mixture in the bowl and clean the instant pot. Cut the chicken breast into 2 servings. Cut the chicken breast in the shape of Hasselback. Fill every Hasselback cut with spinach mixture. Wrap the chicken in the foil. Pour water and insert the steamer rack in the instant pot. Place the wrapped chicken on the rack and close the lid. Cook the meal on steam mode (high pressure) for 10 minutes. When the time is over, allow the natural pressure release and open the lid. Remove the chicken from the foil.
Nutrition: calories 421, fat 25.8, fiber 0.5, carbs 2.2, protein 43.6

Turkey and Spicy Okra

Preparation time: 10 minutes
Cooking time: 30 minutes
Servings: 4
Ingredients:
- 2 cups okra, trimmed
- 1 shallot, chopped
- 1 tablespoon olive oil
- 2 garlic cloves, minced
- 1 turkey breast, skinless, boneless and cubed
- 1 tablespoon chili powder
- 1 cup tomato passata
- A pinch of salt and black pepper
- 1 tablespoon parsley, chopped
- 1 tablespoon oregano, chopped

Directions:
Set the instant pot on Sauté mode, add the oil, heat it up, add the shallot, garlic, turkey and the chili powder and brown for 5 minutes. Add the rest of the ingredients except the parsley and the oregano, put the lid on and cook on High for 25 minutes. Release the pressure naturally for 10 minutes, divide the mix between plates, sprinkle the parsley and oregano on top and serve.
Nutrition: calories 279, fat 9.8, fiber 3.5, carbs 5.6, protein 35.4

Chicken Scarpariello

Preparation time: 10 minutes
Cooking time: 20 minutes
Servings: 2
Ingredients:
- 1 tablespoon olive oil

- ½ teaspoon salt
- 1 Italian sausages link
- 2 chicken thighs, skinless, boneless
- ½ cup bell pepper, chopped
- 1 garlic clove, diced
- ½ cup chicken broth
- 1 chili pepper, chopped
- 1 tablespoon apple cider vinegar
- 1 teaspoon rosemary

Directions:
Pour olive oil in the instant pot. Chop the sausage link and place it in the instant pot. Cook it on sauté mode for 5 minutes. Stir the sausages from time to time with the help of the spatula. After this, remove the sausages from the instant pot. Place chicken thighs in the instant pot and cook them for 3 minutes from each side. After this, add bell pepper, garlic clove, salt, rosemary, and chili pepper. Cook the chicken for 3 minutes more. Then sprinkle it with apple cider vinegar and cook and flip the chicken thighs on another side. Add chicken broth and cooked sausages. Close the lid and cook the meal on manual (high pressure) for 6 minutes. When the time is over, make a quick pressure release and open the lid.
Nutrition: calories 426, fat 21,9, fiber 0.8, carbs 4,5, protein 50.7

Chicken and Balsamic Mushrooms

Preparation time: 10 minutes
Cooking time: 20 minutes
Servings: 4
Ingredients:
- 2 chicken breasts, skinless, boneless and cubed
- 1 tablespoon balsamic vinegar
- 1 pound white mushrooms, sliced
- 1 tablespoon rosemary, chopped
- 1 cup chicken stock
- A pinch of salt and black pepper
- 1 tablespoon avocado oil
- 2 tablespoons tomato passata

Directions:
Set your instant pot on Sauté mode, add the oil, heat it up, add the chicken and the mushrooms and brown for 5 minutes. Add the rest of the ingredients, put the lid on and cook on High for 20 minutes. Release the pressure naturally for 10 minutes, divide everything between plates and serve.
Nutrition: calories 252, fat 9.4, fiber 1.8, carbs 5.1, protein 36.4

Chicken Divan Casserole

Preparation time: 15 minutes
Cooking time: 10 minutes
Servings: 4
Ingredients:
- 1 ½ cup broccoli florets
- 11 oz chicken breast, boiled
- ½ cup Mozzarella, shredded
- 1 garlic clove, minced
- ½ teaspoon salt
- ½ teaspoon white pepper
- ¼ cup heavy cream
- ¼ cup of coconut milk
- 2 tablespoons almond flour
- ¼ teaspoon avocado oil
- 1 cup water, for cooking

Directions:
Shred the chicken with the help of the fork and put it in the big bowl. Add broccoli florets and shredded Mozzarella. Then add garlic clove, salt, white pepper, and heavy cream. Add coconut milk and mix up the chicken mixture until homogenous. After this, brush the instant pot casserole mold with avocado oil and transfer the chicken mixture inside it. Flatten the surface of the chicken mixture with the help of the spatula. Then sprinkle it with almond flour. Pour water and insert the trivet in the instant pot. Place the casserole mold on the trivet and close the lid. Cook the meal on manual mode (high pressure) for 10 minutes. When the time is over, allow the natural pressure release for 10 minutes more.
Nutrition: calories 253, fat 16.1, fiber 2.8, carbs 6.9, protein 22.1

Creamy Turkey and Chard

Preparation time: 10 minutes
Cooking time: 30 minutes
Servings: 4
Ingredients:
- 1 turkey breast, skinless, boneless and cubed
- 1 tablespoon ghee, melted
- 2 garlic cloves, minced
- 1 and ½ cup coconut cream
- 1 cup chard, roughly chopped
- ½ bunch coriander, chopped

Directions:
Set your instant pot on Sauté mode, add the ghee, heat it up, add the meat and the garlic and brown for 5 minutes. Add the rest of the ingredients, put the lid on and cook on High for 25 minutes. Release the pressure naturally for 10 minutes, divide the mix between plates and serve.
Nutrition: calories 225, fat 8.9, fiber 0.2, carbs 0.8, protein 33.5

Orange Chicken

Preparation time: 15 minutes
Cooking time: 22 minutes
Servings: 4
Ingredients:
- 5 tablespoons orange juice
- 1 teaspoon lemon juice
- 1 teaspoon apple cider vinegar
- 1 tablespoon olive oil
- ¼ teaspoon chili flakes
- ½ teaspoon minced ginger
- ¼ teaspoon garlic powder
- 1 tablespoon coconut flour
- 1 teaspoon orange zest, grated
- ½ cup chicken broth
- ½ teaspoon salt
- 15 oz chicken breast, skinless, boneless, roughly chopped

Directions:
In the mixing bowl combine together orange juice, orange zest, lemon juice, apple cider vinegar, olive oil, chili flakes, minced ginger, salt, and garlic powder. Then pour the orange mixture over the chicken and mix up well. Marinate the chicken in the orange mixture for at least 10 minutes. After this, heat up the instant pot on sauté mode for 2 minutes. Add the

chicken mixture and cook it for 5 minutes. After this, stir it well with the help of the spatula and add chicken broth. Close the lid and cook the meal on stew/meat mode for 15 minutes.
Nutrition: calories 182, fat 6.9, fiber 1.4, carbs 4.6, protein 23.9

Duck and Coriander Sauce

Preparation time: 10 minutes
Cooking time: 30 minutes
Servings: 4
Ingredients:
- 1 pound duck legs, boneless, skinless and cubed
- 2 tablespoons ghee, melt
- 2 spring onions, chopped
- 2 garlic cloves, minced
- 1 and ½ cups tomato passata
- 2 tablespoon coriander, chopped

Directions:
Set your instant pot on Sauté mode, add the ghee, heat it up, add the spring onions and the rest of the ingredients except the meat and th tomato passata and brown for 5 minutes. Add the meat and brown for 5 minutes more. Add the sauce, put the lid on and cook on High for 25 minutes. Release the pressure naturally for 10 minutes, divide between plates and serve.
Nutrition: calories 263, fat 13.2, fiber 0.2, carbs 1.1, protein 33.5

Chicken Stroganoff

Preparation time: 10 minutes
Cooking time: 15 minutes
Servings: 3
Ingredients:
- ¼ cup baby Bella mushrooms, sliced
- 1 medium white onion, sliced
- 1 garlic clove, diced
- ¼ teaspoon ground black pepper
- ½ teaspoon ground paprika
- ½ cup of coconut milk
- 1 oz Parmesan, grated
- 1 teaspoon butter
- 8 oz chicken fillet
- ¼ cup chicken broth

Directions:
Place butter in the instant pot. Add white onion, mushrooms, and garlic. Cook the ingredients for 5 minutes on sauté mode. Stir the ingredients from time to time. Meanwhile, cut the chicken fillet into the strips and sprinkle with ground paprika and ground black pepper. Put the chicken strips in the instant pot. Add coconut milk and chicken broth. Then add grated cheese and mix up the ingredients with the help of the spoon. Close and seal the lid. Cook the chicken stroganoff on steam mode for 8 minutes. When the time is over, make a quick pressure release and open the lid. Let the cooked meal rest for 5-10 minutes before serving.
Nutrition: calories 299, fat 18.7, fiber 1.9, carbs 6.8, protein 26.9

Chicken, Baby Kale and Spinach Mix

Preparation time: 5 minutes
Cooking time: 30 minutes
Servings: 4
Ingredients:
- 1 tablespoon ghee, melted
- 1 pound chicken breasts, skinless, boneless and cubed
- 1 pound baby kale
- ½ pound baby spinach
- 1 cup tomato passata
- A pinch of salt and black pepper
- 1 cup chicken stock
- 1 tablespoon chives, chopped

Directions:
Set your instant pot on Sauté mode, add the ghee, heat it up, add the meat and brown for 5 minutes Add the rest of the ingredients except the kale and the spinach, put the lid on and cook on High for 15 minutes Release the pressure fast for 5 minutes, set the pot on Sauté mode, add the kale and spinach, cook for 10 minutes more, divide between plates and serve.
Nutrition: calories 274, fat 12.1, fiber 2.2, carbs 5.6, protein 35.4

Pecan Chicken

Preparation time: 10 minutes
Cooking time: 17 minutes
Servings: 2
Ingredients:
- 6 oz chicken fillet
- 3 pecans, grinded
- 1 egg, beaten
- 1 teaspoon coconut cream
- ½ teaspoon cayenne pepper
- ¼ teaspoon salt
- 1 teaspoon butter
- 1 cup water, for cooking

Directions:
Cut the chicken fillet into 2 servings. Pour water and insert the trivet in the instant pot. Line the trivet with the baking paper. Then rub the chicken fillets with salt and cayenne pepper. Put the chicken on the trivet and close the lid. Cook it for 5 minutes on Steam mode. When the time is over, make a quick pressure release. Open the lid and transfer the chicken on the plate. Clean the instant pot and remove the trivet. Then in the mixing bowl whisk together the egg with coconut cream. Dip the chicken pieces in the egg mixture. After this, coat every fillet in the grinded pecans. Toss butter in the instant pot and melt it on sauté mode (appx.2-3minutes). Place the coated pecan chicken in the instant pot and cook it for 5 minutes from each side.
Nutrition: calories 363, fat 26.1, fiber 2.4, carbs 3.6, protein 29.8

Chicken and Cauliflower Rice

Preparation time: 5 minutes
Cooking time: 30 minutes
Servings: 6
Ingredients:
- 1 and ½ pounds chicken breasts, skinless, boneless and cubed
- 1 and ½ cups cauliflower rice
- 2 tablespoons ghee, melted
- 1 tablespoon sweet paprika
- ½ teaspoon chili powder

- 2 cups chicken stock
- 1 tablespoon cilantro, chopped
- A pinch of salt and black pepper

Directions:
Set the instant pot on Sauté mode, add the ghee, heat it up, add the meat, paprika and chili powder and brown for 5 minutes. Add the rest of the ingredients, put the lid on and cook on High for 25 minutes. Release the pressure fast for 5 minutes, divide everything between plates and serve.
Nutrition: calories 332, fat 15.4, fiber 0.5, carbs 1, protein 34.5

Cayenne Pepper Chicken Meatballs

Preparation time: 15 minutes
Cooking time: 6 minutes
Servings: 3
Ingredients:
- 1 cup ground chicken
- ½ teaspoon cayenne pepper
- 3 tablespoons almond flour
- 1 teaspoon dried dill
- 1 egg, beaten
- 1 onion, minced
- ½ teaspoon minced ginger
- 1 oz Mozzarella, shredded
- ½ teaspoon onion powder
- 2 tablespoons water
- 1 cup water, for cooking

Directions:
In the mixing bowl combine together ground chicken, cayenne pepper, almond flour, dried dill, egg, minced onion, ginger, Mozzarella, and onion powder. When the mixture is homogenous, add 2 tablespoons water and mix up the mixture with the help of the spoon. Then make the meatballs using scooper. Pour water and insert the trivet in the instant pot. Line the trivet with baking paper. Place the meatballs on the trivet in one layer. Close and seal the lid. Cook the chicken meatballs for 6 minutes on manual mode (high pressure). When the time is over, make a quick pressure release and transfer the cooked meatballs in the serving plates.
Nutrition: calories 197, fat 10, fiber 1.7, carbs 6.2, protein 20.1

Turkey and Mustard Greens Mix

Preparation time: 10 minutes
Cooking time: 30 minutes
Servings: 6
Ingredients:
- 2 turkey breasts, skinless, boneless and cubed
- 1 tablespoon olive oil
- 2 garlic cloves, minced
- 1 cup chicken stock
- 1 and ½ cup tomato passata
- 1 pound mustard greens, torn
- 1 tablespoon smoked paprika
- 1 tablespoon cilantro, chopped
- A pinch of salt and black pepper

Directions:
Set the instant pot on Sauté mode, add the oil, heat it up, add the meat, garlic and paprika and brown for 5 minutes. Add the rest of the ingredients except the cilantro, put the lid on and cook on High for 25 minutes. Release the pressure naturally for 10 minutes, divide the mix between plates and serve with the cilantro sprinkled on top.
Nutrition: calories 262, fat 9.8, fiber 4.2, carbs 5.8, protein 34.6

Chicken Cheese Calzone

Preparation time: 15 minutes
Cooking time: 20 minutes
Servings: 4
Ingredients:
- 4 oz chicken breast, shredded
- ¼ cup Mozzarella, shredded
- 1 bacon, slice, cooked, chopped
- 1 tablespoon cream cheese
- 1 tablespoon coconut cream
- 1 egg, beaten
- ½ cup almond flour
- 2 tablespoons flax seeds, grinded
- 1 teaspoon butter, softened
- 1 cup water, for cooking

Directions:
Make the calzone dough: in the mixing bowl combine together butter, flax seeds, almond flour, and egg. Knead the non-sticky dough. Make the calzone filling: in the mixing bowl combine together chicken breast, shredde Mozzarella, bacon, cream cheese, and coconut cream. Roll up the almond flour dough and make 4 rounds with the help of the cutter. Then place the shredded chicken mixture on the dough rounds and fold them. Secure edges of calzones with the help of the fork. After this, pour water and insert the steamer rack in the instant pot. Line the rack with the baking paper and place the calzones on it. Close the lid and cook the calzones for 20 minutes on steam mode (high pressure). When the time is over, make a quick pressure release and open the lid. Transfer the calzones on the plate and cool little.
Nutrition: calories 143, fat 9.7, fiber 1.4, carbs 2.2, protein 11.3

Turkey and Rocket Mix

Preparation time: 5 minutes
Cooking time: 30 minutes
Servings: 4
Ingredients:
- 1 turkey breast, skinless, boneless and sliced
- ½ cup chicken stock
- 2 tablespoons tomato passata
- 1 shallot, minced
- 2 garlic cloves, minced
- 1 cup rocket leaves
- 1 tablespoon avocado oil
- ¼ cup cilantro, chopped

Directions:
Set the instant pot on Sauté mode, add the oil, heat it up, add the meat, shallot and the garlic and brown for 5 minutes Add the remaining ingredients except the cilantro and the rocket, put the lid on and cook on High for 25 minutes. Release the pressure fast for 5 minutes, divide everything between plates and serve with the cilantro and rocket sprinkled on top.
Nutrition: calories 204, fat 6.2, fiber 0,4, carbs 1.6, protein 33.4

Butter Chicken Stew

Preparation time: 10 minutes
Cooking time: 25 minutes
Servings: 4
Ingredients:
- 4 tablespoons butter
- ½ cup asparagus, chopped
- 1 garlic clove, peeled, diced
- ½ teaspoon minced ginger
- 1 teaspoon tomato paste
- ½ teaspoon garam masala
- ½ teaspoon smoked paprika
- ½ teaspoon ground cumin
- ½ cup whipped cream
- 1 teaspoon dried parsley
- 10 oz chicken thighs, skinless, boneless
- ¼ cup chicken broth
- ¼ teaspoon salt
- ¼ teaspoon chili flakes

Directions:
Place butter in the instant pot. Add diced garlic, minced ginger, and garam masala. Cook the ingredients on sauté mode for 4 minutes. Stir the mixture from time to time. Then add ground cumin, parsley, and chicken thighs/ Sprinkle the chicken with salt and chili flakes. Cook it for 3 minutes from each side on sauté mode. Add chicken broth and whipped cream. Close the lid. Cook the chicken for 10 minutes on steam mode (high pressure). Then make quick pressure release and open the lid. Add asparagus and close the lid. Cook the stew for 5 minutes more on stew mode.
Nutrition: calories 291, fat 21.6, fiber 0.6, carbs 2.1, protein 21.9

Chicken and Watercress Mix

Preparation time: 5 minutes
Cooking time: 30 minutes
Servings: 4
Ingredients:
- 2 chicken breasts, skinless, boneless and halved
- 2 spring onions, chopped
- 2 garlic cloves, minced
- 1 tablespoon olive oil
- 1 cup chicken stock
- ½ cup tomato passata
- A pinch of salt and black pepper
- 1 cup watercress, torn

Directions:
Set the instant pot on Sauté mode, add the oil, heat it up, add the spring onions, garlic and the meat and brown for 5 minutes. Add the rest of the ingredients except the watercress, put the lid on and cook on High for 25 minutes. Release the pressure fast for 5 minutes, divide the mix between plates and serve with the watercress on top.
Nutrition: calories 262, fat 12.2, fiber 0.8, carbs 2.9, protein 33.8

Chicken Cauliflower Rice

Preparation time: 10 minutes
Cooking time: 16 minutes
Servings: 3
Ingredients:
- 8 oz chicken fillet, chopped
- 1 small onion, diced
- 1 tablespoon sesame oil
- 1 tablespoon butter
- 1 oz scallions, chopped
- 1 cup cauliflower, shredded
- 1 cup chicken broth
- ½ teaspoon salt
- 1 teaspoon smoked paprika

Directions:
Sprinkle the chopped chicken fillet with salt and smoked paprika. Place it in the instant pot and add sesame oil and onion; sauté the ingredients for 5 minutes on sauté mode. Then add butter, chicken broth, and close the lid. Cook the chicken on Manual (high pressure) for 5 minutes. When the time is over, make a quick pressure release and open the lid. Add shredded cauliflower and mix up well. Cook the meal in manual mode for 1 minute When the time is over, allow the natural pressure release for 5 minutes. Mix up the cooked meal well before serving.
Nutrition: calories 253, fat 14.6, fiber 1.8, carbs 5.3, protein 24.7

Duck, Leeks and Asparagus

Preparation time: 10 minutes
Cooking time: 30 minutes
Servings: 4
Ingredients:
- 2 tablespoons ghee, melted
- 2 duck legs, boneless, skinless and cubed
- 1 shallot, chopped
- 2 leeks, sliced
- ½ pound asparagus, trimmed and halved
- 1 cup chicken stock
- A pinch of salt and black pepper
- 2 teaspoons basil, dried
- 1 teaspoon oregano, dried

Directions:
Set your instant pot on Sauté mode, add the ghee, heat it up, add the shallot, leeks and the meat and brown for 5 minutes. Add the rest of the ingredients, put the lid on and cook on High for 25 minutes. Release the pressure naturally for 10 minutes, divide the mix between plates and serve.
Nutrition: calories 300, fat 13.5, fiber 2.2, carbs 6.7, protein 35.2

Chicken Crust Pizza

Preparation time: 10 minutes
Cooking time: 10 minutes
Servings: 6
Ingredients:
- 1 cup ground chicken
- ½ teaspoon ground black pepper
- ¼ teaspoon salt
- 1 teaspoon smoked paprika
- ½ teaspoon onion powder
- 1 tablespoon coconut flour
- 1 egg, beaten
- 1 tablespoon avocado oil
- 1 teaspoon fresh basil, chopped
- ¼ cup Cheddar cheese, shredded
- ½ cup Mozzarella, shredded
- 2 tablespoons coconut cream

Directions:
In the mixing bowl combine together ground chicken, ground black pepper, salt, smoked paprika, onion

powder, and coconut flour; add Cheddar cheese. Then add egg and mix up the mass until it is homogenous. After this, brush the instant pot bowl with avocado oil and heat up on sauté mode for 2 minutes. Then place the ground chicken mixture in the instant pot bowl and flatten well to get the shape of the pizza crust. Cook it for 5 minutes. Then flip it on another side with the help of 2 spatulas. Sprinkle the chicken crust with fresh basil, coconut cream, and Mozzarella. Close the lid and cook the meal on sauté mode for 5 minutes.
Nutrition: calories 107, fat 6.3, fiber 1.2, carbs 2.4, protein 10.1

Chicken and Garlic Spinach

Preparation time: 10 minutes
Cooking time: 25 minutes
Servings: 4
Ingredients:
- 3 garlic cloves, minced
- 2 tablespoons ghee, melted
- 1 pound baby spinach
- 1 pound chicken breasts, skinless, boneless and cubed
- A pinch of salt and black pepper
- 1 cup chicken stock
- 2 tablespoons cilantro, chopped

Directions:
Set your instant pot on Sauté mode, add the ghee, heat it up, add the garlic and the meat and brown for 5 minutes. Add the rest of the ingredients except the spinach, put the lid on and cook on High for 15 minutes. Release the pressure naturally for 10 minutes, set the pot on Sauté mode again, add the spinach, cook for 5 minutes more, divide everything between plates and serve.
Nutrition: calories 304, fat 15.4, fiber 2.6, carbs 5.1, protein 36.4

Asiago Chicken Drumsticks

Preparation time: 15 minutes
Cooking time: 5 hours
Servings: 4
Ingredients:
- 4 chicken drumsticks, boneless
- 1/3 teaspoon salt
- ¼ teaspoon white pepper
- ½ teaspoon onion powder
- 1 teaspoon minced onion
- 1 teaspoon dried dill
- 1/3 cup chicken broth
- ¼ cup apple cider vinegar
- 2 tablespoons cream cheese
- 5 oz Asiago cheese, grated
- 1 teaspoon arrowroot powder

Directions:
In the big bowl combine together salt, white pepper, onion powder, minced onion, dried dill, chicken broth, and apple cider vinegar. Add cream cheese and 3 oz of Asiago cheese. Whisk the mixture until salt is dissolved. Then add chicken drumsticks and let the ingredients marinate for 10 minutes. Then transfer the chicken drumsticks and ½ part of chicken broth liquid in the instant pot. Close and seal the lid. Cook the meal on Low pressure (manual mode) for 4 hours. When the time is over, open the lid. Combine together the remaining chicken liquid and remaining Asiago cheese. Add arrowroot and stir it. Pour the liquid over the chicken and close the lid. Cook the meal o Low pressure for 1 hour more.
Nutrition: calories 233, fat 14.6, fiber 0.1, carbs 1.6, protein 22.4

Turmeric Duck Mix

Preparation time: 5 minutes
Cooking time: 30 minutes
Servings: 4
Ingredients:
- 1 shallot, chopped
- 1 tablespoon olive oil
- 2 garlic cloves, minced
- 1 pound duck legs, boneless, skinless and cubed
- 1 cup chicken stock
- 1 tablespoon cilantro, chopped
- 1 teaspoon turmeric powder
- A pinch of salt and black pepper

Directions:
Set your instant pot on Sauté mode, add the oil, heat it up, add the shallot, garlic and the meat and brown for 5 minutes. Add the rest of the ingredients except the cilantro, put the lid on and cook on High for 25 minutes. Release the pressure fast for 5 minutes, divide the mix between plates and serve with the cilantro sprinkled on top.
Nutrition: calories 239, fat 10.5, fiber 0.2, carbs 1.1, protein 33.3

Chicken Stuffed Avocado

Preparation time: 15 minutes
Cooking time: 5 minutes
Servings: 2
Ingredients:
- 1 avocado, pitted, halved
- 4 oz chicken fillet, boiled
- 1 tablespoon cream cheese
- ¼ teaspoon minced garlic
- ½ teaspoon dried oregano
- ¼ cup Cheddar cheese, shredded
- ¼ teaspoon ground nutmeg
- 1 teaspoon butter, melted
- 1 cup water, for cooking

Directions:
Shred the boiled chicken and combine it with minced garlic and cream cheese. Then add dried oregano, Cheddar cheese, and ground nutmeg. Scoop ½ part of avocado meat in the chicken mixture. Mix up the chicken mixture well until homogenous. Brush the avocado halves with butter. Then fill every avocado half with chicken mixture. Pour water and insert the steamer rack in the instant pot. Arrange the avocado halves on the rack and close the lid. Cook the meal on manual (high pressure) for 5 minutes. When the time is over, make a quick pressure release and open the lid. Transfer the cooked meal on the plates.
Nutrition: calories 407, fat 32.3, fiber 7, carbs 9.5, protein 22.3

Turkey and Hot Lemon Sauce

Preparation time: 10 minutes
Cooking time: 30 minutes
Servings: 4
Ingredients:

- 2 turkey breasts, skinless, boneless and cubed
- 1 shallot, minced
- 1 tablespoon ghee, melted
- 1 tablespoon lemon juice
- 1 tablespoon lemon zest, grated
- A pinch of salt and black pepper
- 1 teaspoon red pepper flakes
- 1 cup chicken stock

Directions:
Set your instant pot on Sauté mode, add the ghee, heat it up, add the shallot and the meat and brown for 5 minutes. Add the rest of the ingredients, put the lid on and cook on High for 25 minutes. Release the pressure naturally for 10 minutes, divide everything between plates and serve.
Nutrition: calories 227, fat 9.1, fiber 0.2, carbs 0.8, protein 33.5

Chicken Cordon Bleu

Preparation time: 15 minutes
Cooking time: 5 minutes
Servings: 2
Ingredients:
- 6 oz chicken fillet
- 2 ham slices
- 2 Swiss cheese slices
- ¼ teaspoon salt
- ¼ teaspoon white pepper
- 1 teaspoon butter, melted
- ½ cup chicken broth

Directions:
Beat the chicken fillets with the help of the kitchen hammer to make 2 chicken pieces in the shape of the pancake. Then brush every chicken piece with melted butter and top with ham and Swiss cheese. Then sprinkle them with white pepper and salt. Roll the chicken. Pour chicken broth in the instant pot. Place the rolled chicken in the chicken broth and close the lid. Cook the meal on manual mode (high pressure) for 5 minutes. When the time is over, make a quick pressure release and remove the meal from the instant pot.
Nutrition: calories 341, fat 18.8, fiber 0.4, carbs 3, protein 38.1

Oregano Chicken and Dates

Preparation time: 10 minutes
Cooking time: 25 minutes
Servings: 4
Ingredients:
- 1 pound chicken breast, skinless, boneless and cubed
- 1 tablespoon olive oil
- 1 tablespoon oregano, chopped
- 1 cup chicken stock
- 1 cup dates, pitted and chopped
- 1 tablespoon chives, chopped
- 1 tablespoon sweet paprika
- A pinch of salt and black pepper

Directions:
Set your instant pot on Sauté mode, add the oil, heat it up, add the meat and brown for 5 minutes. Add the rest of the ingredients, put the lid on and cook on High for 20 minutes. Release the pressure naturally for 10 minutes, divide everything between plates and serve.
Nutrition: calories 382, fat 12.6, fiber 2.6, carbs 6.6, protein 33.6

Herbed Whole Chicken

Preparation time: 15 minutes
Cooking time: 50 minutes
Servings: 8
Ingredients:
- 3-pound whole chicken
- 1 teaspoon ground cumin
- ½ teaspoon ground nutmeg
- 1 teaspoon fresh thyme
- 1 teaspoon fresh rosemary
- 1 teaspoon smoked paprika
- 1 teaspoon sage
- 1 tablespoon fresh basil, chopped
- ½ teaspoon cayenne pepper
- 1 teaspoon ground turmeric
- 1 teaspoon onion powder
- ¼ cup sesame oil
- 1 teaspoon dried oregano
- 1 teaspoon salt
- 3 garlic cloves, peeled
- 1 ½ cup water, for cooking

Directions:
Pour water in the instant pot and add garlic cloves. Then insert the trivet. In the mixing bowl combine together sesame oil with all spices and herbs from the list above. Rub the chicken with oil mixture well and place it in the instant pot (on the trivet). Close the lid and set manual mode (high pressure). Cook the chicken for 50 minutes. When the time is over, allow the natural pressure release for 10 minutes.
Nutrition: calories 472, fat 35.5, fiber 0.5, carbs 1.5, protein 35.5

White Duck Chili

Preparation time: 10 minutes
Cooking time: 25 minutes
Servings: 4
Ingredients:
- 2 duck legs, boneless, skinless and cubed
- 1 tablespoon ghee, melted
- 1 shallot, chopped
- 1 cup heavy cream
- 1 and ½ teaspoons chili paste
- 1 cup chicken stock
- A pinch of salt and black pepper
- 2 teaspoons thyme, dried

Directions:
Set the instant pot on Sauté mode, add the ghee, heat it up, add the shallot and the meat and brown for 5 minutes. Add the rest of the ingredients, put the lid on and cook on High for 25 minutes. Release the pressure naturally for 10 minutes, divide everything into bowls and serve.
Nutrition: calories 337, fat 21.2, fiber 0.2, carbs 1.4, protein 33.6

Ground Chicken Mix

Preparation time: 10 minutes
Cooking time: 14 minutes
Servings: 3
Ingredients:

- 8 oz ground chicken
- 2 medium celery stalks, chopped
- 2 oz fennel, chopped
- ½ teaspoon ground black pepper
- 1 teaspoon smoked paprika
- 1 tablespoon cream cheese
- 1 teaspoon coconut oil
- 1/3 teaspoon salt

Directions:
Place the coconut oil in the instant pot and melt it. Add celery stalk and fennel. Cook the vegetables for 4 minutes on sauté mode. Stir them after 2 minutes of cooking. Meanwhile, in the mixing bowl combine ground chicken, ground black pepper, smoked paprika, and salt. Add the ground chicken mixture in the instant pot and cook on sauté mode for 3 minutes. After this, add cream cheese, stir well and close the lid. Cook the ground chicken mix for 7 minutes more.
Nutrition: calories 181, fat 8.5, fiber 1.4, carbs 2.9, protein 22.7

Chicken, Radish and Green Beans

Preparation time: 10 minutes
Cooking time: 25 minutes
Servings: 4
Ingredients:
- 2 chicken breasts, skinless, boneless and cubed
- 1 cup radishes, sliced
- 1 pound green beans, trimmed and halved
- 1 and ½ cups chicken stock
- 1 tablespoon tomato passata
- A pinch of salt and black pepper
- 1 teaspoon chili powder
- 1 tablespoon chives, chopped

Directions:
In your instant pot, mix chicken with the radishes and the rest of the ingredients except the chives, put the lid on and cook on High for 25 minutes. Release the pressure naturally for 10 minutes, divide everything between plates and serve.
Nutrition: calories 259, fat 8.7, fiber 4.3, carbs 6.5, protein 35.4

Bacon-Wrapped Chicken Tenders

Preparation time: 15 minutes
Cooking time: 14 minutes
Servings: 6
Ingredients:
- 10 oz chicken breast, skinless, boneless
- 3 bacon slices
- ¼ teaspoon salt
- ¼ teaspoon ground black pepper
- ¼ teaspoon ground turmeric
- 1 cup water, for cooking

Directions:
Rub the chicken breast with ground black pepper, ground turmeric, and salt. Pour water and insert trivet in the instant pot. Arrange the chicken breast on the trivet and close the lid. Cook it on manual mode (high pressure) for 10 minutes. When the time is over, make a quick pressure release and remove the chicken from the instant pot. Shred it with the help of the fork and knife. After this, clean the instant pot and remove the trivet. Cut every bacon slice into halves. Place the bacon halves in the instant pot and cook on sauté mode for 2 minutes from each side. After this, make the small tenders from the shredded chicken mixture with the help of the fingertips. Then wrap every tender in the cooked bacon and secure with the toothpick.
Nutrition: calories 106, fat 5.2, fiber 0, carbs 0.3, protein 13.6

Cinnamon Turkey and Celery Mix

Preparation time: 10 minutes
Cooking time: 20 minutes
Servings: 4
Ingredients:
- 1 turkey breast, skinless, boneless and cubed
- 1 tablespoon sweet paprika
- 1 tablespoon tomato passata
- 1 cup chicken stock
- 1 tablespoon ghee, melted
- 2 celery stalks, chopped
- A pinch of salt and black pepper
- ½ teaspoon cinnamon powder
- 1 tablespoon cilantro, chopped

Directions:
Set instant pot on Sauté mode, add the ghee, heat it up, add the meat and the cinnamon and brown for 5 minutes. Add the rest of the ingredients except the cilantro, put the lid on and cook on High for 15 minutes. Release the pressure naturally for 10 minutes, divide the mix between plates, sprinkle the cilantro on top and serve.
Nutrition: calories 231, fat 9.2, fiber 0.9, carbs 1.6, protein 33.6

Chicken and Spinach Bowl

Preparation time: 10 minutes
Cooking time: 15 minutes
Servings: 4
Ingredients:
- 10 oz chicken fillet, chopped
- ½ teaspoon paprika
- ¼ teaspoon salt
- ¼ teaspoon ground black pepper
- ½ teaspoon cayenne pepper
- 1 tablespoon sesame oil
- 1 red onion, sliced
- 1 cup fresh spinach, chopped
- ¼ cup of water

Directions:
Heat up instant pot on sauté mode for 3 minutes. In the mixing bowl combine together paprika, salt, chicken fillet, ground black pepper, ½ tablespoon of sesame oil, and cayenne pepper. Shake the ingredients gently and place them in the instant pot. Close the lid and sauté them for 5 minutes. Then stir the chicken well and add water. Close the lid and sauté it for 10 minutes more. Meanwhile, mix up together spinach and red onion. Add remaining sesame oil. Place the spinach mixture in the serving bowls and top them with cooked chicken.
Nutrition: calories 179, fat 8.8, fiber 1, carbs 3.2, protein 21.1

Salsa Verde Turkey

Preparation time: 10 minutes
Cooking time: 30 minutes
Servings: 4

Ingredients:
- 1 big turkey breast, skinless, boneless and cubed
- 1 cup salsa Verde
- 1 cup chicken stock
- A pinch of salt and black pepper
- 1 tablespoon chives, chopped

Directions:
In your instant pot, combine all the ingredients, toss, put the lid on and cook on High for 30 minutes. Release the pressure naturally for 10 minutes, divide everything into bowls and serve,
Nutrition: calories 211, fat 6, fiber 0.3, carbs 2.8, protein 34.5

Keto Chicken Burger

Preparation time: 10 minutes
Cooking time: 10 minutes
Servings: 2
Ingredients:
- ½ cup ground chicken
- 1 tomato, sliced
- 4 lettuce leaves
- ¼ teaspoon cayenne pepper
- 1 teaspoon dried dill
- ½ teaspoon onion powder
- ¼ teaspoon garlic powder
- 1 tablespoon almond meal
- ¼ teaspoon salt
- 1 cup water, for cooking

Directions:
Pour water and insert the trivet in the instant pot. In the mixing bowl combine together ground chicken with cayenne pepper, dried dill, onion powder, garlic powder, salt, and almond meal. Stir the ground mixture until smooth. Then make 2 balls from the ground chicken mixture, press them gently in the shape of a burger and place them in the trivet. Close the lid and cook the chicken balls for 10 minutes on manual mode (high pressure). When the time is over, make the quick pressure release. Place the chicken balls on 2 lettuce leaves. Top them with sliced tomato and remaining lettuce leaves.
Nutrition: calories 96, fat 4.2, fiber 1, carbs 3.3, protein 11.3

Basil Chicken Mix

Preparation time: 5 minutes
Cooking time: 25 minutes
Servings: 4
Ingredients:
- 2 chicken breasts, skinless, boneless and halved
- 1 cup chicken stock
- 1 and ½ tablespoons basil, chopped
- ¼ cup red bell peppers, cut into strips
- 4 garlic cloves, minced
- 1 tablespoon chili powder

Directions:
In your instant pot, combine the chicken with the rest of the ingredients, put the lid on and cook on High for 25 minutes. Release the pressure fast for 5 minutes, divide everything between plates and serve.
Nutrition: calories 230, fat 12.4, fiber 0.8, carbs 2.7, protein 33.2

Chicken Liver Pate

Preparation time: 15 minutes
Cooking time: 8 minutes
Servings: 8
Ingredients:
- 2-pound chicken liver
- 1/3 cup butter, softened
- ½ white onion, diced
- ½ teaspoon salt
- ½ teaspoon ground black pepper
- ½ teaspoon dried oregano
- 1 cup water, for cooking

Directions:
Put 1 tablespoon of butter in the instant pot and melt it on sauté mode for 3 minutes. After this, add diced onion and cook it for 5 minutes or until it I golden brown. Then transfer the onion in the big bowl and clean the instant pot. Pour water and insert the trivet in the instant pot. Mix up together chicken liver with salt and ground black pepper. Place the liver on the trivet (you can line the trivet with baking paper) and close the lid. Cook the chicken liver on steam mode for 8 minutes. When the time is over, allow the natural pressure release for 10 minutes and open the lid. Transfer the chicken liver in the food processor and blend it until smooth. Then add smooth liver in the onion; add butter and dried oregano. Stir the pate until homogenous. Store it in the fridge for up to 7 days.
Nutrition: calories 261, fat 15.1 fiber 0.2, carbs 1.8, protein 27.9

Chicken and Hot Endives

Preparation time: 10 minutes
Cooking time: 25 minutes
Servings: 4
Ingredients:
- 2 chicken breasts, skinless, boneless and cubed
- 2 tablespoons ghee, melted
- 2 endives, shredded
- 1 teaspoon hot paprika
- 1 cup chicken stock
- 2 tablespoons tomato passata
- tablespoon dill, chopped

Directions:
Set the instant pot on Sauté mode, add the ghee, heat it up, add the meat and brown for 5 minutes. Add the other ingredients except the dill, put the lid on and cook on High for 20 minutes. Release the pressure naturally for 10 minutes, divide everything between plates and serve with the dill sprinkled on top.
Nutrition: calories 278, fat 15, fiber 0.2, carbs 1, protein 33.3

Coconut Chicken Cubes

Preparation time: 10 minutes
Cooking time: 12 minutes
Servings: 3
Ingredients:
- 10 oz chicken fillet
- 3 tablespoons coconut flakes
- 2 tablespoons coconut flour
- 4 tablespoons butter
- ½ teaspoon salt
- ½ teaspoon turmeric

- ½ teaspoon chili powder
- 2 tablespoons cream cheese

Directions:
Chop the chicken fillet into medium cubes. Then sprinkle them with salt, turmeric, and chili powder. After this, dip every chicken cube in cream cheese. In the bowl mix up together coconut flakes and coconut flour. Coat every chicken cube in the coconut mixture. Melt butter in the instant pot on sauté mode (appx. 3-4 minutes). Then arrange the chicken cubes in the hot butter in one layer. Cook the coconut chicken cubes for 4 minutes and then flip them on another side. Cook the meal for 4 minutes more.
Nutrition: calories 379, fat 27, fiber 2.7, carbs 4.8, protein 28.9

Indian Chicken and Sauce

Preparation time: 10 minutes
Cooking time: 30 minutes
Servings: 4
Ingredients:
- 2 chicken breasts, skinless, boneless and cubed
- 1 cup coconut cream
- A pinch of salt and black pepper
- 2 teaspoons garam masala
- 1 cup chicken stock
- ¼ cup cilantro, chopped

Directions:
In your instant pot, mix the chicken with rest of the ingredients, put the lid on and cook on High for 30 minutes. Release the pressure naturally for 10 minutes, divide everything between plates and serve.
Nutrition: calories 356, fat 22.9, fiber 1.4, carbs 3.6, protein 34.4

Chicken Lettuce Rolls

Preparation time: 10 minutes
Cooking time: 11 minutes
Servings: 4
Ingredients:
- 4 lettuce leaves
- 8 oz chicken, grinded
- 1 garlic clove, diced
- 1 teaspoon dried parsley
- ¼ teaspoon chili flakes
- ¼ carrot, grated
- 1 teaspoon coconut oil
- 1 teaspoon ricotta cheese
- 1 tablespoon heavy cream
- 1 teaspoon apple cider vinegar

Directions:
In the bowl mix up grinded chicken, garlic, parsley, chili flakes, and carrot. Put the coconut oil in the instant pot. Set sauté mode and heat it up for 1 minute. Then add chicken mixture. Cook it on sauté mode 5 minutes. Stir it from time to time with the help of a spatula. After this, add heavy cream and ricotta cheese. Stir well. Add apple cider vinegar. Stir the chicken one more time and cook it for 5 minutes more. Then fill the lettuce leaves with chicken mixture and roll them in the shape of pockets.
Nutrition: calories 114, fat 4.4, fiber 0.2, carbs 1, protein 16.8

Turkey and Creamy Garlic Mix

Preparation time: 10 minutes
Cooking time: 25 minutes
Servings: 4
Ingredients:
- 1 big turkey breast, skinless, boneless and cubed
- 1 tablespoon ghee, melted
- 1 and ½ cups coconut cream
- A pinch of salt and black pepper
- 2 tablespoons tomato passata
- 2 tablespoons garlic, minced
- 1 teaspoon basil, dried

Directions:
Set your instant pot on Sauté mode, add the ghee, heat it up, add the meat and the garlic and brown for 5 minutes Add the rest of the ingredients, put the lid on and cook on High for 20 minutes. Release the pressure naturally for 10 minutes, divide between plates and serve.
Nutrition: calories 229, fat 8.9, fiber 0.2, carbs 1.8, protein 33.6

Turkey Bolognese Sauce

Preparation time: 10 minutes
Cooking time: 17 minutes
Servings: 4
Ingredients:
- ¼ cup carrot, grated
- ½ white onion, minced
- 1 garlic clove, diced
- ¼ teaspoon salt
- 10 oz ground turkey
- 1/3 teaspoon chili flakes
- ½ teaspoon dried thyme
- 1 teaspoon tomato paste
- 1 oz Swiss cheese, grated
- ½ scoop stevia powder
- 1 tablespoon coconut oil
- 1/3 cup water

Directions:
Toss coconut oil in the instant pot and melt it on sauté mode. Then add carrot, garlic, and onion. Cook the ingredients for 5 minutes. Stir them with the help of the spatula after 3 minutes of cooking. Then add salt and ground turkey, Sprinkle the ingredients with chili flakes, dried thyme, and stevia powder. Mix up well and sauté for 3 minutes. After this, mix up water with tomato paste. Pour the liquid over the ground turkey. Stir the sauce well and close the lid. Cook it on manual mode (high pressure) for 4 minutes. When the time is over, make the quick pressure release and open the lid. Top the sauce with Swiss cheese and mix up until the cheese is melted. The sauce is cooked.
Nutrition: calories 205, fat 13.2, fiber 0.6, carbs 2.9, protein 21.6

Chicken Casserole

Preparation time: 10 minutes
Cooking time: 30 minutes
Servings: 8
Ingredients:
- 2 pounds chicken breasts, skinless, boneless and cubed
- A pinch of salt and black pepper
- 2 tablespoons olive oil

- 2 scallions, chopped
- 1 pound Brussels sprouts, quartered
- 1 teaspoon sweet paprika
- 1 teaspoon thyme, dried
- ½ cup almonds, chopped

Directions:
Set your instant pot on Sauté mode, add the oil, heat it up, add the scallions and the meat and brown for 5 minutes. Add the remaining ingredients, put the lid on and cook on High for 25 minutes. Release the pressure naturally for 10 minutes, divide the casserole between plates and serve.
Nutrition: calories 307, fat 15.1, fiber 3.1, carbs 6.6, protein 36.1

Turkey Stuffed Mushrooms

Preparation time: 20 minutes
Cooking time: 10 minutes
Servings: 4
Ingredients:
- 8 white mushrooms
- 1 cup ground turkey
- 1/3 minced onion
- ¼ teaspoon minced garlic
- 1 teaspoon cream cheese
- 1 egg yolk
- 2 oz Mozzarella, shredded
- 2 teaspoons almond meal
- 1 cup water, for cooking

Directions:
In the mixing bowl mix up ground turkey with minced onion, cream cheese, egg yolk, and almond meal. When the mixture is homogenous, add shredded Mozzarella. Trim and clean the mushrooms. Then fill the mushrooms with ground turkey mixture. Pour water and insert the steamer rack in the instant pot. Place the mushrooms in the steamer rack in one layer and close the lid. Cook the mushrooms for 10 minutes on steam mode (high pressure). When the time is finished, allow the natural pressure release for 10 minutes. Carefully transfer the cooked mushrooms on the plate.
Nutrition: calories 281, fat 14.3, fiber 1.4, carbs 6, protein 32.6

Turkey and Cilantro Tomato Salsa

Preparation time: 10 minutes
Cooking time: 20 minutes
Servings: 4
Ingredients:
- 1 big turkey breast, skinless, boneless and cubed
- 1 cup tomatoes, cubed
- 1 tablespoon olive oil
- 1 avocado, peeled, pitted and cubed
- 2 spring onions, chopped
- 1 tablespoon cilantro, chopped
- A pinch of salt and black pepper
- 1 cup chicken stock
- 1 tablespoon smoked paprika

Directions:
Set your instant pot on Sauté mode, add the oil, heat it up, add the meat and brown for 5 minutes. Add the rest of the ingredients, put the lid on and cook on High for 20 minutes. Release the pressure naturally for 10 minutes, divide everything between plates and serve.
Nutrition: calories 343, fat 19.4, fiber 4.3, carbs 5.0, protein 34.5

Cornish Game Hens

Preparation time: 15 minutes
Cooking time: 25 minutes
Servings: 4
Ingredients:
- 1 cornish game hen (8 oz bird)
- ½ teaspoon ground paprika
- ¼ teaspoon ground turmeric
- 1 tablespoon sesame oil
- ½ teaspoon ground black pepper
- ½ teaspoon salt
- 1 cup of water

Directions:
Rub the cornish game hen with ground paprika, turmeric, salt, and ground black pepper. Then brush the bird with sesame oil and transfer in the instant pot. Add water. Close and seal the lid. Cook the bird on manual mode (high pressure) for 25 minutes. When the time is finished, make the quick pressure release and open the lid. Transfer the cooked bird on the serving plate.
Nutrition: calories 211, fat 11.2, fiber 0.4, carbs 0.8, protein 25.8

Chicken and Green Sauté

Preparation time: 10 minutes
Cooking time: 30 minutes
Servings: 4
Ingredients:
- 1 shallot, chopped
- 1 pound chicken breast, skinless, boneless and sliced
- 1 cup kale, torn
- 1 cup mustard greens, torn
- 1 cup Brussels sprouts, shredded
- 1 cup chicken stock
- 2 tablespoons tomato passata
- 2 tablespoons olive oil
- 2 garlic cloves, minced
- A pinch of salt and black pepper

Directions:
Set your instant pot on Sauté mode, add the oil, heat it up, add the shallot and the meat and brown for 5 minutes Add the rest of the ingredients, put the lid on and cook on High for 25 minutes. Release the pressure naturally for 10 minutes, divide the mix between plates and serve.
Nutrition: calories 303, fat 15.7, fiber 1.7, carbs 5.6, protein 34.5

Blackened Chicken

Preparation time: 20 minutes
Cooking time: 60 minutes
Servings: 8
Ingredients:
- 3-pound whole chicken
- 2 tablespoons butter, melted
- 1 tablespoon avocado oil
- 2 tablespoons blackening spice seasoning mix
- 1 tablespoon dried cilantro
- 1 tablespoon apple cider vinegar

- 1 cup water, for cooking

Directions:
Mix up together butter, avocado oil, blackening seasoning mix, dried cilantro, and apple cider vinegar. Then rub the chicken with the oil mixture. Preheat the instant pot on sauté mode for 3 minutes. Then place chicken in the instant pot and cook it for 5 minutes. After this, flip the chicken on another side and cook it for 5 minutes more. After this, remove the chicken from the instant pot. Pour water in the instant pot. Add chicken and close the lid. Cook the chicken on poultry mode for 50 minutes. When the time is over, let the chicken stay in liquid for 30 minutes more.
Nutrition: calories 380, fat 26.5, fiber 0.1, carbs 0.1, protein 35.2

Chicken Meatballs and Spinach

Preparation time: 5 minutes
Cooking time: 30 minutes
Servings: 4
Ingredients:
- 1 pound chicken meat, ground
- 4 garlic cloves, minced
- 1 spring onion, chopped
- ¼ cup cilantro, chopped
- ½ cup coconut flour
- 1 egg, whisked
- A pinch of salt and black pepper
- 1 and ½ cups tomato passata
- tablespoons ghee, melted
- cups baby spinach
- 1 tablespoon parsley, chopped

Directions:
In a bowl, combine the meat with the garlic, onion, flour, cilantro, the egg, salt and pepper, stir well and shape medium meatballs out of this mix. Set the instant pot on Sauté mode, add the ghee, heat it up, add the meatballs and brown them for 2 minutes on each side. Add the sauce and the spinach, put the lid on and cook on High for 25 minutes. Release the pressure fast for 5 minutes, divide everything between plates and serve with the parsley sprinkled on top.
Nutrition: calories 297, fat 16, fiber 0.6, carbs 2, protein 35

Anniversary Chicken

Preparation time: 10 minutes
Cooking time: 21 minutes
Servings: 2
Ingredients:
- 8 oz chicken breast, skinless, boneless
- ½ teaspoon chili flakes
- ½ teaspoon salt
- ½ teaspoon chili powder
- ¼ teaspoon ground turmeric
- ¼ teaspoon garlic powder
- 1 teaspoon coconut oil
- 1 cup water, for cooking

Directions:
Rub the chicken breast with chili flakes, salt, chili powder, turmeric, and garlic powder. Heat up the coconut oil in the instant pot on sauté mode for 3 minutes. Then place the chicken breast in the coconut oil and cook it for 4 minutes from each side; remove the chicken from the instant pot. Clean the instant pot and pour water inside. Insert the trivet in the instant pot. Then place the chicken breast on the trivet and close the lid. Cook the poultry on manual mode (high pressure) for 10 minutes. When the time is over, make the quick pressure release. Slice the chicken breast into servings.
Nutrition: calories 153, fat 5.3, fiber 0.3, carbs 0.8, protein 24.2

Cheesy Turkey

Preparation time: 10 minutes
Cooking time: 25 minutes
Servings: 4
Ingredients:
- 1 turkey breast, skinless, boneless and cubed
- 1 tablespoon avocado oil
- 1 cup mozzarella, shredded
- cups mixed bell peppers, cut into strips
- 1 teaspoon chili powder
- 1 cup chicken stock
- 1 tablespoon cilantro, chopped

Directions:
Set the instant pot on Sauté mode, add the oil, heat it up, add the meat and chili powder and brown for 5 minutes. Add the rest of the ingredients except the cilantro and the mozzarella and toss gently. Sprinkle the mozzarella all over, put the lid on and cook on High for 20 minutes Release the pressure naturally for 10 minutes, divide everything between plates and serve with the cilantro sprinkled on top.
Nutrition: calories 222, fat 7.6, fiber 0.4, carbs 1, protein 35.5

Ajiaco

Preparation time: 10 minutes
Cooking time: 33 minutes
Servings: 5
Ingredients:
- 13 oz chicken breast
- ½ white onion, chopped
- 2 garlic clove, chopped
- 1 teaspoon salt
- ½ teaspoon ground black pepper
- 1 tablespoon sesame oil
- 1 cup green peas, frozen
- 1 tablespoon fresh cilantro, chopped
- 1 teaspoon scallions, chopped
- ½ teaspoon guascas
- 1 ½ cup chicken broth

Directions:
In the bog bowl place white onion, garlic clove, salt, ground black pepper, sesame oil, cilantro, green peas, scallions, and guascas. Mix up the ingredients well and leave for 1 hour to marinate. Then preheat the instant pot on sauté mode for 3 minutes. Put the chicken mixture in the instant pot and cook it for 10 minutes. Stir the ingredients from time to time. Then add chicken broth and close the lid. Cook ajiaco for 20 minutes on poultry mode. Then remove the chicken breast from the instant pot and shred it. Transfer the shredded chicken breast in the serving plates and top with chicken broth from the instant pot.
Nutrition: calories 150, fat 5.1, fiber 1.8, carbs 6.1, protein 18.9

Creamy Chicken Wings

Preparation time: 10 minutes
Cooking time: 30 minutes
Servings: 4
Ingredients:
- 1 pound chicken wings, halved
- 1 tablespoon olive oil
- tablespoons lemon juice
- garlic cloves, minced
- 1 cup chicken stock
- 1 cup heavy cream
- A pinch of salt and black pepper
- 1 tablespoon parsley, chopped

Directions:
Set your instant pot on Sauté mode, add the oil, heat it up, add the garlic and the chicken wings and brown for 5 minutes. Add the rest of the ingredients except the cream and the parsley, put the lid on and cook on High for 20 minutes. Release the pressure naturally for 10 minutes, set the pot on Sauté mode again, add the cream and parsley, toss, cook for 5 minutes, divide into bowls and serve.
Nutrition: calories 358, fat 23.2, fiber 0.1, carbs 2.3, protein 33.8

Ground Turkey Chili

Preparation time: 10 minutes
Cooking time: 35 minutes
Servings: 4
Ingredients:
- 2 cups ground turkey
- 2 oz leek, chopped
- 1 white onion, chopped
- 1 teaspoon salt
- ½ cup crushed tomatoes
- 1 teaspoon chili powder
- ½ teaspoon cayenne pepper
- 1 chili pepper, chopped
- 1 tablespoon avocado oil
- ½ teaspoon ground cumin
- ½ teaspoon dried oregano
- 1 cup of water

Directions:
On the instant pot set sauté mode. Add avocado oil and onion. Then add leek and ground turkey. Stir the ingredients. Add chili powder, cayenne pepper, chili pepper, ground cumin, and dried oregano. Stir it and sauté for 10 minutes. After this, add crushed tomatoes and water. Mix up the chili mixture well and close the lid. Cook the chili for 20 minutes on stew/meat mode.
Nutrition: calories 167, fat 2.9, fiber 2.4, carbs 8.1, protein 27.9

Turkey and Blackberries Sauce

Preparation time: 5 minutes
Cooking time: 30 minutes
Servings: 4
Ingredients:
- tablespoons olive oil
- 1 big turkey breast, skinless, boneless and cubed
- A pinch of salt and black pepper
- 1 cup blackberries
- 1 cup chicken stock
- shallots, minced
- 2 tablespoons chives, chopped

Directions:
Set your instant pot on sauté mode, add the oil, heat it up, add the meat and the shallots and brown for 5 minutes. Add the rest of the ingredients except the chives, put the lid on and cook on High for 25 minutes. Release the pressure fast for 5 minutes, divide everything between plates and serve with the chives sprinkled on top.
Nutrition: calories 271, fat 13, fiber 2, carbs 3.7, protein 33.9

Ethiopian Spicy Doro Wat Soup

Preparation time: 10 minutes
Cooking time: 19 minutes
Servings: 3
Ingredients:
- 3 chicken drumsticks
- 1 teaspoon Berbere spices, divided
- 1/3 teaspoon salt
- 2 tablespoons ghee
- ½ white onion, diced
- 1 teaspoon garlic, diced
- ½ teaspoon fresh ginger, grated
- 1 egg, boiled
- 1 ½ cup chicken broth
- 1 teaspoon tomato paste
- 1 teaspoon lemon juice

Directions:
Set sauté function on your instant pot. Heat up the instant pot for 2 minutes. In the bowl combine together drumsticks and Berbere spices. Add salt. Then put ghee in the instant pot. Add spiced chicken drumsticks and onion. Add garlic and ginger. Cook the chicken for 5 minutes. Stir it well. Add tomato paste and chicken broth. Stir the soup gently. Close and seal the lid and cook it on steam mode (high pressure) for 12 minutes. When the time is over, make the quick pressure release and open the lid. Peel the boiled egg and cut it on 3 servings. Ladle the soup in the bowls and top it with egg and sprinkle with lemon juice.
Nutrition: calories 204, fat 13.3, fiber 0.5, carbs 3.2, protein 17.3

Thyme Duck and Coconut

Preparation time: 10 minutes
Cooking time: 30 minutes
Servings: 6
Ingredients:
- 2 big duck legs, boneless, skinless and cubed
- 1 tablespoon olive oil
- 1 tablespoon thyme, chopped
- ½ cup coconut, unsweetened and shredded
- 1 cup coconut cream
- A pinch of salt and black pepper
- 1 cup chicken stock

Directions:
Set your instant pot on sauté mode, add the oil, heat it up, add the meat and brown for 5 minutes. Add the rest of the ingredients, put the lid on and cook on High for 25 minutes. Release the pressure naturally for 10 minutes, divide everything between plates and serve.
Nutrition: calories 273, fat 18.6, fiber 1.7, carbs 3.7, protein 23.3

Turkey Soup

Preparation time: 10 minutes
Cooking time: 16 minutes
Servings: 4
Ingredients:
- 3 oz turnip, chopped
- 2 celery stalks, chopped
- ¼ cup Edamame beans
- 1 tablespoon cream cheese
- 3 cups chicken broth
- 8 oz turkey breast, skinless, boneless, chopped
- 1 tablespoon sesame oil
- ½ teaspoon salt
- ½ teaspoon chili flakes
- 1 teaspoon dried oregano

Directions:
Pour sesame oil in the instant pot and preheat it for 1 minute on sauté. Then add celery stalk and chopped turkey breast. Sprinkle the chicken with salt and chili flakes. Add the dried oregano. Then add cream cheese and Edamame beans. Cook the ingredients on sauté mode for 10 minutes. Stir them from time to time with the help of a spatula. Then add chicken broth and turnip. Close and seal the lid. Cook the turkey soup for 5 minutes on high-pressure mode (manual mode). When the time is over, make the quick pressure release and open the lid. Ladle the cooked soup in the serving bowls.
Nutrition: calories 135, fat 6.3, fiber 2, carbs 6.9, protein 15.9

Tuscan Chicken

Preparation time: 10 minutes
Cooking time: 25 minutes
Servings: 4
Ingredients:
- 1 pound chicken breast, skinless, boneless and cubed
- A pinch of salt and black pepper
- 1 tablespoon Italian seasoning
- 1 teaspoon oregano, dried
- tablespoons ghee, melted
- 1 cup cherry tomatoes, halved
- cups baby spinach
- 1 cup heavy cream
- ¼ cup parmesan, grated

Directions:
Set the instant pot on Sauté mode, add the ghee, heat it up, add the chicken and brown for 5 minutes. Add salt, pepper and the rest of the ingredients except the parmesan, put the lid on and cook on High for 20 minutes. Release the pressure naturally for 10 minutes, sprinkle the parmesan all over, divide between plates and serve.
Nutrition: calories 339, fat 22.4, fiber 1, carbs 3.8, protein 34.3

Chicken Fricassee

Preparation time: 10 minutes
Cooking time: 28 minutes
Servings: 6
Ingredients:
- 3 bacon slices, chopped
- 6 chicken thighs
- ½ yellow onion, diced
- 1 celery stalk, chopped
- 1 carrot, chopped
- ¼ cup mushrooms, chopped
- 1 teaspoon arrowroot powder
- 3 tablespoons apple cider vinegar
- 2 cups chicken broth
- 1 cup of water
- ½ teaspoon thyme
- 1 bay leaf
- 1 tablespoon lime juice
- 1/3 teaspoon salt
- 1/3 cup heavy cream
- 1 egg yolk

Directions:
Preheat instant pot on sauté mode for 2 minutes and add chopped bacon. Cook it for 4 minutes or until it is crispy. Then remove the bacon in the bowl. Rub the chicken thighs with salt, thyme, and place in the instant pot. Cook it for 3 minutes from each side. Add onion, celery stalk, mushrooms, carrot, arrowroot, and lime juice. Mix up the ingredients and cook them for 6 minutes. Then add bay leaf, apple cider vinegar, chicken broth, and water. Close and seal the lid and cook the meal on manual mode (high pressure) for 10 minutes. When the time is over, make the quick pressure release. Whisk together heavy cream and egg yolk. While stirring the chicken mixture - add the heavy cream liquid. Then sauté the meal for 3 minutes. Place the meal in the bowls. Top the fricassee with cooked bacon.
Nutrition: calories 264, fat 17.3, fiber 0.6, carbs 3.9, protein 21.6

Marinated Turkey Mix

Preparation time: 5 minutes
Cooking time: 30 minutes
Servings: 6
Ingredients:
- 2 pounds turkey breast, skinless, boneless and cubed
- A pinch of salt and black pepper
- yellow bell peppers, cut into strips
- 2 shallots, chopped
- 1 broccoli head, florets separated
- ½ cup olive oil
- Juice of 2 limes
- ¼ cup cilantro, chopped

Directions:
Set your instant pot on Sauté mode, add the oil, heat it up, add the meat, lime juice and the cilantro and brown for 5 minutes. Add the rest of the ingredients, put the lid on and cook on High for 20 minutes. Release the pressure fast for 5 minutes, divide the mix between plates and serve.
Nutrition: calories 310, fat 18.4, fiber 0.4, carbs 2.3, protein 33.4

Chicken Steamed Balls

Preparation time: 10 minutes
Cooking time: 15 minutes
Servings: 2
Ingredients:
- 2 tablespoon almond flour
- 6 oz ground chicken
- 1 teaspoon dried dill
- ¼ carrot, boiled, mashed
- ¼ teaspoon salt
- 1/3 teaspoon ground black pepper

●1 cup water, for cooking
Directions:
In the bowl mix up together almond flour, ground chicken, dill, mashed carrot, salt, and ground black pepper. Then make 2 balls from the chicken mixture. Pour water and insert the steamer in the instant pot. Place the chicken balls inside and cook them for 15 minutes on steam mode (high pressure). When the time is finished, make the quick pressure release and open the lid. The chicken steamed balls are cooked.
Nutrition: calories 209, fat 9.7, fiber 1.1, carbs 2.8, protein 26.3

Tabasco Chicken and Kale

Preparation time: 10 minutes
Cooking time: 25 minutes
Servings: 4
Ingredients:
- 2 chicken breasts, skinless, boneless and cubed
- 2 tablespoons ghee, melted
- 1 tablespoon Tabasco sauce
- 2 cups kale, chopped
- A pinch of salt and black pepper
- 1 tablespoon basil, chopped
- 1 cup chicken stock

Directions:
Set your instant pot on sauté mode, add the ghee, heat it up, add the meat and brown for 5 minutes Add the rest of the ingredients, put the lid on and cook on High for 20 minutes. Release the pressure naturally for 10 minutes, divide everything between plates and serve.
Nutrition: calories 291, fat 14.9, fiber 0.5, carbs 3.8, protein 34.2

South American Garden Chicken

Preparation time: 15 minutes
Cooking time: 17 minutes
Servings: 4
Ingredients:
●1 cup cauliflower, chopped
●1 celery stalk, chopped
●1 tablespoon lemon juice
●4 chicken thighs, skinless, boneless
●1 teaspoon pumpkin puree
●½ teaspoon salt
●1 teaspoon ground black pepper
●½ cup chicken broth
●1 teaspoon ghee
●1 bay leaf
●½ onion, diced

Directions:
Sprinkle the chicken thighs with salt and ground black pepper. Place them in the instant pot. Add ghee. Cook the chicken on sauté mode for 4 minutes. Then flip it on another side and cook for 5 minutes more. After this, add celery stalk and cauliflower. Add diced onion. Then add pumpkin puree, lemon juice, and chicken broth. Close and seal the lid. Cook the meal on manual mode (high pressure) for 8 minutes. Then allow the natural pressure release for 5 minutes.
Nutrition: calories 170, fat 7.4, fiber 1.3, carbs 3.6, protein 23.4

Chicken, Peppers and Mushrooms

Preparation time: 10 minutes
Cooking time: 25 minutes
Servings: 4
Ingredients:
- 2 chicken breasts, skinless, boneless and cubed
- 1 shallot, chopped
- 2 red bell peppers, cubed
- 2 green bell peppers, cubed
- 2 garlic cloves, minced
- 1 pound white mushrooms, halved
- A pinch of salt and black pepper
- 1 cup chicken stock

Directions:
In your instant pot, mix the chicken with the rest of the ingredients, put the lid on and cook on High for 25 minutes. Release the pressure naturally for 10 minutes, divide everything between plates and serve.
Nutrition: calories 283, fat 9.2, fiber 2.8, carbs 4.4, protein 34.5

Chicken Moussaka

Preparation time: 15 minutes
Cooking time: 55 minutes
Servings: 6
Ingredients:
●1 teaspoon avocado oil
●1 cup ground turkey
●1 cup eggplants, peeled, chopped
●1 green bell pepper, chopped
●¼ cup onion, diced
●¼ teaspoon garlic, diced
●½ cup green beans, boiled
●1 tomato, chopped
●½ cup heavy cream
●½ teaspoon salt
●½ teaspoon white pepper
●1 cup water, for cooking

Directions:
Brush the instant pot casserole mold with avocado oil. Then add ground turkey inside and sprinkle it with salt and white pepper. Stir the turkey gently with the help of the fork. After this, top the turkey with eggplants, bell pepper, and onion. Sprinkle the ingredients with garlic, green beans, and chopped tomato. After this, pour the heavy cream over the mixture and cover it with foil. Secure the edges of the casserole mold. Pour water and insert the trivet in the instant pot. Place the casserole mold on the trivet and close the lid. Cook moussaka for 55 minutes on stew/meat mode.
Nutrition: calories 94, fat 4.6, fiber 1.4, carbs 4.3, protein 9.7

Cheddar Turkey

Preparation time: 10 minutes
Cooking time: 30 minutes
Servings: 6
Ingredients:
- 1 tablespoon ginger, grated
- 4 garlic cloves, minced
- 1 tablespoon olive oil
- 1 cup coconut milk
- 1 big turkey breast, skinless, boneless and cubed
- A pinch of salt and black pepper

- 1 cup cheddar cheese, grated

Directions:
Set the instant pot on Sauté mode, add the oil, heat it up, add the garlic, ginger and the turkey and brown for 5 minutes. Add the rest of the ingredients except the cheese and toss. Sprinkle the cheese on top, put the lid on and cook on High for 25 minutes. Release the pressure naturally for 10 minutes, divide everything between plates and serve.
Nutrition: calories 323, fat 22, fiber 1, carbs 3.8, protein 28

Fajita Chicken Casserole

Preparation time: 10 minutes
Cooking time: 16 minutes
Servings: 5
Ingredients:
- 1 cup broccoli, shredded
- 9 oz chicken breast, boneless, skinless, chopped
- ½ teaspoon chili powder
- ½ teaspoon ground black pepper
- ¼ teaspoon salt
- ½ teaspoon chili flakes
- ½ teaspoon ground nutmeg
- 2 bell peppers, roughly chopped
- ½ cup Cheddar cheese, shredded
- ½ cup of coconut milk
- 1 cup chicken broth
- 1 teaspoon ghee

Directions:
Place ghee in the instant pot and melt it on sauté mode. Then add chopped chicken breast. Sprinkle it with chili powder, ground black pepper, salt, chili flakes, and ground nutmeg. Cook the chicken for 8 minutes. Then add bell peppers, broccoli, and coconut milk. Add chicken broth and stir the ingredients with the help of the spoon. After this, top the casserole with Cheddar cheese and close the lid. Cook the meal on manual mode (high pressure) for 6 minutes. Then make the quick pressure release.
Nutrition: calories 198, fat 12.2, fiber 1.8, carbs 6.9, protein 16.2

Chicken and Almonds Mix

Preparation time: 5 minutes
Cooking time: 25 minutes
Servings: 4
Ingredients:
- 1 cup chicken stock
- 2 tablespoons avocado oil
- 2 chicken breasts, skinless, boneless and halved
- 1 tablespoon balsamic vinegar
- tablespoons almonds, chopped
- A pinch of salt and black pepper
- 1 tablespoon chives, chopped

Directions:
Set your instant pot on sauté mode, add the oil, heat it up, add the chicken and brown for 5 minutes. Add the rest of the ingredients, put the lid on and cook on High for 20 minutes. Release the pressure fast for 5 minutes, divide between plates and serve.
Nutrition: calories 254, fat 11.7, fiber 0.9, carbs 1.6, protein 34

Chicken with Black Olives

Preparation time: 10 minutes
Cooking time: 15 minutes
Servings: 2
Ingredients:
- 2 chicken thighs, skinless, boneless, chopped
- ¼ cup black olives, sliced
- ½ cup Mozzarella cheese, shredded
- ½ cup cream
- ½ teaspoon ground black pepper
- 1 teaspoon dried parsley
- ½ teaspoon chili powder

Directions:
Mix up chicken thighs with chili powder, parsley, ground black pepper, and cream. Then put the chicken in the instant pot and cook it on stew mode for 10 minutes. Stir it from time to time with the help of the spatula. Then add black olives and cheese. Stir the ingredients and cook them for 5 minutes more on stew mode.
Nutrition: calories 359, fat 17.3, fiber 0.9, carbs 3.9, protein 45

Turkey, Brussels Sprouts and Walnuts

Preparation time: 5 minutes
Cooking time: 25 minutes
Servings: 4
Ingredients:
- 1 big turkey breast, skinless, boneless and cubed
- 1 tablespoon garlic, minced
- 2 tablespoons olive oil
- A pinch of salt and black pepper
- 1 tablespoon chili powder
- 1 pound Brussels sprouts, shredded
- 1 tablespoon walnuts, chopped

Directions:
Set your instant pot on sauté mode, add the oil, heat it up, add the meat and the garlic and brown for 5 minutes Add the rest of the ingredients, put the lid on and cook on High for 20 minutes. Release the pressure fast for 5 minutes, divide the mix between plates and serve.
Nutrition: calories 323, fat 14.5, fiber 5.4, carbs 6.3, protein 34.9

Indian Chicken Korma

Preparation time: 10 minutes
Cooking time: 15 minutes
Servings: 3
Ingredients:
- 9 oz chicken fillet, chopped
- ½ teaspoon minced ginger
- ¼ teaspoon minced garlic
- ¼ teaspoon Serrano pepper, chopped
- ½ tomato, chopped
- 1 tablespoon peanuts, chopped
- 1 teaspoon ghee
- 1 cup of water
- ¼ teaspoon fennel seeds
- ¼ teaspoon cumin seeds
- ½ teaspoon ground coriander
- ½ teaspoon ground cumin
- ½ teaspoon smoked paprika
- ½ teaspoon salt
- ½ teaspoon ground turmeric

- ¼ teaspoon ground cinnamon
- ¼ teaspoon ground cardamom
- 1 teaspoon garam masala

Directions:
Blend the minced ginger, garlic, Serrano pepper, and tomato until smooth. Then mix up together the blended mixture with chicken. After this, blend peanuts with ¼ cup of water. Place the chicken mixture and ghee in the instant pot. Add fennel seeds, cumin seeds, ground coriander, cumin, paprika, salt, turmeric, cinnamon, cardamom, and garam masala. Carefully stir the chicken with the help of the spatula. Add remaining water and close the lid. Cook the meal on manual (high pressure) for 10 minutes. Then make the quick pressure release and open the lid. Add the blended peanut mixture and close the lid. Cook the chicken korma for 5 minutes on stew mode.

Nutrition: calories 199, fat 9.4, fiber 0.9, carbs 2.1, protein 25.7

Ketogenic Instant Pot Meat Recipes

Garlic and Parsley Pork

Preparation time: 10 minutes
Cooking time: 45 minutes
Servings: 6
Ingredients:
- 2 and ½ pounds pork shoulder, cubed
- 2 garlic cloves, minced
- 2 tablespoons parsley, chopped
- 1 teaspoon garlic powder
- 1 teaspoon oregano, dried
- 1 teaspoon rosemary, dried
- Salt and black pepper to the taste
- 2 cups beef stock

Directions:
In your instant pot, combine the pork with the garlic and the rest of the ingredients, put the lid on and cook on High for 45 minutes. Release the pressure naturally for 10 minutes, divide everything between plates and serve.
Nutrition: calories 454, fat 26.5, fiber 0.3, carbs 1.1, protein 35.6

Rosemary Barbecue Pork Chops

Preparation time: 15 minutes
Cooking time: 18 minutes
Servings: 2
Ingredients:
- 2 pork chops
- 1 teaspoon dried rosemary
- 1 teaspoon avocado oil
- ½ teaspoon salt
- 1 tablespoon BBQ sauce
- 1 tablespoon cream cheese

Directions:
Mix up together dried rosemary and avocado oil. Rub the pork chops with rosemary mixture and leave for 10 minutes to marinate. After this, place them in the instant pot and cook on sauté mode for 4 minutes from each side. Then add BBQ sauce, cream cheese, and salt. Close the lid and cook the pork chops for 10 minutes on sauté mode.
Nutrition: calories 290, fat 22, fiber 0.4, carbs 3.5, protein 18.4

Rosemary and Cinnamon Pork

Preparation time: 10 minutes
Cooking time: 40 minutes
Servings: 6
Ingredients:
- 1 and ½ pounds pork shoulder, cubed
- 1 tablespoon olive oil
- 1 cup beef stock
- 1 tablespoon rosemary, chopped
- 1 tablespoon cinnamon powder
- 2 garlic cloves, minced
- A pinch of salt and black pepper
- 1 teaspoon chili powder

Directions:
Set the instant pot on Sauté mode, add the oil, heat it up, add the meat, chili powder, rosemary and cinnamon and brown for 5 minutes. Add the remaining ingredients, toss, put the lid on and cook on High for 35 minutes. Release the pressure naturally for 10 minutes, divide the mix between plates and serve.
Nutrition: calories 352, fat 26.5, fiber 0.3, carbs 0.7, protein 26.5

Kalua Pork

Preparation time: 25 minutes
Cooking time: 40 minutes
Servings: 4
Ingredients:
- 12 oz pork shoulder, chopped
- ½ teaspoon liquid smoke
- 1 teaspoon salt
- 1 cup water, for cooking

Directions:
In the mixing bowl mix up together chopped pork shoulder with salt and liquid smoke. Leave the meat for 15 minutes to marinate. When the time is over, pour the water and insert the trivet in the instant pot. Line the trivet with baking paper. Place the meat on the trivet in one layer and close the lid. Cook the meal on manual mode (high pressure) for 40 minutes. When the time is over, allow the natural pressure release for 15 minutes. Transfer the cooked meat in the bowls and shred with the help of the fork.
Nutrition: calories 248, fat 18.2, fiber 0, carbs 0, protein 19.8

Curry Pork and Kale

Preparation time: 10 minutes
Cooking time: 35 minutes
Servings: 6
Ingredients:
- 2 pounds pork shoulder, cubed
- 2 tablespoons avocado oil
- 2 tablespoons curry powder
- 1 pound kale, torn
- 2 garlic cloves, minced
- 1 cup beef stock
- 2 tablespoons parsley, chopped
- A pinch of salt and black pepper

Directions:
Set your instant pot on Sauté mode, add the oil, heat it up, add the meat, garlic and curry powder, toss and brown for 5 minutes. Add the rest of the ingredients, put the lid on and cook on High for 30 minutes. Release the pressure naturally for 10 minutes, divide everything between plates and serve.
Nutrition: calories 373, fat 25, fiber 1.6, carbs 6.9, protein 28.8

Parmesan Pork

Preparation time: 10 minutes
Cooking time: 35 minutes
Servings: 4
Ingredients:
- 4 pork chops
- 1 teaspoon white pepper
- 1 teaspoon sesame oil
- ½ cup heavy cream
- 1 teaspoon dried basil
- 4 oz Parmesan, grated

Directions:

Brush the instant pot bowl with sesame oil from inside. Sprinkle pork chops with white pepper and dried basil and put in the instant pot. Then top the meat with Parmesan and heavy cream. Close the lid and cook it on manual mode (high pressure) for 35 minutes. When the time is over, allow the natural pressure release for 10 minutes.
Nutrition: calories 410, fat 32.7, fiber 0.1, carbs 1.8, protein 27.5

Pork and Cilantro Tomato Mix
Preparation time: 10 minutes
Cooking time: 35 minutes
Servings: 6
Ingredients:
- 1 and ½ pound pork stew meat, cubed
- 2 tablespoons olive oil
- 2 garlic cloves, minced
- 1 cup tomato passata
- 1 tablespoon cilantro, chopped
- ½ cup beef stock
- A pinch of salt and black pepper

Directions:
Set your instant pot on Sauté mode, add oil, heat it up, add the meat and the garlic and brown for 5 minutes. Add the rest of the ingredients, put the lid on and cook on High for 30 minutes. Release the pressure naturally for 10 minutes, divide the mix between plates and serve.
Nutrition: calories 285, fat 14.6, fiber 0.6, carbs 3.1, protein 33.9

Garlic Pork Loin
Preparation time: 10 minutes
Cooking time: 60 minutes
Servings: 5
Ingredients:
- 1-pound pork loin, boneless
- 4 garlic cloves, peeled
- 1 white onion, peeled
- 1 teaspoon salt
- 1 teaspoon peppercorns
- 1 bay leaf
- 1 cup chicken broth

Directions:
Put all ingredients in the instant pot and close the lid. Set meat/stew mode and cook the pork loin for 60 minutes. When the time is over, chop the meat into the servings and put in the serving bowls. Add the meat liquid from the instant pot.
Nutrition: calories 241, fat 13, fiber 0.7, carbs 3.4, protein 26.2

Mustard Pork and Chard
Preparation time: 10 minutes
Cooking time: 40 minutes
Servings: 6
Ingredients:
- 1 and ½ pounds pork stew meat, cubed
- 1 tablespoon mustard
- 1 tablespoon ghee, melted
- 1 shallot, minced
- A pinch of salt and black pepper
- 1 pound red chard
- 2 garlic cloves, chopped
- 1 cup beef stock
- 1 tablespoon tomato passata
- 1 tablespoon parsley, chopped

Directions:
Set your instant pot on Sauté mode, add the ghee, heat it up, add the shallot, garlic, the meat and mustard, toss and brown for 5 minutes. Add the rest of the ingredients except the parsley, put the lid on and cook on High for 35 minutes. Release the pressure naturally for 10 minutes, divide the mix between plates, sprinkle the parsley on top and serve.
Nutrition: calories 353, fat 17.4, fiber 0.4, carbs 1.2, protein 34.2

Fragrant Pork Belly
Preparation time: 15 minutes
Cooking time: 65 minutes
Servings: 6
Ingredients:
- 15 oz pork belly
- 1 teaspoon thyme
- 1 teaspoon cumin seeds
- 1 teaspoon fennel seeds
- 1 teaspoon salt
- 1 teaspoon olive oil
- 1 teaspoon garlic, minced
- 1 cup water, for cooking

Directions:
Rub the pork belly with minced garlic, thyme, cumin seeds, fennel seeds, and salt, Then brush it carefully with olive oil. Wrap the pork belly in the foil. Pour water and insert the trivet in the instant pot. Put the wrapped pork belly on the trivet and close the lid. Cook the meal on manual mode (high pressure) for 65 minutes. When the time is over, allow the natural pressure release for 10 minutes. Remove the foil and slice the pork belly into the servings.
Nutrition: calories 337, fat 20, fiber 0.2, carbs 0.6, protein 32.9

Pork, Spinach and Green Beans
Preparation time: 10 minutes
Cooking time: 35 minutes
Servings: 6
Ingredients:
- 1 and ½ pound pork shoulder, cubed
- 1 shallot, minced
- ½ pound baby spinach
- 1 cup green beans, trimmed and halved
- 2 tablespoons olive oil
- A pinch of salt and black pepper
- ½ teaspoon chili powder
- 1 cup tomato passata
- 1 tablespoon parsley, chopped

Directions:
Set your instant pot on Sauté mode, add the oil, heat it up, add the meat, shallot and chili powder and brown for 5 minutes. Add the rest of the ingredients, put the lid on and cook on High for 30 minutes. Release the pressure naturally for 10 minutes, divide the mix between plates and serve.
Nutrition: calories 384, fat 26.5, fiber 1.8, carbs 5, protein 28.4

Parmesan Pork Tenderloins
Preparation time: 10 minutes
Cooking time: 35 minutes

Servings: 4
Ingredients:
- 12 oz pork tenderloin
- ½ white onion, diced
- 1 teaspoon ground black pepper
- ½ teaspoon ground nutmeg
- 1 teaspoon sesame oil
- ½ cup heavy cream
- 2 oz Parmesan, grated
- 1/3 cup water

Directions:
Preheat the instant pot on sauté mode for 4 minutes. Meanwhile, rub the pork tenderloin with ground black pepper and nutmeg. Then brush it with sesame oil from each side. Place the meat in the instant pot and cook it on sauté mode for 3 minutes from both sides. After this, add water and bring it to the boil (appx.5 minutes). Then combine together cream with Parmesan. Pour the liquid over the meat and close the lid. Cook the meat on manual mode (high pressure) for 20 minutes. When the time is over, make the quick pressure release and open the lid. Slice the pork tenderloin and sprinkle it with cheese sauce.
Nutrition: calories 237, fat 12.8, fiber 0.5, carbs 2.7, protein 27.4

Pork, Kale and Capers Mix

Preparation time: 10 minutes
Cooking time: 40 minutes
Servings: 6
Ingredients:
- 2 pounds pork shoulder, cubed
- 1 tablespoon avocado oil
- 1 tablespoon capers, drained
- A pinch of salt and black pepper
- 1 cup beef stock
- 1 pound kale, torn
- ½ teaspoon smoked paprika
- 2 garlic cloves, minced
- 1 tablespoons chives, chopped
- 1 tablespoon oregano, chopped

Directions:
Set the instant pot on Sauté mode, add the oil, heat it up, add the meat, garlic and the paprika and brown for 5 minutes. Add the rest of the ingredients except the chives, put the lid on and cook on High for 35 minutes. Release the pressure naturally for 10 minutes, divide the mix between plates and serve with the chives sprinkled on top.
Nutrition: calories 367, fat 24.5, fiber 1.3, carbs 6.8, protein 28.2

Keto Ham

Preparation time: 10 minutes
Cooking time: 30 minutes
Servings: 4
Ingredients:
- 11 oz spiraled ham
- 1 teaspoon Erythritol
- ¼ teaspoon dried rosemary
- ¼ teaspoon salt
- 1 teaspoon ground cinnamon
- 2 tablespoons butter, melted
- 1 cup water, for cooking

Directions:
Slice the spiral ham and sprinkle it with salt. Then wrap it in foil. Pour water and insert the steamer rack in the instant pot. Place the wrapped ham on the rack and close the lid. Cook it on manual mode (high pressure) for 5 minutes. Then allow the natural pressure release for 10 minutes and open the lid. Transfer the ham in the bowl and clean the instant pot. Place the butter in the instant pot. Add Erythritol, salt, dried rosemary, and ground cinnamon. On sauté mode heat up the liquid. Add the ham and coat it well. Cook the meat on sauté mode for 5 minutes and then flip on another side and cook for 5 minutes more.
Nutrition: calories 218, fat 15.9, fiber 0.3, carbs 4.2, protein 14.8

Pork and Lemon Basil Sauce

Preparation time: 10 minutes
Cooking time: 30 minutes
Servings: 6
Ingredients:
- 2 tablespoons olive oil
- 1 and ½ pounds pork stew meat, cubed
- 2 tablespoons lemon juice
- 1 tablespoon lemon zest, grated
- 1 and ½ cup beef stock
- 2 tablespoons basil, chopped
- A pinch of salt and black pepper

Directions:
In your blender, combine the lemon zest with lemon juice, oil, stock and basil and pulse well. Set the instant pot on Sauté mode, add the basil sauce, heat it up, add the rest of the ingredients, toss, put the lid on and cook on High for 30 minutes. Release the pressure naturally for 10 minutes, divide the mix between plates and serve.
Nutrition: calories 272, fat 14.5, fiber 0.1, carbs 0.3, protein 33.3

Jalapeno Pulled Pork

Preparation time: 10 minutes
Cooking time: 65 minutes
Servings: 2
Ingredients:
- 8 oz pork shoulder, boneless, chopped
- 1 jalapeno pepper, chopped
- 1 teaspoon minced garlic
- 1 cup of water
- 1 teaspoon salt
- 1 teaspoon peppercorns
- ½ teaspoon chili pepper
- 1 teaspoon tomato paste
- ½ teaspoon ground cumin

Directions:
Place the pork shoulder in the instant pot. Add minced garlic, water, salt, peppercorns, chili pepper, and tomato paste. Then add ground cumin and stir the ingredients gently with the help of the spoon. Close the lid. Cook the meat on meat/stew mode for 60 minutes. When the time is over, open the lid and strain the liquid. Then shred the meat with the help of the fork. Add the strained liquid and chopped jalapeno pepper. Close the lid and cook the pulled pork for 5 minutes on sauté mode.
Nutrition: calories 343, fat 24.5, fiber 0.7, carbs 2.4, protein 26.9

Pork and Cauliflower Rice

Preparation time: 10 minutes
Cooking time: 30 minutes
Servings: 4
Ingredients:
- 1 pound pork shoulder, cubed
- 1 cup beef stock
- 1 cup cauliflower rice
- 2 tablespoons chives, chopped
- ½ teaspoon oregano, dried
- A pinch of salt and black pepper
- 2 tablespoons ghee, melted

Directions:
Set your instant pot on Sauté mode, add the ghee, heat it up, add the meat and brown for 5 minutes. Add the rest of the ingredients, put the lid on and cook on High for 25 minutes. Release the pressure naturally for 10 minutes, divide the mix between plates and serve.
Nutrition: calories 393, fat 13, fiber 0.1, carbs 0.2, protein 27.2

Char Siu

Preparation time: 20 minutes
Cooking time: 25 minutes
Servings: 3
Ingredients:
- 7 oz pork butt meat
- 1 teaspoon Erythritol
- 1 tablespoon BBQ sauce (Japanese style)
- 1 teaspoon apple cider vinegar
- ½ teaspoon garlic powder
- 1 tablespoon avocado oil
- ½ teaspoon salt
- 1 cup water, for cooking

Directions:
Make the marinade: in the big bowl mix up together Erythritol, BBQ sauce, apple cider vinegar, garlic powder, avocado oil, and salt. Then brush the meat well and leave to marinate for 20 minutes. After this, wrap the meat in the foil. Pour water and insert the trivet in the instant pot. Place the wrapped meat on the trivet and close the lid. Cook the meat on manual mode (high pressure) for 20 minutes. When the time is over, allow the natural pressure release for 10 minutes. Meanwhile, preheat the oven to 375F. Remove the cooked meat from the foil and slice it. Broil the pork butt in the oven for 5 minutes.
Nutrition: calorie 189, fat 11.6, fiber 0.3, carbs 2.5, protein 17.5

Spicy Pork, Zucchinis and Eggplants

Preparation time: 10 minutes
Cooking time: 30 minutes
Servings: 6
Ingredients:
- 1 and ½ pound pork shoulder, cubed
- 1 tablespoon olive oil
- 2 small zucchinis, sliced
- 2 small eggplants, cubed
- 1 tablespoon chili powder
- A pinch of red pepper flakes
- 2 spring onions, chopped
- 1 and ½ cups beef stock
- 1 tablespoon cilantro, chopped
- 2 tablespoons tomato paste
- A pinch of salt and black pepper

Directions:
Set your instant pot on Sauté mode, add the oil, heat it up, add the meat, chili powder and pepper flakes and brown for 5 minutes. Add the rest of the ingredients, put the lid on and cook on High for 25 minutes. Release the pressure naturally for 10 minutes, divide everything between plates and serve.
Nutrition: calories 396, fat 26.4, fiber 2.3, carbs 5.5, protein 28.5

Chili Spare Ribs

Preparation time: 15 minutes
Cooking time: 25 minutes
Servings: 3
Ingredients:
- 9 oz pork spare ribs
- 1 teaspoon tomato paste
- 2 tablespoons avocado oil
- 1 teaspoon chili powder
- ½ teaspoon chili flakes
- 1 teaspoon apple cider vinegar
- ¼ teaspoon salt
- 1 cup water, for cooking

Directions:
In the shallow bowl whisk together tomato paste, avocado oil, chili powder, chili flakes, salt, and apple cider vinegar. Generously brush the spare ribs with tomato paste mixture and leave for 10 minutes to marinate. Meanwhile, pour water and insert the steamer rack in the instant pot. Place the ribs in the instant pot baking pan. Then place the pan on the rack and close the lid. Cook the spare ribs for 25 minutes on Manual mode (high pressure). When the time is finished, make the quick pressure release and transfer the meal on the plate.
Nutrition: calories 176, fat 12, fiber 0.8, carbs 1.4, protein 15.5

Pork Meatballs and Spring Onions Sauce

Preparation time: 10 minutes
Cooking time: 25 minutes
Servings: 6
Ingredients:
- 2 tablespoons cilantro, chopped
- 1 and ½ pound pork, ground
- 1 cup beef stock
- 2 tablespoons tomato passata
- 1 egg, whisked
- 1 tablespoon olive oil
- ¼ teaspoon red pepper flakes
- A pinch of salt and black pepper
- 3 spring onions, chopped

Directions:
In a bowl, mix the pork with the cilantro, salt, pepper and the egg, stir well and shape medium meatballs out of this mix. Set the instant pot on Sauté mode, add the oil, heat it up, add the meatballs and brown for 2 minutes on each side. Add the rest of the ingredients, put the lid on and cook on High for 20 minutes. Release the pressure naturally for 10 minutes divide the mix between plates and serve.
Nutrition: calories 217, fat 7.4, fiber 0.3, carbs 0.8, protein 35.4

Taiwanese Braised Pork Belly

Preparation time: 15 minutes
Cooking time: 32 minutes
Servings: 6
Ingredients:
- 1-pound pork belly, chopped
- 1 oz shallot, chopped, fried
- 1 teaspoon ginger, sliced
- 1 teaspoon minced garlic
- ½ teaspoon anise
- 1 teaspoon salt
- 1 teaspoon ground cinnamon
- 1 tablespoon apple cider vinegar
- 1 tablespoon avocado oil
- 1 teaspoon swerve
- ½ cup of water

Directions:
Place the chopped pork belly in the instant pot and start to cook it on sauté mode. After 6 minutes stir the pork belly well and add ginger and garlic. Then add avocado oil and stir well. Cook the pork belly on sauté mode for 4 minutes more. After this, add swerve, apple cider vinegar, ground cinnamon, salt, and shallot. Add water and close the lid. Cook the meal on manual mode (high pressure) for 22 minutes. When the time is over, make the quick pressure release.
Nutrition: calories 360, fat 20.7, fiber 0.4, carbs 2, protein 35.2

Raspberry Pork Mix

Preparation time: 10 minutes
Cooking time: 35 minutes
Servings: 4
Ingredients:
- 1 and ½ pounds pork shoulder, cubed
- 1 tablespoon ghee, melted
- 1 cup raspberries
- 1 cup beef stock
- 2 teaspoons sweet paprika
- 1 tablespoon chives, chopped
- 1 tablespoon balsamic vinegar

Directions:
Set your instant pot on Sauté mode, add the ghee, heat it up, add the meat and brown for 5 minutes. Add the rest of the ingredients, toss, put the lid on and cook on High for 20 minutes. Release the pressure naturally for 10 minutes, divide the mix between plates and serve.
Nutrition: calories 357, fat 23.3, fiber 1.2, carbs 2.2, protein 27.6

Korean Style Pork Ribs

Preparation time: 15 minutes
Cooking time: 20 minutes
Servings: 5
Ingredients:
- 1-pound beef chuck short ribs, chopped
- 1 tablespoon chives, chopped
- ½ teaspoon salt
- 2 tablespoons avocado oil
- ½ teaspoon minced garlic
- ¼ teaspoon sesame seeds
- 4 tablespoons apple cider vinegar
- 1 tablespoon Monk fruit
- ½ shallot, chopped
- ½ teaspoon white pepper
- 1 tablespoon butter
- 1 jalapeno pepper, chopped

Directions:
Make the marinade: put shallot in the blender. Add salt, avocado oil, minced garlic, apple cider vinegar, Monk fruit, chopped jalapeno pepper, and white pepper. Blend the mixture until smooth. Then combine together chopped ribs with blended mixture. Coat the ribs well and leave for 15 minutes to marinate. After this, toss the butter in the instant pot and melt it on sauté mode. Place the beef ribs in the instant pot bowl in one layer and cook them for 8 minutes from each side. Then add remaining marinade and sesame seeds. Cook the ribs for 2 minutes from each side more.
Nutrition: calories 282, fat 24, fiber 0.4, carbs 1.3, protein 15.5

Chili Pork Chops

Preparation time: 10 minutes
Cooking time: 25 minutes
Servings: 4
Ingredients:
- 4 pork chops
- 1 tablespoon ghee, melted
- 1 cup beef stock
- 1 tablespoon chili powder
- 1 tablespoon sweet paprika
- 2 garlic cloves, chopped
- A pinch of salt and black pepper
- 1 tablespoon cilantro, chopped

Directions:
Set the instant pot on Sauté mode, add the ghee, heat it up, add the pork chops and brown for 2 minutes on each side. Add the rest of the ingredients, put the lid on and cook on High for 20 minutes. Release the pressure naturally for 10 minutes, divide the mix between plates and serve.
Nutrition: calories 303, fat 23.7, fiber 1.4, carbs 2.8, protein 19.4

Pork and Turnip Cake

Preparation time: 15 minutes
Cooking time: 40 minutes
Servings: 6
Ingredients:
- 6 oz turnip, grated
- 1 cup ground pork
- ½ teaspoon ground black pepper
- 1 teaspoon cumin
- 1 white onion, minced
- ½ teaspoon salt
- 3 tablespoons butter, soften
- ½ cup almond flour
- 1 egg, beaten
- ½ teaspoon baking powder
- 1 cup water, for cooking

Directions:
Make the pie crust: in the big bowl combine together egg, baking powder, almond flour, and butter. Knead the soft and non-sticky dough. Line the instant pot baking mold with baking paper. Roll up the dough with the help of the rolling pin and transfer in the baking mold. Flatten it in the shape of the pie crust. After this, mix up ground pork with grated turnip, ground black pepper, cumin, minced onion, salt, and

transfer the mixture over the pie crust. Flatten it. Then cover the pie with foil. Pour water and insert the trivet in the instant pot. Place the pie on the trivet and close the lid. Cook it on manual mode (high pressure) for 40 minutes. When the time is finished, make the quick pressure release. Cool the pie to the room temperature and slice into servings.
Nutrition: calories 247, fat 18.6, fiber 1.3, carbs 4.6, protein 15.4

Rosemary Pork Chops

Preparation time: 10 minutes
Cooking time: 30 minutes
Servings: 4
Ingredients:
- 4 pork chops
- 2 tablespoons avocado oil
- 2 garlic cloves, minced
- 2 tablespoons rosemary, chopped
- 1 and ½ cups beef stock
- A pinch of salt and black pepper
- 1 tablespoon chives, chopped

Directions:
Set your instant pot on Sauté mode, add the oil, heat it up, add the meat, garlic and rosemary and brown for 5 minutes. Add the rest of the ingredients, put the lid on and cook on High for 25 minutes. Release the pressure naturally for 10 minutes, divide everything between plates and serve.
Nutrition: calories 273, fat 21, fiber 1.1, carbs 2, protein 18.3

Kalua Pig

Preparation time: 15 minutes
Cooking time: 50 minutes
Servings: 6
Ingredients:
- 1 ½-pound pork shoulder, chopped
- 1 teaspoon salt
- 1 tablespoon liquid smoke
- 1 cup of water

Directions:
Sprinkle the meat with salt and liquid smoke. Mix up well. After this, pour water in the instant pot. Place the chopped meat in the instant pot in one layer and close the lid. Cook the meal on chili/beans mode for 50 minutes. When the time is over, allow the natural pressure release for 15 minutes. Open the lid and shred the meat with the help of the forks.
Nutrition: calories 331, fat 24.3, fiber 0, carbs 0, protein 26.4

Pork Chops and Green Chilies Mix

Preparation time: 10 minutes
Cooking time: 25 minutes
Servings: 4
Ingredients:
- 4 pork chops
- 4 garlic cloves, minced
- 1 tablespoon cilantro, chopped
- 1 and ½ cups beef stock
- 2 tablespoons avocado oil
- 2 tablespoons tomato passata
- ½ cup canned green chilies, chopped
- A pinch of salt and black pepper

Directions:
Set your instant pot on Sauté mode, add the oil, heat it up, add the meat and the garlic and brown for 5 minutes. Add the rest of the ingredients, put the lid on and cook on High for 20 minutes. Release the pressure naturally for 10 minutes, divide the mix between plates and serve.
Nutrition: calories 287, fat 21.1, fiber 1.8, carbs 5.1, protein 18.9

Greek Style Pork Chops

Preparation time: 15 minutes
Cooking time: 30 minutes
Servings: 3
Ingredients:
- 3 pork chops
- 1 teaspoon lemon juice
- 1 teaspoon dried oregano
- 1 teaspoon dried cilantro
- ¼ teaspoon onion powder
- ¼ teaspoon garlic powder
- 1/3 teaspoon salt
- ½ teaspoon ground black pepper
- 1 cup water, for cooking

Directions:
In the shallow bowl mix up dried oregano, cilantro, onion powder, garlic powder, salt, and ground black pepper. Then rub every pork chops with the spice mixture. Sprinkle the meat with lemon juice and leave for 5-7 minutes to marinate. Meanwhile, pour water and insert the steamer rack in the instant pot. Then arrange the meat on the steamer rack and close the lid. Cook the pork chops on manual mode (high pressure) for 30 minutes. When the time is over, make the quick pressure release and open the lid.
Nutrition: calories 260, fat 20, fiber 0.3, carbs 0.9, protein 18.2

Sage and Tarragon Pork

Preparation time: 10 minutes
Cooking time: 30 minutes
Servings: 4
Ingredients:
- 4 pork chops
- 2 tablespoons ghee, melted
- A pinch of salt and black pepper
- 1 teaspoon tarragon, dried
- 1 teaspoon sage, dried
- 2 garlic cloves, minced
- 2 cups beef stock
- 2 teaspoons sweet paprika

Directions:
Set your instant pot on Sauté mode, add the ghee, heat it up, add the meat and brown for 5 minutes. Add the rest of the ingredients, put the lid on and cook on High for 25 minutes. Release the pressure naturally for 10 minutes, divide the mix between plates and serve.
Nutrition: calories 328, fat 26.7, fiber 0.5, carbs 1.6, protein 19.7

Curry Pork Sausages

Preparation time: 10 minutes
Cooking time: 20 minutes
Servings: 4
Ingredients:
- 4 pork sausages

- 1 teaspoon curry paste
- ½ cup coconut cream
- 1 tablespoon coconut oil

Directions:
Toss the coconut oil in the instant pot and heat it up on sauté mode until it is melted. Then place the pork sausages in hot coconut oil and cook them on sauté mode for 3 minutes from each side. Meanwhile, in the bowl whisk together curry paste with coconut cream until you get a smooth mixture. When the sausages are cooked from both sides, add curry paste liquid and close the lid. Cook the sausages for 10 minutes on manual mode (high pressure).
Nutrition: calories 178, fat 16.8, fiber 0.7, carbs 2, protein 6.1

Coconut Pork Mix

Preparation time: 10 minutes
Cooking time: 25 minutes
Servings: 6
Ingredients:
- 1 and ½ pounds pork shoulder, cubed
- ½ cup coconut cream
- 2 tablespoons sweet paprika
- 2 tablespoons ghee, melted
- 2 shallots, chopped
- A pinch of salt and black pepper
- 1 tablespoon parsley, chopped

Directions:
Set your instant pot on Sauté mode, add the ghee, heat it up, add the shallots and the meat and brown for 5 minutes. Add the rest of the ingredients, put the lid on and cook on High for 20 minutes. Release the pressure naturally for 10 minutes, divide the mix between plates and serve.
Nutrition: calories 321, fat 25.1, fiber 1, carbs 1.8, protein 21.7

Sage Pork Loin

Preparation time: 10 minutes
Cooking time: 35 minutes
Servings: 12
Ingredients:
- 4-pound pork loin
- 1 tablespoon dried sage
- 1 tablespoon avocado oil
- 1 teaspoon salt
- 1 teaspoon ground black pepper
- 1 teaspoon apple cider vinegar
- 1 teaspoon ground nutmeg
- 1 bay leaf
- 1 cup water, for cooking

Directions:
Pour water in the instant pot. Add bay leaf and insert the steamer rack. Then rub the pork loin with dried sage, salt, ground black pepper, ground nutmeg, and sprinkle the meat with avocado oil and apple cider vinegar. Massage the pork loin with the help of the fingertips and transfer in the steamer rack. Close the lid. Cook the sage pork loin for 35 minutes on manual mode (high pressure). When the time of cooking is finished, make the quick pressure release and open the lid. Slice the cooked meal.
Nutrition: calories 407, fat 23.5, fiber 0.2, carbs 0.4, protein 45.6

Beef, Cauliflower Rice and Shrimp Mix

Preparation time: 10 minutes
Cooking time: 30 minutes
Servings: 4
Ingredients:
- 1 pound beef stew meat, cubed
- A pinch of salt and black pepper
- 2 tablespoons olive oil
- 1 cup cauliflower rice
- ½ pound shrimp, peeled and deveined
- 1 cup beef stock
- 12 ounces tomatoes, chopped
- 2 tablespoons cilantro, chopped

Directions:
Set your instant pot on Sauté mode, add the oil, heat it up, add the meat and brown for 5 minutes Add the rest of the ingredients except the shrimp, put the lid on and cook on High for 20 minutes. Release the pressure naturally for 10 minutes, set the pot on Sauté mode again, add the shrimp, cook for 5 minutes, divide the mix between plates and serve.
Nutrition: calories 358, fat 15.3, fiber 1, carbs 4.2, protein 38.2

Spinach and Fennel Pork Stew

Preparation time: 10 minutes
Cooking time: 40 minutes
Servings: 4
Ingredients:
- 2 cups fresh spinach, chopped
- 8 oz fennel, chopped
- 10 oz pork tenderloin, chopped
- 1 teaspoon salt
- 1 teaspoon onion powder
- 1 teaspoon cumin seeds
- 1 cup chicken broth
- 1 teaspoon dried rosemary
- 1 teaspoon butter

Directions:
Put butter in the instant pot and melt it on sauté mode. Then add the chopped meat and cook it on sauté mode for 3-4 minutes. Stir it well and sprinkle with salt, onion powder, cumin seeds, and dried rosemary. Add chicken broth and close the lid. Cook the meat on sauté mode for 35 minutes. When the time is finished, stir the meat well and add fennel and fresh spinach. Stir the stew and close the lid. Cook the meal on manual mode (high pressure) for 3 minutes. When the time is finished, make the quick pressure release. Allow the cooked stew cool for 5-10 minutes before serving.
Nutrition: calories 145, fat 4.1, fiber 2.3, carbs 5.8, protein 21.1

Spiced Beef

Preparation time: 10 minutes
Cooking time: 30 minutes
Servings: 4
Ingredients:
- 2 pounds beef stew meat, cubed
- 1 tablespoon ghee, melted
- 1 cup veggie stock
- 2 spring onions, chopped
- 2 garlic cloves, minced

- A pinch of salt and black pepper
- 1 teaspoon allspice, ground
- 1 teaspoon turmeric powder
- 1 teaspoon ginger powder
- 1 teaspoon cinnamon powder

Directions:
Set the instant pot on Sauté mode, add the ghee, heat it up, add the meat, allspice, turmeric, ginger and the cinnamon and brown for 5 minutes. Add the rest of the ingredients, put the lid on and cook on High for 25 minutes. Release the pressure naturally for 10 minutes, divide the mix between plates and serve.
Nutrition: calories 306, fat 11.7, fiber 0.4, carbs 1.4, protein 45.4

Garlic Smoky Ribs

Preparation time: 15 minutes
Cooking time: 18 minutes
Servings: 4
Ingredients:
- 11 oz pork ribs
- 1 tablespoon onion powder
- ½ teaspoon minced garlic
- ½ teaspoon salt
- ½ teaspoon chili powder
- 1 teaspoon liquid smoke
- 1 cup water, for cooking

Directions:
Sprinkle the pork ribs with onion powder, salt, and chili powder. Shake the pork ribs and add minced garlic and liquid smoke. Shake them one more time and put in the steamer rack. Pour water in the instant pot. Then place the steamer rack with ribs in water and close the lid. Cook the meal on manual mode (high pressure) for 18 minutes. When the cooking time is finished, allow the natural pressure release for 10 minutes.
Nutrition: calories 220, fat 13.9, fiber 0.2, carbs 1.7, protein 20.9

Beef, Sprouts and Bok Choy Mix

Preparation time: 10 minutes
Cooking time: 30 minutes
Servings: 4
Ingredients:
- 1 and ½ pounds beef stew meat, cubed
- 1 cup bok choy, roughly chopped
- ¼ pound Brussels sprouts, shredded
- 1 cup tomato passata
- 2 garlic cloves, minced
- 2 tablespoons tomato paste
- 1 teaspoon olive oil
- A pinch of salt and black pepper
- 1 tablespoon chives, chopped

Directions:
Set your instant pot on Sauté mode, add the oil, heat it up, add the meat and the garlic and brown for 5 minutes. Add the rest of the ingredients except the chives, put the lid on and cook on High for 25 minutes. Release the pressure naturally for 10 minutes, divide everything between plates, sprinkle the chives on top and serve.
Nutrition: calories 319, fat 10.4, fiber 1.9, carbs 5.9, protein 26.5

Ground Meat Stew

Preparation time: 15 minutes
Cooking time: 40 minutes
Servings: 4
Ingredients:
- 1 cup ground beef
- ½ cup ground pork
- 2 bacon slices, chopped
- 1 onion, diced
- ½ cup celery stalk, chopped
- 1 cup chicken broth
- ½ teaspoon salt
- 1 teaspoon chili flakes
- 1 teaspoon dried dill
- 1 teaspoon dried cilantro
- 1 teaspoon dried parsley
- 1 teaspoon olive oil
- 1 tablespoon heavy cream
- ½ cup broccoli, chopped

Directions:
Pour olive oil in the instant pot. Add bacon and cook it for 3 minutes or until it is light brown, Add ground pork and ground beef. Stir the ingredients and start to cook them on sauté mode. After 5 minutes of cooking, add salt, chili flakes, dried dill, cilantro, and parsley. Then add chicken broth, broccoli, heavy cream, celery stalk, and diced onion. Close the lid and cook the stew on chili/bean mode for 30 minutes.
Nutrition: calories 283, fat 19.2, fiber 1.1, carbs 4.4, protein 22.2

Lamb and Broccoli Mix

Preparation time: 10 minutes
Cooking time: 25 minutes
Servings: 4
Ingredients:
- 1 and ½ cups broccoli florets
- 1 pound lamb shoulder, cubed
- 1 cup beef stock
- ¼ cup tomato passata
- 1 tablespoon dill chopped
- A pinch of salt and black pepper

Directions:
In your instant pot, mix the lamb with the stock and the rest of the ingredients, put the lid on and cook on High for 25 minutes. Release the pressure naturally for 10 minutes, divide the mix between plates and serve.
Nutrition: calories 234, fat 8.6, fiber 1.4, carbs 3.9, protein 34

Pork&Mushrooms Ragout

Preparation time: 10 minutes
Cooking time: 28 minutes
Servings: 4
Ingredients:
- 1 cup shiitake mushrooms, sliced
- ½ cup okra, chopped
- 11 oz pork tenderloin
- 1 teaspoon Erythritol
- ½ teaspoon salt
- 1 tablespoon lemon juice
- 1 teaspoon dried rosemary
- 2 tablespoons olive oil
- 1/3 cup water
- 2 tablespoons cream cheese

Directions:

Cut the pork tenderloin into the strips and put in the instant pot. Add olive oil and stir well. Set sauté mode and cook the meat for 3 minutes. After this, stir the meat and sprinkle it with salt, lemon juice, and dried rosemary. Stir again. Add Erythritol, okra, cream cheese, and mushrooms. Mix up ingredients well. Add water and close the lid. Cook the ragout with the closed lid on stew mode for 20 minutes.
Nutrition: calories 215, fat 11.7, fiber 1.3, carbs 6.3, protein 21.6

Dill Lamb and Tomatoes

Preparation time: 10 minutes
Cooking time: 30 minutes
Servings: 4
Ingredients:
- 1 pound lamb shoulder, cubed
- 1 tablespoon olive oil
- 2 spring onions, chopped
- 2 cups tomato passata
- 2 garlic cloves, minced
- 1 tablespoon dill, chopped

Directions:
Set the instant pot on Sauté mode, add the oil, heat it up, add the lamb and brown for 5 minutes. Add the rest of the ingredients, put the lid on and cook on High for 25 minutes. Release the pressure naturally for 10 minutes, divide the mix between plates and serve.
Nutrition: calories 277, fat 12.1, fiber 2.2, carbs 5.9, protein 33.2

Mesquite Ribs

Preparation time: 10 minutes
Cooking time: 30 minutes
Servings: 2
Ingredients:
- 8 oz pork baby ribs
- ¼ cup apple cider vinegar
- 1 teaspoon soy sauce
- 1 teaspoon mesquite seasonings
- ½ cup of water

Directions:
Pour water in the big bowl. Add apple cider vinegar, soy sauce, and mesquite seasonings. Then put the pork baby ribs in the apple cider vinegar mixture and leave for 5 minutes to marinate. After this, transfer the mixture in the instant pot and close the lid. Cook the meal on manual mode (high pressure) for 30 minutes. When the time is over, make the quick pressure release and remove the ribs from the instant pot.
Nutrition: calories 331, fat 27.2, fiber 0, carbs 0.9, protein 18.3

Curry Lamb and Cauliflower

Preparation time: 10 minutes
Cooking time: 40 minutes
Servings: 6
Ingredients:
- 2 pounds lamb shoulder, cubed
- 1 and ½ cups cauliflower florets
- 2 garlic cloves, minced
- 2 tablespoons ghee, melted
- 1 tablespoon curry powder
- 1 cup beef stock
- A pinch of salt and black pepper
- ½ bunch cilantro, chopped

Directions:
Set your instant pot on Sauté mode, add the ghee, heat it up, add the garlic and the lamb and brown for 5 minutes. Add the rest of the ingredients, put the lid on and cook on High for 35 minutes. Release the pressure naturally for 10 minutes, divide the mix between plates and serve.
Nutrition: calories 335, fat 15.6, fiber 1.2, carbs 2.7, protein 34.5

Keto Pork Posole

Preparation time: 10 minutes
Cooking time: 29 minutes
Servings: 6
Ingredients:
- 1-pound pork shoulder, chopped
- 1 shallot, chopped
- 1 garlic clove, peeled
- ½ cup radish, sliced
- 1 chipotle chili, chopped
- ½ teaspoon dried oregano
- 1 teaspoon chili powder
- ½ teaspoon salt
- 1 cup of water
- 3 tablespoons fresh cilantro, chopped

Directions:
Place all ingredients except cilantro and radish in the instant pot. Close and seal the lid. Cook the meal for 25 minutes on manual mode (high pressure). When the cooking time is finished, make the quick pressure release and open the lid. Add cilantro and radish and stir posole. Close the lid and cook the meal for 4 minutes more on Manual mode (high pressure). When the meal is cooked, make the quick pressure release and open the lid. Cook posole for 5-10 minutes before serving.
Nutrition: calories 231, fat 16.4, fiber 0.7, carbs 1.9, protein 17.9

Garlic Lamb and Chard

Preparation time: 10 minutes
Cooking time: 35 minutes
Servings: 6
Ingredients:
- 2 pounds lamb shoulder, cubed
- 1 cup chard, chopped
- 3 garlic cloves, crushed
- A pinch of salt and black pepper
- 1 cup beef stock
- 2 tablespoons olive oil
- 1 tablespoon rosemary, chopped
- 1 tablespoon chives, chopped

Directions:
Set your instant pot on Sauté mode, add the oil, heat it up, add the garlic and the lamb and brown for 5 minutes. Add the rest of the ingredients except the chives, put the lid on and cook on High for 30 minutes. Release the pressure naturally for 10 minutes, divide the mix between plates and serve with the chives sprinkled on top.
Nutrition: calories 329, fat 16, fiber 0.4, carbs 1.1, protein 34.2

Hoisin Meatballs

Preparation time: 15 minutes
Cooking time: 15 minutes
Servings: 4
Ingredients:
- 1 cup beef broth
- 1 teaspoon hoisin sauce
- 1 egg, beaten
- 1 tablespoon scallions, chopped
- 1 tablespoon white onion, diced
- ½ teaspoon minced garlic
- ¼ teaspoon salt
- ¼ teaspoon ground black pepper
- 2 cups ground beef

Directions:
Pour beef broth in the instant pot. Add hoisin sauce and stir gently with the help of the spoon. After this, in the mixing bowl mix up egg, scallions, white onion, minced garlic, salt, and ground black pepper. Add ground beef and stir the mass until homogenous. Then make the medium size meatballs and put them in the instant pot. Close and seal the lid. Cook the meatballs on manual mode (high pressure) for 15 minutes. When the time is over, allow the natural pressure release for 5 minutes.
Nutrition: calories 160, fat 9.7, fiber 0.2, carbs 1.4, protein 15.8

Coriander Beef and Pork Mix

Preparation time: 10 minutes
Cooking time: 35 minutes
Servings: 6
Ingredients:
- 1 pound beef stew meat, cubed
- 1 pound pork stew meat, cubed
- 2 tablespoons ghee, melted
- 1 tablespoon coriander, chopped
- A pinch of salt and black pepper
- 3 teaspoons turmeric powder
- 2 garlic cloves, minced
- 2 and ½ cups beef stock

Directions:
Set your instant pot on Sauté mode, add the ghee, heat it up, add the beef, the pork and the garlic and brown for 5 minutes Add the rest of the ingredients, put the lid on and cook on High for 30 minutes. Release the pressure naturally for 10 minutes, divide everything between plates and serve with a side salad.
Nutrition: calories 344, fat 16.4, fiber 0.3, carbs 1.1, protein 32.4

Tender Pork Satay

Preparation time: 10 minutes
Cooking time: 15 minutes
Servings: 4
Ingredients:
- 4 pork loin chops
- ½ white onion, sliced
- 2 tablespoons peanut butter
- 1 teaspoon apple cider vinegar
- ½ teaspoon ground black pepper
- ½ cup chicken broth
- ½ teaspoon onion powder
- 1 teaspoon coconut flour
- 1 teaspoon chili powder

Directions:
Place the peanut butter in the instant pot and heat it up on sauté mode for 3-4 minutes. Meanwhile, chop the loin chops roughly. Add the meat in the instant pot. Then add ground black pepper, onion powder, and chili powder. Stir the meat well and cook it for 2 minutes more. Then add apple cider vinegar and chicken broth. Add sliced onion and coconut flour. Stir the ingredients. Close the instant pot lid and cook satay on manual mode (high pressure) for 9 minutes. When the time of cooking is finished, make a quick pressure release. Serve the pork satay with gravy.
Nutrition: calories 320, fat 24.3, fiber 1.3, carbs 4.1, protein 21

Pork Ribs and Green Beans

Preparation time: 10 minutes
Cooking time: 30 minutes
Servings: 4
Ingredients:
- 1 pound pork ribs rack
- ½ pound green beans, trimmed and halved
- 2 tablespoons olive oil
- 1 tablespoon smoked paprika
- 1 teaspoon chili powder
- A pinch of salt and black pepper
- 1 tablespoon rosemary, chopped
- ½ cup beef stock
- 1 tablespoon cilantro, chopped

Directions:
Set your instant pot on Sauté mode, add the oil, heat it up, add the meat, paprika and chili powder and brown for 5 minutes. Add the rest of the ingredients except the cilantro, put the lid on and cook on High for 25 minutes. Release the pressure naturally for 10, divide everything between plates and serve with the cilantro sprinkled on top.
Nutrition: calories 344, fat 21, fiber 3.2, carbs 5.9, protein 33.2

Ham and Cheese Dinner Casserole

Preparation time: 10 minutes
Cooking time: 13 minutes
Servings: 4
Ingredients:
- ½ cup Cheddar cheese, shredded
- 2 oz Jarlsberg cheese, shredded
- 4 eggs, beaten
- 8 oz ham, chopped
- 1 tablespoon butter
- 1 teaspoon ground black pepper
- ½ teaspoon ground paprika
- ½ teaspoon salt
- ½ teaspoon ground turmeric
- 1 teaspoon dried oregano

Directions:
Put butter in the instant pot and melt it. Add chopped ham and sauté it for 4 minutes. Stir it in half the time of cooking. Then sprinkle the ham with ground black pepper, paprika, salt, and dried oregano. Stir well. Add eggs and stir the ingredients until homogenous. After this, add all cheese and close the lid. Cook the meal on manual mode (high pressure) for 4 minutes. Then make the quick pressure release and open the lid. The casserole tastes the best when it is hot.
Nutrition: calories 293, fat 21, fiber 1.2, carbs 3.6, protein 22.2

Lime Pork Chops

Preparation time: 5 minutes
Cooking time: 25 minutes
Servings: 4
Ingredients:
- 4 pork chops
- 2 tablespoons olive oil
- 2 garlic cloves, minced
- 2 tablespoons lime juice
- ½ cup tomato passata
- ½ cup beef stock
- A pinch of salt and black pepper
- 1 tablespoon cilantro, chopped

Directions:
Set your instant pot on Sauté mode, add the oil, heat it up, add the garlic and the pork chops and brown for 5 minutes. Add the rest of the ingredients except the cilantro, put the lid on and cook on High for 20 minutes. Release the pressure fast for 5 minutes, divide everything between plates and serve with the cilantro sprinkled on top.
Nutrition: calories 219, fat 18, fiber 0.3, carbs 1.5, protein 12.4

Blackberry Pork Chops

Preparation time: 10 minutes
Cooking time: 15 minutes
Servings: 2
Ingredients:
- ¼ cup blackberries
- 1 teaspoon Erythritol
- 1 teaspoon butter, melted
- 1 teaspoon cream
- 2 pork chops
- ½ teaspoon ground paprika
- ¼ teaspoon salt
- ½ teaspoon dried cilantro
- 1 cup water, for cooking

Directions:
Pour water and insert the trivet in the instant pot. Then rub the pork chops with cilantro, salt, and ground paprika. Put the pork chops on the trivet and close the lid. Cook the meat on manual mode (high pressure) for 8 minutes Then make the quick pressure release and open the lid. Place the blackberries, Erythritol, and cream in the blender and blend the mixture until smooth. Clean the instant pot and remove the trivet. Pour the blended blackberry mixture in the instant pot. Add butter and bring the liquid to boil on sauté mode. Then add the cooked pork chops. Coat the meat well in the blackberry sauce and cook for 1 minute from each side on sauté mode. Serve the pork chops with remaining blackberry sauce.
Nutrition: calories 283, fat 22.1, fiber 1.2, carbs 2.1, protein 18.4

Pesto Pork and Mustard Greens

Preparation time: 10 minutes
Cooking time: 30 minutes
Servings: 4
Ingredients:
- 1 and ½ pounds pork shoulder, cubed
- 2 tablespoons ghee, melted
- ½ pound mustard greens, torn
- 1 cup beef stock
- 1 tablespoon basil pesto
- 2 garlic cloves, minced
- Salt and black pepper to the taste
- 1 tablespoon parsley, chopped

Directions:
Set the instant pot on Sauté mode, add the ghee, heat it up, add the meat and the garlic and brown for 5 minutes. Add the rest of the ingredients, toss, put the lid on and cook on High for 25 minutes. Release the pressure naturally for 10 minutes, divide the mix between plates and serve.
Nutrition: calories 370, fat 24.5, fiber 1, carbs 1.7, protein 27.5

Pork and Celery Curry

Preparation time: 10 minutes
Cooking time: 35 minutes
Servings: 4
Ingredients:
- 10 oz pork loin, chopped
- 1 cup celery stalk, chopped
- 1 teaspoon curry paste
- 1 tablespoon fresh cilantro, chopped
- ½ cup coconut cream
- ½ cup of water
- 1 teaspoon avocado oil
- ½ teaspoon fennel seeds

Directions:
Pour avocado oil in the instant pot. Add chopped pork loin and cook it on sauté mode for 6 minutes (for 3 minutes from each side). Then add fennel seeds and water. Cook the ingredients for 4 minutes more. Meanwhile, in the bowl whisk together curry paste with coconut cream. When the mixture is smooth, pour it over the meat. Add celery stalk and close the lid. Cook the meal on meat/stew mode for 20 minutes. Then stir it well and add cilantro. Cook the curry for 5 minutes more.
Nutrition: calories 146, fat 10.3, fiber 0.7, carbs 1.7, protein 11.6

Paprika Lamb Chops

Preparation time: 10 minutes
Cooking time: 30 minutes
Servings: 4
Ingredients:
- 4 lamb chops
- 1 tablespoon olive oil
- 1 cup tomatoes, cubed
- 1 cup beef stock
- 1 tablespoon sweet paprika
- A pinch of salt and black pepper
- 1 tablespoon rosemary, chopped

Directions:
Set the instant pot on Sauté mode, add the oil, heat it up, add the lamb and the paprika and brown for 5 minutes. Add the rest of the ingredients, toss, put the lid on and cook on High for 25 minutes. Release the pressure naturally for 10 minutes, divide everything between plates and serve.
Nutrition: calories 292, fat 13.2, fiber 1.6, carbs 3.3, protein 24.2

Beef and Squash Ragu

Preparation time: 10 minutes
Cooking time: 30 minutes

Servings: 4
Ingredients:
- 7 oz beef loin, chopped
- 6 oz Kabocha squash, cubed
- ¼ teaspoon ground cinnamon
- ¼ teaspoon ground nutmeg
- ½ teaspoon salt
- 1 teaspoon ground paprika
- 1 tablespoon cream cheese
- 1 turnip, chopped
- 1 tablespoon almond butter
- ¼ cup chicken broth

Directions:
Melt almond butter in the instant pot on sauté mode. Sprinkle the chopped beef with ground cinnamon, nutmeg, salt, and ground paprika. Put the meat in the hot almond butter and cook it for 3 minutes. Then flip the meat on another side and cook for 2 minutes more. Add turnip and cream cheese. Then add chicken broth and Kabocha squash. Cook the ragu for 20 minutes on sauté mode. Stir it every 3 minutes with the help of the spatula to avoid burning.
Nutrition: calories 154, fat 6.5, fiber 1.8, carbs 6.8, protein 17.3

Pork and Olives

Preparation time: 10 minutes
Cooking time: 30 minutes
Servings: 6
Ingredients:
- 1 and ½ pounds pork shoulder, cubed
- 2 tablespoons ghee, melted
- A pinch of salt and black pepper
- 2 garlic cloves, minced
- 1 cup black olives, pitted and sliced
- 1 cup veggie stock
- ¼ cup tomato passata
- 1 tablespoon cilantro, chopped

Directions:
Set your instant pot on Sauté mode, add the ghee, heat it up, add the meat and the garlic and brown for 5 minutes. Add the rest of the ingredients except the cilantro, put the lid on and cook on High for 25 minutes. Release the pressure naturally for 10 minutes, divide the mix between plates and serve with the cilantro sprinkled on top.
Nutrition: calories 382, fat 23.2, fiber 0.7, carbs 1.7, protein 24.3

Beef Loin with Acorn Squash

Preparation time: 15 minutes
Cooking time: 40 minutes
Servings: 4
Ingredients:
- 8 oz acorn squash, halved, seeded
- 1-pound beef loin
- 1 tablespoon olive oil
- 1 teaspoon salt
- 1 teaspoon ground black pepper
- 2 garlic cloves, peeled
- 1 teaspoon dried rosemary
- 1 cup of water
- ½ teaspoon ground turmeric
- 1 cup water, for cooking

Directions:
Rub the acorn squash with olive oil and dried rosemary. Place the vegetable in the steamer rack. Then pour water in the instant pot and insert the steamer rack inside. Close the lid and cook the squash for 8 minutes. When the time of cooking is finished, allow the natural pressure release for 10 minutes and remove the vegetable from the instant pot. Then cut it into cubes and put it in the serving plate. After this, clean the instant pot and remove the steamer rack. Chop the beef loin into the cubes and put in the instant pot. Add salt, ground black pepper, garlic cloves, water, and ground turmeric. Close the lid and cook the beef on manual mode (high pressure) for 30 minutes. When the time is over, make the quick pressure release. Place the cooked beef over the acorn squash and sprinkle with hot beef gravy.
Nutrition: calories 265, fat 13.1, fiber 1.2, carbs 7.1, protein 31

Beef and Herbed Radish

Preparation time: 10 minutes
Cooking time: 30 minutes
Servings: 4
Ingredients:
- 1 and ½ pound beef stew meat, cubed
- 1 cup radishes, sliced
- 1 tablespoon rosemary, chopped
- 1 tablespoon oregano, chopped
- 1 tablespoon basil, chopped
- 1 tablespoon olive oil
- 1 teaspoon sweet paprika
- 1 cup beef stock
- 1 tablespoon chives, chopped

Directions:
Set your instant pot on Sauté mode, add the oil, heat it up, add the meat and the paprika and brown for 5 minutes. Add the rest of the ingredients except the chives, put the lid on and cook on High for 50 minutes. Release the pressure naturally for 10 minutes, divide the mix between plates, sprinkle the chives on top and serve.
Nutrition: calories 312, fat 12.1, fiber 1, carbs 1.7, protein 24.2

Beef Tips

Preparation time: 10 minutes
Cooking time: 30 minutes
Servings: 3
Ingredients:
- 1 cup turnip, peeled, chopped
- 7 oz beef, chopped
- ¼ cup apple cider vinegar
- 1 tablespoon avocado oil
- 1 white onion, diced
- ½ teaspoon salt
- 1 teaspoon ground black pepper
- 1 cup of water
- 1 teaspoon ground coriander
- 1 teaspoon cream cheese
- 1 teaspoon fresh cilantro, chopped

Directions:
Pour avocado oil in the instant pot. Add beef and onion. Sauté the ingredients for 5 minutes. Then sprinkle them with salt, ground black pepper, and coriander. Mix up with the help of the spatula. Then add apple cider vinegar and water. Insert the steamer rack over the meat and place the chopped turnip on it. Close the lid and cook the meal on manual mode (high pressure) for 15 minutes. When

the time is over, allow the natural pressure release for 10 minutes. Mash the cooked turnip and mix it up with cream cheese. Place the mashed turnip in the serving plates and top with meat, cilantro, and gravy.
Nutrition: calories 166, fat 5.2, fiber 2, carbs 7.1, protein 21.1

Beef and Endives Mix

Preparation time: 10 minutes
Cooking time: 30 minutes
Servings: 4
Ingredients:
- 1 and ½ pounds beef stew meat, cubed
- 1 cup beef stock
- 2 endives, sliced
- 2 tablespoons lime juice
- 2 tablespoons ghee, melted
- 1 tablespoon cumin, ground
- 1 tablespoon sage, chopped
- 1 tablespoon sweet paprika
- A pinch of salt and black pepper

Directions:
Set the instant pot on Sauté mode, add the ghee, heat it up, add the meat and brown for 5 minutes. Add the rest of the ingredients, put the lid on and cook on High for 25 minutes. Release the pressure naturally for 10 minutes, divide the mix between plates and serve.
Nutrition: calories 329, fat 14.2, fiber 0.7, carbs 1.3, protein 23.4

Onion Baby Back Ribs

Preparation time: 10 minutes
Cooking time: 40 minutes
Servings: 6
Ingredients:
- 1-pound pork baby back ribs
- 1 teaspoon onion powder
- 2 white onions, sliced
- 2 tablespoons butter
- ½ cup heavy cream
- 1 teaspoon thyme
- 1 teaspoon dried rosemary
- ½ teaspoon salt

Directions:
Melt butter in the instant pot on sauté mode. Then sprinkle the baby back ribs with onion butter, thyme, and rosemary and put in the hot butter. Cook the meat for 3 minutes and then flip on another side. Add salt, sliced onion, and heavy cream. Close the lid and cook the meal on stew/meat mode for 30 minutes.
Nutrition: calories 362, fat 30.1, fiber 1, carbs 4.3, protein 17.8

Beef and Mushroom Rice

Preparation time: 10 minutes
Cooking time: 30 minutes
Servings: 4
Ingredients:
- 1 and ½ cups beef stock
- 1 tablespoon olive oil
- 1 and ½ pound beef stew meat, cubed
- 1 cup cauliflower rice
- 1 cup white mushrooms, halved
- 2 spring onions, chopped
- 2 teaspoons sweet paprika
- ¼ cup coconut cream
- 1 tablespoon chives, chopped
- A pinch of salt and black pepper

Directions:
Set your instant pot on sauté mode, add the oil, heat it up, add the spring onions, mushrooms and the beef and brown for 5 minutes Add the rest of the ingredients except the chives, put the lid on and cook on High for 25 minutes. Release the pressure naturally for 10 minutes, divide the mix between plates and serve with the chives sprinkled on top.
Nutrition: calories 336, fat 14.4, fiber 0.8, carbs 1.7, protein 23.2

Beef & Cabbage Stew

Preparation time: 10 minutes
Cooking time: 15 minutes
Servings: 4
Ingredients:
- 1 cup ground beef
- 2 cups white cabbage, shredded
- 1 tablespoon coconut oil
- 1 teaspoon salt
- 1 teaspoon ground black pepper
- ½ cup of water
- 1 teaspoon tomato paste
- ½ cup of organic almond milk
- 1 teaspoon dried dill

Directions:
Place cabbage in the big bowl. Sprinkle it with ground black pepper and salt. Shake the cabbage. After this, add dill. Put coconut oil in the instant pot. Melt it on sauté mode. Add ground beef and cook it for 5 minutes. Stir the meat from time to time with the help of the spatula. Add organic almond milk, water, and tomato paste. Stir the ingredients until you get a homogenous mixture. Then add shredded cabbage, mix the ingredients up and close the lid. Cook the stew on manual mode (high pressure) for 10 minutes. Then make the quick pressure release and open the lid. Stir the stew well before serving.
Nutrition: calories 113, fat 7.9, fiber 1.2, carbs 3.8, protein 7.3

Feta Cheese Lamb Mix

Preparation time: 10 minutes
Cooking time: 25 minutes
Servings: 4
Ingredients:
- 4 lamb chops
- 1 tablespoon olive oil
- ½ cup feta cheese, crumbled
- 1 cup kalamata olives, pitted and sliced
- 1 cup veggie stock
- 3 garlic cloves, minced
- 1 tablespoon rosemary, chopped
- 2 tablespoons tomato passata
- A pinch of salt and black pepper

Directions:
Set the instant pot on Sauté mode, add the oil, heat it up, add the lamb chops and brown for 2 minutes on each side. Add the rest of the ingredients except the cheese and the rosemary, put the lid on and cook on High for 20 minutes. Release the pressure naturally for 10 minutes, divide the mix between plates,

sprinkle the cheese and the rosemary on top and serve.
Nutrition: calories 172, fat 13.2, fiber 1.6, carbs 4.6, protein 9.5

Tender Salisbury Steak

Preparation time: 10 minutes
Cooking time: 30 minutes
Servings: 4
Ingredients:
- 1 cup ground beef
- 1 egg white
- 1 tablespoon water
- 1 teaspoon chili powder
- ½ teaspoon salt
- 1 teaspoon olive oil
- 1 cup white mushrooms, sliced
- 1 white onion, sliced
- ½ teaspoon tomato paste
- ½ teaspoon dill, chopped
- ½ cup chicken broth

Directions:
Make the steaks: in the mixing bowl mix up ground beef, egg white, 1 tablespoon of water, chili powder, and salt. Make the medium size steaks from the meat mixture. Then pour olive oil in the skillet. Cook the steaks on medium-high heat for 2 minutes from each side. Meanwhile, place the mushrooms in the instant pot. Add onion, tomato paste, dill, and chicken broth. Then put the steaks over the mushrooms and close the lid. Cook the meal on manual mode (high pressure) for 27 minutes. When the time is over, make the quick pressure release.
Nutrition: calorie 102, fat 5.6, fiber 1, carbs 3.9, protein 9

Mustard and Sage Beef

Preparation time: 10 minutes
Cooking time: 30 minutes
Servings: 4
Ingredients:
- 2 pounds beef stew meat, cubed
- A pinch of salt and black pepper
- 2 tablespoons Dijon mustard
- 1 tablespoon sage, chopped
- 1 tablespoon ghee, melted
- 1 cup tomato passata
- 1 cup beef stock
- 1 tablespoon parsley, chopped

Directions:
Set your instant pot on Sauté mode, add the ghee, heat it up, add the meat and brown for 5 minutes. Add the rest of the ingredients except the parsley, put the lid on and cook on High for 25 minutes. Release the pressure naturally for 10 minutes, divide mix between plates, sprinkle the parsley on top and serve.
Nutrition: calories 323, fat 12, fiber 1.1, carbs 4.3, protein 25.3

Cumin Kielbasa

Preparation time: 7 minutes
Cooking time: 10 minutes
Servings: 4
Ingredients:
- 8 oz kielbasa, sliced
- 1 teaspoon cumin seeds
- 3 tablespoons butter
- 1 tablespoon cream cheese
- ¼ teaspoon salt
- 1 oz Jarlsberg cheese, grated

Directions:
Place butter in the instant pot. Add cumin seeds and salt. Melt the ingredients on sauté mode. Add kielbasa and cook for 3 minutes. Then flip on another side and cook for 3 minutes more. After this, sprinkle the kielbasa with cheese and cream cheese. Stir well and sauté for 4 minutes more.
Nutrition: calories 241, fat 21.6, fiber 0.1, carbs 2.5, protein 9.6

Spiced Lamb Meatballs

Preparation time: 10 minutes
Cooking time: 25 minutes
Servings: 4
Ingredients:
- 1 pound lamb shoulder, ground
- 1 tablespoon olive oil
- A pinch of salt and black pepper
- 1 teaspoon sweet paprika
- 1 and ½ cups tomato passata
- 1 teaspoon cinnamon powder
- 1 teaspoon cumin, ground
- 1 teaspoon coriander, ground
- 1 egg, whisked
- 1 tablespoon dill, chopped

Directions:
In a bowl, mix lamb meat with the rest of the ingredients except the tomato passata and the oil, stir well and shape medium meatballs put of this mix. Set the instant pot on Sauté mode, add the oil, heat it up, add the meatballs and cook them for 2 minutes on each side. Add the tomato passata, put the lid on and cook on High for 20 minutes. Release the pressure naturally for 10 minutes, divide meatballs and sauce between plates and serve.
Nutrition: calories 262, fat 13.1, fiber 0.4, carbs 1.1, protein 33.2

Prosciutto and Eggs Salad

Preparation time: 10 minutes
Cooking time: 6 minutes
Servings: 4
Ingredients:
- 4 eggs
- 5 oz prosciutto, sliced
- 1 cup lettuce, chopped
- 1 tablespoon lemon juice
- 1 teaspoon flax seeds
- 1 tablespoon avocado oil
- ½ teaspoon ground black pepper
- 1 cup water, for cooking

Directions:
Pour water in the instant pot and insert the steamer rack. Place the eggs in the steamer rack and close the lid. Cook the eggs on manual mode (high pressure) for 6 minutes. When the time is over, make the quick pressure release. Open the lid and place the eggs in the cold water. Cool them well and after this peel. Chop the slices prosciutto roughly and put in the salad bowl. Add lettuce, flax seeds, and avocado oil. Then chop the eggs roughly and add in a salad bowl.

Add lemon juice and ground black pepper. Shake the salad gently.
Nutrition: calories 125, fat 7, fiber 0.5, carbs 1.9, protein 13.2

Mint Lamb Chops

Preparation time: 10 minutes
Cooking time: 25 minutes
Servings: 4
Ingredients:
- ½ cup cilantro, chopped
- 4 lamb chops
- 2 green chilies, chopped
- 3 garlic cloves, minced
- Juice of 2 limes
- 2 tablespoons olive oil
- A pinch of salt and black pepper
- ½ cup mint, chopped
- 1 cup veggie stock

Directions:
Set your instant pot on Sauté mode, add the oil, heat it up, add the garlic, chilies and the lamb chops and brown for 5 minutes Add the rest of the ingredients, put the lid on and cook on High for 25 minutes. Release the pressure naturally for 10 minutes, divide the mix between plates and serve.
Nutrition: calories 143, fat 10.9, fiber 0.9, carbs 3, protein 15.6

Mississippi Roast

Preparation time: 10 minutes
Cooking time: 40 minutes
Servings: 3
Ingredients:
- 11 oz chuck roast, chopped
- 1 tablespoon sesame oil
- ¼ cup white onion, chopped
- 1 chili pepper, chopped
- ¼ cup chicken broth
- 1 jalapeno pepper, chopped
- ½ teaspoon peppercorns
- 1 tablespoon coconut oil
- ½ teaspoon salt

Directions:
Set sauté mode and pour sesame oil in the instant pot. Add chopped chuck roast. Sprinkle the meat with peppercorns and cook for 3 minutes from each side. Then add coconut oil, salt, jalapeno, and chili peppers. Then add white onion and chicken broth. Cook the meat on manual mode (high pressure) for 40 minutes. When the time of cooking is finished, make a quick pressure release. Shred the meat gently.
Nutrition: calories 314, fat 17.9, fiber 0.5, carbs 1.6, protein 35

Lamb Chops, Fennel and Tomatoes

Preparation time: 10 minutes
Cooking time: 25 minutes
Servings: 4
Ingredients:
- 4 lamb chops
- 1 tablespoon olive oil
- 4 garlic cloves, minced
- A pinch of salt and black pepper
- Zest of 1 lime, grated
- 2 bay leaves
- 1 tablespoon rosemary, chopped
- 1 fennel bulb, cut into 8 wedges
- ½ cup cherry tomatoes, halved
- 1 teaspoon sweet paprika
- 1 cup veggie stock

Directions:
Set your instant pot on Sauté mode, add the oil, heat it up, add the meat and the garlic and brown for 5 minutes. Add the rest of the ingredients, put the lid on and cook on High for 20 minutes. Release the pressure naturally for 10 minutes, divide everything between plates and serve.
Nutrition: calories 194, fat 7.9, fiber 2.3, carbs 5.3, protein 7.5

Keto Oxtail Goulash

Preparation time: 15 minutes
Cooking time: 80 minutes
Servings: 5
Ingredients:
- 10 oz beef oxtail, chopped
- 2 oz celery root, chopped
- ½ carrot, chopped
- ½ cup onion, chopped
- 1 eggplant, chopped
- 3 oz fennel, chopped
- 1 cup beef broth
- 1 teaspoon salt
- 1 teaspoon ground black pepper
- 1 teaspoon dried oregano
- 2 teaspoons ground turmeric
- ½ teaspoon chili flakes
- 1 tablespoon sesame oil
- 2 tablespoons cream cheese

Directions:
Sprinkle the oxtails with salt and put in the instant pot. Add sesame oil and cook them on sauté mode for 4 minutes from each side. Then add celery root, carrot, onion, eggplant, fennel, ground black pepper, dried oregano, ground turmeric, and chili flakes. Mix up the ingredients with the help of the spoon. Then add beef broth and cream cheese. Close the lid and cook the goulash for 65 minutes on manual mode (high pressure). When the time is over, allow the natural pressure release for 10 minutes.
Nutrition: calories 231, fat 12.2, fiber 4.8, carbs 10.7, protein 20.4

Italian Leg of Lamb

Preparation time: 10 minutes
Cooking time: 40 minutes
Servings: 4
Ingredients:
- 2 pounds leg of lamb, boneless
- 2 tablespoons olive oil
- 4 garlic cloves, minced
- 2 tablespoons rosemary, chopped
- ¼ teaspoon red pepper flakes
- ½ cup walnuts, chopped
- 5 ounces baby spinach
- A pinch of salt and black pepper
- ½ cup mustard

Directions:
Set your instant pot on Sauté mode, add the oil, heat it up, add the garlic, pepper flakes, the lamb and the mustard, toss and cook for 5 minutes. Add all the

other ingredients except the spinach, put the lid on and cook on High for 30 minutes. Release the pressure naturally for 10 minutes, set the pot on Sauté mode again, add the spinach, cook for 5 minutes more, divide the mix between plates and serve.
Nutrition: calories 367, fat 25.3, fiber 3.5, carbs 5.8, protein 25.4

Italian Beef

Preparation time: 15 minutes
Cooking time: 60 minutes
Servings: 8
Ingredients:
- 4-pound beef chuck, chopped
- 3 tablespoons almond butter
- ½ cup shallot, sliced
- 2 garlic cloves, sliced
- ½ cup pepperoncini peppers
- 1 cup chicken broth
- 1 teaspoon Italian seasonings
- ½ teaspoon chili powder
- 1 teaspoon Erythritol

Directions:
Melt almond butter on sauté mode and add sliced shallot and garlic cloves. Cook the vegetables for 5-6 minutes or until they are soft. After this, add chopped beef chuck, pepperoncini, Italian seasonings, and chili powder. Then add Erythritol and chicken broth. Close and seal the lid. Cook the beef on manual mode (high pressure) for 55 minutes. When the cooking time is finished, allow the natural pressure release for 15 minutes. Shred the meat with the help of the fork.
Nutrition: calories 474, fat 17.9, fiber 0.7, carbs 3.5, protein 71

Hot Curry Lamb and Green Beans

Preparation time: 10 minutes
Cooking time: 35 minutes
Servings: 4
Ingredients:
- 4 lamb chops
- 1 pound green beans, trimmed and halved
- Juice of 1 lime
- A pinch of salt and black pepper
- ½ cup beef stock
- 1 teaspoon rosemary, dried
- 1 tablespoon olive oil
- 1 tablespoon curry powder

Directions:
In your instant pot, combine all the ingredients, put the lid on and cook on High for 35 minutes. Release the pressure naturally for 10 minutes, divide the mix between plates and serve.
Nutrition: calories 139, fat 7.7, fiber 3.4, carbs 4.6, protein 8.9

Thyme Braised Beef

Preparation time: 10 minutes
Cooking time: 45 minutes
Servings: 5
Ingredients:
- 1-pound beef loin
- 1 teaspoon dried thyme
- ½ teaspoon salt
- ½ cup butter
- ¼ cup cream cheese
- ½ cup of water

Directions:
Rub the beef loin with dried thyme and salt and put in the instant pot. Add butter and cream cheese. Add water. Close the lid and cook the beef for 45 minutes on manual mode (high pressure). When the meat is cooked, make the quick pressure release. Open the lid and transfer the meat on the chopping board. Chop the meat roughly and put it in the serving plates. Sprinkle the meat with cream cheese gravy.
Nutrition: calories 369, fat 30, fiber 0.1, carbs 0.5, protein 25.4

Lamb and Sun-dried Tomatoes Mix

Preparation time: 10 minutes
Cooking time: 40 minutes
Servings: 6
Ingredients:
- 6 lamb loins
- 2 garlic cloves, minced
- 2 teaspoons thyme, chopped
- A pinch of salt and black pepper
- 2 tablespoons olive oil
- 2 tablespoons balsamic vinegar
- ½ cup parsley, chopped
- ½ cup sun-dried tomatoes, chopped
- 1 cup beef stock

Directions:
Set the instant pot on Sauté mode, add the oil, heat it up, add the lamb and garlic and brown for 5 minutes. Add the rest of the ingredients, put the lid on and cook on High for 35 minutes. Release the pressure naturally for 10 minutes, divide the mix between plates and serve.
Nutrition: calories 353, fat 23.7, fiber 0.5, carbs 1.5, protein 34.2

Butter Lamb

Preparation time: 10 minutes
Cooking time: 3 hours
Servings: 3
Ingredients:
- 11 oz lamb fillet
- 1 teaspoon dried lemongrass
- ½ teaspoon salt
- ¼ cup coconut cream
- 2 tablespoons butter
- ½ cup beef broth
- ½ teaspoon ground paprika

Directions:
Melt butter in the instant pot on sauté mode. Chop the lamb fillet roughly and sprinkle it with dried lemongrass and ground paprika. Place the meat in the instant pot and cook on sauté mode for 2 minutes. Then flip the lamb on another side. Sprinkle it with salt. Add coconut cream and beef broth. Close and seal the lid. Cook the butter lamb for 3 hours on manual mode (low pressure).
Nutrition: calories 315, fat 20.4, fiber 0.6, carbs 1.6, protein 30.6

Cumin Lamb and Capers

Preparation time: 10 minutes
Cooking time: 35 minutes

Servings: 4
Ingredients:
- 4 lamb chops
- 2 tablespoons avocado oil
- A pinch of salt and black pepper
- 2 tablespoons sweet paprika
- 2 tablespoons capers, drained
- 1 cup beef stock
- 2 teaspoons cumin, ground
- 1 tablespoon parsley, chopped
- 1 tablespoon cilantro, chopped

Directions:
Set the instant pot on Sauté mode, add the oil, heat it up, add the lamb chops, paprika and cumin and brown for 5 minutes. Add the rest of the ingredients, put the lid on and cook on High for 30 minutes. Release the pressure naturally for 10 minutes, divide the mix between plates and serve.
Nutrition: calories 110, fat 5.6, fiber 1.9, carbs 4.5, protein 7.9

Coriander Leg of Lamb

Preparation time: 10 minutes
Cooking time: 50 minutes
Servings: 4
Ingredients:
- 1-pound leg of lamb
- 1 tablespoon ground coriander
- 1 teaspoon salt
- 1 cup of water
- 1 tablespoon coconut oil

Directions:
Rub the leg of lamb with salt and ground coriander. Then place the coconut oil in the instant pot and melt it on sauté mode. Put the leg of lamb in the hot coconut oil. Cook the meat for 5 minutes from both sides. Then add water and close the lid. Cook the leg of lamb on manual mode (high pressure) for 40 minutes. When the time is over, make the quick pressure release.
Nutrition: calories 240, fat 11.7, fiber 0, carbs 0, protein 31.9

Herbed Crusted Lamb Cutlets

Preparation time: 10 minutes
Cooking time: 30 minutes
Servings: 4
Ingredients:
- 8 lamb cutlets
- 4 tablespoons mustard
- 3 tablespoons olive oil
- ¼ cup parmesan, grated
- 1 tablespoon parsley, chopped
- 1 tablespoon thyme, chopped
- 1 tablespoon rosemary
- 1 cup tomato passata

Directions:
In a bowl, mix the lamb with the rest of the ingredients except the tomato passata. Add the sauce to the instant pot, add the lamb, put the lid on and cook on High for 30 minutes. Release the pressure naturally for 10 minutes, divide the mix between plates and serve.
Nutrition: calories 162, fat 14, fiber 3.3, carbs 6.5, protein 14.4

Dhansak Curry Meat

Preparation time: 25 minutes
Cooking time: 45 minutes
Servings: 4
Ingredients:
- 1-pound beef sirloin, chopped
- 1 tablespoon nut oil
- ½ teaspoon curry powder
- ½ teaspoon ground paprika
- ½ teaspoon salt
- ½ teaspoon ground turmeric
- 1 teaspoon lemon juice
- 1 teaspoon minced ginger
- ½ cup of water
- ½ teaspoon garam masala
- 1 tomato, chopped
- 1 teaspoon dried cilantro

Directions:
Pour nut oil in the instant pot. Add chopped beef sirloin. Set sauté mode and cook the meat for 5 minutes. Stir it from time to time. After this, add curry powder, ground paprika, salt, turmeric, lemon juice, and minced ginger. Then add garam masala, tomato, and cilantro. Add water and close the lid. Cook the meat on manual mode (high pressure) for 40 minutes. When the time is over, allow the natural pressure release for 25 minutes.
Nutrition: calories 248, fat 10.6, fiber 0.5, carbs 1.4, protein 34.7

Pine Nuts Lamb Meatballs

Preparation time: 10 minutes
Cooking time: 30 minutes
Servings: 6
Ingredients:
- 2 pounds lamb, ground
- ½ cup almond milk
- 2 shallots, minced
- 2 garlic cloves, minced
- 1 tablespoon thyme, chopped
- A pinch of salt and black pepper
- ½ cup pine nuts, toasted
- 1 egg
- 1 tablespoon olive oil
- 12 ounces canned tomatoes, crushed

Directions:
In a bowl, combine the lamb with the rest of the ingredients except the oil and the tomatoes, stir well and shape medium meatballs out of this mix Set the instant pot on Sauté mode, add the oil, heat it up, add the meatballs and cook for 2 minutes on each side. Add the tomatoes, put the lid on and cook on High for 25 minutes. Release the pressure naturally for 10 minutes, divide the mix between plates and serve.
Nutrition: calories 363, fat 26.4, fiber 1.6, carbs 5.5, protein 24.8

Mint Lamb Cubes

Preparation time: 15 minutes
Cooking time: 50 minutes
Servings: 4
Ingredients:
- 1-pound lamb shoulder
- 1 teaspoon dried mint
- 1 teaspoon salt
- 1 teaspoon peppercorns

- 1 bay leaf
- 1 cup beef broth
- 1 teaspoon dried thyme

Directions:
Rub the lamb shoulder with salt and put it in the instant pot. Add dried mint, peppercorns, bay leaf, and dried thyme. Add beef broth and close the lid. Cook the meat on manual mode (high pressure) for 50 minutes. When the time of cooking is finished, allow the natural pressure release for 10 minutes. Then remove the lamb shoulder from the instant pot and slice it. Sprinkle the meat with the beef broth from the instant pot.
Nutrition: calories 224, fat 8.7, fiber 0.3, carbs 1, protein 33.2

Lamb Shoulder Roast

Preparation time: 10 minutes
Cooking time: 35 minutes
Servings: 6
Ingredients:
- 2 tablespoons ghee, melted
- 2 tablespoons olive oil
- 2 shallots, chopped
- 2 garlic cloves, minced
- ½ cup mint, chopped
- 2 pounds lamb shoulder, fat trimmed
- 1 cup veggie stock

Directions:
Set the instant pot on Sauté mode, add the oil and the ghee, heat it up, add the lamb shoulder, garlic and shallots and sear for 2 minutes on each side. Add all the other ingredients, put the lid on and cook on High for 30 minutes. Release the pressure naturally for 10 minutes, slice the roast, between plates and serve.
Nutrition: calories 378, fat 19.2, fiber 0.4, carbs 0.7, protein 27.5

Pork Chops in Sweet Sauce

Preparation time: 10 minutes
Cooking time: 13 minutes
Servings: 2
Ingredients:
- 1 tablespoon Erythritol
- 1 teaspoon butter
- 1 tablespoon heavy cream
- ½ teaspoon ground nutmeg
- ¼ teaspoon salt
- ½ teaspoon cayenne pepper
- ½ tablespoon nut oil
- 2 pork chops
- 4 tablespoons water

Directions:
Sprinkle the pork chops with cayenne pepper, salt, and ground nutmeg. Then pour olive oil in the instant pot. Place the pork chops in the instant pot and cook them on sauté mode for 4 minutes. Then add water and flip the pork chops on another side. Cook the meat for 4 minutes more. Remove the meat from the instant pot. Add butter, heavy cream, and Erythritol. Cook the ingredients on sauté mode for 2-3 minutes or until the mixture is smooth. Add pork chops and coat in the sweet sauce. Sauté the meat for 3 minutes more.
Nutrition: calories 333, fat 28.2, fiber 0.2, carbs 0.7, protein 18.2

Moroccan Lamb

Preparation time: 10 minutes
Cooking time: 30 minutes
Servings: 4
Ingredients:
- 8 lamb chops
- 1 cup Greek yogurt
- 3 tablespoons olive oil
- 1 tablespoon lemon zest, grated
- A pinch of salt and black pepper
- 1 tablespoon cumin, ground
- 1 tablespoon coriander, ground
- 1 tablespoon turmeric powder
- ½ cup mint, chopped
- 4 garlic cloves, minced
- 2 tablespoons lemon juice
- 1 and ½ cups veggie stock

Directions:
Set the instant pot on Sauté mode, add the oil, heat it up, add the meat, cumin, coriander and turmeric and brown for 5 minutes. Add the rest of the ingredients, put the lid on and cook on High for 25 minutes. Release the pressure naturally for 10 minutes, divide everything between plates and serve.
Nutrition: calories 179, fat 14.9, fiber 1.5, carbs 5.5, protein 7.5

Kalua Pork

Preparation time: 15 minutes
Cooking time: 70 minutes
Servings: 3
Ingredients:
- 9 oz pork shoulder
- 2 bacon slices, chopped
- ½ teaspoon of sea salt
- 1 teaspoon ground paprika
- ½ teaspoon liquid smoke
- ½ cup white cabbage, chopped
- ½ cup beef broth

Directions:
Place the chopped bacon in the instant pot and cook it on sauté mode for 5 minutes or until it is light brown. Chop the pork should and mix it up with sea salt and ground paprika. Add the meat in the instant pot. Add liquid smoke and beef broth. Close the lid and cook the meat on manual mode (high pressure) for 60 minutes. When the time is over, make the quick pressure release. Open the lid and add cabbage. Stir it well. Then close the lid again and cook the meal for 10 minutes on manual mode. Make the quick pressure release.
Nutrition: calories 328, fat 23.8, fiber 0.6, carbs 1.4, protein 25.6

Spinach Pork Meatloaf

Preparation time: 10 minutes
Cooking time: 30 minutes
Servings: 6
Ingredients:
- ½ cup almond milk
- ½ cup almond flour
- 1 spring onion, chopped
- A pinch of salt and black pepper
- 2 eggs, whisked
- 1 cup baby spinach

- 2 pounds pork meat, ground
- ½ cup tomato passata
- 1 tablespoon parsley, chopped
- 1 and ½ cups water

Directions:
In a bowl, mix pork with the rest of the ingredients except the tomato passata and the water, stir well, transfer to a loaf pan that fits the instant pot and brush it with the tomato passata. Add the water to your instant pot, add the steamer basket, put the loaf pan inside, put the lid on and cook o High for 30 minutes. Release the pressure naturally for 10 minutes, cool the meatloaf down, slice and serve.
Nutrition: calories 394, fat 26.8, fiber 1, carbs 2.7, protein 35.6

Spoon Lamb

Preparation time: 20 minutes
Cooking time: 65 minutes
Servings: 4
Ingredients:
- 12 oz leg of lamb, boneless, chopped
- ½ teaspoon salt
- ½ teaspoon ground black pepper
- ½ white onion, diced
- 2 oz celery stalk, chopped
- 1 teaspoon minced garlic
- 1 tablespoon lemon juice
- 1 teaspoon lemon zest, grated
- ½ teaspoon coriander seeds
- 1 tablespoon avocado oil
- 1 cup of water

Directions:
Pour avocado oil in the instant pot. Add chopped lamb and cook it on sauté mode for 5 minutes. Then stir the meat well and add ground black pepper and salt. Add minced garlic, lemon juice, lemon zest, and coriander seeds. Stir well and cook for 4 minutes more. Remove the meat mixture from the instant pot. Put onion and celery stalk in the instant pot. Put the meat mixture over the vegetables. Add water and close the lid. Cook the spoon lamb on manual (high pressure) for 55 minutes. When the time is over, allow the natural pressure release for 15 minutes. Mix up the meal with the help of the spoon gently.
Nutrition: calories 174, fat 6.7, fiber 0.8, carbs 2.5, protein 24.3

Ginger Lamb and Basil

Preparation time: 10 minutes
Cooking time: 30 minutes
Servings: 4
Ingredients:
- 1 and ½ pounds leg of lamb, boneless and cubed
- 1 tablespoon olive oil
- 2 tablespoons basil, chopped
- 1 tablespoon ginger, grated
- A pinch of salt and black pepper
- 1 and ½ cups veggie stock
- 1 cup tomato passata

Directions:
Set the instant pot on Sauté mode, add the oil, heat it up, add the meat and brown for 5 minutes. Add the rest of the ingredients, put the lid on and cook on High for 25 minutes. Release the pressure naturally for 10 minutes, divide the mix between plates and serve.
Nutrition: calories 320, fat 13.6, fiber 0.9, carbs 4.4, protein 35.6

Rogan Josh

Preparation time: 15 minutes
Cooking time: 35 minutes
Servings: 4
Ingredients:
- 1 tablespoon ghee
- 1 white onion, diced
- 1-pound beef shoulder
- 1 teaspoon minced garlic
- ½ teaspoon minced ginger
- 1 teaspoon chili pepper
- ½ teaspoon garam masala
- ½ teaspoon ground turmeric
- ½ teaspoon ground paprika
- ½ teaspoon ground cinnamon
- ½ teaspoon ground cloves
- ½ teaspoon ground cumin
- 1 cup of coconut milk
- 1 teaspoon tomato paste

Directions:
Put ghee in the instant pot and preheat it on sauté mode. Chop the beef shoulder into cubes and put in the hot ghee. Then add onion and stir the ingredients. Cook them for 5 minutes. Add minced garlic, ginger, chili pepper, garam masala, ground turmeric, paprika, cinnamon, ground cloves, and cumin. Stir well and sauté for 5 minutes more. Meanwhile, whisk together coconut milk and tomato paste. When the liquid is smooth, add it in the beef and mix up with the help of the spatula. Close and seal the lid. Cook the meal on manual (high pressure) for 25 minutes. When the cooking time is finished, allow the natural pressure release for 15 minutes. Mix up the meal well before serving.
Nutrition: calories 355, fat 25.7, fiber 2.5, carbs 7.5, protein 25.1

Coconut Lamb Chops

Preparation time: 10 minutes
Cooking time: 30 minutes
Servings: 6
Ingredients:
- 6 lamb chops
- 2 tablespoons olive oil
- 1 teaspoon rosemary, chopped
- 1 cup veggie stock
- 1 tablespoon garlic, minced
- A pinch of salt and black pepper
- 1 cup coconut cream
- 1 tablespoon dill, chopped

Directions:
Set the instant pot on Sauté mode, add the oil, heat it up, add the lamb, garlic and rosemary and brown for 5 minutes. Add the rest of the ingredients, put the lid on and cook on High for 25 minutes. Release the pressure naturally for 10 minutes, divide everything between plates and serve.
Nutrition: calories 269, fat 25.1, fiber 1.6, carbs 5.9, protein 7.9

mb Shank

Preparation time: 25 minutes
Cooking time: 45 minutes
Servings: 4
Ingredients:
- 1-pound lamb shank
- 2 garlic cloves, diced
- 3 tablespoon apple cider vinegar
- ¼ cup crushed tomatoes
- 1 teaspoon dried parsley
- 1 teaspoon olive oil
- 4 chipotles in adobo
- 1 cup of water
- 1 teaspoon cayenne pepper

Directions:
Cut the lamb shank into 4 pieces and sprinkle with dried parsley and apple cider vinegar. Add olive oil and diced garlic. After this, sprinkle the meat with cayenne pepper. Mix it up and leave for 10-15 minutes to marinate. Then preheat the instant pot on sauté mode for 5 minutes. Add lamb pieces and all liquid from the meat (marinade). Cook the meat for 2 minutes and flip on another side. Cook it for 2 minutes more. After this, add crushed tomatoes, chipotles in adobo, and water. Close the lid and cook the meat on manual mode (high pressure) for 35 minutes. When the time of cooking is over, allow the natural pressure release for 15 minutes.
Nutrition: calories 245, fat 10.6, fiber 2.7, carbs 3.1, protein 33.4

Spicy Beef, Sprouts and Avocado Mix

Preparation time: 10 minutes
Cooking time: 30 minutes
Servings: 4
Ingredients:
- 1 pound beef stew meat, cubed
- 1 avocado, peeled, pitted and cubed
- 2 cups Brussels sprouts, trimmed and quartered
- ½ teaspoon oregano, dried
- A pinch of salt and black pepper
- 1 tablespoon avocado oil
- 1 cup beef stock
- 1 teaspoon sweet paprika

Directions:
Set the instant pot on Sauté mode, add the oil, heat it up, add the meat, oregano, paprika, salt and pepper and brown for 5 minutes Add the rest of the ingredients except the avocado, put the lid on and cook on High for 25 minutes. Release the pressure naturally for 10 minutes, divide the mix between plates and serve with the avocado on top.
Nutrition: calories 343, fat 17.5, fiber 3.3, carbs 6.7, protein 34.8

White Pork Soup

Preparation time: 15 minutes
Cooking time: 27 minutes
Servings: 2
Ingredients:
- ½ cup ground pork
- ½ shallot, diced
- 1 garlic clove, diced
- 1 teaspoon chili flakes
- 2 oz celery stalk, chopped
- 1 oz leek, chopped
- 1 tablespoon ghee
- ½ teaspoon salt
- ¼ teaspoon ground nutmeg
- 1 tablespoon cream cheese
- 1 cup of water

Directions:
Put ghee in the instant pot and melt it on sauté mode. When the ghee is melted, add ground pork, shallot, garlic clove, chili flakes, and salt. Sprinkle the ground pork with ground nutmeg and stir with the help of the spatula. Cook the meat on meat/stew mode for 10 minutes. Then stir it well and add celery stalk and leek. Add water and cream cheese and close the lid. Cook the soup on manual mode (high pressure) for 10 minutes. Then make the quick pressure release and open the lid. Let the soup rest for 15 minutes before serving.
Nutrition: calories 330, fat 24.6, fiber 0.8, carbs 5.4, protein 21.3

Beef and Creamy Sauce

Preparation time: 10 minutes
Cooking time: 35 minutes
Servings: 6
Ingredients:
- 2 pounds beef stew meat, cubed
- 2 shallots, minced
- 1 cup coconut cream
- ½ teaspoon rosemary, chopped
- 1 tablespoon olive oil
- 1 cup beef stock
- 1 tablespoon dill, chopped
- A pinch of salt and black pepper

Directions:
Set your instant pot on Sauté mode, add the oil, heat it up, add the meat, shallots and the rosemary and brown for 5 minutes. Add rest of the ingredients except the cream, put the lid on and cook on High for 25 minutes. Release the pressure naturally for 10 minutes, set the pot on Sauté mode again, add the cream, toss and cook for 10 minutes more. Divide the mix between plates and serve.
Nutrition: calories 397, fat 21.4, fiber 1, carbs 2.6, protein 32.4

Lamb Pulao

Preparation time: 15 minutes
Cooking time: 35 minutes
Servings: 4
Ingredients:
- 1 cup cauliflower, shredded
- 10 oz lamb loin, chopped
- ¼ cup crushed tomatoes
- ¼ onion, diced
- 1 tablespoon ghee
- ¼ teaspoon ground cardamom
- ¼ teaspoon cumin seeds
- ¼ teaspoon minced garlic
- ¼ teaspoon turmeric
- ¼ teaspoon ground coriander
- ½ cup chicken broth
- ½ teaspoon salt

Directions:
In the shallow bowl mix up together ground cardamom, cumin seeds, turmeric, salt, and ground coriander. Then preheat the instant pot on sauté mode for 2-3 minutes. Place the chopped lamb loin in the hot instant pot bowl and cook on sauté mode for

4 minutes. Then flip the meat on another side and sprinkle with spice mixture. Add ghee. Cook it for 5 minutes more. After this, add diced onion, crushed tomatoes, minced garlic, and chicken broth. Close and seal the lid. Cook the meat on manual mode (high pressure) for 20 minutes. Then make the quick pressure release and open the lid. Stir the meal well and add shredded cauliflower. Stir it again. Close the lid and cook the ingredients for 3 minutes on manual mode. When the cooking time is finished, make the quick pressure release.
Nutrition: calories 287, fat 22.9, fiber 1.1, carbs 3, protein 15.7

Pork and Chives Asparagus
Preparation time: 10 minutes
Cooking time: 30 minutes
Servings: 6
Ingredients:
- 2 pounds pork stew meat, cubed
- 4 garlic cloves, minced
- 1 cup beef stock
- 1 bunch asparagus, trimmed
- A pinch of salt and black pepper
- 1 teaspoon sweet paprika
- 1 teaspoon chives, chopped
- 1 tablespoon olive oil

Directions:
Set your instant pot on sauté mode, add the oil, heat it up, add the garlic and the beef stew meat and brown for 5 minutes Add the rest of the ingredients except the asparagus, put the lid on and cook on High for 20 minutes. Release the pressure naturally for 10 minutes, set the pot on Sauté mode again, add the asparagus, cook for 5 minutes more, divide everything between plates and serve.
Nutrition: calories 347, fat 17.1, fiber 0.2, carbs 0.9, protein 24.7

Meat&Cheese Pie
Preparation time: 25 minutes
Cooking time: 45 minutes
Servings: 8
Ingredients:
- 6 oz ground beef
- 6 oz ground pork
- 3 oz Provolone cheese, grated
- 3 oz Mozzarella cheese, shredded
- 2 tablespoons butter
- 6 tablespoons almond flour
- 1 teaspoon coconut oil
- 1 teaspoon dried parsley
- ½ teaspoon salt
- 1 teaspoon tomato paste
- 1 tablespoon cream cheese
- 1 cup water, for cooking

Directions:
Make the dough: in the mixing bowl mix up butter and almond flour. Knead the ingredients. Then line the instant pot baking pan with baking paper. Pour water and insert the trivet in the instant pot. Roll up the dough into the circle and place it in the baking pan. Flatten the dough circle in the shape of the pie crust. After this, make the pie filling: In the bowl mix up together ground beef, pork, Provolone cheese, coconut oil, parsley, salt, tomato paste, and cream cheese. When the mixture is homogenous, put it over the pie crust and flatten well. Then top the meat filling with Mozzarella. Cover the surface of the pie with foil. Secure the edges. Place the baking pan with pie on the trivet and close the lid. Cook the meal on manual mode (high pressure) for 45 minutes. When the cooking time is finished, make the quick pressure release. Open the lid and immediately remove the baking pan with pie from the instant pot. Remove the foil and cool the pie to the room temperature. Then cut it into the servings.
Nutrition: calories 293, fat 21.2, fiber 2.3, carbs 5.3, protein 22.4

Oregano and Thyme Beef
Preparation time: 5 minutes
Cooking time: 30 minutes
Servings: 4
Ingredients:
- 1 pound beef stew meat, cubed
- 2 garlic cloves, minced
- 1 tablespoon olive oil
- 1 teaspoon thyme, dried
- A pinch of salt and black pepper
- 1 tablespoon oregano, chopped
- 1 and ½ cups beef stock

Directions:
Set your instant pot on Sauté mode, add the oil, heat it up, add the garlic, thyme and the meat and brown for 5 minutes. Add the rest of the ingredients, put the lid on and cook on High for 25 minutes. Release the pressure naturally for 10 minutes, divide the mix between plates and serve.
Nutrition: calories 247, fat 10.7, fiber 0.6, carbs 1.4, protein 34.2

Burger Casserole
Preparation time: 15 minutes
Cooking time: 44 minutes
Servings: 4
Ingredients:
- 1 oz bacon, chopped
- 10 oz ground beef
- ¼ white onion, diced
- 1 teaspoon minced garlic
- 1 tablespoon cream cheese
- ¼ teaspoon mustard
- ¼ teaspoon salt
- 2 eggs, beaten
- 4 oz Cheddar, shredded
- 1/3 cup coconut cream
- 1 teaspoon chili powder
- 1 teaspoon avocado oil

Directions:
Put bacon in the instant pot and cook it on sauté mode for 4 minutes. Flip the bacon on another side after 2 minutes of cooking. When the bacon is cooked, transfer it in the mixing bowl. Then add the ground beef in the mixing bowl. After this, add diced onion, salt, mustard, minced garlic, eggs, chili powder, and cream cheese. Stir the ingredients. Brush the instant pot with avocado oil and arrange the meat mixture inside in the smooth layer. Top the beef layer with shredded Cheddar cheese. Then pour the coconut cream over the cheese and close the instant pot lid. Cook the casserole on manual mode (high pressure) for 40 minutes. When the time is over, allow the natural pressure release for 10 minutes.

Nutrition: calories 314, fat 17.5, fiber 0.9, carbs 3.4, protein 34.7

Almond Lamb Meatloaf

Preparation time: 10 minutes
Cooking time: 30 minutes
Servings: 4
Ingredients:
- 1 and ½ pound lamb, ground
- 2 shallots, minced
- 2 eggs, whisked
- 3 garlic cloves, minced
- 1 tablespoon almonds, chopped
- 1 tablespoon rosemary
- A pinch of salt and black pepper
- 1 cup kale, chopped
- ¼ cup coconut milk
- Cooking spray
- 2 cups water

Directions:
In a bowl, combine the meat with rest of the ingredients except the cooking spray and the water, and stir well. Grease a loaf pan that fits the instant pot with the cooking spray, shape the meatloaf and put it in the pan. Add the water to the instant pot, add the steamer basket, put the meatloaf inside, put the lid on and cook on High for 30 minutes. Release the pressure naturally for 10 minutes, cool the meatloaf, slice and serve.
Nutrition: calories 301, fat 15.1, fiber 1.2, carbs 4.4, protein 35.4

Cauliflower Shepherd's Pie

Preparation time: 15 minutes
Cooking time: 20 minutes
Servings: 4
Ingredients:
- 1 cup cauliflower, chopped
- 1 teaspoon tomato paste
- 1 bell pepper, chopped
- 1 white onion, diced
- 1 teaspoon salt
- ½ cup Cheddar cheese, shredded
- ½ cup chicken broth
- ½ teaspoon ground paprika
- ½ teaspoon dried cilantro
- ½ teaspoon dried basil
- ½ teaspoon dried sage
- 1 teaspoon coconut oil
- ½ cup ground pork
- 1 cup water, for cooking

Directions:
Pour water and insert the steamer rack in the instant pot. Put the cauliflower in the steamer rack and close the lid. Cook the vegetables on manual (high pressure) for 4 minutes. Then make the quick pressure release and open the lid. Transfer the cauliflower in the bowl and mash it with the help of the potato masher. When you get cauliflower puree, add salt and ¼ cup of hot water from the instant pot. You should get a smooth and soft texture of cauliflower puree. After this, place the coconut oil in the instant pot and melt it on sauté mode. Then add bell pepper and white onion. Add ground paprika, cilantro, basil, sage, and ground pork. Mix up the meat mixture with the help of a spatula and sauté for 10 minutes. Stir it from time to time. Then add chicken broth and sauté the ingredients for 2 minutes more. After this, spread the cauliflower puree over the ground pork mixture and close the lid. Cook the meal on manual (high pressure) for 3 minutes. Then make the quick pressure release. Cool Shepherd's pie to room temperature.
Nutrition: calories 217, fat 14.3, fiber 1.8, carbs 6.9, protein 15.4

Pork and Bok Choy

Preparation time: 10 minutes
Cooking time: 35 minutes
Servings: 6
Ingredients:
- 1 and ½ pounds pork stew meat, cubed
- 4 garlic cloves, minced
- 2 tablespoons chili powder
- 1 teaspoon red pepper flakes
- 1 pound bok choy, torn
- 1 tablespoon olive oil
- A pinch of salt and black pepper
- 1 cup beef stock

Directions:
Set the instant pot on sauté mode, add the oil, heat it up, add the garlic, the meat, chili powder and pepper flakes and brown for 5 minutes. Add the rest of the ingredients, put the lid on and cook on High for 30 minutes. Release the pressure naturally for 10 minutes, divide the mix between plates and serve.
Nutrition: calories 365, fat 17.5, fiber 1.8, carbs 3.9, protein 34.6

Big Mac Bites

Preparation time: 10 minutes
Cooking time: 10 minutes
Servings: 2
Ingredients:
- ½ cup ground pork
- ¼ teaspoon white pepper
- ¼ teaspoon salt
- ½ cup lettuce iceberg
- 1 teaspoon flax meal
- 1 pickled cucumber, sliced
- 1 teaspoon coconut oil

Directions:
In the mixing bowl combine together ground pork with salt, flax meal, and white pepper. Then make 2 meatballs from ground pork mixture. Put the coconut oil in the instant pot and melt it on sauté mode. Then put the pork meatballs in the instant pot and cook them for 5 minutes from each side. After this, cool the cooked meatballs to the room temperature. Make the Big Mac bites: place the meatball on the plate and top it sliced cucumber, and lettuce. Pierce the ingredients with a toothpick. Repeat the same steps with the second meatball.
Nutrition: calories 265, fat 17.2, fiber 1.3, carbs 6.5, protein 21.5

Smoked Paprika Lamb

Preparation time: 10 minutes
Cooking time: 30 minutes
Servings: 4
Ingredients:

- 1 and ½ pounds leg of lamb, boneless and cubed
- 1 tablespoon smoked paprika
- 1 and ½ cups tomatoes, cubed
- 3 garlic cloves, minced
- 1 cup veggie stock
- 1 tablespoon ghee, melted
- A pinch of salt and black pepper
- 1 tablespoon cilantro, chopped

Directions:
Set your instant pot on Sauté mode, add the ghee, heat it up, add the meat, smoked paprika and the garlic and brown for 6 minutes. Add the rest of the ingredients except the cilantro, put the lid on and cook on High for 25 minutes. Release the pressure naturally for 10 minutes, divide the mix between plates and serve with the cilantro sprinkled on top.
Nutrition: calories 306, fat 13.4, fiber 0.5, carbs 1.2, protein 43.2

Zoodle Pork Casserole

Preparation time: 20 minutes
Cooking time: 45 minutes
Servings: 4
Ingredients:
- 1 zucchini, trimmed
- 7 oz ground pork
- 1 cup Cheddar cheese, shredded
- 1 teaspoon salt
- 1 tablespoon cream cheese
- 1 teaspoon chili flakes
- ½ teaspoon white pepper
- 1 teaspoon dried sage
- 1 cup water, for cooking

Directions:
Make the zoodles from the zucchini with the help of the spiralizer. In the mixing bowl combine together ground pork with salt, cream cheese, chili flakes, white pepper, and dried sage. Line the instant pot casserole mold with baking paper. Put the ground pork mixture in the casserole mold and flatten it gently with the help of the spatula. Then top it with spiralized zucchini and cream cheese. Sprinkle the casserole with shredded Cheddar cheese. Cover the surface of the casserole mold with foil. Secure the edges of it. Pour water and insert the trivet in the instant pot. Place the casserole mold over the trivet and close the lid. Cook the meal on manual mode (high pressure) for 45 minutes. When the cooking time is over, make the quick pressure release and open the lid. Cool the casserole little before serving.
Nutrition: calories 203, fat 12.1, fiber 0.7, carbs 2.4, protein 20.9

Cajun Beef and Leeks Sauce

Preparation time: 10 minutes
Cooking time: 35 minutes
Servings: 6
Ingredients:
- 2 pounds beef sirloin, cut into steaks
- 1 tablespoon olive oil
- 2 tablespoons Cajun seasoning
- 1 and ½ cups beef stock
- A pinch of salt and black pepper
- 1 teaspoon garlic, minced
- 1 leek, sliced

Directions:
Set your instant pot on sauté mode, add the oil, heat it up, add the garlic, the meat and Cajun seasoning and brown for 5 minutes. Add the remaining ingredients, put the lid on and cook on High for 30 minutes. Release the pressure naturally for 10 minutes, divide the mix between plates and serve.
Nutrition: calories 311, fat 11.8, fiber 0.3, carbs 2.3, protein 25.7

Ground Beef Skewers

Preparation time: 20 minutes
Cooking time: 15 minutes
Servings: 6
Ingredients:
- 2 cups ground beef
- 1 small onion, minced
- 1 garlic clove, minced
- ½ teaspoon ground black pepper
- ½ teaspoon chili flakes
- ½ teaspoon salt
- ½ teaspoon ground paprika
- 1 teaspoon dried cilantro
- 1 egg, beaten
- 1 cup water, for cooking

Directions:
Mix up ground beef with minced onion, garlic clove, ground black pepper, chili flakes, salt, ground paprika, and dried cilantro. Add egg and stir the meat mixture until homogenous. Make 6 balls from the meat mixture and string them on the skewers. Flatten the meat evenly on the skewer. Pour water and insert the trivet in the instant pot. Line the trivet with baking paper and place the skewers with ground beef on it. Close and seal the lid. Cook the meal on manual mode (high pressure) for 15 minutes. Then allow the natural pressure release for 10 minutes. It is recommended to serve the ground beef skewers hot.
Nutrition: calories 103, fat 6.2, fiber 0.4, carbs 1.6, protein 9.8

Beef and Savoy Cabbage Mix

Preparation time: 10 minutes
Cooking time: 25 minutes
Servings: 4
Ingredients:
- 1 pound beef stew meat, cubed
- 1 Savoy cabbage, shredded
- 2 garlic cloves, minced
- 1 tablespoon olive oil
- A pinch of salt and black pepper
- 1 and ½ cups tomato passata
- 1 tablespoon parsley, chopped

Directions:
Set the instant pot on Sauté mode, add the oil, heat it up, add the meat and the garlic and brown for 5 minutes. Add the rest of the ingredients, put the lid on and cook on High for 20 minutes. Release the pressure naturally for 10 minutes, divide the mix between plates and serve.
Nutrition: calories 243, fat 10.6, fiber 0.1, carbs 0.6, protein 34.5

Pastrami

Preparation time: 2 days

Cooking time: 70 minutes
Servings: 4
Ingredients:
- 1 ½-corned beef
- 1 teaspoon Erythritol
- ½ teaspoon ground black pepper
- ½ teaspoon garlic powder
- ½ teaspoon onion powder
- 1 teaspoon ground paprika
- ¼ teaspoon salt
- 1 teaspoon ground coriander
- 1 teaspoon mustard
- 1 teaspoon liquid smoke
- 1 cup water, for cooking

Directions:
Pour water and insert the trivet in the instant pot. Place the corned beef on the trivet and close the lid. Cook the meat on Manual (high pressure) for 70 minutes. When the cooking time is finished, make the quick pressure release and transfer the meat on the plate. After this, in the shallow bowl mix up ground black pepper, garlic powder, onion powder, paprika, salt, and ground coriander. In the separated bowl whisk mustard with liquid smoke. Then brush the corned beef with mustard mixture and rub with the spice mixture generously. Place the meat in the fridge for at least 2 days.
Nutrition: calories 341, fat 24.8, fiber 0.4, carbs 1.3, protein 26.7

Pork and Mint Zucchinis

Preparation time: 10 minutes
Cooking time: 25 minutes
Servings: 6
Ingredients:
- 2 pounds pork stew meat, cubed
- A pinch of salt and black pepper
- 1 cup beef stock
- 1 cup zucchinis, sliced
- 1 tablespoon balsamic vinegar
- 1 tablespoon olive oil
- 1 tablespoon garlic, minced
- 1 tablespoon mint, chopped

Directions:
Set the instant pot on Sauté mode, add the oil, heat it up, add the pork and the garlic and brown for 5 minutes. Add the rest of the ingredients, put the lid on and cook on High for 20 minutes. Release the pressure naturally for 10 minutes, divide everything between plates and serve.
Nutrition: calories 349, fat 17.1, fiber 0.3, carbs 1.2, protein 34.2

Pork Belly Salad

Preparation time: 10 minutes
Cooking time: 8 minutes
Servings: 4
Ingredients:
- 7 oz pork belly, chopped
- ½ cup lettuce, chopped
- 1 teaspoon lemon juice
- 1 teaspoon avocado oil
- ¼ cup cherry tomatoes, halved
- 1 cucumber, chopped
- 1 oz Parmesan, grated
- ½ teaspoon coconut oil

Directions:
Preheat the instant pot on sauté mode for 4 minutes. Toss the chopped pork belly and coconut oil in the instant pot and cook it for 8 minutes – for 4 minutes from each side. Meanwhile, in the salad bowl mix up lettuce with cherry tomatoes and cucumber. Add lemon juice and avocado oil. Shake the salad well. Then top it with the cooked pork belly and grated Parmesan.
Nutrition: calories 273, fat 15.7, fiber 0.6, carbs 3.7, protein 25.8

Beef and Walnuts Rice

Preparation time: 10 minutes
Cooking time: 35 minutes
Servings: 6
Ingredients:
- 1 and ½ pounds beef stew meat, cubed
- 2 garlic cloves, minced
- 1 cup beef stock
- 1 tablespoon walnuts, toasted and chopped
- 1 cup tomato passata
- A pinch of salt and black pepper
- 1 tablespoon basil, chopped
- 1 tablespoon olive oil

Directions:
Set your instant pot on sauté mode, add the oil, heat it up, add the meat and the garlic and brown for 5 minutes. Add the rest of the ingredients, put the lid on and cook on High for 30 minutes. Release the pressure naturally for 10 minutes, divide everything between plates and serve.
Nutrition: calories 329, fat 12.7, fiber 0.9, carbs 4.2, protein 27.6

Pork Salad with Kale

Preparation time: 10 minutes
Cooking time: 15 minutes
Servings: 4
Ingredients:
- ½ cup ground pork
- 1 cup kale
- 1 teaspoon olive oil
- ½ teaspoon chili flakes
- ½ teaspoon onion powder
- 1 teaspoon cream cheese
- ¼ teaspoon salt
- 1 teaspoon peanuts, chopped
- ½ teaspoon sesame oil

Directions:
Pour sesame oil in the instant pot. Add ground pork. Start to cook the meat on sauté mode. After 3 minutes of cooking, stir the ground pork and add chili flakes, onion powder, and salt. Cook the ground pork for 10 minutes. Meanwhile, chop the kale roughly. Add kale in the instant pot and cook the mixture on sauté mode for 2 minutes. Transfer the ingredients in the salad bowl. Add olive oil and peanuts. Stir the salad. The cooked salad should be served warm.
Nutrition: calories 148, fat 10.5, fiber 0.3, carbs 2.1, protein 10.8

Ketogenic Instant Pot Vegetable Recipes

Lime and Paprika Asparagus

Preparation time: 5 minutes
Cooking time: 15 minutes
Servings: 4
Ingredients:
- 2 pounds asparagus, trimmed
- 1 tablespoon lime juice
- 1 tablespoon lime zest, grated
- 1 tablespoon sweet paprika
- 2 cups chicken stock
- A pinch of salt and black pepper

Directions:
In your instant pot, combine the asparagus with the rest of the ingredients, put the lid on and cook on High for 15 minutes. Release the pressure fast for 5 minutes, divide between plates and serve.
Nutrition: calories 56, fat 1.8, fiber 0.4, carbs 0.5, protein 5.6

Garlic and Cheese Baked Asparagus

Preparation time: 10 minutes
Cooking time: 6 minutes
Servings: 4
Ingredients:
- 9 oz asparagus
- 1 teaspoon garlic powder
- ½ cup heavy cream
- ¼ cup of water
- ½ cup Mozzarella, grated
- 1 teaspoon dried oregano
- ¼ teaspoon salt

Directions:
Chop the asparagus roughly. In the mixing bowl combine garlic powder with heavy cream, water, salt, and dried oregano. Then pour the liquid in the instant pot and preheat it on sauté mode for 5 minutes. After this, add chopped asparagus and Mozzarella. Close the lid and cook the meal on manual mode (high pressure) for 1 minute. When the time is over, make the quick pressure release.
Nutrition: calories 78, fat 63, fiber 1.6, carbs 3.8, protein 2.9

Basil Spicy Artichokes

Preparation time: 10 minutes
Cooking time: 20 minutes
Servings: 4
Ingredients:
- 4 big artichokes, trimmed
- A pinch of salt and black pepper
- ¼ cup chicken stock
- 1 teaspoon basil, chopped
- ½ teaspoon hot paprika
- A pinch of red pepper flakes
- A pinch of cayenne pepper

Directions:
In your instant pot, combine the artichokes with the rest of the ingredients, put the lid on and cook on High for 20 minutes. Release the pressure naturally for 10 minutes, divide the artichokes between plates and serve.
Nutrition: calories 10, fat 1.1, fiber 0.8, carbs 1.6, protein 0.6

Brussels Sprouts in Heavy Cream

Preparation time: 10 minutes
Cooking time: 6 minutes
Servings: 3
Ingredients:
- 6 oz Brussels sprouts
- 1/3 teaspoon salt
- ½ teaspoon ground black pepper
- 1 teaspoon butter
- ½ cup heavy cream

Directions:
Melt butter in sauté mode and add Brussels sprouts. Sprinkle them with salt and ground black pepper and cook on sauté mode for 3 minutes. Stir the vegetables and add heavy cream. Close the lid and cook the meal on manual mode (high pressure) for 3 minutes. When the cooking time is finished, allow the natural pressure release for 10 minutes. Stir the vegetables before serving.
Nutrition: calories 106, fat 8.9, fiber 2.2, carbs 5.9, protein 2.4

Coconut Leeks and Sprouts

Preparation time: 5 minutes
Cooking time: 20 minutes
Servings: 4
Ingredients:
- 2 leeks, sliced
- 1 pound Brussels sprouts, halved
- ½ cup chicken stock
- ½ cup coconut cream
- 1 tablespoon dill, chopped
- A pinch of salt and black pepper

Directions:
In your instant pot, combine leeks with the sprouts and the rest of the ingredients, put the lid on and cook on High for 20 minutes. Release the pressure fast for 5 minutes, divide the mix between plates and serve.
Nutrition: calories 148, fat 7.8, fiber 2.9, carbs 5.4, protein 5.5

Wrapped Bacon Carrot

Preparation time: 15 minutes
Cooking time: 4 minutes
Servings: 3
Ingredients:
- 2 large carrots, peeled
- 3 bacon slices
- ¾ teaspoon salt
- ¼ teaspoon ground turmeric
- 1 teaspoon avocado oil
- 1 cup water, for cooking

Directions:
Sprinkle the bacon slices with salt and ground turmeric. Pour avocado oil in the instant pot and heat it up on sauté mode for 2 minutes. Meanwhile, cut the carrots into 6 pieces. Cut the bacon into 6 pieces too. Wrap every carrot piece in the bacon and put in the hot oil in one layer. Cook the vegetables on sauté mode for 1 minute and then flip on another side. Cook the carrot for 1 minute more. Then transfer in the plate. Clean the instant pot and add water. Insert the trivet and put a carrot on it. Close and seal the lid.

Cook the wrapped bacon carrot for 2 minutes. Then make the quick pressure release.
Nutrition: calories 102, fat 7.2, fiber 1.3, carbs 4.9, protein 5.4

Mozzarella Artichokes and Capers
Preparation time: 5 minutes
Cooking time: 15 minutes
Servings: 4
Ingredients:
- 4 artichokes, trimmed
- 1 cup chicken stock
- 1 tablespoon sweet paprika
- 1 tablespoon capers, drained
- 1 tablespoon basil, chopped
- 2 garlic cloves, chopped
- 1 cup mozzarella, shredded

Directions:
In your instant pot, combine the artichokes with the rest of the ingredients except the mozzarella, put the lid on and cook on High for 15 minutes. Release the pressure fast for 5 minutes, divide the mix between plates, sprinkle the mozzarella on top and serve.
Nutrition: calories 106, fat 1.9, fiber 0.2, carbs 0.5, protein 7.8

Caprese Zoodles
Preparation time: 15 minutes
Cooking time: 1 minute
Servings: 6
Ingredients:
- 1 zucchini, trimmed
- ½ cup cherry tomatoes, halved
- ½ cup mozzarella cheese, balls
- 1 teaspoon fresh basil, chopped
- 1 tablespoon lemon juice
- ¼ teaspoon white pepper
- 1 teaspoon sesame oil
- 1 cup water, for cooking

Directions:
Pour water in the instant pot and insert the steamer rack. With the help of the spiralizer make the noodles from the zucchini and put them in the steamer rack. Close and seal the lid and set the timer on "0". Cook the zucchini on high pressure. When the cooking time is finished, make the quick pressure release and open the lid. Transfer the zucchini noodles in the big salad bowl. Add cherry tomatoes, mozzarella balls, and basil. Then sprinkle the ingredients with lemon juice, white pepper, and sesame oil. Shake the meal gently.
Nutrition: calories 22, fat 1.3, fiber 0.6, carbs 1.9, protein 1.2

Asparagus and Tomatoes
Preparation time: 5 minutes
Cooking time: 15 minutes
Servings: 4
Ingredients:
- 1 pound asparagus, trimmed
- 1 cup chicken stock
- A pinch of salt and black pepper
- 2 cups cherry tomatoes, halved
- 1 tablespoon basil, chopped
- 1 tablespoon chives, chopped

Directions:
In your instant pot, mix the asparagus with the stock and the rest of the ingredients, put the lid on and cook on High for 15 minutes. Release the pressure fast for 5 minutes, divide mix between plates and serve.
Nutrition: calories 42, fat 1.2, fiber 0.7, carbs 1, protein 3.5

Cauliflower Florets Mix
Preparation time: 10 minutes
Cooking time: 4 minutes
Servings: 3
Ingredients:
- ½ cup cauliflower florets
- ¼ cup broccoli florets
- 1 tablespoon hazelnuts
- ¼ teaspoon minced garlic
- 1 tablespoon avocado oil
- 1/3 teaspoon salt
- 1 cup water, for cooking

Directions:
Pour water and insert the steamer rack in the instant pot. Put the cauliflower florets and broccoli florets in the steamer. Close and seal the lid. Cook the vegetables on manual mode (steam mode) for 4 minutes. When the cooking time is finished, make the quick pressure release and open the lid. Cool the vegetables to the room temperature and transfer in the big bowl. Chop the hazelnuts and add in the vegetables. Then sprinkle the ingredients with minced garlic, avocado oil, and salt. Shake the well.
Nutrition: calories 23, fat 1.6, fiber 1, carbs 2, protein 0.8

Asparagus and Chives Dressing
Preparation time: 5 minutes
Cooking time: 10 minutes
Servings: 4
Ingredients:
- 1 pound asparagus, trimmed
- 2 tablespoons olive oil
- 2 cups water
- A pinch of salt and black pepper
- 1 teaspoon garlic powder
- 1 cup avocado mayonnaise
- 1 cup Greek yogurt
- 1 and ½ cups basil, chopped
- ½ cup parsley, chopped
- ¼ cup chives, chopped
- ¼ cup lemon juice

Directions:
Put the water in the instant pot, add the steamer basket, add the asparagus inside, put the lid on and cook on High for 10 minutes. Release the pressure fast for 5 minutes, and divide the asparagus between plates. In a blender, mix the avocado mayonnaise with the rest of the ingredients, pulse well, spread over the asparagus and serve.
Nutrition: calories 102, fat 7.5, fiber 3, carbs 6.1, protein 3.4

Balsamic Brussels Sprouts
Preparation time: 10 minutes
Cooking time: 7 minutes
Servings: 3
Ingredients:

- ¼ teaspoon Erythritol
- 1 teaspoon balsamic vinegar
- 2 tablespoons sesame oil
- ¼ teaspoon salt
- ¼ teaspoon chili flakes
- 8 oz Brussels sprouts
- 1 cup water, for cooking

Directions:
Pour water and insert the steamer rack in the instant pot. Put Brussels sprouts in the steamer rack and close the lid. Cook them on steam mode for 2 minutes. Then make the quick pressure release and open the lid. Transfer the vegetables in the bowl and clean the instant pot. Remove the steamer rack. Pour the sesame oil in the instant pot and heat it up on sauté mode for 3 minutes. Add cooked Brussels sprouts. Then sprinkle the vegetables with balsamic vinegar, chili flakes, and salt. Stir them and cook for 2 minutes.
Nutrition: calories 113, fat 9.3, fiber 2.8, carbs 6.9, protein 2.6

Creamy Asparagus Mix

Preparation time: 5 minutes
Cooking time: 10 minutes
Servings: 4
Ingredients:
- 1 bunch asparagus, trimmed
- 2 tablespoons oregano, chopped
- 1 cup heavy cream
- A pinch of salt and black pepper
- 1 cup chicken stock

Directions:
In your instant pot, mix the asparagus with the rest of the ingredients, put the lid on and cook on High for 10 minutes. Release the pressure fast for 5 minutes, divide everything between plates and serve.
Nutrition: calories 121, fat 11.5, fiber 1.8, carbs 4.1, protein 1.9

Tender Sautéed Vegetables

Preparation time: 10 minutes
Cooking time: 8 minutes
Servings: 4
Ingredients:
- ½ cup radish, sliced
- 1 green bell pepper, chopped
- 1 zucchini, chopped
- 1 teaspoon tomato paste
- ½ teaspoon salt
- ½ teaspoon ground coriander
- 3 tablespoons avocado oil
- 1 cup water, for cooking

Directions:
In the shallow bowl mix up avocado oil and tomato paste. Pour water and insert the trivet in the instant pot. In the mixing bowl combine radish, bell pepper, and zucchini. Sprinkle the vegetables with salt and ground coriander. Then add tomato paste mixture. Stir the vegetables. After this, transfer them in the instant pot baking pan and cover with foil. Put the baking pan on the trivet and close the lid. Cook the vegetables on manual mode (high pressure) for 8 minutes. Then make the quick pressure release.
Nutrition: calories 35, fat 1.5, fiber 1.7, carbs 5.2, protein 1.2

Parmesan Radishes and Asparagus

Preparation time: 5 minutes
Cooking time: 10 minutes
Servings: 4
Ingredients:
- 1 bunch asparagus, trimmed
- 2 cups radishes, sliced
- 1 cup chicken stock
- 1 tablespoon chives, chopped
- 1 teaspoon chili powder

Directions:
In your instant pot, combine the asparagus with the radishes and the rest of the ingredients, put the lid on and cook on High for 10 minutes. Release the pressure fast for 5 minutes, divide the mix between plates and serve.
Nutrition: calories 45, fat 0.6, fiber 0.1, carbs 0.4, protein 2

Spaghetti Squash Nests

Preparation time: 20 minutes
Cooking time: 5 minutes
Servings: 4
Ingredients:
- 12 oz spaghetti squash, peeled
- 1 egg, beaten
- ¼ teaspoon salt
- 1 tablespoon coconut flour
- ¼ teaspoon ground cumin
- 1 cup water, for cooking

Directions:
Grate the spaghetti squash and mix it up with egg, salt, coconut flour, and ground cumin. After this, fill the muffin molds with a grated squash mixture Flatten the mixture in the shape of a nest. Use the spoon for this step. Pour water and insert the steamer rack in the instant pot. Arrange the muffin molds with squash nests and close the lid. Cook the meal on manual (high pressure) for 5 minutes. Then make the quick pressure release. Remove the cooked squash nests from the muffin molds.
Nutrition: calories 50, fat 1.9, fiber 0.6, carbs 7, protein 2.2

Artichokes and Bacon Mix

Preparation time: 5 minutes
Cooking time: 10 minutes
Servings: 4
Ingredients:
- 4 artichokes, trimmed
- 2 teaspoons lemon zest, grated
- 1 cup chicken stock
- 1 cup bacon, cooked and crumbled
- 1 teaspoon chili powder
- A pinch of salt and black pepper
- 1 tablespoon basil, chopped
- 1 tablespoon parsley, chopped

Directions:
In your instant pot, combine the artichokes with the lemon zest and the rest of the ingredients except the bacon, put the lid on and cook on High for 10 minutes. Release the pressure fast for 5 minutes, divide the mix between plates, sprinkle the bacon on top and serve.
Nutrition: calories 82, fat 2.5, fiber 1.9, carbs 2.1, protein 5.6

Lemongrass Green Beans

Preparation time: 10 minutes
Cooking time: 1 minute
Servings: 3
Ingredients:
- 8 oz green beans, chopped
- 1 teaspoon dried lemongrass
- 1 teaspoon lime juice
- ¼ teaspoon ground nutmeg
- 1 teaspoon butter, melted
- 1 cup water, for cooking

Directions:
Pour water and insert the steamer rack in the instant pot. Place the green beans and lemongrass in the rack and close the lid. Cook the vegetables on manual mode (high pressure) for 1 minute. Then make the quick pressure release. Transfer the green beans in the bowl. Add lime juice, ground nutmeg, and melted butter. Stir the vegetables well.
Nutrition: calories 37, fat 1.4, fiber 2.6, carbs 5.8, protein 1.4

Balsamic Green Beans and Capers

Preparation time: 10 minutes
Cooking time: 20 minutes
Servings: 4
Ingredients:
- 1 and ½ cups chicken stock
- 1 pound green beans, trimmed and halved
- 1 tablespoon capers, drained
- A pinch of salt and black pepper
- 2 garlic cloves, minced
- 1 tablespoon dill, chopped
- 1 tablespoon balsamic vinegar

Directions:
In your instant pot, combine the green beans with the stock and the rest of the ingredients, put the lid on and cook on High for 20 minutes. Release the pressure naturally for 10 minutes, divide everything between plates and serve.
Nutrition: calories 46, fat 1.7, fiber 0.1, carbs 0.6, protein 2.7

Cucumbers and Zucchini Noodles

Preparation time: 10 minutes
Cooking time: minute
Servings: 4
Ingredients:
- 2 cucumbers
- 1 zucchini, trimmed
- 1 teaspoon fresh dill, chopped
- 1 garlic clove, diced
- 1 teaspoon fresh parsley, chopped
- 1 tablespoon olive oil
- ¼ teaspoon chili powder
- 1 cup water, for cooking

Directions:
Make the noodles from zucchini and put them in the steamer rack. Pour water and insert the steamer rack in the instant pot. Close the lid. Cook the vegetable noodles for 1 minute on steam mode. Then make a quick pressure release and transfer the zucchini noodles in the salad bowl. Make the spirals from the cucumbers and add them to the zucchini. Then add dill, diced garlic, parsley, olive oil, and chili powder. Gently stir the ingredients.
Nutrition: calories 99, fat 0.7, fiber 4.4, carbs 22.8, protein 2.7

Brussels Sprouts and Sauce

Preparation time: 5 minutes
Cooking time: 20 minutes
Servings: 4
Ingredients:
- 1 pound Brussels sprouts, trimmed and halved
- 1 cup chicken stock
- 2 garlic cloves, minced
- A pinch of salt and black pepper
- 1 tablespoon dill, chopped
- 1 tablespoon heavy cream
- 1 tablespoon rosemary, chopped

Directions:
In your instant pot, mix the sprouts with the stock and the rest of the ingredients, put the lid on and cook on High for 20 minutes. Release the pressure fast for 5 minutes, divide the mix between plates and serve.
Nutrition: calories 71, fat 2.1, fiber 1.1, carbs 1.3, protein 4.4

Eggs and Mushrooms Cups

Preparation time: 10 minutes
Cooking time: 7 minutes
Servings: 4
Ingredients:
- 1 cup white mushrooms, grinded
- 2 eggs, beaten
- 2 tablespoons almond flour
- ¼ teaspoon salt
- ¼ teaspoon dried thyme
- 1 teaspoon cream cheese
- 1 teaspoon sesame oil
- 1 cup water, for cooking

Directions:
In the mixing bowl mix up grinded mushrooms, eggs, almond flour, salt, thyme, and cream cheese. Then brush the muffin molds with sesame oil. Put the mushroom mixture in the muffin molds. Then pour water and insert the trivet in the instant pot. Put the muffin molds on the trivet and close the lid. Cook the meal on manual mode (high pressure) for 7 minutes. Then make the quick pressure release. The meal tastes the best when it is cooled to the room temperature.
Nutrition: calories 128, fat 10.7, fiber 1.7, carbs 3.8, protein 6.4

Bell Peppers and Chives

Preparation time: 10 minutes
Cooking time: 20 minutes
Servings: 4
Ingredients:
- 1 pound red bell peppers, cut into wedges
- 1 cup veggie stock
- 1 tablespoon chives, chopped
- 1 tablespoon sweet paprika
- 1 tablespoon chives, chopped

Directions:
In your instant pot, mix the bell peppers with the rest of the ingredients except the chives, put the lid on and cook on High for 20 minutes. Release the

pressure naturally for 10 minutes, divide the mix between plates and serve with the chives sprinkled on top.
Nutrition: calories 70, fat 1.8, fiber 1.1, carbs 1.4, protein 0.6

Kale Skillet with Nuts

Preparation time: 10 minutes
Cooking time: 1 minute
Servings: 4
Ingredients:
- 2 cups Italian dark leaf kale
- 1 teaspoon peanuts, chopped
- 1 teaspoon hazelnuts, chopped
- 1 teaspoon apple cider vinegar
- 1 tablespoon cream cheese
- ½ teaspoon salt
- 1 cup water, for cooking

Directions:
Pour water in the instant pot. Chop the kale roughly and put it in the steamer rack. Arrange the steamer rack in the instant pot and close the lid. Cook the kale on manual mode (steam mode) for 1 minute. Then make the quick pressure release. Transfer the kale in the bowl. Add apple cider vinegar, cream cheese, and salt. Then add hazelnuts and peanuts and mix up the meal well.
Nutrition: calories 35, fat 1.8, fiber 1.4, carbs 3.7, protein 2.3

Cayenne Peppers and Sauce

Preparation time: 5 minutes
Cooking time: 20 minutes
Servings: 4
Ingredients:
- 1 pound mixed bell peppers, cut into wedges
- ½ cup chicken stock
- ½ cup heavy cream
- A pinch of cayenne pepper
- A pinch of salt and black pepper
- 1 tablespoon cilantro, chopped

Directions:
In your instant pot, combine the bell peppers with the stock and the rest of the ingredients, put the lid on and cook on High for 15 minutes. Release the pressure fast for 5 minutes, divide the mix between plates and serve.
Nutrition: calories 63, fat 5.7, fiber 0.4, carbs 2.8, protein 0.7

Shredded Spaghetti Squash with Bacon

Preparation time: 20 minutes
Cooking time: 8 minutes
Servings: 8
Ingredients:
- 4 oz bacon, chopped
- 1-pound spaghetti squash
- 1 tablespoon sesame oil
- 1 teaspoon salt
- 1 cup water, for cooking

Directions:
Pour water and place trivet in the instant pot. Wash and clean the spaghetti squash. Then cut it into halves and put in the trivet. Close the lid and cook it on manual mode (steam mode) for 8 minutes. Then allow the natural pressure release for 15 minutes. Then transfer the spaghetti squash in the plate. Shred it with the help of the fork. After this, transfer the shredded squash meat in the salad bowl. Clean the instant pot and remove the trivet. Add chopped bacon and cook it on sauté mode for 7 minutes. Stir it from time to time. Add the cooked bacon in the shredded spaghetti squash. Then add salt and sesame oil. Stir it.
Nutrition: calories 109, fat 7.9, fiber 0, carbs 4.1, protein 5.6

Bell Peppers and Brussels Sprouts

Preparation time: 5 minutes
Cooking time: 15 minutes
Servings: 4
Ingredients:
- 1 pound mixed bell peppers, cut into wedges
- ½ pound Brussels sprouts, halved
- 1 cup veggie stock
- 1 tablespoon ghee, melted
- 1 teaspoon smoked paprika
- 1 teaspoon cumin, ground
- 1 tablespoon chives, chopped

Directions:
Set the instant pot on Sauté mode, add the ghee, heat it up, add the peppers and the sprouts and cook for 3 minutes. Put the lid on, cook on High for 12 minutes, release the pressure fast for 5 minutes, divide the mix between plates and serve.
Nutrition: calories 68, fat 4.2, fiber 2.3, carbs 3.4, protein 2.4

Green Peas Salad

Preparation time: 10 minutes
Cooking time: 3 minutes
Servings: 2
Ingredients:
- ½ cup green peas, frozen
- ½ teaspoon fresh cilantro, chopped
- ½ teaspoon avocado oil
- ¼ teaspoon ground paprika
- ¾ teaspoon salt
- ½ cup white cabbage, shredded
- 1 cup water, for cooking

Directions:
Pour water and insert the steamer rack in the instant pot. Place the green peas in the steamer rack and close the lid. Cook it on the steam mode (high pressure) for 3 minutes. Allow the natural pressure release for 5 minutes. Transfer the cooked green peas in the bowl. Add cilantro, avocado oil, ground paprika, salt, and white cabbage. Stir the salad well.
Nutrition: calories 36, fat 0.4, fiber 2.4, carbs 6.5, protein 2.2

Bell Peppers and Mustard Greens

Preparation time: 5 minutes
Cooking time: 20 minutes
Servings: 4
Ingredients:
- 1 pound mixed bell peppers, cut into wedges
- ½ pound mustard greens

- A pinch of salt and black pepper
- 1 cup chicken stock
- 1 tablespoon sweet paprika
- 1 teaspoon chives, chopped

Directions:
In your instant pot, combine the bell peppers with the rest of the ingredients, put the lid on and cook on High for 20 minutes. Release the pressure naturally for 5 minutes, divide the mix between plates and serve.
Nutrition: calories 32, fat 3.4, fiber 2.3, carbs 2.9, protein 2.3

Cauliflower Risotto

Preparation time: 10 minutes
Cooking time: 16 minutes
Servings: 4
Ingredients:
- 2 cups cauliflower, shredded
- 1 teaspoon coconut oil
- ¼ cup white onion, diced
- 6 oz white mushrooms, chopped
- ¼ teaspoon garlic powder
- ½ cup of organic almond milk
- 1/3 cup chicken broth
- 1 teaspoon coconut flour
- ½ teaspoon salt

Directions:
Put the coconut oil in the instant pot. Heat up it on sauté mode for 2 minutes. Then add onion, mushrooms, garlic powder, and salt. Stir it and sauté for 10 minutes. After this, add chicken broth and almond milk. Add cauliflower and mix up the risotto. Close the lid and cook it on manual mode (high pressure) for 4 minutes. Then make the quick pressure release. Stir the risotto well.
Nutrition: calories 46, fat 1.9, fiber 2.2, carbs 5.4, protein 3.1

Parmesan Radish

Preparation time: 10 minutes
Cooking time: 10 minutes
Servings: 4
Ingredients:
- 1 pound radishes, sliced
- Juice of 1 lemon
- 1 teaspoon chili powder
- A pinch of salt and black pepper
- 1 cup chicken stock
- 3 tablespoons parmesan, grated

Directions:
In your instant pot, combine the radishes with the lemon juice and the rest of the ingredients, put the lid on and cook on High for 10 minutes. Release the pressure naturally for 10 minutes, divide mix between plates and serve.
Nutrition: calories 38, fat 1.5, fiber 0.2, carbs 0.4, protein 2.5

Collard Greens with Cherry Tomatoes

Preparation time: 15 minutes
Cooking time: 5 minutes
Servings: 4
Ingredients:
- 3 cups collard greens, chopped
- ½ cup cherry tomatoes, halved
- ½ red onion, diced
- 1 teaspoon avocado oil
- ½ teaspoon chili flakes
- ¼ oz Parmesan, grated
- 1 cup water, for cooking

Directions:
Pour water and insert the steamer rack in the instant pot. Place the chopped collard greens in the rack and close the lid. Cook the greens on manual (high pressure) for 5 minutes. When the cooking time is finished, allow the natural pressure release for 10 minutes. Transfer the cooked collard greens in the salad bowl. Add cherry tomatoes and diced red onion. Shake the ingredients gently. Then add chili flakes and avocado oil, and Parmesan. With the help of two spoons or spatulas, mix up the meal.
Nutrition: calories 26, fat 0.8, fiber 1.7, carbs 4.2, protein 1.7

Cheddar Tomatoes

Preparation time: 10 minutes
Cooking time: 20 minutes
Servings: 4
Ingredients:
- 1 and ½ pounds tomatoes, cut into wedges
- 1 cup cheddar cheese, grated
- 1 cup chicken stock
- A pinch of salt and black pepper
- 1 tablespoon dill, chopped
- 1 teaspoon sweet paprika
- 1 tablespoon chives, chopped

Directions:
In your instant pot, mix tomatoes with the rest of the ingredients except the cheese and toss. Sprinkle the cheese on top, put the lid on and cook on High for 20 minutes. Release the pressure naturally for 10 minutes, divide the mix between plates and serve.
Nutrition: calories 161, fat 10.1, fiber 3.1, carbs 4.5, protein 9.6

Cauliflower Gratin

Preparation time: 10 minutes
Cooking time: 25 minutes
Servings: 6
Ingredients:
- 2 cups cauliflower, chopped
- ½ cup mozzarella, shredded
- ½ cup coconut cream
- ½ cup of water
- 1 teaspoon butter
- ½ teaspoon salt
- 1 teaspoon dried oregano
- ½ teaspoon rosemary

Directions:
Grease the instant pot bowl with butter and put the chopped cauliflower inside. Flatten it in one layer if needed. Then in the mixing bowl mix up coconut cream with shredded mozzarella, salt, oregano, and dried rosemary. Pour the liquid over the cauliflower and close the lid. Cook the cauliflower gratin on meat/stew mode for 25 minutes.
Nutrition: calories 68, fat 5.9, fiber 1.4, carbs 3.2, protein 1.8

Creamy Tomatoes

Preparation time: 10 minutes
Cooking time: 10 minutes
Servings: 4
Ingredients:
- 2 cups cherry tomatoes, halved
- 2 spring onions, chopped
- 1 cup coconut cream
- A pinch of salt and black pepper
- 2 tablespoons garlic, minced
- 1 tablespoon dill, chopped

Directions:
In your instant pot, mix the tomatoes with the spring onions and the rest of the ingredients, put the lid on and cook on High for 10 minutes. Release the pressure naturally for 10 minutes, divide the mix between plates and serve.
Nutrition: calories 165, fat 14.5, fiber 2.8, carbs 6.4, protein 2.7

Scalloped Cabbage

Preparation time: 15 minutes
Cooking time: 18 minutes
Servings: 6
Ingredients:
- 2 cups white cabbage, shredded
- 2 tablespoons almond meal
- ½ teaspoon salt
- 1 tablespoon ghee
- 1 teaspoon coconut flakes
- ½ cup Monterey Jack cheese, shredded
- ½ cup of organic almond milk

Directions:
Mix up white cabbage and salt. Stir the cabbage well and leave it for 5-10 minutes. Meanwhile, put the ghee in the instant pot. Melt it on sauté mode. Then add the almond meal and coconut flakes. Cook the ingredients on sauté mode for 2 minutes. Stir well and add almond milk. Then add cabbage and mix up. After this, top the cabbage with shredded cheese and close the lid. Cook the meal on manual (high pressure) for 15 minutes. Allow the natural pressure release for 10 minutes.
Nutrition: calories 72, fat 6.3, fiber 0.9, carbs 2, protein 3.1

Garlic Celery and Kale

Preparation time: 10 minutes
Cooking time: 14 minutes
Servings: 4
Ingredients:
- 2 celery stalks, toughly chopped
- 1 pound kale, torn
- 1 tablespoon olive oil
- 4 garlic cloves, minced
- 1 cup chicken stock
- A pinch of salt and black pepper
- 1 tablespoon parsley, chopped

Directions:
Set your instant pot on Sauté mode, add the oil, heat it up, add the garlic and brown for 2 minutes. Add the rest of the ingredients, put the lid on and cook on High for 12 minutes more. Release the pressure naturally for 10 minutes, divide the mix between plates and serve.
Nutrition: calories 95, fat 3.7, fiber 1.9, carbs 2.4, protein 3.8

Hash Brown Casserole

Preparation time: 10 minutes
Cooking time: 20 minutes
Servings: 4
Ingredients:
- ½ cup cauliflower stalk, shredded
- 2 oz turnip, grated
- ½ cup Cheddar cheese, shredded
- ½ teaspoon onion powder
- ¼ teaspoon ground black pepper
- ¼ teaspoon white pepper
- ¼ teaspoon salt
- 1 teaspoon coconut oil
- 1 cup of coconut milk

Directions:
Place the coconut oil in the instant pot. Heat it up on sauté mode until the oil is melted. Add shredded cauliflower and turnip. Sprinkle the vegetables with onion powder, ground black pepper, and white pepper. Add salt and stir the vegetables. Cook them on sauté mode for 5 minutes. After this, add coconut milk and shredded Cheddar cheese. Close the lid and cook the casserole on meat/stew mode for 15 minutes.
Nutrition: calories 213, fat 20.1, fiber 1.9, carbs 5.4, protein 5.3

Creamy Eggplant Mix

Preparation time: 10 minutes
Cooking time: 15 minutes
Servings: 4
Ingredients:
- 2 tablespoons rosemary, chopped
- 2 eggplants, sliced
- A pinch of salt and black pepper
- 1 cup heavy cream
- 1 teaspoon turmeric powder
- 1 tablespoon dill, chopped

Directions:
In your instant pot, mix the eggplants with the rest of the ingredients, put the lid on and cook on High for 15 minutes. Release the pressure naturally for 10 minutes, divide the mix between plates and serve.
Nutrition: calories 181, fat 11.8, fiber 4.2, carbs 5.9, protein 3.6

Stuffed Mushrooms

Preparation time: 15 minutes
Cooking time: 4 minutes
Servings: 4
Ingredients:
- 1 cup cremini mushrooms, caps
- ¼ cup Mozzarella, shredded
- ¼ teaspoon ground nutmeg
- ¼ teaspoon salt
- 1 tablespoon chives, chopped
- 1 cup water, for cooking

Directions:
Trim the mushroom caps if needed. In the mixing bowl mix up shredded Mozzarella, ground nutmeg, salt, and chives. Fill the mushrooms with the cheese mixture. Pour water and insert the trivet in the instant pot. Then line the trivet with foil. Place the stuffed mushrooms on the trivet. Close and seal the lid. Cook the vegetables on manual mode (high

pressure) for 4 minutes. Make the quick pressure release.
Nutrition: calories 11, fat 0.4, fiber 0.2, carbs 0.9, protein 1

Spicy Eggplant and Kale Mix
Preparation time: 10 minutes
Cooking time: 15 minutes
Servings: 4
Ingredients:
- 4 small eggplants, sliced
- ¼ cup chicken stock
- 1 tablespoon chili powder
- ½ pound kale, torn
- A pinch of salt and black pepper

Directions:
In your instant pot, mix the eggplants with the stock and the rest of the ingredients, put the lid on and cook on High for 15 minutes. Release the pressure naturally for 10 minutes, divide the mix between plates and serve.
Nutrition: calories 65, fat 1.5, fiber 0.3, carbs 0.9, protein 2.8

Green Beans Salad
Preparation time: 15 minutes
Cooking time: 4 minutes
Servings: 2
Ingredients:
- 1 cup green beans, chopped
- 3 oz goat cheese, crumbled
- 1 oz Feta cheese, crumbled
- ¼ teaspoon ground black pepper
- 1 shallot, peeled, sliced
- 1 teaspoon ghee
- ½ teaspoon chili flakes
- 1 cup water, for cooking

Directions:
Pour water and insert the steamer rack in the instant pot. Put the green beans in the steamer rack and close the lid. Cook the vegetables on manual (high pressure) for 4 minutes. Then allow the natural pressure release for 10 minutes and transfer the green beans in the bowl. Clean the instant pot and remove the steamer rack. Toss ghee in the instant pot and melt it on sauté mode. Add shallot and cook it until it is golden brown. Add the cooked shallot in the green beans. Then add crumbled Feta and goat cheese. After this, sprinkle the ingredients with chili flakes and ground black pepper. Mix up the salad well with the help of the spatula.
Nutrition: calories 22, fat 0.8, fiber 0.3, carbs 1.8, protein 2

Tomato and Dill Sauté
Preparation time: 10 minutes
Cooking time: 15 minutes
Servings: 4
Ingredients:
- 1 pound tomatoes, cubed
- 1 tablespoon dill, chopped
- 1 teaspoon garlic, minced
- A pinch of salt and black pepper
- ½ cup chicken stock
- 1 tablespoon parsley, chopped

Directions:
In your instant pot, mix the tomatoes with the dill and the rest of the ingredients, put the lid on and cook on High for 15 minutes. Release the pressure naturally for 10 minutes, divide the mix between plates and serve.
Nutrition: calories 25, fat 1.9, fiber 0.5, carbs 1.4, protein 1.4

Tuscan Mushrooms Sauce
Preparation time: 20 minutes
Cooking time: 10 minutes
Servings: 3
Ingredients:
- 1 teaspoon almond butter
- ½ cup fresh spinach, chopped
- ½ cup white mushrooms, sliced
- 2 tablespoons flax meal
- 1 oz Parmesan, grated
- 1 cup coconut cream
- 1 teaspoon Tuscan seasonings
- ½ cup cherry tomatoes, chopped

Directions:
Heat up the almond butter in the instant pot on sauté mode. Put mushrooms in the hot almond butter and cook them for 3 minutes. After this, stir them and add spinach. Stir well. Sprinkle the vegetables with Tuscan seasonings and flax meal. After this, add coconut cream and cherry tomatoes. Close the lid and cook the sauce on manual (high pressure) for 5 minutes. Allow the natural pressure release for 10 minutes. Open the lid and add Parmesan. With the help of the spatula, mix up the meal until cheese is melted.
Nutrition: calories 279, fat 25.9, fiber 4.2, carbs 9.2, protein 8.1

Mustard Greens and Cabbage Sauté
Preparation time: 10 minutes
Cooking time: 15 minutes
Servings: 4
Ingredients:
- 2 cups mustard greens
- 1 red cabbage, shredded
- 1 tablespoon tomato passata
- A pinch of salt and black pepper
- ¼ cup chicken stock
- 1 tablespoon dill, chopped

Directions:
In your instant pot, mix the mustard greens with the cabbage and the rest of the ingredients, put the lid on and cook on High for 15 minutes. Release the pressure naturally for 10 minutes, divide the mix between plates and serve.
Nutrition: calories 36, fat 1.4, fiber 0.2, carbs 0.4, protein 2

Thyme Cauliflower Head
Preparation time: 15 minutes
Cooking time: 3 minutes
Servings: 3
Ingredients:
- 1-pound cauliflower head, trimmed
- 1 teaspoon thyme
- 2 tablespoons avocado oil
- ¼ teaspoon minced garlic
- 1 cup water, for cooking

Directions:
Pour water in the instant pot and insert the steamer rack. Place the cauliflower head in the steamer rack and close the lid. Cook it on manual mode (high pressure) for 3 minutes. Then allow the natural pressure release for 5 minutes and transfer the cauliflower in the serving plate. In the shallow bowl whisk together avocado oil, minced garlic, and thyme. Brush the cooked cauliflower head with the thyme-oil mixture.
Nutrition: calories 51, fat 1.4, fiber 4.3, carbs 8.8, protein 3.2

Dill Zucchini, Tomatoes and Eggplants

Preparation time: 10 minutes
Cooking time: 15 minutes
Servings: 4
Ingredients:
- 2 cups zucchinis, sliced
- 1 cup tomatoes, cubed
- 1 cup eggplants, sliced
- A pinch of salt and black pepper
- 1 cup tomato passata
- 2 tablespoon dill, chopped

Directions:
In your instant pot, mix the zucchinis with the tomatoes and the rest of the ingredients, put the lid on and cook on High for 15 minutes. Release the pressure naturally for 10 minutes, divide the mix between plates and serve.
Nutrition: calories 41, fat 1.2, fiber 0.2, carbs 0.6, protein 2.4

Stuffed Spaghetti Squash

Preparation time: 20 minutes
Cooking time: 9 minutes
Servings: 6
Ingredients:
- 1-pound spaghetti squash, cleaned, halved
- 5 oz seitan, chopped
- ¼ cup Cheddar cheese, shredded
- 2 eggs, beaten
- 1 tablespoon cream cheese
- ¼ cup heavy cream
- 1 teaspoon butter
- 1 bay leaf
- ½ teaspoon chili flakes
- ¼ teaspoon cayenne pepper
- ½ teaspoon salt
- 1 cup water, for cooking

Directions:
Scoop the squash meat from the spaghetti squash. Then grate the squash meat. In the mixing bowl mix up chopped seitan, grated spaghetti squash meat, shredded cheese, eggs, cream cheese, butter, heavy cream, chili flakes, cayenne pepper, and salt. Fill the spaghetti squash halves with the seitan filling. Wrap the spaghetti squash halves in foil. Then pour water in the instant pot. Add bay leaf. Then insert the trivet in the instant pot. Place the wrapped spaghetti squash on the trivet and close the lid. Cook the meal on manual (high pressure) for 9 minutes. When the cooking time is finished, make the quick pressure release and open the lid. Remove the foil from the spaghetti squash halves.
Nutrition: calories 187, fat 7.6, fiber 1.1, carbs 5.8, protein 21.5

Balsamic Okra

Preparation time: 10 minutes
Cooking time: 15 minutes
Servings: 4
Ingredients:
- 2 cups okra
- 2 spring onions, chopped
- ½ cup chicken stock
- A pinch of salt and black pepper
- 1 tablespoon balsamic vinegar
- 1 tablespoon dill, chopped

Directions:
In your instant pot, mix the okra with the spring onions and the rest of the ingredients, put the lid on and cook on High for 15 minutes. Release the pressure naturally for 10 minutes, divide the mix between plates and serve.
Nutrition: calories 26, fat 1.2, fiber 0.2, carbs 0.7, protein 1.4

Shallot Mushrooms

Preparation time: 10 minutes
Cooking time: 25 minutes
Servings: 3
Ingredients:
- 1 cup cremini mushrooms, chopped
- 3 oz white mushrooms, chopped
- ½ cup shallot, sliced
- 1 tablespoon ghee
- 1 teaspoon Italian seasonings
- 1 teaspoon salt
- 1 teaspoon cream cheese

Directions:
Place the ghee in the instant pot and melt it on sauté mode. Add white mushrooms and cremini mushrooms. Cook the vegetables on sauté mode for 10 minutes. After this, add sliced shallot, cream cheese, salt, and Italian seasonings. Stir the ingredients well and close the lid. Sauté the meal for 15 minutes on sauté mode.
Nutrition: calories 78, fat 5.2, fiber 0.4, carbs 6.6, protein 2.3

Creamy Okra and Collard Greens

Preparation time: 10 minutes
Cooking time: 20 minutes
Servings: 4
Ingredients:
- 1 pound collard greens, trimmed
- 1 cup okra
- 1 cup heavy cream
- ½ cup chicken stock
- 1 tablespoon sweet paprika
- A pinch of salt and black pepper
- 1 tablespoon cilantro, chopped

Directions:
In your instant pot, combine the collard greens with the okra and the rest of the ingredients, put the lid on and cook on High for 20 minutes. Release the pressure naturally for 10 minutes, divide the mix between plates and serve.
Nutrition: calories 151, fat 12.2, fiber 4.3, carbs 6.8, protein 4

Baked Kabocha Squash
Preparation time: 10 minutes
Cooking time: 8 minutes
Servings: 3
Ingredients:
- 2 cups Kabocha squash, peeled, cubed
- ½ teaspoon Erythritol
- ½ teaspoon ground ginger
- ¼ teaspoon ground cinnamon
- 1 tablespoon butter, softened
- 1 cup heavy cream

Directions:
Sprinkle Kabocha squash with Erythritol, ground ginger, and ground cinnamon. Mix up the spices and squash and transfer in the instant pot. Add butter and heavy cream. Close and seal the lid and cook the meal on manual (high pressure) for 8 minutes. Then make the quick pressure release. Carefully transfer the cooked squash in the serving bowls.
Nutrition: calories 200, fat 18.7, fiber 1, carbs 7.7, protein 1.8

Balsamic Savoy Cabbage
Preparation time: 10 minutes
Cooking time: 20 minutes
Servings: 4
Ingredients:
- 1 Savoy cabbage, shredded
- ½ cup chicken stock
- 1 tablespoon dill, chopped
- A pinch of salt and black pepper
- 1 tablespoon balsamic vinegar

Directions:
In your instant pot, mix the Savoy cabbage with the chicken stock and the rest of the ingredients, put the lid on and cook on High for 20 minutes. Release the pressure naturally for 10 minutes, divide the mix between plates and serve.
Nutrition: calories 61, fat 1.3, fiber 0.8, carbs 1, protein 3.2

Sautéed Kohlrabi
Preparation time: 10 minutes
Cooking time: 10 minutes
Servings: 3
Ingredients:
- 1 Serrano pepper, chopped
- 1 teaspoon ground ginger
- 1 tablespoon coconut oil
- 10 oz kohlrabi, chopped
- ½ cup chicken broth
- ½ teaspoon salt

Directions:
Preheat the instant pot on sauté mode for 3 minutes. Then add coconut oil and heat it up for 2 minutes. Add ground ginger and chopped Serrano. Cook the ingredients for 2 minutes. Then add kohlrabi and stir well. Add chicken broth and salt. Close and seal the lid. Cook the meal on manual (high pressure) for 3 minutes. Then allow the natural pressure release for 5 minutes.
Nutrition: calories 74, fat 4.9, fiber 3.6, carbs 6.6, protein 2.5

Cilantro Red Cabbage and Artichokes
Preparation time: 10 minutes
Cooking time: 20 minutes
Servings: 4
Ingredients:
- ½ cup canned artichoke hearts, drained and chopped
- 3 garlic cloves, minced
- 2 small red cabbage heads, shredded
- A pinch of salt and black pepper
- 1 cup chicken stock
- ½ cup tomato passata
- 1 tablespoon cilantro, chopped

Directions:
In your instant pot, combine the artichokes with the garlic and the rest of the ingredients except the cilantro, put the lid on and cook on High for 20 minutes. Release the pressure naturally for 10 minutes, divide the mix between plates and serve with the cilantro sprinkled on top.
Nutrition: calories 141, fat 1.5, fiber 0.2, carbs 1.2, protein 7.3

Butter Edamame Beans
Preparation time: 5 minutes
Cooking time: 1 minute
Servings: 4
Ingredients:
- 1 cup mung beans
- 2 tablespoon butter
- ¼ teaspoon salt
- ¼ cup fresh parsley, chopped
- ½ teaspoon cayenne pepper
- 1 cup beef broth

Directions:
Pour beef broth in the instant pot. Add mung beans, butter, salt, parsley, and cayenne pepper. Close and seal the lid. Set time on 1 minute and cook the Edamame beans on manual (high pressure). Then make the quick pressure release.
Nutrition: calories 110, fat 8.2, fiber 2.2, carbs 4.4, protein 5.7

Dill Fennel and Brussels Sprouts
Preparation time: 10 minutes
Cooking time: 15 minutes
Servings: 4
Ingredients:
- 2 fennel bulbs, cut into wedges
- 1 pound Brussels sprouts, halved
- A pinch of salt and black pepper
- 1 cup chicken stock
- 1 tablespoon dill, chopped
- ¼ cup tomato passata

Directions:
In your instant pot, mix the fennel with the sprouts and the rest of the ingredients, put the lid on and cook on High for 15 minutes. Release the pressure naturally for 10 minutes, divide the mix between plates and serve.
Nutrition: calories 96, fat 1.4, fiber 0.8, carbs 1, protein 5.6

Marinated Tomatillos Paste
Preparation time: 8 minutes
Cooking time: 10 minutes
Servings: 2

Ingredients:
- 1 cup tomatillos
- ½ teaspoon minced garlic
- 1 teaspoon fresh dill, chopped
- ¼ cup of water
- 1 tablespoon avocado oil
- ¼ teaspoon salt
- 1 teaspoon chili powder

Directions:
Finely chop the tomatillos. Heat up the instant pot. When it shows "Hot", add avocado oil and tomatillos. Cook them on sauté mode for 5 minutes. Then add salt, chili powder, and minced garlic. Add water and dill. Close the lid. Cook the ingredients on steam mode for 3 minutes. Then make the quick pressure release. With the help of the immersion blender grind the mixture into a paste.

Nutrition: calories 37, fat 1.8, fiber 2.1, carbs 5.5, protein 1

Cinnamon Green Beans Mix

Preparation time: 10 minutes
Cooking time: 15 minutes
Servings: 4
Ingredients:
- 1 pound green beans, trimmed
- A pinch of salt and black pepper
- ½ cup chicken stock
- 1 teaspoon chili powder
- 1 tablespoon rosemary, chopped
- ½ teaspoon cinnamon powder

Directions:
In your instant pot, combine the green beans with the stock and the rest of the ingredients, put the lid on and cook on High for 15 minutes. Release the pressure naturally for 10 minutes, divide the mix between plates and serve.

Nutrition: calories 41, fat 1.4, fiber 0.1, carbs 0.5, protein 2.3

Tender Rutabaga

Preparation time: 15 minutes
Cooking time: 9 minute
Servings: 4
Ingredients:
- 1-pound rutabaga, chopped
- ½ cup heavy cream
- 2 tablespoons cream cheese
- ½ teaspoon onion powder
- 1 teaspoon ground black pepper
- 1 cup water, for cooking

Directions:
Pour water in the instant pot. Insert the steamer rack. Put rutabaga in the steamer rack. Close the lid. Cook the rutabaga on manual (high pressure) for 9 minutes. Allow the natural pressure release for 5 minutes. Transfer the cooked rutabaga in the big bowl. Bring the heavy cream to boil and add in the rutabaga. Then add cream cheese, onion powder, and ground black pepper. Stir the meal gently with the help of the spoon.

Nutrition: calories 112, fat 7.5, fiber 3, carbs 10.4, protein 2.1

Okra and Olives Mix

Preparation time: 10 minutes
Cooking time: 15 minutes
Servings: 4
Ingredients:
- 2 cups okra
- 1 cup kalamata olives, pitted and sliced
- A pinch of salt and black pepper
- Juice of ½ lime
- ½ cup veggie stock
- 2 tablespoons tomato passata
- 2 tablespoons parsley, chopped

Directions:
In your instant pot, mix the okra with the olives and the rest of the ingredients, put the lid on and cook on High for 15 minutes. Release the pressure naturally for 10 minutes, divide the mix between plates and serve.

Nutrition: calories 64, fat 4, fiber 2.8, carbs 3, protein 1.4

Zucchini Goulash

Preparation time: 5 minutes
Cooking time: 8 minutes
Servings: 4
Ingredients:
- 1 eggplant, chopped
- 2 small zucchini, chopped
- 1 white onion, chopped
- 1 turnip, chopped
- 1 cup chicken broth
- 1 teaspoon tomato paste
- 1 teaspoon fresh thyme
- 1 teaspoon salt
- 1 teaspoon sesame oil
- 1 teaspoon Italian seasonings

Directions:
Put all ingredients in the instant pot and close the lid. Set chili/meat mode (high pressure) and cook the goulash for 8 minutes. Then make the quick pressure release. It is recommended to serve the meal when it reaches room temperature.

Nutrition: calories 73, fat 1.9, fiber 6.2, carbs 13.8, protein 2.5

Olives, Capers and Kale

Preparation time: 10 minutes
Cooking time: 20 minutes
Servings: 4
Ingredients:
- 1 cup black olives, pitted and sliced
- 2 spring onions, chopped
- 1 tablespoon capers, drained
- ½ cup chicken stock
- 1 pound kale, torn
- A pinch of salt and black pepper
- 1 tablespoon parsley, chopped

Directions:
In your instant pot, combine kale with the olives, capers and the rest of the ingredients, put the lid on and cook on High for 20 minutes. Release the pressure naturally for 10 minutes, divide the mix between plates and serve.

Nutrition: calories 99, fat 3.7, fiber 2.3, carbs 3, protein 4

Cheddar Mushrooms

Preparation time: 10 minutes

Cooking time: 15 minutes
Servings: 2
Ingredients:
- 1 cup cremini mushrooms, roughly chopped
- 1 tablespoon cream cheese
- ¼ cup of coconut milk
- 1 teaspoon ground cardamom
- ¼ teaspoon cumin seeds
- ½ teaspoon salt
- 1/3 cup Cheddar cheese, shredded

Directions:
In the mixing bowl mix up coconut milk, cream cheese, ground cardamom, cumin seeds, and salt. Heat up the instant pot. When it shows "HOT", add mushrooms and coconut milk mixture. Close the lid and cook the vegetables on sauté mode for 10 minutes. Then open the lid and stir them with the help of the spatula. Add cheese and close the lid. Cook the mushrooms for 5 minutes more.
Nutrition: calories 176, fat 15.3, fiber 1.2, carbs 4.3, protein 6.8

Eggplants and Cabbage Mix

Preparation time: 5 minutes
Cooking time: 15 minutes
Servings: 4
Ingredients:
- 1 big eggplant, peeled and sliced
- 2 garlic cloves, minced
- A pinch of salt and black pepper
- 1 green cabbage, shredded
- 1 cup chicken stock
- 1 tablespoon dill, chopped
- 1 teaspoon cumin, ground

Directions:
In your instant pot, mix the eggplant with the garlic, cabbage and the rest of the ingredients, put the lid on and cook on High for 15 minutes. Release the pressure fast for 5 minutes, divide the mix between plates and serve.
Nutrition: calories 94, fat 1.5, fiber 0.4, carbs 1, protein 4.5

Garlic Eggplant Rounds

Preparation time: 10 minutes
Cooking time: 10 minutes
Servings: 4
Ingredients:
- 2 eggplants
- 2 tablespoons ghee
- 1 teaspoon minced garlic
- 1 teaspoon salt
- ½ teaspoon cayenne pepper

Directions:
Trim the ends of the eggplants and slice them into the medium rounds. Then sprinkle the vegetables with salt and cayenne pepper. Shake well and leave them for 10 minutes to give the eggplants the opportunity to give juice. Meanwhile, preheat the instant pot. When it shows "HOT", place ghee inside. Melt it. Then put the eggplant rounds in the hot ghee in one layer. Cook the vegetables for 2 minutes from each side. Top the cooked eggplants with minced garlic.
Nutrition: calories 126, fat 6.9, fiber 9.7, carbs 16.5, protein 2.8

Eggplants, Cucumber and Olives

Preparation time: 10 minutes
Cooking time: 12 minutes
Servings: 4
Ingredients:
- 2 and ½ cups eggplant, sliced
- 1 tablespoon avocado oil
- 2 cucumbers, cubed
- 1 shallot, minced
- 1 cup black olives, pitted and sliced
- A pinch of salt and black pepper
- ½ cup chicken stock

Directions:
Set the instant pot on Sauté mode, add the oil, heat it up, add the shallot and cook for 2 minutes. Add the eggplant and the rest of the ingredients, put the lid on and cook on High for 10 minutes. Release the pressure naturally for 10 minutes, divide the mix between plates and serve.
Nutrition: calories 83, fat 4.4, fiber 2.3, carbs 3.4, protein 2

Vegetable Soup

Preparation time: 10 minutes
Cooking time: 3 minutes
Servings: 6
Ingredients:
- 2 tablespoons cream cheese
- ½ cup heavy cream
- 4 cups of water
- 1 cup fresh spinach, chopped
- 1 cup celery stalk, chopped
- 1 zucchini, chopped
- ½ cup green peas
- 1 teaspoon salt
- 1 teaspoon ground black pepper
- ¼ teaspoon chili flakes

Directions:
Put all ingredients in the instant pot bowl. Close and seal the lid. Cook the soup on manual (high pressure) for 3 minutes. When the cooking time is finished, make the quick pressure release and leave the soup with the closed lid for 10 minutes.
Nutrition: calories 66, fat 5, fiber 1.5, carbs 4.1, protein 1.8

Lemon Peppers and Bok Choy

Preparation time: 10 minutes
Cooking time: 20 minutes
Servings: 4
Ingredients:
- 1 pound mixed bell peppers, cut into wedges
- 1 cup bok choy, chopped
- 2 tablespoons sweet paprika
- A pinch of salt and black pepper
- ½ cup chicken stock
- ¼ cup lemon juice
- 1 tablespoon cilantro, chopped

Directions:
In your instant pot, mix the bell peppers with the bok choy and the rest of the ingredients except the cilantro, put the lid on and cook on High for 20 minutes. Release the pressure naturally for 10

minutes, divide the mix between plates, sprinkle the cilantro on top and serve.
Nutrition: calories 34, fat 1, fiber 0.2, carbs 0.5, protein 1.3

Cream of Celery

Preparation time: 10 minutes
Cooking time: 15 minutes
Servings: 4
Ingredients:
- 1 white onion, diced
- 2 green bell peppers, chopped
- 1 cup celery stalk, chopped
- 1 teaspoon white pepper
- ¼ teaspoon salt
- ¼ cup heavy cream
- 1 cup beef broth
- 1 teaspoon ghee

Directions:
Put ghee in the instant pot and heat it up. Then add bell peppers and onion and cook the vegetables on sauté mode for 5 minutes. Stir them from time to time to avoid burning. Then add salt, white pepper, heavy cream, and chicken broth. Add celery stalk and close the lid. Cook the meal on manual mode (high pressure) for 10 minutes. When the cooking time is finished, make the quick pressure release.
Nutrition: calories 80, fat 4.4, fiber 1.9, carbs 8.6, protein 2.5

Tomato Bok Choy Mix

Preparation time: 10 minutes
Cooking time: 15 minutes
Servings: 4
Ingredients:
- 1 pound bok choy, torn
- 1 cup cherry tomatoes, halved
- 2 tablespoons lime juice
- ½ cup chicken stock
- 1 tablespoon ginger, grated
- 1 tablespoon chives, chopped
- 1 tablespoon oregano, chopped
- 1 tablespoon olive oil

Directions:
Set the instant pot on Sauté mode, add the oil, heat it up, add the ginger and sauté for 2 minutes. Add the rest of the ingredients, put the lid on and cook on High for 12 minutes. Release the pressure naturally for 10 minutes, divide the mix between plates and serve.
Nutrition: calories 62, fat 4.1, fiber 2.3, carbs 3, protein 2.5

Steamed Rutabaga Mash

Preparation time: 10 minutes
Cooking time: 5 minutes
Servings: 3
Ingredients:
- 1 teaspoon butter, softened
- ½ teaspoon salt
- 1 teaspoon ground turmeric
- ¼ teaspoon curry powder
- ¼ cup heavy cream, hot
- 2 cups rutabaga, chopped
- 1 cup water, for cooking

Directions:
Pour water and inset the steamer rack in the instant pot. Place the rutabaga in the steamer rack and close the lid. Cook it on manual mode (high pressure) for 5 minutes. Make the quick pressure release. With the help of the potato masher, mash cooked rutabaga. Add salt, butter, ground turmeric, curry powder, and heavy cream. Stir the mashed rutabaga until it is homogenous and will turn color into yellow.
Nutrition: calories 82, fat 5.3, fiber 2.5, carbs 8.4, protein 1.4

Garlic Cabbage and Watercress

Preparation time: 10 minutes
Cooking time: 16 minutes
Servings: 4
Ingredients:
- 1 pound red cabbage, shredded
- 2 garlic cloves, chopped
- 1 tablespoon ghee, melted
- 1 cup chicken stock
- 1 bunch watercress, trimmed
- 1 tablespoon cilantro, chopped

Directions:
Set your instant pot on Sauté mode, add the ghee, heat it up, add the garlic, stir and cook for 2 minutes. Add the cabbage and the rest of the ingredients, put the lid on and cook on High for 14 minutes. Release the pressure naturally for 10 minutes, divide the mix between plates and serve.
Nutrition: calories 63, fat 3.5, fiber 2, carbs 3.1, protein 2

Fragrant Artichoke Hearts

Preparation time: 10 minutes
Cooking time: 20 minutes
Servings: 4
Ingredients:
- 4 artichoke hearts
- ½ teaspoon fennel seeds
- ¼ teaspoon cumin seeds
- 1 tablespoon butter
- ¼ teaspoon salt
- ¼ teaspoon chili powder
- 1 cup water, for cooking

Directions:
Pour water in the instant pot. Place the artichoke hearts in the steamer rack. Arrange the rack in the instant pot and close the lid. Cook the vegetables on steam mode (high pressure) for 15 minutes. Then make the quick pressure release. Open the lid and transfer the artichoke heart in the bowl. Clean the instant pot. Heat it up and when the instant pot display shows "HOT", add butter. Melt it. Add fennel seeds, cumin seeds, salt, and chili powder. Bring the butter to boil and add artichoke hearts. Coat them in the hot butter and cook for 2 minutes on sauté mode.
Nutrition: calories 57, fat 3, fiber 2.2, carbs 7.3, protein 1.1

Mint and Basil Eggplant

Preparation time: 10 minutes
Cooking time: 20 minutes
Servings: 4
Ingredients:
- 1 pound eggplants cubed
- 2 spring onions, chopped

- 1 cup chicken stock
- 1 tablespoon olive oil
- 1 tablespoon mint, chopped
- 1 tablespoon basil, chopped
- 1 teaspoon sweet paprika
- A pinch of salt and black pepper

Directions:
Set your instant pot on Sauté mode, add the oil, heat it up, add the onions and sauté for 2 minutes. Add the eggplants and the rest of the ingredients, put the lid on and cook on High for 18 minutes. Release the pressure naturally for 10 minutes, divide the mix into bowls and serve.
Nutrition: calories 76, fat 3.7, fiber 0.5, carbs 1.2, protein 0.5

Steamed Broccoli Raab (Rabe)
Preparation time: 10 minutes
Cooking time: 7 minutes
Servings: 2
Ingredients:
- 1 ½ cup broccoli rabe, chopped
- 1 teaspoon avocado oil
- 2 oz pancetta, chopped
- ½ teaspoon salt
- 1 teaspoon ground coriander
- ¼ garlic clove, diced
- ¼ cup chicken broth
- 1 cup water, for cooking

Directions:
Pour water and insert the steamer rack in the instant pot. Place the broccoli rabe in the steamer rack and close the lid. Set the timer to "0" and cook the greens on manual (high pressure). When the instant pot beeps, make a quick pressure release and transfer the broccoli rabe in the bowl. Shock the greens with cold water and dry little. Then clean the instant pot and discard the steamer rack. Pour avocado oil inside. Add pancetta. Cook it on sauté mode for 4 minutes. Stir it from time to time. Then sprinkle pancetta with salt, diced garlic, ground coriander, and add broccoli rabe. Stir the mixture well. Add chicken broth and cook it on sauté mode for 1 minute.
Nutrition: calories 177, fat 12.3, fiber 0.1, carbs 3, protein 12.7

Broccoli and Watercress Mix
Preparation time: 10 minutes
Cooking time: 15 minutes
Servings: 4
Ingredients:
- 1 pound broccoli florets
- 1 tablespoon olive oil
- 2 shallots, chopped
- 1 bunch watercress
- 1 tablespoon sweet paprika
- ½ cup tomato passata

Directions:
Set the instant pot on Sauté mode, add the oil, heat it up, add the shallots and cook for 2 minutes Add the rest of the ingredients, put the lid on and cook on High for 13 minutes. Release the pressure naturally for 10 minutes, divide the mix into bowls and serve.
Nutrition: calories 81, fat 4.2, fiber 2.3, carbs 3.5, protein 3.8

Avocado Pie
Preparation time: 20 minutes
Cooking time: 30 minutes
Servings: 6
Ingredients:
- 1 avocado, peeled, pitted
- 2 eggs, beaten
- ¼ cup Cheddar cheese, shredded
- 1 teaspoon cream cheese
- ½ teaspoon cayenne pepper
- ½ teaspoon ground paprika
- 1 teaspoon salt
- ½ cup almond flour
- 2 tablespoons butter, softened
- ½ teaspoon baking powder
- 1 teaspoon lemon juice
- 1 cup water, for cooking

Directions:
Make the pie crust: in the mixing bowl combine almond flour, baking powder, butter, and lemon juice. Knead the soft and non-sticky dough. Then roll it up. Line the instant pot round pan with baking paper and put the pie crust in it. Flatten it with the help of the hands if needed. Chop the avocado roughly and put it in the blender. Add eggs, cream cheese, cayenne pepper, ground paprika, and salt. Blend the mixture until smooth. After this, pour it over the pie crust. Top the filling with Cheddar cheese. Pour water and insert the trivet in the instant pot. Place the pan with pie on the trivet and close the lid. Cook the pie on manual mode (high pressure) for 30 minutes. When the time is over, make the quick pressure release and open the lid. Cool the pie well and then cut it into servings.
Nutrition: calories 159, fat 14.8, fiber 2.6, carbs 4, protein 4.3

Balsamic Bok Choy and Onions
Preparation time: 10 minutes
Cooking time: 20 minutes
Servings: 4
Ingredients:
- 1 pound bok choy, torn
- 2 spring onions, chopped
- 1 cup chicken stock
- 4 garlic cloves, chopped
- 1 tablespoon balsamic vinegar
- A pinch of salt and black pepper
- ¼ teaspoon red pepper flakes
- 1 tablespoon dill, chopped

Directions:
In your instant pot, combine the bok choy with the spring onions and the rest of the ingredients, put the lid on and cook on High for 20 minutes. Release the pressure naturally for 10 minutes, divide the mix between plates and serve.
Nutrition: calories 34, fat 1.2, fiber 0.4, carbs 0.4, protein 2.5

Zucchini Pasta with Blue Cheese
Preparation time: 15 minutes
Cooking time: 5 minutes
Servings: 2
Ingredients:
- 2 zucchini, trimmed
- 3 oz Blue cheese

- ¼ cup heavy cream
- ¼ teaspoon fresh basil, chopped
- ½ teaspoon salt
- 1 teaspoon butter

Directions:
Slice the zucchini into the pasta strips with the help of the potato peeler. Then put the butter in the instant pot and heat it up on sauté mode. When the butter is melted, add heavy cream, fresh basil, and salt. Then add zucchini paste and stir well. Cook the ingredients for 1 minute. Then crumble Blue cheese over the pasta. Cook the meal for 1 minute more.
Nutrition: calories 250, fat 20, fiber 2.2, carbs 8, protein 11.8

Balsamic and Coconut Cabbage

Preparation time: 10 minutes
Cooking time: 14 minutes
Servings: 4
Ingredients:
- ½ cup veggie stock
- 1 pound red cabbage, cut into wedges
- ½ cup coconut aminos
- 2 tablespoons balsamic vinegar
- 1 teaspoon thyme, dried
- A pinch of salt and black pepper
- 2 tablespoons ghee, melted

Directions:
Set the instant pot on Sauté mode, add ghee, heat it up, add the cabbage and sauté for 2 minutes. Add the rest of the ingredients, put the lid on and cook on High for 12 minutes. Release the pressure naturally for 10 minutes, divide the mix between plates and serve.
Nutrition: calories 118, fat 6.8, fiber 2.9, carbs 5.1, protein 1.5

Lemon Artichoke

Preparation time: 10 minutes
Cooking time: 21 minutes
Servings: 4
Ingredients:
- 4 medium artichokes, trimmed
- 4 teaspoons lemon juice
- 2 tablespoons avocado oil
- 1 teaspoon cayenne pepper
- 1 teaspoon minced garlic
- 1 teaspoon salt
- 1 cup water, for cooking

Directions:
In the shallow bowl mix up avocado oil, cayenne pepper, lemon juice, minced garlic, and salt. Whisk the liquid gently. Then brush every artichoke with avocado oil liquid and transfer the vegetables on the trivet. Pour water in the instant pot. Insert the trivet with artichokes in the instant pot and close the lid. Cook the vegetables on manual (high pressure) for 21 minutes. Then make the quick pressure release.
Nutrition: calories 73, fat 1.2, fiber 7.4, carbs 14.4, protein 4.4

Buttery Turmeric Brussels Sprouts

Preparation time: 10 minutes
Cooking time: 10 minutes
Servings: 4
Ingredients:
- 2 pounds Brussels sprouts, halved
- A pinch of salt and black pepper
- 2 tablespoons ghee, melted
- 2 teaspoons turmeric powder
- 1 teaspoon lime zest, grated
- ¼ cup chicken stock
- 2 tablespoons coconut aminos

Directions:
Set the instant pot on Sauté mode, add the ghee, heat it up, add the sprouts and turmeric and coo for 2 minutes. Add the rest of the ingredients, put the lid on and cook on High for 8 minutes. Release the pressure naturally for 10 minutes, divide the mix between plates and serve.
Nutrition: calories 166, fat 7.3, fiber 3.4, carbs 4.4, protein 7.8

Zucchini Boats

Preparation time: 15 minutes
Cooking time: 12 minutes
Servings: 4
Ingredients:
- 2 medium zucchini
- 1 cup Mozzarella cheese, shredded
- 1 teaspoon tomato paste
- 2 teaspoons cream cheese
- ½ cup white mushrooms, chopped
- ½ teaspoon salt
- ½ teaspoon ground black pepper
- ½ teaspoon dried parsley
- ½ teaspoon dried oregano
- 1 teaspoon butter
- 1 cup water, for cooking

Directions:
Heat up butter on sauté mode. Add chopped white mushrooms, salt, ground black pepper, dried parsley, dried oregano, and cream cheese. Cook the ingredients on sauté mode for 5 minutes. After this, add tomato paste and stir the mixture with the help of the spatula until homogenous. Cook it for 3 minutes more. Meanwhile, cut the zucchini into halves and scoop the zucchini meat from them. Then fill the zucchini with mushrooms and top with Mozzarella cheese. Pour water and insert steamer rack in the instant pot. Place the zucchini boats in the steamer rack and close the lid. Cook the meal on manual (high pressure) for 4 minutes. Then make the quick pressure release. Very carefully transfer the zucchini boats in the serving plate.
Nutrition: calories 54, fat 3, fiber 1.4, carbs 4.4, protein 3.7

Lemon and Pesto Broccoli

Preparation time: 5 minutes
Cooking time: 15 minutes
Servings: 4
Ingredients:
- 1 and ½ pounds broccoli florets
- 1 tablespoon lemon juice
- 1 tablespoon lemon zest, grated
- 1 tablespoon basil pesto
- ½ cup chicken stock
- A pinch of salt and black pepper

Directions:
In your instant pot, mix the broccoli with the lemon juice and the rest of the ingredients, put the lid on

and cook on High for 15 minutes. Release the pressure fast for 5 minutes, divide the mix between plates and serve.
Nutrition: calories 81, fat 1.2, fiber 0.5, carbs 1, protein 6.5

Zucchini Fettuccine
Preparation time: 10 minutes
Cooking time: 5 minutes
Servings: 2
Ingredients:
- 1 large zucchini, trimmed
- 1 tablespoon coconut cream
- ¼ teaspoon minced garlic
- ¼ teaspoon ground ginger
- ¼ teaspoon ground black pepper
- ¾ teaspoon salt
- 1 teaspoon coconut oil

Directions:
Slice the zucchini into the ribs with the help of the vegetable peelers. Preheat the instant pot. When it shows "HOT", add coconut oil and melt it. Then add zucchini ribs (fettuccine), minced garlic, ground ginger, and ground black pepper. Stir the vegetables. After this, sprinkle them with coconut cream and close the lid. Cook the meal on sauté mode for 3 minutes.
Nutrition: calories 65, fat 4.4, fiber 2.1, carbs 6.3, protein 2.2

Bok Choy and Parmesan Mix
Preparation time: 5 minutes
Cooking time: 10 minutes
Servings: 4
Ingredients:
- 2 cups bok choy, torn
- ½ cup chicken stock
- 2 tablespoons dill, chopped
- 1 tablespoon tomato passata
- 3 tablespoons parmesan cheese, grated

Directions:
In your instant pot, combine the bok choy with the stock and the other ingredients except the parmesan, put the lid on and cook on High for 10 minutes. Release the pressure fast for 5 minutes, divide the mix between plates, sprinkle the parmesan on top and serve.
Nutrition: calories 24, fat 1.6, fiber 0.6, carbs 1, protein 2.5

Keto Club Salad
Preparation time: 15 minutes
Cooking time: 5 minutes
Servings: 6
Ingredients:
- 4 oz Cheddar cheese, cubed
- ½ cup cherry tomatoes, halved
- 2 cucumbers, chopped
- 4 eggs
- 1 tablespoon heavy cream
- 2 tablespoons coconut cream
- 1 teaspoon dried dill
- 1 teaspoon lemon juice
- ½ teaspoon salt
- 1 cup water, for cooking

Directions:
Pour water and insert the trivet in the instant pot. Place the eggs on the trivet and close the lid. Cook the eggs on manual (steam mode) for 5 minutes. Then make the quick pressure release and open the lid. Cool and peel the eggs. After this, place cheese, cherry tomatoes, and cucumbers in the salad bowl. Make the dressing: in the shallow bowl whisk together heavy cream, coconut cream, dried dill, salt, and lemon juice. Chop the eggs roughly and add them in the salad bowl. Then sprinkle it with dressing.
Nutrition: calories 157, fat 11.5, fiber 0.8, carbs 5.2, protein 9.4

Milky Fennel
Preparation time: 5 minutes
Cooking time: 12 minutes
Servings: 4
Ingredients:
- 2 big fennel bulbs, sliced
- 2 tablespoons ghee, melted
- 2 cups almond milk
- ½ teaspoon nutmeg, ground
- A pinch of salt and black pepper

Directions:
In your instant pot, combine the fennel with the melted ghee and the rest of the ingredients, put the lid on and cook on High for 12 minutes. Release the pressure fast for 5 minutes, divide the mix between plates and serve.
Nutrition: calories 243, fat 20.4, fiber 4.3, carbs 5.7, protein 4.2

Bell Pepper Pizza
Preparation time: 10 minutes
Cooking time: 4 minutes
Servings: 2
Ingredients:
- 1 green bell pepper, halved, seeded
- 1 teaspoon cream cheese
- ¼ teaspoon tomato paste
- ¼ teaspoon dried basil
- 1/3 cup Mozzarella cheese, shredded
- 1 oz Parmesan, grated
- 1 cup water, for cooking

Directions:
In the mixing bowl mix up Parmesan, Mozzarella, and dried basil. In the shallow bowl whisk together cream cheese and tomato paste. Fill the bell pepper halves with cream cheese mixture and top with Mozzarella mixture. Place the pepper halves in the steamer rack. Then pour water in the instant pot. Insert the steamer rack and close the lid. Cook the pepper pizzas on manual (high pressure) for 4 minutes. Then make the quick pressure release.
Nutrition: calories 84, fat 4.6, fiber 0.8, carbs 5.4, protein 6.6

Minty Green Beans
Preparation time: 10 minutes
Cooking time: 15 minutes
Servings: 4
Ingredients:
- 1 pound green beans, trimmed
- 1 green onion, sliced
- 1 tablespoon mint, chopped
- 1 cup chicken stock

- A pinch of salt and black pepper
- 1 tablespoon cilantro, chopped

Directions:
In your instant pot, combine the green beans with the green onion and the rest of the ingredients, put the lid on and cook on High for 15 minutes. Release the pressure naturally for 10 minutes, divide the mix between plates and serve.
Nutrition: calories 40, fat 1.2, fiber 0.4, carbs 0.6, protein 2.4

Peppers & Cheese Salad

Preparation time: 15 minutes
Cooking time: 3 minutes
Servings: 5
Ingredients:
- ¼ cup Parmesan, grated
- ¼ cup Edam cheese, grated
- 4 bell peppers
- 1 tablespoon sesame oil
- 1 black olive, chopped
- ¼ teaspoon salt
- 1 tablespoon avocado oil

Directions:
Pour avocado oil in the instant pot. Pierce the bell peppers with the help of a knife and place in the instant pot. Cook the peppers on sauté mode for 3 minutes from each side. Then remove the vegetables from instant pot and peel them. Remove the seeds and cut the peppers into squares. Place them in the salad bowl. Add chopped olive, sesame oil, and salt. Mix up the peppers with the help of the spoon. Top the salad with Edam cheese and Parmesan cheese.
Nutrition: calories 136, fat 9, fiber 1.4, carbs 8, protein 7.4

Almonds Green Beans Mix

Preparation time: 10 minutes
Cooking time: 15 minutes
Servings: 4
Ingredients:
- 1 pound green beans, trimmed
- 1 tablespoon balsamic vinegar
- A pinch of salt and black pepper
- 2 tablespoons almonds, chopped
- 1 tablespoon dill, chopped
- ½ cup chicken stock

Directions:
In your instant pot, combine the green beans with the vinegar, almonds and the rest of the ingredients, put the lid on and cook on High for 15 minutes. Release the pressure naturally for 10 minutes, divide the mix between plates and serve.
Nutrition: calories 56, fat 1.7, fiber 0.5, carbs 1, protein 2.9

Bok Choy Salad

Preparation time: 10 minutes
Cooking time: 20 minutes
Servings: 4
Ingredients:
- 10 oz baby bok choy, trimmed
- ¼ teaspoon of sea salt
- 1 tablespoon peanut oil
- ½ teaspoon chili flakes
- ½ cup chicken broth
- 1 teaspoon olive oil
- 4 oz prosciutto, chopped

Directions:
Pour peanut oil in the instant pot and preheat it on sauté mode. When the oil is hot, add baby bok choy, sea salt, and chili flakes. Cook the vegetables for 3-4 minutes or until they are light brown. Add chicken broth and close the lid. Cook the bok choy on manual (high pressure) for 4 minutes. Then make the quick pressure release. Transfer the bok choy in the salad bowl. Add prosciutto and olive oil. Mix the salad.
Nutrition: calories 95, fat 6.4, fiber 0.7, carbs 2.1, protein 7.6

Mixed Peppers and Parsley

Preparation time: 10 minutes
Cooking time: 12 minutes
Servings: 4
Ingredients:
- 1 yellow bell pepper, cut into wedges
- 1 green bell pepper, cut into wedges
- 2 red bell peppers, cut into wedges
- 2 garlic cloves, minced
- A pinch of salt and black pepper
- ½ cup chicken stock
- 1 bunch parsley, chopped

Directions:
In your instant pot, combine the bell peppers with the garlic and the rest of the ingredients, put the lid on and cook on High for 12 minutes. Release the pressure naturally for 10 minutes, divide the mix between plates and serve.
Nutrition: calories 25, fat 1, fiber 0.1, carbs 0.5, protein 1

Avocado Pesto Zoodles

Preparation time: 9 minutes
Cooking time: 5 minutes
Servings: 6
Ingredients:
- 1 avocado, peeled, pitted
- 2 medium zucchini, spiralized
- 3 tablespoons pesto sauce
- 1 teaspoon apple cider vinegar
- 1 teaspoon ground black pepper
- 1 teaspoon butter
- 3 tablespoons water

Directions:
Preheat the instant pot. When it shows "hot", add spiralized zucchini, apple cider vinegar, butter, and ground black pepper. Cook the zucchini on sauté mode for 2 minutes. Meanwhile, chop the avocado and put it in the blender. Add pesto and blend the mixture until smooth. Add avocado pesto over the zoodles and mix up well. Cook them for 1 minute more.
Nutrition: calories 119, fat 10.5, fiber 3.2, carbs 5.8, protein 2.2

Peppers, Green Beans and Olives Mix

Preparation time: 10 minutes
Cooking time: 15 minutes
Servings: 4
Ingredients:
- 2 red bell peppers, cut into wedges
- A pinch of salt and black pepper

- 2 garlic cloves, minced
- ½ cup chicken stock
- ¼ pound green beans, trimmed and halved
- 1 cup black olives

Directions:
In your instant pot, combine the bell peppers with the other ingredients, put the lid on and cook on High for 15 minutes. Release the pressure naturally for 10 minutes, divide the mix between plates and serve.
Nutrition: calories 70, fat 3.9, fiber 2.8, carbs 3.2, protein 1.6

Collard Wraps

Preparation time: 10 minutes
Cooking time: 6 minutes
Servings: 4
Ingredients:
- 1 cup scallions, chopped
- 3 eggs
- 2 tablespoon cream cheese
- 1/3 teaspoon salt
- 1 teaspoon chili flakes
- 1 cup collard greens, only leaves
- 1 cup water, for cooking

Directions:
Cook the eggs: pour water and insert the steamer rack in the instant pot. Place the eggs on the rack and close the lid. Cook them in manual mode (high pressure) for 6 minutes. Then make the quick pressure release. Cool and peel the eggs. After this, chop the eggs and mix them up with the scallions. Add cream cheese, salt, and chili flakes. Trim the collard greens if needed. Spread the mixture over the collard greens leaves and wrap them.
Nutrition: calories 76, fat 5.2, fiber 1, carbs 2.9, protein 5.3

Lemon Tomato and Green Beans

Preparation time: 10 minutes
Cooking time: 15 minutes
Servings: 4
Ingredients:
- 1 and ½ pounds green beans, trimmed
- A pinch of salt and black pepper
- 14 ounces canned tomatoes, crushed
- 1 bunch parsley, chopped
- 2 garlic cloves, crushed
- 1 cup chicken stock
- Juice of 1 lemon
- A pinch of red pepper flakes

Directions:
In your instant pot, combine the green beans with the tomatoes and the rest of the ingredients, put the lid on and cook on High for 15 minutes. Release the pressure naturally for 10 minutes, divide the mix between plates and serve.
Nutrition: calories 94, fat 1.4, fiber 0.2, carbs 0.6, protein 5.3

Portobello Toasts

Preparation time: 8 minutes
Cooking time: 8 minutes
Servings: 2
Ingredients:
- 2 medium Portobello mushrooms caps
- 1 oz Parmesan, grated
- 2 tomato slices
- 2 teaspoons butter
- 1 cup water, for cooking

Directions:
Pour water and place the trivet in the instant pot. Line it with baking pan. Put the mushrooms on the trivet. Then put the butter in the mushrooms. After this, add sliced tomato and grated Parmesan. Close and seal the lid. Cook the mushroom toasts for 8 minutes on manual mode (high pressure). Then make the quick pressure release and open the lid. Cool the mushrooms to the room temperature and transfer in the serving plates.
Nutrition: calories 102, fat 6.9, fiber 1.2, carbs 4.1, protein 7.7

Ketogenic Instant Pot Dessert Recipes

Sweet Zucchini Pudding

Preparation time: 10 minutes
Cooking time: 40 minutes
Servings: 4
Ingredients:
- 3 cups zucchinis, grated
- 1 cup swerve
- 1 tablespoon vanilla extract
- 2 eggs, whisked
- 1 cup coconut flour
- Cooking spray
- 1 cup water

Directions:
In a bowl mix the zucchinis with the rest of the ingredients except the water and the cooking spray and whisk well. Grease a pudding pan that fits the instant pot with the cooking spray and pour the zucchini mix inside. Add the water to the instant pot, add the steamer basket, put the pan, put the lid on and cook on High for 40 minutes. Release the pressure naturally for 10 minutes and serve the pudding cold.
Nutrition: calories 176, fat 5.5, fiber 3.4, carbs 4.6, protein 7.8

Chocolate Pudding

Preparation time: 15 minutes
Cooking time: 10 minutes
Servings: 4
Ingredients:
- ½ cup heavy cream
- ½ cup of coconut milk
- 2 tablespoons cocoa powder
- ¼ cup Erythritol
- 2 tablespoons coconut flour
- 1 teaspoon gelatin
- 2 tablespoons water

Directions:
In the shallow bowl whisk together gelatin and water. Leave the mixture. Then pour heavy cream and coconut milk in the instant pot. Add cocoa powder and whisk the liquid until it is homogenous. Add Erythritol and coconut flour. Cook the liquid on sauté mode for 10 minutes. Stir it from time to time with the help of the spoon to avoid burning. When the time is over, cool the liquid for 10 minutes and add gelatin mixture. Stir it until gelatin is dissolved. Transfer the pudding in the serving cups.
Nutrition: calories 148, fat 13.6, fiber 2.7, carbs 5.6, protein 3.5

Almond Strawberry Bread

Preparation time: 5 minutes
Cooking time: 40 minutes
Servings: 6
Ingredients:
- ¾ cup swerve
- 1/3 cup ghee, melted
- 1 teaspoon vanilla extract
- 2 eggs, whisked
- 2 cups strawberries
- 1 teaspoon baking powder
- 1 and ½ cups almond milk
- 1/3 cup almond flour
- 2 cups water
- Cooking spray

Directions:
In a bowl, mix the ghee with the strawberries and the rest of the ingredients except the cooking spray and the water and whisk well. Grease a loaf pan that fits the instant pot with the cooking spray and pour the mix inside. Add the water to your instant pot, add the steamer basket, add the loaf pan inside, put the lid on and cook on High for 40 minutes. Release the pressure fast for 5 minutes, cool the bread, slice and serve.
Nutrition: calories 361, fat 18.2, fiber 3.4, carbs 5.9, protein 5.9

Pumpkin Pie Cups

Preparation time: 10 minutes
Cooking time: 25 minutes
Servings: 4
Ingredients:
- 4 teaspoons coconut flour
- 4 teaspoons almond flour
- 2 teaspoons butter, softened
- ¼ teaspoon vanilla extract
- 2 teaspoons pumpkin puree
- 2 eggs, beaten
- 4 teaspoons Erythritol
- 4 tablespoons flax meal
- 1 tablespoon coconut cream
- 1 cup water, for cooking

Directions:
Mix up together coconut flour, almond flour, butter, and vanilla extract. Then fill the muffin molds with the dough. After this, in the mixing bowl combine together pumpkin puree, eggs, Erythritol, flax meal, and coconut cream. Gently whisk the mixture and pour it over the dough. Pour water and insert the trivet in the instant pot. Place the muffin molds on the trivet and close the lid. Cook the pumpkin pie cups for 25 minutes on manual mode (high pressure). When the time is over, make the quick pressure release and open the lid. Cool the cooked dessert well.
Nutrition: calories 113, fat 8.9, fiber 3.2, carbs 4.5, protein 5.2

Coconut Zucchini Cake

Preparation time: 10 minutes
Cooking time: 40 minutes
Servings: 4
Ingredients:
- 2 egg, whisked
- ½ cup swerve
- 2 tablespoons ghee, melted
- 1 cup coconut milk
- ¼ cup coconut flour
- 2 zucchinis, grated
- ½ teaspoon baking soda
- Cooking spray
- 2 cups water

Directions:
In a bowl, mix the eggs with the zucchinis and the rest of the ingredients except the water and the cooking spray and whisk well. Grease a cake pan with the cooking spray and pour the zucchini mix inside.

Add the water to the pot, add steamer basket, add the cake pan inside, put the lid on and cook on High for 40 minutes. Release the pressure naturally for 10 minutes, cool the cake, slice and serve.
Nutrition: calories 242, fat 23.2, fiber 2.4, carbs 6.8, protein 5.4

Keto Custard

Preparation time: 10 minutes
Cooking time: 15 minutes
Servings: 2
Ingredients:
- ½ cup heavy cream
- 3 egg yolks
- ½ cup stevia powder
- ¼ teaspoon ground cardamom

Directions:
Pour heavy cream in the instant pot. Add ground cardamom. Cook the liquid on sauté mode until it starts to boil (appx 7-8 minutes). Stir it from time to time to avoid burning. Meanwhile, whisk together egg yolks with stevia powder until you get a fluffy mixture. Pour the egg yolk mixture in the heavy cream. Stir it constantly. When the liquid is homogenous, let it boil for 1 minute and switch off the instant pot. Pour the custard in the serving ramekins and let cool well.
Nutrition: calories 185, fat 17.9, fiber 0.1, carbs 1.9, protein 4.7

Vanilla Blackberries Bowls

Preparation time: 10 minutes
Cooking time: 10 minutes
Servings: 4
Ingredients:
- 2 teaspoons vanilla extract
- 3 cups blackberries
- 1 tablespoon swerve
- ½ cup coconut nectar

Directions:
In your instant pot, mix the blackberries with the vanilla and the rest of the ingredients, put the lid on and cook on High for 10 minutes. Release the pressure naturally for 10 minutes, divide the mix into bowls and serve.
Nutrition: calories 70, fat 1, fiber 0.4, carbs 0.9, protein 1.6

Pumpkin Spices Pudding

Preparation time: 10 minutes
Cooking time: 15 minutes
Servings: 4
Ingredients:
- 1 cup coconut cream
- 4 tablespoons coconut flour
- 1 teaspoon pumpkin pie spices
- 1 teaspoon butter
- ½ cup of water
- 4 packets Splenda

Directions:
Pour coconut cream in the instant pot. Add Splenda, butter, and pumpkin pie spices. Cook the liquid on sauté mode until it starts to boil. Meanwhile, whisk together water with coconut flour. Pour the liquid in the boiling coconut cream. Whisk until homogenous. Switch off the instant pot. Pour the pudding in the serving cups and let it cool to room temperature.
Nutrition: calories 208, fat 17.3, fiber 7.4, carbs 13.6, protein 3.4

Plums and Raisins Mix

Preparation time: 10 minutes
Cooking time: 15 minutes
Servings: 4
Ingredients:
- 1 pound plums, pitted and halved
- 1 cup coconut water
- ¼ cup raisins
- ½ cup swerve
- 1 teaspoon vanilla extract

Directions:
In your instant pot, combine the plums with the water and the rest of the ingredients, put the lid on and cook on High for 15 minutes. Release the pressure naturally for 10 minutes, divide the mix into bowls and serve.
Nutrition: calories 50, fat 1.2, fiber 0.1, carbs 0.6, protein 0.8

Molten Brownies Cups

Preparation time: 15 minutes
Cooking time: 10 minutes
Servings: 5
Ingredients:
- 2 oz cocoa powder
- 4 tablespoons coconut butter
- 2 eggs
- 4 teaspoons Splenda
- 4 teaspoons coconut flour
- 1 teaspoon vanilla extract
- 1 cup water, for cooking

Directions:
Crack the eggs in the mixing bowl. Add cocoa powder, coconut butter, Splenda, and vanilla extract. Whisk the mass until it is smooth and homogenous. Then pour the mixture in the small baking cups. Cover every cup with foil. Pour water in the instant pot. Insert the trivet and place the cups on it. Close the lid and cook the molten brownies for 10 minutes on manual mode (high pressure). Then allow the natural pressure release for 10 minutes. Let the cooked dessert cool totally.
Nutrition: calories 151, fat 10.7, fiber 6.1, carbs 13.5, protein 5.3

Berry Chocolate Cream

Preparation time: 5 minutes
Cooking time: 10 minutes
Servings: 4
Ingredients:
- 2 cups heavy cream
- 4 ounces chocolate, cut into chunks and melted
- 1 teaspoon stevia
- 1 cup blackberries
- 2 cups water

Directions:
In a bowl, mix the heavy cream with the chocolate and the rest of the ingredients except the water, whisk well and divide into ramekins. Put the water in your instant pot, add the steamer basket, add the

ramekins inside, put the lid on and cook on High for 10 minutes. Release the pressure fast for 5 minutes, and serve the cream cold.
Nutrition: calories 360, fat 17.2, fiber 2.9, carbs 6.4, protein 3.9

Almond Tart

Preparation time: 15 minutes
Cooking time: 20 minutes
Servings: 6
Ingredients:
- ½ cup almond flour
- 2 tablespoons almond butter
- ¼ teaspoon baking powder
- 1 egg, beaten
- ½ teaspoon ground cinnamon
- 1 tablespoon almond flakes
- ½ cup of organic almond milk
- 3 tablespoons coconut flour
- 2 tablespoons Erythritol
- 1 cup water, for cooking

Directions:
Make the tart crust: mix up together almond flour with almond butter, baking powder, and egg. Knead the dough. Then place the dough in the instant pot tart mold. Flatten it with the help of the fingertips in the shape of the tart crust. Pour water and insert the steamer rack in the instant pot. Place the tart mold on the rack and close the lid. Cook it on manual mode (high pressure) for 8 minutes. Then make a quick pressure release and remove the tart crust from it. Cool it well. After this, clean the instant pot and remove the steamer rack. Pour almond milk in the instant pot. Add coconut flour, Erythritol, and ground cinnamon. Bring the liquid to boil on sauté mode. Stir it constantly. Then switch off the instant pot. Pour the almond milk thick liquid over the pie crust and flatten well. Top the tart with almond flakes and refrigerate for at least 1 hour in the fridge.
Nutrition: calories 122, fat 10.4, fiber 2.8, carbs 5.2, protein 3.8

Strawberries and Pecans Cream

Preparation time: 10 minutes
Cooking time: 10 minutes
Servings: 4
Ingredients:
- 4 ounces strawberries
- 4 ounces coconut cream
- 1 cup stevia
- 1 teaspoon vanilla extract
- 2 tablespoons pecans, chopped
- 1 and ½ cups water

Directions:
In a bowl, mix the strawberries with the cream and the other ingredients except the water, whisk well and divide into 4 ramekins. Add the water to your instant pot, add the steamer basket, add the ramekins inside, put the lid on and cook on High for 10 minutes. Release the pressure naturally for 10 minutes, and serve cold.
Nutrition: calories 129, fat 11.8, fiber 2.3, carbs 5.1, protein 1.6

Chocolate Pudding Cake

Preparation time: 20 minutes
Cooking time: 20 minutes
Servings: 8
Ingredients:
- 2 tablespoons flax meal
- 1 egg, beaten
- ½ cup almond flour
- 4 tablespoons butter, softened
- 1 tablespoon cocoa powder
- 1 cup heavy cream
- 2 tablespoons gelatin
- ¼ cup Erythritol
- 5 tablespoons water
- 1 cup water, for cooking

Directions:
Make the cake crust: mix up together flax meal with egg, almond flour, and butter. Knead the dough. Place it in the non-sticky instant pot cake mold and flatten well. Make the crust with edges. Then pour water and insert the steamer rack in the instant pot. Put the mold with cake crust in the instant pot and close the lid. Cook it on manual mode (high pressure) for 13 minutes When the time is over, make the quick pressure release and open the lid. Cool the cake crust well. Meanwhile, clean the instant pot and remove the rack from it. Pour heavy cream in the instant pot. Add cocoa powder and Erythritol. Cook the liquid on sauté mode for 7 minutes. Meanwhile, whisk water with gelatin together. When the time is over, add gelatin liquid in the cream mixture and switch off the instant pot. Stir the liquid until it is smooth. Then pour it in the bowl and cool to room temperature. Pour the thick liquid over the cake crust and refrigerate for 2 hours.
Nutrition: calories 135, fat 13.5, fiber 0.9, carbs 1.7, protein 3.4

Coconut and Macadamia Chocolate Cream

Preparation time: 10 minutes
Cooking time: 15 minutes
Serving: 4
Ingredients:
- 3 ounces chocolate, unsweetened and melted
- 2 tablespoons macadamia nuts, chopped
- 2 tablespoons coconut, unsweetened and shredded
- 2 eggs, whisked
- 1 cup coconut cream
- ¾ cup swerve
- 2 cups water

Directions:
In a bowl, mix the chocolate with the nuts and the other ingredients except the water, whisk well and divide into ramekins. Add the water to the instant pot, add the steamer basket, put the ramekins inside, put the lid on and cook on High for 15 minutes. Release the pressure naturally for 10 minutes and serve the cream cold.
Nutrition: calories 300, fat 15.8, fiber 2.6, carbs 5.8, protein 6.2

Spice Pie

Preparation time: 10 minutes
Cooking time: 45 minutes
Servings: 8

Ingredients:
- 1 cup coconut flour
- 2 tablespoons butter
- 2 tablespoons cream cheese
- ½ teaspoon ground cinnamon
- ¼ teaspoon ground turmeric
- ½ teaspoon ground cardamom
- ¼ teaspoon ground nutmeg
- 1 teaspoon vanilla extract
- 1 tablespoon peanuts, chopped
- 3 eggs, beaten
- 1 teaspoon pumpkin spices
- 3 tablespoons Splenda
- 1 cup water, for cooking

Directions:
Make the pie batter: whisk together coconut flour, butter, cream cheese, ground cinnamon, ground turmeric, cardamom, nutmeg, vanilla extract, peanuts, eggs, pumpkin spices, and Splenda. When the batter is prepared, pour it in the instant pot pie mold. Flatten the surface of the pie well. Pour water and insert the steamer rack in the instant pot. Place the pie on the steamer rack and close the lid. Cook the pie on manual mode (high pressure) for 45 minutes. When the time is over, make the quick pressure release and open the lid. Cool the pie to the room temperature and cut into the servings.

Nutrition: calories 98, fat 6.3, fiber 0.9, carbs 6.4, protein 2.9

Cantaloupe Pudding

Preparation time: 10 minutes
Cooking time: 15 minutes
Servings: 4
Ingredients:
- 2 and ½ cups coconut milk
- 1 cup coconut cream
- ½ cup swerve
- 1 teaspoon vanilla extract
- 1 egg, whisked
- 1 teaspoon baking powder
- 2 cups cantaloupe, cubed
- 2 cups water

Directions:
In a bowl, combine the coconut milk with the cream and the other ingredients except the water, whisk well and pour into a pudding pan. Put the water in the instant pot, add the steamer basket, put the pan inside, put the lid on and cook on High for 15 minutes. Release the pressure naturally for 10 minutes, divide the pudding into bowls and serve.

Nutrition: calories 184, fat 15.6, fiber 2.1, carbs 7.5, protein 3.4

Keto Cheesecake

Preparation time: 25 minutes
Cooking time: 20 minutes
Servings: 6
Ingredients:
- ½ cup cream cheese
- 2 eggs, beaten
- 2 tablespoons whipped cream
- ¼ teaspoon vanilla extract
- 3 tablespoons Erythritol
- ½ cup almond flour
- 2 tablespoons butter, melted
- 1 cup water, for cooking

Directions:
Mix up almond flour with butter and knead the non-sticky dough. Then put the dough in the baking mold and flatten it in the shape of the pie crust. Pour water in the instant pot and insert the steamer rack. Place the pie crust in the instant pot and cook it on manual mode (high pressure) for 10 minutes. Make the quick pressure release and open the lid. After this, whisk together eggs with cream cheese, whipped cream, vanilla extract, and Erythritol. Pour the liquid over the pie crust and close the lid. Cook the cheesecake on manual mode (high pressure) for 10 minutes. When the time is over, make the quick pressure release and open the lid. Cool the cheesecake for 4 hours in the fridge.

Nutrition: calories 151, fat 14.8, fiber 0.3, carbs 1.3, protein 4

Coconut Raspberries Bowls

Preparation time: 10 minutes
Cooking time: 25 minutes
Servings: 4
Ingredients:
- 1 cup coconut, unsweetened and shredded
- 2 eggs, whisked
- 1 cup coconut milk
- ¾ cup swerve
- 1 teaspoon vanilla extract
- 1 cup raspberries

Directions:
In your instant pot, mix the coconut with the eggs and the rest of the ingredients, whisk well, put the lid on and cook on Low for 25 minutes. Release the pressure naturally for 10 minutes, divide the mix into bowls and serve.

Nutrition: calories 259, fat 22.3, fiber 3.5, carbs 6.8, protein 5.3

Butter Cake

Preparation time: 15 minutes
Cooking time: 35 minutes
Servings: 6
Ingredients:
- ½ cup butter, softened
- 1 egg, beaten
- 1 teaspoon vanilla extract
- ½ teaspoon baking powder
- 1 teaspoon lemon juice
- 2 tablespoons cream cheese
- 1 tablespoon Erythritol
- 1 ½ cup almond flour
- 1 tablespoon Splenda
- 1 cup water, for cooking

Directions:
In the mixing bowl mix up together butter with egg, vanilla extract, baking powder, and lemon juice. Then add almond flour and Splenda. Knead the dough and place it in the baking pan. Flatten it well. Pour water and insert the trivet in the instant pot. Place the dough on the trivet and close the lid. Cook it on manual mode (high pressure) for 35 minutes. When the time is over, make the quick pressure release and open the lid. Whisk together Erythritol and cream cheese. Cool the cooked cake to the room temperature and spread with sweet cream cheese mixture. Cut it into the servings.

Nutrition: calories 330, fat 31.3, fiber 3, carbs 8.5, protein 7.3

Watermelon Cream

Preparation time: 10 minutes
Cooking time: 10 minutes
Servings: 4
Ingredients:
- 2 cups watermelon, peeled and cubed
- 1 cup heavy cream
- 1 tablespoon vanilla extract
- ½ cup swerve
- 1 cup water

Directions:
In a bowl, mix the watermelon and the cream and the other ingredients except the water, whisk and divide into 4 ramekins. Add the water to the instant pot, add the steamer basket, put the ramekins inside, put the lid on and cook on High for 10 minutes. Release the pressure naturally for 10 minutes and serve the mix cold.
Nutrition: calories 136, fat 11.2, fiber 0.2, carbs 7, protein 1.1

Cinnamon Mini Rolls

Preparation time: 15 minutes
Cooking time: 21 minutes
Servings: 10
Ingredients:
- 1 cup almond flour
- ¼ cup coconut flour
- 1 teaspoon baking powder
- 1 teaspoon apple cider vinegar
- 3 tablespoons butter, melted
- 1 tablespoon cream cheese
- ¼ cup Erythritol
- 1 tablespoon cinnamon
- 1 egg, beaten
- 1 teaspoon vanilla extract
- 1 cup water, for cooking

Directions:
In the bowl mix up almond flour, coconut flour, baking powder, and apple cider vinegar. Then add melted butter, cream cheese, egg, and vanilla extract. Knead the soft and non-sticky dough. Roll it up in the shape of a square. In the shallow bowl combine together Erythritol and ground cinnamon. Sprinkle the surface of dough square with ground cinnamon mixture and roll it into the log. Then cut the dough log on 10 pieces. Press ever cinnamon dough piece with the help of the hand palm. Pour water and insert the trivet in the instant pot. Line the trivet with baking paper and place the cinnamon rolls on it. Close the lid and cook the dessert for 21 minutes on manual mode (high pressure). When the time is finished, make a quick pressure release and open the lid. Cool the cooked cinnamon rolls for 5 minutes and remove from the instant pot
Nutrition: calories 72, fat 6, fiber 1.9, carbs 9.5, protein 1.7

Lemon Strawberries Stew

Preparation time: 10 minutes
Cooking time: 20 minutes
Servings: 4
Ingredients:
- 3 cups strawberries
- 1 tablespoon lemon zest, grated
- 1 tablespoon lemon juice
- 1 cup swerve
- 1 teaspoon vanilla extract
- 1 cup water

Directions:
In your instant pot, combine the strawberries with the lemon zest and the rest of the ingredients, put the lid on and cook on High for 20 minutes. Release the pressure naturally for 10 minutes, divide the mix into bowls and serve right away.
Nutrition: calories 82, fat 1.4, fiber 0.5, carbs 1, protein 0.8

Lava Cake

Preparation time: 10 minutes
Cooking time: 15 minutes
Servings: 4
Ingredients:
- 1 tablespoon cocoa powder, unsweetened
- 1 teaspoon Erythritol
- 1/3 teaspoon baking powder
- 1 egg, beaten
- ¼ cup whipping cream
- 1 teaspoon butter
- 1 tablespoon almond meal
- ¼ teaspoon vanilla extract
- 1 cup water, for cooking

Directions:
In the big bowl whisk together egg and cocoa powder. Then add Erythritol and baking powder. Whisk the mixture for 2-3 minutes and add almond meal, vanilla extract, and whipping cream. Stir it until homogenous. Grease the instant pot baking mold with butter and place the cocoa mixture in it. Flatten it with the help of the spatula if needed. Pour water and insert the steamer rack in the instant pot. Place the baking mold with a cocoa mixture on the rack and close the lid. Cook the lava cake for 15 minutes on Manual mode (high pressure). Then make a quick pressure release and open the lid.
Nutrition: calories 59, fat 5.3, fiber 0.6, carbs 2.8, protein 2.1

Egg and Cantaloupe Pudding

Preparation time: 10 minutes
Cooking time: 25 minutes
Servings: 4
Ingredients:
- 4 eggs, whisked
- 1 teaspoon baking soda
- 2 cups heavy cream
- 1 cantaloupe, peeled and cubed
- ½ teaspoon vanilla extract
- 1 cup swerve
- 2 cups water

Directions:
In a bowl mix the eggs with the cream and the rest of the ingredients except the water, whisk well and pour into a pudding pan. Add the water to the pot, add the steamer basket, add the pudding pan inside, put the lid on and cook on High for 25 minutes. Release the pressure naturally for 10 minutes, and serve the pudding cold.

Nutrition: calories 283, fat 11.8, fiber 0.3, carbs 4.7, protein 7.1

Rhubarb Custard

Preparation time: 20 minutes
Cooking time: 6 minutes
Servings: 4
Ingredients:
- 1/3 cup rhubarb, chopped
- 3 eggs, beaten
- 4 packets Splenda
- ½ teaspoon vanilla extract
- 1 cup heavy cream
- 2 tablespoons butter, melted
- 1 cup water, for cooking

Directions:
Whisk together eggs with Splenda. Then add vanilla extract and heavy cream. Add butter and whisk the mass until homogenous. Add chopped rhubarb and mix up the mixture with the help of the spoon. Then pour the mixture into 4 ramekins. Cover every ramekin with foil. Pour water and insert the trivet in the instant pot. Place the ramekins with rhubarb custard on the trivet and close the lid. Cook the meal on manual mode (high pressure) for 6 minutes. When the time is over, allow the natural pressure release for 10 minutes. Remove the foil from the ramekins and let them cool for 5-10 minutes before serving.

Nutrition: calories 205, fat 20.2, fiber 1.2, carbs 3.6, protein 4.9

Cocoa Strawberries Mix

Preparation time: 10 minutes
Cooking time: 15 minutes
Servings: 4
Ingredients:
- 2 cups strawberries
- 1 teaspoon vanilla extract
- 1 tablespoon cocoa powder
- 2 cups coconut water
- 2 tablespoons swerve

Directions:
In your instant pot, mix the strawberries with the vanilla and the rest of the ingredients, put the lid on and cook on High for 15 minutes. Release the pressure naturally for 10 minutes, divide the mix into bowls and serve.

Nutrition: calories 72, fat 1.8, fiber 0.2, carbs 0.7, protein 1.6

Chocolate Mousse

Preparation time: 15 minutes
Cooking time: 3 hours
Servings: 2
Ingredients:
- 2 egg, beaten
- ½ cup heavy cream
- 2 tablespoons cocoa powder
- 1 teaspoon Splenda
- 1 teaspoon butter
- 1 cup water, for cooking

Directions:
Pour heavy cream in the mixing bowl and whisk it until you get strong peaks. Add Splenda and cocoa powder. Whisk the mixture until smooth. After this, whisk the eggs in the separated bowl. Slowly start to add whisked eggs in the whipped cream mixture. Stir it until smooth. Grease the ramekins with butter. Pour the whipped cream mixture in the ramekins. Pour water and insert the steamer rack in the instant pot. Place the ramekins with mousse on the trivet and close the lid. Cook the mousse for 3 hours on Manual (low pressure).

Nutrition: calories 205, fat 18.1, fiber 1.6, carbs 6.1, protein 7.2

Lime Cherry Bowls

Preparation time: 10 minutes
Cooking time: 10 minutes
Servings: 4
Ingredients:
- ½ cup cherries, pitted
- Juice of 1 lime
- Zest of 1 lime, grated
- 1 cup coconut water
- ½ cup coconut, unsweetened and shredded
- ½ teaspoon vanilla extract

Directions:
In your instant pot, mix the cherries with the lime juice and the rest of the ingredients, put the lid on and cook on High for 10 minutes. Release the pressure naturally for 10 minutes, divide the mix into bowls and serve cold.

Nutrition: calories 72, fat 3.4, fiber 1, carbs 1.5, protein 0.5

Cocoa-Vanilla Pudding

Preparation time: 10 minutes
Cooking time: 10 minutes
Servings: 6
Ingredients:
- 1 teaspoon sugar-free maple syrup
- 2 oz hot water
- 1/3 teaspoon vanilla extract
- 9 oz coconut flour
- ¼ tablespoon cocoa powder
- 1/3 teaspoon baking powder
- 4 tablespoons butter, softened
- 2 tablespoons swerve
- 1 egg, beaten
- 1 cup water, for cooking

Directions:
Mix up maple syrup with vanilla extract, coconut flour, cocoa powder, baking powder, butter, and swerve, Add egg and stir the mixture with the help of the fork until smooth. Then transfer the mixture in the round baking mold. Pour water and insert the trivet in the instant pot. Place the mold with pudding on the trivet and close the lid. Cook the pudding on steam mode for 10 minutes. When the time is over, make a quick pressure release and remove the dessert from the instant pot.

Nutrition: calories 212, fat 11.7, fiber 12.8, carbs 20.4, protein 7.2

Zucchini Rice Pudding

Preparation time: 10 minutes
Cooking time: 20 minutes
Servings: 4
Ingredients:
- 2 cups cauliflower rice

- 1 cup zucchinis, grated
- 3 cups coconut milk
- 3 tablespoon swerve
- 1 teaspoon vanilla extract
- 1 tablespoon cinnamon powder

Directions:
In your instant pot, mix the cauliflower rice with the zucchinis and the rest of the ingredients, put the lid on and cook on High for 20 minutes. Release the pressure naturally for 10 minutes, divide the rice into bowls and serve.
Nutrition: calories 122, fat 12.3, fiber 3.1, carbs 4.6, protein 4.5

Keto Carrot Pie

Preparation time: 20 minutes
Cooking time: 35 minutes
Servings: 6
Ingredients:
- 1 tablespoon walnuts, chopped
- 1 carrot, grated
- ½ cup almond butter
- 1 cup almond meal
- 3 tablespoons swerve
- 1 teaspoon psyllium husk powder
- 1 egg, beaten
- 1 teaspoon vanilla extract
- ½ teaspoon ground cinnamon
- ½ teaspoon baking powder
- 1 cup water, for steam mode

Directions:
Put all ingredients in the mixing bowl and stir them with the help of the spoon until you get a homogenous pie mixture. After this, transfer the pie mixture into the baking mold. Flatten the surface of the pie with the help of the spatula. Pour water and insert the steamer rack in the instant pot. Place the pie on the trivet and close the lid. Cook the carrot pie for 35 minutes on manual mode (high pressure). When the time is finished, allow the natural pressure release for 10 minutes and remove the pie from the instant pot.
Nutrition: calories 130, fat 10.2, fiber 3, carbs 6.7, protein 5

Creamy Rice Pudding

Preparation time: 10 minutes
Cooking time: 20 minutes
Servings: 4
Ingredients:
- 2 cups cream cheese, soft
- 2 cups heavy cream
- 3 tablespoons swerve
- 2 cups cauliflower rice
- 1 teaspoon lemon zest, grated
- 1 cup water

Directions:
In a bowl, whisk the cream with the cream cheese and the rest of the ingredients except the water, whisk really well and divide into 4 ramekins. Put the water in your instant pot, add the steamer basket, put the ramekins inside, put the lid on and cook on High for 20 minutes. Release the pressure naturally for 10 minutes and serve the puddings warm.
Nutrition: calories 306, fat 13.4, fiber 0, carbs 2.4, protein 5

Pecan Pie

Preparation time: 15 minutes
Cooking time: 15 minutes
Servings: 4
Ingredients:
- ½ cup coconut flour
- 1 tablespoon butter, melted
- 4 pecans, chopped
- 1 tablespoon Monk fruit powder
- 4 oz coconut milk
- 2 tablespoons almond butter
- 1 cup water, for cooking

Directions:
Make the pie crust: mix up together coconut flour and butter. Knead the non-sticky dough. Place the mixture in the instant pot mold and flatten it with the help of the fingertips in the shape of the pie crust. Pour water and insert the steamer rack in the instant pot. Place the mold with the pie crust on the rack and close the lid. Cook it on manual (high pressure) for 5 minutes. Then make a quick pressure release. Open the lid. In the mixing bowl whisk together milk, Monk fruit, and almond butter. When the mixture is smooth, pour it over the cooked pie crust. Top the pie with chopped pecans and close the lid. Cook the pecan pie for 10 minutes on manual mode (high pressure). When the time is over, make a quick pressure release. Cool the cooked pie well.
Nutrition: calories 297, fat 26.1, fiber 7.9, carbs 13.1, protein 5.9

Berries and Nuts Pudding

Preparation time: 10 minutes
Cooking time: 20 minutes
Servings: 4
Ingredients:
- 1 cup blackberries
- ½ cup blueberries
- 1 egg, whisked
- 1 teaspoon baking soda
- 2 cups coconut milk
- 1 tablespoon macadamia nuts, chopped
- 1 tablespoon pecans, chopped
- 3 tablespoons swerve
- 1 cup coconut cream
- 1 cup water

Directions:
In a bowl, mix the berries with the egg and the rest of the ingredients except the water, whisk well and pour into a pudding pan. Put the water in the instant pot, add the steamer basket, put the pudding pan inside, put the lid on and cook on High for 20 minutes. Release the pressure naturally for 10 minutes and serve the pudding cold.
Nutrition: calories 342, fat 14.8, fiber 3.4, carbs 6.4, protein 6.2

Keto Crème Brulee

Preparation time: 15 minutes
Cooking time: 8 minutes
Servings: 2
Ingredients:
- 1 tablespoon Erythritol
- 2 egg yolks
- 1 cup heavy cream
- ½ teaspoon vanilla extract

- 1 teaspoon Splenda
- 1 cup water, for cooking

Directions:
Whisk egg yolks and Splenda together until smooth. Then add heavy cream and vanilla extract. Whisk the mixture well and pour it into the ramekins. After this, cover every ramekin with foil. Pour water and insert the steamer rack in the instant pot. Place the ramekins on the rack and close the lid. Cook the crème Brulee on manual mode (high pressure) for 8 minutes. Then allow the natural pressure release for 10 minutes and remove the ramekins from the instant pot. Remove the foil and sprinkle the surface of crème Brulee with Erythritol. With the help of the kitchen torch, caramelize Erythritol.
Nutrition: calories 274, fat 26.7, fiber 0, carbs 4.4, protein 3.9

Lime Coconut Vanilla Cream

Preparation time: 10 minutes
Cooking time: 20 minutes
Servings: 4
Ingredients:
- 2 cups coconut cream
- 1 tablespoon lime zest
- 1 tablespoon lime juice
- 4 eggs, whisked
- 2 teaspoon vanilla extract
- 1 cup water

Directions:
In a bowl, combine the coconut cream with the rest of the ingredients except the water, whisk well and divide into 4 ramekins. Put the water in the instant pot, add the steamer basket, put the ramekins inside, put the lid on and cook on High for 20 minutes. Release the pressure naturally for 10 minutes and serve.
Nutrition: calories 342, fat 22.7, fiber 2.7, carbs 7.4, protein 8.3

Lavender Pie

Preparation time: 10 minutes
Cooking time: 40 minutes
Servings: 6
Ingredients:
- ½ cup blackberries
- 1 cup almond meal
- 2 tablespoons flax meal
- 1 teaspoon baking powder
- ½ teaspoon apple cider vinegar
- 3 eggs, beaten
- 1 teaspoon lavender extract
- 1/3 cup cream cheese
- 1/3 cup Erythritol
- 1 teaspoon butter, melted
- 1 cup water, for cooking

Directions:
In the big bowl combine together almond meal, flax meal, baking powder, apple cider vinegar, and eggs. Then add lavender extract, cream cheese, Erythritol, and melted butter. Stir the mixture. In the end you should get a smooth thick batter. Pour it in the non-stick baking mold. Then insert the steamer rack and pour water in the instant pot. Place the mold with pie on the rack and close the lid. Cook the meal on manual mode (high pressure) for 40 minutes. When the time is over, make a quick pressure release and transfer the pie on the plate. Cool it to the room temperature and cut into the servings.
Nutrition: calories 145, fat 11.6, fiber 3.3, carbs 5.8, protein 6.8

Plums Jam

Preparation time: 10 minutes
Cooking time: 30 minutes
Servings: 4
Ingredients:
- Juice of 1 lemon
- 1 tablespoon lemon zest, grated
- 1 cup swerve
- 2 cups plums, pitted and halved
- 1 cup water

Directions:
In your instant pot, mix the plums with the rest of the ingredients, put the lid on and cook on Low for 30 minutes. Release the pressure naturally for 10 minutes, blend the mix using an immersion blender, divide into jars and serve.
Nutrition: calories 42, fat 1.7, fiber 0.2, carbs 0.3, protein 0.4

Blueberry Parfait

Preparation time: 15 minutes
Cooking time: 5 minutes
Servings: 4
Ingredients:
- ½ cup hazelnuts, chopped
- 1 teaspoon flax seeds
- 1 teaspoon chia seeds
- 1 teaspoon pumpkin seeds
- 1 teaspoon coconut oil
- 1 teaspoon liquid stevia
- 1 cup blueberries
- 1 tablespoon Erythritol
- 1 teaspoon water
- 4 tablespoons cream cheese

Directions:
Preheat the instant pot on sauté mode for 3 minutes. Meanwhile, in the mixing bowl combine together flax seeds, chia seeds, pumpkin seeds, and coconut oil. Add liquid stevia and stir it well. Then transfer the mixture in the instant pot and sauté it for 2 minutes. Stir it from constantly. Then transfer the mixture on the baking paper. Whisk together cream cheese with Erythritol and water. When you get a smooth and fluffy mixture, it is cooked. Crush the cooked hazelnut mixture. Then place a small amount of the hazelnut mixture in the glass jars. Add ½ tablespoon of cream cheese mixture and all blueberries in every glass. After this, top the blueberries with remaining hazelnut mixture and cream cheese.
Nutrition: calories 140, fat 11.5, fiber 2.6, carbs 8.2, protein 3

Raspberries and Coconut Puddings

Preparation time: 10 minutes
Cooking time: 25 minutes
Servings: 4
Ingredients:
- 2 cups raspberries
- Zest of 1 lime, grated
- 2 cups coconut cream
- ½ cup coconut, unsweetened and shredded

- 1 teaspoon vanilla extract
- 1 cup water

Directions:
In a bowl, mix the berries with the rest of the ingredients except the water, whisk well and divide into 4 ramekins. Put the water in the instant pot, add the steamer basket, add the ramekins inside, put the lid on and cook on High for 25 minutes. Release the pressure naturally for 10 minutes and serve the puddings cold.
Nutrition: calories 346, fat 15.8, fiber 2.7, carbs 6.5, protein 3.8

Pandan Custard

Preparation time: 10 minutes
Cooking time: 25 minutes
Servings: 3
Ingredients:
- 1 teaspoon pandan extract
- 1 egg, beaten
- 4 tablespoons Truvia
- ½ cup of coconut milk
- 1 cup water, for cooking

Directions:
In the mixing bowl blend together pandan extract, egg, Truvia, and coconut milk. When the mixture is smooth, pour it in the ramekins. Then pour water in the instant pot and insert the rack. Place the ramekins on the rack and close the lid. Cook the custard on manual mode (high pressure) for 25 minutes. When the time is over, make a quick pressure release.
Nutrition: calories 113, fat 11, fiber 0.9, carbs 8.6, protein 2.8

Cinnamon Cream

Preparation time: 10 minutes
Cooking time: 20 minutes
Servings: 4
Ingredients:
- 4 eggs, whisked
- 2 tablespoons lime juice
- 1 teaspoon lime zest, grated
- 1 cup swerve
- 1 and ½ cups coconut cream
- 1 tablespoon cinnamon powder
- 1 and ½ cups water

Directions:
In a bowl, mix the eggs with the lime juice and the rest of the ingredients except the water, whisk well and divide into 4 ramekins. Put the water in the instant pot, add the steamer basket, put the ramekins inside, put the lid on and cook on High for 20 minutes. Release the pressure naturally for 10 minutes, and serve the cream cold.
Nutrition: calories 374, fat 22.1, fiber 3.2, carbs 5.9, protein 8.8

Mug Cake

Preparation time: 10 minutes
Cooking time: 18 minutes
Servings: 2
Ingredients:
- 4 teaspoons butter, softened
- 1 tablespoon cream cheese
- 1 teaspoon vanilla extract
- 2 tablespoons almond flour
- 2 teaspoons Erythritol
- ½ teaspoon baking powder
- 1 egg, beaten
- 1 cup water, for cooking

Directions:
In the mixing bowl, mix up together butter, cream cheese, vanilla extract, almond flour, Erythritol, baking powder, and egg. When the mixture is smooth, pour it into the mugs. Pour water in the instant pot and insert the trivet. Place the mugs on the trivet and close the lid. Cook the cakes on manual mode (high pressure) for 18 minutes. When the time is finished, make a quick pressure release and open the lid.
Nutrition: calories 2846, fat 25.6, fiber 3, carbs 7.2, protein 9.2

Lemon Cantaloupe Stew

Preparation time: 10 minutes
Cooking time: 15 minutes
Servings: 4
Ingredients:
- 2 cups cantaloupe, peeled and cubed
- ½ cup swerve
- 1 cup water
- 1 teaspoon vanilla extract

Directions:
In your instant pot, mix the cantaloupe with the rest of the ingredients, put the lid on and cook on High for 15 minutes. Release the pressure naturally for 10 minutes, divide the stew into bowls and serve.
Nutrition: calories 41, fat 1.7, fiber 0.7, carbs 1, protein 0.8

Coconut Cake

Preparation time: 10 minutes
Cooking time: 30 minutes
Servings: 8
Ingredients:
- 1 cup of coconut oil
- ½ cup coconut flakes
- 1 teaspoon baking powder
- 2 eggs, beaten
- 1 tablespoon flax meal
- ¼ cup heavy cream
- 1 teaspoon butter, softened
- ½ cup Erythritol
- 1 teaspoon vanilla extract
- 1 cup water, for cooking

Directions:
Combine together coconut oil, coconut flakes, and baking powder. Add eggs, flax meal, heavy cream, and butter. After this, add Erythritol and vanilla extract. Stir the mixture with the help of the spoon until you get a smooth and thick batter. Then pour it in the non-stick baking mold. Pour water and insert the steamer rack in the instant pot. Place the baking mold with batter in the instant pot and close the lid. Cook the cake in manual mode (high pressure) for 30 minutes. When the time is over, make a quick pressure release and open the lid. Cool the cake well and after this, remove it from the baking mold and cut into the servings.
Nutrition: calories 291, fat 32.2, fiber 0.7, carbs 1.6, protein 1.8

Ginger Chocolate Cream

Preparation time: 10 minutes
Cooking time: 15 minutes
Servings: 4
Ingredients:
- 4 ounces chocolate, unsweetened and melted
- 2 tablespoons swerve
- 1 tablespoon ginger, grated
- 2 cups coconut cream
- 1 teaspoon vanilla extract
- 1 cup water

Directions:
In a bowl, mix the chocolate with the sugar, ginger and the rest of the ingredients except the water, whisk and divide into 4 ramekins. Put the water in the instant pot, add the steamer basket, put the ramekins inside, put the lid on and cook on High for 15 minutes. Release the pressure naturally for 10 minutes, and serve the cream cold.
Nutrition: calories 235, fat 14.1, fiber 3.8, carbs 4.1, protein 5

Walnut pie

Preparation time: 20 minutes
Cooking time: 5 minutes
Servings: 4
Ingredients:
- 1/3 cup walnuts
- ¼ cup hazelnuts
- 2 tablespoon butter, softened
- 4 tablespoons whipped cream
- 1 teaspoon coconut oil
- 1 oz dark chocolate
- 2 tablespoons swerve

Directions:
Place the walnuts and hazelnuts in the blender and blend until smooth. Add butter and blend for 30 seconds more or until you get the smooth homogenous texture of the mixture. Remove the mixture from the blender and place it in the baking mold. Flatten the mixture in the shape of the pie crust with the help of the fingertips. Place the crust in the freezer. After this, preheat the instant pot on sauté mode for 3 minutes. Add dark chocolate and coconut oil. Then add swerve and sauté the mixture until it is soft and homogenous (appx.for 5 minutes). Stir the mixture constantly to avoid burning. Then whisk together whipped cream and chocolate mixture. When it is smooth, pour the mixture over the frozen walnut pie crust and place it in the fridge. Let the pie rest for at least 3 hours.
Nutrition: calories 236, fat 22.6, fiber 1.4, carbs 6.5, protein 4.1

Macadamia Blackberry Stew

Preparation time: 5 minutes
Cooking time: 20 minutes
Servings: 4
Ingredients:
- 12 ounces blackberries
- 2 tablespoons lime juice
- 2 tablespoons stevia
- 1 and ½ cups coconut nectar
- 1 tablespoon macadamia nuts, chopped
- 1 teaspoon vanilla extract

Directions:
In your instant pot, mix the blackberries with the rest of the ingredients, put the lid on and cook on High for 15 minutes. Release the pressure fast for 5 minutes, divide the mix into bowls and serve.
Nutrition: calories 78, fat 2, fiber 1.2, carbs 1.5, protein 1.4

Keto Chip Cookies

Preparation time: 10 minutes
Cooking time: 8 minutes
Servings: 6
Ingredients:
- 1 teaspoon xanthan gum
- 3 tablespoons butter, softened
- ½ teaspoon vanilla extract
- 1 egg, beaten
- 1/3 teaspoon baking powder
- 1 sugar-free chocolate chips
- 8 oz coconut flour
- 1 tablespoon Erythritol
- 1 cup water, for cooking

Directions:
In the big bowl combine together all ingredients except water for cooking. Knead the smooth dough and cut it into 6 pieces. Make the ball from every dough piece and press gently in the shape of a circle. Pour water and insert the steamer rack in the instant pot. Line the rack with baking paper and place the cookies on it in one layer. Close the lid and cook the chip cookies for 8 minutes on Manual mode (high pressure). When the time is over, make a quick pressure release and remove the cookies from the instant pot. Repeat the same step with remaining cookies.
Nutrition: calories 166, fat 10, fiber 8.4, carbs 15.2, protein 3.8

Plums and Berries Compote

Preparation time: 10 minutes
Cooking time: 20 minutes
Servings: 4
Ingredients:
- 1 cup plums, pitted and halved
- 1 cup blueberries
- 2 tablespoons lemon juice
- 1 and ½ cups water
- ¾ cup swerve
- 1 teaspoon vanilla extract

Directions:
In your instant pot, mix the plums with the berries and the rest of the ingredients, put the lid on and cook on High for 20 minutes. Release the pressure naturally for 10 minutes, divide the compote into bowls and serve.
Nutrition: calories 43, fat 1.2, fiber 0.1, carbs 1, protein 0.5

Keto Vanilla Crescent Cookies

Preparation time: 15 minutes
Cooking time: 19 minutes
Servings: 7
Ingredients:
- 1/3 cup butter, softened
- 3 oz almond flour
- 1.5 oz almonds, grinded

- 2 ½ tablespoons stevia
- ½ teaspoon vanilla extract
- 1 tablespoon Erythritol
- 1 cup water, for cooking

Directions:
Knead the dough from almond flour, butter, almonds, stevia, and vanilla extract. Then roll the dough into the log shape and cut into 7 pieces. Make the shape of crescents. Pour water and insert the trivet in the instant pot. Line the trivet with baking paper and place the crescents on it. Cook the crescent cookies in the manual (high pressure) for 19 minutes. When the time is finished, make a quick pressure release. Sprinkle every crescent cookie in Erythritol.
Nutrition: calories 182, fat 17.8, fiber 2.1, carbs 3.9, protein 3.9

Lime Watermelon Compote

Preparation time: 5 minutes
Cooking time: 10 minutes
Servings: 4
Ingredients:
- 1 and ½ cups watermelon, peeled and cubed
- 2 tablespoons lime juice
- 2 cups water
- 3 tablespoons swerve

Directions:
In your instant pot, mix the watermelon with the rest of the ingredients, put the lid on and cook on High for 10 minutes. Release the pressure fast for 5 minutes, divide the mix into bowls and serve really cold.
Nutrition: calories 40, fat 1, fiber 0.1, carbs 0.2, protein 0.6

Vanilla Muffins

Preparation time: 10 minutes
Cooking time: 15 minutes
Servings: 4
Ingredients:
- 4 tablespoons almond flour
- 1 tablespoon cream cheese
- 1 egg, beaten
- 1 teaspoon vanilla extract
- ¼ teaspoon baking powder
- ¼ teaspoon apple cider vinegar
- 4 teaspoons Erythritol
- 1 cup water, for cooking

Directions:
In the bowl combine together cream cheese, egg, vanilla extract, baking powder, apple cider vinegar, and Erythritol. When the mass is homogenous, add almond flour and stir until smooth. Pour water and insert the trivet in the instant pot. Fill the muffin molds with muffins batter and transfer on the trivet. Close the lid and cook the dessert on manual (high pressure) for 15 minutes. When the time is finished, make a quick pressure release and remove the muffins from the instant pot immediately.
Nutrition: calories 188, fat 16, fiber 3, carbs 6.4, protein 7.6

Heavy Cream and Raspberries Ramekins

Preparation time: 5 minutes
Cooking time: 8 minutes
Servings: 4
Ingredients:
- 2 cups raspberries
- 1 cup heavy cream
- ¼ cup swerve
- 2 tablespoons ghee, melted
- 1 teaspoon vanilla extract
- ½ teaspoon ginger powder
- 1 cup water

Directions:
In a bowl, mix the raspberries with the cream and the rest of the ingredients except the water, whisk and divide into ramekins. Put the water in the instant pot, add the steamer basket, put the ramekins inside, put the lid on and cook on High for 8 minutes. Release the pressure fast for 5 minutes, and serve cold.
Nutrition: calories 195, fat 17.9, fiber 4, carbs 7.5, protein 1.4

Fat Bomb Jars

Preparation time: 8 minutes
Cooking time: 6 minutes
Servings: 4
Ingredients:
- 1 tablespoon coconut oil
- 1 pouch sugar-free chocolate chips
- ½ cup whipped cream
- 3 tablespoons almond butter
- ¼ teaspoon ground cardamom

Directions:
Toss the coconut oil in the instant pot and melt it on sauté mode. After this, add ground cardamom and chocolate chips. Melt the mixture and switch off the instant pot. After this, transfer the chocolate mixture into the bowl. Add whipped cream and almond butter. Stir the mixture until smooth and homogenous. With the help of the scooper place the mixture into the glass jars.
Nutrition: calories 172, fat 15.6, fiber 1.5, carbs 7, protein 3.1

Coconut Pecans Cream

Preparation time: 10 minutes
Cooking time: 15 minutes
Servings: 4
Ingredients:
- 1 cup pecans, chopped
- 1 cup coconut cream
- ½ cup coconut, unsweetened and shredded
- 4 tablespoons swerve
- 1 teaspoon vanilla extract
- 1 cup water

Directions:
In a bowl, mix the pecans with the rest of the ingredients except the water, whisk and divide into ramekins. Put the water in the instant pot, add the steamer basket inside, add the ramekins, put the lid on and cook on High for 15 minutes. Release the pressure naturally for 10 minutes and serve cold.
Nutrition: calories 176, fat 17.6, fiber 2.2, carbs 5, protein 1.7

Blueberry Clusters

Preparation time: 10 minutes
Cooking time: 6 minutes
Servings: 6

Ingredients:
- 1.5 oz dark chocolate
- 1 tablespoon coconut oil
- 1/3 cup blueberries

Directions:
Toss coconut oil in the instant pot. Set sauté mode for 6 minutes and melt the oil. Add dark chocolate and stir well. Cook the mixture until it is homogenous. After this, line the baking tray with baking paper and arrange the blueberries on it into 6 circles. Then sprinkle every "blueberry circles" with melted chocolate mixture and let dry. Store the cooked clusters in the glass jar with the closed lid up to 2 days.
Nutrition: calories 67, fat 5.3, fiber 1.2, carbs 7.9, protein 0.6

Chocolate and Brazil Nuts Bread

Preparation time: 10 minutes
Cooking time: 30 minutes
Servings: 4
Ingredients:
- 1 cup coconut milk
- 2 eggs, whisked
- 2 teaspoons vanilla extract
- 1 cup swerve
- 1 cup brazil nuts, peeled and chopped
- 2 cups coconut flour
- 2 ounces chocolate, melted
- ¼ teaspoon baking powder
- 2 cups water
- Cooking spray

Directions:
In a bowl, combine the coconut milk with the eggs and the rest of the ingredients except the cooking spray and the water and whisk well. Grease a loaf pan with the cooking spray and pour the bread mix inside. Add the water to the instant pot, add the steamer basket, put the loaf pan inside, put the lid on and cook on High for 30 minutes. Release the pressure naturally for 10 minutes, cool the bread down and serve.
Nutrition: calories 253, fat 19.7, fiber 1.8, carbs 6.8, protein 5.2

Strawberry Cubes

Preparation time: 10 minutes
Cooking time: 7 minutes
Servings: 4
Ingredients:
- 4 strawberries
- 1 tablespoon heavy cream
- 1 teaspoon butter
- 1 tablespoon cocoa powder

Directions:
Put the strawberries in the freezer for 5-10 minutes. Preheat the instant pot bowl on sauté mode for 3 minutes. Then add butter and melt it. Add heavy cream and cocoa powder. Whisk the mixture until smooth and turn off the instant pot. After this, let the chocolate mixture cool to room temperature. Dip every strawberry in the chocolate mixture and let to dry it for 3-4 minutes.
Nutrition: calories 28, fat 2.6, fiber 0.6, carbs 1.8, protein 0.4

Greek Pudding

Preparation time: 10 minutes
Cooking time: 30 minutes
Servings: 4
Ingredients:
- 1 and ½ cups coconut flour
- 1 teaspoon baking powder
- ½ teaspoon vanilla extract
- 2 eggs, whisked
- 2 cups Greek yogurt
- ½ cup swerve
- 3 tablespoons coconut flakes
- 2 cups water

Directions:
In a bowl, mix the flour with the baking powder and the rest of the ingredients except the water, whisk well and pour into a pudding pan. Add the water to the instant pot, add the steamer basket, put the pudding pan inside, put the lid on and cook on High for 30 minutes. Release the pressure naturally for 10 minutes and serve the pudding cold.
Nutrition: calories 94, fat 4.3, fiber 0.4, carbs 1.5, protein 4.9

Avocado Brownies

Preparation time: 15 minutes
Cooking time: 14 minutes
Servings: 12
Ingredients:
- 1 avocado, peeled, pitted
- 1 tablespoon cocoa powder
- 1 tablespoon almond butter
- 1 teaspoon vanilla extract
- 1 egg, beaten
- 4 tablespoons almond flour
- ½ teaspoon baking powder
- 3 tablespoons Erythritol
- ½ teaspoon apple cider vinegar
- 1 cup water, for cooking

Directions:
Churn the avocado till the creamy texture. Add cocoa powder, almond butter, vanilla extract, and egg. Mix up the mixture until it is smooth. Then add almond flour, baking powder, Erythritol, and apple cider vinegar. Stir the mass well and pour in the instant pot baking mold. Flatten the surface and cover it with the foil. Pierce the foil with the help of the toothpick. Pour water and insert the trivet in the instant pot. Place the baking mold with a brownie on the trivet and close the lid. Cook the dessert for 14 minutes on manual mode (high pressure). When the time is finished, make a quick pressure release and remove the brownie. Discard the foil and cut the brownie into bars.
Nutrition: calories 103, fat 9.1, fiber 3, carbs 2.4, protein 3.1

Pecans and Plums Bread

Preparation time: 10 minutes
Cooking time: 30 minutes
Servings: 4
Ingredients:
- 1 cup coconut flour
- 3 eggs, whisked
- 1 tablespoon vanilla extract
- 1 and ½ cups swerve

- 2 cups plums, pitted and chopped
- 2 cups coconut milk
- 2 tablespoons pecans, chopped
- ¼ teaspoon baking powder
- 2 cups water
- Cooking spray

Directions:
In a bowl, combine the coconut flour with the eggs and the rest of the ingredients except the cooking spray and the water and whisk well. Grease a loaf pan with the cooking spray and pour the bread mix inside. Add the water to the instant pot, add the steamer basket, put the loaf pan inside, put the lid on and cook on High for 30 minutes. Release the pressure naturally for 10 minutes, cool the bread down, slice and serve.
Nutrition: calories 348, fat 23.5, fiber 3.1, carbs 6.6, protein 7.2

Cheesecake Bites

Preparation time: 15 minutes
Cooking time: 12 minutes
Servings: 2
Ingredients:
- 2 teaspoons cream cheese
- ¼ teaspoon vanilla extract
- 2 tablespoons peanut flour
- ¼ teaspoon coconut oil
- 1 egg, beaten
- 1 teaspoon Splenda
- 1 cup water, for cooking

Directions:
In the mixing bowl mix up cream cheese with vanilla extract, peanut flour, coconut oil, egg, and Splenda. When the mixture is smooth, transfer it in the muffin molds. Pour water and insert the trivet in the instant pot. Place the muffin molds on the trivet and close the lid. Cook the cheesecake bites on manual mode (high pressure) for 12 minutes. When the time is over, allow the natural pressure release for 10 minutes.
Nutrition: calories 76, fat 4.7, fiber 0.6, carbs 3.5, protein 4.3

Chocolate Cheesecake

Preparation time: 10 minutes
Cooking time: 40 minutes
Servings: 6
Ingredients:
- 2 tablespoons ghee, melted
- 1 cup heavy cream
- 2 ounces chocolate, melted
- ½ cup swerve
- 12 ounces cream cheese, soft
- 1 and ½ teaspoon vanilla extract
- 2 eggs, whisked
- Cooking spray
- 1 cup water

Directions:
Grease a spring form pan with cooking spray and leave it aside. In a bowl, mix the ghee with the chocolate, the cream and the rest of the ingredients except the water, whisk well and pour into the pan. Add the water to the instant pot, add the steamer basket, put the pan inside, put the lid on and cook on Low for 40 minutes. Release the pressure naturally for 10 minutes, and serve the cheesecake cold.
Nutrition: calories 282, fat 25.4, fiber 0.2, carbs 5.8, protein 5.5

Coconut Crack Bars

Preparation time: 10 minutes
Cooking time: 8 minutes
Servings: 4
Ingredients:
- 1 cup unsweetened coconut flakes
- 4 tablespoons coconut oil
- 1 egg, beaten
- 2 tablespoons coconut flour
- 2 tablespoons monk fruit

Directions:
In the mixing bowl combine together 3 tablespoons of coconut oil, coconut flour, egg, and coconut flakes. Then add monk fruit and stir the mixture well with the help of the spoon. The prepared mixture should be homogenous. After this, toss the remaining coconut oil in the instant pot and heat it up on sauté mode. Meanwhile, make the small bars from the coconut mixture. Place them in the hot coconut oil in one layer and cook for 1 minute from each side. Dry the cooked coconut bars with a paper towel if needed.
Nutrition: calories 218, fat 21.2, fiber 3.3, carbs 6.1, protein 2.9

Plums and Rice Pudding

Preparation time: 6 minutes
Cooking time: 20 minutes
Servings: 4
Ingredients:
- 2 cups coconut milk
- 1 cup cauliflower rice
- ½ cup plums, pitted and chopped
- ¼ cup heavy cream
- 2 eggs, whisked
- ½ cup swerve
- ½ teaspoon vanilla extract

Directions:
In your instant pot, mix the cauliflower rice with the plums and the rest of the ingredients, put the lid on and cook on High for 20 minutes. Release the pressure fast for 6 minutes, divide the pudding into bowls and serve cold.
Nutrition: calories 339, fat 27.7, fiber 2.7, carbs 6.5, protein 5.7

Keto Blondies

Preparation time: 15 minutes
Cooking time: 30 minutes
Servings: 4
Ingredients:
- 2 oz almond flour
- 2 oz coconut flour
- ½ teaspoon baking powder
- 3 tablespoons Erythritol
- 1 egg, beaten
- 2 tablespoons almond butter, softened
- 1 teaspoon walnuts, chopped
- 1 cup water, for cooking

Directions:
Line the instant pot baking tray with baking paper. After this, in the mixing bowl combine together

almond flour, coconut flour, baking powder, and Erythritol. Add egg, almond butter, and walnuts, With the help of the spoon stir the mass until homogenous. Then transfer it in the prepared baking tray and flatten well the surface of the dough. Pour water in the instant pot and insert the trivet. Place the tray on the trivet and close the lid. Cook the blondies for 30 minutes on manual mode (high pressure). When the time is over, make a quick pressure release. Cool the blondies to the room temperature and cut into serving bars.
Nutrition: calories 180, fat 14, fiber 4.9, carbs 9, protein 7.3

Cinnamon Berries Custard

Preparation time: 10 minutes
Cooking time: 15 minutes
Servings: 4
Ingredients:
- 3 eggs, whisked
- 2 cups coconut milk
- 1/3 cup swerve
- 1 tablespoon ghee, melted
- ½ cup heavy cream
- 1 tablespoon cinnamon powder
- ½ cup raspberries
- 1 teaspoon vanilla extract
- 1 and ½ cups water

Directions:
In a bowl, combine the eggs with the milk and the rest of the ingredients except the water, whisk well and transfer to a pan that fits the instant pot. Add the water to the instant pot, add the steamer basket, put the pan inside, put the lid on and cook on High for 15 minutes. Release the pressure naturally for 10 minutes, divide the mix in bowls and serve really cold.
Nutrition: calories 1276, fat 26.7, fiber 2.4, carbs 6.2, protein 4.9

Low Carb Nutella

Preparation time: 10 minutes
Cooking time: 5 minutes
Servings: 4
Ingredients:
- 3 oz hazelnuts
- 2 tablespoons coconut oil
- 1 teaspoon of cocoa powder
- 1 teaspoon Erythritol
- 2 tablespoons heavy cream

Directions:
Place coconut oil in the instant pot. Set sauté mode and heat it up for 3-4 minutes until the oil is melted. Then add Erythritol and cocoa powder. Whisk it well until homogenous. After this, add heavy cream. Stir the mixture until smooth and switch off the instant pot. After this, grind the hazelnuts. Add melted coconut oil mixture to the grinded hazelnuts. Stir well with the help of the spoon. Store Nutella in the fridge for up to 5 days.
Nutrition: calories 219, fat 22.6, fiber 2.2, carbs 4, protein 3.4

Ginger and Cardamom Plums Mix

Preparation time: 10 minutes
Cooking time: 15 minutes
Servings: 4
Ingredients:
- 3 cups plums, pitted and halved
- 2 cups heavy cream
- 1 tablespoon ginger, grated
- 3 tablespoons swerve
- 2 teaspoons vanilla extract
- ¼ teaspoon cardamom, ground

Directions:
In your instant pot, combine the plums with the cream and the rest of the ingredients, put the lid on and cook on High for 15 minutes. Release the pressure naturally for 10 minutes, divide the mix into bowls and serve cold.
Nutrition: calories 241, fat 22.4, fiber 0.9, carbs 6, protein 1.7

Cheesecake Fat Bombs

Preparation time: 20 minutes
Cooking time: 30 minutes
Servings: 2
Ingredients:
- 1 egg yolk
- 2 tablespoons cream cheese
- 1 teaspoon swerve
- ¼ teaspoon vanilla extract
- 3 tablespoons heavy cream
- 1 teaspoon coconut flakes

Directions:
Whisk the egg yolk with swerve until smooth. Then add heavy cream and pour the liquid in the instant pot. Stir it until homogenous and cook on manual mode (low pressure) for 30 minutes. Meanwhile, mix up together cream cheese with vanilla extract, and coconut flakes. When the time is over and the egg yolk mixture is cooked, open the instant pot lid. Combine together cream cheese mixture with egg yolk mixture and stir until homogenous. Place the mixture in the silicone muffin molds and transfer in the freezer for 20 minutes. The cooked cheesecake fat bombs should be tender but not liquid.
Nutrition: calories 146, fat 14.4, fiber 0.1, carbs 2.4, protein 2.6

Chocolate Cake

Preparation time: 10 minutes
Cooking time: 30 minutes
Servings: 4
Ingredients:
- 1 and ½ cups almond flour
- 1 cup cocoa powder
- Cooking spray
- 1 cup coconut flour
- 2 teaspoons baking powder
- 2 teaspoons baking soda
- ¼ cup flaxseed meal
- ½ cup ghee, melted
- 1 cup swerve
- 4 eggs, whisked
- 1 cup almond milk
- 1 teaspoon vanilla extract
- 2 cups water

Directions:
In a bowl, combine the almond flour with the cocoa, coconut flour and the rest of the ingredients except the cooking spray and the water and whisk really

well. Grease a cake pan with the cooking spray and pour the cake mix inside. Add the water to the instant pot, put the steamer basket, add the cake pan inside, put the lid on and cook on High for 30 minutes. Release the pressure naturally for 10 minutes, cool the cake down, slice and serve.
Nutrition: calories 344, fat 33.1, fiber 3.4, carbs 5.8, protein 8.1

Peanut Butter Balls

Preparation time: 10 minutes
Cooking time: 5 minutes
Servings: 2
Ingredients:
- 1 tablespoon peanuts
- 1 tablespoon butter
- 1 teaspoon Erythritol
- 4 tablespoons coconut flakes

Directions:
Set sauté mode on your instant pot for 5 minutes. Place the butter inside and melt it. Meanwhile, finely chop the peanuts. Add them in the melted butter. After this, add Erythritol and coconut flakes. Stir the mixture until homogenous. With the help of the scooper make 2 balls and chill them in the fridge.
Nutrition: calories 112, fat 11.4, fiber 1.3, carbs 2.3, protein 1.6

Chocolate Cookies

Preparation time: 10 minutes
Cooking time: 30 minutes
Servings: 4
Ingredients:
- 2 eggs, whisked
- ½ cup ghee, melted
- 2 tablespoons heavy cream
- 2 teaspoons vanilla extract
- 2 and ¾ cups almond flour
- ¼ cup swerve
- 1 cup chocolate chips
- Cooking spray
- 1 and ½ cups water

Directions:
In a bowl, mix the eggs with the ghee and the rest of the ingredients except the cooking spray and the water and whisk well. Put the water in the instant pot, add the steamer basket inside, arrange the cookies inside, spray them with cooking spray, put the lid on and cook on High for 30 minutes. Release the pressure naturally for 10 minutes, and serve the cookies cold.
Nutrition: calories 257, fat 21.4, fiber 0.7, carbs 12.5, protein 3.1

Cinnamon Muffins

Preparation time: 10 minutes
Cooking time: 18 minutes
Servings: 4
Ingredients:
- 4 teaspoons cream cheese
- 1 teaspoon ground cinnamon
- 1 tablespoon butter, softened
- 1 egg, beaten
- 4 teaspoons almond flour
- ½ teaspoon baking powder
- 1 teaspoon lemon juice
- 2 scoops stevia
- ¼ teaspoon vanilla extract
- 1 cup of water, for cooking

Directions:
In the big bowl make the muffins batter: mix up together cream cheese, ground cinnamon, butter, egg, almond flour, baking powder, lemon juice, stevia, and vanilla extract. When the mixture is smooth and thick, pour it into the 4 muffin molds. Then pour the water in the instant pot and insert the trivet. Place the muffins on the trivet and close the lid. Cook them for 18 minutes on Manual mode (high pressure). When the time is over, make a quick pressure release and cool the cooked muffins well.
Nutrition: calories 216, fat 19.2, fiber 3.3, carbs 7, protein 7.7

Coffee Cake

Preparation time: 10 minutes
Cooking time: 40 minutes
Servings: 4
Ingredients:
- 1/3 cup brewed coffee
- 1 and ½ cups almond flour
- ½ cup ghee, melted
- 1 and ½ cups swerve
- ½ teaspoon baking powder
- 4 eggs, whisked
- 1 teaspoon vanilla extract
- Cooking spray
- 1 cup water

Directions:
In a bowl, combine the coffee with the flour and the rest of the ingredients except the cooking spray and the water and whisk well. Grease a cake pan with the cooking spray and pour the cake mix inside. Put the water in the instant pot, add the steamer basket, put the cake pan inside, put the lid on and cook on High for 40 minutes. Release the pressure naturally for 10 minutes, cool the cake down, slice and serve.
Nutrition: calories 195, fat 20, fiber 0, carbs 0.5, protein 3.8

Keto Fudge

Preparation time: 10 minutes
Cooking time: 6 minutes
Servings: 5
Ingredients:
- ¾ cup of cocoa powder
- 1 oz dark chocolate
- 4 tablespoons butter
- 1 tablespoon ricotta cheese
- ¼ teaspoon vanilla extract

Directions:
Preheat the instant pot on sauté mode for 3 minutes. Place chocolate in the instant pot. Add butter and ricotta cheese. Then add vanilla extract and cook the ingredients until you get liquid mixture. Then add cocoa powder and whisk it to avoid the lumps. Line the glass mold with baking paper and pour the hot liquid mixture inside. Flatten it gently. Refrigerate it until solid. Then cut/crack the cooked fudge into the serving pieces.
Nutrition: calories 155, fat 13.8, fiber 4.6, carbs 10.7, protein 3.3

Nutmeg Pudding

Preparation time: 10 minutes
Cooking time: 30 minutes
Servings: 6
Ingredients:
- 2 cups water
- Cooking spray
- ½ cup swerve
- 4 eggs, whisked
- 1 cup heavy cream
- ½ cup almond flour
- 1 teaspoon nutmeg, ground
- ½ teaspoon baking soda
- 2/3 cup ghee, melted

Directions:
In a bowl, mix the swerve with the eggs and the rest of the ingredients except the cooking spray and the water and whisk. Grease a pudding pan with the cooking spray and pour the pudding mix inside. Put the water in the instant pot, add the steamer basket, put the pudding pan inside, put the lid on and cook on High for 30 minutes. Release the pressure naturally for 10 minutes, cool the pudding down and serve.
Nutrition: calories 235, fat 24.7, fiber 0.1, carbs 0.7, protein 3.2

Fluffy Donuts

Preparation time: 20 minutes
Cooking time: 14 minutes
Servings: 2
Ingredients:
- 1 tablespoon organic almond milk
- 1 egg, beaten
- ¼ teaspoon baking powder
- ¼ teaspoon apple cider vinegar
- 1 teaspoon ghee, melted
- 1 teaspoon vanilla extract
- 1 tablespoon Erythritol
- ¾ teaspoon xanthan gum
- 1 teaspoon flax meal
- 1 scoop stevia
- ¼ teaspoon ground nutmeg
- 1 tablespoon almond flour
- 1 cup water, for cooking

Directions:
Make the dough for the donut: in the big bowl mix up almond milk, egg, baking powder, apple cider vinegar, ghee, vanilla extract, Erythritol, xanthan gum, flax meal, and almond flour. With the help of the spoon stir the mixture gently. Then knead the non-sticky dough. Cut it into small pieces and put it in the silicone donut molds. Pour water and insert the trivet in the instant pot. Place the silicone molds with donuts on the trivet and close the lid. Cook the donuts on manual mode "high pressure" for 14 minutes. When the time is over, make a quick pressure release and open the lid. In the shallow bowl mix up together ground nutmeg and stevia. Sprinkle every donut with the stevia mixture.
Nutrition: calories 233, fat 18.9, fiber 5.4, carbs 9.3, protein 9.1

Chocolate Chips Balls

Preparation time: 5 minutes
Cooking time: 6 minutes
Servings: 6
Ingredients:
- 1 cup chocolate chips
- 2 tablespoons ghee, melted
- 2/3 cup heavy cream
- 2 tablespoons swerve
- ¼ teaspoon vanilla extract
- 1 cup water

Directions:
In a bowl, combine the chocolate chips with the ghee and the rest of the ingredients except the water, stir well and shape medium balls out of this mix. Put the water in the instant pot, add the steamer basket, put the balls inside, put the lid on and cook on High for 6 minutes. Release the pressure fast for 5 minutes and serve the chocolate balls cold.
Nutrition: calories 350, fat 23.8, fiber 1.4, carbs 6.9, protein 3.6

Coconut Muffins

Preparation time: 15 minutes
Cooking time: 12 minutes
Servings: 6
Ingredients:
- ½ cup coconut flour
- 2 eggs, beaten
- ¼ cup Splenda
- ½ teaspoon vanilla extract
- 3 teaspoons coconut flakes
- ¼ cup heavy cream
- 1 teaspoon baking powder
- 1 teaspoon lemon zest, grated
- 1 cup water, for cooking

Directions:
Make the muffins batter: In the bowl whisk together coconut flour, eggs Splenda, vanilla extract, coconut flour, heavy cream, baking powder, and lemon zest. Use the hand blender to make the batter smooth. Then pour water in the instant pot and insert the trivet. Pour muffins batter in the muffin molds. Then transfer the molds on the trivet and close the lid. Cook the desert on manual mode (high pressure) for 12 minutes. When the time is over, allow the natural pressure release for 5 minutes.
Nutrition: calories 48, fat 3.8, fiber 0.7, carbs 1.9, protein 2.2

Coconut and Cocoa Doughnuts

Preparation time: 10 minutes
Cooking time: 20 minutes
Servings: 4
Ingredients:
- ¼ cup swerve
- ¼ cup flaxseed meal
- ¾ cup coconut flour
- 1 teaspoon baking powder
- 1 teaspoon vanilla extract
- 2 eggs, whisked
- 3 tablespoons ghee, melted
- ¼ cup coconut milk
- 1 tablespoon cocoa powder
- Cooking spray
- 1 cup water

Directions:
In a bowl, mix the swerve with the flaxmeal and the rest of the ingredients except the cooking spray and

the water and stir well. Grease a doughnut pan with the cooking spray and divide the mix. Add the water to the instant pot, add the steamer basket, put the pan inside, put the lid on and cook on High for 20 minutes. Release the pressure naturally for 10 minutes, cool the doughnuts down and serve.
Nutrition: calories 196, fat 17.3, fiber 2.7, carbs 4.5, protein 4.7

Raspberry Pie

Preparation time: 15 minutes
Cooking time: 25 minutes
Servings: 6
Ingredients:
- ¼ cup raspberries
- 1 tablespoon Erythritol
- 3 tablespoons butter, softened
- ¼ teaspoon baking powder
- ½ cup almond flour
- 1 tablespoon flax meal
- 1 teaspoon ghee, melted
- 1 cup water, for cooking

Directions:
Blend raspberries with Erythritol in the blender until smooth. Then in the mixing bowl combine together butter, baking powder, almond flour, flax meal, and knead the dough. Cut it into 2 pieces. Then put one piece of dough in the freezer. Meanwhile, roll up the remaining piece of dough in the shape of a circle. Grease the instant pot baking mold with ghee. Place the dough circle in the prepared baking mold. Then pour the blended raspberry mixture over it. Flatten it with the help of the spoon. Then grate the frozen piece of dough over the raspberries. Pour water and insert the trivet in the instant pot. Cover the pie with foil and put it on the trivet. Close the lid and cook the pie on manual mode (high pressure) for 25 minutes. When the time is finished, make a quick pressure release. Discard the foil from the pie and let it cool to the room temperature.
Nutrition: calories 118, fat 11.6, fiber 1.7, carbs 3, protein 2.4

Chocolate Balls

Preparation time: 5 minutes
Cooking time: 10 minutes
Servings: 10
Ingredients:
- 1 cup ghee, melted
- 3 tablespoons macadamia nuts, chopped
- ¼ cup stevia
- 5 tablespoons unsweetened coconut powder
- 2 tablespoons cocoa powder
- 1 cup water

Directions:
In a bowl, combine the ghee with the macadamia nuts and the rest of the ingredients except the water, whisk really well and shape medium balls out of this mix. Add the water to the instant pot, add the steamer basket, arrange the balls inside, put the lid on and cook on High for 10 minutes. Release the pressure fast for 5 minutes and serve the balls cold.
Nutrition: calories 200, fat 22.4, fiber 0.5, carbs 0.9, protein 0.5

Mint Cookies

Preparation time: 10 minutes
Cooking time: 15 minutes
Servings: 4
Ingredients:
- ¼ cup Erythritol
- ½ teaspoon dried mint
- ¼ teaspoon mint extract
- 4 teaspoons cocoa powder
- 2 egg whites
- ¼ teaspoon baking powder
- ¼ teaspoon lemon juice
- 1 cup water, for cooking

Directions:
Whisk the egg whites gently and add dried mint. Then add Erythritol, mint extract, cocoa powder, baking powder, and lemon juice. Stir the mass until smooth. Pour water in the instant pot. Line the instant pot trivet with the baking paper. Place it in the instant pot. With the help of the scooper make 4 cookies and put them on the trivet. Close the lid and cook the cookies on manual mode (high pressure) for 15 minutes. When the time is over, make a quick pressure release. Open the lid and transfer the cookies on the plate or chopping board. Cool the cookies well.
Nutrition: calories 13, fat 0.3, fiber 0.6, carbs 1.3, protein 2.1

Vanilla and Cocoa Cream

Preparation time: 5 minutes
Cooking time: 5 minutes
Servings: 4
Ingredients:
- 1 and ½ cups heavy cream
- 3 tablespoons swerve
- 2 tablespoons cocoa powder
- 1 teaspoon vanilla extract
- 1 and ½ cups water

Directions:
In a bowl, combine the heavy cream with the rest of the ingredients except the water, whisk well and divide into 4 ramekins. Put the water in the instant pot, add the steamer basket, put the ramekins inside, put the lid on and cook on High for 5 minutes. Release the pressure fast for 5 minutes and serve the cream cold.
Nutrition: calories 216, fat 22.6, fiber 0.8, carbs 3.3, protein 1.7

Coconut Clouds

Preparation time: 10 minutes
Cooking time: 6 minutes
Servings: 2
Ingredients:
- 2 egg whites
- 4 tablespoons coconut flakes
- 1 tablespoon almond meal
- ¼ teaspoon ghee
- 1 teaspoon Erythritol

Directions:
Whisk the egg whites until strong peaks. Then slowly add the almond meal and coconut flakes. Add Erythritol and stir the mixture until homogenous with the help of the silicone spatula. Toss ghee in the instant pot and preheat it on sauté mode for 2

minutes. Then with the help of the spoon, make the clouds from egg white mixture and put them in the hot ghee. Close the lid and cook the dessert on sauté mode for 4 minutes.
Nutrition: calories 74, fat 5.4, fiber 1.3, carbs 2.4, protein 4.6

Plums Pie

Preparation time: 10 minutes
Cooking time: 30 minutes
Servings: 8
Ingredients:
For the crust:
- 1 cup coconut, unsweetened and shredded
- 1 cup pecans, chopped
- ¼ cup ghee, melted

For the filling:
- 8 ounces cream cheese
- 4 ounces strawberries
- 2 tablespoons water
- ½ tablespoon lime juice
- 1 teaspoon swerve
- ½ cup heavy cream
- 1 and ½ cups water

Directions:
In a bowl, combine the coconut with the pecans and the ghee, stir well and press on the bottom of a lined pie pan. In a second bowl, combine the cream cheese with the rest of the ingredients except the water, whisk well, pour over the crust and spread well. Add the water to the instant pot, add the steamer basket, put the pie pan inside, put the lid on and cook on High for 30 minutes. Release the pressure naturally for 10 minutes, cool the pie down, slice and serve.
Nutrition: calories 221, fat 22.4, fiber 1.2, carbs 3.6, protein 2.8

Shortbread Cookies

Preparation time: 15 minutes
Cooking time: 14 minutes
Servings: 6
Ingredients:
- 1 egg, beaten
- ¾ teaspoon salt
- 1 tablespoon almond butter
- 1 teaspoon coconut oil
- ¼ teaspoon baking powder
- ¼ teaspoon apple cider vinegar
- 1 tablespoon Erythritol
- 5 oz coconut flour
- 1 cup water, for cooking

Directions:
Mix up egg with salt, almond butter, coconut flour, and baking powder. Add apple cider vinegar, coconut oil, and Erythritol. Knead the dough and make 6 balls from it. Then press the balls gently with the help of the hand palm and place in the non-sticky instant pot baking tray. Pour water and insert the trivet in the instant pot. Place the tray with cookies on the trivet and close the lid. Cook the cookies on manual mode (high pressure) for 14 minutes. When the time is over, make a quick pressure release and open the lid. Transfer the cooked cookies on the plate and let them cool well.
Nutrition: calories 135, fat 5.5, fiber 10.4, carbs 17.5, protein 4.9

Vanilla Cream Mix

Preparation time: 10 minutes
Cooking time: 20 minutes
Servings: 4
Ingredients:
- 1 tablespoon vanilla extract
- 4 tablespoons butter
- 4 tablespoons sour cream
- 16 ounces cream cheese, soft
- ½ cup swerve
- ½ cup cocoa powder
- 1 cup heavy cream
- 2 cups water

Directions:
In a bowl, combine the vanilla with the butter and the rest of the ingredients except the water, whisk well and divide into 4 ramekins. Add the water to the instant pot, add the steamer basket, put the ramekins inside, put the lid on and cook on High for 20 minutes. Release the pressure naturally for 10 minutes, and serve the cream cold.
Nutrition: calories 330, fat 20.2, fiber 1.6, carbs 5.4, protein 5.8

Lime Bars

Preparation time: 20 minutes
Cooking time: 10 minutes
Servings: 6
Ingredients:
- ½ cup coconut flour
- 2 teaspoons coconut oil
- ¼ teaspoon baking powder
- ½ tablespoon cream cheese
- 1/3 cup coconut cream
- 2 tablespoons lime juice
- 1 teaspoon lime zest, grated
- 2 tablespoons Erythritol
- 1 cup water, for cooking

Directions:
Knead the dough from coconut flour, coconut oil, baking powder, and cream cheese. When the mixture is soft and non-sticky, it is prepared. Then line the instant pot bowl with baking paper. Place the dough inside and flatten it in the shape of the pie crust (make the edges). Close the lid and cook it on sauté mode for 5 minutes. After this, switch off the instant pot. Make the filling: mix up coconut cream, lime juice, lime zest, and Erythritol. Then pour the liquid over the cooked pie crust and cook it on sauté mode for 5 minutes more. When the time is over, transfer the cooked meal in the freezer for 10 minutes. Cut the dessert into bars.
Nutrition: calories 88, fat 6, fiber 4.3, carbs 7.9, protein 1.7

Mascarpone Cheesecake

Preparation time: 5 minutes
Cooking time: 15 minutes
Servings: 6
Ingredients:
- 2 tablespoons butter, soft
- 1 cup heavy cream
- 2 ounces chocolate, melted
- ½ cup swerve
- 12 ounces mascarpone cheese
- 1 and ½ teaspoon cocoa powder

- 1 egg, whisked
- Cooking spray
- 1 cup water

Directions:
In a bowl, combine the butter with the cream and the rest of the ingredients except the cooking spray and the water and whisk well. Grease a cake pan with the cooking spray and pour the mix inside. Add the water to the instant pot, add the steamer basket, put the cake pan inside, put the lid on and cook on High for 15 minutes. Release the pressure fast for 5 minutes, cool the cheesecake down and serve.
Nutrition: calories 263, fat 22.2, fiber 0.3, carbs 6, protein 8.5

Peppermint Cookies

Preparation time: 20 minutes
Cooking time: 5 minutes
Servings: 2
Ingredients:
- ¼ teaspoon peppermint extract
- 2 tablespoons almond flour
- 1 teaspoon heavy cream
- ½ teaspoon butter, softened
- ¼ oz dark chocolate

Directions:
Preheat the instant pot on sauté mode for 3 minutes. Then add almond flour, butter, and heavy cream. Add peppermint extract and dark chocolate. Saute the mixture for 2 minutes. Stir well. Then line the tray with baking paper. With the help of the spoon make the cookies from the peppermint mixture and transfer on the prepared baking paper. Refrigerate the cookies for 20 minutes.
Nutrition: calories 199, fat 17.1, fiber 3.3, carbs 8.1, protein 6.2

Creamy Chocolate Avocado Mix

Preparation time: 5 minutes
Cooking time: 5 minutes
Servings: 4
Ingredients:
- 2 avocados, peeled, pitted and chopped
- 1 cup heavy cream
- ½ cup chocolate chips
- ¼ cup swerve
- 1 teaspoon vanilla extract
- 1 cup water

Directions:
In your food processor, combine the avocados with the rest of the ingredients except the water, pulse well and divide into 4 ramekins. Put the water in the instant pot, add the steamer basket, put the ramekins inside, put the lid on and cook on High for 5 minutes. Release the pressure fast for 5 minutes, and serve the creamy mix really cold.
Nutrition: calories 283, fat 24.6, fiber 4, carbs 4.8, protein 2.2

Macadamia Cookies

Preparation time: 15 minutes
Cooking time: 13 minutes
Servings: 4
Ingredients:
- 1 oz macadamia nuts, chopped
- ½ cup coconut flour
- 2 tablespoons butter
- 1 tablespoon Erythritol
- 1 egg, beaten
- 2 tablespoons flax meal
- 1 cup water, for cooking

Directions:
In the mixing bowl mix up macadamia nuts, coconut flour, butter, Erythritol, egg, and flax meal. Knead the non-sticky dough. Then cut the dough into the pieces and make balls from them. Pour water and insert the trivet in the instant pot. Line the trivet with baking paper and put the dough balls on it. Cook the cookies for 13 minutes on manual mode (high pressure). When the time is over, make a quick pressure release and transfer the cookies on the plate.
Nutrition: calories 193, fat 15.5, fiber 6.6, carbs 10.1, protein 4.8

Vanilla Chocolate Cupcakes

Preparation time: 10 minutes
Cooking time: 20 minutes
Servings: 12
Ingredients:
- ½ cup butter, melted
- ½ cup avocado oil
- ½ cup coconut, shredded
- 2 ounces chocolate, chopped
- ¼ cup cocoa powder
- ¼ teaspoon vanilla extract
- ¼ cup swerve
- 1 cup water

Directions:
In a bowl, combine the butter with the oil and the rest of the ingredients except the water and whisk really well. Line a cupcake pan that fits the instant pot with parchment paper and divide the chocolate mix inside. Put the water in the instant pot, add the steamer basket, add the cupcake pan inside, put the lid on and cook on High for 20 minutes. Release the pressure naturally for 10 minutes and serve the cupcakes cold.
Nutrition: calories 243, fat 23.2, fiber 2.7, carbs 6.8, protein 2

Keto Pralines

Preparation time: 10 minutes
Cooking time: 8 minutes
Servings: 6
Ingredients:
- ½ cup butter
- 5 tablespoons heavy cream
- 2 tablespoons Erythritol
- ¼ teaspoon xanthan gum
- 4 pecans, chopped

Directions:
Place the butter in the instant pot and melt it on sauté mode. Add heavy cream and Erythritol. Stir the mixture well and sauté for 2 minutes. After this, add xanthan gum and pecan. Stir well and cook the mixture for 3 minutes more. Line the baking tray with baking paper. With the help of the spoon, place the pecan mixture in the tray in the shape of circles. Refrigerate the pralines until they are solid.
Nutrition: calories 254, fat 26.6, fiber 3.5, carbs 4.2, protein 1.4

Cream Cheese and Blackberries Mousse

Preparation time: 4 minutes
Cooking time: 4 minutes
Servings: 4
Ingredients:
- 8 ounces cream cheese
- 1 teaspoon serve
- 1 cup heavy cream
- 1 tablespoon blackberries
- 1 cup water

Directions:
In a bowl, mix the cream with the other ingredients except the water, whisk well and divide into 2 ramekins. Put the water in the instant pot, add the steamer basket, put the ramekins inside, put the lid on and cook on High for 4 minutes. Release the pressure fast for 4 minutes and serve the mousse really cold.
Nutrition: calories 202, fat 20.5, fiber 0.1, carbs 1.7, protein 3.3

Blueberry Crisp

Preparation time: 10 minutes
Cooking time: 6 minutes
Servings: 4
Ingredients:
- ¼ cup almonds, blended
- 1 teaspoon butter
- 1 teaspoon flax meal
- 1 tablespoon Erythritol
- ½ cup cream cheese
- ½ cup blueberries
- 1 oz peanuts, chopped

Directions:
Toss butter in the instant pot and melt it on sauté mode. Add almonds and flax meal. Cook the mixture on sauté mode for 4 minutes. Stir it constantly. After this, cool the mixture well. Whisk the cream cheese with Erythritol. Then put ½ of cream cheese mixture in the serving glasses. Add ½ part of the almond mixture and ½ part of blueberries. Repeat the same steps with remaining mixtures. Top the dessert with chopped peanuts.
Nutrition: calories 197, fat 17.8, fiber 2, carbs 6, protein 5.6

Appendix : Recipes Index

A

Ajiaco 137
Almond Cocoa and Strawberries Mix 17
Almond Lamb Meatloaf 164
Almond Strawberry Bread 185
Almond Tart 187
Almonds Green Beans Mix 183
Anniversary Chicken 137
Aromatic Lasagna with Basil 35
Aromatic Swedish Meatballs 83
Artichokes and Bacon Mix 169
Artichokes and Salmon Bowls 79
Artichokes Cream 51
Artichokes Pudding 18
Asiago Cauliflower Rice 69
Asiago Chicken Drumsticks 131
Asian Style Zucchini Soup 37
Asparagus and Chives Dressing 168
Asparagus and Eggs Mix 17
Asparagus and Tomatoes 168
Asparagus Mix 59
Avocado and Broccoli Salad 14
Avocado Boats with Omelet 18
Avocado Brownies 196
Avocado Pesto Zoodles 183
Avocado Pie 180

B

Bacon and Eggs 15
Bacon Artichokes 70
Bacon Avocado Bombs 88
Bacon Bites with Asparagus 75
Bacon Brussels Sprouts 55
Bacon Chowder 36
Bacon Egg Cups 15
Bacon Eggs with Chives 18
Bacon Onion Rings 75
Bacon Radish And Shrimp Salad 93
Bacon Salad with Eggs 28
Bacon Sushi 89
Bacon Tacos 19
Bacon Trout Mix 104
Bacon-Wrapped Chicken Tenders 133
Bacon-Wrapped Shrimps 91
Baked Green Beans 72
Baked Kabocha Squash 176
Baked Snapper 102
Balsamic and Coconut Cabbage 181
Balsamic Artichokes and Capers 68
Balsamic Bok Choy and Onions 180
Balsamic Brussels Sprouts 168
Balsamic Collard Greens 70
Balsamic Curry Chicken 119
Balsamic Eggplant Mix 69
Balsamic Endives 84
Balsamic Green Beans and Capers 170
Balsamic Mushroom and Radish Mix 55
Balsamic Mussels Bowls 80
Balsamic Okra 175
Balsamic Roast Chicken 125
Balsamic Savoy Cabbage 176
Balsamic Spinach 56
Balsamic Turkey and Zucchini 122
Basil Chicken Mix 134
Basil Chili Chicken 118
Basil Eggs Mix 23

Basil Peppers Salsa 90
Basil Shallots and Peppers Dip 88
Basil Shrimp and Eggplants 39
Basil Spicy Artichokes 167
Basil Stuffed Bell Peppers 87
Basil Zucchini and Capers Dip 75
Beef & Cabbage Stew 155
Beef and Cauliflower Stew 48
Beef and Creamy Sauce 162
Beef and Endives Mix 155
Beef and Herbed Radish 154
Beef and Mushroom Rice 155
Beef and Savoy Cabbage Mix 165
Beef and Squash Ragu 153
Beef and Walnuts Rice 166
Beef Cabbage Soup 36
Beef Loin with Acorn Squash 154
Beef Meatballs Stew 50
Beef Soup 42
Beef Tips 154
Beef, Arugula and Olives Salad 92
Beef, Cauliflower Rice and Shrimp Mix 149
Beef, Sprouts and Bok Choy Mix 150
Beet Cubes with Pecans 72
Bell Pepper Cream 45
Bell Pepper Pizza 182
Bell Peppers and Brussels Sprouts 171
Bell Peppers and Cauliflower Salad 12
Bell Peppers and Chives 170
Bell Peppers and Kale Soup 52
Bell Peppers and Mustard Greens 171
Bell Peppers and Olives 68
Berries and Nuts Pudding 191
Berry Chocolate Cream 186
Big Mac Bites 164
Blackberry Muffins 11
Blackberry Pork Chops 153
Blackened Chicken 136
BLT Chicken Wrap 121
Blueberry Clusters 195
Blueberry Crisp 204
Blueberry Muffins 32
Blueberry Parfait 192
Bok Choy and Parmesan Mix 182
Bok Choy Bowls 20
Bok Choy Salad 183
Bone Broth Soup 40
Brazilian Fish Stew 94
Bread Twists 84
Breakfast Avocado Bombs 16
Breakfast Crustless Quiche 22
Breakfast Egg Hash 19
Breakfast Hot Cacao 26
Breakfast Kale Bread 31
Breakfast Spaghetti Squash Casserole 27
Breakfast Stuffed Avocado 25
Breakfast Taco Omelet 22
Broccoli and Almonds Mix 30
Broccoli and Cheese Pancake 15
Broccoli and Watercress Mix 180
Broccoli and Zucchini Soup 42
Broccoli Casserole 12
Broccoli Dip 77
Broccoli Nuggets 68
Bruschetta Chicken 122

Brussels Sprouts and Sauce 170
Brussels Sprouts Casserole 54
Brussels Sprouts in Heavy Cream 167
Buffalo Chicken Soup 40
Burger Casserole 163
Butter Cake 188
Butter Chicken Stew 130
Butter Cod Loin 103
Butter Coffee 85
Butter Crepes 12
Butter Edamame Beans 176
Butter Lamb 158
Butter Scallops 101
Butter Shirataki Noodles 69
Butter Spaghetti Squash 59
Butternut Squash Fries 81
Butternut Squash Soup 37
Buttery Eggplants 69
Buttery Turmeric Brussels Sprouts 181

C

Cabbage and Peppers 67
Cabbage and Spinach Slaw 91
Cabbage and Tomatoes 70
Cabbage Chips 76
Cabbage Hash Browns 12
Cabbage Hash Browns 13
Cabbage Soup 43
Cabbage, Tomato and Avocado Salsa 92
Caesar Salad 120
Cajun Beef and Leeks Sauce 165
Cajun Chicken Salad 119
Cajun Crab Casserole 102
Cantaloupe Pudding 188
Caprese Zoodles 168
Cardamom Walnuts Pudding 23
Catfish and Avocado Mix 106
Cauliflower Bake 20
Cauliflower Cheese 58
Cauliflower Florets Mix 168
Cauliflower Fritters 27
Cauliflower Gnocchi 64
Cauliflower Gratin 172
Cauliflower Hash 13
Cauliflower Mac&Cheese 54
Cauliflower Rice 57
Cauliflower Rice and Olives 61
Cauliflower Risotto 172
Cauliflower Salad with Provolone Cheese 73
Cauliflower Shepherd's Pie 164
Cauliflower Toast 20
Cauliflower Tortillas 70
Cauli-Tatoes 58
Cayenne Pepper Chicken Meatballs 129
Cayenne Pepper Green Beans 67
Cayenne Peppers and Sauce 171
Cayenne Pork and Artichokes Stew 41
Celery and Broccoli Mix 62
Char Siu 146
Chard and Mushrooms Mix 57
Cheddar Mushrooms 177
Cheddar Soup 50
Cheddar Tomatoes 172
Cheddar Tots with Broccoli 66
Cheddar Turkey 140
Cheese Almond Meal Bites 78
Cheese Chips 84
Cheese Egg Balls 21
Cheese Melt 96

Cheesecake Bites 197
Cheesecake Fat Bombs 198
Cheesy Beef Casserole 16
Cheesy Coconut Cream 44
Cheesy Mushroom and Tomato Salad 86
Cheesy Radish 63
Cheesy Radish Spread 93
Cheesy Tomato and Radish Salad 27
Cheesy Turkey 137
Cheesy Zucchini Strips 60
Chia and Blueberries Bowls 17
Chicharrones 92
Chicken & Dumplings Soup 45
Chicken & Mushroom Bowl 50
Chicken & Snap Pea Salad 125
Chicken and Almonds Mix 141
Chicken and Asparagus Soup 45
Chicken and Avocado Mix 40
Chicken and Balsamic Mushrooms 127
Chicken and Brussels Sprouts Stew 49
Chicken and Cauliflower Rice 128
Chicken and Eggplant Mix 119
Chicken and Garlic Spinach 131
Chicken and Green Sauté 136
Chicken and Herbs Sauce 124
Chicken and Hot Endives 134
Chicken and Mustard Sauce 40
Chicken and Oregano Sauce 118
Chicken and Spinach Bowl 133
Chicken and Watercress Mix 130
Chicken Bowls 25
Chicken Cacciatore 124
Chicken Caprese Casserole 119
Chicken Casserole 135
Chicken Cauliflower Rice 130
Chicken Celery Boats 90
Chicken Cheese Calzone 129
Chicken Cordon Bleu 132
Chicken Crust Pizza 130
Chicken Divan Casserole 127
Chicken Enchilada Soup 39
Chicken Fricassee 139
Chicken Fritters 32
Chicken Lettuce Rolls 135
Chicken Liver Pate 134
Chicken Meatballs and Spinach 137
Chicken Moussaka 140
Chicken Paprika 43
Chicken Patties 122
Chicken Provencal 118
Chicken Rendang 123
Chicken Scarpariello 126
Chicken Steamed Balls 139
Chicken Stroganoff 128
Chicken Stuffed Avocado 131
Chicken Tonnato 117
Chicken with Black Olives 141
Chicken with Blue Cheese Sauce 118
Chicken Zucchini Enchiladas 124
Chicken, Baby Kale and Spinach Mix 128
Chicken, Cabbage and Leeks 126
Chicken, Kale and Artichokes 121
Chicken, Peppers and Mushrooms 140
Chicken, Radish and Green Beans 133
Chili Casserole 26
Chili Cauliflower Rice 72
Chili Eggplant and Collard Greens 57
Chili Frittata 16

Chili Haddock and Tomatoes 114
Chili Mushrooms Stew 48
Chili Pork Chops 147
Chili Spare Ribs 146
Chili Tomato and Zucchini Dip 76
Chili Tuna 102
Chili Verde 38
Chipotle Tilapia Mix 115
Chives Broccoli Mash 64
Chives Brussels Sprouts 54
Chocolate and Brazil Nuts Bread 196
Chocolate Balls 201
Chocolate Cake 198
Chocolate Cheesecake 197
Chocolate Chips Balls 200
Chocolate Cookies 199
Chocolate Mousse 190
Chocolate Pudding 185
Chocolate Pudding Cake 187
Cilantro Cauliflower Rice Mix 71
Cilantro Red Cabbage and Artichokes 176
Cilantro-Kale Salad 64
Cinnamon Berries Custard 198
Cinnamon Cod Mix 97
Cinnamon Cream 193
Cinnamon Green Beans Mix 177
Cinnamon Mini Rolls 189
Cinnamon Muffins 199
Cinnamon Pancakes 13
Cinnamon Pancakes 14
Cinnamon Strawberry Oatmeal 31
Cinnamon Turkey and Celery Mix 133
Cinnamon Turkey Curry 38
Clam Chowder 48
Classic Breakfast Casserole 28
Coated Coconut Shrimps 115
Cobb Salad 41
Cocoa Oatmeal 30
Cocoa Strawberries Mix 190
Cocoa-Vanilla Pudding 190
Coconut and Cocoa Doughnuts 200
Coconut and Macadamia Chocolate Cream 187
Coconut Blueberry Pudding 14
Coconut Broccoli Soup 36
Coconut Cake 193
Coconut Chicken and Peppers 117
Coconut Chicken Cubes 134
Coconut Chicken Tenders 125
Coconut Clouds 201
Coconut Crack Bars 197
Coconut Lamb Chops 161
Coconut Leeks and Sprouts 167
Coconut Muffins 200
Coconut Oatmeal 30
Coconut Omelet 32
Coconut Pecans Cream 195
Coconut Pork Mix 149
Coconut Pudding 25
Coconut Raspberries Bowls 188
Coconut Shrimp Platter 83
Coconut Soup 52
Coconut Spinach Mix 56
Coconut Yogurt Mix 18
Coconut Zucchini Cake 185
Cod and Asparagus 110
Cod and Basil Tomato Passata 111
Cod and Broccoli 97
Cod and Cilantro Sauce 94

Cod and Shrimp Stew 49
Cod and Tomato Passata 40
Cod and Tomatoes 94
Cod and Zucchinis 95
Cod in Cream Sauce 103
Coffee Cake 199
Collard Greens and Tomatoes 55
Collard Greens with Cherry Tomatoes 172
Collard Wraps 184
Coriander Beef and Pork Mix 152
Coriander Cod Mix 95
Coriander Leg of Lamb 159
Coriander Seabass 110
Corned Beef with Cabbage 52
Cornish Game Hens 136
Crab Melt with Zucchini 102
Crab Rangoon Dip 110
Crab Rangoon Fat Bombs 112
Crab Salad 42
Crab Spread 91
Crab&Broccoli Casserole 112
Crab, Spinach and Chives 114
Crack Chicken 44
Cranberries Cauliflower Rice 74
Cream Cheese and Blackberries Mousse 204
Cream of Celery 179
Creamy Asparagus Mix 169
Creamy Blueberries and Nuts 23
Creamy Brussels Sprouts Stew 53
Creamy Catfish 116
Creamy Cauliflower 57
Creamy Cauliflower Soup 39
Creamy Chicken Wings 138
Creamy Chocolate Avocado Mix 203
Creamy Eggplant Mix 173
Creamy Eggs Ramekins 14
Creamy Endives 64
Creamy Fennel 66
Creamy Green Beans 58
Creamy Okra and Collard Greens 175
Creamy Rice Pudding 191
Creamy Shrimp and Radish Mix 103
Creamy Tomatoes 172
Creamy Turkey and Chard 127
Creamy Zucchini Pan 22
Crunchy Green Beans 82
Crustless Egg Pie 32
Cucumbers and Zucchini Noodles 170
Cumin Kielbasa 156
Cumin Lamb and Capers 158
Curry Cauliflower Rice Bowls 33
Curry Fish 98
Curry Lamb and Cauliflower 151
Curry Pork and Kale 143
Curry Pork Sausages 148
Curry Tomato Cream 43

D

Dhansak Curry Meat 159
Dill Cherry Tomatoes 60
Dill Fennel and Brussels Sprouts 176
Dill Fennel Mix 63
Dill Halibut 110
Dill Lamb and Tomatoes 151
Dill Zucchini, Tomatoes and Eggplants 175
Dog Nuggets 93
Duck and Coriander Sauce 128
Duck and Fennel 123
Duck and Hot Eggplant Mix 125

Duck, Leeks and Asparagus 130

E

Edamame Hummus 91
Egg & Cheese Salad with Dill 42
Egg and Cantaloupe Pudding 189
Egg Benedict Sandwich 29
Egg Muffins 23
Egg Salad 34
Egg Sandwich 23
Egg Scramble 31
Egg Soup 35
Eggplant and Spinach Dip 83
Eggplant and Zucchini Mix 72
Eggplant Gratin 71
Eggplant Soup 44
Eggplants and Cabbage Mix 178
Eggplants, Cucumber and Olives 178
Eggs and Mushrooms Cups 170
Eggs, Leeks and Turkey Mix 29
Ethiopian Spicy Doro Wat Soup 138

F

Fajita Chicken Casserole 141
Fajita Soup 47
Fat Bomb Jars 195
Fennel and Leeks Platter 84
Feta and Zucchini Bowl 62
Feta Cheese Lamb Mix 155
Fish Casserole 95
Fish Pie 111
Fish Saag 94
Fish Sticks 109
Fluffy Donuts 200
Fluffy Eggs 17
Flying Jacob Casserole 119
Fragrant Artichoke Hearts 179
Fragrant Pork Belly 144
Fried Cauliflower Slices 56
Fried Salmon 98
Frittata with Greens 21

G

Garlic Aioli 87
Garlic and Cheese Baked Asparagus 167
Garlic and Parsley Pork 143
Garlic Beef Mix 34
Garlic Broccoli Mix 55
Garlic Cabbage and Watercress 179
Garlic Celery and Kale 173
Garlic Chicken Drumsticks 118
Garlic Eggplant Rounds 178
Garlic Lamb and Chard 151
Garlic Pork Loin 144
Garlic Smoky Ribs 150
Ginger and Cardamom Plums Mix 198
Ginger Balsamic Chicken 123
Ginger Cabbage and Radish Mix 54
Ginger Cauliflower Rice Pudding 20
Ginger Cauliflower Spread 77
Ginger Chocolate Cream 194
Ginger Halibut 115
Ginger Lamb and Basil 161
Glazed Salmon 107
Gouda Vegetable Casserole 71
Greek Chicken 123
Greek Pudding 196
Greek Style Pork Chops 148
Greek Turkey and Sauce 36
Green Beans and Cod Salad 80
Green Beans and Herbs 61
Green Beans and Kale 67
Green Beans and Rice Mix 34
Green Beans Casserole 59
Green Beans Salad 174
Green Beans Soup 42
Green Beans with Ham 51
Green Hash 16
Green Peas Salad 171
Ground Beef Skewers 165
Ground Chicken Mix 132
Ground Meat Stew 150
Ground Turkey Chili 138

H

Haddock and Cilantro Sauce 109
Halibut and Brussels Sprouts 116
Halibut Ceviche 113
Ham and Cheese Dinner Casserole 152
Ham Roll 17
Hash Brown Casserole 173
Heart of Palm Dip 86
Heavy Cream and Raspberries Ramekins 195
Herbed Asparagus 63
Herbed Crusted Lamb Cutlets 159
Herbed Haddock Mix 112
Herbed Mushroom Mix 21
Herbed Radish Mix 59
Herbed Whole Chicken 132
Hoagie Bowl 120
Hoisin Meatballs 151
Hot Cod Stew 45
Hot Curry Lamb and Green Beans 158
Hot Curry Turkey 125
Hot Jalapeno Poppers Mix 25
Hot Sausages Soup 46
Hot Tempeh 87

I

Indian Chicken and Sauce 135
Indian Chicken Korma 141
Italian Asparagus 84
Italian Beef 158
Italian Beef and Green Beans Mix 21
Italian Leg of Lamb 157
Italian Paprika Chicken 120
Italian Style Salad 42

J

Jalapeno Popper Bread 72
Jalapeno Pulled Pork 145
Jalapeno Soup 34

K

Kale and Bok Choy Muffins 24
Kale Skillet with Nuts 171
Kale Soup 39
Kale Stew 47
Kale Wraps 83
Kale&Parmesan Bowl 57
Kalua Chicken 47
Kalua Pig 148
Kalua Pork 143
Kalua Pork 160
Keto "Potato" Soup 35
Keto Blondies 197
Keto Breadsticks 82
Keto Carrot Pie 191
Keto Cereal Bowl 11
Keto Cheesecake 188
Keto Chicken Burger 134
Keto Chip Cookies 194
Keto Club Salad 182

Keto Crème Brulee 191
Keto Custard 186
Keto Fudge 199
Keto Guacamole Deviled Eggs 87
Keto Ham 145
Keto Jalapeno Bread 80
Keto Lunch Bowl 41
Keto Nachos 90
Keto Oatmeal 24
Keto Oxtail Goulash 157
Keto Pork Posole 151
Keto Pralines 203
Keto Queso Dip 80
Keto Shakshuka 22
Keto Spanakopita Pie Slices 93
Keto Taco Soup 38
Keto Taquitos 89
Keto Vanilla Crescent Cookies 194
Korean Style Pork Ribs 147

L

Lamb and Broccoli Mix 150
Lamb and Sun-dried Tomatoes Mix 158
Lamb Chops, Fennel and Tomatoes 157
Lamb Pulao 162
Lamb Shoulder Roast 160
Lamb Stew 46
Lava Cake 189
Lavender Pie 192
Layered Casserole 25
Lazy Meat Mix 52
Leek Frittata 32
Leek Soup 51
Leeks and Cabbage 73
Leeks and Pork Mix 22
Leeks Sauté 71
Lemon and Pesto Broccoli 181
Lemon Artichoke 181
Lemon Artichokes 62
Lemon Brussels Sprouts and Tomatoes 65
Lemon Cabbage Mix 58
Lemon Cantaloupe Stew 193
Lemon Carnitas 45
Lemon Peppers and Bok Choy 178
Lemon Strawberries Stew 189
Lemon Tomato and Green Beans 184
Lemon Zucchini and Eggplant Spread 75
Lemongrass Green Beans 170
Light Shrimp Pad Thai 114
Lime and Paprika Asparagus 167
Lime Bars 202
Lime Cherry Bowls 190
Lime Coconut Vanilla Cream 192
Lime Cod Mix 109
Lime Glazed Salmon 107
Lime Pork Bowls 36
Lime Pork Chops 153
Lime Salmon Burger 97
Lime Shrimp 96
Lime Spinach and Leeks Dip 76
Lime Watermelon Compote 195
Lobster Bisque 106
Lobster Salad 41
Low Carb Fall Vegetables 65
Low Carb Nutella 198
Low-Carb Flaxseed Brule 29
Lunch Pot Roast 51

M

Macadamia Blackberry Stew 194
Macadamia Cookies 203
Mackerel and Basil Sauce 102
Mackerel and Shrimp Mix 102
Mackerel Pate 111
Marinated Olives 92
Marinated Red Bell Peppers 67
Marinated Shrimp 83
Marinated Tomatillos Paste 176
Marinated Turkey Mix 139
Marjoram Tuna 103
Mascarpone Cheesecake 202
Mashed Brussel Sprouts 56
Mashed Cauliflower 55
Mason Jar Omelet 19
mb Shank 161
Meat & Collard Greens Bowl 49
Meat Muffins with Quail Eggs 13
Meat Sandwich 11
Meat&Cheese Pie 163
Mesquite Ribs 151
Mexican Pork and Okra Salad 37
Mexican Style Keto Rice 57
Milky Fennel 182
Minced Beef Pancakes 17
Mini Casserole in Jars 33
Mini Cheese Pepperoni Pizza 79
Mini Chicken Skewers 82
Mini Frittatas 29
Mini Margharita Pizzas in Mushroom Caps 86
Mint and Basil Eggplant 179
Mint Cookies 201
Mint Lamb Chops 157
Mint Lamb Cubes 159
Mint Salmon and Radish Salad 89
Mint Zucchinis 74
Minty Green Beans 182
Mississippi Roast 157
Mixed Peppers and Parsley 183
Molten Brownies Cups 186
Morning Bacon Bombs 23
Moroccan Lamb 160
Mozzarella and Kale Muffins 24
Mozzarella Artichokes and Capers 168
Mozzarella Broccoli 54
Mozzarella Chicken Fillets 122
Mug Cake 193
Mushroom and Avocado Salad 20
Mushroom and Cauliflower Rice Salad 31
Mushroom and Chicken Soup 39
Mushroom and Okra Omelet 29
Mushrooms and Endives Mix 63
Mushrooms Salsa 86
Mussel Chowder 104
Mussels Casserole 101
Mussels Mariniere 107
Mussels Mariniere 116
Mussels Salad 87
Mustard and Sage Beef 156
Mustard Greens and Cabbage Sauté 174
Mustard Greens Dip 78
Mustard Pork and Chard 144

N

Nutmeg Endives 85
Nutmeg Pudding 200
Nutmeg Zucchini Rice 73
Nutritious Taco Skillet 30

O

Okra and Olives Mix 177

Okra Soup 35
Olives and Spinach Dip 89
Olives Spread 87
Olives, Capers and Kale 177
Onion Baby Back Ribs 155
Orange Chicken 127
Oregano and Thyme Beef 163
Oregano Beef Bites 88
Oregano Chicken 117
Oregano Chicken and Dates 132
Oregano Egg en Cocotte 24
Oregano Fennel Steaks 68
Oregano Green Beans Salsa 75
Oregano Keto Bread Rounds 76
Oregano Tuna 103

P

Pandan Custard 193
Paprika Chicken Wings 117
Paprika Deviled Eggs 79
Paprika Eggs in Pepper Holes 14
Paprika Lamb Chops 153
Paprika Mushrooms 56
Paprika Salmon Skewers 105
Paprika Trout 96
Parchment Fish 113
Parmesan Broccoli Head 73
Parmesan Cauliflower Tots 83
Parmesan Chicken Balls 31
Parmesan Mushroom Spread 76
Parmesan Onion Rings 61
Parmesan Pork 143
Parmesan Pork Tenderloins 144
Parmesan Radish 172
Parmesan Radishes and Asparagus 169
Parmesan Scallops 106
Parmesan Tomatoes Slices 79
Parsley Beef Bowls 35
Parsley Cauliflower Mix 19
Parsley Clams Platter 81
Parsley Meatloaf 48
Pastrami 165
Peanut Butter Balls 199
Pecan Chicken 128
Pecan Pie 191
Pecans and Plums Bread 196
Pepper Pork Chops 49
Peppermint Cookies 203
Peppers & Cheese Salad 183
Peppers, Green Beans and Olives Mix 183
Pesto Chicken Salad 91
Pesto Pork and Mustard Greens 153
Pesto Salmon 95
Pesto Wings 88
Pine Nuts Lamb Meatballs 159
Pine Nuts Savoy Cabbage 59
Pizza Stuffed Chicken 121
Plums and Berries Compote 194
Plums and Raisins Mix 186
Plums and Rice Pudding 197
Plums Jam 192
Plums Pie 202
Poached Cod 114
Popcorn Chicken 81
Pork and Baby Spinach 38
Pork and Bok Choy 164
Pork and Cauliflower Rice 146
Pork and Celery Curry 153
Pork and Chives Asparagus 163

Pork and Cilantro Tomato Mix 144
Pork and Kale Hash 27
Pork and Kale Meatballs 38
Pork and Lemon Basil Sauce 145
Pork and Mint Zucchinis 166
Pork and Olives 154
Pork and Turnip Cake 147
Pork Belly Salad 166
Pork Chops and Green Chilies Mix 148
Pork Chops and Thyme Mushrooms 37
Pork Chops in Sweet Sauce 160
Pork Hash 13
Pork Meatballs and Spring Onions Sauce 146
Pork Pie 19
Pork Ribs and Green Beans 152
Pork Salad with Kale 166
Pork&Mushrooms Ragout 150
Pork, Kale and Capers Mix 145
Pork, Spinach and Green Beans 144
Portobello Toasts 184
Prosciutto and Eggs Salad 156
Prosciutto Shrimp Skewers 97
Provolone Chicken Soup 34
Pumpkin Pie Cups 185
Pumpkin Spices Latte 85
Pumpkin Spices Pudding 186

R

Radish Salsa 78
Raspberries and Coconut Puddings 192
Raspberry Pie 201
Raspberry Pork Mix 147
Red Cabbage and Artichokes 68
Red Chard Spread 90
Rhubarb Custard 190
Roasted Cauliflower Steak 67
Rogan Josh 161
Rosemary and Cinnamon Pork 143
Rosemary Barbecue Pork Chops 143
Rosemary Cauliflower 61
Rosemary Pork Chops 148
Rosemary Radish Halves 62
Rosemary Tilapia and Pine Nuts 114
Rosemary Trout and Cauliflower 97
Rosemary&Butter Mushrooms 54

S

Saffron Bell Peppers 66
Saffron Chili Cod 101
Sage and Tarragon Pork 148
Sage Chicken and Broccoli 121
Sage Chicken and Turkey Stew 51
Sage Eggplants and Green Beans 72
Sage Pork Loin 149
Salmon and Artichokes 98
Salmon and Black Olives Mix 94
Salmon and Coconut Mix 108
Salmon and Cod Cakes 79
Salmon and Dill Sauce 105
Salmon and Eggs Mix 21
Salmon and Endives 101
Salmon and Garlic Spinach 112
Salmon and Green Beans 110
Salmon and Kohlrabi Gratin 104
Salmon and Salsa 100
Salmon and Shrimp Mix 110
Salmon and Swiss Chard Salad 90
Salmon and Tomato Passata 98
Salmon in Fragrant Sauce 99
Salmon Pie 95

Salmon Poppers 108
Salmon Salad 103
Salmon Stew 50
Salmon under Parmesan Blanket 108
Salmon with Lemon 115
Salsa Chicken 44
Salsa Verde Turkey 133
Salty Nuts Mix 85
Sausage Casserole 20
Sautéed Kohlrabi 176
Scallions and Broccoli Mix 13
Scallions and Peppers Bowls 32
Scalloped Cabbage 173
Scotch Eggs and Tomato Passata 18
Sea Bass and Pesto 100
Sea Bass and Sauce 99
Seafood Bisque 106
Seafood Omelet 99
Sesame Chicken 119
Shallot Mushrooms 175
Shortbread Cookies 202
Shredded Chicken Salad 53
Shredded Spaghetti Squash with Bacon 171
Shrimp and Beef Bowls 82
Shrimp and Leeks Platter 80
Shrimp and Lemon Green Beans Mix 112
Shrimp and Mussels Salad 92
Shrimp and Okra Bowls 85
Shrimp and Olives Stew 46
Shrimp Cocktail 100
Shrimp Salad with Avocado 99
Shrimp Tacos 100
Sichuan Style Green Beans 70
Side Dish Cauliflower Ziti 74
Skagenrora 101
Sliced Zucchini Casserole 59
Smashed Cauliflower with Goat Cheese 65
Smoked Crab and Cod Mix 113
Smoked Paprika Lamb 164
Smoky Pulled Pork 45
Soft Eggs 12
Soft Eggs and Avocado Mix 11
Soft Spinach with Dill 57
Soul Bread 77
Sour Cauliflower Salad 43
South American Garden Chicken 140
Southwestern Chili 47
Spaghetti Squash Mac&Cheese 69
Spaghetti Squash Nests 169
Spice Pie 187
Spiced Asparagus 74
Spiced Beef 149
Spiced Chicken Bites 117
Spiced Chicken Carnitas 77
Spiced Hard-Boiled Eggs 16
Spiced Lamb Meatballs 156
Spiced Zucchinis 73
Spicy Beef, Sprouts and Avocado Mix 162
Spicy Eggplant and Kale Mix 174
Spicy Mackerel 98
Spicy Pork, Zucchinis and Eggplants 146
Spicy Tilapia and Kale 107
Spinach and Artichokes Muffins 24
Spinach and Artichokes Spread 78
Spinach and Fennel Mix 60
Spinach and Fennel Pork Stew 149
Spinach and Kale Mix 65
Spinach and Radish Mix 58

Spinach and Tilapia Casserole 111
Spinach Frittata 11
Spinach Mash with Bacon 55
Spinach Pork Meatloaf 160
Spinach Saag 49
Spinach Soup 43
Spinach Stuffed Chicken 126
Spiral Ham 51
Spoon Lamb 161
Squash Casserole 60
Steamed Asparagus 66
Steamed Broccoli 65
Steamed Broccoli Raab (Rabe) 180
Steamed Crab Legs 115
Steamed Rutabaga Mash 179
Strawberries and Nuts Salad 28
Strawberries and Pecans Cream 187
Strawberry Cubes 196
Stuffed Mushrooms 173
Stuffed Pepper Halves with Omelet 15
Stuffed Spaghetti Squash 175
Sweet Baby Carrot 62
Sweet Berries Bowls 29
Sweet Porridge 28
Sweet Shrimp Bowls 81
Sweet Zucchini Mix 27
Sweet Zucchini Pudding 185

T

Tabasco Chicken and Kale 140
Taco Shells 86
Taiwanese Braised Pork Belly 147
Tandoori Salmon 96
Tarragon Chicken Mix 123
Tarragon Lobster 107
Tender Jicama Fritters 77
Tender Pork Satay 152
Tender Rutabaga 177
Tender Salisbury Steak 156
Tender Sautéed Vegetables 169
Thyme Braised Beef 158
Thyme Brussels Sprouts 64
Thyme Cauliflower Head 174
Thyme Cod 116
Thyme Crab and Spinach 113
Thyme Duck and Coconut 138
Thyme Eggplants and Celery Spread 85
Thyme Purple Cabbage Steaks 64
Thyme Tomatoes 65
Tilapia and Capers Mix 106
Tilapia and Olives Salsa 105
Tilapia and Red Sauce 109
Tilapia and Zucchini Noodles 108
Tilapia Salad 104
Tomato and Dill Sauté 174
Tomato and Olives Stew 52
Tomato and Peppers Salad 16
Tomato and Pork Soup 41
Tomato and Zucchini Salad 26
Tomato and Zucchini Salsa 81
Tomato Bok Choy Mix 179
Tomato Turkey and Sprouts 121
Tomatoes and Cauliflower Mix 60
Tomatoes and Olives 69
Tortilla Soup 37
Trout and Eggplant Mix 98
Trout and Radishes 96
Trout and Spinach Mix 99
Tuna and Bacon Cups 113

Tuna and Fennel Mix 104
Tuna and Green Beans Mix 115
Tuna and Mustard Greens 100
Tuna Cakes 107
Tuna Rolls 109
Tuna Salad 96
Tuna Steak Skewers 92
Turkey and Blackberries Sauce 138
Turkey and Cabbage Mix 122
Turkey and Cilantro Tomato Salsa 136
Turkey and Creamy Garlic Mix 135
Turkey and Hot Lemon Sauce 131
Turkey and Lime Dill Sauce 124
Turkey and Mustard Greens Mix 129
Turkey and Rocket Mix 129
Turkey and Spicy Okra 126
Turkey and Spring Onions Mix 120
Turkey Bolognese Sauce 135
Turkey Bowls 26
Turkey Omelet 28
Turkey Soup 139
Turkey Stew 46
Turkey Stuffed Mushrooms 136
Turkey, Brussels Sprouts and Walnuts 141
Turmeric Cabbage Rice 61
Turmeric Cabbage Stew 47
Turmeric Duck Mix 131
Turmeric Shrimp Mix 111
Turnip Creamy Gratin 61
Turnip Cubes 63
Turnip Fries 80
Tuscan Chicken 139
Tuscan Mushrooms Sauce 174
Tuscan Shrimps 105

V

Vanilla and Cocoa Cream 201
Vanilla Blackberries Bowls 186
Vanilla Chocolate Cupcakes 203
Vanilla Cream Mix 202
Vanilla Muffins 195
Vegetable Fritters 66
Vegetable Soup 178
Veggie Soup 50

W

Walnut pie 194
Walnuts Green Beans and Avocado 63
Warm Antipasto Salad 71
Warm Radish Salad 44
Watercress and Zucchini Salsa 88
Watermelon Cream 189
White Cabbage in Cream 58
White Duck Chili 132
White Pork Soup 162
Wontons 30
Wrapped Bacon Carrot 167

Y

Yellow Squash Noodles 68

Z

Zingy Fish 116
Zoodle Pork Casserole 165
Zoodle Soup 46
Zucchini and Lamb Stew 48
Zucchini Boats 181
Zucchini Cheese Fritters 26
Zucchini Fettuccine 182
Zucchini Fries in Bacon 75
Zucchini Goulash 177
Zucchini Meat Cups 15
Zucchini Mix 62
Zucchini Parsley Tots 78
Zucchini Pasta with Blue Cheese 180
Zucchini Rice Pudding 190
Zucchini Spread 25
Zucchinis and Bok Choy 67
Zucchinis and Walnuts Salsa 82

www.ingramcontent.com/pod-product-compliance
Lightning Source LLC
Chambersburg PA
CBHW081108080526
44587CB00021B/3501